CRITICAL SURVEY
OF
SHORT FICTION

CRITICAL SURVEY

OF

SHORT FICTION

Second Revised Edition

Volume 4

Henry James - Ezekiel Mphahlele

Editor, Second Revised Edition
Charles E. May
California State University, Long Beach

Editor, First Edition
Frank N. Magill

SALEM PRESS, INC.
Pasadena, California   Hackensack, New Jersey

Managing Editor: Christina J. Moose
Research Supervisor: Jeffry Jensen
Acquisitions Editor: Mark Rehn
Photograph Editor: Philip Bader
Manuscript Editors: Lauren M. Mitchell
Melanie Watkins
Research Assistant: Jeff Stephens
Production Editor: Cynthia Beres
Layout: Ross Castellano

Library of Congress Cataloging-in-Publication Data

Critical survey of short fiction / editor, Charles E. May.—2nd rev. ed.
    7 v. ; cm.
    First edition edited by Frank Northen Magill.
    Includes bibliographical references and index.
    ISBN 0-89356-006-5 (set : alk. paper) — ISBN 0-89356-007-3 (v. 1 : alk. paper) —
ISBN 0-89356-008-1 (v. 2 : alk. paper) — ISBN 0-89356-009-X (v. 3 : alk. paper) —
ISBN 0-89356-010-3 (v. 4 : alk. paper) — ISBN 0-89356-011-1 (v. 5 : alk. paper) —
ISBN 0-89356-012-X (v. 6 : alk. paper) — ISBN 0-89356-013-8 (v. 7 : alk. paper)
    1. Short story. 2. Short story—History and criticism. 3. Short story—Bio-bibliography.
I. May, Charles E. (Charles Edward) 1941 -   . II. Magill, Frank Northen, 1907-1997.

PN3321 .C7 2001
809.3′1—dc21

00-046384

Fourth Printing

CONTENTS

COMPLETE LIST OF AUTHORS

Volume I

Volume II

Volume III

Volume IV

Volume V

Volume VI

CRITICAL SURVEY
OF
SHORT FICTION

HENRY JAMES

Born: New York, New York; April 15, 1843
Died: London, England; February 28, 1916

PRINCIPAL SHORT FICTION

A Passionate Pilgrim, 1875
Daisy Miller, 1878 (novella)
An International Episode, 1878-1879
The Madonna of the Future, 1879
The Siege of London, 1883
Tales of Three Cities, 1884
The Author of Beltraffio, 1885
The Aspern Papers, 1888
The Lesson of the Master, 1892
The Private Life, Lord Beaupre, The Visits, 1893
The Real Thing, 1893
Terminations, 1895
Embarrassments, 1896
The Two Magics: The Turn of the Screw and Covering End, 1898
The Soft Side, 1900
The Better Sort, 1903
The Novels and Tales of Henry James, 1907-1909 (24 volumes)
The Finer Grain, 1910
A Landscape Painter, 1919
Travelling Companions, 1919
Master Eustace, 1920
Stories of Writers and Artists, 1944
Henry James: Selected Short Stories, 1950
Henry James: Eight Tales from the Major Phase, 1958
The Complete Tales of Henry James, 1962-1965 (12 volumes; Leon Edel, editor)
Tales of Henry James, 1984
The Figure in the Carpet and Other Stories, 1986
The Jolly Corner and Other Tales, 1990

OTHER LITERARY FORMS

Henry James was a prolific writer who, from 1875 until his death, published a book or more every year. Other than short fiction, James wrote novels, dramas, biographies, autobiographies, reviews, travelogues, art and literary criticism, literary theory, and letters. James was a pioneer in the criticism and theory of fiction. Much of his criticism appears in Leon Edel and Mark Wilson's edition of *Henry James: Literary Criticism* (1984). James's creative method and the sources of many of his works are documented in *The Complete Notebooks of Henry James* (1987).

ACHIEVEMENTS

Henry James contributed to the development of the modernist novel, invented cryptic tales that border on the postmodern, and laid the groundwork for the contemporary theory of narrative. He completed twenty novels (two uncompleted novels were published posthumously). He also wrote 112 short stories, 7 travel books, 3 autobiographies, numerous plays, 2 critical biographies, and voluminous works of criticism. James brought the American novel to its fruition and gave it an international flavor. He transformed the novel of physical adventure to one of psychological intrigue. His character studies are probing and intense. His precise use of limited point of view invites the reader to become actively engaged in interpreting events and ferreting out meaning. His works also achieve a masterful blend of summarized action and dramatic scenes. In his short fiction, he created the forerunners of the modern antiheroes and invented metafictional stories about the nature of art and writing. Also, his critical works and many prefaces have given modern critics a vocabulary for discussing character and point of view. James edited a deluxe edition of his complete works, received honorary degrees from Harvard University and the University of Oxford, and was awarded the Order of Merit from King George V. His works have influenced Joseph Conrad, James Joyce, Virginia Woolf, and Graham Greene.

BIOGRAPHY

Henry James's career is usually divided into four periods: his formative years, his apprenticeship, his middle years, and his major phase. James was de-

Henry James (Library of Congress)

scended from Irish Protestants. His grandfather, a poor immigrant, lived out the American Dream and died one of the wealthiest men in the United States. James's father, Henry James, Sr., renounced the Calvinistic work ethic and indulged in the mysticism of Emanuel Swedenborg and the socialism of Charles Fourier.

Through most of his youth, James was shuttled back and forth between Europe and the United States, thus gaining an international perspective on art and life. He learned French and received a European education through a variety of tutors and schools. As a young man, he was exposed to the greatest museums and art galleries in the world. His eye for painting aided him in creating a painterly quality in his work. In 1858, his family moved to Newport, Rhode Island, which was to become the scene of some of his early works of fiction. In 1862, he went to Harvard University to study law but attended Robert Lowell's lectures and decided to pursue a literary career. In 1864, he published his first short story and continued to write stories and criticism for the rest of his life. In 1869, he spent a year abroad. With the death of his fa-

vorite cousin, Minnie, in 1870, he felt that his youth had come to an end.

James entered his apprentice years between 1865 and 1882. During these years, he published his first collection of short fiction, *A Passionate Pilgrim*, and his first significant novel, *Roderick Hudson* (1876). He achieved popular success with *Daisy Miller* and continued to write *The American* (1876-1877), *Washington Square* (1880), and *The Portrait of a Lady* (1880-1881). These works dealt with the international theme and explored the problems of American innocence exposed to the corrupting influence of European society.

In the 1880's, James began to take up some of the themes of the naturalists. With *The Bostonians* (1885-1886) and *The Princess Casamassima* (1885-1886), James began to treat the issues of social reformers. These novels, along with *The Tragic Muse* (1889-1890), were not successful. Between 1890 and 1895, James attempted to establish his reputation as a dramatist, but he was unable to please theater audiences, and his play *Guy Domville* (1894) was booed.

In 1897, James settled down in Lamb House in Sussex, and by 1900 he had entered his major phase and had written three richly textured novels: *The Wings of the Dove* (1902), *The Ambassadors* (1903), and *The Golden Bowl* (1904). He died in 1916 in London and was buried in the United States.

ANALYSIS

Henry James believed that an author must be granted his *donnée*, or central idea, and then be judged on the execution of his material. James's stories are about members of high society. The characters do not engage in dramatic actions but spend much of their time in cryptic conversations, which slowly reveal the intense psychological strain under which they are laboring. James's narrators are often confused individuals trying to puzzle out and evaluate themselves and the people around them. Romance is frequently at the center of James's tales, but his lovers have difficulty coming to terms with their own feelings, and often love goes unrecognized and unfulfilled. Marriage is often rejected by his characters, and when it does appear, it is often the scene of heartaches and hidden resentments. Death and dying are also a part of James's stories. Even though he focuses on the death of women and children, he avoids both the macabre and the sentimental. His stories can be divided into three categories: international romances, tales about writers and artists, and introspective narratives about wasted lives.

James has not been given the same recognition for his short fiction that Nathaniel Hawthorne and Edgar Allan Poe have received; yet James devoted much of his literary life to the creation of short fiction and made many attempts to master the form. Several times in his life he expressed the desire to give up writing novels and to devote himself solely to creating short fiction. For half a century, James employed himself in the writing of 112 pieces of short fiction, beginning with "A Tragedy of Error" in 1864 and ending with "The Round of Visits" in 1910. He began writing stories ten years before he published his first novel, and over his lifetime, his stories appeared in thirty-five different periodicals on both sides of the Atlantic.

James called his short fiction "tales," and he divided his tales into types. The anecdote, which focuses on one character and one incident, is a brief, compact, and highly distilled story comparable to a sonnet. The longer *nouvelle*, which often ran between twenty thousand and forty-five thousand words, allowed James greater development in his short fiction, not for multiplying incidents but for probing the depths of a character's experience. James expanded his stories because he wanted to explore the richness of human experience that lies hidden behind the surface of everyday life.

James's major tales can be divided into three periods: His early stories focus on the international theme; during his middle years, his stories center on writers and artists; and his final stories focus on older characters who have gone through life but never really lived. James's international stories focus on taking characters with set expectations and placing them in foreign environments. *Daisy Miller* is one of James's early novelettes and deals with a young American girl who finds herself out of place in a European environment.

DAISY MILLER

In *Daisy Miller*, young Frederick Winterbourne, an American living in Europe, becomes fascinated with the garrulous Daisy Miller, who is vacationing on the Continent. The free-spirited Daisy amiably flirts with Winterbourne. Although he is attracted to her, he is aware that she and her negligent mother are the source of gossip among European Americans, who are scandalized by the forward ways of the unchaperoned young American. After seeing Daisy in Vevey, he again meets her in Rome, where she is frequently seen with Giovanelli, who is thought to be an Italian adventurer. Ostracized by her American compatriots, she continues to be seen with Giovanelli and risks her life by spending a moonlit night with him at the Colosseum, where she contracts malaria and dies. The puzzled Winterbourne attends her funeral and realizes that she is innocent.

In *Daisy Miller*, James explores the dilemma of an innocent American woman who flouts the social codes of European society. More than that, however, he explores the mind of Winterbourne, a Europeanized American who tries to figure out whether Daisy is naïve or reckless. Like other Jamesean heroes, Winterbourne cannot commit himself to a woman with whom he is falling in love. Finding her attractive but shallow, he is compelled to lecture her on mores, and when he sees her at the Colosseum, he "cuts her dead." Unable to break Winterbourne's stiffness, she sends him a message from her deathbed, noting that she was fond of him. Convinced that he has been unjust to her, Winterbourne escapes into his studies and becomes entangled with a foreign woman.

James's heroine, like Herman Melville's Billy Budd, represents American innocence. Both have found themselves in a world order that puts them at risk, and both are sacrificed by those who should have helped them. In addition to introducing the international theme, *Daisy Miller* introduces two Jamesean types: the sacrificed woman and the egotist who rejects her love. Though James later rejected his subtitle *A Study*, the novelette *Daisy Miller* is a study of the complexity of human relationships. The enigmatic but vivacious Daisy is sacrificed at the Colosseum like the early Christians, while the reticent and regretful lover experiences a sense of loss as he retreats from the world of spontaneity and life.

"The Aspern Papers"

In "The Aspern Papers," James takes the international theme beyond the romance and weaves a darker and more complex tale. In order to obtain the letters of the American poet Jeffrey Aspern, an unnamed American editor takes up residence with Aspern's former mistress Juliana Bordereau and is willing to make love to her middle-aged niece, Miss Tita. He pays exorbitant rent for a room in their Venetian hideaway and spends lavishly to create a garden in their courtyard. Feeling that he is inspired by the mystic presence of Aspern and willing to take any measure to obtain the letters, he breaks into Juliana's drawer and is caught. He retreats, and the dying Juliana hides the papers in her mattress. After Juliana dies, Miss Tita offers to give him the papers if he will marry her. He rejects her proposal only to reconsider it too late, after Miss Tita has burned the papers.

The unnamed narrator goes by an alias. Later, he reveals his name to Miss Tita but not to the reader. He is one version of the unidentifiable American hero who either shuffles names like James Fenimore Cooper's Leatherstocking or assumes various identities like Melville's heroes. He is a man without an identity, a parasite living on the reputation of a famous writer. He is also a typical American monomaniacal quester, fixed on an obsessive quest and willing to sacrifice all in pursuit of it. The narrator sees himself as part of a grandiose scheme; the garden that he plants becomes the symbol of a lost Eden. In Miss Tita, James again sets up woman as a sacrificial victim. Like other Jamesean heroes (and heroes from American literature in general), the narrator rejects marriage. Also, in his quest for knowledge, he is willing to sacrifice the private lives of Juliana and Aspern.

"The Real Thing"

In his next set of stories, which focus on artists and writers, James explores the relationship between life and art, and the conflict between the artist's public and private life. In "The Real Thing," James tells the story of an unnamed artist who hires two highly polished aristocrats forced to earn their living as models. Major Monarch and his wife contrast with the artist's other models, Miss Churm, a feisty cockney, and Oronte, a low-life Italian. The artist discovers that his lower-class models can transform themselves into aristocrats, whereas the real aristocrats present either a static or a distorted picture of reality. He uses the Monarchs to create a set of illustrations upon which his future depends. An old friend tells him to get rid of the aristocrats because they are ruining his work and jeopardizing his career. The artist, however, respects and sympathizes with their plight but eventually has to dismiss them.

In "The Real Thing," James explores not only the relationship between art and life but also the human dilemma of an artist faced with the conflict of saving his career or upholding his responsibility to two people with whom he sympathizes. The story is built on a series of finely balanced contrasts. The Monarchs are pure aristocrats. The artist thinks that they have come to sit for a portrait, but they have come to be hired as models. The Monarchs are aristocrats, yet they cannot model aristocrats, whereas Miss Churm and Oronte are commoners who can easily transform themselves into gentry. Ironically, the Englishwoman models for Italian types, while the Italian model does Englishmen. The servant-class models start out waiting on the Monarchs, but later the Monarchs wait on the servants. Thus, class distinctions are reversed. The artist wants to paint artistic portraits for which the aristocratic Monarchs are suitable, yet he devotes himself to commercial illustrations, using a working woman who can impersonate an empress. The aristocrats display themselves like slaves at an auction, whereas the servants do their job without auditioning. The lower-class models are professionals; the aristocrats are amateurs. The artist friend is supposedly a good judge of models, but he is a second-rate painter. The greatest irony of all is that people who have no sense of self can become transformed into commercial art, while people holding on to their identity, their own clothes, and their own manners become too photographic, too typical, and too much the real thing. Although the artist must rid himself of the two aristocrats, his experience with them has moved him more deeply than his work with the professional models. The story is a gem of balance and contrast that transforms an aesthetic dilemma into an ethical one and explores the relationship of art to life, servant to master, self to role, portraiture to illustration, and commercial art to lived experience. "The Real Thing" is an often-anthologized story and a perfect illustration of James's craft in the anecdote or traditional short story.

"THE FIGURE IN THE CARPET"

The theme of the relationship between art and life is broadened in James's stories about writers. During his middle period, James created a series of stories in which a young would-be writer or critic surveys the life and work of a master writer. In "The Figure in the Carpet," a story about an eccentric writer who has gained significant critical attention, James probes the nature of criticism itself. An unidentified critic trying to gain a name for himself is called upon to review *The Middle*, the latest novel of the famous author Hugh Vereker, because the lead critic, George Corvick, has to meet his fiancé, Gwendolen Erme. The narrator writes a glowing review of Vereker's work, then attends a party in hope of seeing the great author. When a socialite presents Vereker with the narrator's review, he calls it "the usual twaddle." Vereker later apologizes to the critic but says that critics often misunderstand the obvious meaning, which stands out in his novels like a figure in a carpet. The critic probes Vereker for clues, but the author says that the clues run throughout his entire work. After searching for the secret meaning in Vereker's work, the critic gives up the quest as a hoax. His fellow critic Corvick, however, uses the quest for the narrative secret as an excuse to work more closely with his fiancée, Gwendolen. Frustrated in their efforts, Corvick leaves the country. While away, he writes Gwendolen that he has figured out the secret, and he and Gwendolen get married. When Corvick dies, Gwendolen will not reveal the secret to the narrator, who is even willing to marry her to obtain it. Gwendolen does marry a mediocre critic, Drayton Deane. After the deaths of Gwendolen, Vereker, and Vereker's wife, the narrator tries to obtain the secret from Deane, who knows nothing about it.

In "The Figure in the Carpet," James again turns to the monomanical unnamed narrator on a quest for secret knowledge hidden in a text. Like the narrator of "The Aspern Papers," the critic is willing to marry a woman to gain greater knowledge about an author's work. James said that the story was about misunderstood authors and the need for more analytical criticism. Yet, the story sets up typical Jamesean paradoxes. Is Vereker being honest or is "the figure" merely a hoax on critics? Does Corvick really know the secret or is he using his knowledge to win Gwendolen? What is the puzzling connection between interpreting a work and exploring the intimate relationships between men and women? Why do the many so-called possessors of the secret die? This story has been cited as a model for the critical act by many modern critics. Its metafictional qualities and its strange mixture of love and death with the act of interpretation give it a distinctly postmodern quality.

The stories written in James's later years take on a mystical tone. The artist is replaced by a sensitive individual who has alienated himself from the world. The characters are few and often focus on only two people. The characters remain obsessive, but now they are in pursuit of that part of themselves that haunts them. The Jamesean love story is played out into old age, with the woman as a patient bystander, a reflector of the man's battle with himself. The image of the hunt found in Cooper, Melville, and Ernest Hemingway is now symbolic of an internal quest for the terrors hidden within the self. The artists, who in earlier stories sought to gain a second chance or find a next time, now become egocentric gentlemen facing the life that they could have had. The venture into the wilderness becomes a metaphor for the descent into the unconscious.

"THE ALTAR OF THE DEAD"

In "The Altar of the Dead," George Stransom constantly memorializes the death of his bride, Mary Antrim, who died of a fever after their wedding day. Like a character from a Poe short story, he maintains an obsessive devotion to his dead love and is chained to the observance of the anniversary of his wife's death. While remembering his wife, he meets his friend Paul Creston and Paul's second wife. In a strange way, James returns to the international theme by making Creston's new wife an American who has married for money. Stransom meditates on Creston's first wife and idealizes her in her death. Later the same day, Stransom learns of the death of his boyhood friend, Acton Hague, a man who betrayed Stransom in some undisclosed manner. Hague becomes the only dead friend that Stransom rejects, as Stransom becomes more and more absorbed with the dead and creates an altar of candles to them. A mysterious woman becomes a fellow mourner at Stransom's shrine. It takes him months to learn her name and years to find out her address. He finally comes to her apartment after the death of her aunt, only to find that her room is a personal shrine to Acton Hague, who rejected the woman. Since Stransom cannot light a candle for Hague, the relationship ends. The loss of the woman casts a shadow over his daily devotions at his altar. Dismayed, he has a vision of his dead wife, Mary, smiling at him from heaven. Just then, the mysterious woman returns to him as he dies in her arms. The last candle on the altar is lit not only for Acton Hague but also for Stransom.

Stransom has left the world of the living and has become obsessed with the dead. He forms a distant relationship with a fellow mourner, but she is only a part of his isolated world. Her feelings are never considered. Instead of forming a meaningful relationship, he continues to withdraw from human love. Stransom, like other heroes in James's later tales, becomes an example of James's reticent lover, a man who has rejected life and embraced death. The death of Stransom in the woman's arms unites the love and death theme predominant in the later tales.

"THE BEAST IN THE JUNGLE"

"The Beast in the Jungle" is a powerful story about one man's quest for his illusive identity. John Marcher meets May Bartram when they are both in their thirties. Ten years earlier, Marcher revealed to her that he was singled out for a terrible fate. When Marcher recalls that he told her about his premonition, they form a relationship, and May begins to wait with him. Blindly, he rules out love as the strange fate that awaits him and forms a friendship with May, taking her to operas, giving her gifts, and spending hours

talking about his fate. As the years pass, he becomes skeptical that the "beast" will ever come. He feels reluctant to take May along with him on a "tiger hunt." Finally, May becomes ill. She knows his fate but will not tell him because she wants to make him a man like any other. He realizes that he might save her, but he is too preoccupied with his own destiny to become involved with her. She eventually tells him that his fate has already passed him by and that he never recognized it. When she dies, he contemplates that her death might be the terrible fate, but he rules out this premise. Marcher, an outsider at May's funeral, eventually goes abroad only to return to the grave of his friend to see another mourner stricken with grief. Suddenly, the beast leaps out at Marcher, as he realizes that he has failed to love and has been unable to feel deeply about anything. He has been an empty man who has watched his life from the outside but has failed to live it.

Marcher, like Stransom, is held prisoner to an obsession that removes him from the world of human relationships. He cannot give himself to another, so he must await his fate. James called the story a negative adventure. Indeed, Marcher's trek into the wilderness is his own confrontation with his unconscious fears. In his monomaniacal obsession, he sacrifices May, who becomes dedicated to waiting for him to discover his fate, while he prides himself on his disinterestedness. In "The Beast in the Jungle," as in other James stories, the woman becomes useful to the man as a siphon for his own obsessions. Marcher fails to recognize and accept love and wastes his life by projecting all his endeavors onto a nebulous future. He is so wrapped up in his own ego that he fails to believe that the death of a lifelong friend is a terrible fate. In the end, he is brought into the world of the dead. Like Stransom, he has lived outside the present and now has only a lost past on which to look back. Like Winterbourne at the funeral of Daisy Miller, he begins to realize what the woman has meant to him. The cemetery where he stands is compared to a garden, which can be seen as an Eden, where Marcher realizes his own ignorance and comes to a painful awareness of his loss of paradise. The cemetery is also called a wilderness, a wilderness that will take him beyond the settled life and into the terrible recesses of his own heart. Marcher is a version of the American future-oriented pioneer unattached to family and loved ones, an Emersonian hero caught in the void of his own solipsistic world. He also becomes one of the first modern antiheroes, inauthentic men who live outside themselves, men to whom nothing really happens.

"THE JOLLY CORNER"

Stransom becomes absorbed in the past, in the world of the dead, and he neglects to establish a relationship with the woman who mourns with him. Marcher becomes involved in a vacuous destiny, unable to see the love that surrounds him. In "The Jolly Corner," Spencer Brydon, another alienated man who rejects the present, pursues his obsession with a past that might have been. Having lived abroad, Brydon returns to New York after a thirty-three-year absence only to find that the world has changed around him. James again explores what happens to an individual who finds himself in an alien culture. When Brydon comes to settle some property that he owns in the United States, he begins to wonder about his talents as a businessman and contemplates the kind of man he might have been had he stayed in the United States. He eventually develops a morbid obsession with his alter ego, the other self that he might have been. One night, Brydon enters the empty house called the Jolly Corner in search of his *Doppelgänger.* When he finally comes face to face with it, he faints at the monstrous sight. Upon recovery, he finds himself in the lap of Alice Staverton, who reassures him that she does not find his shadow self so horrible. In the end, he rejoices that he has gained knowledge about himself.

Spencer Brydon's return to the United States plays an ironic twist on James's international theme, as a Europeanized American returns to a United States that he feels alienated from and then conjures up an American self that horrifies him. Like Marcher, Brydon finds himself on a hunt stalking his secret self, his fate that might have been. Again, James uses the image of the hunt to symbolize an internal journey into the subconscious mind. As the doors of life's options open and close around Brydon in the haunted house of his lost youth, the monster leaps out at him as it did at Marcher. Both men, like Stransom, collapse upon the women they have neglected. Alice Staverton is the woman who waited and shared his destiny, the way that May Bartram did Marcher's. She not only knew his double but also accepted it. The use of the double figure was popular in romantic and gothic literature, but in "The Jolly Corner," James gave a deeper psychological and philosophical undertone to the motif. In his last group of stories, James used the mystery adventure format to probe the inner psyche of his characters and to examine characters obsessed with living life outside the present.

James brought a greater psychological realism to the genre of short fiction, expanded its length in order to encompass an in-depth range of inner experiences, transformed the mystery story into metafictional narratives that have a distinctly postmodern quality, and reshaped the quest motif of American literature into existential probings about authenticating one's identity.

OTHER MAJOR WORKS

LONG FICTION: *Roderick Hudson,* 1876; *The American,* 1876-1877; *The Europeans,* 1878; *An International Episode,* 1878-1879; *Confidence,* 1879-1880; *Washington Square,* 1880; *The Portrait of a Lady,* 1880-1881; *The Bostonians,* 1885-1886; *The Princess Casamassima,* 1885-1886; *The Reverberator,* 1888; *The Tragic Muse,* 1889-1890; *The Spoils of Poynton,* 1897; *What Maisie Knew,* 1897; *The Awkward Age,* 1897-1899; *In the Cage,* 1898; *The Turn of the Screw,* 1898; *The Sacred Fount,* 1901; *The Wings of the Dove,* 1902; *The Ambassadors,* 1903; *The Golden Bowl,* 1904; *The Outcry,* 1911; *The Ivory Tower,* 1917; *The Sense of the Past,* 1917.

PLAYS: *Daisy Miller,* pb. 1883 (adaptation of his novella); *The American,* pr. 1891 (adaptation of his novel); *Guy Domville,* pb. 1894 (privately); *Theatricals: Tenants and Disengaged,* pb. 1894; *The Reprobate,* pb. 1894; *Theatricals, Second Series: The Album and The Reprobate,* pb. 1895; *The High Bid,* pr. 1908; *The Other House,* wr. 1909, pb. 1949; *The Outcry,* wr. 1909, pr. 1917; *The Saloon,* pr. 1911 (one act); *The Complete Plays of Henry James*, pb. 1949 (Leon Edel, editor).

NONFICTION: *Transatlantic Sketches*, 1875; *French Poets and Novelists*, 1878; *Hawthorne*, 1879; *Portraits of Places*, 1883; *A Little Tour in France*, 1884; *The Art of Fiction*, 1884; *Partial Portraits*, 1888; *Essays in London*, 1893; *William Wetmore Story and His Friends*, 1903; *English Hours*, 1905; *The American Scene*, 1907; *Views and Reviews*, 1908; *Italian Hours*, 1909; *A Small Boy and Others*, 1913; *Notes of a Son and Brother*, 1914 (memoirs); *Notes on Novelists*, 1914; *The Middle Years*, 1917; *The Art of the Novel: Critical Prefaces*, 1934 (R. P. Blackmur, editor); *The Notebooks of Henry James*, 1947 (F. O. Matthiessen and Kenneth B. Murdock, editors); *The Scenic Art*, 1948 (Allan Wade, editor); *The Future of the Novel*, 1956; *Henry James Letters*, 1974-1984 (5 volumes; Leon Edel, editor); *Henry James: Literary Criticism*, 1984; *The Art of Criticism: Henry James on the Theory and Practice of Fiction*, 1986; *The Complete Notebooks of Henry James*, 1987.

BIBLIOGRAPHY

Bell, Millicent. "'The Pupil' and the Unmentionable Subject." *Raritan* 16 (Winter, 1997): 50-63. Claims the story is about that which was once considered almost unmentionable by the genteel: money. James focuses on the extinct code of manners and taste by which refined persons were not supposed to talk much about money.

Gage, Richard P. *Order and Design: Henry James Titled Story Sequences*. New York: Peter Lang, 1988. Gage examines James's published short-story collections, such as *Terminations, Embarrassments*, and *The Soft Side*, in order to show how James collected his stories around a central theme. Focusing on the interrelatedness of James's works, Gage shows how James's stories can be divided into organized units based upon a holistic design.

Heldreth, Leonard. "The Ghost and the Self: The Supernatural Fiction of Henry James." In *The Celebration of the Fantastic*, edited by Donald E. Morse, Marshall B. Tymn, and Csilla Bertha. Westport, Conn.: Greenwood Press, 1992. Discusses two typical patterns in James's ghost stories: In one group, the supernatural force is a trace of the past compelling a character to make a change. In the second group, ghosts constitute an intrusion of the romantic relationship between two characters.

Hocks, Richard A. *Henry James: A Study of the Short Fiction*. Boston: Twayne, 1990. Hocks's book is a good introduction to James's short fiction. The book divides James's stories into three periods: the early social realism, the middle tales dealing with psychological and moral issues, and the later works of poetic expressionism. Detailed analyses of the major works are provided, along with selections of James's writings on short fiction and a collection of critical articles on selected works.

Horne, Philip. "Henry James and the Economy of the Short Story." In *Modernist Writers and the Marketplace*, edited by Ian Willison, Warwick Gould, and Warren Chernaik. London: Macmillan, 1996. Discusses some of the commercial and social constraints and opportunities that affected James's writing of short fiction in the last half of his career.

Kraft, James. *The Early Tales of Henry James*. Carbondale: Southern Illinois University Press, 1969. Kraft briefly covers James's theory of short fiction and gives considerable emphasis to James's little known early stories. He focuses on James's development as a writer of short fiction, beginning with James's first story "A Tragedy of Error" (1864) and ending with "The International Episode" (1879). This book is not for the student interested in James's major works.

Lustig, T. J. *Henry James and the Ghostly*. Cambridge, England: Cambridge University Press, 1994. Discusses James's ghost stories and the significance of the "ghostly" for James's work generally. Among the best-known James stories discussed are "The Jolly Corner" and "The Turn of the Screw." Lustig devotes a third of this study to "The Turn of the Screw," which he argues is a story about reading.

Martin, W. R., and Warren U. Ober. *Henry James's*

Apprenticeship: The Tales, 1864-1882. Toronto: P. D. Meany Publishers, 1994. An analysis of the stories James wrote in the first fifteen years of his career, suggesting how the vision he was creating in those stories prepared for the writing of his first masterpiece, *The Portrait of a Lady.* Discusses the sources of his basic theme of the victimized innocent.

Oates, Joyce Carol. "The Madness of Art: Henry James's 'The Middle Years.'" *New Literary History* 27 (Spring, 1996): 259-262. Discusses the story's buried theme as that of the strange marriage of artist and "greatest admirer."

Pearson, John H. *The Prefaces of Henry James: Framing the Modern Reader.* University Park: Pennsylvania State University Press, 1997. In Chapter 5 of this study, Pearson examines James's preface to volume 17 of his collected works, which contains such stories as "The Altar of the Dead," "The Beast in the Jungle," and "The Birthplace." Provides an intertextual reading of these stories as self-reflective tales in which author and reader are dialectically opposed.

Rawlings, Peter. "A Kodak Refraction of Henry James's 'The Real Thing.'" *Journal of American Studies* 32 (December, 1998): 447-462. Discusses "The Real Thing" and its treatment of issues of representation and reproduction as an allegory in which the tyrannical forces of the real and the vulgar, unless subjected to the processes of selection and idealization, can be all-vanquishing.

Vaid, Krishna Balden. *Technique in the Tales of Henry James.* Cambridge, Mass.: Harvard University Press, 1964. Vaid covers all the major works, gives a comprehensive overview of James's writings on short fiction, and focuses on James's styles of narration and his careful balance of summary and scene. The book contains an excellent chapter on James's later tales.

Wagenknecht, Edward. *The Tales of Henry James.* New York: Frederick Ungar, 1984. The book contains brief analyses of fifty-five of James's major tales as well as thumbnail sketches of other stories. It provides a good reference work for someone looking for short summaries and critical bibliographies (found in the footnotes) but lacks detailed criticism of individual works as well as historical perspective.

Paul Rosefeldt

M. R. JAMES

Born: Goodnestone, Kent, England; August 1, 1862
Died: Eton, England; June 12, 1936

PRINCIPAL SHORT FICTION
Ghost Stories of an Antiquary, 1904
More Ghost Stories of an Antiquary, 1911
A Thin Ghost and Others, 1919
The Five Jars, 1922
A Warning to the Curious, 1925
The Collected Ghost Stories of M. R. James, 1931
    (as *The Penguin Complete Ghost Stories of M. R. James,* 1984)

Book of the Supernatural, 1979 (U.S. title, *The Book of Ghost Stories,* 1979)

OTHER LITERARY FORMS

The scholarly writings of M. R. James were varied and extensive. He cataloged most of the medieval manuscript collections in the Cambridge colleges, the Fitzwilliam Museum, and the Canterbury Cathedral. He was an early researcher in Christian archaeology, contributing dozens of articles and monographs on stained glass, roof bosses, statuary, and wall paintings. James was also one of the foremost biblical scholars of his time and was responsible for producing editions of both old and new testament apocrypha. He edited a number of ancient books in modern translation or in contemporary editions, and researched ancient libraries, as well as works in local history and what might loosely be described as classical studies.

ACHIEVEMENTS

M. R. James won a number of prestigious awards and scholarships at both Eton College and King's College, Cambridge, including the Newcastle Scholarship at Eton and the Eton Scholarship, the Craven Scholarship, the Carus Undergraduate Prize, a Bell Scholarship, the annual Jeremie Septuagint Prize, and the senior Chancellor's Medal for 1886 at King's. He was elected to a fellowship at King's in 1887, became dean in 1889 and provost in 1905. In addition, he served as both assistant director and later director of the Fitzwilliam Museum, Cambridge, was on the syndicate of the library and the university press, and also became vice-chancellor of the university. James became provost of Eton in 1918 and was awarded the Order of Merit in 1930.

BIOGRAPHY

Montague Rhodes James was reared in a family of academics and clerics. His father was a parish priest at Livermore in Suffolk where James grew up. He prepared for Eton at Temple Grove where his father had gone before him, entering Eton in 1876 as a King's scholar. His years at Eton were among the happiest of his life, and he demonstrated a scholarly precocity. He was both a popular boy and a successful student and passed on to King's College, Cambridge, on an Eton Scholarship in 1882. He remained at King's for the next thirty-six years as an undergraduate, fellow, vice-provost, and finally provost. During these years he also fulfilled a number of other academic and administrative posts at the university. He was briefly vice-chancellor of the university during the 1914-1918 war. In 1918, partly in response to various changes taking place at Cambridge, James accepted the provostship of Eton, a position he held until his death in 1936.

ANALYSIS

M. R. James, perhaps the most important practitioner of the ghost story between Joseph Sheridan Le Fanu and the modern scene, was, in the very best sense of the word, an "amateur." An antiquarian, bibliographer, theologian, and educator by profession, his fiction writing was an almost accidental avocation; he made up and told (literally as well as figuratively) ghost stories for his own pleasure and that of his friends. His first two tales, "Canon Alberic's Scrapbook" and "Lost Hearts," were composed to be read aloud at an 1897 meeting of the "Chitchat Society," a short-lived literary club. The group disbanded, but James continued the ritual of reading supernatural narratives to friends every Christmas at eleven o'clock in the evening. Publication of the stories was largely due to the encouragement of these friends and never became more than a minor activity in James's long and full, if uneventful, life.

This is not to say, however, that he was less than completely serious about his ghost stories. Although his oeuvre of thirty-two tales is modest in size, especially when compared with his voluminous nonfiction writings, the quality of the stories is uniformly high, and each has a flavor and style that is distinctly M. R. James. Beyond his own fictions, once he had committed himself to the writing of such narratives, James became both a staunch advocate and an important theorist of the genre.

The primary influence on his work was the mid-nineteenth century master of mystery and horror, Le Fanu. James thought himself a writer in the "Le Fanu tradition" and did everything he could to bring public attention to that neglected predecessor. In 1923, he edited a collection of Le Fanu's best short fiction, *Madam Crowl's Ghost and Other Tales of Mystery*, initiating a "Le Fanu revival" which established that writer as the true father of the modern British horror story. James probably overstated his resemblance to his Irish forebear, but there are enough similarities between them to acknowledge a "Le Fanu-M. R. James tradition"—one that emphasizes familiar, contemporary settings instead of exotic, bygone landscapes; narrative distance and indirection rather than blatant sensationalism; and linguistic precision and subtlety over melodramatic verbal excess.

Although, when asked if he had any "theories as to the writing of ghost stories," James responded "none that are worthy of the name or need be repeated," he did, in fact, have a thorough, if succinct and simple, theory of the genre which he articulated—albeit reluctantly—in a few short essays that preface some of his collections. Most of these principles can be seen operating in "Lost Hearts," the most famous of James's early stories.

"LOST HEARTS"

"Two ingredients most valuable in the concocting of a ghost story are to me," he said, "the atmosphere and the nicely managed crescendo." He begins to create his "atmosphere" and mount his "nicely managed crescendo" in "Lost Hearts" with the picture of a young boy arriving at a very old house; the boy is only sketched in; the house, copied from a real structure, is described in meticulous architectural detail. Like Edgar Allan Poe, a writer in most other respects very different from him, James often endowed his environments and inanimate objects with more reality and vitality than his human characters.

The reader quickly learns that the boy, Stephen Elliott, has come to live with his rich old uncle, Mr. Abney, following the death of his parents. Abney, a bookish scholar, seems benign, if austere and distant. The only odd note in their initial meeting is produced by the old man's insistent repetition of the question: "How old are you?" Abney, however, retreats into the background when Stephen is turned over to Mrs. Bunch, his lively, affectionate, middle-aged housekeeper, who quickly establishes a comfortable setting for the boy—in keeping with James's characteristic strategy.

> Let us, then, be introduced to the actors in a placid way; let us see them going about their ordinary business, undisturbed by forebodings, pleased with their surroundings; and into this calm environment let the ominous thing put out its head, unobtrusively at first, then more insistently, until it holds the stage.

The "ominous thing" makes its unobtrusive entrance into the story when Mrs. Bunch tells Stephen about the mysterious disappearance of two homeless young people, a "gypsy girl" and a "foreign boy," who had also been taken in by Abney. This information is immediately reinforced by a strange and terrible dream Stephen has in which he sees a strange corpselike figure seated in the bathtub, hands over its heart. Two bizarre incidents follow in short order: Stephen awakens one morning to find a series of slits in his nightgown over the heart area, and the butler refuses to go to the wine cellar because he hears voices. James manipulates the ghosts with great skill; the reader cannot be sure whether the rapidly intensifying danger to Stephen comes from these specters or from his uncle, or, perhaps, from both.

The climax of the story is signaled when Abney invites Stephen to an eleven o'clock meeting in his study. Immediately prior to the meeting, Stephen peers out his window and sees two ghosts:

> Whilst the girl stood still, half smiling, with her hands clasped over her heart, the boy, a thin shape, with black hair and ragged clothing, raised his arms in the air with an appearance of menace and of unappeasable hunger and longing. The moon shone upon his almost transparent hands, and Stephen saw that the nails were fearfully long and that the lights shown through them. As he stood with his arms thus raised, he disclosed a terrifying spectacle. On the left side of his chest there opened a black and gaping rent. . . .

Extremely agitated, Stephen rushes to Abney's study, forces the door open, and confronts the horror. The reader, however, is not yet permitted to confront it; instead, he reads an explanation of Abney's actions and motives. Abney was a practicing occultist who attempted to carry out an ancient magic ritual designed to give him almost godlike powers. This required that he consume three hearts taken from "still living human beings" under the age of twenty-one. He had already eaten two (reduced to ashes and mixed with red wine!), and Stephen's was slated to be the third. Abney's fatal mistake was to ignore the "annoyance . . . experienced from the psychic portion of the subjects, which popular language dignifies with the name of ghosts." Only after reading this explanation is the reader allowed to see the picture of

Abney, dead in his chair, his chest slashed open by the dead boy's long fingernails.

The author's reticence in revealing the final assault on Abney is also characteristic of his style. "Lost Hearts" is actually much more direct and visceral than the usual M. R. James story, and it is surprising that Abney's corpse is even described in such detail. The more common technique is to describe the effects of a scene on the observers and leave it to the reader's imagination to fill in the details. When, for example, the unfortunate narrator in "Count Magnus" is found dead, "the jury that viewed the body fainted, seven of 'em did, and none of 'em wouldn't speak to what they see, and the verdict was visitation of God."

For all of its popularity, "Lost Hearts" is atypical of its author in a number of additional ways. The black magic and deliberate malevolence of Mr. Abney are unusual. As a rule, James believed that the machinery of the occult should be left out of a story as much as possible. Although, like Abney, the typical James protagonist is a well-to-do, bookish man of leisure, he is seldom consciously evil. He is more likely to be bored, curious, and a bit naïve, a dangerous combination of qualities. He does not usually summon the dark powers on purpose, but happens on them innocently or in the process of normal scholarly pursuits. Having released the demons inadvertently, he then suffers consequences all out of proportion to his "guilt" (another similarity between the work of James and Le Fanu).

"OH, WHISTLE, AND I'LL COME TO YOU, MY LAD"

Sometimes this hero-victim discovers his error in time to avoid a grisly fate; more often he does not, and the difficulty of dealing with, or even recognizing, the evil forces is compounded by the fact that they are frequently embodied in the most seemingly innocuous and common objects—such things as an old book, a mediocre engraving, a doll house, a swatch of material, a stained glass window, or, as in the case of his best-known story, "Oh, Whistle, and I'll Come to You, My Lad," a small metal whistle.

James's provocative title prepares the reader for a mysterious intruder and is especially effective if he recognizes that it is taken from a Robert Burns song:

"Though father and mother and brother go mad,/ Oh, whistle and I'll come to ye, my lad."

The "lad" of the title is Parkins, a young Professor of Ontography, on a golf-study vacation to the East Coast of Britain. Typically, he is a thorough skeptic who denies the possible existence of ghosts. "Any appearance of concession to the view that such things might exist is equivalent to a renunciation of all that I hold most sacred," he proclaims. Naturally, such an attitude sets him up for what is to follow. A characteristically Jamesian antiquarian, Parkins explores some ancient local ruins where he finds the small bronze whistle hidden in an old altarlike artifact. From the moment Parkins discovers the whistle, he becomes vulnerable.

En route back to his hotel room he sees a presence lurking behind him, "a rather indistinct personage, who seemed to be making great efforts to catch up with him." It is Parkins's own thoughtless curiosity, however, that puts him in real danger. Despite the ambiguous warning etched in Latin on the instrument ("Quis est iste qui venit?"/ "Who is this who is coming?"), he blows the whistle not once, but twice. "Well," he responds aloud to the inscription, "the best way to find out is evidently to whistle for him."

Such minor league hubris is always answered in James; come to Parkins "it" does, but never in a completely recognizable form. The exact nature of the being, its origins, its purposes, and even its capacities, remain unknown. Whatever the creature is, it provokes fear and anxiety in the reader primarily by hint and threat rather than by concrete manifestations of malevolent power.

Skepticism notwithstanding, Parkins's inner emotional security disintegrates as his feelings of being stalked increase. When he first blows the whistle, he sees a mysterious scene of "a lonely figure—how employed he could not tell" and hears a sudden wind crash against the window. Trying to sleep that night, he pictures an agitated man fleeing across a beach, climbing and stumbling over rocks, nervously looking back over his shoulder; then he notices a "figure in pale, fluttering draperies" pursuing in the distance. Parkins also hears the rustling of sheets in a nearby bed and is annoyed by the thinness of the hotel walls.

The next morning the maid notices that both beds in the room have been occupied.

Parkins, however, maintains his skeptical facade, even in the face of the Colonel, his more worldly golf partner. It is the Colonel who relates the whistle and strange winds to old fisherman legends. Then both of the men encounter a young boy who swears to have seen a ghostly figure moving about in Parkins's room. The climax occurs when, late that night, Parkins again hears the rustling and realizes that it comes from the bed next to his. A figure rises and approaches Parkins, who backs up against the window, and closes about him, pushing its "face of crumpled linen" into that of the terrified scholar. At this moment, in the best cliff-hanger tradition, the Colonel bursts into the room and the ghost collapses back into a pile of bedding. The following morning, the Colonel casts the whistle into the sea.

Unfortunately, this bald summary may make the story sound rather tame and perhaps corny, especially to a modern reader familiar with more visceral and vicious specters. No simple plot sketch can convey James's ability to manipulate atmosphere, innuendos, images, allusions, language, and tones and these are what sets "Oh, Whistle, and I'll Come to You, My Lad," apart from the mass of fashionable ghostly tales that proliferated during this period.

James's prose style is precise, economical, and understated. As already noted, he seldom describes violence directly, but relies on suggestion and metaphor. Narrative distance is maintained by an adroit control of tone and point of view, and, unlike Le Fanu, James's detached narrators and his framing devices never get cumbersome or distracting. The effect of all of this is to create a running tension between the intense, disturbing reality of the story and the extremely objective voice that describes it. This tension is most obvious in such overt horror stories as "Lost Hearts," "The Ash-tree," and "Wailing Well" but is perhaps even more effective in subtler tales such as "Oh, Whistle, and I'll Come to You, My Lad," "The Mezzotint," and "The Diary of Mr. Poynter," where it amplifies the underlying ambiguity and unresolved fear which bother the reader long after he has finished the story.

James's influence on the supernatural horror story has been pervasive and continuing. His creative years stretched from the end of the Victorian age almost to the pulp era of H. P. Lovecraft and his contemporaries. Thus, he is the primary transitional figure connecting the late nineteenth century with the modern era. It must be admitted, however, that in tone and style James seems more Victorian than modern. One of the best surveys of this genre gives the appropriate label "elegant nightmare" to the ghost story, and of all such nightmares, those of M. R. James are surely the most elegant.

OTHER MAJOR WORKS

NONFICTION: *Psalms of the Pharisees*, 1891 (with H. E. Ryle); *The Testament of Abraham*, 1892; *The Gospel According to Peter*, 1897; *Ancient Libraries of Canterbury and Dover*, 1903; *Wanderings and Homes of MSS*, 1919; *Apocryphal New Testament*, 1924; *Eton and Kings: Recollections, Mostly Trivial, 1875-1925*, 1926.

BIBLIOGRAPHY

Briggs, Julia. "No Mere Antiquary: M. R. James." In *Night Visitors: The Rise and Fall of the English Ghost Story*. London: Faber & Faber, 1977. This chapter provides a good overview of James's achievements in the genre, with a discussion of his methods of handling locale, the past, domestic terrors, mythology, and even ghosts themselves within his fiction.

Cox, Michael. *M. R. James: An Informal Portrait*. New York: Oxford University Press, 1983. A good, intimate biography that provides a detailed overview of the life of James. Only one chapter is devoted to the ghost stories, "A Peep into Pandemonium."

Joshi, S. C. "M. R. James: The Limitations of the Ghost Story." In *The Weird Tale: Arthur Machen, Lord Dunsany, Algernon Blackwood, M. R. James, Ambrose Bierce, H. P. Lovecraft*. Austin: University of Texas Press, 1990. This critical chapter by an author who acknowledges his dislike for James's ghost stories nevertheless sheds some light on the drawbacks of his method and general narrative strategies.

Mason, Michael A. "On Not Letting Them Lie: Moral Significance in the Ghost Stories of M. R. James." *Studies in Short Fiction* 19 (Summer, 1982): 253-260. This essay discusses how James's ghost stories interweave moral values among the accurate evocations of the past, the subtle manipulations of reality, and the unsettling presence of an objective evil, which characterizes his tales of the supernatural.

Michalski, Robert. "The Malice of Inanimate Objects: Exchange in M. R. James's Ghost Stories." *Extrapolation* 37 (Spring, 1996): 46-62. Argues that James's ghost stories comprise a discourse about objects which have hidden spiritual powers; claims that the exchange of these objects implicitly comments on the exchange of objects in the modern capitalist world; provides a detailed description of the stories "Casting the Runes," "The Treasure of Abbot Thomas," and "A View from a Hill" to support this argument.

Pfaff, Richard William. *Montague Rhodes James.* London: Scolar Press, 1980. Pfaff has written the most comprehensive biography of James as well as the most thorough examination of his writings, especially his academic work. Contains a comprehensive bibliography of James's writings.

Simpson, Jacqueline. "'The Rules of Folklore' in the Ghost Stories of M. R. James." *Folklore* 108 (1997): 9-18. Notes parallels between the ghost stories of James and traditional folklore tales; compares James's stories with Scandinavian folklore motifs.

Sullivan, Jack. "The Antiquarian Ghost Story: Montague Rhodes James." In *Elegant Nightmares: The English Ghost Story from Le Fanu to Blackwood.* Athens: Ohio University Press, 1978. This chapter contains the best analysis of James's ghost stories and their place within the English tradition. Sullivan is especially good in tracing the influence on James. He also traces the influence of James in his chapter "Ghost Stories of Other Antiquaries."

Keith Nelson, updated by Charles L. P. Silet

SARAH ORNE JEWETT

Born: South Berwick, Maine; September 3, 1849
Died: South Berwick, Maine; June 24, 1909

PRINCIPAL SHORT FICTION

Deephaven, 1877 (linked sketches)
Old Friends and New, 1879
Country By-Ways, 1881
The Mate of the Daylight, and Friends Ashore, 1884
A White Heron and Other Stories, 1886
The King of Folly Island, and Other People, 1888
Tales of New England, 1890
Strangers and Wayfarers, 1890
A Native of Winby, 1893
The Life of Nancy, 1895
The Queen's Twin, 1899

Stories and Tales, 1910
The Uncollected Short Stories of Sarah Orne Jewett, 1971

OTHER LITERARY FORMS

Sarah Orne Jewett wrote four novels: *A Country Doctor* (1884), *A Marsh Island* (1885), *The Country of the Pointed Firs* (1896), and *The Tory Lover* (1901). She also published popular books for children, including *Play Days* (1878) and *Betty Leicester* (1890). Her main work of nonfiction was a history, *The Story of the Normans* (1887).

ACHIEVEMENTS

Sarah Orne Jewett is best known as a local colorist who captured with fidelity the life of coastal Maine in the late nineteenth century in sensitive and moving portraits, mainly of women's lives. Except for *The Country of the Pointed Firs*, widely considered her masterpiece, Jewett's long fiction is thought less successful than her short stories. During her lifetime, she was considered one of the best short-story writers in America. Most of her stories appeared first in popular magazines such as *The Atlantic*, under the editorship of William Dean Howells, and *Harper's*. American literary historian F. O. Matthiessen said in his 1929 study of Jewett that she and Emily Dickinson were the two best women writers America had produced. Willa Cather offered Jewett similar praise and credited her with positively changing the direction of her literary career in a brief but rich acquaintance near the end of Jewett's life.

BIOGRAPHY

Sarah Orne Jewett spent most of her life in South Berwick on the Maine coast, where she was born on September 3, 1849. Daughter of a country doctor, she aspired to medicine herself, but moved toward writing because of early ill health (which led her father to take her on his calls, for fresh air), the special literary education encouraged by her family, and her discovery as a teenager of her "little postage stamp of soil" in reading Harriet Beecher Stowe's *The Pearl of Orr's Island* (1862). Her father, especially, encouraged her to develop her keen powers of observation, and her grandfathers stimulated her interest in storytelling. After the death of her father in 1878, she began a lifelong friendship with Annie Fields that brought her into contact with leading writers in America and Europe, such as Henry James and George Eliot. The two friends traveled together in Europe, the Caribbean, and the United States, and after the death of Mr. Fields, they lived together for extended periods.

Jewett began writing and publishing at the age of nineteen. During her career she developed and maintained the purpose of helping her readers to understand and love the ordinary people of her native Maine, and later she told stories about other misunderstood people such as the Irish and southern whites. In her career, she produced more than twenty

Sarah Orne Jewett (Library of Congress)

volumes of fiction for children and adults, history, prose sketches, and poetry. Her short stories show rapidly increasing subtlety and power. Her early books were well received, but beginning with *The Mate of the Daylight, and Friends Ashore*, reviewers routinely praised her collections highly. It was not unusual for a reviewer to be a little puzzled by how much he or she liked Jewett's stories. A frequent response was that the stories seemed to lack plot and action and yet at the same time, they were absorbing and charming. Late twentieth century critics, notably feminist critics, have suggested that Jewett was developing a kind of storytelling in opposition to the popular melodramas with their fast-paced romance or adventure plots. Jewett's stories came more and more to focus on intimate relations of friendship, especially between older women, but eventually in one way or another between all kinds of people.

By the time Jewett wrote her masterpiece, the novella *The Country of the Pointed Firs*, she had fully developed a form of narration that pointed toward the James Joyce of *Dubliners* (1914). This novella, and a number of her best stories such as "Miss Tempy's

Watchers" and "The Queen's Twin," would set up a problem of tact, of how to overcome barriers to communion between two or more people, and then through a subtle process of preparation would make overcoming these barriers possible. The story would end with an epiphany that involved communion between at least two people. Though she wrote a variety of other kinds of stories in her career, this type of development was probably her major accomplishment, and it achieved its fullest realization in *The Country of the Pointed Firs*.

A tragic carriage accident on her birthday in 1902 left her in such pain that she gave up fiction writing and devoted herself to her friends. In the fall of 1908, she met Willa Cather, to whom she wrote several letters that inspired Cather to write about Nebraska. Cather recognized Jewett's help by dedicating to Jewett her first Nebraska novel, *O Pioneers!* (1913). Jewett died at her South Berwick home on June 24, 1909.

ANALYSIS

When a young reader wrote to Sarah Orne Jewett in 1899 to express admiration of her stories for girls, Jewett encouraged her to continue reading:

> You will always have the happiness of finding friendships in books, and it grows pleasanter and pleasanter as one grows older. And then the people in books are apt to make us understand 'real' people better, and to know why they do things, and so we learn sympathy and patience and enthusiasm for those we live with, and can try to help them in what they are doing, instead of being half suspicious and finding fault.

Here Jewett states one of the central aims of her fiction, to help people learn the arts of friendship. Chief among these arts is tact, which Jewett defines in *The Country of the Pointed Firs* as a perfect self-forgetfulness that allows one to enter reverently and sympathetically the sacred realms of the inner lives of others. In her stories, learning tact is often a major element, and those who are successful are often rewarded with epiphanies—moments of visionary union with individuals or with nature—or with communion—the feeling of oneness with another person that for Jewett is the ultimate joy of friendship.

"A WHITE HERON"

"A White Heron," which first appeared in *A White Heron*, is often considered Jewett's best story, perhaps because it goes so well with such American classics as Nathaniel Hawthorne's *The Scarlet Letter* (1850), Herman Melville's *Moby Dick* (1851), and William Faulkner's "The Bear" (1942). With these works, the story shares a central, complex symbol in the white heron and the major American theme of a character's complex relationship with the landscape and society. As a story about a young person choosing between society and nature as the proper spiritual guide for a particular time in her life, however, "A White Heron" is atypical for Jewett. One main feature that marks the story as Jewett's, however, is that the main character, Sylvia, learns a kind of tact during her adventure in the woods, a tact that grows out of an epiphany and that leads to the promise of continuing communion with nature that the story implies will help this somewhat weak and solitary child grow into a strong adult.

Sylvia, a young girl rescued by her grandmother, Mrs. Tilley, from the overstimulation and overcrowding of her city family meets a young ornithologist, who fascinates her and promises her ten dollars if she will tell him where he can find the white heron he has long sought for his collection. Childishly tempted by this magnificent sum and her desire to please the hunter, who knows so much of nature yet kills the birds, she determines to climb at dawn a landmark pine from which she might see the heron leave its nest. She succeeds in this quest, but finds she cannot tell her secret to the hunter. The story ends with the assertion that she could have loved the hunter as "a dog loves" and with a prayer to the woodlands and summer to compensate her loss with "gifts and graces."

Interesting problems in technique and tone occur when Sylvia climbs the pine. The narrative tone shifts in highly noticeable ways. As she begins her walk to the tree before dawn, the narrator expresses personal anxiety that "the great wave of human interest which flooded for the first time this dull little life should sweep away the satisfactions of an existence heart to heart with nature and the dumb life of the forest."

This statement seems to accentuate an intimacy between reader and narrator; it states the position the narrative rhetoric has implied from the beginning and, in effect, asks if the reader shares this anxiety. From this point until Sylvia reaches the top of the tree, the narrator gradually merges with Sylvia's internal consciousness. During the climb, Jewett builds on this intimacy with Sylvia. Both narrator and reader are aware of sharing in detail Sylvia's subjective impressions of her climb and of her view, and this merging of the subjectivities of the story (character, narrator, and reader) extends beyond the persons to objects as the narrator unites with the tree and imagines its sympathy for the climber. The merging extends further yet when Sylvia, the reader, and the narrator see with lyric clarity the sea, the sun, and two hawks that, taken together, make all three observers feel as if they could fly out over the world. Being atop the tallest landmark pine, "a great mainmast to the voyaging earth," one is, in a way, soaring in the cosmos as the hawks soar in the air. At this point of clarity and union, the narrative tone shifts again. The narrator speaks directly to Sylvia, commanding her to look at the point where the heron will rise. The vision of the heron rising from a dead hemlock, flying by the pine, and settling on a nearby bough is a kind of colloquy of narrator and character and, if the technique works as it seems to intend, of the reader, too. This shift in "place" involves a shift in time to the present tense that continues through Sylvia's absorption of the secret and her descent from the tree. It seems clear that the intent of these shifts is to transcend time and space, to unite narrator, reader, character, and the visible scene which is "all the world." This is virtually the same technical device which is the central organizing device of Walt Whitman's "Crossing Brooklyn Ferry," and the intent of that device seems similar as well. The reader is to feel a mystical, "transcendental" union with the cosmos that assures one of its life and one's participation in that life.

A purpose of this union is to make justifiable and understandable Sylvia's choice not to give the heron's life away because they have "watched the sea and the morning together." The narrator's final prayer makes sense when it is addressed to transcendental

nature on behalf of the girl who has rejected superfluous commodity in favor of Spirit, the final gift of Ralph Waldo Emerson's nature in his essay, "Nature." Though this story is atypical of Jewett insofar as it offers a fairly clearly transcendental view of nature and so presents a moment of communion with the nonhuman, it is characteristic of Jewett in that by subtly drawing reader and narrator into the epiphany, the story creates a moment of human communion.

"THE ONLY ROSE"

More typical of Jewett's best work is "The Only Rose," which was first published in *The Atlantic* in January, 1894, and was then collected in *The Life of Nancy*. This story is organized by three related epiphanies, each centering on the rose, and each involving a blooming.

In the first "miracle of the rose," Mrs. Bickford and Miss Pendexter are hypnotized into communion by contemplating the new bloom on Mrs. Bickford's poor bush. In this epiphany, Miss Pendexter enters into spiritual sympathy with Mrs. Bickford, realizing that her silence this time is unusual, resulting not from having nothing to say, but from "an overburdening sense of the inexpressible." They go on to share the most intimate conversation of their relationship. The blooming flower leads to a blooming in their friendship. It also leads, however, to Mrs. Bickford's dilemma: On which of her three dead husbands' graves should she place this single rose? Her need to answer this question points to a deeper need to escape from her comparatively isolated and ineffectual life by shifting from an ethic of obligation to an ethic of love. Her heart has been frozen since her first husband's death, and it is long past time now for it to thaw and bloom again. Miss Pendexter understands something of this and tactfully leaves Mrs. Bickford to work it out for herself.

The second miracle of the rose occurs almost at the end of the story, when John confesses his love for Lizzie to his Aunt Bickford as he drives her to the graveyard. The symbolic rose of young and passionate love moves him to speak, even though he is unsure of the propriety of speaking up to the wealthy aunt from whom he hopes to inherit. His story of young love and hope, however, takes Mrs. Bickford out of herself, and she forgets her troubles in sharing his joy. As a result, he blooms, blushing a "fine scarlet."

The final miracle is that while he is taking the flowers to the graves, she realizes which of her husbands should have the rose. At the same time that John is taking the rose for his Lizzie, Mrs. Bickford is giving it in her heart to Albert, the first husband whom she loved so passionately in her youth. Her realization of this event makes her blush "like a girl" and laugh in self-forgetfulness before the graveyard as she remembers that the first flower Albert gave her was just such a rose.

In the overall movement of the story, Mrs. Bickford is lifted out of herself and prepared for a richer and deeper communion with her friends and relatives. The single rose blossom seems mysteriously to impose an obligation upon her, but probably it really awakens the ancient spring of love within her that was perhaps covered over by grief at losing Albert so young and by the difficult life that followed his loss. When she finally struggles free of the weight of the intervening years, she recovers her hidden capacity for friendship and joy, for forgetting herself and joining in the happiness of others. She has epiphanies, rediscovers tact, and begins again to experience communion.

"Martha's Lady"

"Martha's Lady" first appeared in *The Atlantic* in October, 1897, and was then collected in *The Queen's Twin*. This story illustrates Jewett's mature control over her technique and material. She represents a kind of sainthood without falling into the syrupy sentimentality of popular melodrama.

Into a community beginning to show the effects of a Puritan formalism comes Helena Vernon, a young city woman who is unselfconsciously affectionate and beautiful and, therefore, a pleasure to please. She delights her maiden cousin, Harriet Pyne, charms the local minister, who gives her a copy of his *Sermons on the Seriousness of Life*, and transforms Martha, Harriet's new and awkward servant girl. In fact, Helena transforms to some extent everyone she meets in the village of Ashford, taking some of the starch out of their stiff and narrow way of life. After Helena

leaves to marry, prosper, and suffer in Europe, Martha carries her memory constantly in her heart: "To lose out of sight the friend whom one has loved and lived to please is to lose joy out of life. But if love is true, there comes presently a higher joy of pleasing the ideal, that is to say, the perfect friend." This is the ideal of sainthood that the narrative voice asks the reader to admire. Thanks largely to Martha's living this ideal of always behaving so as to please Helena, she and Harriet live a happy life together for forty years. Helena returns to visit, worn, but with the same youthful spirit, and to reward with a kiss what she recognizes as Martha's perfect memory of the services Helena enjoyed as a girl. This recognition acknowledges Martha's faithfulness to her ideal and creates that moment of communion that is the ultimate reward for such faithfulness.

What prevents this story from dissolving into mush? Nearly all the special features of Jewett's technical facility are necessary. She avoids overelaboration. It is not difficult for an alert reader to notice the parallel to the Christ story type; a liberating figure enters a legalistic society to inspire love in a group of followers, which results in an apotheosis after her departure. The disciple remains true to the ideal until the liberator comes again to claim the disciple. Jewett could have forced this analogy on the reader, but she does not. Only a few details subtly suggest the analogy—character names, calling Martha a saint, and her relics—but these need not compel the reader in this direction, which, in fact, adds only a little to the story's power. While avoiding overelaboration, Jewett also avoids internal views. On the whole, the story is made of narrative summary and brief dramatic scenes. Emotion is revealed through action and speech; this technical choice produces less intensity of feeling than, for example, the intimate internal view of Sylvia in "The White Heron." The result is a matter-of-factness of tone that keeps Martha's sainthood of a piece with the ordinary world of Ashford. This choice is supported by nearly every other technical choice of the story—the attention to detail of setting, the gentle but pointed humor directed against religious formalism, and the emergence of Martha from the background of the story. Jewett's intention seems to be on the one hand to prevent the reader from emoting in excess of the worth of the object, but on the other to feel strongly and warmly the true goodness of Martha's faithfulness to love. Another purpose of this narrative approach is to demonstrate tact. In "A White Heron," both Sylvia and the reader enter the quest for the heron with mixed motives, but the nature of the journey—its difficulties, its joys, the absorption it requires—tends to purify motives and to prepare the spirit for epiphany. Sylvia's vision from atop the pine culminates in communion with the wild bird, a vision she has earned and that she may repeat if she realizes its value.

Jewett's light touch, her own tact in dealing with such delicate subjects, is one of her leading characteristics, and it flowers magnificently in the fiction of the last ten years of her writing career. While the stories discussed above illustrate Jewett's most powerful and moving storytelling, they do not illustrate so fully another of the main characteristics of her stories— humor. Humor is often present in her stories and can be found in more abundance than might be expected in "The Only Rose" and "Martha's Lady." She also wrote a number of funny stories that discriminating readers such as Cather would not hesitate to compare with the work of Mark Twain. "The Guests of Mrs. Timms," though more similar to the stories of Jane Austen than Twain, is a popular story of the humorous ironies that result when a socially ambitious widow calls on another widow of higher status without announcing her visit in advance. Among her best humorous stories are "Law Lane," "All My Sad Captains," "A Winter Courtship," and "The Quest of Mr. Teaby," but there are many others that are a delight to read.

OTHER MAJOR WORKS

LONG FICTION: *A Country Doctor*, 1884; *A Marsh Island*, 1885; *The Country of the Pointed Firs*, 1896; *The Tory Lover*, 1901.

POETRY: *Verses: Printed for Her Friends*, 1916.

NONFICTION: *Letters of Sarah Orne Jewett*, 1911 (Annie Fields, editor); *Sarah Orne Jewett Letters*, 1956 (Richard Cary, editor).

CHILDREN'S LITERATURE: *Play Days: A Book of Stories for Children*, 1878; *The Story of the Normans*, 1887; *Betty Leicester: A Story for Girls*, 1890.

BIBLIOGRAPHY

Auten, Janet Gebhart. "'Nothing Much Happens in This Story': Teaching Sarah Orne Jewett's 'A White Heron.'" In *Short Stories in the Classroom*, edited by Carole L. Hamilton and Peter Kratzke. Urbana, Ill.: National Council of Teachers of English, 1999. Recounts several experiences in teaching the story to high school students, making suggestions about the value of the story to exploring conflicts of interest and expanding the canon.

Blanchard, Paula. *Sarah Orne Jewett: Her World and Her Work*. Reading, Mass.: Addison-Wesley, 1994. Offers biographical information and critical interpretation of the works.

Cary, Richard, ed. *Appreciation of Sarah Orne Jewett: Twenty-nine Interpretive Essays*. Waterville, Maine: Colby College Press, 1973. This book collects a good cross section of the major writing on Jewett from 1885 until 1972. Contains biographical sketches, extended reviews, examinations of her technique, interpretations of some individual works, and evaluations of her career.

_____. *Sarah Orne Jewett*. New York: Twayne, 1962. This critical study of Jewett includes a chronology, a biographical sketch, and descriptive analyses of most of her published works. Cary divides Jewett's works into thematic groups and shows how Jewett is a product of her New England background. Supplemented by annotated bibliographies of Jewett's books and of secondary sources.

Donovan, Josephine. *Sarah Orne Jewett*. New York: Frederick Ungar, 1980. This critical study includes a chronology and an examination of Jewett's literary career, following the development of her major themes through her works. Donovan is especially interested in Jewett's feminist themes. She provides primary and secondary bibliographies.

Graham, Margaret Baker. "Visions of Time in *The Country of the Pointed Firs*." *Studies in Short Fiction* 32 (Winter, 1995): 29-37. Discusses the concept of time in Jewett's book from Julia Kristeva's feminist perspective; argues that Jewett presents masculine, linear time and feminine, cyclical time, yet transcends both to achieve monumental time. Contends the narrator of the stories transcends the notion of superficial change and sees that the mythical and the historical are the same.

Joseph, Philip. "Landed and Literary: Hamlin Garland, Sarah Orne Jewett, and the Production of Regional Literatures." *Studies in American Fiction* 26 (Autumn, 1998): 147-170. Compares some of Garland's early stories with the stories in Jewett's *The Country of the Pointed Firs* to examine ideological conflict within literary regionalism. Argues that while Garland's support for social reform leads him to challenge some of the conventions of late nineteenth century realism, Jewett does not see class differences as a hindrance to U.S. destiny.

Matthiessen, F. O. *Sarah Orne Jewett.* Boston: Houghton Mifflin, 1929. This short biographical study may be the most readily available in libraries. Matthiessen surveys Jewett's life without going into great detail.

Nagel, Gwen L., ed. *Critical Essays on Sarah Orne Jewett.* Boston: G. K. Hall, 1984. This collection includes sixteen contemporary reviews of Jewett's books, reprints of eight critical essays from 1955 to 1983, and eight original essays. These deal with biography as well as interpretation. The introduction surveys the history of critical writing on Jewett.

Nagel, Gwen L., and James Nagel. *Sarah Orne Jewett: A Reference Guide.* Boston: G. K. Hall, 1978. Introduced with a survey of criticism on Jewett, this reference guide lists and annotates writing about Jewett from 1873 to 1976. It is invaluable as a source for secondary writing and for forming impressions of how Jewett's reputation has developed. For discussions of criticism since 1976, see *American Literary Scholarship: An Annual.*

Roman, Margaret. *Sarah Orne Jewett: Reconstructing Gender.* Tuscaloosa: University of Alabama Press, 1992. A survey of Jewett's life and art, focusing on her rejection of the limited role of woman in the nineteenth century. Argues that "The White Heron" presents doubts that men and women can join together and suggests hope for a symbolic androgyny instead. Argues that Jewett rejects male/female sexual categories in her fiction.

Silverthorne, Elizabeth. *Sarah Orne Jewett: A Writer's Life.* Woodstock, N.Y.: Overlook Press, 1993. Silverthorne describes the increasing interest in Jewett's treatment of women, ecology, and regional life. Silverthorne had access to letters and manuscripts unavailable to previous biographers, and she takes full advantage of Jewett scholarship.

Terry Heller

RUTH PRAWER JHABVALA

Ruth Prawer
Born: Cologne, Germany; May 7, 1927

PRINCIPAL SHORT FICTION
Like Birds, Like Fishes, and Other Stories, 1963
A Stronger Climate: Nine Stories, 1968
An Experience of India, 1971
How I Became a Holy Mother and Other Stories, 1976
Out of India: Selected Stories, 1986

East into Upper East: Plain Tales from New York and New Delhi, 1998

OTHER LITERARY FORMS
Ruth Prawer Jhabvala is the author of several novels, including *Heat and Dust* (1975), which won a Booker McConnell Prize and a National Book League award. In screenplay form, that work won an award from the British Academy of Film and Television Arts. Her screenplay adaptation of E. M.

Forster's *A Room with a View* (1908) won a Writers Guild of America Award in 1986 and an Academy Award in 1987. Jhabvala's screenplay *Mr. and Mrs. Bridge* (1990) received a New York Film Critics Circle Award. In 1993, her screenplay adaptation of Forster's *Howards End* (1910) was nominated for an Academy Award.

ACHIEVEMENTS

In addition to the many awards she has won for her fiction, Ruth Prawer Jhabvala received a John Simon Guggenheim Memorial Foundation Fellowship in 1976 and a Neil Gunn International Fellowship in 1979. She was a MacArthur Foundation fellow from 1986 to 1989.

BIOGRAPHY

Ruth Prawer was born in Cologne, Germany, on May 7, 1927, the second child of Marcus Prawer, a Polish-Jewish lawyer, and Eleanora Cohn. The family left Germany in 1939. Most of their relatives perished in World War II.

In England, Prawer was educated at a grammar school and at Queen Mary College, London University. In 1951, she received her M.A. in English literature; her thesis was on the eighteenth century short story. Soon afterward, she married Cyrus S. H. Jhabvala, an Indian Parsi, who had studied architecture at the university. They settled in New Delhi, India, where, with her husband's encouragement, she began producing fiction. Shortly after the birth of their first daughter, Jhabvala completed a novel, *To Whom She Will* (1955). In 1957, her stories began appearing in *The New Yorker*.

In 1961, film producers James Ivory and Ismail Merchant asked Jhabvala to write a screenplay of her novel *The Householder* (1960). Thus began a collaboration that produced some of the most admired films of the twentieth century. In 1975, Jhabvala moved to New York City but continued to maintain a close relationship with her husband.

ANALYSIS

Ruth Prawer Jhabvala's lack of ties to any one place may account for her objectivity as a writer.

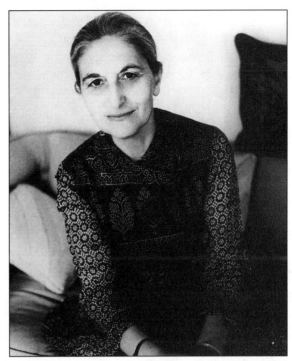

Ruth Prawer Jhabvala (©Jerry Bauer)

However, her detachment does not prevent her from empathizing with her characters, nor does her rootlessness make her less conscious of the importance of place. Jhabvala's experiences may have made her more capable of understanding how feelings of isolation affect individuals, whether they are Indian women, restricted by too many traditions, or Manhattanites, burdened by too many options.

Jhabvala's early stories reflect the delight that, in her story "Myself in India," she describes as a Westerner's initial reaction to India. Like Jane Austen, to whom she was compared by critics, Jhabvala here emphasizes the comic elements in family life, though she does satirize self-deception, snobbery, or pretentiousness. In these lighthearted stories, Jhabvala's characters emerge from their adventures relatively unscathed. For example, the narrator of "My First Marriage," from *Like Birds, Like Fishes and Other Stories*, regards her seduction and abandonment as incidents that merely make her more interesting.

In the 1970's, Jhabvala's short fiction became more pessimistic. Some of her characters seek to escape from the world by following spiritual leaders, as does the protagonist in the title story of *An Experience of India*; others, like the minister in "Rose Petals," from the same collection, have hopes of improving society; still others, such as the minister's wife, dedicate their lives to amusing themselves. Whether they reside in New Delhi or New York, the characters in *East into Upper East* live with the same uncertainties. Although these later stories often end unresolved, one can find satisfaction in their artistic perfection.

"THE OLD LADY"

"The Old Lady" from *Like Birds, Like Fishes and Other Stories* is typical of Jhabvala's early works. Its plot is minimal: The author simply records a few hours of ordinary life in a prosperous Indian family. Besides the servants, the household includes the old lady, her daughter Leila, her son Bobo, and Leila's daughter Munni. Leila's estranged husband Krishna and her older brother Satish, a lawyer, appear for lunch. The household is filled with tension. Leila finds her husband irritating and is annoyed with her mother, her brother, and her daughter for being so fond of him. During their lunch together, Leila embarrasses the inoffensive Krishna and quarrels with Bobo and Satish. Afterward, she criticizes her mother for being too old-fashioned to understand divorce. However, to Satish's annoyance, nothing is decided. The protagonist recognizes this atmosphere as the one that prevailed when her husband was still living. Then she, too, was unhappy; now, however, she has learned from a guru how to distance herself from the emotional turmoil around her. There is a wonderful comic irony in the fact that though her offspring think themselves so much cleverer than their mother, she alone has found the secret of happiness.

"A COURSE OF ENGLISH STUDIES"

One of the recurring subjects of Jhabvala's short fiction is the conflict between East and West. In the early story "A Course of English Studies" from *An Experience of India*, an encounter between East and West is shown as essentially comic. Both of the major characters are worthy targets of satire, the silly Indian girl Nalini, who came to a British university in order to have a literary love affair, and Dr. Norman Greaves, the weak-willed English teacher whom

Nalini chooses as her lover. The story is told from Nalini's perspective, and though it is told in a third-person narrative, the style reflects her breathless enthusiasm. While Nalini has no common sense, she is a brilliant tactician, and as she is unhampered by principles and incapable of feeling shame or embarrassment, Greaves does not stand a chance against her. Nalini thoroughly enjoys the affair; it is Greaves who lives in apprehension. After Nalini pays a visit to his wife and begins planning to take him back to India with her, Greaves terminates the relationship. Nalini recovers rapidly. Convinced that the English poets were wrong about their countrymen's capacity for passion, she decides that she should return to India alone. In other stories, Jhabvala shows cross-cultural adventures as dangerous and potentially tragic, but the lovers in "A Course of English Studies" end up no worse for their affair, though probably no wiser.

"HOW I BECAME A HOLY MOTHER"

The title story from the collection *How I Became a Holy Mother and Other Stories* focuses on a phenomenon which the author finds puzzling, the migrations of Westerners to India in search of spiritual enlightenment. The story is told in the first person by Katie, who at twenty-three tires of her life in London and heads for India. Katie settles down in an ashram, which is relatively clean, has a picturesque setting, and is headed by an energetic but undemanding master. Katie enjoys conversing with the master and with the best looking of his Indian disciples, Vishwa, who eventually becomes her lover. However, she sees right through the master's chief sponsor, the rich, tyrannical "Countess," who plans to take Vishwa to the West with her. Determined not to lose him, Katie lets the Countess discover them making love. The master solves the problem by suggesting that they go on tour together, with Vishwa cast as the Guru and Katie as a Holy Mother. The story is particularly interesting because, unlike so many of Jhabvala's spiritual pilgrims, this protagonist does not allow herself to be overwhelmed by India. Though Jhabvala has said that one can resist India only by escaping from it, here she suggests that common sense may be one's best defense.

"FIDELITY"

Although it is set in Manhattan, "Fidelity," from *East into Upper East*, is much like such stories of one-sided devotion as "Bombay" and "On Bail," from *Out of India*, and the poignant "Expiation," one of the New Delhi stories in *East into Upper East*. In "Fidelity," Sophie loves her self-centered, habitually unfaithful husband, Dave, so much that she will not tell him she has a terminal illness for fear of causing him pain. Sophie knows how easily Dave is driven to tears. She also knows that he is having trouble with the young girl for whom he left her. However, as Dave admits to his sister, he has more than his mistress to worry about. If he does not come up with a significant amount of money, he will be sent to prison for fraud, as happened once before. After his nephew Michael has paved the way for him, Dave appears at Sophie's bedside. Although he pretends concern about her health, Dave is much too focused on himself to notice that she is dying. However, Sophie has decided that the easiest way to give Dave the money he needs is to die as soon as possible. While he holds her, she prepares to take the pills that will end her life, and though Dave has no idea what is really happening, as usual, he prepares to shed his convenient tears. "Fidelity" demonstrates Jhabvala's power to reveal the very souls of her characters without intruding into the narrative.

OTHER MAJOR WORKS

LONG FICTION: *To Whom She Will*, 1955 (U.S. edition, *Amrita*, 1956); *The Nature of Passion*, 1956; *Esmond in India*, 1958; *The Householder*, 1960; *Get Ready for Battle*, 1962; *A Backward Place*, 1965; *A New Dominion*, 1972 (U.S. edition, *Travelers*, 1973); *Heat and Dust*, 1975; *In Search of Love and Beauty*, 1983; *Three Continents*, 1987; *Poet and Dancer*, 1993; *Shards of Memory*, 1995.

SCREENPLAYS: *The Householder*, 1963; *Shakespeare Wallah*, 1965 (with James Ivory); *The Guru*, 1968 (with Ivory); *Bombay Talkie*, 1970; *Autobiography of a Princess*, 1975 (with Ivory and John Swope); *Roseland*, 1977; *Hullabaloo over Georgie and Bonnie's Pictures*, 1978; *The Europeans*, 1979 (with Ivory); *Quartet*, 1981 (with Ivory); *The Cour-*

tesans of Bombay, 1983; *Heat and Dust*, 1983; *The Bostonians*, 1984 (with Ivory); *A Room with a View*, 1986 (based on E. M. Forster's novel); *Madame Sousatzka*, 1988 (with John Schlesinger); *Mr. and Mrs. Bridge*, 1990; *Howards End*, 1992 (based on Forster's novel); *The Remains of the Day*, 1993; *Jefferson in Paris*, 1995, *Surviving Picasso*, 1996; *A Soldier's Daughter Never Cries*, 1998; *The Golden Bowl*, 2000.

TELEPLAY: *Jane Austen in Manhattan*, 1980.

BIBLIOGRAPHY

Chakravarti, Aruna. *Ruth Prawer Jhabvala: A Study in Empathy and Exile*. Delhi: B. R. Publishing, 1998. Discusses other European authors who have written about India, and Jhabvala's role as expatriate. Useful for scholars and students approaching Jhabvala for the first time. Includes bibliographical references and an index.

Crane, Ralph J. *Ruth Prawer Jhabvala*. Twayne's English Authors Series 494. New York: Twayne, 1992. In a chapter entitled "Sufferers, Seekers, and the Beast That Moves: The Short Stories," Jhabvala's first five volumes of short fiction are discussed. Crane maintains that the differences among Jhabvala's stories reflect her own ambivalence toward India. Includes biographical chapter, chronology, notes, and bibliography.

Crane, Ralph J, ed. *Passages to Ruth Prawer Jhabvala*. New Delhi: Sterling, 1991. Only one of the essays in this volume deals specifically with short stories. However, much of what is said about theme in the analyses of the novels is applicable to the short fiction as well.

Godden, Rumer. "A Cool Eye in a Parched Landscape." *The New York Times Book Review*, May 25, 1986, 1, 20. Points out stories in *Out of India* that exemplify the internal struggle that Jhabvala discusses in "Myself in India."

Gooneratne, Yasmine. *Silence, Exile, and Cunning: The Fiction of Ruth Prawer Jhabvala*. New Delhi: Orient Longman, 1983. Argues that several related themes inform all of Jhabvala's fiction. Includes extensive bibliography.

Gray, Paul. "Tributes of Empathy and Grace." *Time*

127 (May 12, 1986): 90. In *Out of India*, women repeatedly sacrifice themselves for undeserving men. However, Jhabvala's Western women choose to immerse themselves in India, while her Indian women have fewer options.

Jhabvala, Ruth Prawer. "The Artistry of Ruth Prawer Jhabvala." Interview by Bernard Weinraub. *New York Times Magazine*, September 11, 1983, 64. An important interview/profile, in which Jhabvala explains why she left India for New York City.

_____. "Introduction: Myself in India." In *Out of India: Selected Stories*. New York: William Morrow, 1986. Jhabvala defines the "cycle" of reactions to India which all Westerners seem to experience. Essential reading.

Mason, Deborah. "Passage to America." *The New York Times Book Review*, November 29, 1998, 20, 22-23. The stories in *East into Upper East* prove once again that Jhabvala is a "spellbinding urban fabulist," whose rootless characters escape from reality in various ways. "The Temptress" is the only story of true redemption.

Sucher, Laurie. *The Fiction of Ruth Prawer Jhabvala: The Politics of Passion*. New York: St. Martin's Press, 1989. Utilizes four novels and nine short stories to prove that Jhabvala's detachment masks her real romanticism, as seen in her interest in feminine sexual politics. Includes bibliography.

Urstad, Tone Sundt. "Protecting One's Inner Self: Ruth Prawer Jhabvala's 'Rose Petals.'" *Studies in Short Fiction* 33 (Winter, 1996): 43-49. "Rose Petals" exemplifies what Jhabvala has stated about how different people react to India's overwhelming social problems. An excellent starting point for the study of Jhabvala's short fiction.

Rosemary M. Canfield Reisman

CHARLES JOHNSON

Born: Evanston, Illinois; April 23, 1948

PRINCIPAL SHORT FICTION
The Sorcerer's Apprentice, 1986

OTHER LITERARY FORMS

Charles Johnson worked as a cartoonist from 1965 to 1972 before turning to prose fiction. His first novel, *Faith and the Good Thing*, was published in 1974, followed by *Oxherding Tale* (1982), *Middle Passage* (1990), and *Dreamer* (1998). *Being and Race: Black Writing Since 1970* (1988) includes essays on literary theory and culture, while *I Call Myself an Artist* (1999) has essays, interviews, reviews, and an autobiographical sketch.

ACHIEVEMENTS

Middle Passage won the National Book Award for Fiction in 1990. *Booker*, a Public Broadcasting Service (PBS) teleplay, received a Writer's Guild Award and the Prix Jeunesse in 1985. *The Sorcerer's Apprentice* was a finalist for the 1987 PEN/Faulkner Award. The story "Kwoon" was reprinted in 1993's *Prize Stories: The O. Henry Awards*.

BIOGRAPHY

Charles Johnson was born in the Chicago suburb of Evanston, Illinois, on April 23, 1948. A voracious reader who resolved to complete one book per week when he entered high school, Johnson aspired to be a visual artist and took a two-year correspondence course in cartooning while still in school. He entered Southern Illinois University in 1966, majoring in journalism, and began a lifelong study of martial arts in 1967. Johnson published his first book of political drawings, *Black Humor*, in 1970, followed by *Half-Past Nation Time* in 1972, while producing a show called *Charlie's Pad* for PBS, which was to run for ten years starting in 1969.

Johnson married Joan New in 1970 and began the first of six novel-length manuscripts that he wrote during the next two years, while working toward a master's degree in philosophy at Southern Illinois. He entered a doctoral program at the State University of New York at Stony Brook in 1973, published the novel *Faith and the Good Thing* in 1974, and in 1976 accepted a position in the English Department of the University of Washington.

Oxherding Tale, the novel that elevated Johnson to national prominence as a writer, appeared in 1982 after being rejected by twenty-five publishing houses. The short stories that Johnson had been placing in magazines since 1977 were collected as *The Sorcerer's Apprentice* in 1986, and his theoretical overview of African American literature, *Being and Race: Black Writing Since 1970*, was issued in 1988. Johnson's novel *Middle Passage* won the National Book Award, making Johnson the second black man (after Ralph Ellison) to be so honored. In spite of his success in several fields, Johnson has continued what he describes as "the same life and labor—that of devoting myself to a genuinely philosophical black American fiction."

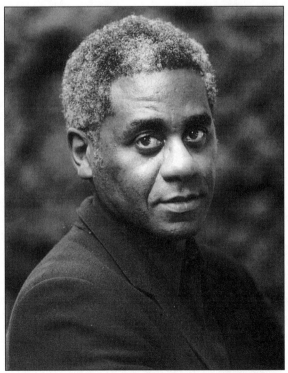

Charles Johnson (©Miriam Berkley)

ANALYSIS

From the beginning of his writing life, Charles Johnson sought to combine a deep interest in the dominant aesthetic and philosophical concerns of the Western intellectual tradition with the specific issues and historical consequences of three centuries of chattel slavery and economic discrimination. In response to the numerous stereotypes and misconceptions about African American life that have accumulated in American culture, Johnson observed, "Good fiction sharpens our perception; great fiction *changes* it." Assuming that pioneering black writers like Richard Wright, Ralph Ellison, and Zora Neale Hurston have shattered the silence surrounding the black experience, Johnson has attempted to open the field, further asserting, "We know, of course, more than oppression and discrimination." Describing his objective as "whole sight," Johnson has worked toward a "cross-cultural fertilization" in his fiction, which draws on the full range of technical strategies, which he calls "our inheritance as writers."

One of the most influential people in Johnson's development was the writer and theorist John Gardner, who stressed the importance of what Johnson calls "imaginative storytelling reinforced by massive technique." In his short fiction collection, *The Sorcerer's Apprentice*, Johnson's technical facility is evident in stories that range from straight realism to fable, fantasy, folktale, allegory, and quasi-autobiographical confession, mingling modes within stories, while establishing an authentic, convincing narrative voice that reflects the psychological condition of his protagonists. The pattern of development in his stories is from what he calls "ignorance to knowledge, or from a lack of understanding to some greater understanding." This understanding is often an aspect of the character's quest for identity, a kind of progression in which Johnson resists a fixed notion of the self in favor of what he calls the "expansive." The stories in the collection touch on some of the most fundamental aspects of African American life to reveal what Rudolph Byrd calls "the richness of the black world."

"THE EDUCATION OF MINGO"

Each of the stories in *The Sorcerer's Apprentice* has a specific philosophic concept at the core of the narrative. "The Education of Mingo," which opens the collection, is informed by the argument that humans are ultimately not responsible for their actions if there is an omniscient deity in control of the universe. The story is grounded in a very down-to-earth situation involving a white man, Moses Green, who has trained an African slave, Mingo, to echo all of his desires, attitudes, preferences, and predilections. As Mingo begins to act beyond the specific instructions of his master, anticipating Green's subconscious and instinctual urges, the servant/master relationship is presented as a reciprocal form of entrapment, in which neither is truly free or completely himself. The costs of this arrangement are Green's permanent connection to his slave and Mingo's restriction to his status as menial, no matter how skilled or accomplished he becomes. The story is both a commentary on three centuries of slavery and a vivid expression of the inner conflicts of an essentially good man, whose well-meaning attempt to educate someone he regards as completely ignorant must lead to a disastrous, violent conclusion due to his own massive ignorance of Mingo's mind. The interlocking destiny of Green and Mingo, the secret sharers of each others' lives, points the story toward an indeterminate future, in which the racial clash of American life remains to be resolved. As the writer Michael Ventura has observed, the stories in *The Sorcerer's Apprentice* often "reveal the underside of the last or next," so that the brothers in the succeeding story, "Exchange Value," Cooter and Loftis, are also trapped in an interlocking relationship that wrecks their ability to think with moral clarity or any sense of self-preservation.

"CHINA"

Located at the center of the collection, "China" is the most energetically affirmative story in *The Sorcerer's Apprentice*, closer in mood to Johnson's celebrated novels, *Oxherding Tale* or *Middle Passage*, than to his short fiction. Rudolph Lee Jackson, the protagonist, is a middle-aged man whose entire life has been a catastrophe of caution and avoidance. His marriage is devoid of passion or communication, he is physically feeble, psychically terrified, and steadily deteriorating from even this diminished condition. The story is not an open allegory, but Jackson is presented as an emblem of the frightened, semi-bourgeois, not-quite-middle-class black man, nearly completely emasculated by a retreat from the daily assaults of a racist society and further discouraged by the constant critical sarcasm of his wife Evelyn, whose disappointment and fear is understandable in terms of Jackson's apparent acceptance of defeat.

Johnson has criticized novels in which "portraits of black men . . . are so limited and one-sided" that they seem immoral. The direction of "China" is an opening away from what Johnson calls "an extremely narrow range of human beings"—exemplified by Jackson, who has a "distant, pained expression that asked: *Is this all?*"—toward a kind of self-actualization and fulfillment, which Jackson achieves through a difficult, painful but energizing course in the philosophy and practice of martial arts. In some of his most engaging, vivid writing, Johnson describes the revitalization and growth that leads to Jackson's symbolic rebirth as a man, as he becomes more and more involved in the life of the kwoon. Initially, Evelyn resists everything about Jackson's enthusiastic, disciplined transformation, but at the story's conclusion, she is, despite her reservations and fears, awakened to the possibility of a life without the artificial, self-imposed limits that African Americans have adopted as a kind of protection from the pain of a three-centuries-long legacy of racial oppression. The story "Kwoon" is a further exploration of the mental condition at the heart of true physical power that martial arts can provide, and it illuminates the genuine humility that the strongest people know when they have moved beyond the ego trap of resistance to enlightenment.

"ALĒTHIA"

"ALĒTHIA" is the most explicitly philosophical of Johnson's short stories. It is narrated by a book-ruled professor, whose ordered, intellectually contained life is fractured when a student pulls him into a forest of uncontrolled passion, the necessary complement to his mental fortress. The two sides of human existence are expressed in the contrast between the professor's measured discourse and the raw reality of the netherworld to which his guide takes him. The word "alēthia" is drawn from the philosopher Max

Scheler's term concerning a process that "calls forth from concealedness," and it stands for the revelation of an inner essence that has been previously suppressed—the "ugly, lovely black life (so it was to me) I'd fled so long ago in my childhood." Johnson's presentation of the professor is a commentary on the retreat that a preoccupation with the purely mental may produce and a statement about the futility of repressing aspects of the true self.

OTHER MAJOR WORKS

LONG FICTION: *Faith and the Good Thing*, 1974; *Oxherding Tale*, 1982; *Middle Passage*, 1990; *Dreamer*, 1998.

TELEPLAYS: *Charlie Smith and the Fritter Tree*, 1978; *Booker*, 1984.

NONFICTION: *Black Humor*, 1970 (cartoons and drawings); *Half-Past Nation Time*, 1972 (cartoons and drawings); *Being and Race: Black Writing Since 1970*, 1988; *Black Men Speaking*, 1997; *Africans in America: America's Journey Through Slavery*, 1998; *I Call Myself an Artist*, 1999.

BIBLIOGRAPHY

African American Review 30, no. 4 (Winter, 1996). A special issue of the journal devoted to Johnson's work. Most of the essays consider Johnson's novels, but there are some references to the short fiction. The strength of the issue is the variety of viewpoints it presents, ranging from political assessments to philosophical excursions. Uneven but often informative.

Byrd, Rudolph P., ed. *I Call Myself an Artist: Writings by and About Charles Johnson*. Bloomington: Indiana University Press, 1999. An intelligently chosen, eclectic collection of works by Charles Johnson, which includes an autobiographical essay and several essays explaining his aesthetic perspective and theories of literary composition. There are also two interviews with Johnson and an extensive section of critical discussions of Johnson's work, including an essay by the editor on *The Sorcerer's Apprentice*, which explains Johnson's employment of the philosophical perspectives of Alfred North Whitehead.

Gleason, William. "The Liberation of Perception: Charles Johnson's *Oxherding Tale*." *Black American Literature Forum* 25 (Winter, 1991): 705-728. One of the most perceptive critiques of the spiritual dimension of Johnson's writing, an important component often overlooked by other commentators.

Little, Jonathan. *Charles Johnson's Spiritual Imagination*. Columbia: University of Missouri Press, 1997. A critical study of Johnson's work, with a chapter on *The Sorcerer's Apprentice*, arguing that the short fiction, in contrast to novels like *Oxherding Tale* and *Middle Passage*, offers a pessimistic view of human existence, dwelling on the "nightmarish and destructive side of his (Johnson's) integrative aesthetic and social vision." The individual stories are approached with insight and are effectively related to Johnson's other work. Little concludes the chapter with an assertion that "the short stories often resonate with more power, depth and ambiguity" than the longer books.

Ventura, Michael. "Voodoo and Subtler Powers." *The New York Times Book Review*, March 30, 1986, 7. Ventura's thoughtful essay contends that *The Sorcerer's Apprentice* might best be understood as a "good short novel" in that each story works as a commentary or extension of the next or previous one. His sense of central themes and ongoing concerns is illuminating.

Leon Lewis

DENIS JOHNSON

Born: Munich, Germany; July 1, 1949

Jesus' Son, 1992

OTHER LITERARY FORMS

Denis Johnson has published several volumes of poetry, the best known being *"The Incognito Lounge" and Other Poems* (1982), and a number of novels, such as *Angels* (1983) and *Already Dead: A California Gothic* (1997). He has also written book reviews, a screenplay, news copy, and essays ("School's Out," 1999).

ACHIEVEMENTS

Denis Johnson has received a National Poetry Series Award and a Whiting Writers Award from the Whiting Foundation for "exceptionally promising emerging talent." *Jesus' Son* was ranked eighth in a list of the top one hundred short-story collections in modern fiction and has been made into a film by Evenstar Productions, directed by Alison Maclean.

BIOGRAPHY

Denis Johnson, the son of a United States diplomat, was born in Munich, West Germany, in 1949. He grew up in countries such as the Philippines and Japan, wherever his father was posted. These frequent moves inculcated in Johnson a sense that relationships and life were unsustainable. In the United States, he went to school in Washington, D.C., and while overseas he attended the American School. Later, Johnson attended the Iowa Writers' Workshop at the University of Iowa. His first marriage produced one son but ended in divorce. Years later, he remarried. Johnson, intermittently a teacher and a journalist, has always been a writer and often alludes to a troubled period when he was addicted to heroine and alcohol. In 1969, when he was only twenty, he published his first volume of poetry, which received immediate acclaim. In 1983, he began writing the first of his novels. He has also been a foreign news correspondent, covering such hot spots as the war in Somalia. Johnson is well traveled and has made homes in such disparate places as Washington, D.C., Iowa, Massachusetts, and Arizona. He settled in Good Grief, Idaho, with his wife, Cindy, and their two children, Lana and Daniel.

ANALYSIS

Denis Johnson writes about lost souls, who have faint hopes of finding, if not God, at least some meaning in their lives. His themes and violent descriptions echo the works of Flannery O'Connor and Robert Stone, two of his major influences. Johnson portrays the marginal in American society: the addicts, alcoholics, homeless, beggars, and crooks, as well as those who simply cannot or will not adapt to mainstream culture, a culture that itself is crumbling and has helped create the characters it rejects. Johnson's characters seem able to survive on hope and human resilience, no matter how outcast or alienated they may be. Ultimately, Johnson's themes are metaphysical. The alienation of his characters implies a someone or a something from which to be alienated.

Johnson's finely detailed works are often episodic and surreal but told in a colloquial, almost intimate manner. He balances a wry detachment from his characters with a tenderness for even the most criminal of them. Johnson's narrators are often addicts. Therefore, the narrator's voice is alternately dreamy and brutally factual, shifting from a detachment, which speaks casually of bullets and blood, to an unexpected, intimate recognition of the characters' common humanity. The sudden intrusion of compassion in otherwise cold narratives has the effect of producing both Christlike and pathological states within the same character.

By juxtaposing fact and fantasy, realism and surrealism, saintliness and destructive craziness, Johnson flirts with altering the short-story form itself, producing a variation which intrigues as well as appalls. As the reader watches losers spiral downward through the consciousness of a narrator, who is also "not all there," he or she feels empathy for them and recognizes the implicit suggestion that, through a shared humanity, the difference between Johnson's misfits and the rest of society is one of degree only, that in some respects everyone is "not all there."

"CAR CRASH WHILE HITCHHIKING"

The narrator, high on drugs, hitches a ride in an Oldsmobile and senses an imminent crash the minute he hears the "sweet voices of family inside it." After the wreck, the narrator, holding the family's baby, wanders toward the other car that was involved in the accident. Seeing that the broadsided car has been smashed, he assumes all inside are dead and walks past it. Flagging down a passing truck, he tells the truck driver to go for help. Because the truck driver cannot turn around on the narrow bridge, the narrator leaves the truck, sees another car nearing the scene, and approaches it. Then he perceives that the man in the smashed car is not dead but soon will be. At the hospital, he hears the wife shriek when she learns of her husband's death. The narrator remarks her scream made him "feel wonderful to be alive" and that he had "gone looking for that feeling everywhere," exhibiting the addict's relentless search for a rush.

Years later, in a hospital detoxification ward, the narrator experiences a flashback to the accident scene. The ambiguous last phrase, "you ridiculous people, you expect me to help you," expresses either contempt for those who might count on him or the self-loathing and guilt beneath an addict's thrill-seeking veneer.

"EMERGENCY"

The narrator, working as a hospital clerk, befriends Georgie, an emergency room orderly, who steals pills (which the narrator takes) and is always high. Terrence Weber comes in with a knife stuck in his one good eye. Explaining that his wife stabbed him, Weber claims the knife has affected his brain because his body will no longer do what his mind directs it to do. The emergency room physician calls for the best eye surgeon, brain surgeon, and anesthetist, then orders Georgie to prepare Weber for surgery, even though he knows Georgie is "not right."

As the specialists argue over how best to remove the knife, Georgie returns from preparing the patient

with the knife in hand. Stunned, no one says anything. When the narrator asks how Weber is doing, Georgie replies, "Who?"

Later, Georgie and the narrator, still high, become lost. When Georgie hits a rabbit, he cries, "Rabbit stew," picks up the rabbit and skins it with Weber's knife. When he finds tiny rabbit fetuses inside the corpse, he declares, "We killed the mother but saved the children," then hands them to the narrator, who warms them in his shirt. As darkness approaches, the two stumble upon what the narrator hallucinates is a military graveyard with large angels hovering overhead. In a rare lucid moment, Georgie recognizes the place as a drive-in movie theater. When the screen goes blank, they argue over whether or not to go home. Georgie resists driving until he remembers that the rabbits need milk. The narrator tells him to forget about the rabbits, which have been crushed inside his shirt. The rabbits' deaths provoke Georgie's wrath, but the narrator acknowledges he is unclear about how or when the deaths occurred. His only clear memory is of the morning's mystical beauty.

Before Georgie and the narrator return to the hospital, they pick up a friend of the narrator, a serviceman named Hardee, who is absent without leave and headed for Canada. Georgie declares that he will take Hardee to Canada. When asked what he does for a living, Georgie replies, "I save lives." Ironically, despite Georgie's drug-crazed recklessness, he probably could get Hardee to Canada, just as he succeeded in removing Weber's knife. The reader does not learn anything more about Hardee because of the drugged narrator's fragmented narration, which, like their lives, is in a state of emergency.

When they return to work, the Lord's Prayer is playing over the intercom. Weber, miraculously unscathed, comes to say goodbye to Georgie, who does not recognize him. The infusion of the sacred into this story implies that the protagonists' successes may be providential.

"BEVERLY HOME"

Living in Phoenix, the narrator decides to look for a job because members of his Narcotics Anonymous group think he should. He finds work at the Beverly Home, an old-age home that also houses the disabled, some of whom are so deformed they make "God look like a senseless maniac." During his free time, the narrator rides the bus and strolls in the desert. One evening, he hears a woman singing in the shower. Entranced, he hides behind some greenery and peeps at her. The narrator reveals his cowardice and violence when he states that he would break in and rape the woman if he had a mask to wear. Peeping at the woman becomes an obsession for him, particularly after he discovers that the woman and her husband are Amish, an oddity in Phoenix. Hoping to see them make love (he never does), he watches their daily movements, including an extraordinary act of contrition: a foot washing by the repentant husband.

When not working or peeping, the narrator dates first a dwarf, then a woman whose childhood encephalitis has left her with spasms and who is thus "unwholesome and very erotic." The narrator thirsts for, but is afraid of, making connections of either a spiritual or an earthly nature. Beverly Home's hall seems a room for souls waiting to be reborn. He has sex with the dwarf with the television on so he will not have to get to know her. The closest he gets to either God or a real relationship is peeping at the Amish couple. The parallels between the Beverly Home misfits and the narrator are obvious to the reader but not to the narrator, who gratefully concludes that he is improving, despite living among "weirdos."

"DIRTY WEDDING"

"Dirty Wedding" deals with the narrator's anguish over his girlfriend's abortion. As he and Michelle approach the abortion clinic, picketers sprinkle holy water on them and pray, and the narrator wishes he knew their prayer. Hating himself, he tells lies to make Michelle leave him, but she stays until, as the narrator says, "She really knew me."

Thrown out of the abortion clinic for making wisecracks, the narrator aimlessly rides the city's public transportation. As in "Beverly Home," when the narrator illustrates his alienation by peeping through the window at the married couple, on the train he peers into the windows of buildings as the train rushes past.

After Michelle's abortion, he cannot look strangers in the eye. Fixating on one man, who seemingly has an appointment, the narrator follows him. When the man confronts him, the narrator thinks the man is Jesus Christ. Later, the narrator says that he would have felt the same way about anyone he followed, thus revealing his need for direction.

Back on the train, the narrator muses on what motel maids stuff into trash dumpsters; thoughts about throwaways lead him to thinking about Michelle's fetus. He reveals his sense of loss as he wonders if the fetus could imagine a world outside the womb, if its darkness would get darker in death, and if it would know or care about being aborted.

Abruptly the narrator shifts the subject to Michelle. Michelle ran off with a man named John Smith, then died from a drug overdose. Afterward, Smith heard her ghost calling to him and also died. Illustrating his convenient sense of victimization, the narrator brands Michelle a traitor and a killer. Once she shot him five times, not to kill him but to "eat his heart," to wound him the way a mother can devastate a child. He concludes that arguments about the morality of abortion are beside the point. "It," the wrong, in this situation is not the abortion. "It" is "What the mother and father did together," implying destructive personal relations and motives, as well as premarital sex. The narrator's union with Michelle is dirty not because they aborted their child but because of the way they treated each other.

OTHER MAJOR WORKS

LONG FICTION: *Angels*, 1983; *Fiskadoro*, 1985; *The Stars at Noon*, 1986; *Resuscitation of a Hanged Man*, 1991; *Already Dead: A California Gothic*, 1997; *The Name of the World*, 2000.

SCREENPLAY: *Hit Me*, 1998.

POETRY: *The Man Among the Seals*, 1969; *Inner Weather*, 1976; *"The Incognito Lounge" and Other Poems*, 1982; *The Veil*, 1987; *The Throne of the Third Heaven of the Nations Millennium General Assembly*, 1995.

BIBLIOGRAPHY

Donnelly, Daria. "Flannery O'Connor in Reverse— *Jesus' Son*." *Commonweal*, August 13, 1993. This review alleges that Johnson's *Jesus' Son* owes much to Flannery O'Connor. Unlike similar allusions in the work of O'Connor, the spiritual allusions in *Jesus' Son* rest on incertitude, rather than on faith. The passive spiritual hopefulness of Johnson's fiction is reflected in the addicted narrator of *Jesus' Son*. Through the nonlinear, drunken narrative, reality is rendered both comically and tragically. Donnelly thinks that much of the power of *Jesus' Son* is in the complex rendering of the narrator, who exhibits both lust and indifference, as well a longing for love and God.

Gates, David. *Newsweek*, February 8, 1993, 67. Reviews *Jesus' Son* positively, calling it "masterfully bleak." Gates particularly stresses the narrative form, praising Johnson's depiction of the narrator's drugged, hallucinatory mind as he tells his stories. The surreal tone is exhilarating, according to Gates, for it reflects the irrational lives of the addicts. In the same way, the stories' enigmatic forms are appropriate to the subject matter.

Kristulent, Steve. Review of *Already Dead*, by Denis Johnson. *Oyster Boy Review* 9 (May-August, 1998). This review deals not only with this particular novel but also with Johnson as a social critic. Kristulent compares Johnson to such European novelists as Milan Kundera and Robert Musil, who believe that every personal choice is also a political one. He also considers Johnson's work to be particularly American, comparing him to John Dos Passos in his emphasis on contemporary fringe groups.

McManus, James. Review of *Jesus' Son*, by Denis Johnson. *New York Times Book Review*, December 27, 1992, 5. *Jesus' Son* is a masterpiece of moral deterioration. Its disjointed narrative illustrates both diseases and Christlike states of mind, as well as a condition in which salvation remains possible but improbable.

Miles, Jack. "An Artist of American Violence." *The Atlantic*, June, 1993, 121-127. Praises Johnson's skill in portraying the mind of the addict and criminal, but thinks the characters' poetic language is linguistically unrealistic. Miles calls the characters' spiritual longings "pre-religious," a yearning for God, a result of having lost faith in people. Johnson's most innovative contribution is the narrator's intermittent, direct addresses to the reader. These intimate asides bring the reader closer not only to the narrator but also to the more shattering moments in the narrative.

Wiggins, Marianne. *The Nation* 256 (February 15, 1993): 121. Praises *Jesus' Son* for depicting characters with serious flaws and scars, such as addictions and craziness. What makes the book memorable is that Johnson at times endows the characters with an essential, shared humanity. Claims that reading the stories is like reading subconscious ticker tape.

Woodrell, Daniel. Review of *Jesus' Son*, by Denis Johnson. *Washington Post Book World*, February 21, 1993, C1. Comments on the strengths and weaknesses of *Jesus' Son*. Woodrell praises the fragmentary style that reflects the narrator's mindset and states that in the best stories the narrator's disjointed consciousness is portrayed so that his anguish conveys a kind of majesty. The stories fail to reveal much more of the character of the narrator than the reader is shown in the beginning, and the characters in *Jesus' Son* are not as large of heart as the characters in *Angels*.

Mary Hanford Bruce

SAMUEL JOHNSON

Born: Lichfield, Staffordshire, England; September
18, 1709
Died: London, England; December 13, 1784

PRINCIPAL SHORT FICTION

The Rambler, 1750-1752
The Adventurer, 1753-1754
The Idler, 1758-1760
Rasselas, Prince of Abyssinia: A Tale by S. John-
son, 1759 (originally published as *The Prince of*
Abissinia: A Tale)

OTHER LITERARY FORMS

The range and quality of Samuel Johnson's literary output is almost unparalleled in either English or
American literature. He wrote tragedy, poetry, biography, periodical essays, and travel books. He is most
famous for his *A Dictionary of the English Language:*
To Which Are Prefixed, a History of the Language,
and an English Grammar (1755), *Rasselas, Prince of*
Abyssinia, his critical edition, with notes and a preface, of *The Plays of William Shakespeare* (1765), and
his collection of essays *The Lives of the Poets* (1779-
1781). Johnson was also known as a brilliant conversationalist, and James Boswell, in his *The Life of*
Samuel Johnson, LL.D. (1791), fortunately preserves
this fascinating side of Johnson as a critic and verbal
artist.

ACHIEVEMENTS

As the widely used historical label "Age of Johnson" reveals, Samuel Johnson was the most famous
man of letters in the second half of the eighteenth century. His neoclassicism, his Christian humanism, and
his political conservatism were thoroughly grounded
in the rational aesthetic of his predecessors, but he
was no slave to the formal standards of his era. He is
considered a pioneer in modern scholarship and practical criticism as well as a neoclassical poet. His dictionary, produced almost single-handedly; his introductory essays on English poets, which use the works
to illuminate the poet's life and the life to interpret

the poet's works; and the combination of philosophy,
allegory, and travel adventure in his short novel—all
combine to secure his special place in the history of
English literature, regardless of literary trends.

BIOGRAPHY

The son of a bookseller in Lichfield, Samuel Johnson failed as a school teacher and settled in London,
where for years he barely survived as a hack writer.
The first work published in his name was *The Vanity*
of Human Wishes: The Tenth Satire of Juvenal Imi-
tated in 1749. The same year witnessed the production of his tragedy, *Irene*, by his friend and former
student David Garrick; but his *The Rambler* essays
first brought him general public notice, and his massive *A Dictionary of the English Language* made him
the preeminent man of letters of his age. This work
was followed by his 104 *The Idler* essays, *Rasselas*,
his edition of *The Plays of William Shakespeare, A*
Journey to the Western Islands of Scotland (1775),
and *The Lives of the Poets* (1779-1781). Johnson was
physically a huge and uncouth man, with tics and personal eccentricities which amused some and frightened others. He was profoundly melancholy, fully
aware of his extraordinary intellectual gifts, and terrified of the damnation he could expect from God if he
did not use his talents well. He was indolent, tending
to procrastinate until his work could be put off no
longer and then writing with incredible rapidity. He
was a social man in a very social age, the greatest
conversationalist of an age of brilliant conversation,
but despite his international reputation and his royal
pension of three hundred pounds a year, he was constantly beleaguered by debt. His relationship with the
Scotsman James Boswell has long intrigued biographers: They have depended greatly on Boswell's record of Johnson amid his circle of friends in an age
known for its interest in conversation. His appetite for
food, company, knowledge, and ideas was as voracious as his fear of death and judgment for the work
he left undone. He died in 1784 at the age of seventy-
five.

ANALYSIS

Samuel Johnson is primarily thought of not as a fiction writer but as a critic, and since his criticism explains so much about the peculiar form which his own fiction was to take, it is wise to discuss his views on criticism. The subject of *The Rambler* 4 is modern fiction. Johnson recognized that fiction underwent a profound change in his lifetime. Gone were the improbabilities of the romantic fiction of the past, expressed in its giants, knights, ladies, hermits, and battles. Contemporary works of fiction, Johnson wrote, "exhibit life in its true state, diversified only by accidents that daily happen in the world, influenced by passions and qualities which are really to be found in conversing with mankind." With this new verisimilitude, fiction acquires a new power, and consequently, a new responsibility. Since these works are chiefly read by the "young, the ignorant, and the idle, to whom they serve as lectures of conduct, and introductions into life," writers must be very careful in choosing their subjects and characters:

> It is . . . not a sufficient vindication of a character, that it is drawn as it appears, for many characters ought never to be drawn; nor of a narrative, that the train of events is agreeable to observation and experience, for that observation which is called knowledge of the world, will be found much more frequently to make men cunning than good.

Fiction, then, has a didactic purpose, whether a writer wishes it or not: Readers imitate the behavior of the characters their authors offer as admirable, and authors therefore have a moral responsibility to select their characters and incidents carefully. They must also distinguish the "good and bad qualities in their principal personages," lest, as readers became more involved with these characters, they "lose the abhorrence of their faults, . . . or, perhaps, regard them with some kindness for being united with so much merit."

The type of fictional hero Johnson advocates is virtuous, although not angelic. In the plot, his virtue, "exercised in such trials as the various revolutions of things shall bring upon it, may, by conquering some calamities, and enduring others, teach us what we may hope, and what we can perform." Vice must be

shown, but it "should always disgust; nor should the graces of gaiety, or the dignity of courage, be so united with it, as to reconcile it to the mind." The final purpose of fiction is to teach this moral truth:

> That virtue is the highest proof of understanding, and the only solid basis of greatness; and that vice is the natural consequence of narrow thoughts, that it begins in mistake, and ends in ignominy.

Johnson was acutely sensitive to the power which people's lives, both fictional and historical, have on the reader. In *The Rambler* 60, he stresses the fundamental "uniformity in the state of man," insisting that "there is scarce any possibility of good or ill, but is common to human kind. . . . We are all prompted by the same motives, all deceived by the same fallacies, all animated by hope, obstructed by danger, entangled by desire, and seduced by pleasure."

An examination of Johnson's fiction reveals that these beliefs about character and the moral function of fiction appear again and again. Many of *The Rambler, The Adventurer*, and *The Idler* essays take the form of short fictional letters, didactic and moral in

Samuel Johnson (Library of Congress)

their intent, which recount more or less artificial tales of hope and misfortune. They are not really what is considered fiction: Plot is stylized, truncated, and undramatic; characterization is minimal; and both are subordinated to the moral lesson. Johnson does not create individual personalities but displays states of minds, generalized experiences, and moral decisions common to all. Carey McIntosh has pointed out that Johnson's fiction characteristically contradicts the pattern of conventional novels: His characters begin in prosperity and success and end as sadder but wiser victims of their own folly or the world's cruelty. These letters commonly take the form of confessions (in which the narrator admits to a fault or mistake), complaints (tales of misfortune told by a victim), or quests (in which the hero goes through a number of opportunities, all of which prove specious). In all three types, the reader is led to a sense of Johnson's usual theme—the vanity of human wishes.

Johnson creates not individuals, but character types, and the character's name, expressed in Latin or English, is frequently the key: Verecundulus (bashful), Hyperdulus (super slave), Misella (miserable), Squire Bluster, Prospero, Suspirius the screech owl. Some papers are sketches of characters in the Theophrastan sense, such as Prospero, the *nouveau riche* (*The Rambler* 200), and Dick Minim, the critic (*The Idler* 60 and 61), typifying a quality, vice, or virtue. Others are moral fables, such as the story of Seged's futile attempt to make one week happy (*The Rambler* 204 and 205). Through each character the reader sees reality generalized and abstracted; the reader is not expected to believe the reality of the character or the fiction, but rather to recognize, in the formalized patterns and choices depicted, similar patterns and choices of his own life.

RASSELAS

Although some of the periodical essay-fictions are obvious, clumsy personifications of moral ideas, *Rasselas* is a powerfully realized book-length fiction, and, while *Rasselas* shares many characteristics with the essay-fiction, these characteristics work together to make it a model of its kind. Johnson wrote this "Eastern tale," as he called it, capitalizing on the popularity of those he had written in *The Rambler* (such

as the fable of Seged), to make money to cover the expenses of his eighty-nine-year-old mother, who was dying. He told Sir Joshua Reynolds that he "composed it in the evenings of one week, sent it to the press in portions as it was written, and had never since read it over." His mother died the week of its composition, and the 125 pounds he was paid for the work were used, Boswell was told, to "defray the expense of his mother's funeral, and to pay some little debts she had left."

The sober tale is certainly suited to the occasion. It tells of the inexorable disillusioning of a prince and princess who, unhappy despite their riches and security, search the world to discover what "choice of life" makes people happy. Prince Rasselas of Abyssinia lives in the Happy Valley, a secret earthly paradise walled off from the outside world by mountains and reserved for the successors to the throne and those teachers, artists, and servants whose duties are to make the confinement delightful. The first fourteen chapters are set in this paradise. At the age of twenty-six, growing increasingly dissatisfied, Rasselas contrasts himself with the animals and wonders what is wrong with him. They are content when their physical needs are satisfied; he is not. "Man has surely some latent sense for which this place affords no gratification, or he has some desires distinct from sense which must be satisfied before he can be happy." When an old sage remarks, "if you had seen the miseries of the world, you would know how to value your present state," Rasselas sets his mind on escaping to see for himself. He spends many months dreaming and planning, and although he is unsuccessful, he nevertheless discovers some satisfaction in striving for a goal: One is happier knowing what one wants.

The prince meets Imlac, a poet and man of learning, who tells of his own quest for happiness in the world and eventual retreat to the valley; Imlac, however, is also eager to leave now, and agrees to help Rasselas find a means of escape. They are joined by Rasselas's sister, Nekayah, and with Imlac as their guide through the world, the brother and sister and her maid leave the valley. The next thirty-five chapters recount their futile search for earthly happiness.

Indulgence of the senses proves unsatisfactory, but so does stoic control of the passions. The group leaves the city to examine country life: The romance of the pastoral world is quickly dispelled when they discover that shepherds are rude, ignorant, and envious savages; the prosperous country gentleman, although more cultured, lives in constant fear of his life and his possessions; and the wise hermit, about to abandon his own solitude, returns with them to Cairo.

The prince and princess then divide their search; he examines the courts and places while she peruses the middle stations of life. They both discover that no station or state of life, not even virtuousness, makes people particularly happy. On a visit to the pyramids, Nekayah's maid, Pekuah, is abducted, and the progress of grief is described. When Pekuah returns at last, she recounts not a romantic Eastern adventure (such as *The Arabian Nights' Entertainments* might depict) but a constant battle with ennui.

When Rasselas then turns to academic studies, Imlac warns him about the dangers of intellectual life by telling the story of an astronomer whose solitary studies led to madness. From this point, however, the book becomes more hopeful since Pekuah and Nekayah's visits to the astronomer gradually free him from his delusions. Then, when Imlac takes them all to the catacombs, he convinces them of the immortality of the soul: "To me, said the princess, the choice of life [has] become less important; I hope hereafter to think only on the choice of eternity." This clearly is the moral lesson of the book, and in the final chapter, "The Conclusion, in Which Nothing Is Concluded," they decide to return to Abyssinia.

Rasselas possesses some of the qualities of the Asian tale, a form very popular in the eighteenth century. Most such tales were not Asian at all, and although Johnson had translated Father Lobo's *A Voyage to Abyssinia* in 1735, he is not attempting to depict a real Eastern society in *Rasselas*. Johnson uses Asianism, in McIntosh's words, "to simplify and exaggerate experience and thereby clarify its meaning," to create an environment "almost hypothetically pure," and "to raise and ennoble his argument." The language is thus elevated to a level of dignity and generality without any incongruity, and the imaginary setting equally corresponds. At the same time, one has the impression of exploring every mode of existence—high, low, urban, rural, married, single, young, old, social, solitary, ancient, modern—in a formal, ordered, almost scientific way.

Because *Rasselas* is a novel-length piece of fiction, some readers make the mistake of judging it as a novel. It is not, and the reader who expects realistic characterization, vivid settings, suspense, or plot probably will be disappointed. Johnson intended none of these things. *Rasselas* is an apologue, a fictional representation of a moral statement. According to Sheldon Sacks, the statement *Rasselas* dramatizes is that "earthly happiness does not exist, but its absence does not result in unbearable misery in this world for the reasonably virtuous who . . . may turn their eyes with hope toward heaven." As an apologue it is made up of formal, fablelike episodes, which are organized for rhetorical effect rather than for fictional probability; all characters, events, and relationships are subordinated to the theme they exemplify. Consequently, there is almost no characterization. Rasselas, like the remaining characters, has only enough plausibility and individuality to make the episodes convincing fictional examples of the apologue's premise but no more. Interest in the characterization of Rasselas himself would divert attention from the central idea which must always dominate and shape the fiction. Thus, the reader never knows the color of his hair, his height, or the tone of his voice. He represents a kind of eighteenth century Everyman in whom, despite the elevation of his language and the artificiality of his circumstances, every reader recognizes himself.

In a famous passage, Imlac explains to Rasselas the business of a poet, and in so doing, also explains the purpose of such generality in Johnson's fiction:

> The business of a poet . . . is to examine, not the individual, but the species; to remark general properties and large appearances: he does not number the streaks of the tulip, or describe the different shades in the verdure of the forest. He is to exhibit . . . such permanent and striking features, as recall the original to every mind. . . .

He must also "consider right and wrong in their abstracted and invariable state; he must disregard present laws and opinions, and rise to general and transcendental truths, which will always be the same. . . ." Johnson believed that such truths shaped existence, and therefore he made them the center of all his fiction. In *Rasselas*, they are given a form which convinces and moves the reader long after such beliefs have gone out of vogue. The central character, then, is not Rasselas or Imlac, but rather the reader himself, who recognizes his own particular experience in the generalized situations of the book and perceives his own life take shape around the truths he finds therein.

OTHER MAJOR WORKS

PLAY: *Irene: A Tragedy*, pr. 1749.

POETRY: *London: A Poem in Imitation of the Third Satire of Juvenal*, 1738; *The Vanity of Human Wishes: The Tenth Satire of Juvenal Imitated*, 1749; *Poems: The Yale Edition of the Works of Samuel Johnson*, 1965 (E. L. McAdam, Jr., and George Milne, editors, volume 6).

NONFICTION: *Marmer Norfolciense*, 1739; *A Compleat Vindication of the Licensers of the Stage*, 1739; *The Life of Admiral Blake*, 1740; *An Account of the Life of Mr. Richard Savage, Son of the Earl Rivers*, 1744; *An Account of the Life of John Philip Barretier*, 1744; *Miscellaneous Observations on the Tragedy of Macbeth*, 1745; *The Plan of a Dictionary of the English Language*, 1747; *A Dictionary of the English Language: To Which Are Prefixed, a History of the Language, and an English Grammar*, 1755; preface and notes to *The Plays of William Shakespeare*, 1765 (8 volumes); *The False Alarm*, 1770; *Thoughts on the Late Transactions Respecting Falkland's Islands*, 1771; *The Patriot: Addressed to the Electors of Great Britain*, 1774; *Taxation No Tyranny: An Answer to the Resolutions and Address of the American Congress*, 1775; *A Journey to the Western Islands of Scotland*, 1775; *Prefaces, Biographical and Critical, to the Works of the English Poets*, 1779-1781 (10 volumes; also known as *The Lives of the Poets); The Critical Opinions of Samuel Johnson*, 1923, 1961 (Joseph Epes Brown, editor).

TRANSLATIONS: *A Voyage to Abyssinia*, 1735 (of Jerome Lobo's novel); *Commentary on Pope's Principles of Morality*, 1739 (of Jean Pierre de Crousaz).

BIBLIOGRAPHY

Bate, Walter Jackson. *The Achievement of Samuel Johnson*. New York: Oxford University Press, 1955. An essential place to begin a general study of the accomplishments, the personal life, and the influence of Johnson. Johnson's achievements in both the literary world and the social world are set in their eighteenth century context. Bate provides enough detail to offer a well-rounded picture of a great scholar who was able to speak convincingly of the human world of pain and weakness as well as to write knowingly of poets and poetic achievement in his era.

Folkenflik, Robert. "*Rasselas* and the Closed Field." *The Huntington Library Quarterly* 57 (Autumn, 1994): 337-352. Claims the satire in *Rasselas* results from the gap between the endlessness of human quest and the closed field of human scope.

Foy, Roslyn Reso. "Johnson's *Rasselas*: Women in the 'Stream of Life.'" *English Language Notes* 32 (September, 1994): 39-53. Examines Johnson's depiction of women in *Rasselas*; argues that the work may be viewed as an equitable portrayal of the potentialities of human beings without making distinctions between the sexes.

Greene, Donald J. *The Politics of Samuel Johnson*. 2d ed. Athens: University of Georgia Press, 1990. Divided into sections on his early years, first books, London career, and the reign of George III. Greene updated the scholarship of the first edition (1960) and included detailed notes and bibliography. Indispensable background reading for the Johnson student, written by one of the great Johnson scholars of the twentieth century.

_____. *Samuel Johnson*. New York: Twayne, 1970. An appreciation of Johnson's literary achievement emphasizing its variety and depth and including commentary on the scholar's contributions to the development of modern journalism. The concept of Johnson as a man of letters, with an emphasis on critical theory and practical criticism, is addressed. Individual works by Johnson are also treated, and bibliographies are included.

Holmes, Richard. *Dr. Johnson and Mr. Savage*. New York: Pantheon, 1993. This distinguished biographer provides a fascinating insight into the origins of Johnson's prose by conducting a keen psychological investigation of Johnson's relationship with the controversial poet Richard Savage. This short book is ideal for the beginning student of Johnson, immersing him in Johnson's period and making Johnson a vivid presence as man and writer. Holmes provides a succinct and very useful bibliography.

Lipking, Lawrence. *Samuel Johnson: The Life of an Author*. Cambridge, Mass.: Harvard University Press, 1998. In Lipking's terms, he is writing a life of an author, not the life of a man—by which he means that he concentrates on the story of how Johnson became a writer and a man of letters. A superb work of scholarship, Lipking's book reveals a sure grasp of previous biographies and should be read, perhaps, after consulting Bate.

Miller, Stephen. "Why Read Samuel Johnson?" *The Sewanee Review* 107 (Winter, 1999): 44-60. Argues that Johnson's work is of more than historical interest; claims his writing reveals a profound understanding of the perplexity of man's passions and that he was a great prose stylist.

Smith, Duane H. "Repetitive Patterns in Samuel Johnson's *Rasselas*." *Studies in English Literature 1500-1900* 36 (Summer, 1996): 623-639. Argues that two aspects of the text, facts and meaning, are complementary rather than contradictory and that Johnson affirms the value of the narrative as entertainment even as he denies its value as a moral tale.

Wimsatt, William K. *The Prose Style of Samuel Johnson*. New Haven, Conn.: Yale University Press, 1941. This standard work continues to shed light on the sentence structure, the Latinate diction, the rhetorical devices, and other elements that identify Johnson's prose style. The study of rhetoric in the eighteenth century provides the background for this careful analysis, but the treatment is quite contemporary in approach. This volume is essential for a newcomer in understanding how Johnson composed—often in his head—his often lengthy and complex sentences in order to achieve a clarity of meaning.

James W. Garvey, updated by
Emma Coburn Norris

JAMES JOYCE

Born: Dublin, Ireland; February 2, 1882
Died: Zurich, Switzerland; January 13, 1941

PRINCIPAL SHORT FICTION
Dubliners, 1914

OTHER LITERARY FORMS

James Joyce's name is synonymous with twentieth century fiction, to a revolution in which he devoted himself with remarkable single-mindedness. The results are to be found in three extremely influential works of fiction—*A Portrait of the Artist as a Young Man* (1914-1915, serial; 1916, book), *Ulysses* (1922), and *Finnegans Wake* (1939). Though his work in other genres is of much less significance, Joyce also wrote two books of poetry, *Chamber Music* (1907) and *Pomes Penyeach* (1927), as well as one play, *Exiles* (pb. 1918). His youthful critical essays, crucial to an understanding of his artistic origins, were collected posthumously and edited by Richard Ellmann and Ellsworth Mason as *The Critical Writings of James Joyce* (1959). The raw material for *A Portrait of the Artist as a Young Man*, edited by Theodore Spencer, was also published posthumously as *Stephen Hero* (1944).

James Joyce (Library of Congress)

ACHIEVEMENTS

James Joyce is acknowledged by many as the twentieth century's greatest prose artist and is also, arguably, that century's most famous author. Despite his small output and the increasing difficulty of his works, Joyce's name stands as a monument to commitment and artistic integrity. Since the end of World War II, there has hardly been a novelist in the West who has not felt Joyce's influence. Continuing interest in his complex mind and work is sustained by a vast array of academic commentators.

The reasons for Joyce's eminence are not hard to find. Each of his works, beginning with the short stories of *Dubliners*, is notable for its startling originality of language and conception. His fiction, moreover, placed his native city, Dublin, indelibly on the map of the world's culture. His life, a continual struggle against ill health, exile, and the almost total neglect of publishers, has come to be perceived as an eloquent expression of self-determination in an age of totalitarian conformity.

BIOGRAPHY

James Augustine Joyce was born on February 2, 1882, the eldest child of John Stanislaus and Mary Jane (May) Murray Joyce. The family was typical of the growing ranks of the Irish Catholic middle class of the day, socially confident, politically optimistic, though less than well established economically. During Joyce's early years, however, the family remained in comfortable circumstances, and at the age of six, Joyce was enrolled in Clongowes Wood College, an elite Jesuit boarding school outside Dublin. After two years at Clongowes, Joyce's education was interrupted because of a decline in family fortunes, the result in large part of John Joyce's improvidence. In 1893, Joyce began to attend Belvedere College, another Jesuit school, in Dublin, where, in addition to undergoing a thorough exposure to the narrow Catholicism of the day, he won a number of academic prizes. In 1898, Joyce entered University College, Dublin, from which he was graduated in 1902.

Throughout the 1890's, the Joyce family continued to experience hard times. Their setbacks had a parallel in the reversal of Ireland's political fortunes during the same period. In 1891, Charles Stewart Parnell, the disgraced leader of the Irish cause, died. This event was the occasion of Joyce's first-known literary work, an accusatory poem directed against the foremost of Parnell's lieutenants, who had turned against him, entitled "Et tu, Healy." The 1890's also saw the rise of a literary and intellectual movement in Ireland. By the time Joyce had begun his undergraduate career, this movement was sufficiently evolved to be criticized, a task that Joyce took upon himself, most notably in a pamphlet entitled "The Day of the Rabblement." While at college, Joyce also distinguished himself by other literary essays, most notably with an article on Henrik Ibsen—an important early influence—which appeared in the prestigious *Fortnightly Review.*

In 1902, Joyce left Ireland for Paris, intending to study medicine in order to secure an income to support his writing. This unsuccessful trip was abruptly curtailed by news of his mother's terminal illness. After her death in 1903, Joyce spent an unproductive year in Dublin, relieved only by writing poems and the initial versions of some of the *Dubliners* stories and by meeting Nora Barnacle, his wife-to-be. With her, he left Ireland in 1904, remaining abroad, with a few brief exceptions, for the rest of his life.

Joyce and his wife began life in Pula, then a backwater in the Austro-Hungarian Empire, later known as the town of Pulj in Yugoslavia. Most of their lives before World War I, however, were spent in Trieste. There, their two children were born, Giorgio in 1905 and Lucia two years later. Joyce earned an uncertain and reluctant living teaching English as a foreign language and worked on the stories of *Dubliners* and *A Portrait of the Artist as a Young Man*. A number of prospective publishers deemed the stories to be too scandalous to issue, and *Dubliners* languished in limbo until 1914.

That year was to prove decisive to Joyce's development as a writer. Through the good offices of the Irish poet William Butler Yeats, the American poet Ezra Pound contacted Joyce and arranged for *A Portrait of the Artist as a Young Man* to be serialized. In that year, also, Joyce started his most celebrated work, *Ulysses*, and moved with his family to Zurich, where they lived for the duration of the war. Briefly returning to Trieste in 1919, the family moved to Paris, where *Ulysses* was published in 1922. Beset by ill health and by the mental illness of his daughter, though immune from financial difficulties through the generosity of a patron, Harriet Shaw Weaver, Joyce remained in Paris working on his opaque masterpiece, *Finnegans Wake*, until World War II obliged him to resettle in Zurich. There, Joyce died of complications arising from perforated ulcers on January 13, 1941.

ANALYSIS

In August, 1904, James Joyce wrote to his friend C. P. Curran: "I am writing a series of epicleti. . . . I call the series *Dubliners* to betray the soul of that hemeplegia or paralysis which many consider a city." This note announces, in effect, a transformation of the short story as a form. The note's pretentious jargon reveals the attitude of the young Joyce's artistic demeanor. In addition, it calls attention to some of the main technical and thematic characteristics of a volume that had to wait a further ten years for a publisher to consider it acceptable.

There is still some scholarly debate over the term "epicleti," whose etymology remains obscure. It is clear, however, that Joyce's use of the term shows him to be in pursuit of an aesthetic method. This self-conscious search for a method reveals Joyce as a preeminently twentieth century modernist author. As with his eminent contemporaries and advocates T. S. Eliot and Pound, to write was to articulate a theory of writing. Moreover, the search was successfully concluded, as the closing chapter of *A Portrait of the Artist as a Young Man* records. It culminated in the "epiphany," which means "showing forth" and which describes not only Joyce's method but also his objectives in using one.

Joyce used the term "epiphany" to describe some of his own early artistic efforts in prose. These sketches sometimes resemble prose poems, calibrating moments of intense perception and emotional heightening. At other times, they take the form of life studies of banal moments in everyday life. The overall intention is one of unmasking hidden states, whether of the exalted or humdrum variety. In both instances, the pieces are marked by a fastidious language, which clearly anticipates the "style of scrupulous meanness" in which Joyce said *Dubliners* is written.

DUBLINERS

Artistic theory is not the only novelty of *Dubliners*. Joyce's note to Curran also draws attention to his subject matter. From a strictly historical point of view, Joyce's characterization of his birthplace is to some extent misleading. The stories of *Dubliners* tend to overlook those factors that distinguished the city in Joyce's time. The impact and significance of the establishment in Dublin of Ireland's national theater, the Abbey, for example, which opened in 1904, may be lost on non-Irish readers of Joyce's stories. In general, Joyce is at pains to belittle the various attempts at cultural self-renewal, which were a marked feature of Dublin life in the early years of the twentieth century, as the satire of the story "A Mother" shows—although in "The Dead" this satirical attitude is significantly modified. Joyce also fails to provide a cross section of the city's social composition, there being no stories featuring the upper echelon. The city was not quite the paraplegic of Joyce's diagnostic imagination.

The stories' emphasis is on what Joyce asserts to be typical of his city. This democratic vision of his brings to the reader's notice a range of marginalized citizens. These include children, the alienated, the helpless and hopeless, and particularly women—*Dubliners* has a feminist undercurrent, all the more noteworthy because of its time. These citizens, often known merely by a single name, represent the social, cultural, and moral cost of living in a city that was less a capital than one of the British Empire's provincial administrative centers. The fact that their humdrum and unpromising lives should be subjected to the artistic and intellectual powers that Joyce possessed is significant on a number of counts. From the standpoint of literary history, *Dubliners* combines the two prevailing literary modes of Joyce's day. In a refinement of an approach pioneered by the great French novelist Gustave Flaubert, Joyce subjects material that had hitherto been the artistic property of the naturalists to the aesthetic commitments of the Symbolists. One way of describing the function of the epiphany is to note its author's organization of commonplaces in such a manner that they ultimately yield possibilities of meaning greater than their culturally preconditioned, or factual, appearances admit.

From the point of view of Irish literary history, the stories of *Dubliners* eloquently, though untypically, participate in the overall effort of the Irish Literary Revival to address national realities. The careful delineation of lost lives, which characterizes most of *Dubliners*, is a unique contribution to the spirit of the critique, which informs much of the stories' Irish cultural context. It is not surprising to learn that they were considered too controversial to publish with impunity, or that, by virtue of being so, they confirmed their author's belief that they constituted "a chapter in the moral history of my country."

A further notable feature of the book is that, unlike many collections of short stories, particularly those of that period, *Dubliners* is a collection of stories that, however limited in range, is disparate while at the same time functioning as a coherent whole. Its coherence is not merely a matter of Joycean cunning, whereby the collection's opening story is entitled "The Sisters" and centers on a death, while the final story is called "The Dead" and takes place at a party hosted by sisters. The history of the book's composition, to which must be added a recognition of the complications brought about by publishers' lack of commitment, precludes any such facile observation, since "The Dead" was conceived and written after Joyce's initial version of *Dubliners* had been completed and submitted for publication. Two other stories were added to the original dozen, "Two Gallants" and "A Little Cloud." Rather more subtly, the collection achieves coherence by numerous overlapping means. These include the integrity of its style, its thematic consistency, the largely uniform character of its *dramatis personae*, and its use of a major device in the overall scheme of Joyce's aesthetic, repetition and variation.

In addition, Joyce himself had an integrated vision of the work's coherence, one whereby the whole would be seen to be greater than the sum of the parts. This view holds good particularly when applied to the twelve stories of the initial *Dubliners*, where it describes a mode of symmetrical organization as well as a principle of thematic development, so that a case can readily be made for the work as a whole comprising a "moral history." According to Joyce, *Dubliners* may be divided into four consecutive sections. The first of these consists of the three opening stories, "The Sisters," "An Encounter," and "Araby." These are followed by a sequence of stories dealing with adolescence, "The Boarding House," "After the Race," and "Eveline." Three stories of mature life come next, "Clay," "Counterparts," and "A Painful Case." Finally the volume closes with a trio of stories devoted to public life, "Ivy Day in the Committee Room," "A Mother," and "Grace."

While the symmetry of this quartet of trios is disrupted by the introduction of further stories, two of the new additions, both written in 1906, enlarge rather than negate their respective categories. The range of the stories of adolescence is considerably broadened by the addition of "Two Gallants." Similarly, the motifs of entrapment and disillusion, typical of the stories of mature life, are further adumbrated in the history of Chandler, the protagonist of "A Little Cloud." In "The Dead," written in 1907, Joyce's artistry as a writer of short fiction is seen to best advantage. In addition, this story crystallizes and elevates to a higher plane of intellection and feeling many of the themes of *Dubliners*, the result being what is generally acknowledged to be one of the finest short stories in the English language.

The titles of the stories of *Dubliners* offer a clue to the nature of their contents. Such titles as "An Encounter," "A Painful Case," "Counterparts," "A Mother," and "The Dead"—to take some of the most obvious cases in point—seem deliberately to offer little or nothing to the reader, neither a sense of expectation nor a sense of anything particularly distinctive within the material, even though Joyce insisted to his publishers that presenting his fellow citizens to the world at large had undoubted novelty value. Yet the very anonymity of many of the titles points with precision to both their character and their method. The stories' protagonists are for the most part colorless, unpromising, defeated, and lacking in interiority. For the most part, they are unaware of these facts about their personalities and conditions, and the stories evolve somewhat remorselessly to a point where these hapless characters are on the threshold of recognizing, or deliberately overlooking, their morally abject lives. The fact, therefore, that the stories' titles frequently evoke generic types or states is a pointer to one of their prominent attributes. The stories that do not conform to this general rule have titles that are extremely localized and opaque in a different sense. Few readers will know automatically that the ivy day referred to in "Ivy Day in the Committee Room" refers to the custom of commemorating the Irish political leader Charles Stewart Parnell, or that "Araby," in addition to its generic connotations, refers to an actual bazaar that was held in Dublin in mid-May, 1894. This obscure fact makes the story's protagonist the same age as Joyce was when the bazaar was held.

The sense of comparative anonymity and insignificance suggested by the titles is replicated in the case of the protagonists, a large number of whom are either anonymous or known by a single name, as though they had not yet succeeded in attaining the measure of identity required to merit being fully named. The very title *Dubliners* is clearly generic, and Joyce, approaching his material from such a standpoint, reveals his interest in the typical, the representative, and the norm. In this sense, Joyce shows his deep sense of the short-story form, with its traditional emphasis on the delineation of representative characters in representative contexts. Such an interest is amplified with great deftness and versatility in the language of the stories, which frequently draws on official, generic codes of utterance. Gabriel's speech on hospitality in "The Dead" is an important example of one such code, particularly when contrasted with the highly wrought meditation that closes the story. The sermon that concludes "Grace" is another, despite being rendered in the narrative mode known as free indirect style for satirical purposes. A third example is the mimicry of the newspaper report of police evidence in "A Painful Case." The collection as a whole is saturated by formal and informal exploitation of the characters' various modes of utterance from which a sense of their cultural orientation and impoverishment may be extrapolated.

As with all Joyce's works, the latently satirical manipulation of cliché is a crucial feature of *Dubliners*. In addition, by virtue of the author's uncanny ear not merely for the demotic but for the quality of consciousness that such utterances reveal, the stories possess a convincing patina of objectivity, as though it is the restless but unobtrusive activity of their language that produces their effects, rather than anything as unrefined as the author's direction and intentions. Thus, the doctrine of the artist's impersonality, which has numerous important implications for modernist aesthetics and which Joyce, possibly following the example of Gustave Flaubert, invokes in *A Portrait of the Artist as a Young Man*, is utilized in *Dubliners* to telling effect.

It is in the matter of the stories' presumed objectivity that *Dubliners* fell foul of the publishing industry of the day. Joyce freely availed himself of the civic furniture of his native city, including by name actual business premises—pubs and hotels, notably—as well as churches and other well-known amenities and distinctive features of the social life of his birthplace. By so doing, he not only went further in his pursuit of documentary verisimilitude than the vast majority of even naturalistic writers of Joyce's generation but also revealed a conception of language—or of what happens to language once it is written—which, in its mature development in *Ulysses* and *Finnegans Wake*, provided a complex, integrated code of cultural semiotics. Joyce's use of place-names, the names of businesses, and most notoriously the names of English royalty, shows his understanding that a name is a word, not a supposedly photographic facsimile of the entity it denotes. *Dubliners* is replete with names chosen with a sensitivity to their artistic and cultural resonance as well as to their geographical precision. For example, the North Wall, Eveline's terminus in the story that bears her name, is both correct in a documentary sense and thematically appropriate. A subtler instance is Mr. Duffy's residence at Chapelizod, a short distance outside Dublin. Not only does the choice of residence underline Duffy's standoffish nature, but also the name of where he lives is a corruption of Chapel Iseult. This name invokes the legend of the lovers Tristan and Iseult, of whose tragic love Duffy's affair is a banal but nevertheless heartfelt shadow. Use of the legend is an anticipation of the method in *Ulysses*, where the heroic stuff of epic forms an ironic but by no means belittling counterpoint to the trial of twentieth century human beings.

Neither of Joyce's English and Irish publishers was very interested in the long-term consequences or subtle immediacies of Joyce's art. Both feared that his use of actual names would lead them into serious legal difficulties, which would be compounded by what was considered a use of blasphemous language and an impersonation of the thoughts of Edward, Prince of Wales, in "Ivy Day in the Committee Room," Joyce's favorite story in the collection. Joyce, against his better judgment, toned down the impersonation and made a number of other minor adjustments, while basically upholding his right of documentary representation in the service of artistic integrity and objectivity.

The most conclusive evidence for the stories' objectivity, however, is provided by their use of the epiphany. Much critical ink has been consumed in attempting to explicate this device. Undoubtedly it is a key concept not only in the appreciation of the art of Joyce's short stories but also in the comprehension of the form's development under the influence of *Dubliners*. At the same time, the reader who does not possess a firm grasp of the concept may still read *Dubliners* with satisfaction, insight, and sympathy. The epiphany makes its presence felt, typically, at the conclusion of a *Dubliners* story. It is here that the reader is likely to experience a certain amount of distancing from the action, which cannot be accounted for merely by the foreignness of the characters and their locale. These, in themselves, do not inhibit either the forward movement of the narrative or that movement's potential for significance. At the point when that potential might well be expected to be realized, however, it may strike the reader as being deferred or repressed.

This discovery is intended to alert the reader that the narrative technique of a *Dubliners* story only superficially conforms to the introduction-development-denouement model of story organization. Early critics of the work, indeed, complained that for the most part, through their lack of dramatic issue or intriguing theme, the stories were no more than sketches, not seeing that what Joyce was interested in was as much manner as matter, and that only a minimalist approach of the kind he used would grace with art the marginal conditions of his characters and articulate, in a mode that did not violate the impoverished spirit of his paralyzed raw material, its worthiness and the value of bringing it to the reader's attention. Concern for the reader's attention is therefore critical, since so much of what Joyce was writing about had already been effectively written off socially, culturally, politically, and spiritually. The comprehensive nature of this silencing is spelled out in the collection's opening story, "The Sisters."

The strain placed on the reader's attention by the typical conclusion of the stories is Joyce's method of expressing his concern that the material's impact not be diminished by meeting the preconditioned expectations of how its conflicts might be resolved. Rather than have the story reach a conclusion, with its connotations of finality and mastery, Joyce ends the story, breaks off the action before all its implications and ramifications have been extrapolated. He thereby extends to the reader an invitation, which may also be a duty, to draw out the inferences of this act of narrative termination. The development of inferences is the means whereby the story achieves the statement of itself, an achievement that describes the epiphany in action.

In order to participate in the activity of revelation that the term "epiphany" connotes, the reader will note that not only does a *Dubliners* story conventionally, if loosely, observe the Aristotelian unities of time, place, and action, but also that unity is achieved by the tissue of correspondences, insinuations, nuances, echoes, and general interplay that exists among the various phases of a given story's action and the language. The introduction of the train at the end of "A Painful Case" is an obvious example of Joyce's cunning and tacit strategies. One of the outcomes of these effects is to offset any purely deterministic sense of plot. The compulsiveness and irreversibility of action, on a sense of which plot tends to be based, is offset, modified, or at the very least has its crudely dramatic character diminished by Joyce's effects. As a result, the reader is placed in a position of assembling what the story's fabric of data signifies. It is the reader, typically, rather than the protagonist, who recognizes the epiphanic moment, the moment at which the tendencies of the action become undeniably clear. At this moment, the reader attains the point of maximum perspective. It is a moment of closure but of reinvestment, of withdrawal and of sympathy, of estrangement and acceptance. Its result is to make the reader morally complicit with the material, since were it not for the epiphany's appeal to the reader the material's significance, or rather its ability to signify, would be moot. The empowered reader becomes the type of citizen whom the representative protagonist of a *Dubliners* story cannot be. The stories represent a mastery over material and circumstances with which the reader is called upon to identify, but which the characters cannot embody.

While it is possible to consider the stories of *Dubliners* from many different artistic, cultural, and moral perspectives, the theme of independence or the lack of it is the one that seems most central to Joyce's concerns. His preoccupation with the paralyzed condition of his native city may be described as an awareness of how little the spirit of independence moved there. The numerous implications of this lack are addressed in story after story. The typical trajectory of the story is the optimistic going out, the counterpart of which is the disillusioned return. In even such a simple story as "An Encounter," the youngster's naïve dream of adventure and access to the adult world is both realized and made unrecognizable and unacceptable by the form it takes. Encounters with worldly others, such as the flirtatious couples at the bazaar at the end of "Araby," or Frank in "Eveline," the sophisticated foreigners in "After the Race," or Ignatius Gallaher in "A Little Cloud," all leave the protagonists reduced and defeated. The world is a more complex and demanding environment than their dreams of fulfillment might have led them to believe. The self withdraws, pained that the world is not a reflection of its needs. As in "Two Gallants," when the world can be manipulated to serve the ego, the process is crude, exploitative, and morally despicable.

Some of the most far-reaching implications of the independence theme may be seen in "Ivy Day in the Committee Room." There, the heirs of a dramatically successful political movement for a constitutional form of Irish independence are depicted as bemused, opportunistic, devoted to rhetoric rather than action, stagnant in thought and deed. Their conspicuous lack of will is matched by their inconsistency of thought. Yet, while satire is a pronounced feature of the story, Joyce also makes clear that the characters cannot be merely scorned. The poem that affects them is certainly not a fine piece of writing, as the story's closing comment would have readers believe. On the contrary, it is a heartfelt performance, genuine in its feeling and authentic in its response. The negative elements of these characters' lives and the bleak outlook for the productive commissioning of their human potential become, in Joyce's view, as compelling a set of realities as the triumph of the will or worldly fulfillment.

"THE DEAD"

This view receives its most comprehensive expression in "The Dead," making the story, for that reason alone, the crowning achievement of *Dubliners*. From the playful malapropism of its opening sentence to its resonant closing periods, this story provides, in scale, thematic variety, psychological interest, and narrative tempo, a complete and enriched survey of Joyce's artistic and moral commitments at the close of the first phase of his writing career. Whereas previously, the collection's stories were representations of a quality, or poverty, of consciousness to which the characters were unable to relate, in "The Dead" Gabriel achieves an awareness of his particular consciousness. The moment of recognition, the epiphany, in which Gabriel realizes what his wife's story of lost love says about his own emotional adequacy, is not an experience whose meaning the reader infers. It is a meaning whose articulation by Gabriel the reader overhears. Unlike many of the other stories, however, "The Dead" does not end on this note of recognition. Gabriel, for all that "The Dead" has shown him having difficulty in being self-possessed and autonomous, acknowledges the force and significance of Gretta's revelation. He relates to those limitations in himself, which the story of Michael Furey underlines. In doing so, he attains a degree of sympathy, honesty, and freely chosen solidarity with the finite, mortal nature of human reality, his mind enlarging as its sense of defeat becomes a central and constraining fact of life. The balance achieved in "The Dead" between subjective need and objective fact, between romance and reality, between self-deception and self-awareness gives the story its poise and potency and makes it a persuasive recapitulation of the other *Dubliners* stories' concerns.

It is by the conclusive means of "The Dead" that Joyce's *Dubliners* identifies itself with the critique of humanism, which was a fundamental component of the revolution in the arts at the beginning of the twentieth century. The invisibility of the author's personality, the tonal and stylistic restraint with which the stories are told, and the aesthetic subtlety of the epiphany add up to rather more than simply a revolution in short fiction. They also, by their nature, draw attention to the force of the negative as a reality in the lives of the characters, a reality that Joyce, by refusing to overlook it, helped place on the agenda of twentieth century consciousness.

OTHER MAJOR WORKS

LONG FICTION: *A Portrait of the Artist as a Young Man*, 1914-1915 (serial), 1916 (book); *Ulysses*, 1922; *Finnegans Wake*, 1939; *Stephen Hero*, 1944 (edited by Theodore Spencer).

PLAY: *Exiles*, pb. 1918.

POETRY: *Chamber Music*, 1907; *Pomes Penyeach*, 1927.

nonfiction: *The Critical Writings of James Joyce*, 1959; *Letters*, 1957-1966 (3 volumes); *Selected Letters of James Joyce*, 1975 (Richard Ellmann, editor); *The James Joyce Archives*, 1977-1979 (64 volumes).

BIBLIOGRAPHY

Beck, Warren. *Joyce's "Dubliners": Substance, Vision, Art.* Durham, N.C.: Duke University Press, 1969. An extremely comprehensive study of *Dubliners*. After a lengthy introduction, each of Joyce's stories is examined in turn. The author's approach is essentially that of the New Critics. The texts are combed thoroughly for their verbal possibilities, resulting in both exhaustive and dutiful readings.

Benstock, Bernard. *Narrative Con/Texts in "Dubliners."* Urbana: University of Illinois Press, 1994. Includes analyses of narrative principles, symbolic systems, theological contexts, and a variety of themes and techniques in *Dubliners*.

Bosinelli, Rosa M. Bollettieri, and Harold F. Mosher, Jr., eds. *ReJoycing: New Readings of "Dubliners."* Lexington: The University Press of Kentucky, 1998. Fourteen new essays on *Dubliners* that argue Joyce questioned literary, cultural, and political developments of his time. The essays examine themes, style, intertexuality, politics, linguistics, and gender conflicts in Joyce's stories.

Brunsdale, Mitzi M. *James Joyce: A Study of the Short Fiction.* New York: Twayne, 1993. A general introduction to Joyce's stories, focusing on the five most familiar stories from *Dubliners*. Also includes excerpts from Joyce's own nonfiction criticism and from other critics.

Cheng, Vincent J. *Joyce, Race, and Empire*. Cambridge, England: Cambridge University Press, 1995. A study of race and imperialism, ethnicity and political power, in Joyce's works. Argues that the religious, patriarchal, and racist metaphors in *Dubliners* represent Ireland's colonial relationship with England. Discusses stories as dramatizations of how the colonized yearn to replicate the colonizers; scolds Gabriel in "The Dead" for his patriarchal alliance with the British.

Ellmann, Richard. *James Joyce*. 1959. 2d ed. New York: Oxford University Press, 1984. The definitive biography, generally regarded as the last word on its subject's life and widely considered as the greatest literary biography of the twentieth century. Copiously annotated and well illustrated, particularly in the 1984 edition. Contains a considerable amount of informative background on the characters of *Dubliners* and their contexts. Of particular interest is the chapter entitled "The Backgrounds of 'The Dead.'"

Fargnoli, Nicholas, and Michael P. Gillespie. *James Joyce A to Z: The Essential Reference to the Life and Work*. New York: Oxford University Press, 1995. A dictionary-type reference book with approximately eight hundred entries on characters, concepts, locales, terminology, and critics of Joyce.

Hart, Clive, ed. *James Joyce's "Dubliners": Critical Essays*. New York: Viking, 1969. Arguably the single most helpful full-length work on *Dubliners*. It consists of essays on each of the stories, each by a different author. The authors are frequently well-known Joyce scholars, such as A. Walton Litz and the editor. Inevitably, the manner of critical approach in the case of a number of the essays is somewhat outdated.

Leonard, Garry M. *Reading "Dubliners" Again: A Lacanian Perspective*. Syracuse, N.Y.: Syracuse University Press, 1993. Using Lacan's Freudian approach to language's role in creating our experience of reality, Leonard examines the stories in *Dubliners*, urging readers to explore their kinship with the moral paralysis of the characters.

Schwarz, Daniel R., ed. *"The Dead" by James Joyce*. New York: St. Martin's Press, 1994. A casebook of essays on "The Dead," from such critical perspectives as reader-response theory, new historicism, feminism, deconstruction, and psychoanalysis.

Studies in Short Fiction 32 (Summer, 1995). A collection of sixteen new essays on *Dubliners*, along with eleven reviews of new books on Joyce. Includes general essays on techniques and themes of *Dubliners* as well as analyses of "Araby," "The Sisters," "Grace," "The Dead," and discussions comparing Joyce's stories with those of William Trevor and Edna O'Brien.

George O'Brien

K

FRANZ KAFKA

Born: Prague, Czechoslovakia; July 3, 1883
Died: Kierling, Klosterneuburg, near Vienna, Austria; June 3, 1924

Principal short fiction

Betrachtung, 1913 (*Meditation*, 1948)
Das Urteil, 1913, 1916 (*The Sentence*, 1928; also as *The Judgment*, 1945)
Die Verwandlung, 1915 (novella; *The Metamorphosis*, 1936)
Ein Landarzt: Kleine Erzählungen, 1919 (*The Country Doctor: A Collection of Fourteen Short Stories*, 1945)
Ein Hungerkünstler: Vier Geschichten, 1924 (*A Hunger Artist*, 1948)
Beim Bau der Chinesischen Mauer: Ungedruckte Erzählungen und Prosa aus dem Nachlass, 1931 (*The Great Wall of China and Other Pieces*, 1933)
Erzählungen, 1946 (*The Complete Stories*, 1971)
The Penal Colony: Stories and Short Pieces, 1948
Selected Short Stories, 1952

Other literary forms

Franz Kafka did not attempt to write drama or poetry. His métier was prose. He was a perfectionist who apparently intended only a portion of what he had written for publication. The three novels and several more volumes of short stories were prepared for publication posthumously by the executor of his literary estate, Max Brod.

Kafka also wrote voluminously in other categories of prose that bear the same distinctive style as his creative work. His diaries and letters contain many comments that aid in the understanding of his stories, and his meticulous legal reports are exemplary professional documents.

Achievements

Every year, more secondary literature is published about Franz Kafka than about almost any other author except William Shakespeare. This attests the extraordinary power and alluringly enigmatic content of his works. While his inimitable prose style describes everything as if it were self-evident, he invariably introduces elements of the fantastic and surreal and portrays the demise of his characters as inevitable. His works are imbued with a sense of horror as isolated characters struggle futilely against malign forces that they do not understand.

Kafka unintentionally became the voice of the age. Coming after the philosophers Martin Heidegger and Edmund Husserl, and being contemporary with the founder of psychoanalysis, Sigmund Freud, he captured the existential angst of the generation. As a result of the Industrial Revolution, the father no longer worked from the home but dominated the family from a distance. The figure of authority was a stranger.

Biography

Franz Kafka's literary achievements are all the more remarkable when one considers that he lived to be only forty, was increasingly ill with tuberculosis during the last seven years of his life, and up until two years before his death held a full-time position as a lawyer.

While his lifestyle was in keeping with that of his mother's bachelor brothers, one of whom was a country doctor, Kafka and his father were very different in personality. The efforts of the robust, self-confident, and sometimes abusive businessman to rear a frail, insecure, and sensitive son led to a constant state of friction between the two. Unlike his younger sisters, who married and established families of their own,

Kafka lived mainly with his parents, attempting always to relate to the father who could not understand him.

Kafka's parents had a strong marriage but did not have much time for their children, who were cared for by household help. During the day, the parents worked together in their store. In the evening, the two of them played cards. Kafka did well in school, contrary to his fears, and received a good education, especially in Latin, from dedicated teachers.

In 1901, Kafka entered the German University in Prague and obtained his doctorate in law in 1906. He resigned from his first position, stating as his reason that he was upset by the cursing and swearing, even though it had not been directed at him. Through the intercession of a friend, he then obtained a position with the Workers' Accident Insurance Institute and remained with the firm from 1908 to 1922, when his declining health necessitated an early retirement. His work was appreciated, and he received many benefits from the firm.

Kafka was never without friends, and he had a good sense of humor—something that could be emphasized more in the interpretation of his works. He liked to read his stories aloud and sometimes broke down in uncontrollable laughter over the plots that he had invented. Marriage was something that Kafka both desired and feared. He was engaged twice to Felice Bauer, a woman who lived in another city. He had met her briefly through a friend and soon afterward initiated an epistolary relationship. This became a pattern that he repeated with two other women, always being reluctant to be with them in person. Only in the last year of his life did he overcome his inhibitions enough to live for a few months with a woman half his age, Dora Dymant.

Dymant did not realize the value of Kafka's literary works and at his request burned many manuscripts. Kafka also stipulated in his will that his friend and executor, the author Max Brod, was to burn everything not published during Kafka's lifetime. It was an ambivalent request, because Brod had said he would never do so.

Although Jewish, Kafka was relatively unaffected by anti-Semitism. The gravestone for him and his

Franz Kafka (Archive Photos)

parents is in the Strasnice Cemetery in Prague. His three sisters were later killed in concentration camps.

ANALYSIS

Franz Kafka's stories are not about love or success. They do not leave the reader feeling comfortable. Writing was, for him, a necessity. On August 6, 1914, Kafka wrote in his diary: "My talent for portraying my dreamlike inner life has thrust all other matters into the background; my life has dwindled dreadfully, nor will it cease to dwindle. Nothing else will ever satisfy me." The meaning of the images from his dreamlike inner life was not always clear to him at the time of writing. Sometimes he realized only several years later what he may have subconsciously meant. Toward the end of his life, he decided that psychoanalysis was a waste of time and abandoned that approach in retrospective reading. Critics may not be of the same opinion.

"THE JUDGMENT"

Kafka wrote "Das Urteil" ("The Judgment") in one sitting through the night of September 22-23, 1912. It was an eminently satisfying experience, the only one of his works that he said came out of him like a birth. When he sat down to write, he had intended to depict a war scene. Then, the story took its own direction, and when he finished, early in the morning, he was not sure what it meant. He knew only that it was good.

In the course of "The Judgment," the main character, Georg Bendemann, experiences a complete reversal in his plans. At the outset, he announces his engagement to Frieda Brandenfeld. At the end, he commits suicide. The transition from good news to bad and the descent from normalcy into apparent madness are subtly accomplished. With hindsight, one can see that warning signs are held up all the way. Yet none of these signs is in itself shocking enough to alienate the reader. Only their cumulative effect is overwhelming. Kafka's stories wield their powerful influence over the reader's mood by always remaining plausible. While never losing the semblance of logical reportage, Kafka creates scenes of horror, which both spring from and give rise to psychological suffering. Anything resembling such scenes has come to be called "Kafkaesque."

Kafka writes metaphorically, letting characters, actions, and objects represent emotional and psychological states. Thus, the works are understood best not as narrative advancing a plot but in terms of the protagonist's attempts to transcend absurdity, depersonalization, and alienation. There is a strong autobiographical element in all the stories.

Most critics equate Georg Bendemann with Kafka, and Georg's father with Kafka's father. The issue to be dealt with, then, is why the father would violently oppose the son's engagement to a woman from a well-to-do family. To accept that, one has to subscribe to an inverse standard. Kate Flores interprets this aspect of "The Judgment" in an anthropological way, explaining that for precivilized man it was an act of insubordination to supplant the dominant male. Certainly, "The Judgment" does contain elements of a primal struggle. Also consistent with

this reading is the father's tenacious hold on Georg's watch chain, as if to halt the inexorable advance of time and the aging process. There is also the fact that Kafka's father did indeed deride one of his engagements, although at a much later date than when "The Judgment" was written.

Kafka's stories support many interpretations. It is important, when reading "The Judgment," that one not concentrate on the apparent polarity of father and son to the exclusion of the curious figure of the friend in Russia, to whom the first third of the story is devoted. In fact, preposterous though it may seem, the most comprehensive reading results from considering all three male figures—the friend in Russia, Georg Bendemann, and his father—to be different aspects of the same person, namely Kafka. It is significant that only one name is provided.

The friend in Russia immediately becomes associated with writing, because Georg has been writing to him for years. This association is reinforced when the father, surprisingly, also claims to have been writing to the friend. After Georg has brought up the matter of an engagement on three separate occasions, the friend in Russia responds by showing some interest, but as with his emotionless reaction to the death of Georg's mother, the friend's interest in human affairs seems perfunctory. He has few social contacts, has let his business slide, and seems to be in a general state of ill health and decline. His life has dwindled dreadfully. This identifies him with Kafka the writer.

Georg Bendemann's business seems to have been operating in inverse proportions to that of his friend in Russia. It is thriving, and he has recently become engaged. The thriving business and the engagement go hand in hand in "The Judgment." Both are traditionally recognized outward signs of success. Kafka, at the time of writing "The Judgment," was already a successful lawyer, well established in his firm and becoming interested in Felice Bauer, who seems to be represented in the story by her close namesake, Frieda Brandenfeld. Frieda makes a remark to Georg that, on the surface, is very puzzling. She tells him that since he has friends such as the one in Russia, he should never have gotten engaged. This is the warning sign that either Frieda or the friend in Russia will have to go. The application to Kafka's life seems clear: Either Felice or the writing will have to go.

The most interesting and complex of the three male figures is the father. While appearing to oppose Georg, the older man can, in this case, actually be relied on to say what Georg wants to hear. Faced with the irreconcilable conflict between loyalty to his longtime friend in Russia and loyalty to his new fiancé, Georg finds himself inexplicably going to his father's room, where he has not been for some time. The sunlight is blocked by a wall, the father is surrounded by ancient newspapers, and the window is shut. It is a trip into the dark and the past, which is sealed off from the outside world. The father represents the subconscious. He is also the progenitor, and he is still, despite some deceptive signs of senility, the figure of authority.

The father's first remark, which points beyond the frame of the surface story, is his question of whether Georg really has a friend in St. Petersburg. What the father really seems to be asking is whether the friend can continue to be called a friend when he has been so neglected. Georg at this point is still inclined to decide in favor of Frieda and an outwardly successful life, so he endeavors to quell the troubling reference to his friend by carrying his father from the dark out into the light and then covering him up, thereby forcibly suppressing the question of the friend.

Contrary to Georg's intent, this results in the father's exploding into action. In an extraordinarily dramatic scene, he hurls off the blankets, leaps to his feet, and, standing upright on the bed and kicking, denounces Georg's plans for marriage and accuses him of playing the false friend all these years. Georg realizes that he should be on his guard against attack but then forgets again and stands defenseless before his father.

The father's second remark that seems rather incredible in terms of the surface story is that the friend in Russia has not been betrayed after all, because he, the father, has also been writing to him all along and representing him. Suppressed talents are only strengthened in the subconscious. The father now unquestionably has the upper hand and pronounces his judgment over Georg: He was an innocent child, but

he has been a devilish human being. Presumably, it was during childhood that Georg cultivated the friend now in Russia. As an adult, getting ever more into business and thoughts of marriage, Georg has been devilish by denying his true self, the writer. The father finishes by sentencing Georg to death by drowning. To drown is to be plunged into the creative element.

Georg confirms the validity of his father's verdict by carrying out the sentence. It is important for the reader to remember that as the father crashes on the bed exhausted, the subconscious having asserted itself, and as Georg lets himself fall from the bridge, effectively ending the business career and the engagement, it is the formerly faded and foreign true self, the writer, who remains. Thus, what seems on first reading to be a horror story of insanity and suicide is actually not a disaster at all but an exercise in self-preservation. No sooner had Kafka become romantically involved with Felice than he had worked out subconsciously how detrimental such a relationship would be to his career as a writer. With such personal material, it is no wonder the writer in Kafka felt inspired to finish "The Judgment" in one sitting. Ironically, his conscious mind was at that point still so far behind the insights of the subconscious that he dedicated the story to none other than Felice Bauer.

The subtitle of Heinz Politzer's book on Kafka, *Parable and Paradox*, evokes the elusive nature of Kafka's story lines, which are charged with opposing forces seeking synthesis. Although most of the stories are grim, the reader cannot help but be amused at the outrageous, at times burlesque turns of events. Only the bleak and disquieting desperation of the characters contradicts the humor inherent in their situations. Also, many of the stories end with the main character dead or reduced to a state of utter hopelessness. Many of the longer stories, such as "The Judgment," are so complex that they can be confusing. Kafka's shorter stories, consisting of only a paragraph or a page or two, sometimes leave a more lasting impression, because they each center on one main event.

"GIVE IT UP!"
Politzer begins his study with a lengthy discussion of a 124-word commentary that Kafka wrote late in 1922. In the commentary, which has become known

as "Give It Up!," a traveler heading for the train station early one morning becomes disconcerted when he checks his watch against a clock tower and thinks that he must be late. In his haste, he becomes uncertain of the way and has to ask a police officer. The officer repeats the question, then tells the man to give up and turns away from him. The police officer's reply is both hilarious and profoundly unsettling. It is hilarious because it is completely out of line with what a police officer would say. It is unsettling because it lifts the story out of the mundane into a world where not only time but also, apparently, place have lost their relevance and it is impossible to determine one's way. The issue has become existential.

"BEFORE THE LAW"

Kafka innately distrusted figures of authority and frequently portrayed them maliciously misleading and abusing those who came under their power. The 1922 commentary is simply a lighter variation on the theme that Kafka stated unforgettably in 1914 in his parable "Vor dem Gesetz" ("Before the Law"). This moving and perfect piece of writing was later incorporated into chapter 19 of Kafka's novel *Der Prozess* (1925; *The Trial*, 1937).

In the two-page parable, a man from the country seeks access to the law. He is told by the doorkeeper that he may not enter at the moment but possibly later. The man is deterred from entering without permission by the doorkeeper's telling him that this is only the first of many doors that are guarded by increasingly powerful doorkeepers. The man spends the rest of his life there waiting for admittance and gives away everything he owns in unsuccessful attempts to bribe the doorkeeper. Finally, in his dying hour, he asks why no one else has come to that door, only to hear the doorkeeper say: "This door was intended only for you. I am now going to shut it."

The parable is not enlightening. By the time the man finds out that he should go through the door after all, it is shut in his face. The story seems, rather, to be a comment on the human condition as Kafka experienced it in early twentieth century Europe. The rise of science and industry had displaced but could not replace religion, with the result that human beings could no longer find their way. The human institu-

tions, the apparent absolutes represented by the law, prove to be fallible, imperfect, and unreliable. Nothing now can fill the human need for direction in life. Reality has become fragmented and disjunctive. "Before the Law" is particularly poignant because the reader cannot help but believe that, before the law, human beings are all people from the country, simple, helpless creatures who have lost their way.

"THE BUCKET RIDER"

The way out of this impossible situation is brilliantly described with humor and sadness in Kafka's three-page story "Der Kübelreiter" ("The Bucket Rider"), written during a coal shortage in the winter of 1916. The main character has no coal, and it is bitterly cold. He also has no money but goes to the coal dealer anyway, to ask for only a shovelful. To show how desperate he is, he rides there on his empty coal bucket, sailing through the air and calling down from high above the dealer's house. The dealer is deeply moved by the voice of an old customer, but it is his wife who goes to the street to investigate. Once she finds that the bucket rider cannot pay immediately, she claims to see no one and waves him away with her apron. The bucket is too light to offer any resistance. The rider ascends "into the regions of the ice mountains" and is "lost for ever."

This story contains the delightful, dreamlike element of the fantastic that is a source of great beauty in Kafka's works. The moment the main character decides to ride on his bucket, which occurs at the beginning of the second paragraph, he is lifted out of everyday reality, in which he would surely have frozen to death. Kafka shows, once again, that it is useless to plead with others, especially those who have some authority. Rather than send his main character on an empty bucket back to his freezing room, Kafka has the bucket whisk him away into the ice mountains, never to return. Coal and indeed all mundane concerns cease to be a problem as the bucket rider leaves behind the human habitat. Thwarted by everyday pettiness, he has moved instead into a timeless mental space that seems infinitely more interesting. In "The Bucket Rider," Kafka represents that space with the image of distant ice mountains. In his fifty-second aphorism, he writes a literal description of that saving space: "There is only a spiritual world; what we call the physical world is the evil in the spiritual one, and what we call evil is only a necessary moment in our endless development." The bucket rider has transcended the evil phase.

"A COUNTRY DOCTOR"

The winter of 1916 was one of Kafka's most prolific periods and one in which he seemed especially visually oriented and inclined toward the fantastic. His seven-page masterpiece "Ein Landarzt" ("A Country Doctor") is one of his most involved works. It contains all Kafka's main themes and the salient features of his style.

As in "The Bucket Rider," the setting of "A Country Doctor" is an icy winter, and the mood is one of confused, melancholy desperation. The situation is hopeless, and the doctor sees no way out of it. Unlike "The Bucket Rider," which has only one main event, "A Country Doctor" is a richly textured work. The most rewarding interpretive approach is that employed here in examining "The Judgment." There are three main male characters: the country doctor, the groom, and the sick boy. They seem to represent different aspects of the same person, and the story, once again, seems to be autobiographical.

The country doctor is an older man who has been working for a long time in his profession, and he is disillusioned. The local people, while placing many demands on him, do nothing to help him. Not one of the neighbors would lend him a horse in an emergency. In keeping with the spirit of the age, the people have lost their faith in religion and look instead to science and medicine to perform the miracles, backing up the doctor's efforts with choral chanting as if he were a medicine man. He is the only one sadly aware of the limitations of his profession but plays out the charade in a resigned fashion, eventually lying outright to the boy by minimizing the severity of his fatal wound.

Kafka was a professional as well, a lawyer who in 1916 had already worked nine years after articling. Although he was a dedicated and valued member of his firm, he regarded his work as a necessary evil, as his means of earning a living so that he could write in his spare time. He was not disillusioned with law, but neither did he harbor any cherished illusions about his distinguished profession. He believed that, as it did to the man from the country in "Before the Law," law was wearing him out. Readers will equate the country doctor with Kafka the lawyer.

In order of appearance, the second male character in "A Country Doctor" is the groom. That he belongs to the country doctor or is part of him is evidenced by the servant girl's remark, "You never know what you're going to find in your own house." Certainly, the groom represents a source not tapped in a long time—so long, in fact, that the country doctor is surprised when the man emerges from the abandoned pigsty. By association with the steaming horses, by the birthlike nature of their emergence, and by his rape of Rose, the groom stands for vitality, sensuality, and sex. He is also associated with savagery and filth.

At the time of writing "A Country Doctor," Kafka had broken off his first engagement to Felice Bauer and had had several short-lived affairs. He was attracted to women but still felt that marriage and his work as a writer were mutually exclusive. His belief that marriage was not for him was based also on his perception of the sexual act as something terrible. Just as the groom represents a repressed aspect of the country doctor, who had all but ignored Rose, so too he represents the sexual fulfillment that Kafka decided again and again to sacrifice in order to continue his writing. Readers will equate the groom with Kafka the lover.

The groom and the two horses emerge from the pigsty together, then go off in different directions. While the groom was pursuing Rose, the unearthly horses transported the country doctor to the sick boy. Perhaps the boy was only to be reached by supernatural means. There is a fairy-tale quality to the ten-mile journey. It took only a moment, and the blinding snow was gone, replaced by clear moonlight. The nature of the journey is significant for the reader's interpretation of the boy. Kafka has placed him in the spiritual world.

Whereas the country doctor is only one of many, as stressed by the indefinite article in the title, the boy is unique. His father, family, and the villagers have no understanding of the boy's condition. Clearly, the boy is having a hard time of it in these surroundings. Even the doctor feels ill "in the narrow confines of the old man's thoughts." Disheartened, the boy at first wants to die. So does the doctor. Once the doctor becomes aware of the unique nature of the boy's great wound, however, which is both attractive and repulsive, rose-colored and worm-eaten, the boy decides that he wants to live. By then, though, it is too late. The blossom in his side is destroying him.

Like the friend in Russia in "The Judgment," the boy in "A Country Doctor" appears sickly but turns out to be of supreme importance. Kafka was not physically strong. In 1916, his tuberculosis had not yet been diagnosed, but he suffered from stomach problems. He lived with his parents, who were concerned that the long hours he spent writing were ruining his health. It is therefore fitting that those characters in his stories who represent Kafka the writer appear to be sickly. Readers will equate the boy with Kafka the writer.

Like the surface level of "The Judgment," the surface level of "A Country Doctor" reads like a tragedy of unequaled proportions. Unable to help the boy, the country doctor finds himself also unable to get home, for the trip away from the boy is as slow as the trip to him was fast. "Exposed to the frost of this most unhappy of ages," the doctor realizes that, as a result of this trip, he has not only sacrificed his servant girl but also lost his flourishing practice to his successor. What this translates into, though, is a triumph. Kafka the writer has subjugated Kafka the lawyer and Kafka the lover. The famous, peremptorily fatalistic last line of the story reveals its double meaning. "A false alarm on the night bell once answered—it cannot be made good, not ever." Once Kafka accepted his gift as a writer, he could never abandon that link with the spiritual world.

Kafka's works show, simultaneously and paradoxically, not only the existential angst inherent in the human condition but also a way out of that hopeless state. If the various characters are considered as elements of a personality seeking integration, the stories end not bleakly but on a transcendent note. Kafka's refuge was in his writing, in the spiritual world, and in laughter.

OTHER MAJOR WORKS

LONG FICTION: *Der Prozess*, 1925 (*The Trial*, 1937); *Das Schloss*, 1926 (*The Castle*, 1930); *Amerika*, 1927 (*America*, 1938, better known as *Amerika*, 1946).

NONFICTION: *The Diaries of Franz Kafka*, 1948-1949; *Tagebücher, 1910-1923*, 1951; *Brief an den Vater*, 1952 (written 1919; *Letter to His Father*); *Briefe an Milena*, 1952 (*Letters to Milena*, 1953); *Briefe, 1902-1924*, 1958; *Briefe an Felice*, 1967 (*Letters to Felice*, 1974); *Briefe an Ottla und die Familie*, 1974 (*Letters to Ottla and the Family*, 1982).

MISCELLANEOUS: *Hochzeitsvorbereitungen auf dem Lande und andere Prosa aus dem Nachlass*, 1953 (*Dearest Father: Stories and Other Writings*, 1954; also known as *Wedding Preparations in the Country, and Other Posthumous Prose Writings*, 1954).

BIBLIOGRAPHY

Ben-Ephraim, Gavriel. "Making and Breaking Meaning: Deconstruction, Four-Level Allegory, and *The Metamorphosis*." *The Midwest Quarterly* 35 (Summer, 1994): 450-467. Argues that Kafka's ability to combine oppositions without resolving them enables him to simultaneously build and dismantle an allegorical ladder ascending the four levels of traditional interpretation.

Bloom, Harold, ed. *Franz Kafka*. New York: Chelsea House, 1986. A collection of essays, on Kafka himself and on themes that pervade his oeuvre, by distinguished scholars. Includes essays on the short stories "Up in the Gallery," "A Country Doctor," "Der Bau" ("The Burrow"), and "Die Verwandlung" ("The Metamorphosis"). Contains an excellent index that itemizes specific aspects of the works.

Boa, Elizabeth. *Kafka: Gender, Class, and Race in the Letters and Fictions*. New York: Oxford University Press, 1996. An excellent study. Includes bibliographical references and an index.

Corngold, Stanley. *Franz Kafka: The Necessity of Form*. Ithaca, N.Y.: Cornell University Press, 1988. Chapter 3 (43 pages) contains what is very likely the definitive analysis of "The Metamorphosis." Also includes excellent analysis of "The Judgment," in chapters 2 and 7, discussions of form and critical method, and comparisons with other authors. Corngold also wrote a critical bibliography of "The Metamorphosis" in *The Commentator's Despair* (1973).

Flores, Angel, ed. *The Problem of "The Judgement": Eleven Approaches to Kafka's Story.* New York: Gordian Press, 1976. An English translation, followed by a valuable collection of essays on the short story that Kafka considered his best. Harmut Binder reveals a surprising number of background sources in literature and legend. Kate Flores writes a convincing analysis based on the nature of human fatherhood. Walter Sokel provides an extensive interpretation. Very worthwhile.

Hayman, Ronald. *K: A Biography of Kafka.* London: Weidenfeld & Nicolson, 1981. More than a biography, this study contains many helpful discussions of the literary works, showing how they arose in response to specific situations and linking them with contemporary passages from Kafka's diary and letters. A moving portrayal particularly of Kafka's last days, when his steps toward liberation coincided tragically with the final stages of tuberculosis.

Heinemann, Richard. "Kafka's Oath of Service: 'Der Bau' and the Dialectic of Bureaucratic Mind." *PMLA* 111 (March, 1996): 256-270. Analyzes "Der Bau," as a literary representation of what Kafka called the bureaucratic mind, which reflects both the acceptance of authority as a foundation for attachment to a community and the paralysis of a restlessly critical consciousness that makes impossible any reconciliation between self and other.

Oz, Amos. "A Log in a Freshet: On the Beginning of Kafka's 'A Country Doctor.'" *Partisan Review* 66 (Spring, 1999): 211-217. Argues that the story is not a story of crime and punishment, nor is it a fable about making the wrong decision. The feelings of guilt the doctor experiences are not the result of any action. Under the terms of Kafka's contract, the doctor is guilty a priori, convicted from the start, despite his innocence.

Pawel, Ernst. *The Nightmare of Reason: A Life of Franz Kafka.* New York: Farrar, Straus & Giroux, 1984. An excellent biography, remarkable in that Pawel's meticulous research has extended beyond Kafka to include the fates of all those lives he touched. Conveys detailed knowledge of the school and university systems of the time and of the stages of social and political unrest in Prague. Beautifully written.

Politzer, Heinz. *Franz Kafka: Parable and Paradox.* Revised and expanded edition. Ithaca, N.Y.: Cornell University Press, 1966. A seminal work in Kafka scholarship. Proceeding from a detailed analysis of one paragraph, Politzer discusses several of the short stories at length ("The Judgment," "The Metamorphosis," and "In the Penal Colony") and touches on all the stories. Entertains many alternative readings and compares the works with one another.

Spann, Meno. *Franz Kafka.* Boston: Twayne, 1976. Spann's familiarity with the 250 books in Kafka's library enables him to identify sources and influences. He corrects many misleading errors in the English translations, provides lucid overviews of diverse critical approaches, and offers his own concise readings of the works. Good discussions of the major short stories.

Speirs, Ronald, and Beatrice Sandberg. *Franz Kafka.* New York: St. Martin's Press, 1997. Chapters on "a writer's life" and on the novels and short stories. Provides detailed notes and extensive bibliography.

Jean M. Snook

DAVID MICHAEL KAPLAN

Born: New York, New York; April 9, 1946

PRINCIPAL SHORT FICTION

Comfort, 1987
Skating in the Dark, 1991

OTHER LITERARY FORMS

David Michael Kaplan's book-length *Revision: A Creative Approach to Writing and Rewriting Fiction* (1997) shows writers how to be their own editors, offers strategies, and points out common errors.

ACHIEVEMENTS

David Michael Kaplan's stories have been anthologized in publications such as *American Short Fiction*, *The Best American Short Stories*, *Prize Stories: The O. Henry Awards, Sudden Fiction International*, and *The Sound of Writing*. Kaplan has received awards from the National Endowment for the Arts, the Yaddo Corporation, the Illinois Arts Council, the Pennsylvania Council on the Arts, and the CINE New York International Film and Television Festival.

BIOGRAPHY

David Michael Kaplan was born in New York City on April 9, 1946, to Sidney and Minnie Marie Henson Kaplan. He married twice, the second time to Joyce Winer in 1988. He earned his bachelor's degree at Yale University (1967) and his master's of fine arts at the University of Iowa (1987). Before teaching at the latter institution (1985-1987) and thereafter at Loyola University, Chicago, Kaplan was the creative director of Shadowstone Films, Durham, North Carolina (1971-1976) and the production director of National Television News, Los Angeles (1976-1984).

Prior to the publication of his collections, Kaplan's short stories appeared individually in *The Atlantic*, *Playboy*, *Redbook*, *Triquarterly*, *Fiction Network*, *Ohio Review*, *The Wooster Review*, *Shankpainter*, *Yellow Silk*, *Doubletake*, and elsewhere. His stories have also been broadcast on National Public Radio's *The Sound of Writing* series.

ANALYSIS

The stories in David Michael Kaplan's first collection, *Comfort*, have two primary themes: difficult, often sad, parent-child relationships and the magical or mystical. The former theme focuses on children physically and/or emotionally estranged from a parent through abandonment, divorce, misunderstanding, or death, followed by a search for reconciliation. Stylistically, Kaplan tries to practice what he teaches in his writing workshops. As his course descriptions read, "Revision is where the story gets made: we all know this hoary maxim from writers' workshops and creative writing books." Kaplan emphasizes the need to engage the reader's interest right from the start, to create the imaginative "reality" of the fictional world, and to establish the authority of the narrative voice so that the reader may willingly suspend disbelief. Kaplan does not always offer a resolution to the strange connections and the unbridgeable distances between the characters he creates. For instance, in "Summer People," which was revised for his second collection, an estranged and divorced son, who has spent his adult life trying to get away from his father's excessively judgmental attitude, is reunited with his widower parent. Long-standing conflicts and resentments flare up, and the son has a confrontation with the father after they close up their old summer house for the last time. Still, there is no reconciliation.

"Love, Your Only Mother," in the first collection, is the most typical variation on Kaplan's primary theme. It is about a mother who left her daughter with the girl's father thirty years earlier and whose only contact with her daughter, who is now married with a daughter of her own, has been the occasional bizarre and untraceable postcard from various locations in the West. The postcards—sixty-three in all—have never revealed where the mother is, only where she was sometime before. Thus, the postcards are more terrifying than comforting.

In another story, "In the Realm of the Heron," a father takes his eleven-year-old daughter on a lakeside vacation in the wake of his wife's sudden, accidental death. The young widower has not been able to cope with his daughter's unexpressed rage and refusal to accept her loss. One day, the father insists on taking his daughter to an old deserted house that he discovered while rowing in a nearby lake. Instead of the idyllic retreat that he envisioned, the girl finds a dead heron nailed to a wall. In this instance, the experience provides the daughter with the opportunity to deal with her bereavement.

In "Elisabetta, Carlotta, Catherine," a young woman, abandoned by her mother long ago, searches for a girl in a picture, which also depicts her prematurely deceased father. She thus presumes the girl in the photograph to be his illegitimate daughter. In searching for a posthumous reconciliation with her dead parent, the daughter goes to Barbados and watches a strange ritual, a voodoo ceremony involving the raising of a demon, who is supposed to be able to reveal one's heart's desire in exchange for something the petitioner treasures. Elisabetta offers the demon the photograph of her father and the child, for whom she has been searching on the island. The photograph is consumed in the demon's flames, but Elisabetta does not get her wish. This story, then, like "Doe Season," touches base with both major themes.

Indeed, Kaplan uses the surreal or the supernatural as a plot device and as a way to enrich the understanding of his stories. This becomes apparent in his treatment of dreamlike fantasies, levitation, voodoo, witchery, transformation, ghostly visitations, and the like, as in "A Mexican Tale" or "Elias Schneebaum," two horror tales in which the supernatural provides the plot itself.

"COMFORT"

The title story of domestic realism in Kaplan's first collection is about two young women, Laurie and Michaela, former Skidmore College classmates now sharing an apartment in Saratoga, New York, while holding down nondescript jobs. On this warm spring evening, the girls are expecting a visit from the current boyfriend of Laurie's mother, Ted Bremmer. Laurie has a generally low opinion of her parent's consorts, including Ted Bremmer, who is currently on assignment in Saratoga. Laurie had met him on a previous occasion and disapproved of his behavior then. Michaela suggests that Laurie test his faithfulness by trying to seduce him. When Laurie objects, Michaela jokingly volunteers.

Potent drinks followed by Ted's wine and Michaela's attraction for the middle-aged man do the rest. The more Michaela makes a play for Ted, the more incensed Laurie feels. When it becomes evident to Laurie that Ted, in fact, has spent a good part of the night in Michaela's room, and thus has failed the "test," she calls him at his motel but hangs up after uttering an expletive.

The tension of the story flows from whether Laurie will now become even more estranged from her mother, given the evidence that the woman's current boyfriend is no better than her previous "jerks." In addition, there is a question of whether Laurie and Michaela will continue to be friends or Laurie's strong sense of betrayal by her roommate will end their earlier close ties. Accordingly, there is little comfort to be found in this or several other stories in the collection.

"DOE SEASON"

Widely considered to be the showpiece of Kaplan's first collection, *Comfort*, this fantasy story is about a precocious nine-year-old girl, Andy, who is initiated into the adult world of sexuality and death on the occasion of a deer hunt. On a cold winter morning in the Pennsylvania woods, she witnesses the gutting of a doe, which she reluctantly accepted an invitation to kill the previous day. It is the only one bagged by an otherwise all-male party of three—her father, his friend Charlie, and the latter's eleven-year-old son Mac.

That night Andy experiences a surreal, dreamlike vision of herself stepping out of the tent just as the doe's ghost enters the hunters' camp. The animal helplessly allows the girl to approach closely enough to touch it and palpate the inside of its gaping wound. As Andy cups the doe's beating heart, its warmth nearly sears her hand. She is struck by the horror and beauty of it all. The next morning, when the hunting party finds the dead doe and her father begins to eviscerate it, Andy runs away.

Here, as in several other stories, Kaplan deals with the complicated ties between parents and children. In this case, the conflict revolves around how Andy relates to her mother, who makes only a brief appearance in the story, as well as how Andy resists her father's teasing of her hoydenish qualities. In fact, the story ends with her not responding to her boyish nickname Andy but insisting on the use of her full name, Andrea. The deer hunt has hastened the girl's passage from tomboyhood to premature womanhood.

Skating in the Dark

This is a collection of twelve interrelated stories presented as a novel. It traces the coming of age, marriage, and divorce of Frank Kresky over a forty-year period, from 1951 to 1990. During that time he tries to find out who he is. Frank first appears at age seven, growing up in a small western Pennsylvania town and dreading piano lessons from a nun ("Piano Lessons"). By age fifteen he likes to break into houses, including the one he shares with his parents ("Break-In"). Age twenty-five finds him in Crete ("Governotou") agonizing over what he should be and whether he should marry Jena. It is the summer of 1969, and he has supposedly been deferred from the Vietnam War draft because of his job as an "educator" writing standardized achievement tests. Seven years later, now married, Frank takes Jena back to Crete to visit his old haunts and do what had been enjoyable the first time around, but the fun has gone out of it ("Tombs"), and the couple is evidently drifting apart.

In the title story, "Skating in the Dark," set in January, 1972, when Frank is twenty-eight years old, he and his wife of three years, now living and working in Southern California, travel back east for a family visit and break into his parents' summer home, where they learn they are doomed to say things they do not mean and that deceptions and lies are bound to mark their future conjugal life.

The remaining stories deal with the aftereffects of Frank's divorce, as well as the ill health, decline, and death of his parents. The final tale, "In the Night," set in August, 1990, when Frank is forty-six, shows him trying to help a girlfriend, Allie, out of a major crisis in her life, affording him some kind of redemptive quality.

Thus, this collection is about a sterile, childless marriage and about parent-child relationships. At the close, Frank still seems to be trying to find himself. He is still afraid of life and of growing up; for him, looking back—skating in the dark—is at best a sad, elegiac experience. Reading *Skating in the Dark*, then, is a little like thumbing through a photo album from which most of the happy pictures are missing, a series of episodes recording the sadder and more troublesome moments of a man's life. The stories of the unengaging hero's coming of age as he fumbles through his rough-and-tumble life, searching for a persona he can accept, do not lead to anything pleasurable. Accordingly, as in Kaplan's first collection, *Comfort*, the atmosphere is morose.

Other major works

nonfiction: *Revision: A Creative Approach to Writing and Rewriting Fiction*, 1997.

Bibliography

Cameron, Peter. "Melancholy in the 50's." Review of *Skating in the Dark*, by David Michael Kaplan. *The New York Times*, September 8, 1991, sec. VII, 41. A short-story writer's book review of Kaplan's second collection finds that the protagonist's prolonged sensitivity to hurt seems more like unchecked moping.

Hall, Sharon K., ed. "David Michael Kaplan." *Contemporary Literary Criticism: Yearbook 1987* 50 (1988): 55-58. A profile and various review synopses of Kaplan's first short-story collection, *Comfort*.

"*Skating in the Dark*." Review of *Skating in the Dark*, by David Michael Kaplan. *Kirkus Reviews* 59 (August 1, 1991): 956. A critical reading of Kaplan's second collection finds it a little too calculating and, with two or three exceptions, lacking in real power.

"*Skating in the Dark*." Review of *Skating in the Dark*, by David Michael Kaplan. *Publishers Weekly* 238 (August 2, 1991): 62. A laudatory review of the collection sees it as neatly sidestepping "muzzy nostalgia traps" in the protagonist's movement toward a more redeemable life.

Wood, Susan. "Children Without Parents." Review of

Comfort, by David Michael Kaplan. *The New York Times*, June 4, 1987, sec. VII, 41. A review of Kaplan's first collection finds its stories "affecting" because of their common focus on the ex- traordinary moments of recognition in ordinary lives.

Peter B. Heller

ANNA KAVAN

Helen Woods
Born: Cannes, France; April 10, 1901
Died: London, England; December 5, 1968

PRINCIPAL SHORT FICTION
Asylum Piece and Other Stories, 1940
I Am Lazarus, 1945
The House of Sleep, 1947
A Bright Green Field and Other Stories, 1958
Julia and the Bazooka and Other Stories, 1970
My Soul in China: A Novella and Stories, 1975

OTHER LITERARY FORMS

Anna Kavan wrote novels early in her career under the name Helen Ferguson, including *A Charmed Circle* (1929), *The Dark Sisters* (1930), and *Let Me Alone* (1930), which was reprinted under the name Anna Kavan in 1979. As Anna Kavan she wrote several other novels, among them *A Scarcity of Love* (1956), *Eagles' Nest* (1957), and *Ice* (1967), which is highly regarded as a work of science fiction.

ACHIEVEMENTS

Largely unrecognized in her lifetime, Anna Kavan has become something of a cult figure since her death. She has been compared to such figures as Franz Kafka, Virginia Woolf, Sylvia Plath, D. H. Lawrence, John Fowles, and Anaïs Nin (who was one of her greatest admirers), and her writing has been classified variously as science fiction, feminist fiction, and surrealist fiction. Her greatest achievement lies in the portrayal of the subjective emotional states of mental illness, drug dependency, and the paranoia that accompany them, as well as the loneliness and the general sense of isolation that many individuals in contemporary society suffer at one time or another. Employing vivid imagery to portray the vague line separating dreams and reality, she is, as Gunther Stuhlmann writes, "one of the most hauntingly remarkable artists of modern English literature."

BIOGRAPHY

A knowledge of Anna Kavan's life is essential to understanding and appreciating her literature, for she is a profoundly autobiographical writer. Echoes of her unhappy childhood, mental illness, and drug addiction appear repeatedly in her stories, and her protagonists are frequently versions of the author herself.

Kavan lived virtually two separate and distinct lives: first as Helen Woods, Helen Woods Edmonds, and Helen Ferguson; and, second, as Anna Kavan. The author was born Helen Woods in Cannes, France, to a wealthy upper-middle-class couple, and details of her early years are sketchy. Little is known about her father, except that he disappeared early in her life. She traveled extensively with her glamorous mother, Helen (Bright) Woods, who eventually remarried a wealthy South African and died young. Kavan's relationship with her mother, who was by all accounts aloof and distant with her young daughter, strongly influenced her life and writing.

In the 1920's, Helen Woods married Donald Ferguson, a successful Scottish businessman, and they settled in Burma, where Helen began writing. Her first book, *A Charmed Circle*, was published in 1929, and by 1937, she had produced twelve novels. The couple had a son, who was eventually killed in World War II, and the marriage ended in divorce, with Helen later marrying painter Stuart Edmonds. Although reportedly happier than her first marriage, this relationship also ended in divorce.

After the dissolution of each marriage, Helen stayed in sanatoriums in Switzerland and England, experiences that she later chronicled in her fiction. By the end of the 1930's, she had also become addicted to heroin, registering as an addict just prior to World War II. This period marked drastic changes in her life, including a name change by deed poll to Anna Kavan (Anna for the protagonist of her novel *Let Me Alone* and Kavan after Kafka's "K") and a complete change in physical appearance from matronly brunette to thin, nearly emaciated, silver blond (a hair color shared with most of her heroines). Her fiction also changed markedly from the more conventional novels of Helen Ferguson, and she enjoyed a measure of critical success when her first book as Anna Kavan, *Asylum Piece and Other Stories*, appeared in 1940.

During the war years, she lived briefly in New York, worked as a researcher in a military psychiatric unit in London, and beginning in 1942 served as an assistant editor on the literary journal *Horizon*, which also published several of her stories. Her critical reputation declined after the war, and by 1956, she was reduced to paying a vanity press to publish *A Scarcity of Love*, while *Eagles' Nest* and *A Bright Green Field and Other Stories* appeared in 1957 and 1958. She spent these years in London, renovating and selling old homes, as well as designing and building a home of her own. Always impeccably groomed, shy, and reclusive, she was given to bizarre behavior, as, for example, when she threw a roast duck across the table during a dinner party.

More than one attempted suicide and bouts with severe depression marked her later years, as well as the humiliation of mandatory attendance at sessions for drug addicts sponsored by National Health, promoting the fear and distrust of authority that play such a prominent role in her stories. She continued writing, including the novel *Who Are You?* (1963) and the well-received *Ice*, which began to revive interest in her career. She died at age sixty-seven, with a loaded syringe, her "bazooka" as she called it, in

her hand. Her later stories were published posthumously, collected in *Julia and the Bazooka and Other Stories*, which details her drug addiction, and *My Soul in China: A Novella and Stories*.

ANALYSIS

Anna Kavan's dominant theme, the isolation of the individual in contemporary society, is usually expressed through intensely personal tales of loneliness, mental anguish, and despair set against ominous foreign or institutional backdrops. Her characters, often nameless or merely initialed young women, are psychologically unstable, existing in a vague world where the bounds of dream and reality continually shift. The themes of madness, drug addiction, repressive authority, lost love, and loneliness weave a common thread through each volume of her stories. Although often criticized for speaking to her personal despair rather than to a more universal humanity, Kavan's fiction cannot help striking a deeply responsive and sympathetic chord in the reader.

"THE BIRTHMARK"

The stories in *Asylum Piece and Other Stories* explore various states of madness, paranoia, and estrangement from the inside out. In the first story, "The Birthmark," a nameless narrator, away from home for the first time, develops a strong affinity for a girl, known only as H, whom she meets at boarding school. A typical Kavan character, H has "a face unique, neither gay nor melancholy, but endued with a peculiar quality of apartness" which is further accentuated by her peculiarly shaped birthmark, "a circle armed with sharp points and enclosing a tiny shape very soft and tender—perhaps a rose." Despite the attraction they feel for each other, neither can overcome her sense of "apartness" to form a bond with the other. Years later, while touring an ancient fortress in a foreign country, the narrator believes that she sees H, whom she has never forgotten, imprisoned in a subterranean cell, but feels powerless to help her. Typically, the gulf between the two is too great to bridge.

"GOING UP IN THE WORLD"

"Going Up in the World" also involves an alienated figure, here a lowly petitioner who begs her Patron and Patroness to "share a little . . . sunshine and warmth." The unnamed narrator can no longer bear her "lonely, cold and miserable" existence and petitions her "patrons" to admit her into the inner sanctum of their luxuriously warm world. Typically, the exact nature of the Patron and Patroness's authority over the narrator remains vague. Possessing the power to banish her to a miserable existence, they speak like scolding parents exhorting their child to "give up [her] rebellious ways." Well-dressed, smug, self-satisfied figures such as these, whether doctors, parents, or unspecified "officials," appear regularly in Kavan's stories, issuing capricious orders that can ruin a life in an instant.

"ASYLUM PIECE"

"Asylum Piece," the longest story of the volume, is divided into eight parts, the first of which presents an outsider's view of a mental institution, which looks deceptively like a scene "upon which a light comedy, something airy and gay, is about to be acted." The setting is pastoral, calm, and beautiful and "flooded with dazzling midsummer sunshine." Part 2, however, shifts the perspective to that of a patient, a frightened young woman committed against her will, and the succeeding sections shift to an omniscient view of the inmates' daily lives.

An atmosphere of impotence, imprisonment, and isolation predominates in these sections. In one, a young man, determined to row across the lake to freedom, comes to realize that he is trapped, not just by the physical boundaries of the asylum, but by the boundaries of his own mind. In another, a young woman, perhaps the narrator from part 2, is committed by her husband who "longs to disassociate himself from the whole situation." Lonely and deserted, she is briefly comforted by a sympathetic young cleaning woman. In a later episode, a young woman (again perhaps the same one) spends a holiday from the asylum with her visiting husband, a stern and inflexible man who cannot wait to end the visit and return home. Crushed by her husband's rejection, the young woman is left to the comfort and understanding of a fellow inmate. Unlike many of Kavan's stories, "Asylum Piece" holds out some possibility for human contact, however brief and transitory.

"THERE IS NO END"

The volume comes full circle with the last story, "There Is No End," which harks back to the motif of imprisonment from "The Birthmark." A nameless woman, imprisoned by "unseen and impassable" walls in a place where there is "no love . . . nor hate, nor any point where feeling accumulates," wonders if it is "life then, or death, stretching like an uncolored stream behind and in front of me?" For this narrator and for many of Kavan's characters, prison is only an outer manifestation of an inner sense of isolation, from which no escape is possible.

I AM LAZARUS

I Am Lazarus continues the themes of psychological turmoil, paranoia, and isolation introduced in *Asylum Piece and Other Stories* and explores the devastating effects of war on the psyche and the cruelly dehumanizing techniques employed by mental institutions to "rehabilitate" their patients. In the title story, set in an idyllic pastoral sanatorium, "every tree pruned to perfection, . . . brilliant with flowers," a young, aristocratic Englishman has been reduced to an automaton by insulin shock treatments. Although outwardly a model citizen, Mr. Bow is inwardly confused and frightened, feeling in control only while working on his leather belt in craft class. He functions successfully when clear-out rules exist to guide his behavior but is otherwise debilitated. Although his doctor remarks that "he doesn't know how lucky he is . . . We've pulled him back literally from a living death," the opposite is in fact true. The pathetic young man has been doomed to a living death, not rescued from one.

"THE PALACE OF SLEEP"

In "The Palace of Sleep," another victim of destructive "rehabilitative" techniques, drugged to unconsciousness by her doctors, looks "absolutely lifeless, void" and appears to have "forfeited humanity and given . . . over prematurely to death." Her doctor, smug in the knowledge that he has extinguished her pain, fails to perceive a look of "wild supplication, of frantic abysmal appeal" on her lifeless face. Like Mr. Bow, this fair-haired young woman, apparently cured of her madness, no longer a bother to society, is inwardly suffering as intensely as before.

THE HOUSE OF SLEEP

In the novella *The House of Sleep*, referred to by one reviewer as an "autobiography of dreams," Kavan alternates brief bits of "daytime life" with detailed dream sequences, believing that in the "tension between the two polarities night and day, night, the negative pole, must share equal importance with the positive day." This work chronicles a young girl's progressive retreat from the reality of a "remote and starry" mother who seldom had time for her and died young and a distant father who refused to explain her mother's death. Relegated to the "crowded ugliness" of boarding school, the girl regresses ever further into herself, until, living almost entirely in her dream life, she is institutionalized. Although praised for its brilliant dream imagery reminiscent of a Salvador Dalí painting, a critic remarked that "one never feels any desire to read on . . . because Anna Kavan has given too much importance to the negative pole, and thereby destroyed the tension between day and night."

JULIA AND THE BAZOOKA AND OTHER STORIES

Julia and the Bazooka and Other Stories, perhaps Kavan's best collection of stories, transcends the merely autobiographical to achieve the status of art. Continuing to explore the themes of isolation, loneliness, and mental illness, this volume also deals with drug addiction. Unlike *Asylum Piece and Other Stories* and *I Am Lazarus*, in which she occasionally ventures outside herself to explore other characters, this collection is almost entirely self-referential, most stories told by a first-person narrator, all seemingly about the same character.

"THE OLD ADDRESS"

In the first story, "The Old Address," the narrator is released from an institution for drug rehabilitation into a threatening and ominous world peopled with "hordes of masks, dummies, zombies" where "everything look[s] sinister." A short-lived feeling of freedom is soon overtaken by the sense of permanent imprisonment within her. Remembering that "I am alone, as I always am" and that "there's to be no end to my incarceration in this abominable, disgusting world," she hails a taxi to drive to the "old address," back to the haven of her drug addiction.

Several stories in this volume use the automobile to symbolize, paradoxically, both the individual's sense of estrangement from her world and her means of dealing with that estrangement. Often used as a symbol of drug addiction, the car represents the syringe or "bazooka" that brings temporary relief from the narrator's suffering. In "The Fog," the narrator, driving in a drug-induced haze, runs down a teenager because she sees him as a "teenage mask," a "dummy made of stuffed clothes and umbrellas," not a real person. As she reasons, "I wasn't really here, so [he] couldn't be either." The narrator longs to be "no more than a hole in space, not here or anywhere at all, for as long as possible, preferably forever."

"THE WORLD OF HEROES"

"The World of Heroes" again deals with cars, this time the world of racing. The narrator finds a sense of security and belonging among the ranks of drivers of high-powered cars. To her a car is "a very safe refuge . . . the only means of escape from all the ferocious and cruel forces lurking in life and in human beings." She finds love with various drivers, moving from one to another, living a "fairy tale" existence. The car, however, which provides this exciting, satisfying life, also takes it away when the narrator is seriously and disfiguringly injured in a race. Her friends disappear, her lovers are gone, and she, like all Kavan's heroines, winds up alone, "back where [she] was as a child, solitary, helpless, unwanted, frightened."

"JULIA AND THE BAZOOKA"

"Julia and the Bazooka," one of Kavan's most critically well-regarded stories, is a moving account of a young woman's drug addiction. As one reviewer commented, "The whole volume has great documentary interest, but 'Julia and the Bazooka' turns the truth of a life into art." Julia's drug addiction is foreshadowed by her childhood love of poppies, although she is told to "throw the poppies away" because they "make a mess dropping their petals all over the house." Even as a little girl, she "feels cut off from people . . . afraid of the world," and by the time of her marriage, she is addicted, carrying her syringe along with her wedding bouquet. Like many of Kavan's heroines, Julia is a good driver, who laughs at danger because "[nothing] can frighten her while she has the syringe." She dies in a bomb blast during the war, lying "in her red-stained dress, her bag, with bazooka inside, safely hooked over one arm," and "[t]here is no more Julia anywhere. Where she was there is only nothing."

MY SOUL IN CHINA: A NOVELLA AND STORIES

My Soul in China: A Novella and Stories, also published posthumously, contains the title novella and several stories in a lighter vein than her previously published work, leaning more toward science fiction and commentary on contemporary society. The novella, much more characteristic of the body of her work, features a typical Kavan heroine, here named Kay, who, like the heroine in "The Old Address," has just been released from an institution. Estranged from her husband, she meets an Australian who offers to take her to California for six months of recuperation before he returns to his wife and family. *My Soul in China* offers one of Kavan's most moving accounts of a tormented soul, a woman who cannot escape her madness no matter how hard she tries to lose herself in others. Kay feels she is "on a narrow bridge without handrails, hair-raisingly suspended above nothingness." At one end lies "security, familiarity . . . a safe vegetable life without risks or emotions . . . while the other end vanishes into dangerous and unknown, stern cloud shapes there coldly assembling." Kay soon discovers, after a brief idyll, that her Australian lover cannot shield her forever from her demons, and as their time together winds down she feels "as indifferent, as vacant as the uninhabited world, the blank empty eye of infinite space stares me down; and the blue unblemished arch of a godless eternity has no consolation to offer me, none at all."

Kay's fear that "the self I inherited from my ancestors, the person I should have been, has been irremediably mutilated and pulled apart, its fragile balance of thoughts and feelings destroyed," echoes the fears of nearly all Kavan's lost, tormented souls. Looking outside themselves, her protagonists find neither love nor faith nor a sense of belonging. Looking inside, they find even less; a soul so destroyed and tortured that they cannot bear to contemplate it. The only hope lies in the oblivion of drugs, madness, or the final oblivion of death.

OTHER MAJOR WORKS

LONG FICTION: *A Charmed Circle*, 1929 (as Helen Ferguson); *The Dark Sisters*, 1930 (as Ferguson); *Let Me Alone*, 1930 (as Ferguson; reprinted under Anna Kavan, 1979); *A Stranger Still*, 1935 (as Ferguson); *Goose Cross*, 1936 (as Ferguson); *Rich Get Rich*, 1937 (as Ferguson); *Change the Name*, 1941; *A Scarcity of Love*, 1956; *Eagles' Nest*, 1957; *Who Are You?*, 1963; *Ice*, 1967; *Mercury*, 1994; *The Parson*, 1995.

MISCELLANEOUS: *My Madness: The Selected Writings of Anna Kavan*, 1990 (edited by Brian W. Aldiss).

BIBLIOGRAPHY

Aldiss, Brian. Introduction to *Ice*. Garden City, N.Y.: Doubleday, 1970. Aldiss, who met and corresponded with Kavan, discusses *Ice* as a work of science fiction and Kavan's reaction to being regarded as a science-fiction writer: "She was surprised. At first, she rejected the idea. Slowly, she came to like it. . . . I fancy she always liked anything that was a novelty." He also offers biographical details and interesting insights into her character.

Byrne, Janet. "Moving Toward Entropy: Anna Kavan's Science Fiction Mentality." *Extrapolation* 23 (Spring, 1982): 5-11. One of the few critical articles available on Kavan, it centers on *Ice* rather than her short fiction, but it nevertheless provides valuable insights into Kavan's fictional style and concerns. Byrne discusses the novel in the context of Kavan's earlier work, in which she "consistently saw the world as peopled by characters who treated each other cruelly or foolishly, or were so lost in their own private hells that they had no relation to each other."

Callard, D. A. *The Case of Anna Kavan: A Biography*. London: Peter Owen, 1992. An excellent study of the life of Kavan.

Davies, Rhys. Introduction to *Julia and the Bazooka and Other Stories*. New York: Alfred A. Knopf, 1975. Davies, a good friend of Kavan, reflects on the close relationship between the circumstances of her life (particularly her drug addiction) and her fiction, in particular the story "Julia and the Bazooka." His valuable psychological insights clarify readings of her fiction.

Garrity, Jane. "Nocturnal Transgressions in *The House of Sleep*." *Modern Fiction Studies* 40 (Summer, 1994): 253-277. Claims that the work illustrates the critical need to reevaluate Kavan's experimentalism within a context that foregrounds the conjunction of feminist literary discourse and modernist practice.

Lessing, Doris. "Ice-Maiden Stung by a Spider: 'Change the Name.'" *The Independent*, June 5, 1993, p. 28. Lessing provides a short biographical sketch of Kavan and briefly discusses three of her novels: *Ice*, *Change the Name*, and *My Soul in China*. Comments on the relationship between fiction and autobiography.

Owen, Peter. "Publishing Anna Kavan." *Anais* 3 (1985): 75-76. Owen, Kavan's publisher, offers interesting personal insights ("Anna Kavan was a lonely person, aloof with strangers, who relaxed only with a few intimate friends. . . . She was an excellent hostess and a good cook") and a valuable insider's look at Kavan's publishing history.

Stuhlmann, Gunther. "Anna Kavan Revisited: The Web of Unreality." *Anais* 3 (1985): 55-62. Stuhlmann's valuable, well-written overview of Kavan's life and career includes many biographical facts unavailable elsewhere and some discussion of her literary influences and fiction. The article also discusses Anaïs Nin's interest in Kavan and her work and includes a photograph of Kavan in her garden.

Wakeman, John, ed. "Anna Kavan." In *World Authors: 1920-1925*. New York: H. W. Wilson, 1980. The entry in this volume provides good background material on Kavan's life and career, placing her fiction in the context of her life, particularly noting the critical reaction to her work as it appeared. The article contains a photograph of Kavan and a bibliography of her principal works, as well as a listing of critical articles and reviews.

Mary Virginia Davis

YASUNARI KAWABATA

Born: Osaka, Japan; June 11, 1899
Died: Zushi, Japan; April 16, 1972

PRINCIPAL SHORT FICTION
Shokonsai ikkei, 1921
Suishō gensō, 1934
Jōjōka, 1938
Shiroi mangetsu, 1948
Maihime, 1951
Bungei tokuhon Kawabata Yasunari, 1962
The House of the Sleeping Beauties and Other Stories, 1969
Kōgen, 1969
Tenohira no shōsetsu, 1969
Shui yueh, 1971
Honehiroi, 1975
Tenjū no ko, 1975
Palm-of-the-Hand Stories, 1988

OTHER LITERARY FORMS

Besides approximately two hundred short stories and fictional vignettes (or short, short stories), Yasunari Kawabata wrote both "serious" novels, which earned for him a Nobel Prize, and "popular" novels, which gained for him financial security. The latter, considered by some critics as vulgarizations, are not included in editions of his complete works. His serious works include juvenile fiction, travel accounts, journalism, letters, reviews, translations, editions, plays, and lectures.

Yasunari Kawabata, Nobel Laureate for Literature in 1968
(©The Nobel Foundation)

ACHIEVEMENTS

Known throughout the world as the only writer from his country to have received the Nobel Prize in Literature, Yasunari Kawabata was also awarded every major Japanese literary honor, including membership in the Japanese Academy of Arts (1954). In 1972, he was posthumously awarded the First Class Order of the Rising Sun. In his work, Kawabata combines universal themes with literary techniques and conventions typical of Japanese culture. His eminence as a writer of fiction is based on this characteristic of fusing contrary, although not antithetical, elements. He draws upon the East and the West as well as the traditional and the modern, juxtaposes mimetic precision with symbolic evocation, joins the erotic and the spiritual, and fluctuates between dream and reality. In like manner, he cultivated and perfected both long and short genres of fiction and in a sense brought them into conjunction, since many of his long works can be broken down into short, independent elements. His themes embrace both the mundane

and the esoteric, his narrative style ranges from the graphic to the lyrical, and his highly original plots and situations touch upon fundamental moral and aesthetic issues of modern life.

BIOGRAPHY

Orphaned at the age of four, Yasunari Kawabata was reared by his grandparents and later by an uncle. Originally attracted by painting, he later decided to follow writing as a career, and at the age of sixteen he published in a little magazine an account of carrying his teacher's coffin. Two years earlier, he had written reminiscences of his grandfather, which he later published under the title "Jūrokusai no nikki" ("Diary of a Sixteen-Year-Old"). In 1921, he received his first payment for a literary work, a review, and published in a student literary magazine an account of a memorial day commemoration that drew the favorable attention of a prolific novelist, Kikuchi Kan, a dominating force in Japanese literary circles of the time. The themes of death and loneliness of Kawabata's mature years appeared early in his career and may have been influenced by the loss of his parents and grandparents. During his youth, he came briefly under the influence of a Japanese avant-garde clique that advocated the adoption of novel Western movements such as Dadaism, Futurism, and Surrealism. These tendencies were wrapped up in the term *Shinkankakuha*, which embraces neoperceptionism or neosensualism, but Kawabata's allegiance to this extremely many-sided coterie was only temporary and irresolute. His major work in the experimental mode, "Suishō gensō" ("Crystal Fantasy"), utilizes the stream-of-consciousness technique.

Kawabata established his reputation as a creative writer with the publication in 1926 of his story "Izu no Odoriko" ("The Izu Dancer") and acquired both critical and popular acclaim with his novel *Yukiguni* (1947; *Snow Country*, 1956). In 1941, he visited Manchuria twice, spending a month in the ancient capital of Mukden and returning to Japan shortly before the breaking out of the Pacific War. Throughout the conflict, Kawabata's publications consisted in large measure of childhood recollections, and he immersed himself in the study of traditional Japanese culture. In the aftermath of his country's defeat, Kawabata announced that he would henceforth write only eulogies, a promise not fulfilled unless his major themes of death, loneliness, and opposition to the Westernization of Japan could be considered elegiac. These themes dominated the first two of his great postwar novels, *Sembazuru* (1949-1951, serial; 1952, book; *Thousand Cranes*, 1958) and *Yama no oto* (1949-1954, serial; 1954, book; *The Sound of the Mountain*, 1970), and another novel, *Kyoto* (1962; *The Old Capital*, 1987).

The Old Capital, which has as protagonists virginal twins who meet for the first time in their late teens after being separated as infants, has received relatively little critical attention in English, perhaps because of the innocence of the characters and the extensive descriptions of the woodland scenery surrounding Kyoto. Western critics have been more attracted by the novella *The House of the Sleeping Beauties*, concerning an unusual brothel in which old men spend the night with naked girls, who are voluntarily drugged into unconsciousness. The love of nature in the one and the eroticism in the other are both typical of Kawabata and are often coalesced in his other works.

In 1948, Kawabata became president of the PEN Club of Japan, a position he utilized to continue his perennial occupation of encouraging and promoting the careers of young writers. In 1957, he was the guiding spirit behind the twenty-ninth congress of PEN, held in Tokyo, and in 1959, he was elected vice president of that organization, attending three of its congresses in other countries.

In his Nobel Prize acceptance speech, Kawabata remarked that he neither admired nor was in sympathy with suicide. It was a great shock to his associates and to the world at large, therefore, when in April, 1972, he took his own life by inhaling gas.

ANALYSIS

The short story or the vignette is the essence of Yasunari Kawabata's literary art. Even his great novels were written piecemeal. Not only were they originally published in serial form, the parts frequently presented as separate stories, but also many segments were rewritten and revised for both style and content. Japanese tradition has applied the term *shosetsu*, loosely "fiction," to both novels and short stories, and as a result, such works as "The Izu Dancer," consisting of only thirty pages, and *The House of the Sleeping Beauties*, forming less than a hundred, have been treated critically as novels.

"DIARY OF A SIXTEEN-YEAR-OLD"

Kawabata composed his first work "Jūrokusai no Nikki" ("Diary of a Sixteen-Year-Old") at that age and published it eleven years later. The work describes the humiliating last days and suffering of his grandfather and foreshadows the themes of aging and death in his later works. Comparing the diary with his recollections at a later date, Kawabata maintained that he had forgotten the sordid details of sickness and dying portrayed in his narrative and that his mind had since been constantly occupied in cleansing and beautifying his grandfather's image.

"THE IZU DANCER"

With "The Izu Dancer," his first work to obtain international acclaim, the opposite is true. Here, he idealizes a somewhat commonplace autobiographical incident and group of characters. The story, told in the first person, concerns the encounter of a nineteen-year-old youth on a walking tour of the Izu Peninsula with a group of itinerant entertainers, including a young dancer, who appears to be about sixteen. The young man accompanies them on their way, spurred with the hope that he would eventually spend a night with the young dancer. One morning, as he prepares to enter a public bath, he sees her emerging naked from the steam and realizes that she is a mere child, and a feeling akin to a draught of fresh water permeates his consciousness. Learning that she is only thirteen years of age, he, nevertheless, remains with the players and is accepted by them as a pleasant companion until they reach their winter headquarters. There, he takes a boat back to Tokyo, and his eyes fill with tears as the dancer bids him farewell, floating in a "beautiful emptiness."

The situation of a young man joining forces with a group of itinerant entertainers resembles that in Johann Wolfgang von Goethe's *Wilhelm Meisters Lehrjahre* (1795-1796; *Wilhelm Meister's Appren-*

ticeship, 1824), perhaps the reason that the work was translated into German in 1942, more than twenty years before being rendered into any other Western language. Some years after the original publication, Kawabata revealed that the portrayal of his youthful journey is highly idealistic, concealing major imperfections in the appearance and behavior of the actual troupe. Presumably in real life, moreover, the young age of the dancer would have been no deterrent to his amorous inclinations, since he later portrayed a thirteen-year-old prostitute as the heroine of one of his popular novels concerning Asakusa, the amusement section of Tokyo. The longing for virginal innocence and the realization that this degree of purity is something beyond ordinary attainment is a recurrent theme throughout Kawabata's work, portraying innocence, beauty, and rectitude as ephemeral and tinged with sadness. The sentimental ending of "The Izu Dancer" is considered to symbolize both the purifying effect of literature upon life as well as Kawabata's personal passage from misanthropy to hopefulness.

"THE MAN WHO DID NOT SMILE"

Kawabata pursues the theme of the psychological effect of art and nature in another autobiographical story, "Warawanu otoko" ("The Man Who Did Not Smile"), representing his middle years. The author of a screenplay, impressed by the beauty of the dawn in the countryside, where the script is being filmed, rewrites the last scene with the intention of wrapping "reality in a beautiful, smiling mask." The rewriting is inspired by his notion of having every one of the characters in a mental hospital, locale of the film, wear a laughing mask. On returning to Tokyo, the author visits his own wife in a hospital, where she playfully places one of these masks on her own face. He is horrified by perceiving the ugliness and haggardness of her features in contrast with the beauty of the mask. He meditates on the commonplace that life is ugly but art is beautiful, and he concludes that everyone's smile may be artificial, but he cannot decide whether art in itself is a good thing.

"OF BIRDS AND BEASTS"

Kawabata gives another unflattering view of life and his own personality in "Kinjū" ("Of Birds and Beasts"). The misanthropic protagonist en route to at-

tend the dance recital of a discarded mistress reflects on a pair of dead birds that he had left at home. Musing that the "love of birds and animals comes to be a quest for superior ones, and so cruelty takes root," he finds a likeness in the expression of his former mistress, at the time of her first sexual yielding, to the placid reaction of a female dog while giving birth to puppies. When he encounters the dancer as she is being made up in her dressing room, he envisions her face as it would be in the coffin. Although the story reveals, as he later admitted, that it was written in a fit of cantankerousness, it embodies the serious theme that human and animal kingdoms share the final destiny of death.

"THE MOLE"

In "Hokuro no Tegami" ("The Mole"), Kawabata looks at life from a woman's perspective, delineating a wife's obsession with a physical flaw. Designed to reveal how the process of loving and being loved differs in men and women, "The Mole" consists of a letter from a wife to her separated husband, describing the disintegration of their marriage in which a bodily blemish acts as a catalyst. Ever since childhood, the wife had played with the mole, shaped like a bean, a female sex symbol in Japan. The habit had at first merely irritated the husband, later driven him to beat her, and eventually induced his indifference. On one occasion, the wife dreamed that the mole came off and she asked him to place it next to a mole on his own nose, wondering whether it would then increase in size. This image of gender reversal suggests what is wrong with the marriage. Her obsession with the mole represents an expression of love that proved counterproductive because the husband failed to recognize its true nature. Although the wife's dilemma arouses the reader's sympathy, Kawabata may have had opposite intentions, since he had originally given the story the title "Bad Wife's Letter."

"THE MOON ON THE WATER"

The feminine perspective is dominant also in "Suigetsu" ("The Moon on the Water"), a story of reciprocated love combining the themes of death, beauty, and sexuality. The story concerns a hand mirror that a dying husband uses while lying in bed to watch the processes of nature outside of his window.

The moon as such appears in the narrative in only two sentences, where it is seen in the mirror as itself the reflection of a reflection, thereby introducing the philosophical problem of the nature of reality. The moon in the water is without substance, but in Zen Buddhism, the reflected moon is conversely the real moon and the moon in the sky is the illusion. The moon is also a symbol of virginity, relevant to the wife's continence, enforced by the husband's illness during nearly the entire period of her marriage. After the husband dies, the woman remarries and no longer feels shy when a man praises the beauty of her body. At the same time, she realizes that human anatomy prevents her from seeing her own face, except as a reflection in a mirror. She had loved her first husband because she imagined while he was dying that he had been a child inside her, and she is puzzled because she does not feel an equal degree of devotion toward her second husband. She, nevertheless, becomes pregnant and then revisits the area where she had lived during her first marriage. At the end of the story, she asks, "What if the child should look like you?" leaving the reader with uncertainty concerning the antecedent of the pronoun. The reveries of this paradoxically innocent woman in a second marriage combine and recombine the sexual, the aesthetic, and the metaphysical.

THE HOUSE OF THE SLEEPING BEAUTIES

The same elements form Kawabata's somewhat sensational novella *The House of the Sleeping Beauties*, combining lust, voyeurism, and necrophilia with virgin worship and Buddhist metaphysics. The house is an imaginary brothel in which the patrons, old men approaching senility, sleep with naked virgins who are drugged into insensibility. The protagonist is exceptional in that he still has the physical capacity of breaking a house rule against seeking ultimate sexual satisfaction, but he resists the impulse. The circumstances of the story array the beauty of youth and purity against the ugliness of old age and death. Further contrasts are introduced in the protagonist's subsequent visits to the house, in each of which a different girl evokes erotic passages from his early life. The various beauties could be interpreted as composite recollections or dreamlike fanta-

sies from his past. In the three last visits, his sexual meditations are intermixed with thoughts of death, and he asks to be given for his own use the potent drug administered to the girls. The five visits as a whole suggest the human life span, the first featuring a lovely girl, representing "life itself" and giving off the "milky scent of a nursing baby," and the last portraying the actual death and abrupt carrying away of one of the sleeping beauties.

"ONE ARM"

A related story, "Kataude" ("One Arm"), can be interpreted as either more bizarre or more delicate in its eroticism. A young virgin takes off her arm and gives it to a somewhat older man, who takes it home and carries on a conversation with it as he lies in bed, a conversation that makes him recollect the sexual surrender of a previous acquaintance. Along with the erotic descriptions of the arm in contact with parts of the man's body, the narrative introduces New Testament quotations concerning pure and sacrificial love. On one level, the arm is simply a symbol of a woman giving herself sexually to a man, but it may also represent the loneliness of a man who is deprived of a companion with whom to share his thoughts.

OTHER MAJOR WORKS

LONG FICTION: *Izu no odoriko*, 1926 (*The Izu Dancer*, 1955); *Asakusa kurenaidan*, 1930; *Matsugo no me*, 1930; *Kinjū*, 1933 (*Of Birds and Beasts*, in *The House of the Sleeping Beauties and Other Stories*, 1969); *Yukiguni*, 1935-1937 (serial), 1947 (book; *Snow Country*, 1956); *Hana no warutsu*, 1936; *Hokura no nikki*, 1940 (*The Mole*, 1955); *Meijin*, 1942-1954 (serial), 1954 (book; *The Master of Go*, 1972); *Utsukushii tabi*, 1947; *Otome no minato*, 1948; *Sembazuru*, 1949-1951 (serial), 1952 (book; *Thousand Cranes*, 1958); *Yama no oto*, 1949-1954 (serial), 1954 (book; *The Sound of the Mountain*, 1970); *Asakusa monogatari*, 1950; *Hi mo tsuki mo*, 1953; *Saikonsha*, 1953; *Suigetsu*, 1953 (*The Moon on the Water*, 1958); *Kawa no aru shitamachi no hanashi*, 1954; *Mizuumi*, 1954 (serial), 1955 (book; *The Lake*, 1974); *Tokyo no hito*, 1955; *Nemureru bijo*, 1960-1961 (serial), 1961 (book; *The House of the Sleeping Beauties*, in *The House of the Sleeping Beauties and*

Other Stories, 1969); *Utsukushisa to kanashimi to*, 1961-1963 (serial), 1965 (book; *Beauty and Sadness*, 1975); *Kyoto*, 1962 (*The Old Capital*, 1987); *Kataude*, 1965 (*One Arm*, 1967); *Shōsetsu nyumon*, 1970; *Aru hito no sei no naka ni*, 1972; *Tampopo*, 1972.

NONFICTION: *Jurūkosai no nikki*, 1925; *Shinshin sakka no shinkeikō kaisetsu*, 1925; *Bungakuteki jijoden*, 1934; *Rakka ryusui*, 1966; *Bi no sonzai to hakken/The Existence and Discovery of Beauty*, 1969 (bilingual); *Utsukushii nihon no watakushi/Japan, the Beautiful, and Myself*, 1969 (bilingual); *Isso ikka*, 1973; *Nihon no bi no kokoro*, 1973.

TRANSLATIONS: *Ocho monogatari shū*, 1956-1958 (of ancient Japanese stories); *Isoppu*, 1968 (of *Aesop's fables*).

MISCELLANEOUS: *Kawabata Yasunari zenshū*, 1948-1969.

BIBLIOGRAPHY

Gessel, Van C. *Three Modern Novelists: Soseki, Tanizaki, Kawabata*. New York: Kodansha International, 1993. Concentrates on Kawabata's detachment from modernity. Contains excellent biographical background and detailed notes but no bibliography.

Keene, Donald. *Dawn to the West: Japanese Literature of the Modern Era*. New York: Holt, Rinehart and Winston, 1984. Fifty-nine pages by this eminent critic and translator of Japanese fiction are devoted to Kawabata. Traces many of Kawabata's themes to his childhood experiences and gives the circumstances of publication and reception of his major works. Keene believes that Kawabata's main preoccupations were Japanese landscapes, Japanese women, and Japanese art. Contains a bibliography and extensive notation.

Morris, Mark. "Orphans." *The New York Times*, October 12, 1997. A review of *The Dancing Girl of Izu*, discussing the title story and the "palm-of-hand" stories in the collection; generally praises the stories as excellent examples of Kawabata's early short fiction.

Napier, Susan J. *The Fantastic in Modern Japanese Literature: The Subversion of Modernity*. New York: Routledge, 1996. See chapter 3, "Woman Lost: The Dead, Damaged, or Absent Female in Postwar Fantasy," and especially the separate discussion of "Sleeping with the Dead: Kawabata's *House of Sleeping Beauties* and *One Arm*."

Palmer, Thom. "The Asymmetrical Garden: Discovering Yasunari Kawabata." *Southwest Review* 74 (1989): 390-402. Discusses Kawabata's small fictions called "palm-of-the-hand stories"; asserts they are stylized, intuitive studies of the tension, mystery, and beauty of being alive in an "ephemeral, unfathomable universe."

Petersen, Gwenn Boardman. *The Moon in the Water: Understanding Tanizaki, Kawabata, and Mishima*. Honolulu: University Press of Hawaii, 1979. An excellent critical study, emphasizing nuances of Japanese style and culture. Includes a chronology, a bibliography and explanatory notes.

Starrs, Roy. *Soundings in Time: The Fictive Art of Kawabata Yasunari*. Richmond, England: Japan Library, 1998. A good study of Kawabata's fiction.

Swann, Thomas E., and Kinya Tsuruta. *Approaches to the Modern Japanese Short Story*. Tokyo: Waseda University Press, 1982. Analyzes "The Izu Dancer," *The House of the Sleeping Beauties*, and "One Arm."

Ueda, Makoto. *Modern Japanese Writers and the Nature of Literature*. Stanford, Calif.: Stanford University Press, 1976. Devoting forty-five pages to Kawabata, this distinguished Japanese scholar emphasizes the elements of positive thought and action, vitality, beauty, and purity in Kawabata's work. Complemented by a bibliography and an index.

A. Owen Aldridge

GARRISON KEILLOR

Born: Anoka, Minnesota; August 7, 1942

OTHER LITERARY FORMS

Garrison Keillor began his literary career in 1960 as a radio comedian appearing on Minnesota Public Radio. From 1974 to 1987, he hosted a live weekly radio show based in St. Paul, Minnesota, entitled *A Prairie Home Companion*, a variety format that included original monologues that he called "News from Lake Wobegon." Offered as a premium to Minnesota Public Radio contributors, Keillor's *The Selected Verse of Margaret Haskins Durber* (1979) includes fourteen poems about Minnesota that he had read or sung on the air. The short fiction that he subsequently published is largely rooted in the twenty-minute monologues that he composed for his radio shows and that revolve around the places and characters of the mythical Lake Wobegon, Minnesota, in Mist (missed) County. Some of his monologues have also been released on audiocassette tapes, videocassettes, and compact-disc recordings. Beginning in 1989, Keillor hosted from New York City the weekly radio broadcast *American Radio Company of the Air*, a variety format, which likewise included original monologues, some of which have been anthologized in print or on tape. In 1999, Keillor published the novel *Me, Jimmy (Big Boy) Valente, Governor of Minnesota*.

ACHIEVEMENTS

Garrison Keillor, along with Spalding Gray and Eric Bogosian, achieved fame as one of the most accomplished monologuists in the last half of the twentieth century. His written production initially grew out of both his live and his recorded performances and succeeded largely because his reputation as a performer preceded the publications. He is a homespun humorist with a droll, low-key, tongue-in-cheek style. His rambling tales emanated from poking fun at the fictional characters of his mythical Lake Wobegon, Minnesota, "the little town that time forgot and that decades cannot improve."

Besides having created and hosted nationally acclaimed radio shows and published best-selling books, Keillor has continued to be a regular contributor to *The New Yorker*. He received a Grammy Award for his recording of *Lake Wobegon Days* and two Awards for Cable Excellence for the Disney Channel productions of *A Prairie Home Companion*. He has also received a George Foster Peabody Broadcasting award and an Edward R. Murrow award. He has appeared with the Chicago, Minnesota, Milwaukee, San Francisco, Pittsburgh, and National symphony orchestras, and in a performance entitled "Lake Wobegon Tonight," at the Apollo Theatre in London. He has received a Gold Medal Award for spoken English from the American Academy of Arts and Letters in 1990 and was inducted into the Museum of Broadcast Communications and the Radio Hall of Fame in 1994.

BIOGRAPHY

Garrison Keillor's roots in small-town Minnesota provided him with the particular brand of midwestern humor that brought him fame and on which he continued to capitalize even after relocating to New York City. Born Gary Edward Keillor, he was the third of six children in the family of John P. Keillor, a railway mail clerk and carpenter, and Grace Denham Keillor. When he was in the eighth grade, he adopted the pen name "Garrison" in place of his given names because, he said, he believed that it sounded "more formidable." He grew up just north of Minneapolis, Minnesota, south of the small town of Anoka in what has since become Brooklyn Park. After his 1960 graduation from Anoka High School, he enrolled in the University of Minnesota, authored a regular column, published stories in the student magazine *The Ivory Tower*, which he later edited, and was student announcer for KUOM, the university radio station. He received a B.A. in English and journalism in 1966, went to New York in an unsuccessful attempt to land a job as a writer, returned to work on a master's degree in English, and then took a job with KSJR-FM in Collegeville, the first station in the Minnesota Public Radio network.

Keillor spent fourteen years on and off, from 1968 to 1982, as a disc jockey in St. Paul, Minnesota. His earliest program, *The Prairie Home Morning Show*, eventually included anecdotes about a mythical Midwestern place that he called Lake Wobegon, situated in the similarly mythical Mist County. One of the hallmarks of the program was inclusion of advertisements from bogus sponsors: Powdermilk Biscuits, Jack's Auto Repair, Bertha's Kitty Boutique, and Ralph's Pretty Good Grocery, among others. Besides broadcasting, Keillor was busy writing. He sold his first story, "Local Family Keeps Son Happy," to *The New Yorker* in 1970, then moved with his wife and

small son to a farm near Freeport, Minnesota. He was divorced in 1976.

Modeled after the Grand Ole Opry in Nashville, Tennessee, Keillor's first live segment of *A Prairie Home Companion* aired on July 6, 1974. The monologues, advertisements, and musical entertainment were highlights of the program. Eleven years later, one of the show's monologues concerned a twenty-fifth high school class reunion in which the narrator, Keillor, rekindles an acquaintance with a foreign exchange student that blossoms into a romance. The monologue was biographical in the sense that, at his own class reunion at Anoka High School, Keillor established a real-life relationship with Ulla Skaerved, Danish exchange student twenty-five years earlier, and they were married on December 29, 1985, in Denmark.

A Prairie Home Companion continued in weekly radio broadcasts for thirteen years, culminating in a farewell performance on June 13, 1987. During these years, Keillor anthologized his monologues in recordings and in books. Perhaps a disenchantment with his celebrity status and an irritation with newspaper reporters in St. Paul, who printed what Keillor believed to be private information about himself, resulted in Keillor and his new wife relocating to Denmark for a short while, then settling in New York City. There, he continued to write for *The New Yorker* and host a weekly radio broadcast entitled *American Radio Company of the Air*.

In the mid-1990's, Garrison Keillor resumed live broadcasts of *A Prairie Home Companion*, but for his return to radio he began touring the United States and no longer limited himself to performing his shows in Minnesota. He still continued to tell witty stories about the residents of the fictional town of Wobegon, Minnesota. In 1999, Garrison Keillor wrote a fictional autobiography of a resident of Wobegon and a witty satire of Governor Jesse Ventura of Minnesota. The similarities between the

Garrison Keillor (©Miriam Berkley)

fictional governor named Jimmy Valente and Jesse Ventura are so striking that Keillor felt the need to state that readers should not assume that his book, a satire of the state of American politics in the late twentieth century, has anything to do with Jesse Ventura.

ANALYSIS

Garrison Keillor's upbringing in a small town in central Minnesota is the single greatest influence on his work. Many of the experiences and characters that appear in his short fiction are rooted in memories of events that happened to him there or of people whom he knew. In fact, the name for his radio show *A Prairie Home Companion* is taken from a cemetery in Moorhead, Minnesota, called Prairie Home Lutheran Cemetery.

The theme of religion—specifically Christianity—is the most frequently explored concept in Keillor's work. He has, in fact, described *A Prairie Home Companion* as "a gospel show." Growing up, Keillor and his family were members of the Plymouth Brethren, a Protestant sect of Anglican dissenters that closely resembles the "fundamentalists" and the "Sanctified Brethren" in his published works. His upbringing was a conservative one, in which drinking, smoking, dancing, attending movies, and watching television were frowned upon; consequently Keillor writes with a conservative, instructional, and highly moral tone. A piece in one of his early books is entitled "Your Wedding and You: A Few Thoughts on Making It More Personally Rewarding, Shared by Reverend Bob Osman." Here, Keillor offers, tongue in cheek, prudent advice and practical suggestions on how to tailor a wedding ceremony to fit the personalities of the bride and groom. A couple he calls Sam and Judy, for example, "chose to emphasize their mutual commitment to air and water quality, exchanging vows while chained to each other and to the plant gate of a major industrial polluter."

LAKE WOBEGON STORIES

Throughout his writing, Keillor writes about ordinary events that evoke a natural piety, *memento mori*, along with an awareness of the transience of all things. His philosophy is consistent with the Chris-

tian doctrine that life is basically good. Some of the pieces, for example, offer metaphors for the Christian promise of eternal life. A quotation from "State Fair," a piece that appears in *Leaving Home*, perhaps best illustrates this. In it, the narrator remembers riding the Ferris wheel as a child:

> We go up and I think of people I knew who are dead and I smell fall in the air, manure, corn dogs, and we drop down into blazing light and blaring music. Every summer I'm a little bigger, but riding the ferris wheel, I feel the same as ever, I feel eternal. . . . The wheel carries us up high, high, high, and stops, and we sit swaying, creaking, in the dark, on the verge of death. . . . Then the wheel brings me down to the ground. We get off and other people get on. Thank you, dear God, for this good life and forgive us if we do not live it enough.

In other pieces, however, rebellion against his repressive upbringing surfaces in sarcasm, not all of it gentle or good-humored. The most notable example of this is an extended complaint, the "longest footnote in American fiction," entitled "95 Theses 95," which appears in *Lake Wobegon Days*. One of Keillor's important themes here is righteous anger at how the Midwest has shaped him. Keillor uses the character Johnny Tollefson, a fictional, angry son, who returns to Lake Wobegon with a new wife from Boston, intent on nailing a set of written complaints about the repressive effects of putative parents and neighbors to the door of the Lutheran church, but "something in his upbringing made him afraid to pound holes in a good piece of wood." So, instead, the treatise becomes "lost" on the overloaded desk of the town's newspaper editor and ultimately appears as a footnote that spans twenty-three pages.

In this complaint, Keillor rails against religious strictures, fear of sexuality, fastidiousness, and his resultant ineptness at sustaining interpersonal relationships. A milder complaint is thesis 7, which states,

> You have taught me to fear strangers and their illicit designs, robbing me of easy companionship, making me a very suspicious friend. Even among those I know well, I continue to worry: what do they *really* mean by liking me?

These complaints become increasingly bitter; thesis 14, for example, states:

> You taught me to trust my own incompetence and even now won't let me mash potatoes without your direct supervision. "Don't run the mixer so fast that you get them all over," you say, as if in my home, the walls are covered with big white lumps. I can't mow a lawn or hang tinsel on a Christmas tree or paint a flat surface in your presence without you watching, worried, pointing out the unevenness.

Thesis 21 shows Keillor's anger at having been brought up to feel guilty. "Suffering was its own reward, to be preferred to pleasure. As Lutherans, we viewed pleasure with suspicion. Birth control was never an issue with us. Nor was renunciation of pleasures of the flesh. We never enjoyed them in the first place."

This is an imposing example of Keillor's sarcasm, but it is just as important to bear in mind his knack for comedy, which is, ultimately, more prevalent in his work. With deliberate pacing and mild surprise, many of his stories are gentle, nostalgic, and quiet. Finally, he celebrates, rather than satirizes, the Sanctified Brethren. He believes that, despite ridiculous situations and smallness or meanness in certain people, "life is a comedy" because "God is the author, and God writes an awful lot of comedy." Although he laughs at how foolish humankind can be, it is a good-natured laughter which has his characters' best interests at heart.

When one of Keillor's characters, Clarence Bunsen, discovered that what he thought was a heart attack in the shower one day really was not, he was so grateful that he dropped a check into the collection plate at church the following Sunday, only to realize moments later that he had mistakenly made it out for three hundred dollars instead of thirty, thus cleaning out his bank account.

Lake Wobegon's visitation by twenty-four Lutheran ministers ends in a disaster that is really humorous. Pastor Inqvist had arranged an outing for the clergy on a pontoon boat owned by Wally of the Sidetrack Tap, but the combined weight of all the earnest ministers each holding a can of beer was too much for the *Agnes D.* She took on more water than Wally could bail out, forcibly introducing eight of the clergy to the Baptist heresy of full immersion. Soon, all the ministers were standing chin deep in water, faces uplifted, unable to call out for help "because their voices were too deep and mellow," and "trying to understand this experience and its deeper meaning."

Family gatherings at which his great uncle and aunt told long tales were also influential on Keillor. Keillor often calls himself a "shy person," and, in fact, humorously advocates "shy rights" in some of his tales. His quietly reserved and remote personality is immediately evident in listening to his radio broadcasts. Not surprisingly, one of Keillor's main themes is an idealization of home and family relationships, and another is the evanescence of home. Many of his tales, as well as the title of one of his books, concern his relationship with home.

HAPPY TO BE HERE

Happy to Be Here collected witty and urbane pieces that Keillor initially wrote for periodical publication. Though the book includes no Lake Wobegon material, it pokes fun at small-town life in its sly humor and bucolic optimism. Keillor uses an ordinary Minnesota farm as his setting for the ideal "home": "Found paradise. Here it is, and it is just what I knew was here all along. . . . I'm happy to be here." Here also Keillor parodies the styles of writing in magazines such as *Life* and *Rolling Stone*, the swagger of political figures and the unchecked optimism, grand designs, and little moral dilemmas of his midwestern characters. Two of the pieces, "WLT" and "The Slim Graves Show," draw on his radio experience, and many offer rules to live by or recount lessons that he has learned from life.

LAKE WOBEGON DAYS *and* LEAVING HOME

Prompted by the popularity of the monologues in *A Prairie Home Companion* broadcasts, Keillor offered in *Lake Wobegon Days* an extended history and geography of the mythical town of Lake Wobegon. Although giving abundant detail of a specific place, Keillor insists on the universality of his myth because he believes that places like it exist everywhere. The book has a pattern of development that is both chronological and seasonal. It chronicles the founding of the town by early settlers and the establishment of its traditions. Emphasizing the cycle of seasons, it also recounts the personal story of a little boy growing up among the Sanctified Brethren, envious of Catholics and Lutherans, who becomes a restless adolescent.

Leaving Home: A Collection of Lake Wobegon Stories is the title of Keillor's second book of Lake Wobegon stories, published after Keillor ended his association with Minnesota Public Radio and moved to Denmark and then, soon afterward, to New York City. If *Lake Wobegon Days* defined the stable and slightly sentimentalized mid-American town, *Leaving Home* portrays it in flux and recombination, emphasizing the transience of all things. Every story recounts some kind of leave-taking or homecoming: a waitress quitting her job at the Chatterbox Café, a boy joining the army, Father Emil retiring from Our Lady of Perpetual Responsibility Catholic Church, family members returning to Lake Wobegon for Christmas. During the time of the book's writing, Keillor himself married a second time and left Minnesota, so the book is significant biographically as well as artistically. Keillor laments in the book's introduction that his home territory, Minneapolis and St. Paul, had changed, and not for the better. The Met Stadium, he notes, had been replaced by "a polyester ball field with a roof over it, a ghostly greenish plastic baseball mall, and all those lovely summer nights were lost." The book ends with Keillor himself taking leave of his characters: "This is my last view of [the residents of Lake Wobegon] for a while. If you see them before I do, say hello from me and give them my love."

WE ARE STILL MARRIED

We Are Still Married: Stories and Letters is a challenging set of essays about life on the edge. The stories are cryptic, cynical, suave, and aggressive. In several, Keillor expresses explicit anger at the media. "My Life in Prison" is a vicious parody about what journalists have done to him. The title story is the piece that closes the book, which describes the near destruction of an ordinary marriage once the media move in to examine it. There is violence in the book as well as sadness and some midcareer anxiety. The

rest rooms in New York City's subways are described as a hell unmatched by even the most primitive rural Minnesota gas stations, "full of garbage, filth, killer bees, Nazis, crack heads, [and] flies who carry AIDS." Annie Szemanski is a tobacco-spitting, brass-kneed feminist baseball player in "What Did We Do Wrong?" who insults and abuses her ardent fans. Even the five sketches devoted to Lake Wobegon characters are more complicated and sophisticated than his earlier stories had been, depicting raw emotion and a bit of meanness.

A PRAIRIE HOME COMPANION

In 1997, Garrison Keillor's fictional autobiography of a male resident of Wobegon was published. Readers sense that this narrator represents the persona created by Keillor for the monologues he gave in performances of *A Prairie Home Companion*. Each chapter is a touching story told by the narrator. Perhaps the most moving story is the one Keillor entitled "The Wake." Keillor evokes the universal use of humor as a defense mechanism by family members attending a wake and the difficulty that people have in talking about the lives of recently deceased family members. In this story, the narrator's father has just died and he has returned to Wobegon for the funeral. As they are approaching the cemetery, the narrator tells his friend Diana that his dad is not in the coffin but in Buenos Aires. This remark represents a clear effort to deny reality, but many people who are grieving seek to deny reality. Keillor also describes a curious group of strange characters, including a retired senator who now lives in a trailer park in Florida and several cousins who tell tall tales. This story illustrates very nicely how people use humor to get through painful experiences such as a wake or a burial.

More than one critic of Keillor's work has compared his particular brand of humor and storytelling with that of Mark Twain. Both authors are distinctly American, offering homespun profundities and cracker-barrel philosophy that are regional in inception and origin. Both tell tall tales with digressive anecdotes. Both mock pretense, portray comic suffering, and reveal the near-universal indignities of youth. As platform performers, both share the belief that a good tale should be heard as well as read, and both pose as overeager, inept but perceptive witnesses to life experiences. The rich imagination evident in the writings of both authors can be enjoyed by scholars of humor as well as ordinary people who simply want to laugh.

OTHER MAJOR WORKS

LONG FICTION: *WLT: A Radio Romance*, 1991; *Wobegon Boy*, 1997; *Me, Jimmy (Big Boy) Valente, Governor of Minnesota*, 1999.

POETRY: *The Selected Verse of Margaret Haskins Durber*, 1979.

CHILDREN'S LITERATURE: *Cat, You Better Come Home*, 1995.

RECORDINGS: *A Prairie Home Companion Anniversary Album*, 1980; *News from Lake Wobegon*, 1983; *Ten Years on the Prairie: "A Prairie Home Companion" Tenth Anniversary*, 1984; *Gospel Birds and Other Stories of Lake Wobegon*, 1985; *A Prairie Home Companion: The Final Performance*, 1987; *A Prairie Home Companion: The Second Annual Farewell Performance*, 1988; *A Prairie Home Companion: The Third Annual Farewell Performance*, 1989; *More News from Lake Wobegon*, 1989; *Local Man Moves to the City*, 1991; *Lake Wobegon U.S.A.*, 1992; *Rhubarb*, 1993; *A Prairie Home Companion: Twentieth Anniversary Collection*, 1994; *Guy Noir, Radio Private Eye*, 1994; *Fertility*, 1995; *Patience*, 1995; *A Prairie Home Christmas with Garrison Keillor and Hundreds of Friends and Aquaintances*, 1995; *Youth*, 1995; *Horrors!: A Prairie Home Companion*, 1996; *Mother, Father, Uncle, Aunt: Stories from Lake Wobegon*, 1996; *The Old Man Who Loved Cheese*, 1997; *Life These Days: Stories from Lake Wobegon*, 1998.

BIBLIOGRAPHY

Fedo, Michael. *The Man from Lake Wobegon*. New York: St. Martin's Press, 1987. Fedo's biography of Keillor, from early childhood until his departure from Minnesota, is an unauthorized biography. Keillor refused to be interviewed by Fedo and encouraged his staff and the performers on his show to do likewise. Still, Fedo reveals close particulars of Keillor's personal life, his interests and influences, and the phenomenon of his popularity. Particularly useful is Fedo's four-page bibliography, which includes published interviews and articles about Keillor.

Lee, Judith Yaross. *Garrison Keillor: A Voice of America*. Jackson: University Press of Mississippi, 1991. Analysis of Keillor's stories in *Lake Wobegone Days*, *Leaving Home*, and other uncollected short fictions. Examines Keillor's methods of composition and such literary ancestors of his creation of Lake Wobegone as William Faulkner's Yoknapatawpha, James Joyce's Dublin, and Sherwood Anderson's Winesburg.

Narveson, Robert D. "Catholic-Lutheran Interaction in Keillor's *Lake Wobegon Days* and Hassler's *Grand Opening*." In *Exploring the Midwestern Literary Imagination*, edited by Marcia Noe. Troy, N.Y.: Whitston, 1993. Compares descriptions of Catholic and Lutheran interaction in small towns in Keillor's fiction with anthropological studies. Suggests that such social interactions in fiction may be conditioned more by the demands exerted by fiction's thematic significance and related symbolic patterns than by their correspondence to external reality.

Scholl, Peter A. *Garrison Keillor*. New York: Twayne, 1993. Examines Keillor's humorous and pastoral fiction and the place of Minnesota in literature. Includes a bibliography and an index.

_____. "Garrison Keillor." In *Dictionary of Literary Biography, 1987 Year-Book*, edited by J. M. Brook. Detroit: Gale Research, 1988. A very good introduction to Keillor's life and works, giving insights into Keillor's personality, motivation, and career. Recounts the early influences of his literary heroes and of the Grand Ole Opry. Discusses Keillor's childhood, education, and individual published works in some detail and chronicles Keillor's involvement in radio broadcasting.

_____. "Garrison Keillor and the News from Lake Wobegon." *Studies in American Humor* 4 (Winter, 1985-1986): 217-228. Comparing Keillor to Will Rogers and Mark Twain, Scholl stresses the regional, homespun character of Keillor's work. He also draws a distinction between two Keillors, "that of wandering storyteller in exile from Lake Wobegon and that of the urbane wit and writer for *The New Yorker.*" Scholl discusses the unique brand of storytelling that Keillor uses in his monologues, a combination of spontaneity and studied elegance that is evident in the oral narratives as well as on the printed page. He stresses Keillor's focus on the "continuity and resilience of human life" and on the belief that "God is good."

Skow, John. "Let's Hear It for Lake Wobegon!" *Reader's Digest* 128 (February, 1986): 67-71. The inviting and immediate tone of this article makes it very engaging. It details a public performance of a segment of *A Prairie Home Companion* and, in doing so, relates explicitly the tone and mood that infuses all Keillor's work. Some biographical information gives insight into Keillor's career as a performer.

Traub, James. "The Short and Tall Tales of Garrison Keillor." *Esquire* 97 (May, 1982): 108-117. This article, in part an interview, contains an early yet detailed look at Keillor's performance techniques. Formative influences from childhood, college, and adulthood are recounted. Much attention is paid to Keillor's method and technique of written composition as well as the evolution of *A Prairie Home Companion.*

Jill B. Gidmark, updated by Edmund J. Campion

BENEDICT KIELY

Born: Dromore, County Tyrone, Northern Ireland; August 15, 1919

PRINCIPAL SHORT FICTION

A Journey to the Seven Streams: Seventeen Stories, 1963

A Ball of Malt and Madame Butterfly: A Dozen Stories, 1973

A Cow in the House and Nine Other Stories, 1978

The State of Ireland: A Novella and Seventeen Stories, 1980

A Letter to Peachtree and Nine Other Stories, 1987

God's Own Country, 1993

OTHER LITERARY FORMS

Benedict Kiely has published several novels, a number of which are set in his native Northern Ireland; others are set mainly in Dublin or in a mixture of Northern Ireland and Ireland. *There Was an Ancient House* (1955) is based on his year as a Jesuit novice; *Proxopera* (1977) deals with violence in Northern Ireland in the 1970's. His nonfiction includes *Counties of Contention* (1945), on Northern Ireland; *Poor Scholar: A Study of the Works and Days of William Carleton, 1794-1869* (1947), a life of the nineteenth century Irish novelist; *Modern Irish Fiction: A Critique* (1950), literary criticism; *A Raid into Dark Corners: And Other Essays* (1999); and *The Waves Behind Us: Further Memoirs* (1999). For many years Kiely has written weekly travel pieces for the *Irish Times*; he has also published numerous book reviews and critical essays. He is the editor of several anthologies and has published children's literature, such as *The Trout in the Turnhole* (1995).

ACHIEVEMENTS

Benedict Kiely is a member of the Irish Academy of Letters. He also received an honorary doctorate of letters from the National University of Ireland in 1984.

BIOGRAPHY

Benedict Kiely grew up in Omagh, County Tyrone, and was graduated from the Christian Brothers School. He began writing for publication in 1936, entered a Jesuit novitiate in 1937, but resigned with a back injury in 1938. He was graduated from University College, Dublin, in 1943. In addition to being a prolific writer of fiction, Kiely had a distinguished career as a newspaper reporter in Dublin, holding among other influential positions that of literary editor of *The Irish Press*, a national daily. Much of the material for his short fiction is drawn from his days as a working journalist. He has also held various teaching positions in the United States. Kiely settled in Dublin, where his reputation as a broadcaster, raconteur, and a man of letters exceeds his artistic renown.

ANALYSIS

Benedict Kiely's approach to short fiction is typically discursive, episodic, and anecdotal, because of the nature of his material as well as his artistic apprehension of it. Kiely's material is drawn less from his own imagination than from the things people say, write, or sing. His artistic rendering of the material comes from his well-developed sense of oral tradition. This sense is alert not only to the delight of utterance but also to the ways in which utterance stimulates memory and how stories, like shadow plays, illustrate the trials of loss and love that characterize the human journey.

The outcome of these orientations is a body of short fiction that speaks to the rich verbal integument of Irish culture. The adaptation of oral tradition to the context of a society's growing pains is one of Kiely's most significant contributions to modern Irish writing. In addition, his fiction identifies strata of myth in the adventures and careers of its protagonists. This mythic dimension concerns journeying, unearthing, restoring, and the rituals of arrival and departure. Kiely's sense of landscape wistfully evinces this dimension. The presence of an archetypal undertow is another means by which Kiely's work reinvigorates certain important strains of Irish literary culture. The flexible and informal conservatism of Kiely's artistic strategies constitutes a distinctive accomplishment in what has been a time of rapid and unnerving change in Irish culture and society.

His Northern Ireland background, his attachment to both Ireland and Northern Ireland, his reminiscences about Ireland, his love of poetry, his humor and irony—all can be found in his favorite stories, in-

cluding "A Cow in the House," "A Ball of Malt and Madame Butterfly," "Down Then by Derry," "A Journey to the Seven Streams," "Bluebell Meadow," and "Maiden's Leap." All of these stories were written between 1960 and 1975; the last three were first published in *The New Yorker*.

"A COW IN THE HOUSE"

"A Cow in the House" relates a childhood experience of Kiely on his first trip from Omagh to Dublin when the journey was prepared for by an amateurish and embarrassing haircut by a local barber who, for further humiliation, kept a cow in his house. From such adverse beginnings, the child must also clack through Dublin with a loose heel; and his self-consciousness causes him to make another mistake when he sings a bawdy song for a group of nuns. The day's series of disasters turns only when he visits a hall of mirrors, where he becomes conscious of the imperfections of other people; all have "big noses, red faces, legs too long or short, behinds that waggled, clothes that didn't fit. Every one of them had a cow in the house."

"A JOURNEY TO THE SEVEN STREAMS"

Perhaps Kiely's penchant for travelogues derives from his father, who had traveled to South Africa to fight in the Boer War. Kiely reminisces about him in "A Journey to the Seven Streams," in which the father conducts the family among Northern Ireland towns in the vicinity of Omagh and recites history as he points out important features of the landscape. A rickety car, in the days when cars were few, and the family's wry comments on it provide much of the humor of this story. To the owner the car is "human," but it stops and refuses to start without being pushed uphill; it frightens livestock and attracts congregations. Returning to Omagh, the family decides that decorum demands they alight from the car at the town's entrance and walk the rest of the way home.

"A BALL OF MALT AND MADAME BUTTERFLY"

At the opposite extreme from youthful remembrance is "A Ball of Malt and Madame Butterfly." To write about his queen of the streets, Kiely chooses the ancient and beautiful symbol of female erotica, the butterfly, and surrounds his Madame Butterfly with attitudes of humor and endearment. This Butterfly owes little to her counterpart in the opera by Giacomo Puccini except a slightly Japanese appearance; her basic occupation, to Guy de Maupassant's story "Ball of Suet." The place she frequents in Dublin is a pub called the Dark Cow, and "What she is her mother was before her, and proud of it."

The story begins with just a touch of prejudice against prostitutes, unpopular though such sentiment is among Butterfly's loyal followers, the men of the fire brigade. A ladder raised to a smoking upstairs window focuses attention on a partly dressed male who shoves a woman back into the room so that he can escape first. Indignation turns to laughter when Butterfly emerges, and the firemen subsequently make certain that the ungallant man's wife and hometown hear about his deeds.

Images of flight now focus on birds, which, like cows, are favored in Irish mythology but, unlike cows, have the further advantage of romantic enhancement by the poet William Butler Yeats and all his entourage of poetry enthusiasts, one of whom is a lonely, shy, forty-year-old Dublin bachelor named Pike Hunter. Painfully self-conscious, he passes through Stephen's Green, where women on park benches seem as "gracefully at rest as the swans on the lake." Then Pike sees the poet himself and observes a touching meeting of Yeats and Maud Gonne in their old age and all their majesty; the sight of Maud Gonne recalls for Pike the poem "When You Are Old" and that "one man loved the pilgrim soul in you, and loved the sorrows of your changing face." His knowledge of a former meeting on Howth Head and the poems "His Phoenix" and "The White Birds" furthers his romantic inclinations, for next he walks into the Dark Cow, frequented by dockers, and into the acquaintance of Butterfly. She will become his personal "phoenix" as in Yeats's poem, the means for him of his transformation and his pilgrimage. The lines "I would that we were, my beloved, white birds on the foam of the sea" will lead later to Butterfly's flight away from Pike. Although Pike knows other poets as well, it is Ireland's greatest that causes his downfall.

Drunk on poetry, views, and visions, Pike buys champagne for Butterfly and meets her fireman friend, Austin, who knew Butterfly's dance-hall mother and who always orders "A ball of malt" and adds "and Madame Butterfly" as a joke. Pike becomes acquainted with Jody, the pub owner, and with Butterfly's "stable of girls," all of whom have never before seen the like of Pike Hunter. His lovemaking reminds Butterfly of a Christian Brother: He soon has her "puked" with his continual recitations of poetry, and he loves her with a singularity of devotion that interferes with her normal trade. Nor does she appreciate his efforts to transform the relationship from a mercenary one by failing to pay her for every performance. Meanwhile, Butterfly invests Jody's five-pound note at the races and then buys with the profits a musquash coat of such elegance that she wears it for everything, including a trip to Howth Head to walk around the mountain as the poet had done with Maud Gonne. She could have tolerated the rough walk in high-heeled shoes (topped with a broken heel), the hot sun running sweat under her fur coat, the delays for mending the heel, and the resultant shivers when the sun sank but that the shy Pike should—under the inspiration of poetry—turn into a violent rapist and attempt to flatten her on Howth proves too much indignity for Butterfly, who prefers the privacy of a rumpled bed. The resultant quarrelsome fault-finding ends the relationship.

Thereafter, Pike returns drunk, only once, to the Dark Cow, where efforts to cheer him up fail and evoke from him only a comment, "Boys, Beethoven when he was dying, said: Clap now, good friends, the comedy is done." His aunts, who had presided over his extended virginity, soon find him impossible to live with and place him in Saint Patrick's Hospital, where another Irish writer, Dean Swift, "died roaring." Jody dies and his successor ousts all the girls from the Dark Cow. Austin meets Butterfly some time later on O'Connell Street under the Nelson Pillar and tells her the story of the slavey whom Lord Nelson took for a wife and made Lady Emma Hamilton. From this Butterfly apparently takes inspiration and eventually marries a dock worker. In this way Kiely blends two of his favorite themes: the literary and historic past of his country and the literary-minded character who quotes poetry, mostly at inopportune moments to unappreciative audiences.

"MAIDEN'S LEAP"

In "Maiden's Leap" the protagonist is a writer, Robert St. Blaise Macmahon, whose pride in superiority to his maidenly cousin suffers a rude fall. Kiely sets this story in his hometown of Omagh, a garrison town whose people Robert Macmahon despises for their pettiness; but then Robert regards nearly everything as somewhat beneath him: the United States, which he visited and in which he was the only person with sense enough to admire the alligators; Yeats and James Joyce, who are "colossal bores"; the town, because his father had "as good as owned it"; his housekeeper and cousin-once-removed Miss Hynes; and any fleshly contact with other people. He has pride of ancestry and no desire for progeny. At age forty-one with a spinsterish and impoverished housekeeper two years older than he is, he condescends to the civic guard until the man's mission—to inform him of a dead body in the spinster's bed—registers in his consciousness. Yet the dead man, having died "Unhouselled, unappointed, unannealed," as Robert says, evokes from the guard a comment that Robert mentally concedes is worthy of repetition elsewhere: The dead man could not expect the company of a resident chaplain. Robert's thinking in quotations leads him to urge the guard, in the words of Henry James, to "try to be one of those on whom nothing is lost"; yet the supreme irony of the story is that much is lost on Robert. While awaiting removal of the corpse, Robert learns from the guard good, human stories about the deceased: He once bought and lost—through the open back door of a van—two hundred hens; his brother, a gardener, had died on a lawnmower when it exploded beneath him—lives that would make good writing and that other people live while Robert looks down his nose; yet, again ironically, he despises the Cyrano de Bergerac nose of the corpse. His chief concern about the corpse in his housekeeper's bed is that he, Robert, will be laughed at by the community, "clods he had always regarded with a detached and humorous, yet godlike, eye."

As the guard departs, Robert sits in the room of Miss Hynes and remembers when he tried to kiss her at age sixteen and she slapped him. That she has for many years concealed a lover in his ancestral mansion fails to change his pitying opinion of her. She had come to him an orphan from the cliffs of Glenade, north of Manorhamilton in County Literim, where legend described a woman who had leaped from a cliff to save her virtue and was dashed to her death on the rocks below; Robert imagined his housekeeper having made a similar leap to his hearthside, where, as a poor relation, she lived a death of all romantic hopes. He also imagines their liaison when he was sixteen to have been her last prospect for romantic entanglement.

Now he begins reading her diary, however, and finds that, much to his chagrin, instead of admiring him as he deserves to be admired, instead of playing the role of a poor relation grateful to her benefactor, she has always ridiculed and satirized every aspect of his being—his handmade shoes; his writing books that no one reads; his arrogance and aloofness, which kept him from knowing anything interesting; and his fondness for alligators in Florida. Yet the diary reveals her to be a good writer and a good critic, for she sees that "he was twisting life to suit his reading." She scourges him for his thoughtful criticism of the Irish for not marrying young; to her this belies his ignorance of the conditions of their existence. Finally, he learns, she had rejected his advances when she was eighteen and he sixteen not because of what he was doing but because of the "stupid way he was trying to do it."

Miss Hynes, meanwhile, has made her escape early to report to the civic guard and kept herself at the guard's barracks, but she telephones back long enough to comment on Robert and on her diary. She proves in this conversation that she is in reality more than the housekeeper he has known, and, certainly, she is the witty and insightful writer he has discovered in the diary. She calls him, for his talking in quotations, a two-footed gramophone. Later, when as an employer he tries to demand her return to her duties, the guard informs him she has taken the train to Dublin. Her lover died, he concedes, "looking at the roses," and the two had met as growers of roses. Her second maiden's leap to Dublin is Macmahon's fall into wrenching, dismaying self-knowledge.

"BLUEBELL MEADOW"

In a different perspective, the process by which adults impose their political and religious differences on the otherwise unifying factors of children's friendships is the theme of "Bluebell Meadow," set in Kiely's hometown of Omagh, dominated by the opposing symbols of the British army barracks and the Catholic church spires. From events and ways of the previous centuries, Catholics are called papishes and support the Free State (now the Republic of Ireland) to the south; Protestants are called Black Protestants and remain loyal to the Union (with Britain). Those moderates who would bridge the gap still have a sensitivity to the more intense feelings of others and let discretion dominate social interaction.

Kiely tells this story from the viewpoint of a sensitive teenage girl restricted by a leg brace and her blue convent school costume, but she reads much and has a mind that ranges far beyond this Northern Ireland town. Where she reads in a park, Lofty emerges from the nearby river and gives her one of his fresh-caught trout. His seeking her out she treats as mostly casual friendship; that he is "of the other persuasion" does not immediately occur to her, nor does it especially matter. She remembers a year earlier when Lofty's mother, whom she met on a train to and from Bundoran, seemed "great fun" as she recited jokes and rhymes against both papishes and Protestants, laughed as she smuggled sugar from the Free State, conversed with the girl's uncle and agreed—Protestant and Catholic—on the defects of jerry-built houses.

The girl becomes acquainted with a sense of humor in Lofty and a sensitivity corresponding to her own: his knowing without asking that, in a leg brace, she would not choose to walk with him; his enjoyment of his three sisters, who love the company of the British soldiers; his sisters' teasing him about a nursemaid whose pram he pushed up a hill and who mistook him for a Catholic. Upon her accusation that he would not associate with her in public view, he did not correct her because she might not like her pram pushed by a Presbyterian.

Such pleasantries between Lofty and the girl are permitted to continue only from April to August, when a black man (not a person of African descent,

but rather here a member of the Black Perceptory of the Orange Order who wears a black sash in the July 12 Protestant parade) sits beside her on her park bench. After some agreeable conversation, he launches into the day's business—to separate her, in the names of God and country and for her own good, from Lofty. The reason, he explains, is that Lofty's uncle is a tiler, "a big man in the Orange Order," one who keeps intruders out and who is responsible to the Worshipful Master, which is himself. Lofty, he says, is a B-Special, a member of the British army pledged "to hold Ulster against the Pope and the Republic of Ireland," one who visits Catholics at night to ascertain their registration. In an irate moment, he adds, "The B-Specials are sworn to uphold Protestant liberty and beat down the Fenians and the I.R.A." It makes no difference to him that she is not a Fenian or a member of the Irish Republican Army, nor that she and Lofty are not thinking of marriage. With further warnings he departs on the terms of a big, friendly man trying to help her. Lofty's friendliness ceases.

At home a sergeant questions her about bullets Lofty had given her and she had placed in an earthenware jug, and she must accompany him to the station. To her uncle, who had seen bullets used in the United States, harboring bullets without a gun seems as harmless as it does to her, but the confiscation of the bullets given in friendship marks the vast division between the two families. Under British rule in the past, no Irish person was allowed to own a knife or gun or weapon of any kind. In spite of tolerance among individuals, the ships of church and state sail divided seas.

"DOWN THEN BY DERRY"

The most thoroughly autobiographical of Kiely's stories is "Down Then by Derry," in which the "he" or "dad" of the story is clearly an elderly Kiely, returning to scenes of childhood, recalling a letter from an American correspondent who also had lived in the area, visiting his eighty-five-year-old mother, and having for company a son and daughter. Here is Omagh, with its church spires and army barracks, the town where the rivers Drumragh and Camowen meet and go on "under the name of Strule," and a song about the Strule recurs in the visitor's thoughts. Memories of the past and of people who have traveled elsewhere merge with many nostalgic sights—a sycamore planted a hundred years before; a man who cut down a white-thorn, then saw two ghostly children and died that night with no other forewarning; his mother's habit of spitting after mention of the devil. Some persons did not leave Omagh, however, and the remembered childhood romances climax in the appearance of an aged face, from which comes a stranger's recognition: "We saw you on the teevee." Her brother now sits in a wheelchair; she dismisses a childhood friend with a brief comment and goes away.

The main story concerns Omagh without military and civil strife. It differs from the reality of the 1970's that Kiely confronted at the close of "Bluebell Meadow": "There are burned-out buildings in the main streets, and barricades and checkpoints at the ends of the town. . . . Still, other towns are worse. Strabane, which was on the border and easy to bomb, is a burned-out wreck—and Newry. . . . And Derry is like Dresden on the day after." The bluebells were appropriate to the life described in "Down Then by Derry," and this former life is the life to remember.

OTHER MAJOR WORKS

LONG FICTION: *Land Without Stars*, 1947; *In a Harbour Green*, 1949; *Call for a Miracle*, 1951; *Honey Seems Bitter*, 1952; *The Cards of the Gambler*, 1953; *There Was an Ancient House*, 1955; *The Captain with the Whiskers*, 1960; *Dogs Enjoy the Morning*, 1968; *Proxopera*, 1977; *Nothing Happens in Carmincross*, 1985.

NONFICTION: *Counties of Contention*, 1945; *Poor Scholar: A Study of the Works and Days of William Carleton, 1794-1869*, 1947; *Modern Irish Fiction: A Critique*, 1950; *All the Way to Bantry Bay and Other Irish Journeys*, 1978; *Dublin*, 1983; *Ireland from the Air*, 1985; *Drink to the Bird: A Memoir*, 1991; *A Raid into Dark Corners: And Other Essays*, 1999; *The Waves Behind Us: Further Memoirs*, 1999.

CHILDREN'S LITERATURE: *The Trout in the Turnhole*, 1995.

EDITED TEXTS: *The Penguin Book of Irish Short Stories*, 1981; *Yeats' Ireland: An Enchanted Vision*, 1989; *And as I Rode by Granard's Moat*, 1996.

BIBLIOGRAPHY

Casey, Daniel J. *Benedict Kiely*. Lewisburg, Pa.: Bucknell University Press, 1974. In this introductory essay, the author tends to cast Kiely as a traditional Irish storyteller. This approach is a reliable guide to one of Kiely's most important characteristics, but it needs to be developed more fully than in this rather generalized work.

Dunleavy, Janet Egleson. "Mary Lavin, Elizabeth Bowen, and a New Generation: The Irish Short Story at Midcentury." In *The Irish Short Story: A Critical History*, edited by James F. Kilroy. Boston: Twayne, 1984. The new generation in question is the one which emerged in the 1950's. Kiely is correctly identified as one of its important members. The case for Kiely's distinctive contribution to the genre is plausibly, if briefly, advanced. A sense of that contribution is clarified by Kiely being seen in the context of the Irish short-story's development.

Eckley, Grace. *Benedict Kiely*. Boston: Twayne, 1972. The most comprehensive account of Kiely's work. In particular, the significance of the relationship between his fiction and nonfiction is discussed. Kiely's novels also receive an attentive reading. Supplemented by a useful chronology and a bibliography.

Foster, John Wilson. *Forces and Themes in Ulster Fiction*. Dublin: Gill and Macmillan, 1974. The most incisive criticism of Kiely's work is to be found here, especially in pages 72 to 81 and 91 to 100. The author relates Kiely's work both to its social and literary backgrounds. In particular, the tendency of Kiely's fiction toward the mythic is the subject of much valuable discussion. The main focus of the discussion is Kiely's short fiction.

Kiberd, Declan. *Inventing Ireland: The Literature of the Modern Nation*. Cambridge, Mass.: Harvard University Press, 1996. An important study of the development of Irish literature from Oscar Wilde to the present day.

Kiely, Benedict. Interview by Richard H. Brown. *Publishers Weekly* 228 (November 22, 1985): 54. A brief biographical sketch, including an interview in which Kiely discusses his career and his novel *Nothing Happens in Carmincross*; Kiely talks about the influence of Yeats, Joyce, Ernest Hemingway, and William Faulkner on his work.

O'Grady, Thomas B. "Echoes of William Carleton: Benedict Kiely and the Irish Oral Tradition." *Studies in Short Fiction* 28 (Summer, 1991): 321-330. Discusses similarities between Carleton's and Kiely's stories, particularly their narrative voice of the old storyteller or fireside *seanchaí* of the Irish peasantry. Discusses Kiely's first-person narratives, his creation of a storytelling occasion, and his artful manner of telling.

Scanlan, Margaret. "The Unbearable Present: North-ern Ireland in Four Contemporary Novels." *Études Irlandaises: Revue Française d'Histoire, Civilisa-tion, et Littérature de l'Irlande* 10 (1985): 145-161. Among the works considered is Kiely's novella about civil strife in Northern Ireland, *Proxopera*. Kiely is not generally considered a Northern Irish writer which distorts his achievement in certain key respects. The article isolates the distinct con-tribution made by *Proxopera* to contemporary writ-ing about Northern Ireland.

Grace Eckley, updated by
George O'Brien

JAMAICA KINCAID
Elaine Potter Richardson

Born: Saint Johns, Antigua; May 25, 1949

PRINCIPAL SHORT FICTION
At the Bottom of the River, 1983

OTHER LITERARY FORMS

In addition to her short stories, Jamaica Kincaid has written the novels *Annie John* (1985), *Lucy* (1990), *The Autobiography of My Mother* (1996); a book-length essay concerning her native island Antigua entitled *A Small Place* (1988); a children's book, *Annie, Gwen, Lilly, Pam, and Tulip* (1986), with illustrations by Eric Fischl, and the nonfiction works *My Brother* (1997) and *My Garden (Book)* (1999). In 1998, she edited *My Favorite Plant: Writers and Gardeners on the Plants They Love.*

ACHIEVEMENTS

Jamaica Kincaid's short-story collection *At the Bottom of the River* received the Morton Dauwen Zabel Award from the American Academy of Arts and Letters in 1983. Her novel *Annie John* was one of three finalists for the international Ritz Paris Hem-ingway Award in 1985. Her short story "Xuela" was included in *The Best American Short Stories 1995*; "In Roseau" was included in *The Best American Short Stories 1996.*

BIOGRAPHY

Born in 1949, Jamaica Kincaid, then Elaine Potter Richardson, lived with her homemaker mother and carpenter father on Antigua, a small West Indian is-land measuring nine by twelve miles. The family was impoverished: Their house had no running water or electricity. The young girl's chores included drawing water from a community faucet and registering with the public works so that the "night soil men" would dispose of the family's waste. Even so, her childhood was idyllic. She was surrounded by the extraordinary beauty of the island, was accepted by her community, and was loved and protected by her mother. When Kincaid was nine, however, her mother gave birth to the first of three more children—all boys. At that point, the closeness that Kincaid had enjoyed was at first disturbed and then destroyed. She credits the lies that she began to tell her mother as the catalyst for her fiction writing: "I wasn't really lying. I was pro-tecting my privacy or protecting a feeling I had about something. But lying is the beginning of fiction. It was the beginning of my writing life." Also at this time, she began to comprehend the insidious impact of colonialism. (Antigua was a British colony until 1967, and only in 1981 did it receive full independence.) The Antiguans' docile acceptance of their inferior status enraged her. Thus the serenity she had known as a child was displaced by loneliness and anger.

In 1966, Kincaid, seeking to disassociate herself from her mother, left Antigua not to return for nineteen years and then only after she was a naturalized citizen of the United States and an established writer. Arriving in Scarsdale, New York, the seventeen-year-old Kincaid worked as a live-in baby-sitter. She did not open her mother's letters, and when, after a few months, she took an au pair position in New York City, she did not send her mother her new address. For the next three years, she cared for the four young girls of Michael Arlen, a writer for *The New Yorker* and a future colleague when she herself would become a staff writer for the magazine. Her childhood and early New York experiences are fictionalized in *At the Bottom of the River*, *Annie John*, and *Lucy*.

During her first few years in New York, she wanted to continue her education at a university but found her Antiguan schooling to be inferior; instead, she first studied for a high school diploma, took a few photography courses at a community college, and then attended Franconia College in New Hampshire on scholarship, leaving after a year because, although only in her twenties, she felt too old. After jobs as a secretary and receptionist, she wrote for a teen magazine. In 1973, she changed her name to Jamaica Kincaid, perhaps suggesting that she had achieved her own identity. Associating with New York writers and artists, she met George Trow (*Lucy* is dedicated to him), who wrote "Talk of the Town" for *The New Yorker*. She collaborated on a few columns, and eventually one of her pieces was accepted by editor William Shawn, who was known for encouraging fledgling writers. In 1978, the magazine published her first short story, "Girl." Soon after, she married Allen Shawn, the editor's son. In 1983, her first collection, *At the Bottom of the River*, was published to generally favorable reviews, as was her subsequent work,

Jamaica Kincaid in 1990 (Sigrid Estrada)

which has earned for her a devoted following. She continued to write short stories, usually published in *The New Yorker*, and give lectures and readings. She and Allen Shawn, a composer and professor at Bennington College, along with their two children—Annie, named after her mother, and Harold—settled in Bennington, Vermont.

ANALYSIS

Jamaica Kincaid is noted for her lyrical use of language. Her short stories and novels have a hypnotic, poetic quality that results from her utilization of rhythm and repetition. Her images, drawn from her West Indian childhood, recall Antigua, with its tropical climate, Caribbean food, local customs, and folklore laced with superstitions. Many of her stories move easily from realism to surrealistic fantasy, as would a Caribbean folktale. She is also praised for her exploration of the strong but ambiguous bond between mother and daughter and her portrayal of the transformation of a girl into a woman. Thus her work touches upon the loss of innocence that comes when one moves out of the Eden that is childhood. These are the features that are found not only in her short fiction but also in her novels, the chapters of which *The New Yorker* originally published as short stories, and in *Annie, Gwen, Lilly, Pam, and Tulip*, a children's book that was part of a project designed by the Whitney Museum of American Art, the original publisher, who sought to bring together contemporary authors and artists for a series of limited editions aimed primarily at collectors.

Kincaid's concern with racism, colonialism, classicism, and sexism is rooted in her history: "I never give up thinking about the way I came into the world, how my ancestors came from Africa to the West Indies as slaves. I just could never forget it. Or forgive it." She does not hesitate to tackle these issues in her writing. In her nonfictional *A Small Place*, she directs the force of her language toward an examination of her native island of Antigua, presenting the beauty as well as the racism and corruption rooted in its colonial past. In her fiction, these same issues are not slighted; for example, *Annie John* and *Lucy* address various forms of oppression and exploitation.

Jamaica Kincaid's short stories, strongly autobiographical, are often set in the West Indies or incorporate images from the islands and include many events from her youth and young adulthood. In general, her stories chronicle the coming-of-age of a young girl. Because the mother-daughter relationship is central to the process, Kincaid often examines the powerful bond between them, a bond that the child must eventually weaken, if not break, in order to create her own identity. Kincaid has been accurately called "the poet of girlhood and place."

"GIRL"

The first of the ten stories in *At the Bottom of the River* is the often praised and quoted "Girl." Barely two pages in length, the story outlines the future life of a young girl growing up on a small Caribbean island. The voice heard belongs to the girl's mother as she instructs her daughter in the duties that a woman is expected to fulfill in a culture with limited opportunities for girls. Twice the girl interrupts to offer a feeble protest, but her mother persists.

The girl is told how to wash, iron, and mend clothes; how to cook fritters and pepper pot; how to grow okra; and how to set the table—in short, everything that will enable her to care for a future husband. She is told how to smile, how to love a man, and how to get rid of an unborn baby should it be necessary. Most important, however, her mother warns her about losing her reputation because then the girl (and this is unsaid) loses her value as a potential wife. Almost as a refrain, the mother cautions, "On Sundays try to walk like a lady and not like the slut you are so bent on becoming" or "This is how to behave in the presence of men who don't know you very well, and this way they won't recognize immediately the slut I have warned you against becoming." On the island, the girl's most important asset is her virginity.

The language is a prime example of Kincaid's ability to work a hypnotic spell. The story consists of a series of variations on particular instruction: "This is how to sew on a button; this is how to make a buttonhole for the button you have just sewed on; this is how to hem a dress when you see the hem coming down and so to prevent yourself from looking like the slut I know you are so bent on becoming." The rhythm and repetition create a lyric poetic quality that is present to some degree in all Kincaid's fiction. Her prose demands to be read out loud.

"Girl" suggests the child's future life on the island, but several stories in the collection re-create the atmosphere of her present existence. The story "In the Night" recounts her daily experiences. Thus, details such as crickets or flowers that would be important to her are recorded, often in the form of lists or catalogs: "The hibiscus flowers, the flamboyant flowers, the bachelor's buttons, the irises, the marigolds, the whiteheadbush flowers, lilies, the flowers on the daggerbush," continuing for a full paragraph. Here cataloging, a familiar feature of Kincaid's prose, represents a child's attempt to impose an order on her surroundings. The young narrator does not question her world but only reports what she observes. Thus witchcraft exists side by side with more mundane activities: "Someone is making a basket, someone is making a girl a dress or a boy a shirt . . . someone is sprinkling a colorless powder outside a closed door so that someone else's child will be stillborn." This melding of the commonplace with the supernatural occurs frequently in Kincaid's fiction. The narrator's troubles, such as wetting the bed, are those of a child and are easily resolved by her mother. Her plans for the future, marrying a woman who will tell her stories, also are typical of a child. This is an idyllic world before the fall from innocence, a world in which everything is ordered, listed, and cataloged. Nothing is threatening, since the all-powerful mother protects and shields.

"HOLIDAYS"

In several other stories, including "Wingless" and "Holidays," the girl is again shown to be occupied by the usually pleasant sensations of living: walking barefoot, scratching her scalp, or stretching, but sometimes, as illustrated in "Holidays," experiencing pain: "spraining a finger while trying to catch a cricket ball; straining a finger while trying to catch a softball; stepping on dry brambles while walking on the newly cut hayfields." The trauma, however, is clearly limited to physical sensations. When the child thinks of the future, the images are those of wishful thinking, similar to daydreams. This tranquil state of youth, however, is only temporary, as "Wingless" implies. The narrator, wingless, is still in the "pupa stage."

"THE LETTER FROM HOME"

In "The Letter from Home," the narrator's growing awareness makes it impossible for her to maintain the comforting simplicity of her child's world. Questions about life and death intrude: "Is the Heaven to be above? Is the Hell below?" These inquiries, however, are set aside in favor of the present physical reality—a cat scratching a chair or a car breaking down. Even love and conception are reduced to the simplest terms: "There was a bed, it held sleep; there was movement, it was quick, there was a being." She is not ready to confront the idea of death, so when death beckons, she "turned and rowed away."

"WHAT I HAVE BEEN DOING LATELY"

Just as the philosophical questions about life and death disrupt the bliss of childhood, so does the journey toward selfhood, which Kincaid symbolically represents as a journey over rough or impassable terrain or water. In "What I Have Been Doing Lately," the obstacle is water: "I walked for I don't know how long before I came to a big body of water. I wanted to

get across it but I couldn't swim. I wanted to get across it but it would take me years to build a boat. . . . I didn't know how long to build a bridge." Because the journey is difficult, as any passage to adulthood would be, the narrator is hesitant, afraid of finding the world not beautiful, afraid of missing her parents, so she goes back to bed: She is not ready yet. Soon, however, she will not have the option of retreating and waiting.

"MY MOTHER"

The journey toward selfhood necessitates a separation from the mother, as is suggested in the story "My Mother." The protection that was vital during childhood becomes stifling in adolescence: "Placing her arms around me, she drew my head closer and closer to her bosom, until finally I suffocated." Furthermore, the girl's feelings are ambiguous. Realizing that she has hurt her mother, she cries, but then she utilizes those tears to create a pond, "thick and black and poisonous," to form a barrier over which they "watched each other carefully." The all-protecting mother of the earlier stories transforms herself into a mythic monster and thus threatens the emerging selfhood of the daughter. The daughter, however, also grows "invincible" like her mother, and she, too, metamorphoses into a similar beast. Strong as the daughter has become, however, she can never vanquish her mother: "I had grown big, but my mother was bigger, and that would always be so." Only after the daughter completes her own journey toward selfhood is her mother no longer a threat: "As we walked along, our steps became one, and as we talked, our voices became one voice, and we were in complete union in every way. What peace came over me then, for I could not see where she left off and I began, or where I left off and she began."

"AT THE BOTTOM OF THE RIVER"

The concluding and title story is also the longest in the collection, at about twenty pages. "At the Bottom of the River" suggests answers to the questions raised in the other stories. Again, Kincaid employs the symbol of a journey through forbidding terrain to suggest traveling through life. What is the purpose of the journey, for what does one ultimately face but death? One man, overwhelmed, does nothing. Another discovers meaning in his family, his work, and the beauty of a sunrise, but still he struggles and "feels the futility." How can one live with the paralyzing knowledge that "dead lay everything that had lived and dead also lay everything that would live. All had had or would have its season. And what should it matter that its season lasted five billion years or five minutes?" One possible response is suggested in the life of "a small creature" that lives in the moment, aware only of the sensation of grass underfoot or of the sting of a honeybee.

The narrator, who at first knew only the love of her mother, suffers from its necessary withdrawal. Adrift, she embarks on a symbolic journey in which she submerges herself in a river-fed sea. Discovering a solution at the bottom of the river, she emerges with a commitment to the present. Death, because it is natural, cannot be destroyed, but the joys derived from the commonplace—books, chairs, fruit—can provide meaning, and she "grow[s] solid and complete."

"XUELA"

Kincaid's story "Xuela" became the first chapter of her novel *The Autobiography of My Mother* (1996). Like many of her other stories, it is set against a rich description of the botany and geography of tropical Dominica, and it continues Kincaid's meditation on the theme of mothers and daughters. Xuela, the daughter who shares her mother's name, also shares with many Kincaid women an anger at the mother who has rejected her and a fury at the world which little understands—and little cares—about her needs.

In the story's first sentence, the reader learns that Xuela's mother died in giving her birth, and the rest of the story is the record of the first seven years of Xuela's life. Her father places the infant in the care of Eunice, his laundry woman and visits her every two weeks when he delivers the dirty clothes he can care for as little as he can care for his baby daughter either physically or emotionally, oblivious as he is to his laundrywoman's lack of affection for her foster child.

The child, however, knows very well that her foster mother has no use for her, and she grows ever more bitter and withdrawn. When she breaks Eunice's treasured china plate, she cannot bring herself to utter

the words "I'm sorry." Like the turtles she captures and carelessly kills, Xuela has withdrawn into a shell which threatens to destroy her with enforced isolation.

At that point her father sends Xuela to school. The few other students are all boys; like their teacher they are "of the African people" and unable to respond to the powerful element of Carib Indian in Xuela's ancestry. The teacher wears her own African heritage like a penance and is quick to label Xuela's intelligence as a sign of her innate evil. When the child is found writing letters to her father, he removes her from the school and takes her to live with him and his new wife, another woman who has no love for the child. Like her insensitive teacher, her father's power as a jailer seems to suggest the destructive powers of colonialism, another Kincaid theme.

Through all these trials, the child is sustained by a vision of her mother, who appears to her in sleep. In the dream, she sees her true mother descending a ladder to her, but always the dream fades before she can see more than her mother's heels and the hem of her robe. Frustrating as it is, the dream also comes to represent the presence of the only person outside herself that Xuela can identify with unreserved love.

The story's themes of the mother who, from the child's point of view, has willfully withdrawn her love joins with the theme of the child's wakening to the use of sexuality to replace her lost mother's love, linking this story to the rest of Kincaid's work.

Kincaid's stories are praised for their strong images, poetic language, and challenging themes, and they are criticized for their lack of plot and sometimes obscure symbolism. Any reader, however, who, without reservations, enters Kincaid's fictive world will be well rewarded.

OTHER MAJOR WORKS

LONG FICTION: *Annie John*, 1985; *Lucy*, 1990; *The Autobiography of My Mother*, 1996.

NONFICTION: *A Small Place*, 1988; *My Brother*, 1997; *My Garden (Book)*, 1999.

CHILDREN'S LITERATURE: *Annie, Gwen, Lilly, Pam, and Tulip*, 1986 (with illustrations by Eric Fischl).

EDITED TEXTS: *The Best American Essays 1995*, 1995; *My Favorite Plant: Writers and Gardeners on the Plants They Love*, 1998.

BIBLIOGRAPHY

Als, Hilton. "Don't Worry, Be Happy." Review of *Lucy*. *The Nation* 252 (February 18, 1991): 207-209. Als compares the novel with *A Small Place*, since both are concerned with oppression. Als emphasizes Kincaid's importance as a Caribbean writer who is not afraid to tackle the issues of racism and colonialism at the risk of alienating readers.

Bloom, Harold, ed. *Jamaica Kincaid*. Philadelphia: Chelsea House, 1998. A collection of individually authored chapters on Kincaid, this critical study includes bibliographical references and an index.

De Abruna, Laura Nielsen. "Jamaica Kincaid's Writing and the Maternal-Colonial Matrix." In *Caribbean Women Writers*, edited by Mary Condé and Thorunn Lonsdale. New York: St. Martin's Press, 1999. Discusses Kincaid's presentation of women's experience, her use of postmodern narrative strategies, and her focus on the absence of the once-affirming mother or mother country that causes dislocation and alienation.

Ellsberg, Peggy. "Rage Laced with Lyricism." Review of *A Small Place*. *Commonweal* 115 (November 4, 1988): 602-604. In her review of *A Small Place* with references to *At the Bottom of the River* and *Annie John*, Ellsberg justifies the anger that is present in *A Small Place*, anger that is occasioned by exploitation.

Emery, Mary Lou. "Refiguring the Postcolonial Imagination: Tropes of Visuality in Writing by Rhys, Kincaid, and Cliff." *Tulsa Studies in Women's Literature* 16 (Fall, 1997): 259-280. Emery uses one of Jean Rhys's novels to illustrate a dialectical relationship between the European means of visualization and image-making in postcolonial literatures as something not just of the eye. Argues that the use of the rhetorical trope of ekphrasis (an artistic hybrid) reflects the cultural hybrid nature of postcolonial literature.

Ferguson, Moira. *Jamaica Kincaid: Where the Land Meets the Body*. Charlottesville: University Press of Virginia, 1994. Includes bibliographical references and an index.

_____. "A Lot of Memory: An Interview with Jamaica Kincaid." *The Kenyon Review*, n.s. 16 (Winter, 1994): 163-188. Kincaid discusses the inspiration for her writing and the reasons she wrote her first book in an experimental style; describes the influence of the English tradition on fiction in the Caribbean; comments on the nature of colonial conquest as a theme she explores through the metaphor of gardening.

Garis, Leslie. "Through West Indian Eyes." *The New York Times Magazine* 140 (October, 7, 1990): 42. Based on an interview with Kincaid, this six-page article is the best source of information about Kincaid's life. Contains details about her childhood in Antigua, her relationship with her mother, her early interest in books, her early years in New York, and her marriage to Allen Shawn. Includes illustrations.

Milton, Edith. "Making a Virtue of Diversity." Review of *At the Bottom of the River*, by Jamaica Kincaid. *The New York Times Book Review*. (January 15, 1984): 22. Milton presents the major criticism of Kincaid's fiction—that the stories are obscure, plotless, and too visionary. Milton also discusses the strong Caribbean folktale influence evident in Kincaid's stories.

Onwordi, Iki. "Wising Up." Review of *At the Bottom of the River* and *Annie John*, by Jamaica Kincaid. *The Times Literary Supplement* (November 29, 1985): 1374. A brief review in which Onwordi discusses the works' similarities, especially in language and themes.

Simmons, Diane. *Jamaica Kincaid*. New York: Twayne, 1994. Includes bibliographical references and an index.

Barbara Wiedemann, updated by
Ann Davison Garbett

STEPHEN KING

Born: Portland, Maine; September 21, 1947

PRINCIPAL SHORT FICTION

Night Shift, 1978
The Dark Tower: The Gunslinger, 1982
Different Seasons, 1982
Skeleton Crew, 1985
Dark Visions, 1988 (includes stories by Dan
    Simmons and George R. R. Martin)
Four Past Midnight, 1990
Nightmares and Dreamscapes, 1993
Hearts in Atlantis, 1999

OTHER LITERARY FORMS

Stephen King is best known for his horror novels, which he is known for publishing at the rate of approximately one per year, several under the name Richard Bachman. His most notable are *Carrie: A Novel of a Girl with Frightening Power* (1974), *Pet Sematary* (1983), and *Misery* (1987). Several of his novels have been made into films, and he has written several screenplays himself, including original works specifically for the screen, such as *Cat's Eye* (1984) and *Stephen King's Sleepwalkers* (1992). His teleplay *Storm of the Century* (1999) was also published in novel form the same year. A few of his poems have been included in his short-story collections, and he has written an analysis of horror fiction entitled *Danse Macabre* (1981).

ACHIEVEMENTS

Stephen King became, in a relatively short time, one of the most popular writers in the United States. Nearly every book he has published has reached the best-seller lists, whether in hardback or paperback, and has often remained there for months. He is respected in the field of horror fiction, and several of his books have received World Fantasy Award nominations. He has received the World Fantasy Award for his short story "Do the Dead Sing?" (1981), a British Fantasy Award for *Cujo* (1981), and a Hugo Award for his nonfiction work *Danse Macabre*. He has won special recognition for his contributions to horror fiction by both the British Fantasy Awards and the World Fantasy Awards. In 1986 *Skeleton Crew* won the Locus Award for best collection. The short story "The Man in the Black Suit" won a World Fantasy Award in 1995.

BIOGRAPHY

Stephen Edwin King was born in 1947 in Maine, where he lived the majority of his life. His parents had adopted his elder brother, David, several years before King was born, since his mother was told that she would be unable to have children. King's father abandoned the family when King was two years old. After his parents' separation, King's mother moved the family to Indiana, then Connecticut, and finally, in 1958, back to Maine to be near her aging parents. King's mother was a strict Methodist with fundamentalist leanings, and David and Stephen attended church and Bible school several times a week.

King began to show an interest in writing at age seven or eight, partly to amuse himself during frequent periods of illness. His mother often read to her sons, including some of Classic Comics' adaptations of famous novels; King was impressed by H. G. Wells's *The Time Machine* (1895) and *The War of the Worlds* (1898). He was always an avid reader and loved adventure stories and science fiction; thus, even his juvenile work was influenced by fantasy and horror. At the age of twelve, he sent stories to the magazines *Fantastic* and *Fantasy and Science Fiction*; soon afterward, he discovered the stories of H. P. Lovecraft and began reading a range of horror fiction, including the works of Lovecraft, Edgar Allan Poe, several gothic novelists, and Richard Matheson, whose horror novels, set in modern times, greatly influenced King.

King entered high school in 1962, and in 1965 his story "I Was a Teenage Grave Robber" appeared in *Comics Review*, a fan magazine. He wrote all through high school and printed several of his stories on his brother's offset printing press. In 1966, he entered the

Stephen King (Archive Photos)

University of Maine at Orono and made his first professional sale, of "The Glass Floor," to *Startling Mystery Stories*. He also began work on two manuscripts that were eventually published under the pseudonym Richard Bachman in the 1970's. At the university, he received encouragement from several of his professors and was influenced by such naturalist writers as Thomas Hardy and Theodore Dreiser. He wrote a column, "King's Garbage Truck," for the university newspaper and was active in campus politics. In his senior year, while he was working at the college library, he met fellow student Tabitha Spruce, whom he married in 1971. King graduated from the University of Maine in 1970 with a degree in English and a teaching certificate; unable to find work as a teacher, however, he took a job in an industrial laundry, an experience on which he drew for several of his stories. In 1971, he was hired to teach high school English at Maine's Hampden Academy, where he spent two years.

In 1973, King sold his first novel, *Carrie: A Novel of a Girl with Frightening Power*, to Doubleday. New American Library's purchase of the paperback rights allowed King to quit teaching and write full time. In 1976, the film version of *Carrie* gave King's popularity a boost, but he was already selling quite well and producing virtually a novel per year. In 1979, King wrote his first screenplay, *Creepshow* (1982), and in 1986, Metro-Goldwyn-Mayer/United Artists released *Maximum Overdrive*, which King had both scripted and directed. The reading world was shocked in June of 1999 when King was struck by a vehicle while he was taking a stroll near his summer home in Lewiston, Maine. He sustained multiple fractures to his right leg and hip, broken ribs, and a collapsed lung. Although grateful to be alive, King regretted most not being able to write during his long recuperation.

ANALYSIS

Stephen King credits writers Richard Matheson and Robert Bloch, in addition to Lovecraft and Poe, with showing him that the horror story could be brought out "of the foggy moors and the castles and into those 7-Eleven stores and suburbia." He said, "The [horror] genre exists on three basic levels, separate but independent, and each one a little bit cruder than the one before. There's terror on top, the finest emotion any writer can induce; then horror; and, on the very lowest level of all, the gag instinct of revulsion." King's stories easily fit the various levels of horror that he describes. Not particularly worried about style, he aims for the impact of plot. Not all King's stories can be labeled solely horror; many have elements of science fiction, and many of his best stories contain a strong sense of psychological tension. Most of the stories, however, even those that cannot neatly be pegged as belonging to a particular genre, attempt to create a sense of uneasiness. King explains their popularity by how they serve as emotional releases for his readers: "When you've got a lot of free-floating anxieties, the horror story or movie helps to conceptualize them, shrink them down to size, make them concrete so they're manipulable. . . . [T]here's probably some minor catharsis involved."

"JERUSALEM'S LOT"

The kind of horror with which King is most often associated, that of things that go bump in the night, is well represented in his short-story collections. Two of the stories, "Jerusalem's Lot" and "One for the Road," are connected by setting and plot elements to King's novel *'Salem's Lot* (1975). In "Jerusalem's Lot," set in 1850 and told in a series of letters and journal entries, Charles Boone, hoping to regain his strength after a serious illness, moves into his ancestral home along with his friend Calvin McCann. They hear noises in the walls and attribute them to rats, but they soon learn that the townspeople of Preacher's Corners believe otherwise. Between the stories they glean from a townswoman and a journal that McCann finds in the house, Boone and McCann discover that Boone's mad great-uncle, Philip Boone, had joined with a malign preacher to unleash the evils found in a satanic bible called *The Mysteries of the Worm*. Boone tries to eradicate the evil by burning the book, but while he starts to set the pages on fire, his friend McCann is killed by an enormous worm. Boone commits suicide, and the story ends with a note written in 1971 by a distant Boone relative who disbelieves the evidence of the letters of Charles Boone but mentions hearing rats behind the walls of the ancestral home.

"Jerusalem's Lot" has all the trappings of horror in the gothic tradition: a house shunned by the townspeople, inexplicable noises behind the walls, an abandoned town, religion that has been twisted to serve evil, and a monster in the cellar. The tale, written originally for a college class in gothic fiction, is perhaps the only King story that takes place not in modern suburbia but in the past, in a setting somewhat akin to the lonely moors and castles of the gothic writers.

"ONE FOR THE ROAD"

"One for the Road," though also set in Jerusalem's Lot, is a modern vampire story. The car Gerard Lumley and his family are in has gone off the road near Jerusalem's Lot in a bad snowstorm. Lumley leaves his wife and child to find help. When he returns, both his wife and daughter have become vampires. King commented that "I've always believed that if you think the very worst, then, no matter how bad things get . . . they'll never get as bad as *that*. If you write a novel where the bogeyman gets somebody else's children, maybe they'll never get your own children." Fear for loved ones is a common theme in King's stories. Because Lumley is afraid for his wife and daughter, he risks his own life to get help for them. While he is gone, the worst happens to his wife and daughter: They have become something alien, something that no longer loves him.

"THE MONKEY"

In "The Monkey," King creates a high level of tension from the protagonist's fear for his family, especially for his youngest son. When Hal was young, he discovered a toy monkey with a worn-out mechanism for clanging the cymbals strapped to the monkey's paws. When someone near Hal is about to die, the monkey clashes the cymbals. Hal attempts several times to get rid of the monkey, finally throwing it down his aunt's well. Years later, when Hal and his family are clearing the attic of his aunt's house after her death, Hal's eldest son finds the monkey. In a desperate attempt to be rid of the maniacal toy, Hal rows out to the middle of the lake and drops the monkey into the water, nearly drowning as his boat breaks up, while his younger son watches. "The Monkey" is an effective story that evokes terror, the highest on King's list of horror-story levels. Like all King's stories, it is intensely visual. His settings and characters are familiar and easy to empathize with, and King forcefully uses the monkey as a symbol of evil that survives despite all efforts to keep away from it.

"TRUCKS" AND "THE MANGLER"

Numerous King stories deal with the destruction wrought by mechanical devices. "The Monkey" is perhaps the most effective, as the monkey is never *seen* to do anything other than strike its cymbals when it should not be able to do so. The connection between the clash of cymbals and death is made in the mind of Hal, and though it seems to be supported by the evidence, the connection could be pure coincidence. In "The Mangler" and "Trucks," however, the machines are clear agents of wholesale destruction. "The Mangler" is set in an industrial laundry: A mangler is a machine that irons and folds material fed into it. This mangler develops a taste for blood and sucks several workers into its internal mechanism: "A devil had taken over the inanimate steel and cogs and gears of the mangler and had turned it into something with its own life." After two men unsuccessfully attempt to exorcise the machine, the mangler tears itself loose from its moorings and moves toward the town.

"Trucks" concerns vehicles that turn against their owners, running them down when they try to escape. The trucks encircle a diner, crashing into it after their human hostages refuse to acknowledge a Morse code signal beeped out on a horn to refuel the vehicles. Both "Trucks" and "The Mangler" envisage machines that were built to serve human beings, turning to demand sacrifice and service themselves. King has commented that he finds machines frightening because he does not understand how they work. Both stories, too, while they play on one's fear of death and mutilation, are also rather amusing in a dark sort of way.

"THE WOMAN IN THE ROOM"

In many of his stories, however, King treats death in a far more realistic manner, and in some ways these stories are more disturbing than stories such as "The Mangler." While "The Mangler" graphically describes violent death—fitting into King's third level in the horror genre, the "gag instinct of revulsion"—the plot is clearly unrealistic. It is one of those stories that takes the fear of death and makes it manipulable and even laughable. Industrial accidents do happen but not because machines turn malevolent. A story such as "The Woman in the Room," however, is more introspective and is based on King's own feelings when his mother was dying of cancer. It is highly realistic in both plot and emotion. In it, a son visits his mother in the hospital, where she has just had a "cortotomy," an operation to destroy the pain center in her brain so that she will not be in agony from the cancer in her stomach. The operation has also destroyed 60 percent of her motor control. Seeing her weak, unable to move freely, and with no hopes of recovery, the protagonist, Johnny, considers giving her some Darvon pills that he found in her medicine cabinet at home to end her suffering and her life. During his visit, his mother says, "I wish I was out of this. I'd do anything to be out of this." Finally, he brings the pills to the hospital, shows his mother the box, and

shakes six pills into his hand. She looks at them and tacitly agrees to end her life by swallowing all six. Her last request is for Johnny to see if her legs are together: She wants to die with some dignity. She also tells Johnny that he has always been a good son.

"The Woman in the Room" reflects on a very personal, touching level the incredible difficulty of watching a loved one experience a painful death. King's style is as plain and as colloquial as ever; he does not try to elevate it to suit the subject. The story is told in the present tense, and the very artlessness and transparency of King's style give the story an air of honesty. It is by no means a horror story, yet it evokes what King calls "the finest emotion any writer can induce"—terror: fear that one's own parents will get cancer; fear that one will be faced with the same painful dilemma as Johnny; or ultimately, fear that oneself will end up lying in agony in a hospital bed, as Johnny's mother did.

"THE BODY"

Another psychologically honest story is "The Body," which became the 1986 film *Stand by Me*. In it, four twelve-year-old boys walk along a railway track in search of the corpse of a boy who has been hit by a train. The intense friendship between the boys, their silly jokes and twelve-year-old bravado, strikes the reader as real and true to life. Because they are young, the idea of finding the body excites them, making this trip an adventure. It is not until they actually see the boy's body that they finally confront the reality of death:

> The kid was dead. The kid wasn't sick, the kid wasn't sleeping. The kid wasn't going to get up in the morning anymore . . . or catch poison ivy or wear out the eraser on the end of his Ticonderoga No 2 during a hard math test. The kid was dead.

Their quest and their discovery of the body are a rite of passage to which each of the boys reacts slightly differently; soon after they return to town, to their usual lives and to school, they drift apart, growing up in different directions, affected in different ways by what they experienced on that brief trip. King's plain, unornamented style again renders a believable and realistic story.

"THE BALLAD OF THE FLEXIBLE BULLET"

"The Ballad of the Flexible Bullet" is quite different from most of King's other short stories. It is not horror, but neither is it completely realistic. The story concerns a paranoid writer who believes that a "Fornit" inhabits his typewriter to help him write. His editor, humoring him, goes along with the idea and says that he has a Fornit too. Soon, the editor, who has begun to drink heavily, begins finding messages on his typewriter from his Fornit when he wakes up from his periodic blackouts. The last message warns him that the writer's Fornit is about to be killed. When the writer hears this warning, he buys a gun to protect his Fornit but ends up killing himself after he watches his Fornit die. The flexible bullet of the title is madness; it kills just as surely as a lead bullet does, but in an unpredictable way. The story walks a neat tightrope between dismissing the Fornits as products of a deranged mind and admitting their existence: The writer's wife wonders if madness is catching when she thinks she hears the dying screams of the Fornit from inside the typewriter.

"The Ballad of the Flexible Bullet" ends in violent death. The writer attempted to kill his wife and the housekeeper and her son before shooting himself. No matter what type of story King is writing, he usually seems to return to terror, horror, or the gag reflex. King has commented that "the horror story makes us children. That's the primary function of the horror story—to knock away all this stuff . . . to take us over taboo lines, to places we aren't supposed to be." King does not limit this function of his stories to those of the horror genre; whether his characters are confronting death by mutilation from a mad mangler or death by cancer, King takes his readers over taboo lines, making them confront by proxy such subjects as madness, fear, and death.

"THE MAN IN THE BLACK SUIT"

With the publication of "The Man in the Black Suit" in the October 31, 1993, issue of *The New Yorker*, Stephen King created what might be considered one of his most "literary" stories. This story received both popular and critical acclaim, both camps voicing appreciation for King's storytelling ability and his perceptiveness in delving into the deep recesses of humanity. More important, "The Man in the Black Suit" creates a psychological depth that many of King's other stories lack.

"The Man in the Black Suit" is the story of a nine-year-old boy coming face to face with the devil. The story is recounted as the boy, now eighty, faces quickly approaching death in his nursing-home bed. The further one moves into the narrative, the more apparent the complexity of the situation becomes, and how it fits into the Stephen King canon is appreciated.

In the classical American tradition, King allows his protagonist, Gary, to make a decision that will have lasting consequences for his sanity and spirituality. When Gary goes off on an afternoon fishing expedition, he must promise his parents that he will go no further than where "Castle Stream forks." However, like poet Robert Frost's traveler, Gary decides to go further, and his decision governs the remainder of his life. As he moves deeper into the wilderness, Gary becomes more apprehensive, indicating to the reader that something evil lives here in the wild. After catching two fish, Gary decides to take a nap. Awakening from his nap by a bee on his nose, Gary comes into contact with "the man in the black suit," very out of place in the wilderness. Gary knows immediately that the man is the devil and is afraid of him. The demon threatens Gary, but the young boy is able to escape, eventually meeting his father who had come to join him fishing. The father intimates that Gary may have merely dreamed his encounter with the devil, but the boy knows the truth.

Although he does write a psychologically complex work, King retains many devices that tie this story to earlier ones. The boy remembers this particular event many years after it occurred, a plot device used in *It* (1986), *The Green Mile* (1996), and "The Body." His protagonist is a teacher and writer of sorts, the type of character prominent in numerous other works. King allows wickedness to emerge from a setting that houses stored-up evil, as happened in *It*, *'Salem's Lot*, and *Pet Sematary*. However, the most prevalent King element is the old man's realization that "what you write down sometimes leaves you forever," echoing King's own argument that by writing about the things that terrify us the most, we are able to elude them.

OTHER MAJOR WORKS

LONG FICTION: *Carrie: A Novel of a Girl with Frightening Power*, 1974; *'Salem's Lot*, 1975; *The Shining*, 1977; *Rage*, 1977 (as Richard Bachman); *The Stand*, 1978 (unabridged version 1990); *The Dead Zone*, 1979; *The Long Walk*, 1979 (as Richard Bachman); *Firestarter*, 1980; *Cujo*, 1981; *Roadwork*, 1981 (as Richard Bachman); *The Running Man*, 1982 (as Richard Bachman); *Christine*, 1983; *Pet Sematary*, 1983; *Cycle of the Werewolf*, 1983 (novella; illustrated by Berni Wrightson; also published as *Silver Bullet*, 1985); *The Talisman*, 1984 (with Peter Straub); *The Eyes of the Dragon*, 1984, 1987; *Thinner*, 1984 (as Richard Bachman); *The Bachman Books*, 1985 (omnibus edition, includes *Rage*, *The Long Walk*, *Roadwork*, and *The Running Man*); *It*, 1986; *Misery*, 1987; *The Tommyknockers*, 1987; *The Drawing of the Three*, 1987 (illustrated by Phil Hale); *The Dark Half*, 1989; *Needful Things*, 1991; *Gerald's Game*, 1992; *Dolores Claiborne*, 1993; *Insomnia*, 1994; *Rose Madder*, 1995; *The Green Mile*, 1996 (six-part serialized novel); *Desperation*, 1996; *The Regulators*, 1996 (as Bachman); *Wizard and Glass*, 1997 (illustrated by Dave McKean); *Bag of Bones*, 1998; *Storm of the Century*, 1999 (originally written for television); *The Girl Who Loved Tom Gordon*, 1999.

SCREENPLAYS: *Creepshow*, 1982 (with George Romero; adaptation of his book); *Cat's Eye*, 1984; *Silver Bullet*, 1985 (adaptation of *Cycle of the Werewolf*); *Maximum Overdrive*, 1986 (adaptation of his short story "Trucks"); *Pet Sematary*, 1989; *Stephen King's Sleepwalkers*, 1992.

TELEPLAYS: *The Stand*, 1994 (based on his novel); *Storm of the Century*, 1999.

NONFICTION: *Danse Macabre*, 1981; *Black Magic and Music: A Novelist's Perspective on Bangor*, 1983; *Bare Bones: Conversations on Terror with Stephen King*, 1988 (edited by Tim Underwood and Chuck Miller); *On Writing: A Memoir of the Craft*, 2000.

MISCELLANEOUS: *Creepshow*, 1982 (adaptation of the D. C. Comics); *Nightmares in the Sky*, 1988.

BIBLIOGRAPHY

Beahm, George W. *The Stephen King Story*. Kansas City, Mo.: Andrews and McMeel, 1992. A good, updated biography of King. Includes bibliographical references and an index.

Hohne, Karen A. "The Power of the Spoken Word in the Works of Stephen King." *Journal of Popular Culture* 28 (Fall, 1994): 93-103. Discusses the tension in King's work between slang speech, which codifies a knowledge rejected by those in power, and monologic orality, which embodies that power; claims his works illustrate the tension between official and unofficial languages and ideologies that exists not only in literature but also throughout society.

King, Stephen. *Bare Bones: Conversations on Terror with Stephen King*. Edited by Tim Underwood and Chuck Miller. New York: McGraw-Hill, 1988. Though many of the interviews collected in this volume become somewhat repetitive, they provide a good sense, in King's own words, of what he is trying to do in his fiction and why he does it. The interviews were held between 1979 and 1987; the opening transcript of a talk King gave at the Billerica Public Library is most useful.

_____. *Danse Macabre*. New York: Everest House, 1981. King researched and wrote this critical work on horror fiction and film at the instigation of his editor. He focuses on works since the 1940's and discusses novels, B-films, and horror comics to support his thesis that monsters such as Godzilla are a way of making tangible the fear of such things as nuclear war.

Magistrale, Tony. *Stephen King: The Second Decade, Danse Macabre to the Dark Half*. New York: Twayne, 1992. Discusses King's work in the 1980's, including his nonfictional analysis of the horror genre in *Danse Macabre*, his Richard Bachman books, *Misery*, and the novellas of the *Dark Tower* saga. Also includes a 1989 interview in which King discusses fairy-tale references in his work, as well as his treatment of sexuality, masculinity, and race; discusses critical and popular reaction to his fiction.

Miller Power, Brenda, Jeffrey D. Wilhelm, and Kelly

Chandler, eds. *Reading Stephen King: Issues of Censorship, Student Choice, and Popular Literature*. Urbana, Ill.: National Council of Teachers of English, 1997. Examines issues at the heart of horror fiction. Includes bibliographical references and an index.

Spignesi, Stephen J. *The Complete Stephen King Encyclopedia: The Definitive Guide to the Works of America's Master of Horror*. Chicago: Contemporary Books, 1991. First published with the title *The Shape Under the Sheet*, this is an important guide for all students of King. Includes bibliographical references and indexes.

Underwood, Tim, and Chuck Miller, eds. *Fear Itself: The Horror Fiction of Stephen King, 1976-1982*. San Francisco: Underwood-Miller, 1982. This is another collection of articles on King's work. The articles vary in quality, with Ben Indick's "King

and the Literary Tradition of Horror" providing a good introduction to the history of the horror genre. Douglas Winter's essay, "The Night Journeys of Stephen King," discusses several of the short stories. Includes a bibliography.

Winter, Douglas E. *The Art of Darkness: The Life and Fiction of the Master of the Macabre, Stephen King*. 1984. Rev. ed. New York: New American Library, 1989. Winter's work provides a perceptive critical overview of King's work, with long articles on each novel up to *The Talisman* and a chapter on the short stories in *Night Shift* and *Skeleton Crew*. Winter also includes summaries of King's short stories, a short biography of King, and extensive bibliographies both of King's work and of books and articles written about him.

Karen M. Cleveland Marwick,
updated by Tom Frazier

BARBARA KINGSOLVER

Born: Annapolis, Maryland; April 8, 1955

Principal short fiction
Homeland and Other Stories, 1989

Other literary forms

Barbara Kingsolver is known primarily for her longer fiction, which includes *The Bean Trees* (1988), *Animal Dreams* (1990), *Pigs in Heaven* (1993), *The Poisonwood Bible* (1998), and *Prodigal Summer* (2000). She also writes travel articles, book reviews, essays, and poetry. Her nonfiction work *Holding the Line: Women in the Great Arizona Mine Strike of 1983* (1989) compellingly presents the plight of miners in southern Arizona's copper mining "company towns." She has authored a collection of poetry entitled *Another America* (1992, 1998). The volume's form invites awareness of diverse perspectives, with Kingsolver's poetry and its Spanish translations printed on facing pages. A selection of her essays in *High Tide in Tucson: Essays from Now*

or Never (1995) offers thoughts on parenting, home ownership, cultural habits, travel, and writing. Her observations on the natural order of things, from child rearing to exploring a volcanic crater in Hawaii, range from self-deprecatingly humorous to awe-inspired. All celebrate one's connection to and citizenship of the world.

Achievements

Barbara Kingsolver has won many writing awards. In 1986 the Arizona Press Club gave her its feature-writing award. She received American Library Association awards for *The Bean Trees* in 1989 and for *Homeland and Other Stories* in 1990. The Edward Abbey Ecofiction award (1990) for *Animal Dreams* and the prestigious PEN/West Fiction Award (1991) added to her reputation. In 1993 and 1994 respectively, she received the Los Angeles Book Award and the Mountain and Plains Booksellers Association Award for *Pigs in Heaven*. Her first three novels were *New York Times* Notable Books and she also received an Enoch Pratt Library Youth-to-Youth Book Award for *The Bean Trees*. In 1995, an honorary doctorate was conferred on her by DePauw University. True to her activist principles, she founded the Bellwether Prize, given in support of literature promoting social change.

BIOGRAPHY

Barbara Kingsolver was born in Annapolis, Maryland, on April 8, 1955. Her childhood was spent mostly in eastern Kentucky's rural Nicholas County. She began writing before she entered high school. In 1977 she earned her undergraduate degree magna cum laude in biology from DePauw University in Indiana. Work toward her master's of science degree at the University of Arizona at Tucson included a creative writing class. Between her stints as a student, she lived for a time in Greece and France. After completing her master's degree, she worked as a science writer for the University of Arizona and began to write feature articles, which have appeared in national publications such as *Smithsonian*, *Harper's*, and *The New York Times*. In 1985 she married Joseph Hoffman and wrote *The Bean Trees* in insomniac interludes during her pregnancy with her daughter Camille. She settled in Tucson, Arizona, with husband Steven Hopp, Camille, and Lily. Kingsolver has been a political activist all of her adult life.

ANALYSIS

Barbara Kingsolver's short stories are notable for their clear-eyed, sometimes ironic, and always empathic look at the daily lives of ordinary people. Her narrators are mostly female or compassionate omniscient voices telling stories of homecomings, intergenerational misunderstandings, and mundane events such as scheduling errands or getting to know one's neighbors. She pays close attention to the tensions that control events like Thanksgiving dinners and accurately captures the dynamics of husband and wife and of mother and daughter. In her stories, characters struggle to understand who they are in the context of family history and their present circumstances. The epiphanies of Kingsolver's women are small but searingly personal. They range from deciding not to

have a child to a sudden understanding of a mother's point of view. In a News Hour online interview with David Gergen, editor-at-large for *U.S. News and World Report*, Ms. Kingsolver explained her fascination with the quotidian episodes in families' and couples' lives:

> We need new stories. We need stories that can help us construct, reconstruct the value of . . . solidarity, of not . . . the lone solo flier, but the family, the community, the value of working together.

Kingsolver's short fiction is not minimalist. She belongs to generations of storytellers who create settings rich in sensual and situational detail. Her characters are clearly situated and her stories have a satisfying beginning, middle, and end as do the stories of nineteenth century writers such as Sarah Orne Jewett and Mary E. Wilkins Freeman. She is also distinctly contemporary because her characters reach an episode's end when they achieve some insight or understanding of their condition. They do not, however, find sentimental or easy answers. Each story con-

Barbara Kingsolver (Seth Kantner)

cludes with characters more able to cope with the literal and emotional landscapes of their lives.

Like poet and essayist Adrienne Rich, Kingsolver embraces the political. She believes art should reflect the world she sees daily, so she writes, for example, about the plight of mine workers in the American Southwest and the displacement of American Indians. College professors, aging hippies, and small-town eccentrics all wrestle with bigotry and stereotyping as they move through their lives. Kingsolver's characters avoid the cynicism of many contemporary fictional voices, seeking instead a synthesis that will see them through or the moral vision that will allow them to rise above prejudices they cannot control. She combines the narrative structure of nineteenth century realists with the frank look at life espoused by John Steinbeck, one of her inspirations. Ms. Kingsolver's characters offer an alternative to ironic, angry characters. They struggle with the inequities of American life without losing their ability to maintain human connection. Kingsolver creates characters who confront life without relinquishing hope. Her vision is distinctive and welcome.

HOMELAND AND OTHER STORIES

Barbara Kingsolver's collection is divided between stories in which the difficulties of small-town life are controlled by the fears and sensibilities of people wed to the status quo and those in which the clash between alternative lifestyles and the ordinary routines of existence is prominent. With one exception, the narrators are women or feature omniscient narrators, whose voices elucidate women's lives and points of view. The stories frequently have a postmodern view of time, jumping nonchronologically from one episode or memory to the next, the changes marked by spaces in the text as well as by narrated events. Kingsolver interestingly blurs the line between character and narrator by interspersing narrative passages with snippets of dialogue. Often the narrator's contributions could just as easily be spoken by the main character; this shared quality underlines the universal relevance of private stories. Kingsolver's stories, built around family routines, usually emphasize a thoughtful female character grappling with a problem. These range from spending quality time with a child ("Quality Time"), facing the need to break off a love affair ("Stone Dreams"), coping with suffering the failure of a long-standing relationship ("Blueprints"), and fighting economic and social injustice ("Why I Am a Danger to the Public") to deciding whether or not to have a child ("Covered Bridges"). Another theme is how one comes to terms with one's past. "Survival Zone" and "Extinctions" have dual tensions: The eternal city/country dilemma surfaces differently in each story, and each considers the opportunities for a life in the larger world as opposed to a well-known existence. "Rose Johnny" tackles the divisive and mean-spirited affects of racial prejudice in a small southern town. A young girl, curious and kindhearted, tells the story, which highlights the socially sanctioned cruelty of adults. Kingsolver's characters realize the beginnings of personal solutions or they relate histories that reveal insights won after the scrutiny of their pasts. Either way, readers know life always goes on in its complicated and demanding way. Survival is mandatory; understanding possible.

"HOMELAND"

The title story of Kingsolver's collection *Homeland and Other Stories* retrospectively tells the tale of an aging Cherokee grandmother's last days. Gloria St. Clair, Great Mam's granddaughter, a grown woman with her own grown children, narrates a family history that begins with the Cherokee Trail of Tears. Great Mam's band had eluded relocation by hiding and was finally allowed to settle where they chose. Still, they called the refugee years "The Time When We Were Not." Gloria's reference initiates the reader into history as a personal experience. A reminiscence of the family's trip back to Great Mam's birthplace, the Hiwassee Valley in Tennessee, follows. Gloria's father, a coal miner just back to work after a season of wildcat strikes, decides this trip is necessary for his mother, who is in her waning days; he plans it despite his wife's skepticism.

Great Mam and Gloria's special relationship evolves along with the story. During lazy afternoons or quiet evenings in the dark, Great Mam tells Gloria stories of the animals "as if they were relatives [her] parents had neglected to tell [her] about." The trip, with the three children bumping along in the back of a pickup truck, as well as the fact that they slept three to a bed, reveals the family's economic situation. Gloria's mother represents a third dynamic, the social status quo; she is thankful God spared her children a "Cherokee nose." Mrs. Murray rises above the common-law, racially mixed marriage of her husband's parents. Gloria balances between her mother and her love for the soft-spoken woman, who tells her how the world began and calls her Waterbug. She fatalistically laments her lack of attention to stories she now knows were rare treasures. The trip fails, the home of a once-proud people houses a troop of sideshow Indians in Cherokee Park. Great Mam does not get out of the truck but remarks to Gloria, "I've never been here before." Great Mam's death is unremarkable, personal, and poignant for Gloria and a troublesome irritation for her mother—the three of them a perfect metaphor for the pain of America's position on "the Indian question."

"ISLANDS ON THE MOON"

Annemarie and her mother Magda are intimate antagonists because Annemarie thinks her mother "doesn't seem mid-forties, she seems like Grandma Moses in moonstone earrings." Annemarie has been alienated from her mother, an aging hippie with wild hair, since her father's death, and her aggravation only increases when Magda turns up pregnant at the same time that she does. As it turns out, Annemarie is not presently married and is contemplating remarrying her first husband. Her own son, Kevin, is moving steadily beyond her reach. Magda breaks her practice of keeping her distance because she wants Annemarie to accompany her when she has amniocentesis, a test to which she would not have agreed had her doctor not threatened to drop her as a patient if she refused. On the way to the clinic, the two have an automobile accident and are rushed to the hospital. The shock of the accident and their time side by side in the hospital free a torrent of resentments from Annemarie. Her persistence prompts Magda to say, "I never knew what you expected from me, Annemarie. I never could be the mother you wanted." When Annemarie

makes the ultimate accusation, that Magda does not miss her husband, Magda recounts her husband's obsessive attempts to try to think of all the things she would need to remember to do after he was gone. Stunned, Annemarie understands her error. "How could I not ever have known that, that it wrecked your life, too?" she asks her mother. At the story's end, Annemarie reaches over to touch her unborn sister, establishing a tenuous bond which now has a chance to flourish.

OTHER MAJOR WORKS

LONG FICTION: *The Bean Trees*, 1988; *Animal Dreams*, 1990; *Pigs in Heaven*, 1993; *The Poisonwood Bible*, 1998; *Prodigal Summer*, 2000.

POETRY: *Another America*, 1992, 1998.

NONFICTION: *Holding the Line: Women in the Great Arizona Mine Strike of 1983*, 1989; *High Tide in Tucson: Essays from Now or Never*, 1995.

BIBLIOGRAPHY

Fleischner, Jennifer, ed. *A Reader's Guide to the Fiction of Barbara Kingsolver: "The Bean Trees," "Homeland and Other Stories," "Animal Dreams," "Pigs in Heaven."* New York: Harper Perennial, 1994. A good resource for the student new to Kingsolver's work.

Gaard, Greta. "Living Connections with Animals and Nature." In *Eco-Feminism: Women, Animals, Nature*, edited by Greta Gaard. Philadelphia: Temple University Press, 1993. Discusses the implications of a personal/political commitment to the natural world.

Kingsolver, Barbara. Interview by Lisa See. *Publishers Weekly* 237 (August 31, 1990): 46. Kingsolver discusses her early literary influences and her research and writing methods.

Marshall, John. "Fast Ride on 'Pigs.'" Review of *Pigs in Heaven*, by Barbara Kingsolver. *Seattle Post-Gazette*, July 26, 1993, p. 1. This review gives an overview of Kingsolver's writing.

Karen L. Arnold

MAXINE HONG KINGSTON

Born: Stockton, California; October 27, 1940

OTHER LITERARY FORMS

Maxine Hong Kingston has written the novel *Tripmaster Monkey: His Fake Book*, 1989; her essays include the collection *Hawai'i One Summer* (1987). She acted as an adviser on a 1994 stage adaptation of her *The Woman Warrior* and *China Men*.

ACHIEVEMENTS

Maxine Hong Kingston's accolades include the National Book Critics Circle award for best nonfiction work for *The Woman Warrior* in 1976, *Time* magazine's listing of *The Woman Warrior* in its top ten nonfiction works of the decade in 1979, the American Book Award for nonfiction for *China Men* in 1981, inclusion of *China Men* in the American Library Notable Books List, the *Mademoiselle* magazine award in 1977, the Ainsfield-Wolf Race Relations Award in 1978, a National Education Association writing fellowship in 1980, National Endowment for the Arts Writers Awards in 1980 and 1982, a Stockton Arts Commission Award in 1981, a Hawaii Award for Literature in 1982, a Hawaii Writers Award in 1983, a PEN/West Fiction Award for *Tripmaster Monkey* in 1989, a California Governor's Art Award in 1989, a Major Book Collection Award in 1990, an American Academy of Arts and Letters award in 1990, a Brandeis University National Women's Committee award, and a John Simon Guggenheim Memorial Foundation grant.

BIOGRAPHY

Born the daughter of Chinese immigrants Tom and Ying Lang Hong in Stockton, California, Maxine Hong Kingston grew up torn between her parents' traditional East Asian culture and the culture of America. While her parents worked to support their family by operating a laundry, Kingston suffered, according to the autobiographical information in her books, much conflict over simultaneous identity as an American and a Chinese person. She addressed her struggles through writing, an activity begun at age nine. She benefited from immersion in Chinese traditional tales as she projected herself into roles of strong female figures from Chinese mythology.

Kingston earned a bachelor of arts degree from the University of California at Berkeley, then married Earl Kingston in 1962. Following the birth of their son, Joseph, Kingston taught high school English and later taught at the Honolulu Business College. While teaching at the Mid-Pacific Institute in Honolulu from 1970 to 1977, she wrote for publications and engaged in a long but ultimately successful search for a literary agent to represent *The Woman Warrior*. It appeared in print in 1976, won several awards, and was eventually published by Alfred A. Knopf. Kingston relocated to the mainland, where she became the McAndless Distinguished Professor in the Humanities at Eastern Michigan University, and in 1990 she became the Chancellor's Distinguished Professor at the University of California at Berkeley. In 1987 a limited edition (150 copies) of an eleven-essay collection, *Hawai'i One Summer*, appeared through a San Francisco press. She joined the American Academy of Arts and Sciences in 1992.

Kingston then spent approximately eighteen months helping the Berkeley Repertory Theatre prepare a stage presentation based on *The Woman Warrior* and *China Men*. Coproduced by the Huntington Theatre Company in Boston and the Center Theatre Group in Los Angeles, the presentation, by playwright Deborah Rogin, opened to mixed reviews.

ANALYSIS

Maxine Hong Kingston's first two books defied conventional categorization. While the grantors of several critical awards labeled them nonfiction, their format is that of traditional short fiction with each

Maxine Hong Kingston (Franco Salmoiraghi)

chapter able to stand alone as its own story. Kingston's use of Chinese mythology to chronicle her life and those of her ancestors not only entertains but also provides a gritty, often disturbing, education in Chinese culture, particularly in its regressive attitudes toward women. One *Washington Post* critic labeled Kingston's stories "intense" and "fierce," noting that they form "a strange, sometimes savagely terrifying and, in the literal sense, wonderful" reading. Feminist critics find themes such as the marginalization of women and their routine sacrifice to social ideals of great interest. Also intriguing is the theme of mother/daughter relationships. While Kingston's mother seems at moments ruthless and even cruel, at other times she stands as a paragon of emotional strength, a figure well worth Kingston's imitation. The fact that Kingston dedicates *The Woman Warrior* to her parents reveals her overall positive feelings toward their influence and her Chinese background.

Kingston notes Chinese literary classics as influences on her writing along with works by Mark Twain, Gertrude Stein, Virginia Woolf, and William Carlos Williams. While Stein's works affect Kingston's use of dialogue, Kingston looks to Woolf for expertise in handling large expanses of time. She does not rely on the traditional use of chronology for continuity but rather on the strong individual voices of her mythological characters juxtaposed with her own modern, or postmodern, voice as narrator and sometimes as protagonist. She also cites as important her viewing of Chinese opera as a child, in which the application of a mixture of the fantastic and the realistic greatly impressed her.

"No Name Woman"

"No Name Woman" originally appeared as a chapter of *The Woman Warrior* in 1976. It has since been anthologized, most notably by feminist critics Sandra M. Gilbert and Susan Gubar in *The Norton Anthology of Literature by Women: The Tradition in English* (1985). Kingston uses legend to complement and inform fact as she relates select childhood experiences, one of which involves her hearing the story of an aunt who first shames her Chinese family by becoming pregnant by a man who is not her husband, then commits suicide. Horrifying details recall the ransacking by neighbors of the family home as "punishment" for her aunt's immoral act:

> At first they threw mud and rocks. . . . Then they threw eggs and began slaughtering our stock. We could hear the animals scream their deaths.

With a terrifying lack of emotion, the narrator's mother adds,

> Your aunt gave birth in the pigsty that night. The next morning when I went for the water, I found her and the baby plugging up the well.

Ostensibly, the story proves a cautionary tale; having begun menstruation, Kingston stands warned of the shame that may result from her body's reproductive capability. However, she focuses instead on the injustice faced by females within traditional Chinese society. More important, Kingston recognizes multiple benefits to her mother's story. When her mother cautions her not to tell her father that she knows this tale, that act of confidence mitigates the seeming lack of respect for Kingston on the part of her mother. The story supports the theme of cultural conflict made apparent in the narrator's thought that her aunt's true punishment was not death, "but the family's deliberately forgetting her." It also allows Kingston's emphasis on the importance of writing: "My aunt haunts me—her ghost drawn to me because now, after fifty years of neglect, I alone devote pages of paper to her."

"WHITE TIGERS"

The narrator begins this chapter by summarizing the Chinese myth of Fa Mu Lan, a sword fighter and heroine of China. She contemplates the possible roles that Chinese women may assume and the power of the woman warrior, quickly adding the thought that helps perpetuate Kingston's emphasis on the power of words: "At last I saw that I too had been in the presence of great power, my mother talking-story." Then the narrator's voice becomes that of a girl who tells of her quest to become a sword fighter, beginning with a journey up a mountain and into the sky, where she receives training from two guide figures familiar to the traditional quest. Various symbols important to Chinese mythology find their way into the tale: the white heron for valor, the dragon for challenge, and the walnut tree, an Oriental symbol of life.

As she meets the call to adventure that marks the beginning of most quest stories, the girl journeys through a barren land, representing the loss of fertility stolen from her country by marauders. Various trickster figures appear in the form of animals, all important to the future sword fighter's heroic development. Kingston imbues the story with multiple mystical elements:

> When I could point at the sky and make a sword appear, a silver bolt in the sunlight, and control its slashing with my own mind, the old people said I was ready to leave.

However, she herself has stated that readers should not focus on Chinese stereotypes in her writing. She places the story early in her collection to "show that the childish myth is past. . . . The White Tigers is not a Chinese myth but one transformed by America." This story continues Kingston's contemplation of the female role, her own in particular, within her traditional and her modern culture.

CHINA MEN

Kingston's *China Men* may be viewed as a work complementary to her *The Woman Warrior.* It echoes the first book's approach to grounding narrative in history and has been categorized variously as nonfiction and as historical fiction. Those supporting the second view defend the label "historical fiction" by arguing that Kingston's portrayal of China exceeds mere history. Rather, her "truths" she grounds in the individual experiences of her characters, all members of her own family, rather than in facts found in historical accounts. Of the six chapters and twelve stories/anecdotes, only one varies from this approach. "The Laws" offers a summary of laws that discriminated against Chinese immigrants beginning in 1868. For example, a 1924 immigration law excluded all Chinese females from entry into the United States. Furthermore, marriage to a Chinese female by an American male, or vice versa, would cause the American to lose his or her citizenship.

Kingston employs this story to clarify the aspirations that first drew the Chinese to America, a country imbued with mystical characteristics and labeled the "Gold Mountain" by those who idealized its appeal. She illuminates the ordeals suffered by Chinese immigrants, including the physical quest that brought them to America, through nonlinear narratives of their experiences in World Wars I and II and in the Vietnam War. "On Discovery," the title of her first chapter, refers to her own discovery of her heritage as well as to the discovery made by a Chinese mythical male scholar, Tang Ao, of the "Land of Women." In a role reversal illuminating gender expectations, Tang Ao undergoes the painful process of having his feet bound as he becomes a slave to the females who rule the land. Critics note that by locating her mythical land in America, Kingston comments both on American culture's "demasculinization" of the Chinese immigrant and on China's demoralizing and often inhumane treatment of women. In the story "The Adventures of Lo Bun Sun," she adopts Daniel Defoe's familiar tale of *The Life and Strange Surprizing Adventures of Robinson Crusoe, of York, Mariner, Written by Himself* (1719) to expose Crusoe, and by extension other English speakers, as trickster imperialists, whose motivations remain based on greed leading to a desire for power.

The collection acts as an homage not only to Kingston's family members, made clear in the chapters "The Father from China" and "The American Father," but also to all male Chinese immigrants and their second- and third-generation offspring. The twelve tales celebrate their native culture, their adopted culture, and their physical, spiritual, and intellectual contributions to both. Throughout her collection, Kingston entertains and informs, while also criticizing racist behavior and systems that co-opt social relationships to form hierarchies in which one group assumes the right to control another based on an arbitrary and capricious cultural order.

OTHER MAJOR WORKS

LONG FICTION: *Tripmaster Monkey: His Fake Book*, 1989.

NONFICTION: *Hawai'i One Summer*, 1987.

BIBLIOGRAPHY

Cheung, King-Kok. *Articulate Silences: Hisaye Yamamoto, Maxine Hong Kingston, Joy Kogawa*. Ithaca: Cornell University Press, 1993. A discussion of all three authors' use of what Cheung terms "double-voiced discourse" as they demonstrate the arbitrary nature of "truth" and "history" through appropriation and subversion of their culture's dominant discourse.

Gao, Yan. *The Art of Parody: Maxine Hong Kingston's Use of Chinese Sources*. New York: Peter Lang, 1996. Discusses all of Kingston's works, emphasizing her skill in avoiding mythological stereotypes as she adapts Chinese stories to shape her vision of American culture.

Kingston, Maxine Hong. *Conversations with Maxine Hong Kingston*, edited by Paul Skenazy and Tera Martin. Jackson: University Press of Mississippi, 1998. Collection of interviews of Kingston by various interviewers.

Ludwig, Sami. *Concrete Language: Intercultural Communication in Maxine Hong Kingston's "The Woman Warrior" and Ishmael Reed's "Mumbo Jumbo."* Cross Cultural Communication 2. New York: Peter Lang, 1996. This study of intercultural communication includes a bibliography.

Simmons, Diane. *Maxine Hong Kingston*. New York: Twayne, 1999. Complete biography, discussion of works, chronology, conversations with Kingston, and bibliography.

Skandera-Trombley, Laura, ed. *Critical Essays on Maxine Hong Kingston*. New York: G. K. Hall, 1998. An interesting and informative collection made all the more valuable by the inclusion of an interview with, and a statement by, Kingston that elucidates her view of the critical reception of her works.

Smith, Jeanne Rosier. *Writing Tricksters: Mythic Gambols in American Ethnic Literature*. Berkeley: University of California Press, 1997. Discusses Kingston's three major works as focused on Chinese trickster myths and figures, particularly the monkey, stressing the trickster nature of Kingston's narrative itself, which remains subversive and paradoxical.

Virginia Brackett

W. P. KINSELLA

Born: Edmonton, Alberta, Canada; May 25, 1935

PRINCIPAL SHORT FICTION

Dance Me Outside, 1977
Scars, 1978
Shoeless Joe Jackson Comes to Iowa, 1980
Born Indian, 1981
The Moccasin Telegraph and Other Stories, 1983
The Thrill of the Grass, 1984
The Alligator Report, 1985
The Fencepost Chronicles, 1986
Red Wolf, Red Wolf, 1987
The Further Adventures of Slugger McBatt, 1988
The Miss Hobbema Pageant, 1989
The Dixon Cornbelt League and Other Baseball Stories, 1993
Brother Frank's Gospel Hour and Other Stories, 1994

OTHER LITERARY FORMS

W. P. Kinsella is best known for his novel, including *Shoeless Joe* (1982) and *The Iowa Baseball Confederacy* (1986), which combine baseball with fantasy, and *If Wishes Were Horses* (1996) and *Magic Time* (1998). *Shoeless Joe* is the basis of the popular 1989 film *Field of Dreams*. Because of its use in the film, Kinsella's line "If you build it, he will come" has become a catchphrase. Kinsella has also written poetry, plays, and the nonfiction *A Series for the World* (1992), about the 1992 World Series between the Toronto Blue Jays and the Atlanta Braves.

ACHIEVEMENTS

W. P. Kinsella received the Books in Canada First Novel Award, the Canadian Authors Association Prize for Fiction, the Alberta Achievement Award for Excellence in Literature, the Stephen Leacock Medal for Humor, and the Canadian Book Publishers' Author-of-the-Year Award.

BIOGRAPHY

William Patrick Kinsella was born May 25, 1935, in Edmonton, Alberta, Canada. His father was a con-

tractor; his mother, a printer. An only child, Kinsella spent his early years in a log cabin near Lac Ste.-Anne, sixty miles northwest of Edmonton. He rarely saw other children and completed grades one through four by correspondence. His parents, grandmother, and aunt read to one another and told stories, and Kinsella began writing fantasies when he was five or six. The family moved to Edmonton when he was ten, and his father, a former semiprofessional baseball player, began taking him to baseball games. In the eighth grade, Kinsella won a prize for "Diamond Doom," a baseball mystery. At eighteen, he published his first story, a science-fiction tale about a totalitarian society, in *The Alberta Civil Service Bulletin*.

Kinsella worked as a government clerk, manager of a retail credit company, account executive for the City of Edmonton, owner of an Italian restaurant, and taxicab driver, the last two while attending the University of Victoria, where he received a B.A. in 1974. He then attended the Writers' Workshop at the University of Iowa, earning a master of fine arts degree in 1978. He taught at the University of Calgary from 1978 to 1983, but he hated the academic life, quitting to write full time. Kinsella was married to Mildred Clay from 1965 to 1978. From 1978 to 1983, he taught creative writing at the University of Calgary. He then resigned from teaching to spend his time writing. He married the writer Ann Knight in 1978, and they settled in White Rock, British Columbia, and Iowa City, Iowa, when not traveling to attend major league baseball games. Kinsella has two daughters, Shannon and Erin. In 1997 Kinsella was hit by a car and suffered a concussion and the loss of taste and smell. His injuries, which also included difficulty concentrating, put his writing career on hold.

ANALYSIS

W. P. Kinsella said that his storytelling skills resulted from growing up in an oral tradition. He and his Yugoslavian grandmother swapped stories, hers set in the hills near Dubrovnik, his in rural Alberta. Through this process, he learned to entertain by making his listener eager to hear what will happen next. Kinsella is a serious writer who sees the writer's first duty as entertainment and thus makes his characters less cynical and angry than he is. He considers himself a realist who does not believe in magic, yet many of his stories are tall tales or fantasies. While his fiction is sometimes sentimental, it is nevertheless effective because of the compassion that he feels for characters confronted by the absurdities of a seemingly meaningless world.

Kinsella calls his short, surrealistic stories "Brautigans" because of the influence of writer Richard Brautigan on his life and career. According to Kinsella, whose favorite book is Brautigan's *In Watermelon Sugar* (1968), "Brautigan's delicate, visual, whimsical, facetious writing appealed to a whole generation of us who were able to identify with the gentle, loving losers of his stories." Typical of Kinsella's Brautigans is "Syzygy," about Grabarkewitcz, a European immigrant to Vancouver whose cat sleeps in the bathroom sink and disappears down the drain when its owner is shaving: "'Cats are independent devils,'" said Grabarkewitcz. 'They never come when you call them.'" The Brautigans are Kinsella's most self-consciously literary stories, a fact that he acknowledges in "The Secret" by having Grabarkewitcz confess to the crime of "bookfondling."

"THE BOOK BUYERS"

One of the longest and best of the Brautigans is "The Book Buyers," which satirizes his native country's eccentricities. The narrator wonders why, if most Canadians seem chained to television sets or computers, statistics show that they are buying more books than ever before. Finding himself in Toronto, he decides that this is the perfect place to investigate this phenomenon since "as we all know, there is nothing either west or east of Toronto."

Going to the only bookstore in Toronto that sells books by Canadians, he spots a typical Canadian reader: "He had a bottle opener and ski lift tickets attached to the zipper of his parka." The customer buys $102 worth and says he has to deliver them somewhere. The narrator eventually discovers that the books go to a warehouse, where they are shredded and recycled as packing cases by the government to

W. P. Kinsella in 1984 (AP/Wide World Photos)

keep the book business alive. He threatens to make the practice public unless at least one book he has written is included in each pickup. He describes the boxes containing computers and video cassette recorders as representing "the essence of Canadian literature." "The Book Buyers" is typical of Kinsella's satire since instead of becoming angry over Canada's neglect of its writers and his compatriots' general antiintellectualism, he turns the whole matter into a benign joke.

"EVANGELINE'S MOTHER"

"Evangeline's Mother," one of the best of his realistic stories, deals with typical Kinsella subjects such as loneliness and class differences. The ambitious Henry Vold goes to work for a savings and loan company after high school, meets Rosalie on a blind date, and impregnates and marries her. Rosalie, who lives for the moment, leaves the dull Henry for a service-station attendant when their daughter, Carin, is a year old. Henry remarries, choosing someone like himself this time—Mona, a financial analyst—and they have a son as practical and unadventurous as they are.

Carin becomes a rebellious, promiscuous teenager and comes to live with Henry when Rosalie can take her behavior no longer. Henry loves Carin uncritically, forgiving her anything. Mona warns him that Carin cannot be trusted and is manipulating him. Despite himself, Henry is attracted to Carin's exotic, vivacious friend Evangeline. He is branch manager of a large savings and loan association and expects to be promoted into senior management, but he allows Evangeline to seduce him. Even meeting her slovenly mother, who once must have been as young and attractive as her daughter, does not deter Henry. He quits his job, withdrawing half his seventy thousand dollars in savings, and the three of them run away together.

Henry makes a mistake in getting involved with Rosalie, since she hardly fits into the carefully planned, conservative world he envisions for himself. His well-ordered world is perhaps too well ordered. He misses the adventure, the risk, and the sex that he associates with a certain type of woman. His world is empty and too lonely without it. Kinsella presents Henry's decision as the fulfilling of a psychological need but does not sentimentalize it. The story ends with a hint of danger: "as he glanced down at Vangy's sepia hand, it seemed to him that the nails . . . curled frighteningly. Images of talons filled Henry's mind." Henry can have order or adventure but not both. Kinsella explores this same theme of longing to recapture the spirit of the past in the equally poignant "Mother Tucker's Yellow Duck" and "K-Mart."

"The Thrill of the Grass"

As with his baseball novels, magic and spirituality are at the center of most of Kinsella's baseball stories. These tales are remarkable for the author's ability to find so many ways of looking at how the ritual of baseball can impose order on a chaotic universe and bring a sense of wholeness to shattered lives. In "The Thrill of the Grass," the narrator misses major league baseball during the lengthy players' strike of 1981 and goes to the empty stadium where he is a season-ticket holder. On impulse, he breaks the law for the first time in his forty years as a locksmith by letting himself into the stadium. In love with the game but repelled by the artificial turf, he enlists another fan to replace the turf with sod, square foot by square foot. Each invites a friend to take part, and soon dozens of men armed with sod, sprinklers, rakes, and hoes work each night until dawn to restore the field to its natural beauty, its divinity. With the transformation complete, the narrator feels "like a magician who has gestured hypnotically and produced an elephant from thin air." For Kinsella, the magic of baseball inspires other magical acts.

"The Thrill of the Grass" is one of the best examples of Kinsella's presentation of baseball as a substitute religion. The men's journeys to the stadium are called pilgrimages, and the narrator does not even confide in his beloved wife, since the restoration of the grass is "a ritual for true believers only." Kinsella does not attempt to explain or justify this attitude toward baseball; it must be accepted on faith. The locksmith always watches games from the first-base side and mistrusts anyone, even his daughter, who prefers to sit elsewhere: "The positions fans choose at sporting events are like politics, religion, or philosophy: a view of the world, a way of seeing the universe. They make no sense to anyone, have no basis in anything but stubbornness." Kinsella expresses deep suspicion of organized religion (as well as politics, bureaucracies, academics, and reformers) throughout his fiction, especially in his Native Canadian stories. Baseball is infinitely superior to religion, for it allows the possibility of regaining Eden.

"The Last Pennant Before Armageddon"

Religion also plays a part in "The Last Pennant Before Armageddon." Al Tiller is considered the stupidest manager in major league baseball. The fifty-five-year-old has never had a winning record as either player or manager in professional baseball. Suddenly, however, he is an apparent genius. The Chicago Cubs, who have not won a National League pennant since 1945, have been in first place all season, and Al should be on top of the world. Managers are essentially lonely people, but Al is lonelier than most, since he has an enormous burden that he is unable to share.

In June, he is listening to a radio sports program in St. Louis, when a caller who says he is an archangel announces that the Chicago Cubs will win the last pennant before Armageddon. Since early August, Al has a nightly dream in which petitioners plead with God to allow the Cubs to win. God replies that the Cubs will win the last pennant before Armageddon. (*The Iowa Baseball Confederacy* also involves the Cubs and apocalyptic events.) Not a religious man, Al is concerned because the Soviet Union has troops in Sri Lanka and the American president has threatened to use force to remove them. Al calls the host of the radio program, but he does not remember anyone claiming to be an archangel.

Al has been faced with a difficult decision before. As a minor leaguer, he fell in love with the perfect woman, but she married someone else. After Al became engaged to a less exciting woman from his hometown, his first love left her husband and asked Al to take her back. He did the honorable thing but always wondered what his life would have been like with his first love, even though she died at thirty. Now, as the Cubs approach the final game of the National League play-offs with the Los Angeles Dodgers, Al has to endure a final dream. In it, a woman petitioner who has always had her back to him turns and is his first love: "Now I have the most important reason of all to manage to win, something beyond honour, beyond duty. For surely, when all is said and done, love is more important." Like Henry Vold in "Evangeline's Mother," Al needs to take a chance for once. Playing it safe has made him a loser. Just as baseball and honor may be more important than religion and politics, love is superior to anything. Kinsella uses baseball and magic or the supernatural to comment on basic human issues.

THE SILAS ERMINESKIN STORIES

Kinsella has written dozens of stories about the Cree Indian reserve near Hobbema, Alberta. He writes about Native Canadians with sensitivity and understanding of their unique culture. The characters are generally poor, semiliterate, unemployed, and alcoholic, with little hope for improvement. While these problems lurk in the background of most of the stories—and are the main concern of several—the predominant tone of the tales narrated by Silas Ermineskin is comic. Kinsella comments on racism, social injustice, and political indifference, while creating entertainment through the absurdities and even slapstick surrounding these issues.

The stories originate when twenty-year-old Silas is given a writing assignment in an English class at the technical school that he attends and where he continues with the encouragement of his teacher. Because the teacher corrects only spelling and punctuation, the tales are written in an unlettered, colloquial style. They usually center on the misadventures of Silas; his best friend, the uncouth and uncontrollable Frank Fencepost; Mad Etta, a four-hundred-pound medicine woman; and Bedelia Coyote, the local feminist and political activist. Mad Etta is often a Jeeves to Silas's Bertie Wooster, advising him about how to extract himself and his friends from complicated situations. Silas's stories deal with such subjects as a Native Canadian automobile salesman who cheats other Native Canadians, a father who forces his daughter into prostitution, Silas and Frank's trip to Las Vegas, a Native Canadian politician who tries to be white, a Mexican who poses as a Native Canadian doctor, the staging of a buffalo hunt for Prince Philip, and Mad Etta's playing hockey. Silas describes disease, death, and despair and is often bitter: "Sometimes when I have to put up with the Government or the Church I feel so helpless, I get so mad my hands shake." The harsh reality of the Native Canadians' situation is counterbalanced by Kinsella's use of mysticism, as when Mad Etta rights a series of wrongs by turning three men into weasels.

Silas's most memorable stories are the comic ones. In one of the best, "The Killing of Colin Moosefeathers," Silas and Frank invent a fellow student at the technical school as a prank, giving him "the silliest name we can come up with." A chain of events leads to Colin's being registered for classes. Silas, Frank, and Bedelia eventually manage to get a credit card for him, making purchases up to the credit limit. Silas quickly learns why they can get away with it all: "People is real greedy and will take a chance if it gonna mean a sale for them." When the bill collectors start arriving, they say Colin is dead. To get liquor for Colin's wake, they allow a white man in a suit to use the credit card: "Those kind be the most anxious to make quick money because they all the time have to pay for expensive clothes." Silas and his friends even come up with a grave, cross, and wreath to prove to the police that Colin is dead. The police dig up the grave only to be told that Colin has been cremated.

Throughout Silas's stories, white people ignore, distrust, and hate Native Canadians. Colin Moosefeathers gives them the opportunity for revenge and fun at the same time that they exploit a socioeconomic system from which they have been excluded. Their pranks escalate because of the whites' gullibility and greed, and their faceless bureaucracy. Anyone can use Colin's credit card, since Anglo-Canadians think all Native Canadians have funny names and look alike. Whites almost always lose in such confrontations with Kinsella's Native Canadians because they underestimate them.

These Native Canadian stories succeed primarily because of Kinsella's virtuosity as a storyteller, and "The Kid in the Stove" celebrates the art of storytelling. Silas entertains his little brothers and sisters with the story that he learned from their mother about how, in 1907, Lazarus Bobtail and four of his five children were murdered by a white man. The fifth child escaped by crawling into a stove: "For such a sad story it almost make a happy ending when you hear at the end that one child got away." Since he is interested in the history of Native Canadians in Alberta, Silas wants to find out more about the murder and locates a newspaper account that fails to mention the fifth child. He learns that Mrs. Bobtail, who was away at the time of the killings, gave birth a few weeks later. Her having "one in the oven" has evolved in the Native Canadians' oral tradition into a more positive account of what happened. Silas is eager to correct the mistake, until he realizes that the misconstrued version serves a much better purpose than the truth.

The Silas Ermineskin stories often verge on sentimentality because Kinsella, like his hero Brautigan, forces himself to find some virtue arising out of sorrow. "The Kid in the Stove" stands out for reflecting Kinsella's apparent theory of art by acknowledging the healing power of fiction. The audience wants the thrill of the horrifying murders but needs some redemption resulting from their fears. The constant good humor of Silas and his friends in the face of despair is life-affirming.

"BULL"

Ever since the colonial period, Native Canadians have been largely excluded from well-paying jobs and often have been forced to live on reservations. In his 1994 book of short stories entitled *Brother Frank's Gospel Hour and Other Stories*, Kinsella describes how different Native Canadian characters deal with Anglo-Canadians who treat them condescendingly. In the short story "Bull," the protagonist Frank is portrayed as a rather simpleminded Native Canadian who tries to stay away from bill collectors and the police. Frank gets a job as a foreman on Manley Cartstairs's large ranch by claiming that he has extensive experience on large ranches throughout Alberta; Frank is such a slick talker that Manley Carstairs does not bother to check his false references. Frank is summarily fired from his job when Manley Carstairs finds him sleeping with his daughter. He is very surprised when he receives a subpoena to testify in a civil court case brought by the employer who had fired him, for this will be his first time in court as a witness and not as a defendant. Frank resents losing his job and wants to get back at his former boss.

As the civil trial begins, Frank is confused because there is no criminal defendant; he does not understand that courts hold both civil and criminal trials. Manley Carstairs raises Charolais cattle, and he had hired Ace Artificial Insemination, Inc., to inseminate his prize cattle, but something went wrong and the new calves were a mixed breed. He is suing the company for his losses. During his testimony, Frank pretends that he does not understand questions from the judge and the lawyers, and they conclude that he is an honest simpleton. When the lawyer for the insemination company asks Frank how the error could have happened, Frank recognizes a clear opportunity to get back at his former boss. Frank swears under oath that because of his anger toward his former boss he opened the gate around the Charolais cattle, thus allowing other cattle to mate with them. The judge then absolves the animal insemination company of all responsibility. After the trial, Frank's friend Silas tells him that his testimony was filled with lies because Silas, not Frank, had opened the gate around the Charolais cattle on the Carstairses' ranch. Manley Carstairs treated his workers so badly that they were all patiently waiting for an opportunity to cause him financial loss.

"BROTHER FRANK'S GOSPEL HOUR"

The final short story in this collection is "Brother Frank's Gospel Hour." In this story, Frank is still the main character, but this time he is an employee of a poorly funded radio station for Native Canadians called KUGH. For reasons Frank and his friends do not understand, the Canadian federal government moves their radio station from the town onto the reservation. Frank is upset because this move will mean that KUGH will receive less revenue for commercials from local businesses. Frank creates an ingenious get-rick-quick scheme, pretending he is a clergyman who mixes Christianity with traditional Native Canadian myths, which he makes up during his broadcasts. He promises on the air to send gifts to poor people who ask him for help, and he simply asks his listeners to send him money so he can help those who are suffering. Frank is so persuasive that the money begins to flow into KUGH. He keeps a hefty profit for himself and his friends, but he does send gifts to people in need. Wealth has finally come to this impoverished reservation. Frank skillfully negotiates contracts with a national company that agrees to pay him very well to syndicate his show, but Frank insists on maintaining control over all contributions. Frank has become a celebrity, but this fame has changed him. He now dresses like a white man, and other residents of the reservation feel alienated from him, although he does share his new wealth with his friends and other Native Canadians.

OTHER MAJOR WORKS

LONG FICTION: *Shoeless Joe*, 1982; *The Iowa Baseball Confederacy*, 1986; *Box Socials*, 1991; *The Winter Helen Dropped By*, 1995; *If Wishes Were Horses*, 1996; *Magic Time*, 1998.

PLAYS: *The Thrill of the Grass: Three Plays About Baseball*, pb. 1988.

POETRY: *Rainbow Warehouse*, 1989; *Even at This Distance*, 1994 (with Knight).

NONFICTION: *Two Spirits Soar: The Act of Allen Sapp, the Inspiration of Allan Gonor*, 1990.

BIBLIOGRAPHY

Aitken, Brian. "Baseball as Sacred Doorway in the Writing of W. P. Kinsella." *Aethlon* 8 (Fall, 1990): 61-75. Aitken looks at the spiritual aspects of Kinsella's baseball novels and two of his stories, "Frank Pierce, Iowa" and "K-Mart." He concludes that Kinsella shows how North Americans can find as much spiritual fulfillment in sports as in formal religion.

Cameron, Elspeth. "Diamonds Are Forever." *Saturday Night* 101 (August, 1986): 45-47. Cameron shows how most of Kinsella's fiction centers on adolescent males who, unencumbered by women, pursue quests as if they were knights errant.

Horvath, Brooke K., and William J. Palmer. "Three On: An Interview with David Carkeet, Mark Harris, and W. P. Kinsella." *Modern Fiction Studies* 33 (Spring, 1987): 183-194. Kinsella explains how he came to write about baseball and his attitude toward literary criticism.

Kinsella, W. P. "Interview." *Short Story*, n.s. 1 (Fall, 1993): 81-88. Kinsella discusses baseball as the chess of sports and why it serves him so well in his fiction. Talks about the transformation of the book *Shoeless Joe* into the film *Field of Dreams*. Discusses those contemporary short-story writers he likes best, his own collections of short stories, and what he thinks the future of short fiction will be.

_____. "W. P. Kinsella, the Super-Natural." Interview by Sheldon Sunness. *Sport* 77 (July, 1986): 74. Kinsella discusses his fondness for baseball, his disdain for Canada's native game of hockey, and his wish to be a major league baseball player in another life.

Murray, Don. *The Fiction of W. P. Kinsella: Tall Tales in Various Voices*. Fredericton, New Brunswick, Canada: York Press, 1987. This brief but excellent study provides an overview of Kinsella's fiction, placing emphasis on the short stories. Murray includes three interviews with Kinsella, a bibliography, and an index.

_____. "A Note on W. P. Kinsella's Humor." *The International Fiction Review* 14, no. 2 (1987): 98-100. Humor is the basic ingredient in Kinsella's fiction, according to Murray. He argues that anarchy is justified and funny in Kinsella's works.

Michael Adams, updated by Edmund J. Campion

RUDYARD KIPLING

Born: Bombay, India; December 30, 1865
Died: Hampstead, London, England; January 18, 1936

Principal short fiction

In Black and White, 1888
Plain Tales from the Hills, 1888
Soldiers Three, 1888
The Story of the Gadsbys, 1888
The Phantom 'Rickshaw and Other Tales, 1888
Under the Deodars, 1888
Wee Willie Winkie, 1888
Life's Handicap, 1891
Many Inventions, 1893
The Jungle Book, 1894
The Second Jungle Book, 1895
Soldier Tales, 1896
The Day's Work, 1898
Stalky and Co., 1899
Just So Stories, 1902
Traffics and Discoveries, 1904
Puck of Pook's Hill, 1906
Actions and Reactions, 1909
Rewards and Fairies, 1910
A Diversity of Creatures, 1917
Land and Sea Tales for Scouts and Guides, 1923
Debits and Credits, 1926
Thy Servant a Dog, 1930
Limits and Renewals, 1932

Other literary forms

Rudyard Kipling's literary career began in journalism, but his prose sketches and verse brought him early fame. He wrote several novels, most lastingly *Kim* (1901), and he also wrote works of history, including a study of his son's military regiment from World War I. In his lifetime as well as posthumously, however, his fame depended upon his poetry and short stories, both of which he wrote for adult audiences and for children. Kipling's autobiography, *Something of Myself: For My Friends Known and Unknown* (1937), was published after his death.

Achievements

By his early twenties, Rudyard Kipling had become one of the best-known writers in the English language. His first poems and stories were written and published in India, but his popularity quickly spread throughout the English-speaking world and beyond. Although he published several novels, the short-story form proved to be his most successful métier. Drawing upon his experiences in India, many of his early stories featured the adventures of ordinary soldiers, junior officers, and civil officials, and his use of dialect was a recognized feature of his literary technique. Awarded the Nobel Prize in Literature in 1907, he also received honorary degrees from many universities.

Kipling wrote extensively about the benefits of the United Kingdom's paramount position in the world, and over time his public persona was perceived to be that of a political reactionary. Although some of his finest short stories were written in the last two decades of his life, by that time, to many of his contemporaries, he had become yesterday's man, irrevocably associated with political imperialism, a dying creed even before his death in 1936. After his death, however, his stories received much critical study and acclaim, and Kipling is considered to be one of the major practitioners of the short-story art ever to write in English.

Rudyard Kipling, Nobel Laureate for Literature in 1907
(©The Nobel Foundation)

BIOGRAPHY

Joseph Rudyard Kipling was born in Bombay, India, in 1865. His father, John Lockwood Kipling, was an artist and teacher. His mother, Alice Macdonald Kipling, was from a family of exceptional sisters. One married the Pre-Raphaelite painter, Sir Edward Coley Burne-Jones, and another was the mother of Stanley Baldwin, the British prime minister in the years between the two world wars.

As was customary at the time, Rudyard and his younger sister remained in England when their parents returned to India, and Kipling dramatized his misery at being left behind in his later writings. He attended a second-rank private school that prepared middle-class boys for careers in the military; small, not athletic, and forced to wear glasses, Kipling was not an outstanding or popular student, but his literary interests proved a defense and a consolation. The university was not an option for him, primarily for financial reasons, and he returned to India, where his parents had found a position for him on an English-language newspaper.

Kipling was fascinated by India. Often unable to sleep, he spent his nights wandering the streets. He had written some poetry as a schoolboy and continued to do so, while also composing newspaper sketches featuring his Anglo-Indian environment. By the end of the 1880's, he had already published several volumes of short stories and poems. No British writer since Charles Dickens had become so well known, and Kipling was only in his mid-twenties. His works were often satiric, and some readers believed that he cast aspersions upon the British army and imperial authorities in India, but the opposite was closer to Kipling's own feelings. He doubted that the English at home understood the sacrifices that the average soldier, the young officer, and the district commissioners were making to preserve Great Britain's prosperity and security.

Kipling left India in 1889 and established himself in London, where he became acquainted with the major literary figures of the day, including Thomas Hardy and Henry James. In 1890, he published his first novel, *The Light That Failed*. With the American Wolcott Balestier, Kipling, in spite of his previous unwillingness to attach himself to any literary partnership, wrote a second novel, *The Naulahka: A Story of East and West* (1892). Kipling's relationship with Balestier was very close, and, after the latter's death, he married Balestier's sister, Caroline (Carrie), in 1892. Kipling subsequently settled in Vermont, near his wife's family. Although residing there for four years before returning to England, Kipling never admired the United States and had difficulty with Carrie's family.

His fame reached its pinnacle in the years before the South African Boer War broke out in 1899. His portrayal of the Empire struck a chord in the British psyche during the 1890's; a changing political climate, however, began to make Kipling's public posture as an imperialist less acceptable. Still, he continued to write, both for children and for adults. In 1902, he purchased Bateman's, a country house in Sussex, which remained his home for the rest of his life.

Long a frustrated man of action and a Francophile from his schoolboy years, he vehemently opposed Germany during World War I. His only son was killed in action in 1915. Kipling's health had begun to decline, his marriage was less than fulfilling, and although he received much formal praise, his later stories were not widely read. He died in 1936 and was buried in Westminster Abbey, more a recognition for his earlier than his later career. Only after his death was it possible to separate the public man—imperialist and antiliberal—from the literary artist whose best stories have continued to survive.

ANALYSIS

Many of Rudyard Kipling's earliest short stories are set in the India of his early childhood years in Bombay and his newspaper days in Lahore. The intervening years at school in England had perhaps increased his sensitivity to the exotic Indian locale and British imperial presence. Kipling was a voracious reader of English, French, and American writers, trained by his newspaper experience in the virtues of conciseness and detail. His art arrived almost fully revealed in his earliest works. Kipling focused, however, not on the glories and conquests of empire but on the lives—work and activities, passions and emotions—of ordinary people responding to what were often extraordinary or inexplicable events. Love, especially doomed love, terror and the macabre, revenge and its consequences—these were the elements upon which his stories turned, even later when the settings were often English. His fame or notoriety was almost instantaneous, in part because of the locations and subject matter of the stories, because of his use of dialect in re-creating the voices of his nonestablishment characters, and because Kipling's early writings appeared at a time when England and Western civilization as a whole were caught up in imperial dreams and rivalries.

A number of his stories pivot around the relations between men and women. Kipling has been called a misogynist, and often his characters, particularly those in the military, blame women for their own and others' misfortunes. Most of his stories employ a male voice, and many critics agree that Kipling's women are not often fully realized, particularly in his early years. The isolation of British soldiers and officials in India could itself explain these portrayals.

There were boundaries in that esoteric environment—sexual, social, racial—that were violated only at a cost, but in Kipling's stories they are crossed because his characters choose to do so or cannot help themselves.

"BEYOND THE PALE"

In "Beyond the Pale," Christopher Trejago seduces and is seduced by a fifteen-year-old Hindu widow, Bisea, before misunderstanding and jealousy cause the lovers to terminate the relationship. Later, Trejago returns to their place of rendezvous only to discover that Bisea's hands have been cut off at the wrists; at the instant of his discovery, he is attacked by a sharp object that injures his groin. One of Kipling's shortest stories, it exhibits several of his continuing concerns. Love, passion, even understanding are often doomed, whether between man and woman or between British and Indians, while horror and unexpected shock can occur at any time and have lasting effects; revenge is a human quality. Stylistically, the story is rich in the descriptive detail of the dead-end alley where Bisea and Trejago first met but is enigmatic in explaining how the affair became known, leading to Bisea's maiming. The story does not end with the assault on Trejago. As often with Kipling, there is a coda. Trejago is forced to carry on, with a slight limp and the remembrance of horror leading to sleepless nights.

"LOVE-O'-WOMEN"

Dangerous boundaries and illicit relationships also feature in his "Love-o'-Women," the story of Larry Tighe, a gentleman who had enlisted as a common soldier, a gentleman-ranker who stepped down out of his proper world. Kipling often used the technique of a story-within-a-story, told by a narrator who may or may not be telling the total truth but whose own personality and perception are as important as the plot itself, accomplished most notably in "Mrs. Bathurst." Here, in "Love-o'-Women," the tale opens with Sergeant Raines shooting one of his own men, Corporal Mackie, who had seduced Mrs. Raines. After Raines's trial, several soldiers ruminate on the dead Mackie's fate. One of them, Terrence Mulvaney, comments that Mackie is the lucky one: He died quickly. He then tells the story of Tighe, who claimed the nickname of Love-o'-Women and made a career in the military of seducing daughters and wives, governesses and maids. When Tighe attempts to commit suicide by exposing his body to enemy fire during a battle, Mulvaney saves him and learns that Tighe deeply regrets what he has done, including his treatment and loss of his only real love, a woman named Egypt who turned to prostitution. Dying of syphilis, Tighe collapses in Egypt's arms; she then shoots herself. Kipling did not necessarily believe in justice in the world, and, although reared a Christian, he was not orthodox in his religious beliefs but believed that there was a mortality for which one must answer. In "Love-o'-Women," sin required confession, contrition, and penance.

"THE PHANTOM 'RICKSHAW"

Ghosts or phantoms also often played a role in Kipling's stories. In "The Phantom 'Rickshaw," Jack Pansay, an English official in India, begins a shipboard flirtation with a married woman, Mrs. Keith-Wessington, while returning from England. The affair continues in India, but Pansay grows tired of her, becoming engaged to someone else. Mrs. Wessington refuses to accept the termination of the romance and subsequently dies after losing control of her rickshaw while attempting to renew the affair. Soon, as a ghostly presence, she and her rickshaw begin to appear to Pansay, and feeling that his rejection had killed her, he himself sinks into decline. Although his doctor believes that his illness is merely the result of overwork, Pansay believes otherwise: His death is the payment required for his treatment of Mrs. Wessington.

"THE WISH HOUSE"

From the beginning of his literary career, Kipling was considered to be a master in the use of dialect. Mulvaney's telling of Tighe's tale was rendered in an Irish dialect. In Kipling's Indian stories, Mulvaney's Irish was joined by characters speaking London Cockney, Yorkshire in northern England, and others. In many of his later stories, Kipling incorporated various English dialects, such as the Sussex dialect spoken by Grace Ashcroft and Liz Fettley in "The Wish House." He generally used dialect when portraying the speech of persons from the undereducated classes or foreigners—persons different from his middle-class readers—and his treatment is often successful, even though some critics have claimed that his dialect re-creations were not entirely accurate. It has also been argued that, at times, the use of dialect gets in the way of the reading and understanding of the story itself, although this is more true of his early stories than his later ones.

"THE BRUSH-WOOD BOY"

On occasion, Kipling attempted to create the speaking style of the middle or upper classes. Here the use of words and phrases can be disconcerting to the reader, particularly after the diction and slang of an era has become dated. In "The Brush-Wood Boy," George Cottar, the perfect public-school graduate and heroic young officer, resorts to "By Jove" on a regular basis. Possibly accurate then, it is artificial and stereotyped to a later generation. The same might be said about Kipling's attempts to re-create the voices of children: Sometimes they are successful, sometimes not. If dialogue and dialect can deepen and extend the meaning and quality of a story, they can also date a story and detract from it.

In the 1890's, after his marriage to Carrie and the birth of his three children, Kipling, although continuing to write short stories and novels for an adult audience, also turned his hand to works for children. Kipling had an empathetic feeling for children; some critics suggest that he never entirely outgrew his own childhood, with its traumas and rewards. *The Jungle Book* was published in 1894 and *The Second Jungle Book* the following year. The series of stories of the baby Mowgli reared by wolves in the jungle is perhaps the most enduring of Kipling's many short-story collections. Several generations of children read about Father and Mother Wolf, the tiger Shere Khan, the sleepy bear Baloo, the panther Bagheera, and Kaa, the python. In later decades, other children came to know them through the Walt Disney cartoon feature, but there is a quality in the Kipling stories that did not translate fully to the screen. Like authors of other animal stories, Kipling anthropomorphized his creatures, and they exhibit recognizable human characteristics, but his jungle contains a quality of danger, of menace, which was not replicated in the Disney production.

"THE KING'S ANKUS"

Kipling's City of the Cold Lair in "The King's Ankus," inhabited only by the evil White Cobra, places the reader in a dark, dangerous, and claustrophobic building, a house of fear and death. A continuing motif in the stories involves references to the Law of the Jungle—Charles Darwin's survival of the fittest—an ideology very prominent in the imperialist years of the late nineteenth century. The villainous Shere Khan, Mowgli's rival who is always eager to put Mowgli to death, belonged to that jungle world, while the Monkey-People as portrayed in "Kaa's Hunting" and human beings, driven from their village in "Letting in the Jungle," did not. Both species did not properly follow the law; both were cowardly, vindictive, thoughtless, greedy, and irrational.

JUST SO STORIES

The *Just So Stories* were published in 1902. These were composed for an audience younger and more innocent than the readers of *The Jungle Book* stories. The teller of the tales, or fables, addresses his hearer as "O My Best Beloved," who was Kipling's eldest child, Josephine, who died at the age of six, in 1899. The *Just So Stories* appeal on two levels. First, they purport to answer some of the eternal questions of childhood such as "How the Camel Got His Hump" and "How the Leopard Got His Spots." In so doing, Kipling's genius for specific details captivates the reader. From "How the Whale Got His Throat" comes the following:

> If you swim to latitude Fifty North, longitude Forty West (that is magic), you will find sitting *on* a raft, *in* the middle of the sea, with nothing on but a pair of blue canvas breeches, a pair of suspenders (you *must* not forget the suspenders, Best Beloved), and a jack-knife, one shipwrecked Mariner.

Second, the settings of the tales enchant with their exotic locale, such as the Howling Desert of the camel, the High Veldt of the leopard, and "the banks of the turbid Amazon" in those High and Far-Off Times.

PUCK OF POOK'S HILL

The fourth collection of Kipling's children's stories was *Puck of Pook's Hill*, published in 1906. Now ensconced in the English countryside at Bateman's, Kipling turned to the history of England. Puck, "the oldest Old Thing in England," appears to two young children, Dan and Una, and through the use of magic conjures up for them various past eras from pre-Roman times onward. The nationalistic bias of the tales is not heavy-handed, and generally the narrative and the conversations of the characters are appropriate for children, while Puck's world, if not Puck himself, is more familiar and less exotic than Kipling's earlier children's books. Among re-created practical Romans, patriotic Saxons, and archetypal peasants, the most evocative tale is "Dymchurch Flit," recited by the narrator in a Sussex dialect. In the aftermath of Henry VIII's Protestant Reformation, England's fairies ("pharisees") wished to flee from the land, and a peasant woman gives her two disabled sons through a "pure love-loan" to ferry them to the Continent. At the end of each conjuring of the past, however, Puck causes the children to forget him and his creations; he and his magic belong in the stories, not in so-called real life. Although Puck uses magic, the stories themselves are more realistic, being grounded in history, than either the fables of *The Jungle Book, The Second Jungle Book*, or *Just So Stories*.

"MRS. BATHURST"

One of Kipling's most successful short stories was "Mrs. Bathurst," published in 1904 and set in South Africa. On one level, the story is told through an unidentified first-person narrator. He and his friend Inspector Hooper, a railway investigator who had just returned from surveying railway equipment in the interior, are passing time drinking beer on a hot day. Hooper has something in his pocket for which he occasionally reaches but never quite removes. They are shortly joined by Pycroft, a sailor, and Sergeant Pritchard, whom the narrator knows but Hooper does not. Pycroft and Pritchard begin to reminisce about sailors whom they have known: Boy Niven who led them astray in the forests of British Columbia supposedly searching for his uncle's farm, Spit-Kit Jones who married "the cocoanut-woman," and Moon, who had "showed signs o'bein' a Mormonastic beggar" and who deserted after sixteen years of service. The talk then turns to "V," who had disappeared just recently while up-country, only eighteen months before his pension. "V" was also known as Click because of his false teeth, which did not quite fit. Hooper is interested in what Pycroft and Pritchard have to say about "V" and asks them if "V" has any tattoos. Pritchard takes umbrage, believing that Inspector Hooper is seeking information in order to arrest his friend "V." Apologies are made, and then Hooper asks to hear more about "Vickery," though until that moment only "V" had been used in the discussion.

The narrator asks why Vickery ran away, and Pycroft, through a smile, lets it be known that there was a woman involved. Mrs. Bathurst, a widow, owned a hotel in New Zealand frequented by sailors and others. Asked to describe her, Pycroft answered that "'Tisn't beauty, so to speak, nor good talk necessarily. It's just It." Pycroft has now become the primary narrator, and Vickery and Mrs. Bathurst are filtered through his memories and perceptions. According to Pycroft, Mrs. Bathurst had "It," and Vickery was captivated although he did not let that be known to Pycroft at the time. Last December, as Pycroft tells the story, while on liberty in Cape Town, he ran into Vickery who, visibly disturbed, demanded that Pycroft accompany him to a biograph or cinematograph. This early motion picture—a recent novelty—featured scenes from England. Sitting in the front row, Vickery and Pycroft watched various London views appear on the "magic-lantern sheet." The scene shifted to London's Paddington Station, and among the passengers who came down the platform in the direction of the camera was Mrs. Bathurst, who "looked out straight at us with that blindish look. . . . She walked on and on till she melted out of the picture—like a shadow jumpin' over a candle."

At Vickery's urging, Pycroft accompanies him for five consecutive evenings to the cinematograph. On one occasion, Vickery agitatedly claims that Mrs. Bathurst is looking for him. Then, under obscure circumstances, Vickery is assigned up-country, and before he leaves he tells Pycroft that the motion picture of Mrs. Bathurst would appear again in a town where he would be able to see her once more. Vickery also abruptly informs Pycroft that he is not a murderer, for his wife had died during childbirth after Vickery had shipped out. Confused, Pycroft asked for the rest of the story but was not enlightened: "'The rest,' 'e says, 'is silence,'" borrowing from *Hamlet* (c. 1600-1601). Pycroft heard no more from Vickery.

At this point Hooper again reaches into his pocket and makes a reference to false teeth being acceptable evidence in a court of law. He then tells of his recent experience in the interior. Told to watch for a couple of tramps, Hooper recites how he could see them from a long way off, one standing and one sitting. They were dead.

> There'd been a bit of a thunderstorm in the teak, you see, and they were both stone dead and black as charcoal. That's what they really were, you see—charcoal. They fell to bits when we tried to shift 'em. The man who was standin' up had the false teeth. I saw 'em shinin' against the black. . . . Both burned to charcoal.

Again, Hooper reaches to his pocket, and again he does not bring forth anything. Although no other evidence appears, Pritchard for one seems to assume that the other body, unidentified by Hooper, is Mrs. Bathurst. Pycroft concludes that he for one is glad that Vickery is dead, wishing only to drink the last of the beer.

Throughout the story, Mrs. Bathurst is perceived through a series of images, as seen and related by Pycroft and Pritchard, who had known her in New Zealand, as told by Vickery to Pycroft, as she appears flickering on the motion-picture screen and as the unidentified narrator recites these varying images to the reader. If one theme in "Mrs. Bathurst" is the difficulty of perceiving the reality behind the images, another is the compulsive and destructive power of love. This was not a new aspect in Kipling's work, but perhaps never before had the woman, and even the man, Vickery, been quite so filtered from the reader through the various narrators and now including her image on the screen. Vickery's death apparently resulted because of his experience with Mrs. Bathurst. What was that experience? Was he escaping from her or seeking her out? Was he guilty of something? Apparently he was not guilty of murdering his wife. Had love or its consequences driven him mad? One critic has pointed out the element of "synchronicity," or the significant coincidence as an element in "Mrs.

Bathurst." Many twentieth century writers, from James Joyce to Anthony Powell, have employed this device. In "Mrs. Bathurst," the most notable example was the coincidence of Vickery and then Pycroft discovering Mrs. Bathurst on the motion-picture screen. The story is of seemingly disjointed events, like individual scenes in a motion picture. Combined they may have a coherence, but what that coherence is, or means, remains obscure, merely flickering images. Readers have puzzled over "Mrs. Bathurst" ever since the story first appeared.

"THEY"

Several of Kipling's later stories continue to develop his earlier themes. In 1904, Kipling wrote "They." A ghost story, or perhaps a fantasy, its setting is a beautiful, isolated country house in England inhabited by a young blind woman who, through her sheer need, has been able to bring back the spirits of dead children and thus to transcend the grave, the ultimate barrier. Like Mrs. Bathurst and other of Kipling's female characters, the blind woman has a power that profoundly affects the world around her. In "The Wish House," Grace Ashcroft goes to an abandoned house, inhabited by wraiths, where it was possible to take on the pain of some loved one; for her, it was her former lover. Like the blind woman in "They," however, she is driven by a love that is ultimately a selfish one: She is willing to accept his pain as hers not only because she loved him but also because she hopes that he will never marry and find happiness with anyone else.

"MARY POSTGATE"

"Mary Postgate," a powerful story of repression and revenge, portrays a middle-aged spinster and companion who passively accepts the abuse of the young boy of the house, Wyndham Fowler. He treated her shabbily for years, throwing things at her, calling her names such as "Posty" and "Packhead," and belittling her abilities. Then, while in training as a pilot in World War I, Wynn is accidentally killed. Postgate has long repressed and denied any feelings and does so again when his death is announced; her only regret is that he died before he had the chance to "kill somebody." While she is in town getting paraffin to burn Wynn's effects, a building collapses, killing a

young girl; although the local doctor tells her that the crash occurred from natural causes, she refuses to accept it, convinced that the Germans have bombed the house. Returning home to light the fire, she comes across an injured pilot in the garden and, assuming that he is German, refuses to summon a doctor, electing instead to watch him die. In choosing the pilot's death, Postgate not only is having her revenge for the death of Wynn and the girl killed supposedly at the hands of the hated German enemy but also is gaining her personal revenge for the hollowness of her own life. The pilot in the garden might well be German, but for Mary it makes no difference: It could be anyone. As he dies and as the fire consumes Wynn's effects, Mary experiences a rush of ecstasy comparable to a sexual release. "Mary Postgate" is a deeply felt exploration of a damaged human psyche.

"DAYSPRING MISHANDLED"

"Dayspring Mishandled" is one of Kipling's last and finest stories. It too is a story of revenge, but revenge ultimately not taken. It tells of two writers, Manallace and Castorley, cynically writing for pulp publication: "If you save people thinking you can do anything with 'em." After they quarrel, Castorley decides to write real literature and becomes a pseudo-expert on Geoffrey Chaucer; Manallace, who does have literary abilities, chooses not to pursue his talent and continues the easy path. Over an unspecified insult by Castorley to a woman for whom Manallace has been caring—typically in Kipling, much is left unsaid—Manallace vows revenge, creating a fake Chaucerian manuscript that Castorley publicly proclaims as legitimate, thus earning a knighthood. Manallace plans to reveal the fake, perhaps to the press, perhaps to Castorley himself to drive him insane, but he delays his plan as Castorley's health begins to fail and as he is put under the care of a doctor Gleeag, who Manallace later suspects is poisoning Castorley. Lady Castorley urges Manallace to help Castorley assemble his collected works for publication and implies that she knows about the forgery; Manallace believes that she is having an affair with Gleeag, the doctor, and that she wants knowledge of the fake Chaucer manuscript to come out in hopes that the shock will kill her husband. On his deathbed,

Castorley confesses his fears to Manallace: The manuscript was "*too* good," and his wife has reminded him that "a man could do anything with anyone if he saved him the trouble of thinking," which is exactly what Manallace has done with Castorley by allowing him to validate the fake without really thinking. Castorley dies of what Gleeag, Lady Castorley's paramour, said was "Malignant kidney-disease—generalized at the end."

Like most of Kipling's best stories, "Dayspring Mishandled" explores the recurring themes of passion and revenge, the failure of human nature, the confusion in relationships, frustrated ambition, and the inability to see clearly, even in the understanding of oneself. It is rich in allusions and references that remain unexplained and are left for the reader to explore. Kipling's most popular stories were the product of his early life, but some of his greatest stories—too often ignored for a time—were written toward the end.

OTHER MAJOR WORKS

LONG FICTION: *The Light That Failed*, 1890; *The Naulahka: A Story of East and West*, 1892 (with Wolcott Balestier); *Captains Courageous*, 1897; *Kim*, 1901.

POETRY: *Departmental Ditties*, 1886; *Barrack-Room Ballads and Other Verses*, 1892; *The Seven Seas*, 1896; *Recessional and Other Poems*, 1899; *The Five Nations*, 1903; *The Years Between*, 1919; *Rudyard Kipling's Verse*, 1940 (definitive edition).

NONFICTION: *American Notes*, 1891; *Beast and Man in India*, 1891; *Letters of Marque*, 1891; *The Smith Administration*, 1891; *From Sea to Sea*, 1899; *The New Army in Training*, 1914; *France at War*, 1915; *The Fringes of the Fleet*, 1915; *Sea Warfare*, 1916; *Letters of Travel, 1892-1913*, 1920; *The Irish Guards in the Great War*, 1923; *A Book of Words*, 1928; *Something of Myself: For My Friends Known and Unknown*, 1937; *Uncollected Prose*, 1938 (2 volumes); *Rudyard Kipling to Rider Haggard: The Record of a Friendship*, 1965 (Morton N. Cohen, editor).

MISCELLANEOUS: *The Sussex Edition of the Complete Works in Prose and Verse of Rudyard Kipling*, 1937-1939 (35 volumes).

BIBLIOGRAPHY

Battles, Pau. "'The Mark of the Beast': Rudyard Kipling's Apocalyptic Vision of Empire." *Studies in Short Fiction* 33 (Summer, 1996): 333-344. A reading of Kipling's story as his most powerful critique of the Empire; argues that "The Mark of the Beast" is an allegory of the relationship between the colonizer and the colonized.

Bauer, Helen Pike. *Rudyard Kipling: A Study of the Short Fiction*. New York: Twayne, 1994. Discusses the themes of isolation, work, the Empire, childhood, the supernatural, and art in Kipling's short stories. Includes Kipling's comments on writing and excerpts from a formalist and a postcolonial analysis of Kipling.

Birkenhead, Lord. *Rudyard Kipling*. London: Weidenfeld & Nicolson, 1978. This work was initially completed in 1948 but was not published until much later because of the opposition of Elsie Bambridge, Kipling's daughter. It contains some information from documents later destroyed.

Carrington, C. E. *The Life of Rudyard Kipling*. Garden City, N.Y.: Doubleday, 1956. The first major published study of Kipling's life, the author succeeded with Elsie Bambridge where Lord Birkenhead did not. Also contains some material later destroyed. Sympathetic but not entirely uncritical of Kipling's politics.

Coates, John. *The Days's Work: Kipling and the Idea of Sacrifice*. Madison, N.J.: Fairleigh Dickinson University Press, 1997. Explores one of Kipling's favorite themes.

Daniel, Anne Margaret. "Kipling's Use of Verse and Prose in 'Baa Baa, Black Sheep.'" *Studies in English Literature 1500-1900* 37 (Autumn, 1997): 857-875. Argues that the story relies on a literary self-consciousness to bring under artistic control the possible untruths and chaos of memory; claims that Kipling's use of both prose and poetry creates a comfortable connection with his audience.

Hai, Ambreen. "On Truth and Lie in a Colonial Sense: Kipling's Tales of Tale-Telling." *ELH* 64 (Summer, 1997): 599-625. Argues that construction of the lie (as fiction) became a specific, serious mode for Kipling to rethink and re-present re-lations between empire and his own fiction, between power and (self-)censorship, and a coded form to negotiate the boundaries of the unspeakable; suggests that for Kipling the lie is an alternative form of truth-telling.

Mallett, Phillip, ed. *Kipling Considered.* New York: St. Martin's Press, 1989. This collection contains essays on *Plain Tales from the Hills, Stalky & Co.,* Kipling and Conrad, and "Mrs Bathurst." The most helpful for readers interested in Kipling's short stories is Clare Hanson's discussion of the meaning of form in Kipling's short stories; Hanson establishes a theoretical framework for the short story as a genre and discusses Kipling's "Mary Postgate" to illustrate her concepts.

Orel, Harold, ed. *Critical Essays on Rudyard Kipling.* Boston: G. K. Hall, 1990. Sections on Kipling's poetry, his writing on India, his work as a mature artist, his unfinished memoir, and his controversial reputation. Introduced by a distinguished critic. No bibliography.

Paffard, Mark. *Kipling's Indian Fiction.* New York: St. Martin's Press, 1989. A discussion of the influence of India on Kipling's writing. Analyzes the development of Kipling's style along with his treatment of India and the literary and historical context of this treatment.

Pinney, Thomas. *In Praise of Kipling.* Austin: Harry Ransom Humanities Research Center, The University of Texas at Austin, 1996. A volume of criticism that is mostly positive.

Rutherford, Andrew, ed. *Kipling's Mind and Art.* Stanford, Calif.: Stanford University Press, 1964. Subtitled *Selected Critical Esays,* it includes commentaries by Edmund Wilson, George Orwell, and Lionel Trilling, among others.

Seymour-Smith, Martin. *Rudyard Kipling.* New York: St. Martin's Press, 1989. The author of this provocative and controversial work probes deeply into Kipling's personality and sexuality and argues that they are the key to the understanding of Kipling's writings.

Tompkins, J. M. S. *The Art of Rudyard Kipling.* Lincoln: University of Nebraska Press, 1965. First published in 1959, this major critical study of Kipling's literary work should be consulted in any discussion of Kipling's art.

Wilson, Angus. *The Strange Ride of Rudyard Kipling: His Life and Works.* London: Martin Secker & Warburg, 1977. Wilson, literary critic and novelist, sees Kipling's ability to remain in part a child as the key to his imagination. Wilson's own background in fiction gives insight into Kipling's own works.

Eugene S. Larson

DANILO KIŠ

Born: Subotica, Yugoslavia; February 22, 1935
Died: Paris, France; October, 15, 1989

PRINCIPAL SHORT FICTION

Rani jadi, 1970 (*Early Sorrows: For Children and Sensitive Readers*, 1998)
Grobnica za Borisa Davidoviča, 1976 (*A Tomb for Boris Davidovich*, 1978)
Enciklopedija mrtvih, 1983 (*The Encyclopedia of the Dead*, 1989)

OTHER LITERARY FORMS

Danilo Kiš wrote prose, drama, poetry, and essays. His prose works include many uncollected short stories and the novels *Mansarda* (1962), *Psalam Forty-four* (1962), *Bašta, pepeo* (1965; *Garden, Ashes*, 1975), and *Peščanik* (1972; *The Hourglass*, 1990). He also wrote literary essays: *Po-etika* (1972), *Po-etika, knjiga druga* (1974), *čas anatomije* (1978), *Homo Poeticus* (1983), *Gorki, talog, iskustva* (1990), *Skladište* (1995), and *Homo Poeticus: Essays and Interviews* (1995), edited by Susan Sontag. His works have been translated into French, Hungarian, German, and other languages.

ACHIEVEMENTS

Danilo Kiš won many awards, national and international, including the *Nedeljne Informativne Novine* prize for Novel of the Year (1972); the Ivan Goran Kovači Prize (1977); Grand Aigle de la Ville de Nice (1980); Skender Kulenovi Prize (1986); Premio di Tevere (1988); Preis des Literaturmagazins (1988), and the Bruno Schulz Prize (1989). He was also distinguished with titles: Munka Erdmerend Arany (1978) and Chevalier des Arts et des Lettres (1986).

BIOGRAPHY

Danilo Kiš deliberately obscured his biography. It is certain, though, that he was born to a Hungarian father and a Montenegrin mother in the land bordering Hungary in present-day Serbia. In the view of his life

that he personally sanctioned, he focuses only on his childhood in his parents' home.

He graduated from the University of Belgrade in the newly formed department of comparative literature. His novel *Mansarda* is titled a *poema*, meaning epic, which embodies Kiš's predilection for paradox by intermingling genres.

Kiš himself wrote prolifically about his literary works and about literature itself. He also translated from Russian, Hungarian, English, and French into Serbo-Croatian. He died of lung cancer in 1989.

ANALYSIS

Danilo Kiš is most notable for reaching an international audience in non-"world language," which both distinguishes him from and unites him with other writers of Central Europe. Seldom does a Western sensibility, centered on its own historical importance, perceive a resonance with a voice from a country as small as the state of Wyoming. Yet Kiš's stories are relatively well known and widely read among Americans.

Kiš's narrative stance is the defining characteristic of his prose and even of the way he relates his own biography. He situates the discourse somewhere between the acute pain of his character and the view of the coldest bystander, relating the most intimate of sensations as though from a great distance and relegating the historical sweep of enormous cataclysms in terms of everyday, quotidian existence.

His stories are told with significant intrusion from many narrators, some of whom seem to be the author, some of whom relate "documentation" from various, principally "written," sources. Often, there are footnotes reemphasizing the effect of documentation. The validity of any statement in a story is always put in question, unlike most fiction, which requires the reader to suspend disbelief. Kiš often subverts linear logic using fantastic and improbable events related in simple journalistic style, creating a sense of the surreal as an ordinary existence, and mundane, everyday life as unexpected or too good to be true.

Danilo Kiš (©Miriam Berkley)

Kiš's characters seemingly act out of feelings that they never express. Their emotions are described externally by information such as physical description or gestures or through stream-of-consciousness narration. This emotional ventriloquism emphasizes the feeling of emptiness in life and the meaninglessness of activity. Still, it is not the pessimistic that carries his narrative but the small talk of his characters, each of whom, despite the near certainty of a reductive demise, seems fully desirous of life.

EARLY SORROWS

Early Sorrows, despite its English subtitle, *For Children and Sensitive Readers*, is nothing like the genre known as children's literature in the West. The character acting through all the stories, Andreas Sam, has gone back to his childhood neighborhood after a time of separation through war. There he visits his old memories, people long dead, houses long gone, and tries to re-create a world that is lost or, perhaps alternatively, to create a rationale for having no more of the old world but a new one instead. This reexamination of fate is probably what Joseph Brodsky had in mind when he wrote that Kiš's writing "erodes our

sense of death's impenetrability." Kiš does not defer to the inevitable; he has his character stand on street corners and on people's porches, questioning the past, questioning death itself as well as present circumstances.

However, it is in "fording the stream between dreams and life," as the character Andy himself feels, that the crossing between the palpable and the perceivable is achieved. The direction of the stream of narration in the stories moves seamlessly between the two conventionally perceived contradictory modes of consciousness. What is more real, the reader must ask—what stands now in the street or what is left behind, perhaps hidden by the wall or between the bed sheets in a dreamy slumber? Kiš seems to believe that it is all equally real, equally a dream, as though all of life is a dream—except sometimes, motion intervenes and resets the path of the dream.

One of the more realistic stories, "Pages from a Velvet Album," seems directly autobiographical, with Andy greeted with the news of his father's death by a relative who has just returned from Adolf Hitler's extermination camps. Here, too, the pathos is more direct in Andy's imagination—as he construes the last moments his father lived—than in the reality of life lost. Crossing between ordinary life and the dream, Andy's reality blurs the boundaries most believably, and his apprehension of the facts, with their transposition into fantasy, makes sense to the reader.

The likeness of this story to Kiš's autobiographical statement, included as the last chapter in this edition, is manifest: "In 1944 my father and all our relatives were taken off to Auschwitz, and almost none returned," perhaps his most quoted comment. The horror of the years of Nazi atrocity begins and ends in one short sequence, stated in a single sentence. The fictionalized version Andy relates seems more realistic, fleshed out, more in human terms. Perhaps literature, at its best, really can be more "true" than life.

A TOMB FOR BORIS DAVIDOVICH

A Tomb for Boris Davidovich, a collection of seven stories, includes the one that gave the collection its name; the book has been dubbed a novel, evidently by Kiš's publishers, and it won a prize for novel of the year. Each story centers on the climactic ending, in which the characters meet their inevitable denouement. The stories vary in setting and time, although most occur around World War II and involve the worldview of people, often of the Jewish faith, in a predicament that could euphemistically be described as between a rock and a hard place: between Adolf Hitler's barbarousness and Joseph Stalin's insensate domination.

Some of Kiš's favorite narrative ploys involve introducing his characters as though through a first-person narrator, who often will intrude into the subsequent omniscient narration as though supplying historical facts. An interesting aspect of these stories is the frame, setting the narrative up as though it were documented history, using footnotes purportedly as reference to other materials. The vacillation between documentary and fantasy, between first-person and omniscient narration, between humdrum atrocity and fabulously unreal everyday life, is like a pendulum, only less predictable and always unsettling.

The characters inhabiting these stories are often quite base, and seemingly the more real for their bad demeanor. The opening story, "The Knife with the Rosewood Handle," for example, introduces no positive character whatsoever, only murderers, gangsters, racketeers and the like, who involve themselves in different types of nefarious deeds. There is no sense of justice served, only random violence which is made to seem like an emblem of the time rather than an innately human characteristic. In the second story, "The Sow That Eats Her Farrow," the lengthy digressions on moral philosophy and literary history set up a sounding board for the raucous invasion of loud noise which, like accompaniment, sets the story in motion. The story that gives the collection its name in like manner centers on the mystery of life by way of chronicling Boris Davidovich's biography through elaborate pseudo-documentation which is then, seemingly, reread in the final chapter.

"Encyclopedia of the Dead"

"Enciklopedija mrtvih" ("Encyclopedia of the Dead") comes from a collection by the same name, and perhaps represents Kiš's finest accomplishment. Narrated as though by a woman, the protagonist is taken to a great library in Sweden and left to discover the book "Encyclopedia of the Dead," which contains information only about people who are not included in other encyclopedias. There she reads about the most intimate details of her recently deceased father, a man who lived, in principle, a rather unremarkable life. Yet the encyclopedia is "the sum of human destinies, the totality of ephemeral happenings," and the compilers are obsessed with "the idea that every human being is unique and every event singular"; thus all the details are related as though "nothing in the history of mankind is ever repeated, things that at first glance seem the same are scarcely even similar . . . everything happens always and never." Hence this man who could probably never be found in any other encyclopedia on any account, is chronicled in extraordinary detail. Kiš effectively turns the rules of history upside down, leaving all the "important" people out and concentrating on the most ordinary events. He also sets the philosopher Friedrich Nietzsche on his head with his idea of the "never-return, no matter what it could be said to look like" as though in refutation of the famous idea of "eternal recurrence." Through the device of this fantastic encyclopedia, the spiritual and emotional lives of ordinary people resist obliteration and retain meaning and human dignity, despite the sweeping events of global history.

Other major works

LONG FICTION: *Mansarda*, 1962; *Psalam 44*, 1962; *Bašta, pepeo*, 1965 (*Garden, Ashes*, 1975); *Peščanik*, 1972 (*Hourglass*, 1990).

TELEPLAYS: *Noč i magla*, 1968; *Papagaj*, 1969; *Drveni sanduk Tomasa Wulfa*, 1974.

NONFICTION: *Po-etika*, 1972; *Po-etika, knjiga druga*, 1974; *čas anatomije*, 1978; *Homo Poeticus*, 1983; *Gorki, talog iskustva*, 1990; *Homo Poeticus: Essays and Interviews*, 1995; *Skladište*, 1995.

Bibliography

Birnbaum, M. D., and R. Trager-Verchovsky. *History, Another Text: Essays on the Fiction of Kazimierz Brandys, Danilo Kiš, György Konrád, and Christa Wolf*. Ann Arbor, Mich.: University of Michigan, 1988. A good critical study of these authors and their works.

Horvath, Brooke. "Danilo Kiš: An Introduction." *Review of Contemporary Fiction* 14, no. 1 (1994): 97-208. A good source for background on Kiš's major writing and the longest critical and bibliographic work on Kiš in English. Here thoughts and ideas are posited to place Kiš in the context of Central European literature and literary history. It is also useful as a view on the author himself.

Christine D. Tomei

HEINRICH VON KLEIST

Born: Frankfurt an der Oder, Prussia; October 18, 1777

Died: Wannsee bei Potsdam, Prussia; November 21, 1811

PRINCIPAL SHORT FICTION

Die Marquise von O—1808 (novella; *The Marquise of O*—1960)

Michael Kohlhaas, 1810 (novella; English translation, 1844)

Erzählung, 1810-1811 (2 volumes; *"The Marquise of O," and Other Stories*, 1960)

OTHER LITERARY FORMS

Heinrich von Kleist considered himself primarily a dramatist, and each of his several plays is recognized in the twentieth century as a masterpiece of its type. *Der zerbrochene Krug* (1808; *The Broken Jug*, 1930), Kleist's comedy of unmasking, is one of the liveliest exhibitions of comic misunderstanding and double entendre in European drama. In *Penthesilea* (1808; English translation, 1959), Kleist restructures a Greek myth as a psychological tragedy. Under the spell of a Dionysian frenzy, Penthesilea murders Achilles when she misinterprets his gesture of reconciliation and love. When she realizes what she has done, she wills herself to die. *Das Käthchen von Heilbronn* (1810; *Cathy of Heilbronn*, 1927) and *Penthesilea* are paired by Kleist as opposite expressions of identical inner impulses. *Cathy of Heilbronn* is a fairy tale in which the heroine's forbearance and inner surety guided by dream win her a life of true happiness. Kleist also wrote a family tragedy, *Die Familie Schroffenstein* (1803; *The Schroffenstein Family*, 1916), a patriotic play, *Die Hermannsschlacht* (1821), and *Amphitryon* (1807; English translation, 1962), an adaptation of Molière's comedy of the same name. Kleist's fragmentary tragedy, *Robert Guiskard* (1808; English translation, 1962), prompted Wieland's celebrated comment that the play, if finished, would unite the spirits of Aeschylus, Sophocles, and Shakespeare. Kleist's last play, the internationally known *Prinz Friedrich von Homburg* (1821; *The Prince of Homburg*, 1875), follows the career of a young prince whose dream of future glory is playfully encouraged by the Elector and his guests, who come on the prince walking in his sleep. The prince wins a military victory but is sentenced to death for violating orders. When he sees his grave being dug, he recoils in horror and begs for his life. Later he accepts his guilt and passionately yearns for death. When he is pardoned and celebrated as a hero after all, reality seems more illusory than the dream which opens the play.

Kleist was also a journalist, and he wrote a group of war poems and several aesthetic and political essays. These along with several of his stories first appeared in newspapers.

ACHIEVEMENTS

Although he received little recognition during his lifetime, Heinrich von Kleist is considered a masterful writer of fiction and one of the greatest German dramatists. Critics rank his work second only to that of his great contemporaries, Johann Wolfgang von Goethe and Friedrich von Schiller. His short fiction (novellas), as well as his dramas, all confront the central problem of the elusive quality of truth, and even his highly individual writing style and syntax seem to reflect that problem by using an objective tone and a complex pattern of a clause within a clause, breaking the logical sequence of the reader's thoughts. The world is presented as problematic or "torn," bereft of its logical or sensible wholeness, and his characters are confronted with an irrational universe, barring the possibility of justice and happiness. Kleist's tragic view of the contradictions in the world present an essentially modern viewpoint, a forerunner of the feelings of isolation and alienation in an unpredictable world so often presented by twentieth century writers.

BIOGRAPHY

Following the military tradition of his family, Heinrich von Kleist joined the Prussian army at the age of fifteen, but he resigned his commission in 1799, declaring that he had wasted seven valuable years. He returned to Frankfurt an der Oder, the city of his birth, where he entered the university. Kleist plunged himself into a rigorous study of mathematics and philosophy, believing that through virtuous discipline and knowledge, one could achieve moral perfection and happiness. He became engaged to a general's daughter, Wilhelmine von Zenge, and began teaching her his eudaemonistic precepts by letter. In 1801, Kleist announced the total collapse of his convictions, which he claimed resulted from reading Kant's philosophy. This so-called Kant crisis set Kleist forth on the erratic and intense search for meaning that was to characterize the remaining eleven years of his life.

Kleist traveled to France, hoping to accomplish "something good, absolutely." When his decision to become a Swiss farmer came to naught, he began to write. In 1803, he outlined several plays and finished a draft of *The Schroffenstein Family*. Favorable reviews of the play encouraged him, and he probably outlined several stories as well. Kleist's exhilaration soon gave way to despondency; he broke his engagement, journeyed through Switzerland and Italy, and returned to Paris, where he burned the fragment of *Robert Guiskard*. He then left Paris to join Napo-

leon's forces in hope of dying during the invasion of England, but he was located by a friend and sent back to Germany.

In 1804, Kleist was given work by the Finance Minister of Berlin. He held that post and others like it for two years, and, despite continual bouts of illness, he completed several stories and plays. While traveling to Dresden in 1807, Kleist and several friends were arrested as French spies. Kleist continued writing in prison and upon his release was celebrated by the literary society of Dresden. He met Adam Müller there, and the two founded the literary journal, *Phöbus*, which, after a promising start, failed. Disillusioned with the instability of the literary world, Kleist moved to Austria and then to Prague where he tried to found a patriotic journal called *Germania*. His political activism and publishing plans came to nothing when Austria fell to Napoleon.

In 1810, Kleist appeared back in Berlin. His first volume of *Erzählungen* was published that year, and he founded the *Berliner Abendblätter*, Germany's first daily newspaper. The *Abendblätter* became an immediate popular success, but the government soon censored much of its news. The last issue appeared just six months after the first.

Kleist appealed to the king for a civil service post or a stipend but got no response. A second volume of five of Kleist's *Novellen* appeared later that year, but his dramas and stories did not earn him a living. As a final resort, Kleist turned again to the military. He joined the Prussian army just as an alliance was signed with France. Once again French victories signaled Kleist's defeats. With his last resource exhausted, Kleist appealed to his family but found that they were no longer willing to help. Weary and embittered by the years of struggle and rejection, Kleist feared that his love of art was beginning to wane. In 1811, he met a terminally ill young woman, and the two made a suicide pact. On November 21, 1811, on the shores of Wannsee near Berlin, Heinrich von Kleist shot Henrietta Vogel and then himself.

ANALYSIS

"Das Erdbeben in Chili" ("The Earthquake in Chile") was the first of Heinrich von Kleist's

Novellen to appear in print, and in many ways it is emblematic of all of his tales. The refugees from the earthquake, which hit Santiago in 1647, experience in literal fashion what Kleist regards as the general condition of human existence—people are set adrift from the regular order of their days, and the visible framework of the world falls into unexpected collapse. Life's cataclysms, be they geological or psychological, are not inevitable, but they are unpredictable. Kleist's stories are fraught with accidents and unexpected reversals which confound human response.

When Jeronimo hears the bells signaling his lover's execution, he vows to die with her. He is preparing to hang himself when the earthquake hits, destroying the prison and setting him free. Each lover thinks the other is dead, but they find each other, and Josepha has their baby with her. In the company of other refugees, they experience a night of Edenic calm, convinced they have been saved by divine miracle. Those who have fled with them do not mention their illicit love, which had sentenced Josepha to death and Jeronimo to prison. Drawn together in extremity, the human family is as one. By morning the tremors stop, and Josepha is eager to go to the cathedral to give thanks. As she and Jeronimo enter, they hear the priest describing the earthquake as a punishment for moral laxity, and he mentions the young lovers by name. They try to leave but are recognized. The outraged crowd turns murderous and beats them to death in front of the cathedral.

Kleist's later protagonists do not fall victim to the sort of direct, unanswerable force which destroys Jeronimo and Josepha. Later characters are more active and articulate; their fates are more complex. No matter how involved their stories, however, all Kleist's heroes share a native ingenuousness with the two young lovers in "The Earthquake in Chile." These characters attempt to keep a strange world at bay by allegiance to an inner certainty which is precarious and enigmatic but deeply felt. Such convictions may produce suffering and confusion or, on occasion, redemption. Kleist's characters ask questions, faint, describe the world or themselves as mad, but they cling to their own sense of truth as best they can. This haphazard bravery has its wellspring in human feeing, which in Kleist's world endows it with a sort of purity and honor.

"THE MARIONETTE THEATER"

In "Über das Marionettentheater" ("The Marionette Theater"), Kleist describes the difference between a marionette and a human dancer. Because the puppet is built around a center of gravity, its limbs move effortlessly and in harmony; it is possessed of every grace. Perfectly controlled from above, it is so light its feet barely touch the earth. Human dancers, although free from strings and able to move as they desire, are weighted to the earth. Their motions are typically awkward and artificial attempts to mime the weightless grace of the marionette. Characters such as Littegarde and Friedrich in "Der Zweikampf" ("The Duel") and several of Kleist's heroines intimate that some dancers can locate the center of gravity and dance with intuitive grace.

THE MARQUISE OF O—

The Marquise of O— is one such character. She is a young widow rearing her children quietly in the shelter of her father's house. To her great disbelief, she learns that she is pregnant. Her parents are shocked and then mortified when she denies any knowledge of how such a condition could have arisen. An examining doctor makes jokes at her expense; she is scorned by her brother and driven from the house by her father. Retaining her dignity and poise, the marquise settles herself and her children in new quarters and advertises in the newspaper for the unknown man to come forth.

A few months before, Count F—, commander of forces which had the marquise's father's castle under siege, had rescued the young widow from a band of his own men. She called the count her angel and fainted, but the commander himself then took advantage of her. Count F— returns months later and asks to marry the marquise. He is in love with her and ashamed of his deed, but he does not admit to the rape. By then, the marquise has discovered her pregnancy and rejects him, declaring herself unworthy.

In great embarrassment, Count F— answers the newspaper ad. The family is happily relieved. Ashamed of their past conduct, they are anxious to put the embarrassing incident aside. They welcome the count into the family and make wedding plans. It is the marquise who hesitates. Her trust had been betrayed, and she is too honorable to capitulate immediately to the count's advances; she is also too honest to deny love for the sake of revenge. She marries Count F—, and the two produce a houseful of children and live happily ever after. The marquise, who answers to no force except her own honorable convictions, is one of the strongest heroines in all of short fiction. Toni, the heroine of "Die Verlobung in St. Domingo" ("The Engagement in Santo Domingo") is a similar character, but her faith and confident actions cost her her life.

"THE FOUNDLING"

Tension between inner convictions and the confusions of the external world is at the center of most of Kleist's stories. Only in "Der Findling" ("The Foundling") does Kleist allow unexpected tragedy to assume the proportions of perverse malevolence. "The Foundling" is an oddity in Kleist's corpus, and it lacks the authenticity of his other tales, which present life as paradox.

MICHAEL KOHLHAAS

Kleist's finest and most complex study of ambiguity is *Michael Kohlhaas* (1810), which purports to be the story of one man's search for justice. While taking a group of horses to market, Kohlhaas is illegally detained at the Brandenburg-Saxony border and charged a tax. He is forced to leave two horses as substitute payment and also a man to tend them. When he has proof that the tax is illegal, he presses charges. On his return, he finds that his horses have been abused and his man is missing. He is still patient, confident that the law will redress his grievances. Kohlhaas presses his case further, but it is ignored by the magistrates. When his wife is accidentally killed while trying to bring his case to an authority's attention, Kohlhaas vows to take things into his own hands. His fervor for justice turns to self-righteousness and violence when he attacks a nunnery and begins burning towns. His band of marauders is feared throughout the land, and Kohlhaas, swept up by his own sense of power, names himself an emissary of the Archangel Michael and has himself carried by porters. Justice and revenge become inseparable.

Martin Luther issues a proclamation declaring Kohlhaas's actions evil and appeals to him to stop. Since he respects no man more than Luther, Kohlhaas goes to him and humbly follows his directives. A series of unfortunate events follow which eventually cost Michael Kohlhaas his life. The incompetence and inattention of government authorities turn out to be the horse dealer's greatest enemies. Kohlhaas is an earnest individual who is unable to elicit honorable redress from a disorganized bureaucratic system. In his quest for individual justice, he resembles many a twentieth century protagonist. This theme appears to be the central one of *Michael Kohlhaas* until the last several pages of the story, at which point the plot is riven in two.

As the story reaches its conclusion, the reader is told that Michael Kohlhaas carries a locket around his neck in which is contained a piece of paper which reveals the fate of the House of Saxony. Kohlhaas was given the paper by a Gypsy Woman at a carnival shortly after his wife died, although this event is not reported in the narrative. When the Elector of Saxony learns that Kohlhaas is the man with the prophecy, he offers to spare the doomed man's life if he will give him the paper. The Gypsy Woman visits Kohlhaas in prison and warns him that the Elector will take the amulet from him after death if he does not relinquish it. She also tells him that the bit of paper can save his life. Kohlhaas, however, does not give up the paper. He reads it, peers straight into the Elector's eyes, places it in his mouth and swallows it. Then he walks to the scaffold to meet his death.

This unexpected turn of events has a disorienting effect on the entire story. What seemed to be a complex tale of an unfortunate individual in a bureaucratic society is redirected into another realm of human experience. The Gypsy Woman makes a reader reexamine all the earlier events of the story. Is it the government which is disordered and disorienting to an individual like Michael Kohlhaas or is it the nature of life itself? Human foolishness and sloth cause government's inconsistencies, but what causes universal inconsistencies? The Gypsy Woman is a supernatural force associated with irrationality and accident. Her presence is evidence that magic and mystery are at large in the cosmos whether man recognizes them or not.

Kleist's themes are remarkably echoed by his prose style. His language is objective in tone and apparently sequentially presented, but what is connected in the orderly schemata of the German sentence is often neither logical nor sequential.

"THE BEGGARWOMAN OF LOCARNO"

"Das Bettelweib von Locarno" ("The Beggarwoman of Locarno"), Kleist's briefest story, illustrates the power the author could create almost solely from the force of language. The plot per se is but the sketchiest of anecdotes. An Italian count orders an old woman to sleep behind the stove. As she crosses the room, she slips and hurts her back but does manage to get behind the stove. The next morning she is dead. Some time later a prospective purchaser of the castle is hosted in the room where the beggarwoman died. During the night, he hears a ghost and leaves the next morning. The count and countess spend a night in the room themselves. They hear scratchings as if someone is crossing the room. The countess rushes away and the count, "weary of life," burns down the castle. The reader is never told whether there is a ghost or whether the count believes there is. The old woman's ghost prompts all the action and yet her presence is questionable. She might be called a palpable sense of nothingness. If her spirit is present, the reader has no sense of what it is, what its motives are, or what it means. Such moments of complete and eloquent silence are a hallmark of Kleist's narrative style.

"ST. CECILIA"

In Kleist's stories, supernatural power is visible in every human turning, but its meaning seems to pose the same questions for the narrator as it does for his readers and his characters. At best, the artist can describe a multiplicity of perceptions which might be regarded as true. Kleist calls one of his stories a legend and draws further attention to its ambiguous meaning when he names it "Die heilige Cäcilie: Oder, Die Gewalt der Musik" ("St. Cecilia: Or, The Power of Music.")

During a period when iconoclasm is rife, four brothers take it upon themselves to rid the world of one particularly obvious popish relic, the convent of St. Cecilia. They gather a band of like-minded protesters and, on the Feast of Corpus Christi, enter the church intending to reduce it to rubble. The nuns, although outwardly composed, are quite undone. The men are milling around awaiting a signal from their leaders when a pale nun enters and approaches the orchestra. The other sisters are surprised to see the orchestra conductor, whom they believe to be deathly ill. As the first notes of the glorious festival music sound, the four brothers fall on their knees before the altar and remain motionless throughout the concert. Their baffled followers wait in vain for a signal. Hours later the four have to be removed to a lunatic asylum. There they keep their prayerful attitude which is broken only when they bellow the *gloria in excelsis* each night at midnight.

Six years later their mother arrives in Aachen. She hears the festival described by one of the protesters as a youthful misadventure. The Mother Superior describes the feast as a miracle, since St. Cecilia herself apparently conducted the music. No one, however, accounts for her insane sons whose ghostly singing still splits the night. Such is the pitch of Kleist's miracles and mysteries. They have as many meanings as observers, and one meaning as good as cancels out the others. Paradox remains at the center: Count F— is a devil and an angel, Michael Kohlhaas is an honorable and terrible man, and the miracle of St. Cecilia is both glorious and horrible. Contradiction is life's basic truth.

OTHER MAJOR WORKS

PLAYS: *Die Familie Schroffenstein*, pb. 1803 (*The Schroffenstein Family*, 1916); *Amphitryon*, pb. 1807 (English translation, 1962); *Penthesilea*, pb. 1808 (English translation, 1959); *Der zerbrochene Krug*, pr. 1808 (*The Broken Jug*, 1930); *Robert Guiskard*, pb. 1808 (English translation, 1962); *Das Käthchen von Heilbronn: Oder, Die Feuerprobe*, pr., pb. 1810 (*Cathy of Heilbronn: Or, The Trial by Fire*, 1927); *Prinz Friedrich von Homburg*, pr., pb. 1821 (*The Prince of Homburg*, 1875); *Die Hermannsschlacht*, pb. 1821.

BIBLIOGRAPHY

Allen, Richard. "Reading Kleist and Hoffmann." In *Romantic Writing*, edited by Stephen Bygrave. London: Routledge, 1996. Discusses irony, characterization, and the cultural and political context of Kleist's story "The Betrothal on Santo Domingo."

Brown, H. M. *Heinrich von Kleist: The Ambiguity of Art and the Necessity of Form*. New York: Oxford University Press, 1998. A thoughtful study on Kleist's style.

Brown, Robert H. "Fear of Social Change in Kleist's 'Erdbeben in Chili.'" *Monatshefte* 84 (1992): 447-458. Argues that "The Earthquake in Chile" explores contemporary social conflicts with no simple solutions. Discusses the story as being focused on the collapse of the old order and the disintegration behind reform movements of the eighteenth century; the story's subtext deals with modern challenges to harmonious cooperative hierarchy.

Dutoit, Thomas. "Rape, Crypt, and Fantasm: Kleist's *Marquise of O.*" *Mosaic* 27 (September, 1994): 45-64. Discusses the implications of impregnation in Kleist's story; argues that the story suggests a gap between the fact that something happened and the description of the event.

Dyer, Denys. *The Stories of Kleist: A Critical Study*. New York: Holmes & Meier, 1977. An excellent study of Kleist's masterpieces of short fiction, intended for students and general readers with little knowledge of German literature. After a chapter on Kleist's life and works, Dyer treats the stories individually so that each chapter is a self-contained interpretation. Chapter 8 summarizes the main points about Kleist's themes and style. Contains an index and a bibliography, including some sources on individual stories (many in German).

Gearey, John. *Heinrich von Kleist: A Study in Tragedy and Anxiety*. Philadelphia: University of Pennsylvania Press, 1968. A helpful and readable study of Kleist's life and works. In studying the works, Gearey focuses on the problem of conflict, which he believes is caused by Kleist's own puzzlement over the problem of human experience. Includes

plot summaries and analyses of Kleist's early dramas, some of his novellas, and his later major works. Supplemented by a chronology of Kleist's life and a bibliography.

Grandin, John M. *Kafka's Prussian Advocate: A Study of the Influence of Heinrich von Kleist on Franz Kafka*. Columbia, S.C.: Camden House, 1987. This study tracks parallels of style and theme in the works of the two writers. It is Grandin's belief that much of Kafka can be better understood through "Kleistian eyes" and that some Kleist stories can be read "from the more modern Kafka perspective." The comments on *Michael Kohlhaas* are particularly helpful. Complemented by an index and a bibliography.

Guenther, Beatrice Martina. *The Poetics of Death: The Short Prose of Kleist and Balzac*. Albany: State University of New York Press, 1996. Examines the short fiction of Kleist and Honoré de Balzac. Includes bibliographical references and an index.

Maass, Joachim. *Kleist: A Biography*. Translated by Ralph Manheim. New York: Farrar, Straus & Giroux, 1983. A comprehensive biography of Kleist including detailed information about his family background, life, and attitudes. His works are also discussed in context. Includes photographs, a select bibliography, and an index of works and names.

Mehigan, Timothy J. *Text as Contract: The Nature and Function of Narrative Discourse in the "Erzählungen" of Heinrich von Kleist*. Frankfurt am Main: Peter Lang, 1988. A discussion of Kleist's short fiction from the point of view of language and communication. Mehigan believes that the narratives have a "strong sense of structure," even when describing disorder, and he uses a narrative paradigm to show the relationship between pattern and disorder in the individual works. Contains an extensive bibliography.

Silz, Walter. *Heinrich von Kleist: Studies in His Works and Literary Character*. Philadelphia: University of Pennsylvania Press, 1961. A collection of essays on various works and aspects of Kleist's literary expression. Includes separate chapters on

"Das Erdbeben in Chili," *Amphitryon*, "Über das Marionettentheater," *Michael Kohlhaas*, and *Prinz Friedrich von Homburg*, and an excellent chapter on the recurrence of certain concepts and expressions in Kleist's work. Supplemented by notes to each chapter, bibliographical references, and an index of names.

Ugrinsky, Alexej, et al., eds. *Heinrich von Kleist Studies*. New York: AMS Press, 1980. A collection of studies prepared for the Heinrich von Kleist bicentennial (1777-1977) and published in both English and German. After an introduction on Kleist's life by Ilse Graham, the discussions are divided into various headings: drama; novellas; marionettes; comparative studies; education, linguistics, and science; and new perspectives. In-

cludes an index and a reprint of the catalog of materials available on Kleist.

Werlen, Hans Jakob. "Seduction and Betrayal: Race and Gender in Kleist's 'Die Verlobung in St. Domingo.'" *Monatshefte* 84 (1992): 459-471. Discusses how the story reflects the struggle between the races in the seduction of Toni and her recasting into the image of Gustav's dead bride. Uses Sigmund Freud's concept of "suggestion" to discuss the effect of Gustav on Toni. Claims that the end of the story removes Gustav and Toni from their previous historical-political and racial context and erases its own central issues of race, sexuality, and culture.

Helen Menke, updated by Susan L. Piepke

JOHN KNOWLES

Born: Fairmont, West Virginia; September 16, 1926

PRINCIPAL SHORT FICTION

Phineas: Six Stories, 1968

OTHER LITERARY FORMS

In addition to his short fiction, John Knowles published a volume of nonfiction, *Double Vision: American Thoughts Abroad* (1964), and several novels, including *A Separate Peace* (1959), *Indian Summer* (1966), *Spreading Fires* (1974), *A Stolen Past* (1983), and *The Private Life of Axie Reed* (1986). He also wrote articles for *Saturday Evening Post, Story, New World Writing, Reader's Digest*, and *Holiday* and a memoir, *Backcasts: Memories and Recollections of Seventy Years as a Sportsman* (1993).

ACHIEVEMENTS

John Knowles established his literary reputation in the 1960's when *A Separate Peace* won the William Faulkner Foundation Award for a first novel, the Rosenthal Award of the National Institute of Arts and

Letters, and an Independent Schools Education Board award. *A Separate Peace* explores the process of growing up, and it became a favorite with younger people in the 1960's, along with William Golding's *Lord of the Flies* (1954) and J. D. Salinger's *The Catcher in the Rye* (1951). In the novel, Knowles reveals the typical precise craftsmanship and handling of characteristic themes that run throughout all of his later work.

BIOGRAPHY

John Knowles, the third of four children of James Myron and Mary Beatrice Shaw Knowles, was born in the coal mining town of Fairmont, West Virginia, in 1926. After attending public schools in Fairmont through the ninth grade, Knowles left home at fifteen to attend Phillips Exeter Academy in New Hampshire. He entered the prestigious preparatory school in the fall of 1942 as a "lower middler," or sophomore. He found Phillips Exeter very challenging. In 1943 he attended a special summer wartime session there and joined a group called the Suicide Society, the members of which jumped from a tall tree on the campus into a river below. Because of a bad fall from this tree, Knowles was on crutches for a while with a foot injury. After graduating from Exeter in 1945, he enlisted in the U.S. Army Air Forces' Aviation Cadet Program, qualifying as a pilot.

Subsequently, he attended Yale University, where he majored in English and was on the editorial board of the *Yale Daily*. While at Yale he also submitted stories to the *Yale Record*, the university's humor magazine, was invited to join Yale's Wiffenpoofs, and was a member of the varsity swimming team. For his senior essay at Yale he wrote a novel. He graduated from Yale in 1949 and went to work as a reporter and drama critic for the Hartford *Courant*. In 1952 he became a freelance writer and lived for the next several years in Europe. There he wrote a novel called "Descent to Proselito," which was accepted for publication but withdrawn by Knowles on the advice of writer Thornton Wilder, and published his first story, "A Turn in the Sun," in *Story* magazine.

When he returned to the United States in 1955, he settled in New York City. A year later he published the story "Phineas" in *Cosmopolitan* (one which was the germ of his critically acclaimed, award-winning, and extremely popular *A Separate Peace*) and moved to Philadelphia, where he worked as an associate editor of *Holiday* magazine. There he started writing *A Separate Peace*, his first published novel.

When it was clear that *A Separate Peace* was a very successful novel, Knowles resigned his position at *Holiday* to travel abroad again. During this two-year trip he gathered material for a travel book and published another novel. Now an established writer, Knowles returned from Europe to live in New York City. Throughout the 1960's he traveled, served as writer-in-residence at the University of North Carolina and at Princeton University, and completed another novel and a book of short fiction entitled *Phineas: Six Stories*. After his father died in 1970, Knowles moved to Southampton on Long Island, where he wrote five novels and was part of a coterie of writers that included Truman Capote and Irwin Shaw. In 1988 Knowles moved to Fort Lauderdale, Florida.

John Knowles (Kimberly Dawson Kurnizki)

ANALYSIS

John Knowles writes about environments he himself has experienced, and his descriptive technique is one of his most appealing qualities. Frequently he uses place description to indicate the environmental shaping of his protagonists' personalities. He ties this to the themes in his work. Knowles is interested in the self-knowledge derived from his protagonists' continual attempts to integrate the two elements of the American character, savagery and cautious Protestantism, into a reasonable whole. His later novels continue to explore the strategies his protagonists invent to reconcile this dualism.

PHINEAS

Phineas consists of six stories, "A Turn with the Sun," "Summer Street," "The Peeping Tom," "Martin the Fisherman," "Phineas," and "The Reading of the Will," which are not linked thematically but which possess a universality that leaves the reader with an insight into the condition of man. Structurally, all the stories are orthodox and follow the traditional plot structure, but their final effect is aimed at more than one level, a symbolic timelessness coming from the context of each story. The plot is only half of each story; the other half is the matrix of the earth from which the author, the story, and the phenomenon of life emerge.

"A Turn with the Sun"

The first story in the volume, "A Turn with the Sun," is set in New Hampshire, and, although the immediate locale is Devon, a sophisticated prep school, nature plays a larger role in the story. The plot is simple and concerns the attempts of Lawrence Stewart to break the barrier of the "foggy social bottomland where unacceptable first year boys dwell" and to win a close friend. Lawrence, the protagonist, has entered Devon in the fall in the fourth form and instantly finds out that he possesses nothing distinct to make him accepted by his "sophisticated" peers. Like Knowles himself, he is from an unknown and small West Virginia town, he does not have outstanding athletic ability, his clothes are wrong, his vocabulary is common, and he engages in conversation about the wrong things. He is assigned to live in a small house with "six other nebulous flotsam," and as early as his fourth day at school, Lawrence shows signs of becoming a person to be considered. Lawrence is standing on the bridge and does not have anything in mind when he dives from it. He is similar to other Devon students when he initially plunges from the bridge, an unknown newcomer, but his dive is so remarkable that when he breaks the surface of the water he has become to his peers a boy to be regarded. His achievement is capped by an invitation to dinner from Ging Powers, a senior from his own town who, previous to his dive, has religiously avoided him.

The dinner that evening is Lawrence's waterloo. In his own mind he is sure that this is the beginning of a new career at Devon. As he walks into the dining room, he sees his host and his friends huddled at a corner table. Ging then introduces him to Vinnie Ump, the vice-chairman of the senior council, and Charles Morrell, the sportsman laureate of Devon, an outstanding football, baseball, and hockey player.

During the course of the conversation, Lawrence realizes that Ging is a social climber and immediately feels superior to him. He also understands by looking at Morrell that the important aspect of the athlete is not his ability but his unique personality, the "unconscious authority" that his diverse skills give him. Then his own visions of being the next Captain Marvel get the better of him, and he lies, "I have some cousins, two cousins, you know—they're in clubs at Harvard. . . ." Suddenly aware that the others are interested, Lawrence goes on with his diatribe on the clubs of Harvard, capping it eventually with a restatement of his dive from the bridge. When Morrell asserts that "I saw you do it," Lawrence is overwhelmed because the most important athlete in school saw him in his moment of triumph. He envisions the distinct possibility of becoming Morrell's protégé and jumps at the chance by talking continuously about his house and family and anything he can think of to make himself sound important.

His downfall occurs when he asks which of the men at chapel the first day of school was the dean; when the other boys describe him, Lawrence responds in his loudest voice, "Like my beagle, that's the way he looks, like the beagle I've got at home, my beagle looks just like that right after he's had a bath." The consternation of the three seniors calls Lawrence's attention to the elderly couple making their way toward the door; his questions ("Was that the dean? . . . Did he hear me?") go unanswered momentarily, and Lawrence responds symbolically by slipping under the table. Only then does Lawrence realize the ridiculousness of his position, "under a table in the Anthony Wayne Dining Room of the Devon Inn, making a fool of himself." Immediately Ging, Morrell, and Vinnie make excuses and begin to leave. Morrell asks Lawrence, "Are you British?" and "Is that why you talk so queer?" Numbed, Lawrence can only smother his sobs and keep his anguish to himself.

After this evening, all Lawrence's attempts to be "regarded" backfire, until suddenly with the change of seasons he is redeemed to an extent. He plays intramural football and makes the junior varsity swimming team; that winter his housemates start accepting him and calling him "Varsity." Yet there are still sensitive incidents, and he has confrontations with several of his housemates regarding his undistinguished background.

When Lawrence returns to Devon after the spring break, the bleakness of winter has given way to the peripheral beauty of spring. Then unexpectedly he begins to slip in his studies. For two successive French classes he is unprepared, but the undercutting from his peers does not bother him. Soon after this he achieves a "minor triumph" when he scores his first goal for his intramural team, but the event is actually of little magnitude and does nothing to further his quest to be "regarded." The day of this "minor triumph" turns out to be the final day of his life. After a shower Lawrence goes to the trophy room and fantasizes that 1954 will be the year that he will win the Fullerton Cup, the trophy awarded to the outstanding athlete of each year. Then he suddenly realizes the "finiteness of the cup" and that with the passage of time the cup and the inscriptions on it will all fade from human memory. The room suddenly feels like a crypt, and he steps outside to the freshness and aroma of spring. That night Lawrence, a good swimmer, accidentally drowns in the river that flows between the playing fields. Bruce and Bead, who have gone swimming with him, try to save him, but fail. At a conference two days later Bruce remembers distinctly that Lawrence "had looked different, standing up there on the bridge." The dean asks if Lawrence had looked happy. "Something like that. He wasn't scared, I know that," Bruce answers, unable to fathom the enigma.

Structurally "A Turn with the Sun" is a modern short story following in the mode of such writers as Katherine Mansfield, James Joyce, and Sherwood Anderson and sharply distinct from the contemporary mode of stories with a surreal surface structure. The story begins *in medias res* with Lawrence scoring a winning goal in a spring lacrosse game. Then the story recounts how he made a remarkable dive the previous September on his fourth day at Devon. There is no formal introduction or exposition. The positioning of words in the first sentence, however, together with the punctuation and the soft vowel

sounds grouped together, suggests the softness of dusk and is in direct contrast to Lawrence's experience. Moreover, the serene setting sets the area of thematic concern. The atmosphere created in the first sentence is maintained throughout the story. Everything that Lawrence does or experiences is set against a backdrop of changing seasons, of a beautiful nature indifferent to the upheavals around it. The important images and recurring motifs—the steamy heat, the bridge and the stream, the quest for athletic glory—come together at the end of the story to symbolize how Lawrence never "found" himself during his short stay at Devon. Thus "A Turn with the Sun" achieves microcosmic proportions not through the story line, but by repetitive patterns. Parallel scenes (the two dives), motifs, and events juxtaposed with each other create metaphors and achieve symbolic levels; thus Lawrence's accidental death assumes universal meaning.

"PHINEAS"

The narrative technique of flashback which Knowles deploys in "A Turn with the Sun" is also used in the title story of the volume. The flashback in "Phineas" is framed by a prologue and an epilogue in the present tense designed to link the narrative to the present moment. The setting is Devon, the same as that used in the earlier story, and the cast of characters includes the narrator and his roommate, Phineas or "Finny." Thematically the focus in this story is more on the process of initiation of the young narrator than on the quest to be "regarded." When the narrator arrives at Devon during the summer session, he is thrown off by the outgoing attitude of his roommate, Phineas. At the very moment of arrival, Finny lectures him on all subjects, "beginning with God and moving undeviatingly through to sex." The narrator chooses not to reveal his own confidences, however, because he takes an immediate dislike to Phineas.

Phineas is an excellent athlete. He excels in soccer, hockey, and lacrosse and has the queer notion that an athlete is "naturally good at everything at once." When the narrator asks him why he chose these teams, he replies nonchalantly that they give him the freedom to develop and display his individual talent—"to create without any imposed plan." This lack of discipline makes Finny a weak student, and the narrator begins to suspect that Finny is interfering with his studies because "He hated the fact that I could beat him at this. . . . He might be the best natural athlete in school, the most popular boy, but I was winning where it counted." The narrator suddenly feels that he is equal to Finny and that Finny has human frailties after all.

One evening in summer, five students, including Finny and the narrator, go to the river with the intention of jumping into it from a tree which leans out slightly over the river's edge. Finny jumps into the river impetuously, expecting the others to follow. Everybody refuses except the narrator, who "hated" the idea but jumps anyway because he does not want to "lose" to Phineas. A similar tree episode is the central incident in Knowles's novel *A Separate Peace*. Soon after this event, Phineas draws up a charter for the *Super Suicide Society of the Summer Session*, inscribing his name and the narrator's as charter members and enrolling Chet, Bobby, and Leper as trainees. The society meets almost every evening and all members are required to attend and jump.

On a Thursday evening, the day before a French examination, Phineas goes over to the narrator's room and asks him to attend a meeting of their select society because Leper has finally agreed to jump. The narrator is visibly irritated and says sarcastically, "Okay, we go. We watch little lily-liver Leper not jump from a tree, and I ruin my grade." Finny is taken aback at this and says simply, "I didn't know you needed to study. . . . I thought it just came to you." The narrator realizes for the first time that Phineas has assumed that the narrator's intellectual capacity comes as easily as his own natural ability at sports. Truth dawns on the narrator and he realizes that Phineas has never been jealous of him or considered him a rival—he has simply considered himself a far "superior" person. This realization causes the narrator, as they both climb the tree by the river, to shake the limb, and Phineas falls into the river with a "sickening natural thud." One of his legs is shattered in the fall and he is maimed for life.

Later, when the narrator goes to see Phineas at the infirmary, his guilt almost makes him reveal the truth.

When he asks Phineas if he remembers how he fell, Phineas answers "I just fell, that's all." The narrator finally has a total conception of Phineas's character and realizes that he has not been jealous of Phineas's popularity, background, or skill at sport—he has envied Finny's total and complete honesty.

"Phineas" also has a universal quality stemming from its classic initiation theme. The narrator is initiated into the ways of men within three months of his first meeting with Phineas. Phineas himself is not only the touchstone but also a symbol of an ideal state of being. His lack of human frailties sets him apart from the snobbish class struggle and the Machiavellian quest for athletic fame which Knowles satirizes in "Phineas" and in "A Turn with the Sun." This quest is responsible for the undertone of pessimism in both stories, for it makes victims not only of the involved, but also of the innocent. Thus Lawrence is drowned and Phineas is maimed for life, a victim of his roommate's moment of jealousy in a self-seeking, hostile world.

This negative view of human striving contrasts sharply with the serenity of nature in Knowles's stories. Unlike Thomas Hardy's nature, which reflects the aimlessness of human life, Knowles's nature is beautiful, peaceful, and distant. "Phineas" opens with a nostalgic description of an old Massachusetts town with its "ancient impregnable elm" and proceeds to Devon where the pace of summer is sketched in a beautiful metaphor: "Summer moved on in its measureless peace." The story ends with the approach of dusk, which seems to have a special meaning for Knowles; similarly, "A Turn with the Sun" opens with a soothing detailed description of the sun going down, and "Martin the Fisherman" ends with the "warm crimson glow" of the sun setting over the ocean. This peaceful beauty is in stark contrast to the social and moral conflict in the stories and symbolizes the other half of life—the latent allure beneath the external conflagration of life.

Epiphany is an element common to all of Knowles's stories. The sudden realization, the dawning of the truth, is quite marked in "Phineas" but is more subtle in "Martin the Fisherman," a short vignette in which the patron of a Basque fishing boat finally sees the problem of his crew from their perspective after he gets an accidental dunking in the sea. In "The Reading of the Will," Christopher Curtin realizes that his father did not leave him anything because he, Christopher, did not need any help. Everything was left to Christopher's mother, except a mysterious manila envelope. This was left to Ernie, Christopher's older brother. When Christopher brings the envelope to Ernie's hospital room in Cairo, he has to sit outside while Ernie opens it.

OTHER MAJOR WORKS

LONG FICTION: *A Separate Peace*, 1959; *Morning in Antibes*, 1962; *Indian Summer*, 1966; *The Paragon*, 1971; *Spreading Fires*, 1974; *A Vein of Riches*, 1978; *Peace Breaks Out*, 1981; *A Stolen Past*, 1983; *The Private Life of Axie Reed*, 1986.

NONFICTION: *Double Vision: American Thoughts Abroad*, 1964; *Backcasts: Memories and Recollections of Seventy Years as a Sportsman*, 1993 (memoir).

BIBLIOGRAPHY

Bryant, Hallman Bell. *A Separate Peace: The War Within*. Boston: Twayne, 1990. One of Twayne's masterwork studies, this is a helpful guide for the student of the novel. Includes bibliographical references and an index.

Degnan, James. "Sex Ex Machina and Other Problems." *The Kenyon Review* 31 (Spring, 1969): 272-277. By analyzing "Phineas," the source of material for *A Separate Peace*, Degnan shows how Knowles succeeds when he adheres to treating the torments of the sensitive intelligent male adolescent. In other novels, however, he fails because he leaves this theme.

Holborn, David G. "A Rationale for Reading John Knowles' *A Separate Peace*." In *Censored Books: Critical Viewpoints*, edited by Nicholas J. Karolides, Lee Burress, and John M. Kean. Metuchen, N.J.: Scarecrow Press, 1993. An essay championing the novel and its importance in the literary canon.

McEwen, Fred. "John Knowles: Overview." In *Twentieth-Century Young Adult Writers*, edited by Laura Standley Berger. London: St. James Press, 1994. A standard introduction to the author and his works.

Weber, Ronald. "Narrative Method in *A Separate Peace*." *Studies in Short Fiction* 3 (Fall, 1965): 63-72. To show how Knowles's narrative method relates to his themes, Weber explores comparisons with J. D. Salinger's *The Catcher in the Rye* (1951). He shows how, because he is such a precise craftsman, Knowles provides the clearer statement about life.

Zia Hasan, updated by Louise M. Stone and
James Norman O'Neill

MILAN KUNDERA

Born: Brno, Czechoslovakia; April 1, 1929

OTHER LITERARY FORMS

Milan Kundera began his literary career as a poet, playwright, and critic before turning to short fiction. In the late 1960's, he began devoting himself almost exclusively to long fiction, publishing several highly acclaimed novels and a miscellany, *L'Art du roman* (1986; *The Art of the Novel*, 1988), as well as a dramatic "variation" on a favorite eighteenth century novel, entitled *Jacques et son maître: Hommage à Denis Diderot* (pr. 1970; *Jacques and His Master*, 1985). With director Jaromil Jires, he wrote a screenplay, adapted from his first novel *Žert* (1967; *The Joke*, 1969).

ACHIEVEMENTS

Included among Milan Kundera's many literary honors are the Prix Médicis for *La Vie est ailleurs* (1973; *Life Is Elsewhere*, 1974), the Prix Europa for literature, 1982; *The Los Angeles Times* Book Prize for fiction for *L'Insoutenable Légèreté de l'être* (1984, *The Unbearable Lightness of Being*, 1984); Académie Française Critics prize, 1987; Nelly Sachs prize, 1987; *Independent* Award for foreign fiction, 1991, and the Jerusalem Prize for Literature on the Freedom of Man in Society, 1985. His writing has been translated into many languages including Japanese, Spanish, Serbian, Finnish, and Greek.

BIOGRAPHY

Milan Kundera's life has followed as curious and circuitous a course as the plots of his polyphonic novels. He worked as a laborer and jazz musician. Influenced by his father, Ludvík, a noted pianist and musicologist, Kundera attended Charles University and the Academy of Music and Dramatic Arts in Prague, where he studied piano, composing, film directing, and screenwriting. He joined the Communist Party in 1948, was expelled in 1950, and was reinstated in 1956. He published three volumes of poetry during the 1950's, joined the academy's film faculty in 1958, and began writing plays and stories in the early 1960's.

The year 1967 proved to be an especially momentous one in Kundera's life. That year saw his marriage to Vera Hrabankova; the publication and immediate success of his first novel, *The Joke*; and his provocative speech at the fourth Writers Union meeting. Warning against the threat political repression posed to Czech literature, he spearheaded efforts to speed reform and extend freedom. The reformers carried the day. Antonín Novotný fell from power; Alexander Dubček rose, and with him the Prague Spring of 1968, which ended when the Soviet army, "legitimized" by the token participation of its Warsaw Pact allies, invaded Czechoslovakia on August 20. Kundera was soon branded a counterrevolutionary; he was dismissed from his faculty position, was expelled from the party for a second time, and found his plays banned and his books removed from libraries and bookstores.

Silenced in his own country, Kundera soon began to be heard abroad. In 1975, two years after his second novel, *Life Is Elsewhere*, won France's prestigious Prix Médicis, Kundera was allowed to leave Czechoslovakia to accept a faculty appointment at the Université de Rennes as a professor of comparative literature from 1975 to 1979. The Communist government proved less generous in responding to the publication of his fourth novel, *Le Livre du rire et de l'oubli* (1979; *The Book of Laughter and Forgetting*, 1980), revoking his citizenship. In 1980, he accepted a position at a university, Écoles des Hautes Études in Paris, and became a naturalized French citizen one year later. Although comfortable in France—largely, he said, because of his early interest in, and affection for, Denis Diderot, François Rabelais, and the French Surrealists—Kundera has been as critical of Western forms of censorship as of Communist ones. Asked in 1987—two years before the Velvet Revolution led by playwright-president Václav Havel, which ended Communist rule in Czechoslovakia—whether he believed he would ever be allowed to return to his native land, Kundera said he would not want to: "One emigration suffices for a lifetime."

ANALYSIS

That the West expects writers from Eastern (or what Milan Kundera prefers to call Central) Europe to be political was something Kundera learned the hard way when an English publisher, in the wake of the Soviet invasion, restructured and to some extent even rewrote *The Joke* to make it into what Kundera subsequently claimed it was not: a political protest against communism rather than a work of fiction (or, as Kundera countered at the time, a love story only). In terms of ideological preference, Kundera describes himself as "an agnostic" no more interested in a literature of politics than in a literature of the author's personality. He is, in other words, no more and no less opposed to communist ideology than he is to capitalist (or communist) "Imagology," as he terms the assault upon individual freedom in his sixth novel, *Nesmrtelnost* (1990; *Immortality*, 1991). His

Milan Kundera (©Vera Kundera)

fiction is neither political nor didactic (moralistic), autobiographical nor journalistic. Rather, it is deeply meditative—more an exploration than an explanation.

Kundera traces his literary lineage back to Miguel de Cervantes, Rabelais, Diderot, Laurence Sterne, and more recently to the great twentieth century Central European writers Hermann Broch, Jaroslav Hašek, Franz Kafka, Robert Musil, and Witold Gombrowicz. What attracts him to the first four is their sense of play, and to the latter five their "search for new forms," a search that is at once "impassioned" yet "devoid of any avant-garde ideology (faith in progress, revolution, and so on)." "The great Central European novelists ask themselves what man's possibilities are in a world that has become a trap," or, as Kundera explained to fellow novelist Philip Roth, a pair of traps: fanaticism on one side, absolute skepticism on the other, with human beings attempting to negotiate the narrow path between the two. Kundera conceives of his negotiation not in terms of mimetic plots but instead as existential inquiries that raise questions rather than offer answers, preferring the demystifying "wisdom of uncertainty" to the "noisy foolishness" of received ideas. Thus, instead of the plot and characters of conventional fiction, Kundera offers a theme and variation approach, with characters who are not mimetic representations but instead "experimental egos" and the author's "own unrealized possibilities." Yet for all the open-ended complexity of Kundera's fiction, his writing proves remarkably clear and concise, almost classically chaste in style despite its often erotic subject matter. It is also a prose that strives to be what Kundera believes Sterne's *The Life and Opinions of Tristram Shandy, Gent.* (1759-1767) and Diderot's *Jacques le fataliste et son maître* (wr. c. 1771; *Jacques the Fatalist and His Master*, 1797) are: "absolutely irreducible" and "totally unrewritable," qualities as necessary in the media-maddened West as they were in an eastern police state.

Kundera, along with Havel, is one of contemporary Czechoslovakia's two most important writers and, after Franz Kafka, the country's most interesting, influential, and international novelist—"the other

K," as Mexican novelist Carlos Fuentes called him. Such flattering comparisons are fully merited, for not only is Kundera, in his own largely apolitical and anti-ideological way, as devoted as Havel to resisting totalitarianism in its various guises, but also, as Kafka did before him, he has changed the very shape and scope of the twentieth century novel, giving it a new form and a new importance. For a writer so intellectually complex and aesthetically uncompromising, he has achieved a surprisingly large but wholly deserved following increased by, perhaps, but certainly not owing to, the popularity of Philip Kaufman's 1987 film version of Kundera's fifth novel, *The Unbearable Lightness of Being.*

LAUGHABLE LOVES

Kundera's stories have received little critical attention, overshadowed by his better-known and more ambitious novels. He began writing the stories as a way of relaxing while working on his first play. He soon realized, however, that fiction would serve him far better than drama or poetry as a means for dealing with the "fascinating and enigmatic" reality in which he then found himself and his compatriots. Just as important, only when he began to write the first of his stories was Kundera able to find "my voice, my style, and myself." Kundera, who completed the last of the stories only three days before the Soviet invasion, said that *Laughable Loves* is the book that he is "fondest of because it reflects the happiest time of my life." *Laughable Loves* is important for another reason, for in these early stories one finds the wellsprings of Kundera's later novels (which some convention-bound reviewers have complained are not novels at all but instead story collections). The form of the novel as Hermann Broch and Kafka practiced it and as the Soviet critic Mikhail Bakhtin came to define it provided Kundera with the scope and flexibility that his imagination required, but a scope and flexibility already manifest in miniature as they were in *Laughable Loves.* In them, the reader finds ample evidence of Kundera's early interest in, and mastery of, the theme and variation approach, which would provide him with a potent means for countering what Terry Eagleton has called "the totalitarian drive of literary fiction."

Laughable Loves is more than the title of three slender volumes published during the 1960's and of the collection of eight of the ten original stories published in 1970 (seven in the French and English editions, 1970 and 1974 respectively). *Laughable Loves* refers as well to the theme on which each of the stories plays its variations—a theme that Kundera also treats in each of his six novels. Love figures prominently and ambiguously throughout Kundera's fiction: partly as a release from everyday reality, partly as a way of achieving at least a momentary personal freedom, partly as a revelation of character, and partly as an epistemological delusion (in *Immortality* Kundera writes that love gives one "the illusion of knowing the other"). Love then, is not so much a state of being as it is the intersection of various social, sexual, political, and epistemological forces, a struggle against power that all too often—and perhaps all too predictably—turns into the exercise of power over another. In *The Book of Laughter and Forgetting,* for example, "love is a constant interrogation," and in *La Valse aux adieux* (1976; *The Farewell Party,* 1977), an unfaithful yet in his own way loving husband is "always suspecting his wife of suspecting him." The relation between love and totalitarianism proves both close and comic, "laughable," a word that here means more than simply "amusing." Kundera conceives of laughter as the antidote to the seriousness that he believes characterizes the modern, journalistic age. As he explains in his introduction to *Jacques and His Master,* taking the world seriously means "believing what the world would have us believe." Not surprisingly, given the complexity of his meditative style of fiction making, Kundera defines laughter in a twofold way: as an expression of the sheer joy of being and as a more or less existential negation of the world's seriousness. Kundera as hedonist and kitsch destroyer approves of both and also understands that, taken to the extreme, each poses its own danger: the fanaticism of the totalitarian idyll often associated with a youthful lyrical (poetic) idealism and the absolute skepticism of the unbeliever.

"NOBODY WILL LAUGH"

Both extremes manifest themselves in the opening story of *Laughable Loves.* "Nikdo se nebude smát"

("Nobody Will Laugh") bears a striking resemblance to Kundera's slightly later first novel. The story's main character (and narrator), Klima, receives a pleading and obsequious letter from a stranger, Mr. Zaturetsky, asking him to read and recommend his enclosed essay for publication in the *Visual Arts Journal*, which, unbeknown to Zaturetsky, rejected the narrator's "controversial" study which that very day appeared in a less orthodox but also less prestigious publication. Seeing that Zaturetsky's essay is unoriginal to the point of being unintentionally plagiaristic but on the other hand unwilling to do the hatchet work of the very editor who rejected his essay, Klima decides to amuse himself by writing a long and cynically sympathetic letter in which he manages to make no final evaluation whatsoever. Klima has, however, underestimated his petitioner's desperation and persistence. Zaturetsky repeatedly appears at the university and even shows up at Klima's attic apartment, where he finds not Klima but the beautiful Klara, who has been sleeping with Klima while he fulfills his promise of finding her a better job. Klima's efforts to elude Zaturetsky prove as desperate and humorous as Zaturetsky's attempts to locate him: Klima changes his teaching schedule, pretends to be in Germany, dresses up a student in his hat and coat, has the department secretary lie for him, and finally, when at last confronted by his nemesis, charges Zaturetsky with having made sexual advances toward Klara.

Following the zany yet terrifying logic of Kundera's fiction and Eugène Ionesco's plays, the consequences of Klima's little joke grow more and more serious, even as Klima continues to believe that everyone will laugh once his story is told. Klima, however, is wrong: "Nobody will laugh." The local committee finds him lacking in seriousness; he will lose his faculty position and with it his future and Klara, who has already found someone better suited—and more powerfully placed—to get her what she wants. Klima does find some comfort in the knowledge that his story "was not of the tragic, but rather of the comic variety." Humor such as this comes perilously close to horror, particularly the horror of absurdity without end, an absurdity that permeates every corner of existence, including Mrs. Zaturetsky's dedication to her husband and his essay, which she has never even read. "It wasn't a question of willful plagiarism," Klima realizes, "but rather an unconscious submission to those authorities who inspired in Mr. Zaturetsky a feeling of sincere and inordinate respect" of the very same kind that the woefully inadequate and inept Mr. Zaturetsky inspires in his utterly sexless, wholly humorless, and therefore laughable wife.

"THE HITCHHIKING GAME"

Submission of a different kind plays a key role in "Falešný autostop" ("The Hitchhiking Game"). Here, instead of Klima's friendly first-person narration, Kundera adopts an emotionally distant prose reminiscent of the existential gaze described by Jean-Paul Sartre. A "young man," twenty-eight, and a "girl," twenty-two, lovers, are driving toward the resort where they will spend the next two weeks on vacation. He values her modesty; she wishes she were more open about her body. Making clear that she does not enjoy his little game of running out of fuel and making her hitchhike to the nearest station, she makes him stop for gasoline. Instead of precluding their usual game, however, this stop enables him to play a variation on it. He pretends that she is a hitchhiker to whom he is giving a ride. Although there are still only two bodies in the car, there are now at least four "possible selves": the young man, the girl, the young man whom the young man is pretending to be, and the hitchhiker whom the girl is pretending to be. The dizzying proliferation of fictive selves signals considerably more than narrative gamesmanship; there arises the complex question of whether, and to what degree, these pretended, or possible, selves conceal or reveal the nameless and perhaps identityless young man's and the girl's actual selves (and the related question of whether a phrase such as "actual self" can now be said to mean anything at all). No longer on the road to their planned destination (the resort where they had reserved a room), they discover that "fiction was suddenly making an assault upon real life" and, worse, that "there's no escape from a game," least of all a game involving the politics of sexual power and identity. Just as "the game merged with life," multiple images merge, stacked one upon the other in the eye of the lover turned beholder. Freed to play the part of whore, the girl ironically achieves a greater sexual freedom and pleasure than she had known before, but she immediately feels she has paid too high a price: her self. Hearing her repeat her plaintive and "pitiful tautology"—"I am me, I am me"—the young man understands "the sad emptiness of the girl's assertion." This emptiness recalls Klíma's recognition of his comical fate at the end of "Nobody Will Laugh," but the last lines of "The Hitchhiking Game" are bleaker still: "There were still thirteen days' vacation býefore them."

"LET THE OLD DEAD MAKE ROOM FOR THE YOUNG DEAD"

Similarly bleak prospects, coupled with a dizzying array of possible selves, characterize "At ustoupí starí mrtví mladým mrtvým" ("Let the Old Dead Make Room for the Young Dead"). The title suggests an ironic take of the familiar *carpe diem* theme. Two lovers meet after ten years. He is now thirty-five, divorced, living alone in a provincial town, working at a job that affords him no satisfaction. She is now nearly fifty, a widow who has just discovered that she has forgotten to renew the lease on her husband's grave. Thus she takes the cemetery administrator's words to her, which form the story's title, first as a reproach and then as her rationale for having sex with her former lover. No act in Kundera's fiction is ever quite so simply motivated, however, and hers involves as much revenge as love—revenge against the son who has forced her to play the widow's role—and it involves, too, as much self-assertion as self-accusation. The lovemaking proves no less ambiguously motivated for the man who wishes to possess at last the woman who has eluded him (along with so much else in his inconsequential life) for so long, even though he knows that their encounter will end in disgust. Yet he finds this prospect oddly exciting:

> . . . he, whether he realized it or only vaguely suspected it, could not strip all these pleasures that had been denied him of their significance and color (for it was precisely their colorfulness that made his life so sadly dull), he could reveal that they were worthless, that they were only appearances doomed to destruc-

tion, that they were only metamorphosed dust; he could take revenge upon them, demean them, destroy them.

"SYMPOSIUM"

Kundera's two Dr. Havel stories treat much the same theme but in a far more playful way. "Symposion" ("Symposium") draws its title from Plato and its five-act structure from drama. Its five characters—the chief physician, Havel, the aging Nurse Alzbeta, the attractive thirty-year-old woman doctor, and the young intern Flaishman—offer a host of sexual possibilities (permutations based as much on misreadings, misstatements, and expectations as on sexual preferences). The story focuses on Nurse Alzbeta's efforts to attract Havel's attention, efforts that nearly result in her death (variously read—and misread—as a suicide attempt). Her striptease becomes an apt metaphor for the story itself insofar as the story reveals more and more of the characters' deceits and self-deceptions while nevertheless managing, like any good striptease, to conceal the very mystery it entices the viewer/reader into believing will be exposed (revealed as well as made vulnerable). In "Dr. Havel Twenty Years Later," Havel is made to play Alzbeta's part, with, however, considerably more success, thanks to his established position, his reputation as a Don Juan, and especially his marriage to a beautiful and well-known actress. As in "Symposium," there is a youth (here it is a young editor, and in "Symposium" it is the intern) willing to take one of Havel's little jokes seriously because the joke appeals to his naïve sense of self-importance and his need to have his identity validated by someone older and more authoritative.

"EDWARD AND GOD"

Edward, in "Eduard a Buh" ("Edward and God"), proves less naïve and more manipulative though perhaps no less self-deluded. A joke played at the expense of the ultra-Stalinist Miss Chekachkova costs Edwárd's brother his job but indirectly helps secure for Edward a teaching position at the school that she now runs. Far more self-aware than either Flaishman or the editor, Edward divides his life into two spheres: the serious and obligatory on the one hand

and the unserious and nonobligatory on the other (teaching he places in the latter category). Edward, however, is not nearly as free as he thinks. His pursuit of Alice, a churchgoer, jeopardizes his position at the state school; in parallel fashion, his radical skepticism, cynical in nature, jeopardizes his relationship with Alice (whose religious fervor is more political than spiritual in origin, a fact of which she remains serenely unaware). During his private reeducation session, Edward turns the tables on the spinsterish Miss Chekachkova, ordering this ardent communist to strip, kneel, and recite the Lord's Prayer. Finding her humiliation sexually exciting, he carries her off to bed. He also—and again under false pretenses—overcomes Alice's very different scruples (she mistakenly believes Miss Chekachkova and the other communists are persecuting him for his religious beliefs). Although he finds any God that would forbid extramarital sex "rather comical," Edward becomes angry when Alice consents to his sexual advances, believing that she has betrayed her God too easily. In "Edward and God," as in all Kundera's stories and novels, reversals and incongruities such as these abound, nowhere more ambiguously than in this story's closing paragraphs. Edward, still a nonbeliever, sits in a church, "tormented with sorrow, because God does not exist. But just at this moment his sorrow is so great that suddenly from its depth emerges the genuine *living* face of God." In describing Edward as having "a sorrow in his heart and a smile on his lips," the narrator is drawing on the poetry of the Czech writer Karel Hynek Mácha and the romantic lyricism that Kundera has often criticized for making a value of feeling and the excesses it engenders. "For my part," Kundera has explained, "I'm always tempted to reverse the terms, 'a faint sadness on one's lips and a deep laugh in one's heart.'" From such a depth of heart—"and art"—Kundera's "laughable loves" emerge as early variations on a persistent theme.

"THE GOLDEN APPLE OF ETERNAL DESIRE"

"Zlaté jablko vecné touhy" ("The Golden Apple of Eternal Desire") is divided into such mini-chapters as "The Insidious Nature of Excessive Faith" and "In Praise of Friendship," offering a structured approach to a central character whose life revolves around the obsessive pursuit of women. His friend, the narrator, a university professor of Greek culture, is swept along by the much more self-confident Martin, as Martin obsessively flirts with women and collects their names and numbers. Only one of several problems is the fact that Martin is married and claims to revere his wife. In an effort to snag a beautiful girl at a cafe, Martin gives her a book on Estruscan culture belonging to the narrator. They arrange to meet the girl, a nurse at a country hospital, the following day. Martin calls the initial view of a woman a "sighting," explaining,

> it is not as difficult, for someone with numerical requirements, to *seduce* a girl as it is to *know* enough girls one hasn't yet seduced . . . it is necessary always . . . to sight women, that is, to record in a notebook . . . the names of women who have attracted us and whom we could one day *board*.

Boarding is the next step in getting in touch with a potential conquest by gaining access to her. The narrator trusts Martin's taste better than his own, believing that he merely plays "at something Martin lives." With only a few hours to wait for the nurse and a female friend to get off work, Martin persists in flirting with other women just for boarding practice. He even goes so far as to tell a girl whom he wishes to impress that he is the film director Milos Forman. The tables turn when this girl-child stands the men up. As Martin has assured his wife he will be home early that evening, they have only one hour to pick up and seduce the nurse and her friend. They wait outside the hospital, and Martin becomes extremely anxious. Finally, as the women approach the car, Martin inexplicably drives off. The narrator later repents for not believing in Martin's "divine power of . . . womanizing." He lies to Martin about a woman he is close to seducing. They concoct a scenario where Martin will pass himself off as someone not associated with his friend and "board" the same woman. Such a delicious possibility, the narrator proposes, is the Golden Apple of Eternal Desire. There is both a tenderness and a compassionate sense of humor with which Kundera handles Martin. However, it is the narrator for whom one feels the most as he has little sense of his ability to attract women and lives through the more assured power of another man's prowess. In the end, he must invent an imaginary woman with whom they both fantasize a sensual experience. Kundera has said that *Laughable Loves* represents one of the happiest times in his own life. While "The Golden Apple of Eternal Desire" reflects a double life of sorts, the spirit of conquest certainly can be a joyous one at times.

OTHER MAJOR WORKS

LONG FICTION: *Žert*, 1967 (*The Joke*, 1969, revised 1982); *La Vie est ailleurs*, 1973 (*Life Is Elsewhere*, 1974; in Czech as *Život je jinde*, 1979); *La Valse aux adieux*, 1976 (*The Farewell Party*, 1976; in Czech as *Valčik no rozloučenou*, 1979; revised as *Farewell Waltz*, 1998); *Le Livre du rire et de l'oubli*, 1979 (*The Book of Laughter and Forgetting*, 1980; in Czech as *Kniha smíchu a zapomnění*, 1981); *L'Insoutenable Légèreté de l'être*, 1984 (*The Unbearable Lightness of Being*, 1984; in Czech as *Nesnesitelná lehkost bytí*, 1985); *Nesmrtelnost*, 1990 (*Immortality*, 1991); *La Lenteur*, 1995 (*Slowness*, 1996); *L'Identité*, 1997 (*Identity*, 1998).

PLAYS: *Majitelé klíčů*, pr. 1961; *Ptákovina, čili Dvojí uši—dvojí svatba*, pr. 1968; *Jacques et son maître: Hommage à Denis Diderot*, pr. 1970 (*Jacques and His Master*, 1985).

SCREENPLAY: *Žert*, 1969.

POETRY: *Člověk zahrada širá*, 1953; *Poslední máj*, 1955, revised 1963; *Monology*, 1957, revised 1964.

NONFICTION: *Umění románu: Cesta Vladislava Vančury za velkou epikou*, 1960; *L'Art du roman*, 1986 (*The Art of the Novel*, 1988); *Les testaments trahis*, 1993 (*Testaments Betrayed*, 1995).

BIBLIOGRAPHY

Aji, Aron. *Milan Kundera and the Art of Fiction: Critical Essays*. New York: Garland, 1992. Critical essays by Ilan Stavans, John O'Brien, Octavio Paz, Charles Molesworth, Nina Pelikan Straus, and many others. Well-established essayists discuss "Kundera and the Eighteenth Century English Novel," "The Cyclic Form of Laughable Loves," and Kundera's contribution to the novel form. There is also an essay by Carlos Fuentes, "The Other K." This collection is a powerful tribute to the writer.

Banerjee, Maria Nemcová. *Terminal Paradox: The Novels of Milan Kundera*. New York: Grove Weidenfeld, 1990. A critical study of Kundera's long fiction. Includes a bibliography.

Boyers, Robert. "Between East and West: A Letter to Milan Kundera." In *Atrocity and Amnesia, The Political Novel Since 1945*. New York: Oxford University Press. 1985.

_____. "Milan Kundera: Meaning, Play, and the Role of the Author." *Critique* 34 (Fall, 1992): 3-18. Argues that Kundera's role as intrusive author is not as diametrically opposed to Roland Barthes's announcement of the death of the author as one might suppose. Uses Barthes's ideas as a theoretical tool to examine Kundera's authorial stance and the kind of play that characterizes his fiction.

Brand, Glen. *Milan Kundera: An Annotated Bibliography*. New York: Garland, 1988. The starting point for any serious student of Kundera's work. Includes an excellent introduction, an exhaustive primary bibliography, and a well-annotated bibliography of reviews and criticism.

Gaughan, Richard T. "'Man Thinks; God Laughs': Kundera's 'Nobody Will Laugh.'" *Studies in Short Fiction* 29 (Winter, 1992): 1-10. An analysis of "Nobody Will Laugh" as one of the best examples in Kundera's short stories of how comedy and laughter help resist the deadening effects of forced beliefs and reveal a common ground of understanding and solidarity.

Gopinathan Pillai, C. *The Political Novels of Milan Kundera and O. V. Vijayan: A Comparative Study*. New Delhi: Prestige, 1996. Includes a bibliography and an index.

Kundera, Milan. *Testaments Betrayed: An Essay in Nine Parts*. New York: HarperCollins, 1995. Kundera's discussion of the novel as a genre throws much light on his own fiction, both long and short. Kundera argues for a fiction of moral judgment, discusses the importance of humor in fiction, and examines the ways he thinks that critics have misunderstood great works of fiction.

Misurella, Fred. *Understanding Milan Kundera: Public Events, Private Affairs.* Understanding Modern European and Latin American Literature. Columbia: University of South Carolina Press, 1993. In what is clearly a labor of deep admiration for Kundera's body of work, Misurella lays out an approach to his novelistic forms, examining in each chapter such topics as the human possibilities of Kafka and Diderot, the "Longing for Paradise in *The Unbearable Lightness of Being*," among others. He concludes with "The Art of the Novel" and a comprehensive bibliography.

Nemcova Banerjee, Maria. *Terminal Paradox: The Novels of Milan Kundera.* New York: Grove Press. 1992. A critical study of Kundera's novels.

O'Brien, John. *Milan Kundera and Feminism: Dangerous Intersections.* New York: St. Martin's Press, 1995. A look female characters in Kundera's fiction.

Petro, Peter, ed. *Critical Essays on Milan Kundera.* New York: G. K. Hall, 1999. A critical study of Kundera's fiction. Includes a bibliography and an index.

Plimpton, George, ed. *Writers at Work: "The Paris Review": Interviews.* New York: Viking Penguin, 1986. An interview with Kundera.

Pochoda, Elizabeth. Introduction to *The Farewell Party.* New York: Viking Penguin, 1977. Pochoda situates Kundera's fiction and the private lives of his characters within a larger political context. Their lives are marked by helplessness and a sense of missed opportunities. Instead of freeing them from political oppression, love seems to refigure the system of political oppression on a more intimate scale.

Porter, R. C. *Milan Kundera: A Voice from Central Europe.* Århus, Denmark: Arkona Press, 1981. In separate chapters, Porter discusses *Laughable Loves*, Kundera's three plays, *The Joke, Life Is Elsewhere*, and *The Book of Laughter and Forgetting*. The introduction is especially useful for establishing the political context of Kundera's writings.

The Review of Contemporary Fiction 9 (Summer, 1982). This special issue devoted to Kundera and

Zulfikar Ghose includes Lois Oppenheim's interview with Kundera, Glen Brand's "Selective Bibliography of Kundera Criticism," and Maria Nemcova Banerjee's "The Impossible Don Juan" on the Don Juan theme in *Laughable Loves*. An expanded version of Banerjee's essay appears in her *Terminal Paradox: The Novels of Milan Kundera* (New York: Grove Weidenfeld, 1990).

Rorty, Richard. "Heidegger, Kundera, and Dickens." In *Essays on Heidegger and Others: Philosophical Papers.* Cambridge: Cambridge University Press, 1991. Compares the fiction of Kundera to that of Martin Heidegger and Charles Dickens.

Roth, Philip. "Milan Kundera." In *Reading Myself and Others.* New York: Farrar, Straus & Giroux, 1975. First published as "Milan Kundera, The Joker" in *Esquire*, in April, 1974, and as "Introducing Milan Kundera" in *Laughable Loves*. Roth provides a capsule biography, a brief history of contemporary Czechoslovakia, discusses the relation between "erotic play and power" (the Don Juan theme), and offers brief but interesting comments on specific stories, "The Hitchhiking Game" and "Edward and God" in particular.

Salmagundi, no. 73 (Winter, 1987). This special issue devoted to Kundera is framed by two indispensable interviews and includes seven important essays on his work, chiefly the novels. "Estrangement and Irony," by Terry Eagleton, and "On Milan Kundera," by Clavin Bedient, are especially noteworthy.

Sturdivant, Mark. "Milan Kundera's Use of Sexuality." *Critique: Studies in Modern Fiction* 26 (Spring, 1985): 131-140. Sturdivant offers a detailed reading of the sexual theme first raised by Elizabeth Pochoda and Philip Roth, examining *The Joke, The Book of Laughter and Forgetting*, "Symposium," "The Hitchhiking Game," and "Edward and God."

Updike, John. *Hugging the Shore: Essays and Criticism.* "Czech Angels" Ecco Press. 1994. This collection was the winner of the National Book Critics Circle Award for Criticism.

Robert A. Morace, updated by Nika Hoffman

L

PÄR LAGERKVIST

Born: Växjö, Sweden; May 23, 1891
Died: Lidingö, Sweden; July 11, 1974

PRINCIPAL SHORT FICTION

Människor, 1912 (novella)
Två sager om livet, 1913
Järn och människor, 1915
Det eviga leendet, 1920 (novella; *The Eternal Smile*, 1934)
Onda sagor, 1924
Gäst hos verkligheten, 1925 (novella; *Guest of Reality*, 1936)
Kämpende ande, 1930
Bödeln, 1933 (novella; *The Hangman*, 1936)
I den tiden, 1935
The Eternal Smile and Other Stories, 1954
The Marriage Feast and Other Stories, 1955
The Eternal Smile: Three Stories, 1971

OTHER LITERARY FORMS

Pär Lagerkvist's first literary success was a volume of poetry, *Ångest* (1916; anguish). He dominated the Scandinavian theater with plays such as *Han som fick leva om sitt liv* (1928; *The Man Who Lived His Life Over*, 1971) and *De vises sten* (1947; *The Philosopher's Stone*, 1966). His international reputation was established by the novels written in his later life, particularly *Barabbas* (1950).

ACHIEVEMENTS

Pär Lagerkvist received the prestigious literary prize from Samfundet De Nio in 1928. He was elected one of eighteen "Immortals" of the Swedish Academy in 1940 and was awarded an honorary Ph.D. from the University of Gothenburg in 1941. He received the Bellman Foundation Award in Fiction in 1945 and the Nobel Prize in Literature in 1951.

BIOGRAPHY

Pär Fabian Lagerkvist was born May 23, 1891, in Växjö, Sweden, to Anders Johan and Johanna (Blad) Lagerkvist, an orthodox Lutheran couple, who stressed religious training. In 1910, he matriculated at the University of Uppsala, where he briefly studied the humanities. Lagerkvist began his literary career with a novella, *Människor*. In 1913 he traveled to Paris, where he was influenced by the visual arts. He applied the boldness of Fauvism, the simplicity of Primitivism, and the contrasting perspectives of cubism to literature in his first critical essay, *Ordkonst och bildkonst* (1913; *Literary Art and Pictorial Art*, 1982).

In 1915 Lagerkvist moved to Denmark, where he remained throughout World War I, establishing his literary reputation with a volume of poetry, *Ångest*, which is considered the first expressionistic work in Swedish. In Copenhagen, he turned his literary attention to the theater and in 1918 married Karen Dagmar Johanne Sørensen. Returning to Stockholm, he became a drama critic for *Svenska Dagbladet*, writing his final review in June, 1919. Thereafter he sustained himself writing fiction.

Lagerkvist traveled a great deal during the 1920's, especially to France and Italy, his pessimism dissipating as he observed Europe recovering from the war. His autobiographical novella *Guest of Reality* was published in 1925, the same year that he divorced his wife and married a Swedish widow, Elaine Luella Hallberg. In the 1930's he became an outspoken critic of totalitarianism and fascism in such works as *The Hangman*. This work was revised as a play in 1934 and became the most significant Scandinavian play of the decade. His final collection of short stories, *I den tiden*, was published in 1935.

As Europe again became engulfed in war, Lagerkvist wrote his first mature novel, *Dvärgen* (1944;

The Dwarf, 1945). His international reputation was established when he was awarded the Nobel Prize in Literature following the publication of *Barabbas*. He continued writing allegorical novels until he suffered a stroke, passing away July 11, 1974.

ANALYSIS

Pär Lagerkvist is the preeminent Swedish literary figure of the mid-twentieth century. He employed elements of myth and fable, combined with simple language and direct storytelling to explore the internal struggle between modern humankind and God. The quest to answer life's eternal questions permeates his writings as he explores the relationship between good and evil, faith and despair, the purpose of life and the meaning of death. The strength of Lagerkvist's storytelling lies in the dichotomy of yearning for the conservative religion of his youth and finding that religion has forsaken humanity in its blind struggle to find meaning in a scientific age. He described himself as a "religious atheist," believing in a deity that is obscured by religion.

As a young writer, Lagerkvist repudiated the decadence of late nineteenth literature and the naturalism of nineteenth century Norwegian playwright Henrik Ibsen in favor of the radical French artistic aesthetic and the "dream plays" of August Strindberg. Lagerkvist's pessimistic early works are colored by the cruelty of World War I and are critically linked to German expressionists. Following the war, Lagerkvist grappled with the reasons for mortal existence in both allegorical and autobiographical short stories, novellas, and plays. As Europe once again became a battleground, Lagerkvist became an outspoken critic of totalitarianism and strong supporter of "heroic humanitarian idealism." Following World War II he created a cycle of short novels wherein he demonstrates a more optimistic belief that good can ultimately conquer evil and that love can prevail. A major achievement is Lagerkvist's ability to grapple with philosophical issues without resorting to sermonizing or moralizing. He clearly depicts characters struggling with the contradictory ambiguities of life but allows his readers to draw their own conclusions.

Pär Lagerkvist, Nobel Laureate for Literature in 1951 (©The Nobel Foundation)

THE ETERNAL SMILE

In the novella *The Eternal Smile*, the dead pass the eternities discussing the meaning of life. Ordinary people fondly remember the simple pleasures derived from living ordinary lives while others tell of their misfortunes or untimely deaths. Lagerkvist's search for spiritual meaning is explored through the voices of three "saviors." The first savior claims to be the Son of God who gave his life for the world. In death, however, he became disillusioned, a man like everyone else. The second savior recalls that life meant helpless confusion and that it did not afford peace even to those who were happy. He concludes that the meaning of life is so simple, nothing can be said about it. The third savior decries their current monotonous existence, in which there is no joy because there is no confusion or misery. He proclaims that they must seek out God and demand the restitution of life's riches and pains. They wander for centuries, finally coming upon a clearing in which an old man is cutting wood. When they recognize that he is God, they ask what he meant by life. God explains that he is a simple man and that he only did the best that he knew how. He reveals that he never requested anything for himself and that they should be content with their lives. Lagerkvist reveals his philosophy of God when his characters understand that God is like them, only more so. He concludes that happiness and fulfillment are to be found in this life.

"FAR OCH JAG"

"Far och jag" (1923; English translation, 1955) appeared in the collection *Onda sagor* and has been included in all three English-language collections. It tells of the terrifying moment when a child realizes that his world will not be the safe, simple world that his father knew. A ten-year-old boy goes for a walk in the forest with his father. The boy becomes terrified when night falls, afraid even to breathe for fear of losing his life. His father comforts him with the assurance that there is a God. As they walk along a railroad track, they are surprised by the monstrous appearance of an unscheduled train. They must leap down an embankment to avoid being killed. As the train roars by, the boy realizes that it is a symbol of his own and perhaps the world's future. It is the anguish of the unknown, with which his father is unacquainted; his life will not be like his father's secure existence.

THE HANGMAN

The novella *The Hangman* embodies the aesthetic, political, and philosophical aspects of Lagerkvist's stories. A hangman sits alone in a medieval tavern, dressed in bloodred attire, drinking his beer. One by one, the men in the tavern tell their tales of the mystical powers of the hangman, depicted as both executioner and scapegoat. The tavern is in fascist Germany, where the hangman is revered by the revelers as a distorted ideal of humankind. However, they are not certain they recognize him because they have each accepted the role of executioner themselves. When they beg to know his identity he finally speaks, admitting to them that he is the hangman. He con-

demns them for their murderousness by confessing that when he was required to execute Jesus Christ, he discovered that human beings had turned their God to stone and had treated their Savior as they would any other man. Lagerkvist's contrasting perspectives create a composite that condemns violence and racism, ultimately causing the readers to ask if they, indeed, destroyed their own god.

"DET LILLA FÄLTTÅGET"

The short story "Det lilla fälttåget" (1935; English translation, 1954) from *I den tiden* is included in both *The Eternal Smile and Other Stories* and *The Marriage Feast and Other Stories*. The story is a devastating antiwar tale, which capitalizes on the image of Adolf Hitler's youth troops and the fascist love of parades and spectacle. It is an account of warfare from training through combat, carried out by six- to fourteen-year-old children, who are more capable and successful than any army of adults could ever hope to be. The war stories are as preposterous as the child army itself. One lieutenant is spanked by a washerwoman, who demands to know why he is not home with his family. A battle ends with exactly 12,924 casualties on each side and the remaining troops in precisely the same positions they held at the beginning of the campaign. Eventually the enemy is outflanked in a maneuver that is studied by generals for generations. Hearts swell with pride as these "little men," less the thousands lost in battle, celebrate their victory with a great parade. The cheering is loudest for those marching at the rear, blind and with small, artificial limbs in place of those amputated in service to their country. In what is perhaps his most ironic fable, Lagerkvist clearly demonstrates that the atrocities of war are not honorable but horrible, and that war is childish.

OTHER MAJOR WORKS

LONG FICTION: *Dvärgen*, 1944 (*The Dwarf*, 1945); *Barabbas*, 1950 (English translation, 1951); *Sibyllan*, 1956 (*The Sibyl*, 1958); *Ahasverus död*, 1960 (*The Death of Ahasuerus*, 1962); *Pilgrim på havet*, 1962 (*Pilgrim at Sea*, 1964); *Det heliga landet*, 1964 (*The Holy Land*, 1966); *Mariamne*, 1967 (*Herod and Mariamne*, 1968).

PLAYS: *Sista människan*, pb. 1917; *Teater: Den svåra stunden*, pr., pb. 1918 (*The Difficult Hour*, I-III, 1966); *Himlens hemlighet*, pb. 1919 (*The Secret of Heaven*, 1966); *Den osynlige*, pb. 1923; *Han som fick leva om sitt liv*, pr., pb. 1928 (*The Man Who Lived His Life Over*, 1971); *Konungen*, pb. 1932 (*The King*, 1966); *Bödeln*, pb. 1933 (adaptation of his novella; *The Hangman*, 1966); *Mannen utan själ*, pb. 1936 (*The Man Without a Soul*, 1944); *Seger i mörker*, pb. 1939; *Midsommardröm i fattighuset*, pr., pb. 1941; *Midsummer Dream in the Workhouse*, 1953; *De vises sten*, pb. 1947 (*The Philosopher's Stone*, 1966); *Låt människan leva*, pr., pb. 1949 (*Let Man Live*, 1951); *Barabbas*, pr., pb. 1953 (adaptation of his novel).

POETRY: *Ångest*, 1916; *Den lyckliges väg*, 1921; *Hjärtats sånger*, 1926; *Vid lägereld*, 1932; *Genius*, 1937; *Sång och strid*, 1940; *Dikter*, 1941; *Hemmet och stjärnan*, 1942; *Aftonland*, 1953 (*Evening Land*, 1975).

NONFICTION: *Ordkonst och bildkonst*, 1913 (*Literary Art and Pictoral Art*, 1982); "Modern teater: Synpunkter och angrepp," 1918 ("Modern Theatre: Points of View and Attack," 1966); *Teater*, 1918; *Det besegrade livet*, 1927; *Den knutna näven*, 1934 (*The Clenched Fist*, 1982); *Den befriade människan*, 1939; *Antecknat: Ur eferlämnede dagböcker och anteckningar*, 1977.

MISCELLANEOUS: *Motiv*, 1914 (poetry, essays, and prose sketches); *Kaos*, 1919 (poetry and the play *The Secret of Heaven*); *Modern Theatre: Seven Plays and an Essay*, 1966.

BIBLIOGRAPHY

Block, Adele. "The Mythical Female in the Fictional Works of Pär Lagerkvist." *The International Fiction Review* 1, no. 1 (January, 1974): 48-53. An examination of the mythical mother figure in Lagerkvist's short fiction.

Brantly, Susan. "Tradition Versus Innovation: The Cradle of Swedish Modernism—Pär Lagerkvist." In *A History of Swedish Literature*, edited by Lars G. Warme. Vol. 3. Lincoln: University of Nebraska Press, 1996. A general overview of Lagerkvist's work, including discussion of "The Eternal Smile."

Scobbie, Irene. *Pär Lagerkvist: Gäst hos verkligheten*. 3d ed. Hull: University of Hull, 1981. Despite the title, this work, which includes bibliographical references, is in English.

Sjöberg, Leif. *Pär Lagerkvist*. New York: Columbia University Press, 1976. A definitive short overview of Lagerkvist's primary works. Four major examples of his short fiction, "The Eternal Smile," "Father and I," *Guest of Reality*, and *The Hangman* are examined in depth.

Spector, Robert Donald. *Pär Lagerkvist*. New York: Twayne, 1973. A full-length study of Lagerkvist's complete works in English. Spector examines structure, point of view, and symbolism and finds a fundamental unity in Lagerkvist's prose, drama, and poetry. Excellent bibliography.

White, Ray Lewis. *Pär Lagerkvist in America*. Atlantic Highlands, N.J.: Humanities Press, 1979. This is an index of reviews of Lagerkvist's works published in America, however, it includes only one short-story collection, *The Eternal Smile and Other Stories*.

Gerald S. Argetsinger

JHUMPA LAHIRI

Born: London, England; July 11, 1967

PRINCIPAL SHORT FICTION

The Interpreter of Maladies, 1999

OTHER LITERARY FORMS

In addition to her short fiction collection, Jhumpa Lahiri has written a nonfiction work, *Accursed Palace: The Italian Palazzo on the Jacobean Stage (1603-1625)*, which was published in 1997.

ACHIEVEMENTS

Despite her modest output, Jhumpa Lahiri has received an impressive number of awards and honors. Recipient of the Henfield Award and the Fiction Prize (from *Transatlantic Review* and *Louisville Review* respectively), she has been hailed in *The New Yorker*'s "Future of American Fiction" issue as one of the country's best young writers, has had one story, "The Interpreter of Maladies," selected for both *The Best American Short Stories 1999* and *Prize Stories: The O. Henry Awards*, and was appointed the 1999 Margaret Bridgman Fellow in Fiction at the Bread Loaf Writers' Conference.

BIOGRAPHY

Although her parents were from Calcutta, Jhumpa Lahiri was born in London on July 11, 1967, and raised in Rhode Island, where she began writing while still in grade school. After completing her undergraduate education at Barnard College in New York City (B.A., 1989), she worked as a research assistant at a nonprofit organization before enrolling in Boston University's writing program (M.A., 1993); "The Interpreter of Maladies" first appeared in the program's literary magazine, *Agni*. In the course of earning a doctorate in Renaissance studies (Boston University, 1997), Lahiri realized that she had considerably more interest in imaginative writing than in scholarship. A two-year fellowship at the Fine Arts Work Center in Provincetown (1997-1999) gave her time to write as well as to secure an agent, a coveted

acceptance from *The New Yorker*, and a book contract from Houghton Mifflin. Her apprenticeship complete and the making of her international reputation under way, Lahiri settled in New York City.

ANALYSIS

The publication of Salman Rushdie's Booker McConnell Prize-winning novel, *Midnight's Children* (1980), generated an enormous Western interest in and appetite for contemporary Indian writing, albeit chiefly fiction written in English by writers living outside India. In Britain, the new generation of Indian writers is large and varied. In the United States, where the Indian population is proportionately much smaller and less visible, the kinds of Indian writing favored by publishers and readers are in general limited to the exotic and the poignant. Much to her credit, Lahiri has avoided exploiting the former while investing the latter with an emotional depth made all the more effective by a restrained, Chekhovian style that is worlds away from both the Rabelaisian extravagance of Rushdie and the mere cleverness of his many imitators.

Lahiri's roots, in fact, predate Rushdie, extending back to another transplanted Bengali writer, Bharati Mukherjee, whose early stories also concern the complexities of the Indian immigrant experience. In dealing with the lives of the Americanized offspring of that earlier immigrant generation, Lahiri is interested less in the clash of cultures than in the commonplace disasters that slowly erode the fragile foundations of her characters' everyday lives. It is for this new generation of young, well-educated Indian Americans that Lahiri's stories provide a shock of recognition not unlike Hanif Kureishi's films and fictions have in Britain and Philip Roth's early fiction did for young American Jews in the 1950's, the sense that "someone understands us!" The cultural displacement that Lahiri's characters experience so acutely has wider implications, however, insofar as it serves as an "index of a more existential sense of dislocation."

"THE INTERPRETER OF MALADIES"

The title story of Lahiri's debut collection offers an excellent introduction to her highly accomplished but unassuming art. At first glance "The Interpreter of Maladies" looks like a case of yet another Indian writer exploiting a distant homeland to satisfy the American appetite for the foreign and faraway. The story does not exploit, however; it explores. Its Indian setting acts as a necessary backdrop for a complex portrayal of that sense of disappointment and displacement central to Lahiri's vision. A young, thoroughly Americanized Indian couple, Mr. and Mrs. Das, both born in the United States, pay a visit to the Sun Temple in Konarak, under the watchful eye of their guide and driver, Mr. Kapasi, from whose perspective, but not in whose voice, the story is told. Thus, it is the couple, not the country, that appears strange to Mr. Kapasi, who takes note of, and quiet exception to, a family that acts as if "they were all siblings." Although appalled by their effusive, even excessive informality, Mr. Kapasi also finds himself attracted, especially as they take pains to include him in their little circle and even more when Mrs. Das pays him an unexpected compliment, saying how important his regular, weekday job is, interpreting patients' maladies for a doctor.

Lahiri quickly sketches Mr. Kapasi's life as a series of disappointments. Having once dreamed of becoming a scholar of languages, he has had to settle for much less: first, as a teacher of English at a local grammar school, and then, in order to pay his dead son's medical bills, as an interpreter of maladies and weekend tour guide. Not surprisingly, Mrs. Das's compliment goes to his head. Her promise to send him a copy of the group photo that her husband has just taken leads this otherwise hopeless husband of an embittered wife to fantasize a chaste but satisfying epistolary relationship with the attractive, twenty-eight-year-old Mrs. Das. It is an imaginary airmail affair of the heart that appears at once touching and ridiculous, especially as played against the backdrop of the temple's erotic friezes. However, when Mrs. Das, whose own marriage is none too happy, tells Mr. Kapasi of her secret symptoms—the child fathered by another man, the "terrible urges to throw things away"—he proves inadequate, even "insulted that Mrs. Das should ask him to interpret her common, trivial little secret." Failing to understand the depth of her despair, he responds in a way that serves as the ironic measure of his own failures of nerve and compassion. "'Is it really pain you feel, Mrs. Das, or is it guilt?'" Even the scrap of dignity he salvages from rescuing her son from hungry monkeys is quickly stripped away when he alone sees the paper on which he had written his address (and pinned his hopes) fall from Mrs. Das's bag and blow away in the wind.

"A TEMPORARY MATTER"

"A Temporary Matter" is an even more painful rendering of what Lahiri has described as "the dilemma, the difficulty and often the impossibility of communicating emotional pain to others, as well as expressing it to ourselves." The title refers to a disruption in electrical service while workmen repair a damaged line. "'It's good of them to warn us,'" says the wife, Shoba. There had been no warning months before when her child was stillborn and she and her husband had been left to drift apart even while living together, she into her job as a proofreader (correcting other people's mistakes), he, "still a student at thirty-five," into a still unfinished dissertation on agrarian revolts in India. Darkness forces them together, dining together by candlelight and passing the time telling stories that become "an exchange of confessions—the little ways they'd hurt or disappointed each other, and themselves." The experience is painfully intimate, fraught with risk as well as possibility, but when the line is repaired, it is the reader's turn to be caught off guard, unprepared first for Shoba's declaring that she is leaving Shukumar, then for the way he avenges himself, telling his rebellious wife what she had neither known nor wanted to know: their child's sex. It was a secret he had kept even after holding their dead son "because he still loved her then, and it was the one thing in her life that she had wanted to be a surprise." The story ends with the two together yet alone, each weeping "for the things they now knew."

"WHEN MR. PIRZADA CAME TO DINNER"

Lahiri found writing "When Mr. Pirzada Came to Dinner" difficult because it draws on two aspects of her own experience. One is the way her parents' lives in America were largely defined by their Indianness, which caused them to look back, and occasionally travel back, to India, in part to compensate for the "malnourished version of family" they experienced as immigrants. (This is a subject more fully rendered in "Mrs. Sen's.") The other is the way that as the daughter of Indian immigrants, Lahiri came to feel that she could never really be at home either in the India her parents yearned for or in America. "When Mr. Pirzada Came to Dinner" is not so much about its title character, then, as it is about its Lahiri-like narrator, a woman in her early thirties looking back to 1971, when she was ten and Mr. Pirzada, a visiting researcher from Dacca, was a frequent guest in her home. It is a time when East Pakistan becomes Bangladesh and ten-year-old Lilia comes to feel her Indianness in much more complex terms than before. She learns, for example, that despite language and appearance, the "impeccably suited" and formal-sounding Mr. Pirzada is not Indian and that the war in East Pakistan that her parents and their guest follow so intently on television has no place at her school, where she and her classmates study the American Revolution. Seemingly, all ends well: India comes to the Bangladeshis' aid; Mr. Pirzada is reunited with his family in a homeland at once familiar and new; and Lilia grows up, learning along the way from books about a war halfway around the world that had once mystified her. Nonetheless, the story ends elegaically, with Lilia's feeling the "absence" that haunts all of Lahiri's characters.

"THE THIRD AND FINAL CONTINENT"

"The Third and Final Continent" is another story Lahiri found difficult to write, not because it is autobiographical (though it does draw on her parents' experiences) but because of the challenge of narrating the story in a man's voice. Although it is her restrained style, Indian characters, and immigrant themes that have attracted most attention, it is Lahiri's virtuoso handling of narrative voices and points of view that is arguably the most impressive feature of her writing: the Faulkner-inspired "we" of "The Treatment of Bibi Haldar," the young white boy in "Mrs. Sen's," the young (again white) woman from

Michigan in "Sexy" who feels so displaced in a Boston in which her well-off Indian lover feels so at home. Perhaps the greater challenge Lahiri faced in writing this story was to avoid sounding sentimental, which is just what "The Third and Final Continent" did seem when it first appeared in *The New Yorker*. As the last of the nine stories in *The Interpreter of Maladies*, however, "The Third and Final Continent" leaves a very different impression. Here, the artful simplicity of the narrator's seemingly uneventful odyssey from Calcutta to London in 1964 and then to Boston on the very day in 1969 when men first set foot on the Moon, seems quietly triumphant rather than sentimental. The story's and the narrator's modesty and humility compel the reader's attention, focusing not on the narrator's travails but instead on the summer he rented a room in the home of an elderly and cantankerous lady whom he treated with typically Indian formality and sincere if understated affection. His subsequent life, humbly and briefly narrated at story's end, is ordinary enough—marriage, job, home, children—yet it leads the reader to wonder whether in marveling at achievements such as the Moon landing the reader may have missed entirely the kinds of commonplace triumphs that "The Third and Final Continent" celebrates—triumphs so conspicuously absent in Lahiri's other stories.

OTHER MAJOR WORKS

NONFICTION: *Accursed Palace: The Italian Palazzo on the Jacobean Stage (1603-1625)*, 1997.

BIBLIOGRAPHY

Bellafante, Ginia. "Windows into Life." *Time* 154 (August 2, 1999): 91. Bellafante maintains that Lahiri and Gish Jen—*Who's Irish: Stories* (1999)—are two of the best of the young writers who have published collections of short stories this summer. Lahiri's strength is her "gift for illuminating the full meaning of brief relationships" of various kinds.

Crain, Caleb. "Subcontinental Drift." *The New York Times Book Review*, July 11, 1999, 11-12. In Lahiri's seductive, "elegantly constructed" stories, "the pang of disappointment turns into a sudden hunger to know more" on the part of both characters and readers.

Curtis, Sarah. "Strangers and Neighbours." *The Times Literary Supplement*, October 22, 1999, 25. In these stories of "isolation and displacement," Lahiri goes well beyond typical Indian-immigrant fiction, utilizing her "ability to delineate in telling detail the mores of both [Indian and American] societies" in order to "illuminate human nature" in general.

Kakutani, Michiko. "Liking America, but Longing for India." *The New York Times*, August 6, 1999, p. E48. Praising Lahiri's "wonderfully distinctive new voice" and "eloquent and assured style," Kakutani contends that the "cultural displacement" that connects Lahiri's stories serves as "a kind of index of a more existential sense of dislocation."

Keesey, Anna. "Four New Collections Show the Elastic Quality of Short Fiction." *The Chicago Tribune*, August 8, 1999, p. 4. Lahiri's fiction "deals tenderly with the difficulties of the expatriate." Although not averse to including "vivid, aromatic details" of Indian life, she is most effective when most retrained and austere.

O'Grady, Megan. Review of *The Interpreter of Maladies*, by Jhumpa Lahiri. *The Village Voice* 104 (April 19, 1999): 59-60. According to O'Grady, *The Interpreter of Maladies* "speaks to anyone who has ever felt like a foreigner—at home or abroad." Although marriage may be her "richest domain," the "awe she invokes in her characters as they cross barriers of nations and generations" is present in all nine stories.

Todd, Tamsin. "At the Corner Delhi." *The Washington Post*, October 7, 1999, p. C8. After Arundhati Roy (*The God of Small Things*), Lahiri has been anointed "the next subcontinental sensation"; fortunately her fiction proves her a worthy candidate: original, "accomplished, insightful and deeply American."

Robert A. Morace

TOMMASO LANDOLFI

Born: Pico, near Frosinone, Italy; August 9, 1908
Died: Rome, Italy; July 7, 1979

PRINCIPAL SHORT FICTION

Dialogo dei massimi sistemi, 1937
Il Mar delle Blatte, 1939
La spada, 1942
Le due zitelle, 1945 (*The Two Old Maids*, 1961)
Cancroregina, 1950 (*Cancerqueen*, 1971)
Ombre, 1954
Se non la realtà, 1960
Racconti, 1961
In società, 1962
Gogol's Wife and Other Stories, 1963
Tre racconti, 1964
Racconti impossibili, 1966
Cancerqueen, and Other Stories, 1971

Le labrene, 1974
A caso, 1975
Landolfi: Le più belle pagine, 1982 (partially translated in *Words in Commotion and Other Stories*, 1986)

OTHER LITERARY FORMS

While Tommaso Landolfi wrote mainly short stories and short works called *novelle*, he also published some long fiction. Examples include *La pietra lunare* (1937; the moonstone) and *Un amore del nostro tempo* (1965; a love story of our time). He wrote for the theater: *Landolfo VI di Benevento* (1958; Landolph VI) and *Faust '67* (1969). He published two highly regarded volumes of poetry: *Viola di morte* (1972; the violet shade of death) and *Il tradimento* (1977; betrayal). In Italy, he also enjoyed a reputation as an observant literary critic and a witty and ironic essayist. A selection of critical essays are gathered in *Gogol a Roma* (1971; Gogol in Rome), while *Del meno* (1978; this and that) is a collection of columns which Landolfi published over the years on the "terza pagina" (the literary page) of the *Corriere della Sera*. To this steady and voluminous activity must be added the writer's numerous translations from French, German, and Russian literature.

ACHIEVEMENTS

Tommaso Landolfi is a unique and eccentric writer who fits into no obvious category of Italian literature, past or present. Italian fiction in the twentieth century follows the tradition laid down by the nineteenth century masters, Alessandro Manzoni and Giovanni Verga, both of whom dealt directly with the historical forces at work on human society and who emphasized realistic description of the social backdrop. Landolfi appears to have had no interest in dealing overtly with those historical crises of his time which had such a formative influence on his own generation (fascism and World War II). Instead, Landolfi's cosmopolitanism is reflected in his continuous output as a translator—mainly from Russian, but also from French and German literature, which always paralleled his literary production.

In the 1930's, Landolfi was associated with the hermetic movement in Italian poetry and prose, as a part of that generation of writers who, in response to the pressures of the fascist regime, turned in on themselves to rediscover a poetic voice or simply to maintain private integrity, while they also looked to foreign traditions in search of stylistic and thematic mentors. In those years, Landolfi, who had taken a degree in Russian literature at the University of Florence, continued to reside in that city and published his early fiction in reviews such as *Letteratura* and *Campo di Marte*. The hermetics made their antifascist comments obliquely, never attacking the regime directly but rather withdrawing from its vulgarity, militancy, and stridency.

The hermetics had attracted Landolfi most, not for their political attitude but rather for their exploration of the metaphysical, especially as expressed in the humble and the mundane. Increasingly obsessed with the spiritual and existential, Landolfi became more and more isolated during the postwar period, when the intellectual climate became intensely political, with mounting claims made on writers for commitment and partisan allegiance. He consciously neglected issues he deemed outside his own art, and an important consequence of his withdrawal from fashion was the delayed recognition of his work. His columns in the *Corriere della Sera*, however, earned him a wider audience, and he won repeated recognition in Italy for his achievements over a broad area of the literary landscape. To list only a few of his awards: the Premio Viarregio for fiction; the Bagutta and Elba (1966) awards; the Premio D'Annunzio (1968, 1974); the Pirandello Theater Award (1968, for *Faust '67*); the Premio di poesia Fiuggi (1972); and the Strega Prize for fiction (1975, for *A caso*).

BIOGRAPHY

The biographical facts pertaining to Tommaso Landolfi can be briefly stated. His life was without major incidents, and he chose to live in obscurity, away from the glare of publicity. Landolfi is known for consciously establishing barriers between himself and any would-be biographer. This jealously guarded privacy amounted to something of an obsession.

He was born in Pico (in the province of Frosinone) in 1908. His mother died in his second year, and as a young adolescent he was sent away to boarding school. He later attended the University of Florence, from which he was graduated, having specialized in Russian literature. He spent most of the 1930's in Florence, participating in the literary activities of the time, publishing his early fiction. It is known that, on the eve of World War II, he was arrested and spent some time in prison for activities deemed inappropriate by the regime. Landolfi's political demeanor, however, took the form of a rather generic antifascism rather than that of an overt militancy. During the war, he lived with his father in his ancestral home in Pico, which at different times during the war was occupied both by German forces and by Moroccan troops of the Free French Army. Landolfi married later in life, fathered two children, and devoted himself to literature. He divided the years after the war between Pico and Rome, where he died in 1979.

ANALYSIS

It is appropriate to begin with a psychological portrait of the man before proceeding to an analysis of the writer's principal themes and works. For one who made such a cult of privacy, Tommaso Landolfi proved remarkably confessional, revealing much of a complicated inner life, the details of which are far richer than the external events of his career. In this respect, the critic's task was made much easier with the publication in the 1950's and the 1960's of such autobiographical works as *La Bière du pecheur* (1953; the sinner's bier/coffin), *Rien va* (1963; no more), and *Des mois* (1968; months). These works are not strictly diaries; they are more like private jottings in which the writer reminisces but also attempts to define personal responses to crises in his own life and to clarify his position vis-à-vis all human experience. These volumes have their nineteenth century antecedents in Giacomo Leopardi's *Zibaldone* (1898-1900; notebooks) and Charles Baudelaire's *Mon cœur mis à nu* (1887; *My Heart Laid Bare*, 1950).

The following psychological patterns are quite visible in Landolfi's personality and in the fiction that they have nourished. The loss of his mother before his second birthday left scars on the psyche of the child and adolescent that were to stay with him the rest of his life, bestowing on him a profound sense of privation and an equally strong sense of guilt. To the child's trauma one can trace the origins of an ambivalence toward women, who, on the one hand, stirred in the writer erotic and even violent impulses, and, on the other, as repositories of a sacred motherhood suggested an ineffable purity accessible only through dream and memory. In the absence of the mother stood the father—in reality an affectionate if gruff man with a taste for solitude and a forthright antifascist. The fictional father figure loomed menacingly over vulnerable offspring, often in a gloomy manor in an abandoned corner of the provinces. The son may never have fully pardoned the father for sending his hypersensitive child to a private boarding school at the age of twelve: For the second time in his young life, Landolfi felt rejected, cast off and set afloat in a hostile universe. Thereafter the fiction bristled with the theme of Oedipal conflict and incestuous temptation. In the novella *La morte del re di Francia* (the death of the King of France, published in *Gogol's Wife and Other Stories*,) the father, So-and-So, broods over his daughter Rosalba's ripening adolescence and supervises her daily bath, while he is also the object of her erotic dream. In the fable *Racconto d'autunno* (1947; *An Autumn Story*, 1989), an old man keeps his daughter imprisoned in an isolated villa, where she serves as a high priestess to an almost necrophiliac cult of his dead wife. The Landolfian antihero is solitary and impotent in a much larger than sexual sense: His essential form of communication is the monologue, which he commits to the page of his diary. He is convinced of his own uselessness in an existence that he finds insufficient.

THE TWO OLD MAIDS

The Two Old Maids, published just after the war, offers few concessions to the fashion of contemporary realism. Both the setting and the style of this novella place it within the tradition of nineteenth century fiction, which Landolfi acknowledges, and from which he detaches himself in the second sentence. The reader can be thankful, he writes, that he (the author) would not dream of describing this house and district in every detail. His satire of a literature to which he remains devoted and of a way of life that he knows rather too intimately remains unerring. The district is "disheartening"; dust lies on the buildings and trees. In the apartment which the reader is invited to enter, the old maids Lilla and Nena sacrifice their lives to their seemingly indestructible mother, who dominates them to her dying day.

The hero of this tale is the monkey, the family pet, more or less domesticated and living, as all objects of love do (says Landolfi), in a large cage. The sisters have inherited him from their brother, a sea captain, who brought him back from one of his voyages; and they lavish on him an affection that is their memorial to the departed mariner. The monkey is the only male in the house, summing up in his diminutive frame the roles of father, brother, even husband, and certainly that of the children the barren sisters never bore. Like a child or lover, he likes to sleep in Lilla's lap and sometimes clutch her breasts when she lies down for a nap. The animal introduces a contrapuntal principle of virility and spontaneity into a shared existence predicated on a pious suppression of instinct.

The crisis comes when the monkey, Tombo, is accused by the Mother Superior of the convent next door of stealing the consecrated host and drinking the communion wine from the chapel. Nena vehemently denies these charges, but on closer inspection she learns that the ingenious Tombo can indeed unlock his cage, make his way over the wall into the convent garden, and pay a visit to the chapel. Following him, Nena hides herself in that sacred place together with a young nun and observes with her own eyes the sacrilegious trespass of the monkey. What she sees horrifies her far more than the accusations of stealing heard from the Mother Superior. Every gesture that the little creature makes—the way he wraps himself in the holy corporal as if it were a stole, the pouring of the wine into the chalice, the salutation to a nonexistent congregation—can spell only one thing: "Tombo was saying Mass!" For such desecration he is immediately condemned. Nena declares, "He must die."

If the tale is read simply as social satire, then the monkey's comic imitations of the gestures of the priest do not go beyond a parody of the mass and the devalued rituals of the Church. Tombo, however, is not the damnable heretic for which he is mistaken. In effect, his visits to the chapel are his way of following in his mistresses' footsteps, of identifying with their faith, of adoring their God as best he might. Tombo's gibbering and untidy imitation, had Nena the charity or piety to stop and reflect, is rather a reminder, or memory, of masses conducted under primitive conditions in the distant colonies under missionary supervision. Improvised and scruffy, garbled but sincere, it is the sort of thing Lilla and Nena's sea captain brother—and his pet monkey—might have witnessed many times in his travels. It is within this simple probability that much of the tale's irony, and tragedy, lie.

The demise of the monkey is finally consummated. Landolfi communicates the terror of an animal that knows no guilt but knows it is about to die, betrayed for having dared to love. Nena victoriously snuffs out a flickering life, and in her victory achieves a terrible irony. By his crucifixion she elevates the blasphemer Tombo to actual martyrdom. The last event in the sisters' life is over, and until their death all can return to normal, or, as Landolfi puts it, a gray dust can settle over everything once more.

CANCERQUEEN

Cancerqueen is linked thematically to Landolfi's previous fiction in that it explores the human search for freedom along with the foundering of that quest. It marks at the same time an anticipated development in his career and a point of crisis. It is in part an exercise in science fiction which suggests that the writer's imagination was finally working its way free of earthbound experience and needed to test itself against the dimensions of space. The tale is divided into two parts. The first recounts the author's meeting with a mad scientist who invites him on a voyage to the moon aboard his spaceship, christened *Cancerqueen*. This fantasy is told in chronological order in punctilious detail, as if it belonged to the tradition of narrative realism. Part 2 is a diary in which the protagonist, marooned alone in the spaceship, jots down his thoughts on his isolation, on life in general, on his fears and obsessions. Artistically this part marks a rupture with the first forty pages of the tale; it also provides an interesting indication of the diaristic direction of Landolfi's prose less than three years before the publication of *La Bière du pecheur*. This diary also indicates the growing inversion of Landolfi's point of view and his preference to write in the first person singular and to adopt the form of the monologue.

The protagonist is a failed writer forced to return to his native village and house as a result of gambling debts and disappointments in love. He receives a visit from an escapee from the local insane asylum, who tries to interest him in a bizarre story of his invention of a wonderful machine designed to fly them to the moon. Can there be any method in this madman? Is he the victim of the prejudice of rival professionals jealous of his superior genius? Is he the expression of human fears of science and fascination with the forces beyond human control—the fears that humanity's moral development has not kept pace with technological advance? Might this maniac not represent the gambler's instinct in Landolfi come to whisper in his ear that it is better to risk all for a flight through the cosmos than to accept stagnation and death in a moldering mansion without hope or a future?

The author is tempted, and the two men rush out of the house to embark on their "singular excursion" into the mountains in search of the treasured creation of Filano (the mysterious visitor and architect of *Cancerqueen*). The remarkable description of this journey by moonlight up steep slopes, across vertiginous peaks, and over dizzying chasms is another example of Landolfi's fascination with the wild nature of his native hills around Pico. They are built into the texture of many of his tales, and he invests them with a strange, gothic beauty, attractive and terrifying. The journey ends with a descent into a cave at the pit of which is the miraculous *Cancerqueen*, a creation of almost mythic dimension and faith more than of scientific calculation. She—and she must be granted her sex—is presented not as a triumph of physics but rather is anthropomorphized as an extension of the human imagination now poised to conquer space.

The human imagination, however, is impeded by human paranoia. Filano goes mad and, concluding that the voyage will be jeopardized by the extra weight of his companion, determines to jettison him. In the ensuing struggle it is Filano who is plunged into the void, with the protagonist facing space alone. Not quite alone, however, for the laws of physics decree that the ejected Filano cling eternally to the sides of his beloved craft, and he is transformed into an irremovable mute companion on a voyage without end.

"THE MUTE"

Characters in Landolfi's stories who resort to violence are obliged to live with the consequences of their acts. The child murderer in "La muta" ("The Mute") must await the arrival of his executioners. Kafka, imagined in "Il babbo di Kafka" (Kafka's father) as killing his father, who has assumed the form of a spider, can never be certain whether the spider he

killed really did contain his father's soul. In like manner, the protagonist of *Cancerqueen* must live forever with the image of Filano grimacing at him from space beyond the window. In seeking to liberate himself, the protagonist has turned himself into a prisoner. Would it not have been better to stay amid the ugly confusion of human society than to seek the rarefied purity of space? The final irony is that the writer has begun to write again, but there is no audience. No one will recover the manuscript. His works are like Filano's corpse, empty husks cast into space.

"GOGOL'S WIFE"

Passing from the eventual madness of the writer lost in space to that of another, unable to free himself from an obsession, the reader encounters similar concerns in Landolfi's best-known short story, "La moglie di Gogol" ("Gogol's Wife"). This story first appeared in the 1954 collection of short stories and autobiographical pieces entitled *Ombre* (shadows). The title and protagonist are a reminder of Landolfi's lifelong interest in the author of the 1842 novel *Dead Souls* (a study of Gogol is included in Landolfi's critical essays, in *Gogol a Roma*), to whom he was drawn for a narrative style that depended less on meticulous observation than on audacious leaps of the imagination. Undoubtedly, Landolfi was also interested in Gogol as an example of an unbalanced mind that descended into religious mania and a fatal melancholy that led to his early death. Like his Gogol, many of Landolfi's heroes fall victim to hallucinations and obsessions, and the author deals convincingly with acute states of psychological isolation, undoubtedly similar to his own.

The tale reads like a surrealistic joke conceived as an entertainment which ultimately reveals much more about its author than was originally intended. Gogol's wife is an inflatable rubber doll which can be blown up to the size and dimensions chosen by her spouse. She possesses a rudimentary spine and rib cage for rigidity. She is nude at all times, and the narrator, in the guise of an intimate of the great Nikolai, draws attention to the remarkable anatomical exactitude of her exposed genitalia. Yet what appears to be a perfect human replica is only an epidermis, with no inner organs, no mind, no character of her own.

What is the reader to make of this simulacrum of a wife? Since this Gogol is an invention of Landolfi, one is to assume that some of the observable fetishes and the transference of affection from people to objects belong to him. A doll is preferred to a proper wife out of the fear of a real woman's independence and judgment. The doll, naked and placid, with her changes of wigs, able to assume a variety of shapes according to the caprice of the inflater, is quite literally a sex object, ready at all times to satisfy the whims of the husband. The fact that she cannot answer back makes her always passive, subservient, and obedient. (The narrator, however, recalls one occasion when she does appear to talk, childishly expressing a desire to go to the lavatory, which throws Gogol into a fit of rage, causing him to deflate her for the evening.) The doll also brings out sadistic impulses in the male; indeed, she seems designed to be humiliated. To inflate her, a pump is inserted in her anus, and she is deflated by forcing one's hand down her throat to release a nozzle.

Subservient as she is, her master is convinced of a stubborn insubordination in her nature, a kind of passive resistance to his whims, perhaps even an unspoken mockery, which he interprets as a challenge to his authority. The wife-doll, Caracas, represents a taunting sexual presence to Gogol which his growing religious mania persuades him to eradicate from his life. She must suffer the same fate as the manuscript of the second part of *Dead Souls*, and in the final conflagration one sees a murderous assault on female sensuality, the world of the flesh and even art (in that Caracas is part muse and the inspirer of the literature of love). In addition, Gogol throws into the flames what appears to be a baby doll of the same material as Caracas, identified as her son. Once more, a father exerts a fearful, fatal authority over his offspring.

Landolfi's symbolism is rich and suggestive, never formulaic or precise. Caracas is a projection of a host of male fears of the female, of the ambiguous relations between the sexes. She offers both physical partnership and challenge to her companion, but the reader can never say with certainty that she equals one value or meaning rather than another. Furthermore, each reading of the tale will yield different levels of interpretation. The story goes well beyond a psychological portrait of Gogol. The fears of the eternal feminine, the impotence of the protagonist, the failure to establish a relationship with another, the sadism of the father—all are familiar themes in Landolfi's fiction. The reader is directed to "La beccaccia" (the woodcock), also in *Ombre*, which focuses on a hunter's cruelty toward an innocent creature following his disappointment in love.

The thematic links between these stories offer a guide to a complete reading of Landolfi's work. In different ways, they deal with aspects of freedom in psychological and aesthetic terms. Tombo introduces into the house of the old maids disturbing motifs of vitality and an alternative form of religious expression. His death is the price he must pay for their lives to remain unruffled. The association of space flight with artistic freedom is quite clear in *Cancerqueen*, but the dream runs into conflict with human limitations, leaving the artist-protagonist suspended in the void. Gogol may immolate his wife to free himself of a degrading dependence, but his creative will is not restored by that brutal expedient. The fate or crisis of the artist is a serious matter for Landolfi.

In *Cancerqueen*, he reveals the ultimate isolation of the writer, who passes with tragic inevitability from dialogue to monologue to silence. Two fellow writers whom he includes in his tales, Franz Kafka and Nikolai Gogol, are presented as being insane, suggesting that this condition accompanies that of the artist. Either one risks mental balance by choosing art as a way of life, or one must be part mad in order to write (or paint or compose). Either way, life in art amounts more to tyranny than to freedom. The caverns and labyrinthine mansions where many of Landolfi's dramas occur suggest that he is interested only in the hidden experience. What lies below the surface of life alone is worth writing about, revealing secret truths of which we are unaware, including destructive impulses that society has a right to control. Landolfi is by no means an aesthete who has chosen literature as a means of refining a style for the pleasure of a handful of insiders. He is a disturbing writer who reveals the cracks in the human façade.

OTHER MAJOR WORKS

LONG FICTION: *La pietra lunare*, 1937; *Racconto d'autunno*, 1947 (*An Autumn Story*, 1989); *Ottavio di Saint-Vincent*, 1958; *Un amore del nostro tempo*, 1965.

PLAYS: *Landolfo VI di Benevento*, pb. 1959; *Scene della vita di Cagliostro*, pb. 1963; *Faust '67*, pb. 1969.

POETRY: *Viola di morte*, 1972; *Il tradimento*, 1977.

NONFICTION: *Un paniere di chiocciole*, 1968; *Gogol a Roma*, 1971; *Del meno*, 1978.

MISCELLANEOUS: *La Bière du pecheur*, 1953; *Rien va*, 1963; *Des mois*, 1968.

BIBLIOGRAPHY

Brew, Claude. "The 'Caterpillar Nature' of Imaginative Experience: A Reading of Tommaso Landolfi's 'Wedding Night.'" *Modern Language Notes* 89 (1974): 110-115. Although focusing on one story, Brew's attentive analysis of narrative technique, cryptic imagery, and surreal action—especially as these apply to imagined rather than literal experience—illuminates many other stories by Landolfi.

Calvino, Italo. "Introduction: Precision and Chance." *Words in Commotion and Other Stories*. New York: Viking, 1986. Master fantasist and personal acquaintance of Landolfi, Calvino utilizes Landolfi's real-life obsession with gambling to identify and analyze his "rules" for the "game" (literature) between writer and reader. As described by Calvino, necessity, chance, uncertainty, and suffering are as significantly interwoven for Landolfi the man as they were for Landolfi the artist.

Cancogni, Annapaola. "Confronting Phantoms." *The New York Times*, November 30, 1986. A review of *Words in Commotion and Other Stories*. Claims that Landolfi's stories bring us face to face with the netherworld of phantoms and fears that we often repress in the name of reality. Asserts that he is an anomaly in Italian fiction with no clear literary ancestor or descendant.

Capek-Habekovic, Romana. *Tommaso Landolfi's Grotesque Images*. New York: Peter Lang, 1986. Landolfi's stories are analyzed through their grotesque imagery, which the author claims he uses to combat the toll of scientific logic and modern technology on humanity: too much perfection produces dehumanization. Excerpts in Italian; notes; thorough bibliography.

Elder, Richard. "An Author Whose Mind Is Elsewhere." *Los Angeles Times*, October 8, 1986. A review of *Words in Commotion and Other Stories*. Elder contends that the stories have a Poe-like sense of the grotesque, but that they are told with such an offhandedness that their effect is sabotaged; claims that Landolfi is an artist, but one who chooses deliberately to mar what he writes.

Rosenthal, Raymond. "A Note on Landolfi." In *Cancerqueen, and Other Stories*. New York: Dial Press, 1971. A short but lucid essay. Rosenthal emphasizes the creative effort both reader and author must exercise in confronting Landolfi's works. Paradox, ambiguity, and doubt are highlighted as primary aspects of the stories, both because of the experience of reading and because of Landolfi's own obsession with conflict and the reality of the spirit.

Weales, Gerald. "Fiction Chronicle." *The Hudson Review* 24, no. 4 (1971-1972): 716-730. Weales's very short review of *Cancerqueen* reveals an unanticipated disappointment: "What I find at work in Landolfi is a professional story-teller, one who uses the traditional materials—loss, death, cruelty—sometimes to explore humanity in its greatest pain, at others simply to play games with the reader."

Harry Lawton, updated by Terri Frongia

RING LARDNER

Born: Niles, Michigan; March 6, 1885
Died: East Hampton, New York; September 25, 1933

PRINCIPAL SHORT FICTION
Bib Ballads, 1915
Gullible's Travels, 1917
Treat 'Em Rough, 1918
The Real Dope, 1919
Own Your Own Home, 1919
How to Write Short Stories, 1924
The Love Nest and Other Stories, 1926
Round Up: The Stories of Ring Lardner, 1929
Lose with a Smile, 1933

OTHER LITERARY FORMS

Ring Lardner is known chiefly as a short-story writer, but in his own time was better known as a sportswriter, columnist, and humorist. He also wrote two novel-length works, *You Know Me Al* (1915) and *The Big Town* (1921), and he tried his hand at writing musical comedies, *June Moon* (1929; in collaboration with George S. Kaufman) being his only successful one. Most of Lardner's nonfictional prose remains uncollected, although a few works have appeared in book form, including an early piece about the return of the Chicago White Sox from a worldwide tour, a book of verse about successful business and professional men (*Regular Fellows I Have Met*, 1919), three humorous essays, "The Young Immigrunts," "Symptoms of Being Thirty-five," and "Say It with Oil," and a burlesque autobiography, *The Story of a Wonder Man* (1927).

ACHIEVEMENTS

Ring Lardner added significantly to a tradition dating back at least as far as Mark Twain's *The Adventures of Huckleberry Finn* (1884). Using first-person monologue (usually humorous, always steeped in colloquialisms, occasionally in the form of correspondence), Lardner allowed his characters to reveal themselves, warts and all. As such, the superficiality and insincerity of his narrators is starkly con-

trasted with the often harsh truths they unintentionally reveal. This allowed Lardner to illustrate some of the less edifying aspects of American society and human nature in general. He also captured the spoken language (and slang) of ordinary people, rendering it as an art form unto itself. Thus, in addition to their entertainment value, Lardner's stories provide a telling picture of American manners and morals during the first third or so of the twentieth century. Finally, Lardner was a pioneer in the fruitful marriage between the game of baseball and American letters, laying the foundation for later works by prominent authors such as Mark Harris (*Bang the Drum Slowly*, 1956), W. P. Kinsella (*Shoeless Joe*, 1982, filmed as *Field of Dreams*, 1989), Bernard Malamud (*The Natural*, 1952), and Philip Roth (*The Great American Novel*, 1973).

BIOGRAPHY

Ring Lardner was born into a wealthy, genteel family and educated at home by his mother and a tutor before he attended the public high school. After a brief stay at the Armour Institute in Chicago, where his father sent him to study mechanical engineering, he held a series of jobs with newspapers, chiefly as a sportswriter, which led him into writing fiction about ball players and athletes. He married Ellis Abbott in 1911; they had four sons. He died in 1933 of a heart attack.

ANALYSIS

The question that inevitably arises in any discussion of Ring Lardner's stories is: What is Lardner's attitude toward his characters and by extension toward the culture out of which they come? Is Lardner, in other words, a misanthrope who hated not only his own characters but also himself, or is he, rather, a disappointed idealist who found in the world of his immediate experience constant instances of cruelty, vulgarity, and insensitivity? Those who point to Lardner's sheltered upbringing and the apparently happy family life both of his early years and of his

Ring Lardner (Library of Congress)

later married life favor the latter view, while those who wish to find in his fiction some affirmation of the goodness of human beings prefer the former. Obviously, no final answer to the question is possible.

"CHAMPION"

If one reads an early story such as "Champion," one sees a heavy-handed author stacking the cards against his brutal hero, Midge Kelly. Midge beats his crippled brother to steal his half dollar and, when their mother objects, beats her too. Thereafter Midge's life is a succession of victories and brutalities: He becomes a prizefighter who wins fight after fight and, at the same time, does in those who have befriended him. Although his crippled brother is sick and unable to get out of bed and longs to have a letter from his famous brother, Midge refuses to write. When his wife and son are ill and destitute, he tears up a letter from his wife begging for help. He fires the manager who has helped make him a champion fighter and heaps money on a woman who is obviously using him, although he later casts her off, too, and then takes for himself the wife of his new manager. Through the obvious card-stacking one sees Lardner's intention. He hates brutality and he hates

the way brutality is not only ignored but also rewarded in our society. Midge Kelly is not a believable character; he is a symbol on which Lardner heaps all of the abuse he can muster. If it were not for the brutality, "Champion" would be a maudlin tearjerker.

The truth seems to be that, underneath the pose of the realist, observer, and reporter of American crudities, Ring Lardner was a sensitive, even a sentimental man. The monologue form exactly suited his need to keep the sentimentality out of sight while letting his crude, vulgar, insensitive types condemn themselves out of their own mouths, but it was also a way of allowing the victims of the bullies to engage the reader's sympathies without having to make them stereotyped victims: cripples who are beaten, mothers knocked down by their sons, abandoned wives and babies. Lardner's best stories present the reader with a story in which the real author has all but disappeared while his narrator tells his ironically revealing, self-condemning tale.

"HAIRCUT"

One of the best of Lardner's stories, "Haircut," is told by a barber who is giving a haircut to an unnamed stranger in a small Midwestern town. The hero of the barber's tale is Jim Kendall, a practical joker, whom the barber describes as "all right at heart" but whom the reader quickly sees as a man who enjoys inflicting pain on other human beings under the guise of being funny. To pay his wife back for getting his paycheck (he gives her no money to run the household), Kendall tells her to meet him with their children outside the tent of a visiting circus. Instead of joining her there with the tickets as he promised, he hides out in a saloon to savor the joke he is playing on his family. Meanwhile, a new doctor in the town, "Doc" Stair, appears on the scene, and feeling sorry for the mother with the crying children, buys the tickets for them. When Kendall hears how Doc Stair spoiled his fun, he gets furious and vows revenge. He tricks a young woman, Julie Gregg, who is "sweet on" Doc Stair, into coming into the doctor's office late at night. No one is there but Kendall and his friends hiding in the dark. When Julie calls out the doctor's first name, "Oh, Ralph," Kendall and his crowd leap out and mimic her. When she retreats, they chase her home. Another frequent victim of Kendall's jokes, a "cuckoo" named Paul who is fond of Julie and the doctor and who hears the doctor say that a man like Kendall ought not to be allowed to live, invites himself to go duck hunting with Kendall. Kendall gives Paul his gun to hold, the gun goes off, and Kendall is killed. Doc Stair, the coroner, rules the shooting accidental. Although in this story the chief villain is given his comeuppance, a subtler cruelty is revealed by the barber who says of Kendall that in letting a man like Paul hold his gun, he probably got what he deserved.

"GOLDEN HONEYMOON"

Another of Lardner's best stories, "Golden Honeymoon," is a gentler satire; indeed, critics have disagreed about whether this is the portrait of a happy marriage or a vicious attack on marriage in general. Doubtless the truth lies somewhere in between, for the old man who tells the story of his and his wife's trip to Florida on their golden honeymoon is a boring windbag. He is impressed with himself and his son, who is "high up in rotary"; with the commonplace, vulgar details of their trips to cafeterias, church socials, card games, and movies; and with their encounter with his wife's old beau. The main action of the story concerns the conflict that arises between the couple over the reappearance fifty years later of the suitor, who is married to a woman the narrator describes as a rotten cardplayer. Although he is not as brutal or despicable as other Lardner narrators, he has many of the same faults: insensitivity, vanity, pettiness, and even a little cruelty. When he wins a game of checkers, he gloats; when he loses at horseshoes, he pouts. When his wife hurts her back on the croquet court, he laughs at her, and when he is beaten at horseshoes, he quarrels with his wife and she quits speaking to him. The story ends "happily"—that is, the two make up and get "kind of spoony"—but the essential portrait remains that of a boring, vain, pompous old man.

"SOME LIKE THEM COLD"

"Some Like Them Cold" is a story told through the exchange of letters between a young woman named Mabelle Gillespie who allows herself to be picked up by a young man in the La Salle Street Sta-

tion in Chicago. Chas. F. Lewis (as he signs his letters) is on his way to New York to break into the songwriting business. He is a typical Lardner monologuist—vain, crude, and cruel—and Mabelle is the familiar Lardner victim—sensitive, trusting, and foolish. Her letters to Lewis play up her virtues as a "home body"; his become increasingly short, emphasizing how well he is getting on in the Big Town and offering accounts of women who chase him. After he announces his marriage to a woman whom he had earlier described as cold and indifferent to home life, he advises Mabelle not to speak to "strange men who you don't know nothing about as they may get you wrong and think you are trying to make them." "Some Like Them Cold" was later converted by Lardner into the successful musical comedy *June Moon*.

"EX PARTE"

A story technically subtler is "Ex Parte," told in the first person by a man attempting to justify his part in the breakup of his marriage. As he tells it, he and his wife were happy on their honeymoons but as soon as they moved into the house he had bought as a surprise for her (he had promised they would choose a house together), their marriage began to go bad. The trouble is that the house and furniture (picked out by a decorator) are too shiny and new-looking to suit his wife; she hates the house and admires the converted barn and early American furniture of her school friend. Even the nicks and burns on her friend's dining room table seem beautiful to her. So the narrator, after consuming a large quantity of "early American Rye," goes home and mutilates their table with a blow torch. His wife leaves him, and he is now trying to get his friends to take his side in the quarrel.

What is unusual about this story is that, instead of the typical opposition of bully and victim, there is rather a battle between two people equally insensitive and shallow: the husband who likes bright, shiny new things and the wife who likes antiques. For both, marriage is simply a matter of having the right things.

To call Ring Lardner either a misanthrope or a humorist, or even a realist who observed American manners, is to miss the point. Lardner was a moralist, like his friend F. Scott Fitzgerald, and, although at times he could be merely funny or sentimental or tiresome, his best stories are homilies, camouflaged by humor, on meanness, cruelty, and vanity. Lardner had a remarkable ear for a certain kind of native American speech, and he used that talent for giving his stories the ring of truth and passing on to succeeding generations a small but enduring collection of excellent short stories.

OTHER MAJOR WORKS

LONG FICTION: *You Know Me Al*, 1915; *The Big Town*, 1921.

PLAY: *June Moon*, pr. 1929 (with George S. Kaufman).

NONFICTION: *My Four Weeks in France*, 1918; *Regular Fellows I Have Met*, 1919; "The Young Immigrunts," 1920; "Symptoms of Being Thirty-five," 1921; "Say It with Oil," 1923; *What of It?*, 1925; *The Story of a Wonder Man*, 1927.

BIBLIOGRAPHY

Blythe, Hal, and Charlie Sweet. "Lardner's 'Haircut.'" *The Explicator* 55 (Summer, 1997): 219-221. Poses the question of why Whitey would tell his tale of homicide to a stranger; argues that Whitey feels guilty because he has been involved and thus, like the Ancient Mariner, stops strangers to tell his tale.

Bruccoli, Matthew J., and Richard Layman. *Ring Lardner: A Descriptive Bibliography*. Pittsburgh: University of Pittsburgh Press, 1976. This highly accessible and useful summary of Lardner's work provides a good starting point for getting a sense of Lardner's overall achievements, range, and productivity.

Cowlishaw, Brian T. "The Reader's Role in Ring Lardner's Rhetoric." *Studies in Short Fiction* 31 (Spring, 1994): 207-216. Argues that readers of Lardner's stories perceive a set of corrective lessons conveyed satirically by an implied author. Readers who accept the role of implied reader and thus align themselves with the implied author as perceptive and intelligent people accept these lessons and thus fulfill the basic purpose of satire, which is social correction.

Elder, Donald. *Ring Lardner*. Garden City, N.Y.: Doubleday, 1956. This early biography is helpful because it includes much firsthand testimony from those who knew Lardner throughout his career, including the very early days when his affection for baseball and overall philosophy of life were formed.

Friedrich, Otto. *Ring Lardner*. Minneapolis: University of Minnesota Press, 1965. An admirably concise work that discusses Lardner's command of different dialects. Puts the darker side of Lardner's psyche into the context of myths and misconceptions popular at the time he wrote. An expert on the historical period both in the United States and Europe, Friedrich provides a lucid and insightful introduction to Lardner's main themes and techniques.

Geismar, Maxwell. *Ring Lardner and the Portrait of Folly*. New York: Thomas Y. Crowell, 1972. Probably the most ambitious work of literary criticism devoted entirely to Lardner. Geismar draws a full blown critique of American materialism out of Lardner's work, arguing that Lardner's sarcasm and satire masked a deeply felt idealism.

Lardner, James. "Ring Lardner at 100—Facing a Legacy." *The New York Times Book Review* 90 (March 31, 1985): 3. James Lardner reflects on the life and work of his grandfather, Ring Lardner, and describes the Ring Lardner Centennial Conference held at Albion College in Michigan; discusses Lardner's satire, although he contends he gives his characters more depth than one usually associates with satire.

Lardner, Ring. *Letters of Ring Lardner*. Edited by Clifford M. Caruthers. Washington, D.C.: Orchises, 1995. Lardner's correspondence reveals biographical elements of his life.

Lardner, Ring, Jr. *The Lardners: My Family Remembered*. New York: Harper & Row, 1976. Lardner's third son, a successful screenwriter, provides a charming portrait of the Lardner family. As portrayed here, Ring Lardner, Sr., was humble and completely unpretentious about his work. He was also a good family man and had an interesting circle of friends, including F. Scott Fitzgerald.

Robinson, Douglas. *Ring Lardner and the Other.* New York: Oxford University Press, 1992. Examines Lardner's themes in his fiction. Includes bibliographical references and an index.

Yardley, Jonathan. *Ring.* New York: Random House, 1977. This well-written, thorough biography is especially good at drawing the very strong connec-tion between Lardner as journalist and Lardner as short-story writer. According to Yardley, the journalistic desire of unadorned facts that Lardner had to present leads logically to an unflinching examination of human nature and American society through the medium of fiction.

W. J. Stuckey, updated by Ira Smolensky

MARGARET LAURENCE

Born: Neepawa, Manitoba, Canada; July 18, 1926
Died: Lakefield, Ontario, Canada; January 5, 1987

PRINCIPAL SHORT FICTION

The Tomorrow-Tamer, 1963
A Bird in the House, 1970

OTHER LITERARY FORMS

Margaret Laurence's best-known books are the series of four novels and the short-story collection that have been called the Manawaka works, named after the fictional town in central Canada from which all the major characters originate. The series consists of *The Stone Angel* (1964), *A Jest of God* (1966), which was made into the motion picture *Rachel, Rachel* in 1968, *The Fire-Dwellers* (1969), *A Bird in the House*, and *The Diviners* (1974). Although this is not a series in the sense of sequels, the characters are related through their birthplace and memories, as well as some by birth, as in William Faulkner's imaginary Yoknapatawpha County.

Laurence also translated Somali folktales and poetry, published as *A Tree for Poverty: Somali Poetry and Prose* in 1954, the first collection of Somali literature ever published in English. The novel *This Side Jordan* (1960) tells the story of Ghanna's emergence as a nation. *New Wind in a Dry Land* (1964) is an account of Laurence's first two years in Somaliland, describing both her experiences and the life of Somali nomads; it was also published under the title *The Prophet's Camel Bell*. In the field of literary criti-cism, Laurence wrote *Long Drums and Cannons: Nigerian Dramatists and Novelists, 1952-1966* (1968), a study of Nigerian novelists and dramatists writing in English. She also wrote four novels for children.

ACHIEVEMENTS

Margaret Laurence is not only a great Canadian writer but also a universal voice for understanding, independence, and brave experimentation with life. Her African work helps to point up the evils of colonization, whether of a country, a people, or an individual. Her Manawaka series more specifically looks at the oppression of women by societal expectations that are irrational and sexist and that result also in the lessening of individual men.

In 1967, Laurence became an Honorary Fellow of United College, University of Winnipeg; she was the first woman and the youngest person to be honored in this way. The novel *This Side Jordan* won for her Canada's Beta Sigma Phi Award, a prize for the best first novel by a Canadian, in 1960. In 1971, Laurence was made a Companion of the Order of Canada; in the following years, she was awarded seven honorary degrees. Her novel *The Diviners* won the Governor General's Medal for Fiction in 1974 and the Molson Prize. She received the Woman of the Year Award from B'nai B'rith Toronto Women's Branch in 1976 and won the Periodical Distributor's Award for the mass paperback edition of *A Jest of God* in October of 1977.

BIOGRAPHY

Jean Margaret Wemyss was born on July 18, 1926, in Neepawa, Manitoba, Canada. She began writing at the age of eight, and at age thirteen she sent a story to a *Winnipeg Free Press* competition; in that story, she first used the name Manawaka for a town similar to her native Neepawa. She contributed stories to her school magazines and later to the university magazine when she attended United College in Winnipeg. She completed a B.A. in honors English from that institution in 1947 and went to work as a reporter on the *Winnipeg Citizen*. She married Jack Laurence, an engineer, and moved with him to England in 1949. In 1950, her husband was offered a job in Somaliland to build dams in the desert, and so the Laurences moved to Africa, a place that would have a strong effect on Margaret Laurence's writing career. It was there that she began to write seriously.

In 1952, the couple moved to Ghana, where Jocelyn was born. Laurence had been translating Somali folktales and poetry, which were published as *A Tree for Poverty: Somali Poetry and Prose* by the Somali government in 1954. That same year, the Laurences' son David was born. In 1957, the family returned to Vancouver, Canada.

In 1960, her novel *This Side Jordan* was published simultaneously in Canada, England, and the United States. Two years later, she separated from Jack Laurence and moved with her children to Buckinghamshire, England. There, she published her first collection of short stories, *The Tomorrow-Tamer*, begun while she was in Africa and based on her experience of that continent. It was while she was in Great Britain that she began to write her Canadian or Manawaka books, the group of five great works centered on the prairies. The first book in this series, *The Stone Angel*, established her as a leading Canadian novelist.

Beginning in 1970, Laurence wrote for *The Vancouver Sun* and, in 1971, for *Maclean's* magazine. In 1973, she moved back permanently to Canada, where she was writer-in-residence at the University of Western Ontario. In 1974, she was writer-in-residence at Trent University and published *The Diviners*, her last adult novel and the final in the Manawaka cycle. In

Margaret Laurence (John Reeves Photographer)

1976, she published *Heart of a Stranger*, a collection of essays.

For the last twelve years of her life, Laurence wrote no more novels but focused on children's stories and an autobiography, which was incomplete at the time of her death, on January 5, 1987, in Lakefield, Ontario.

ANALYSIS

Margaret Laurence's short stories are collected in two volumes, which display the two major places of her concern: *The Tomorrow-Tamer* is set in Africa and explores the effect of imperialism and colonialism on the people there, while *A Bird in the House* is a part of the Manawaka cycle, telling the story of a young Canadian girl and her family in a series of interconnected stories. Both collections, however, display Laurence's ongoing concerns with the dignity of the individual; the effects of societal events on families; the politics of dominance; the themes of death, freedom, and independence; and racial, social, and gender inequities. The collections also display her skillful control of narrative voice, her ability to render the dialects of English-speaking people from a broad range of places and ages, her imaginative use of metaphor, and her delight in wordplay.

THE TOMORROW-TAMER

The Tomorrow-Tamer was written out of Laurence's experience of living in Ghana just before it gained its independence from the British, and the major themes are the pains of imperialism and the problems of independence. These are explored in stories that alternate between the tragic or ironic and the comic. While she worked on these stories, she read *Psychologie de la colonization* (1950; *Prospero and Caliban: The Psychology of Colonization*, 1956) by Dominique O. Mannoni, a French ethnographer, and later acknowledged his work as the only theoretical influence on her fiction.

Some of the stories in this collection would seem to have their roots in the oral tradition of the Somali works that Laurence had recently translated for her book *A Tree for Poverty*. For example, the title story, "The Tomorrow-Tamer," focuses on a young man, Kofi, who has grown up in a traditional village setting, made a traditional marriage, and expects to live as his ancestors did. The government, however, has brought in a crew to build a bridge over the Owura River, seen as a god by Kofi's people, and he is chosen by the village to be the first to work on it. In the process, he transposes his loyalties from his ancestral gods to those of the bridgemen, among whom he wishes to be counted. He knows, however, how to give of himself only as he has been taught, so that when the ironically named Emmanual, a bridgeman who travels from place to place living only for the earning of money and the spending of it, asks him what he will do next, he decides that he will be the priest of the bridge. Indeed he becomes so, as, in a moment of transcendence, he gazes at the sun while painting the peak of the bridge and as a result falls into the water. The village people see his drowning as a sacrifice from the bridge to the river. What gives the story a talelike, oral feel is that the death of Kofi becomes a legend in the village, and even his bereaved father is proud, for "a man consumed by the gods lives forever." This thought leaves the reader with a feeling of completion, despite the tragic nature of the story.

Another story in a similar vein is "The Voices of Adamo," which is also a tale of the inability of disparate cultures to communicate, despite good intentions. In it, Adamo is an almost epic heroic character who loses his whole village in an epidemic yet manages to survive incredible odds in the jungle, only to end up in a British regimental band as a drummer. He is taken on by Captain Fossey, the bandmaster, and he transposes his tribal loyalties to the captain. As independence nears, however, the captain, totally unable to read Adamo in any way but in terms of his own British culture, tries to find Adamo a better place in the world, while Adamo, who has very little grasp of English, thinks that Fossey is trying to dismiss him. All he can sense is that he is being sent off, another loss, like the loss of his village, his family, his place in the scheme of things, and so in despair, he kills Fossey. This is the only peace that he can obtain, the knowledge that he will be allowed to stay in his new home until he dies, which unfortunately will be very soon under the end of British rule.

In contrast to the tragic sense of the imperialistic contribution to the African continent is the story "The Perfume Sea," which tells the tale of two people without a home, Archipelago and Doree, who run a beauty salon for European women. With the coming of independence, their livelihood is destroyed: Not only are they penniless, but also they have no resources to fall back on, like strangers in a strange land. Both misfits—one small and round (the Italian man, Archipelago), the other tall and gawky (the woman from no one knows where, Doree)—they face a bleak future until, in a moment of epiphany, they realize that there is a whole new market out there, that of African women who desire to look like city women. Their new shop begins to prosper only after Mercy, the daughter of their African landlord, tries their services and is immensely satisfied; thus they are saved, as Archipelago says, by an act of Mercy, one of the delightful puns in which Laurence occasionally indulges herself.

All the stories in this collection deal with outsiders, either native Africans who have been dispossessed by Europeans, Europeans who have settled in Africa but are forced by the independence movement to recognize that they do not belong, or colonizers who believe that they are in the right but have never been a part of the real life of the country. Archipelago and Doree are unusual outsiders, touching in their delicate affection for each other, unacceptable to the European community because they are service class and have possibly shady backgrounds but viewed by the Africans as a part of the European community. It is only when they are completely down on their luck that the African community accepts them. A number of the other stories in the collection display more typical colonial types, although never in the form of stereotype.

In "The Drummer of All the World," Matthew, the son of a missionary, grows up playing with an African child, nursed by an African woman. His Africa is exotic, warm, and exciting, but when he returns after schooling in England, he learns that his Africa has disappeared. Although he regrets this, he realizes that he never saw the disease (and dis-ease) below the surface of his experience. Matthew is a typical European in love with an unreal image of an African world, but at the same time he is more in touch with the reality of that world than his father, an iconoclast in a nearly literal sense, since he destroys the fetishes of the people. Matthew thinks, "Moses broke the idols of his own people."

A BIRD IN THE HOUSE

In contrast, *A Bird in the House* is peopled by characters who grew up in the fictional small town of Manawaka, Manitoba, Canada. Unlike the African stories, in which Laurence employs either the first-person or the third-person voice, these Canadian stories are all told in the first person by a single narrator, Vanessa, whose voice is a true accomplishment; although she ranges in age from a very young child to a young adult, the voice simultaneously presents the experience appropriate to her age with insights of the adult mind. Also, as Vanessa is preparing herself to be a writer, she sees things from a writer's vantage point, even though she is also involved. She is also constantly gathering material, which means that she listens closely to, even eavesdrops on, adult conversations, thus allowing her to know more of what is happening in her world than many first-person narrators

would, particularly a child. Laurence has admitted that *A Bird in the House* is the most autobiographical of her works.

Vanessa's world is a restricted one, hemmed in by the power of adults, particularly her maternal grandfather, who is a patriarch of the most oppressive sort, and by the breakdown of society, which results in wars (both World Wars I and II touch Vanessa's life) and depression. She escapes this world by writing stories of the most lurid, romantic, and impossible sort; at least, she does this as a youngster, but exposure to the reality of the world around her gradually forms a more mature approach to life.

The title story, "A Bird in the House," like many of the stories in the collection, centers on the theme of death. Vanessa's father dies of pneumonia, and the young girl loses her faith, thus feeling more isolated from her community. Another story, "The Mask of the Bear," depicts the loss of her grandmother and her anger and anguish over her grandfather's implacable patriarchal coldness and selfishness. Both of these stories have epilogues in which a more mature Vanessa recognizes the disappointments and humanity of these men in her life, and how they too were trapped by their societies.

Margaret Laurence is a major world author whose compassionate understanding of what forms the individual character and the character of nations, combined with her ability to render this knowledge in clear, distinctive prose so that all who read her will feel the same (at least while reading), has added to the wealth of the global reading community.

OTHER MAJOR WORKS

LONG FICTION: *This Side Jordan*, 1960; *The Stone Angel*, 1964; *A Jest of God*, 1966; *The Fire-Dwellers*, 1969; *The Diviners*, 1974.

NONFICTION: *The Prophet's Camel Bell*, 1963 (published in the United States as *New Wind in a Dry Land*, 1964); *Long Drums and Cannons: Nigerian Dramatists and Novelists, 1952-1966*, 1968; *Heart of a Stranger*, 1976.

CHILDREN'S LITERATURE: *Jason's Quest*, 1970; *Six Darn Cows*, 1979; *The Olden Days Coat*, 1979; *The Christmas Birthday Story*, 1980.

EDITED TEXT: *A Tree for Poverty: Somali Poetry and Prose*, 1954.

BIBLIOGRAPHY

Buss, Helen M. *Mother and Daughter Relationships in the Manawaka Works of Margaret Laurence.* Victoria, B.C.: University of Victoria, 1985. A Jungian reading of the four Manawaka novels and *A Bird in the House*, this book raises some interesting issues about the mother-daughter relationships that Laurence depicts, although at times the archetypal readings can be somewhat dense. Includes a select bibliography of criticism on Laurence and some later feminist criticism that informs the critic's work.

Hind-Smith, Joan. *Three Voices: The Lives of Margaret Laurence, Gabrielle Roy, Frederick Philip Grove.* Toronto: Clarke, Irwin, 1975. Designed for students and the general reader, this volume is very helpful as an introduction to Laurence's work. It includes biographical information, at the same time providing narrative summaries of the major works.

Irvine, Lorna M. *Critical Spaces: Margaret Laurence and Janet Frame.* Columbia, S.C.: Camden House, 1995. Irvine provides chapters on early review and critiques, maturing opinions, biographical and critical studies, and the role of politics, gender, and literary study. Includes a detailed bibliography.

Morley, Patricia. *Margaret Laurence.* Boston: Twayne, 1981. An extremely helpful and complete study of Laurence's work, which the author approaches by first arguing that Laurence, despite the fact that her work tends to focus on two very disparate places, Africa and Canada, has shown a consistent development of ideas and themes. She then looks at the African works, followed by the Manawaka cycle. Includes a complete chronology up to 1980, biographical information, an index, and an annotated select bibliography. A useful reference tool.

New, William, ed. *Margaret Laurence: The Writer and Her Critics.* Toronto: McGraw-Hill, 1977. This volume is an anthology of criticism on Laurence and interviews with her. Contains an informative introduction by the editor and, most important, three central essays by Laurence herself, which are invaluable aids to the understanding of her fiction.

Nicholson, Colin, ed. *Critical Approaches to the Fiction of Margaret Laurence.* Vancouver: University of British Columbia Press, 1990. An excellent collection of critical essays on Laurence, most written specifically for this book. They cover such topics as Laurence's place in the Canadian tradition in fiction, her work on Africa, close readings of specific works, comparison with Tillie Olsen and Jack Hodgins, and the use of autobiography in her writing. Includes a helpful preface and an index.

Riegel, Christian, ed. *The Writing of Margaret Laurence: Challenging Territory.* Edmonton: University of Alberta Press, 1997. Essays on Laurence's African stories, the novels, and Laurence's Scots Presbyterian heritage and other early influences. Includes a bibliography.

Thomas, Clara. *The Manawaka World of Margaret Laurence.* Toronto: McClelland and Stewart, 1976. A close reading of the works in the Manawaka cycle combined with an argument that although Laurence's characters talk Canadian, Laurence cannot be restricted to the category of Canadian or prairie writer, as her concerns, experiences, and philosophy are far from limited to one nation, or even one continent. Supplemented by a complete bibliographic checklist.

Woodcock, George. *Introducing Margaret Laurence's "The Stone Angel": A Reader's Guide.* Toronto: ECW Press, 1989. A close reading of the novel *The Stone Angel*, the first of the Manawaka series. Examines the novel's plots, characters, themes, origins, comparisons, and critical reception, as well as Laurence's work as a whole. Includes a useful chronology of Laurence's life, a brief biography, and an index.

Mary LeDonne Cassidy

MARY LAVIN

Born: East Walpole, Massachusetts; June 11, 1912
Died: Dublin, Ireland; March 25, 1996

PRINCIPAL SHORT FICTION

Tales from Bective Bridge, 1942
The Long Ago and Other Stories, 1944
The Becker Wives and Other Stories, 1946
At Sallygap and Other Stories, 1947
A Single Lady and Other Stories, 1951
The Patriot Son and Other Stories, 1956
Selected Stories, 1959
The Great Wave and Other Stories, 1961
The Stories of Mary Lavin, 1964-1985 (3 volumes)
In the Middle of the Fields and Other Stories, 1967
Happiness and Other Stories, 1969
Collected Stories, 1971
A Memory and Other Stories, 1972
The Shrine and Other Stories, 1977
A Family Likeness and Other Stories, 1985
In a Café, 1995

OTHER LITERARY FORMS

Mary Lavin's novel *Gabriel Galloway* was serialized in *The Atlantic Monthly* in 1944 and was later published as a book under another title, *The House in Clewe Street* (1945). *The House in Clewe Street* and the novel *Mary O'Grady* (1950, 1986) are a loosely connected series of episodes in family life, structured to dramatize the lives of family members over several generations. Without an overall unity, the novels lack direction and force; there are, however, numerous examples within the novels of the social mores and restrictive attitudes more artfully handled in the short stories. Lavin's fine children's stories, *A Likely Story* (1957) and *The Second-Best Children in the World* (1972), capture the imaginative life of children.

ACHIEVEMENTS

As a major Irish writer, Mary Lavin is a realist in the tradition of Frank O'Connor and Seán O'Faoláin. The resemblance to those important Irish writers, however, stops there. Her characters are usually sol-

idly middle class, and they tend to be shopkeepers and clerks, a population that is, perhaps, less "submerged" than that of O'Connor's fiction. For Lavin, social class is a determining factor in a character's behavior and fate. She stresses the limitations imposed by a character's social role. In addition, she does not use humor as a major fictional device. Instead of humor, there is often an ironic twist to the plot. Lavin's plots also tend to avoid the simple solution provided by techniques such as reversal and recognition. Instead, she closely examines the problems that her characters encounter. If there is a resolution, it is by no means a simple one.

Lavin is the recipient of numerous awards and honors, including the James Tait Black Memorial Prize in 1944, the Katherine Mansfield-Menton Prize in 1962, the Ella Lynam Cabot Fellowship in 1971, the Gregory Medal in 1974, and the American Irish Foundation Award in 1979. Lavin was president of the Irish Academy of Letters from 1971 to 1973, and she received the American Irish Foundation award in 1979.

Lavin was honored at the Kells Heritage Festival in County Meath in 1993, when a Irish television documentary about her life and work, *An Arrow in Flight*, was screened. Also in 1993, Aosdana, the Irish body that honors writers, musicians, and visual artists, granted her its highest distinction by electing her to the rank of Saoi, "in recognition of creative work which has made an outstanding contribution to the arts in Ireland." The Irish President at the time, Mary Robison, praised Lavin's ability to "catch the tones of the Irish family and the tensions therein."

BIOGRAPHY

Born in East Walpole, Massachusetts, on June 11, 1912, and the only child of Irish-born Nora Mahon and Tom Lavin, Mary Lavin emigrated to Ireland in her ninth year. Educated at Loreto Convent in Dublin and University College, Dublin, she wrote her M.A. thesis on Jane Austen; she then taught French at Loreto Convent for two years while preparing her unfinished Ph.D. thesis on Virginia Woolf. In 1942, she married William Walsh, and they had three daughters: Valentine, Elizabeth, and Caroline. After the death of her husband in 1954, Lavin had little time to write fiction since she had to bring up her children and run the farm at Bective. A John Simon Guggenheim Memorial Foundation Fellowship in 1959, however, and another in 1962, gave her the time and confidence to create fiction once more. She published a number of stories that were then collected in *The Great Wave and Other Stories*. Thereafter, the years became serene and productive. Lavin received a number of awards and prizes, including a third Guggenheim Fellowship, in 1972, and a D.Litt. from the National University of Ireland in 1968. In 1969, she married an old friend from her university days, Michael MacDonald Scott, a laicized Jesuit.

Lavin, who had been living in a nursing home in Blackrock, a southern suburb of Dublin, died March 24, 1996, at the age of eighty-three. She was praised by both the president of Ireland, Mary Robison, and the Taoiseach, John Bruton, who said her life was characterized by the ability to "make the ordinary extraordinary." She was eulogized in Irish and English newspapers by many of the most famous Irish critics and authors, such as William Trevor, Clare Boylan, W. J. McCormack, and Maurice Harmon. Publication of the first full-length biography of Lavin was stalled in May, 1998, because one of her daughters was unhappy with her portrayal in the book.

ANALYSIS

Neither national nor international events find their way into Mary Lavin's fiction, which is crammed with incidents from the lives of Dublin shopkeepers, country people, island fishermen and their families, nuns, priests, her parents, her children, and her husbands. Lavin's characters, much more important than the plots, which are rather mundane, are usually autobiographical. They represent the author and her acquaintances at various stages in her lifetime: childhood, student life, marriage, motherhood, and widowhood.

Whereas James Joyce was haunted by a father-son conflict, Lavin was plagued by a mother-daughter conflict, resulting in what might be called an Electra complex. It partially accounts for the frequent revelations of unhappy marriages between mismatched couples although the differences were a source of attraction before the birth of children or the assumption of responsibilities. More often than not, the wife characters are domineering, unhappy, practical slaves to social mores. Some other women characters—nuns, spinsters, sisters, and widows—are vain, flighty, insecure, and emotionally labile. Husband characters, in contrast, no matter how beaten they are by their wives and circumstances, have a certain poetic vision, while the priests, bachelors, brothers, and widowers appear robust, in command of life and their emotions.

"MISS HOLLAND"

"Miss Holland," Lavin's first short story, published in *Dublin Magazine* and reprinted in *Tales from Bective Bridge*, is the story of a typical spinster. Agnes Holland, lonely and ill prepared to face life, traveled for years with her father, who made all the decisions. At his death, Agnes must adjust to the world without anyone to help her. The story, set in England, begins with Agnes searching for a place to live; she finally decides to live at the guest house of Mrs. Lewis because of a playful cat.

Also living there are two men and three women with whom Agnes has nothing in common. She is not a conversationalist and cannot join in the spirited exchanges held during dining hours. Since the other boarders are younger, age is a further obstacle. Agnes feels trapped by her surroundings; there is nothing from the past that she can recollect which will bridge the gap between her and the boorish boarders. Agnes thinks she must try to enter this strange world and wants to discover something to share with the group, needing to be part of her environment.

The black cat affords the opportunity. Agnes sees him jumping in the sun after running through the flower bed where he plucked one red carnation; the image is like that of a Spanish dancer, and she can hardly wait to tell the group. At dinner she and a male guest begin to speak simultaneously, so Agnes waits to let him tell his story. To her horror, she learns that he has shot the cat. Amused, the other guests begin to laugh. Agnes is silent, withdrawing from the boisterous group; no longer can she associate with such people. Having no place else to go because she must live on the small amount of money left to her by her father, she determines to live on past memories of more genteel days. All the ugly characteristics of the uncultured men and women rush to her mind, separating her from them. Loneliness will become a fixed part of life, borne with dignity. Agnes's emotional drama is the conflict of the story. Forever opposed to vulgarity, Agnes realizes she can no longer use her imagination to disguise poor taste and must protest "because my people before me went that way."

"AT SALLYGAP"

Annie Ryan in "At Sallygap" and Ella in "A Happy Death" are typical examples of the wife characters who pressure their husbands. Childless, Annie is a real terror. Artistic Manny Ryan, a fiddler who years earlier was heading to Paris with a band, jumped ship for Annie. He thought she was loving, fragile, and in need of him. Their marriage, however, symbolizes the paralysis and stagnation of Irish urban life. After years of labor, they have nothing more tangible than a tiny Dublin shop where they work and live. Manny knows that "All the Dublin people were good for was talking." Annie was no exception. Her tongue lashes out at Manny usually because he is not aggressive enough in commercial dealings. Annie dominates him while wishing he would be the dominant spouse. Manny's gentility, unfortunately, serves as a red flag for Annie's temper.

By ordering him to go to Sallygap to set up a trade in fresh eggs, Annie gives him a brief escape from his hateful marriage. A lover of nature, Manny draws strength from the rural scenes. On missing the last bus, he walks home, free "at last from the sordidness of the life he led." While Manny feels elated, however, Annie, accustomed to her husband's regularity, goes through a variety of emotions awaiting his return. First, she plans to taunt him. Then thinking he is out drinking to get the courage to fight back, she relishes that prospect and prepares herself for a grand battle. Next, fear overcomes her: Perhaps Manny is dead. No, he would be brought home alive with a "latent mutinous instinct" activated, which she hopes will enliven their relationship. On hearing his foot-

step, however, Annie realizes nothing has changed. Manny is sober and servile, "imprisoned forever in her hatred."

"A HAPPY DEATH"

In "A Happy Death," Ella, with three daughters to rear, has to control her emotions in dealing with her dying husband Robert. To supplement their income, Ella rents rooms in their home, using some of the money to buy clothes for Robert so he can get a better job at the library. Outraged when he is demoted from clerk to porter because of his coughing, she demands that he quit, but he refuses and works as a porter. Ella cannot comprehend Robert's need to work and bring her his wages, so she convinces herself that he works to spite her and lower the family's social class. The emotional charges between Ella and Robert build up until his death and explode in Ella afterward.

Through a series of flashbacks, a device Lavin uses in most of her stories, the reader learns of Ella's happy courtship with Robert, her admiration of his white skin and his interest in poetry, and their elopement against her parents' wishes. Their happiness is fleeting. After they are married, she burns his poetry books, sees his white skin as a sign of weakness, and understands why her shopkeeping parents opposed her marriage to unemployed Robert. When Robert is hospitalized, with a flush of excitement, Ella insists on keeping up appearances. He must have the best ambulance, a private ward, a new nightshirt, and oranges which he cannot eat.

The daughters are embarrassed by their mother's vain fussing over Robert; it is unnatural to send out for grapes, apples, and newspapers when they know he can neither eat not read. Ella, however, wants everyone to know Robert is a person of importance with people who care for him. More fruit, biscuits, and sweets are brought to him, making it difficult for the nurses to find space for the thermometer.

Eventually, Ella realizes that the unconscious Robert is dying and prays for his happy death; meanwhile, her prayers and behavior at the bedside are a continued source of distress to her daughters. Thrusting a crucifix in Robert's face, Ella tries to get him to say an act of contrition; he does not. Then he regains his senses long enough to call out for Ella with the lovely golden hair. Misunderstanding her request for him to repeat "I am heartily sorry," Robert thinks she is sorry for having offended him and says, "There's nothing to be sorry about. You always made me happy, just by being near me." Robert's delirious mind recollects their youth and plans for "just the two of them," ignoring the daughters, and a look of "rapturous happiness" returns to his face before he dies. Bewildered, Ella refuses comfort from the priest, nurse, and her daughters. Screaming and sobbing, she is led from the ward, disbelieving God's refusal to answer her prayers for Robert's happy death. Ironically, she does not know that her prayers have been answered.

"SAY COULD THAT LAD BE I"

The young boy in "Say Could That Lad Be I," an early story in the first collection, *Tales from Bective Bridge*, and Tom in "Tom" from the collection *The Shrine and Other Stories*, are portraits of Lavin's father. The farm boy, mischievous and carefree, has a dog, White Prince, the greatest fighter in the countryside. On a visit to his grandmother, the boy takes along White Prince. It is a great mistake to lock him in the cottage when he goes on an errand for his grandmother, since the dog jumps through a closed window and follows his master to the village. After a disturbance in a shop, White Prince flies through its window, causing even greater destruction. Pretending that it is not his dog, the boy walks back to his grandmother. On the road, White Prince, dragging a leg of mutton in his mouth, joins his master. There is not much the lad can do but wash the mutton, present it to his grandmother, and head home before the townspeople pounce on him.

"TOM"

In "Tom," Lavin opens the story by saying, "My father's hair was black as the Devil's, and he flew into black, black rages." Everything about him was black except for "the gold spikes of love with which he pierced me to the heart when I was a child." The author leaves little doubt about the affection she held for her father. In this story she recounts with pride his exploits at school, his walks under a sky filled with birds, his travels to Dublin, Liverpool, Scotland, and America, plus his return to Ireland.

Her portrait of her mother is quite different. Lavin states with disinterest that her mother had numerous memories filling her head, but they could all be reduced to her mother at the piano with her singing sisters and their beaux about her. Her courtship with Tom was more ardent on his part than hers. Yet she, at thirty years old, realized she had snared a desirable fifty-year-old bachelor even though she disliked him at first because of his coarseness, ignorance, and arrogance. Lavin surmises her mother would have preferred her Protestant suitor, Mr. Barrett, a land agent on a large estate. Because of the age difference, Nora lived twenty-four years after Tom's death; Lavin agrees it was an unfair relationship. Her father had her "mother's beauty when he could proudly display it but she did not have his support when she needed it most."

Mary, in contrast, had Tom's support when she needed it. While at the university, he took her to Roscommon, revisiting his boyhood haunts and sharing his memories. Ignoring the material changes, he points out the unchanging mounds, stone walls, and streams running over mossy stones. Although he recognizes old friends, very aged and worn, they do not recognize him. A childhood friend, Rose Magarry, on seeing him says he is Tom's son, "Sure, you're the dead spit of him!" Silently, they leave without correcting the woman.

"SENILITY"

Tom does not follow the same rules that Nora does, and Mary accepts his lifestyle without complaint. If he was ever a burden to her, it does not appear in her fiction. Incidentally, the old mother in "Senility" from the same collection is an exquisite portrait of a widowed woman who lives with her daughter. The emotional tension between them is acute, and neither mother nor daughter will release it. The son-in-law acts as a referee in a continuing war of nerves.

When not writing about her family, Lavin presents other people's problems. Always busy with her own difficulties as the correspondence with Lord and Lady Dunsany reveals, she records some fresh insights about psychotic behavior in a tightly structured society. In writing about insanity, she is more comprehensive in *Mary O'Grady*, her second novel, with a description of Patrick's withdrawal from his family and its effect on the members, but the short stories also document the exploits of schizophrenic people, giving the impression that such people are an integral part of Irish society.

"ETERNA"

Eterna, the nun in "Eterna," is an excellent example of a woman who cannot face life. A young doctor called to treat the novice Eterna finds her arrogant despite an outward appearance of humility. He discovers that her infected arm was caused by turpentine soaking through the bandage over a cut which she received by falling off a ladder. Eterna, he learns, is an artist. As the eldest of ten from a poor family, she was educated by the nuns because of her talent and joined the order to continue her work; she could not remain with her impoverished family, and the doctor learns that in time she could not remain with the order.

Years after his calls at the convent in a provincial town, he sees Eterna again at the national Gallery in Dublin. She has a crazed look, wears outlandish clothes, and fixes her daft gaze on him. It brings back his memories of her former life and his brief, questioning visits with her. He flees from the gallery and rushes to his car to await his wife. She, who also knew Eterna, is nonchalant about his encounter with the artist, saying, "If she'd gone a bit cracked, what about it . . . she was probably headed that way from the start." She then tells her husband that people have to clip their wings in order to keep their feet on the ground.

The many widows in Lavin's fiction have their feet on the ground, representing their author after the death of her first husband. Mary and Maudie from "In a Café," Brede from "Bridal Sheets," the unnamed widow from "In the Middle of the Fields," and Vera Traska from "The Cuckoo-Spit," "Happiness," "Trastevere," and "Villa Violella" trace Lavin's battle against loneliness and her eventual adjustment to another self and remarriage. Vera in "Happiness" is a central widow character. Her story is told in the first person by her eldest daughter, an unusual technique for Lavin, who generally uses the omniscient third-person point of view. Kate, the eldest daughter in

"The Will," the novice in "My Vocation," the neighbor-narrator in "The Small Bequest," the niece-narrator in "A Wet Day," the daughter in "The Mouse," and the husband in "My Molly" are other exceptions to the omniscient viewpoint.

"HAPPINESS"

The daughter in "Happiness" describes Vera's thoughts about happiness and how it must not be confused with pleasure or perceived as the opposite of sorrow. The narrator then introduces her younger sisters, Bea and Linda (the latter was only a year old at their father's death), Father Hugh (Michael Scott), a family friend filling the place of the lost father, and Grandmother, who "God Almighty couldn't make happy." This is a portrait of Lavin's family. Episodes from Lavin's life with husband Robert (William Walsh) and grandfather Tom reveal happy moments. The black period immediately after Robert's death is an unhappy period when the narrator and Bea guard against their mother's suicide. Their trips to Europe are in vain because Vera cannot forget her husband, but since the children learn geography and history, the trips are not completely a waste. In rearing her daughter after returning home, Vera rejects advice from relatives, friends, and strangers who want her to accept life as a vale of tears.

By accepting life's chaos, symbolized by her disordered study, Vera painfully pursues life. Father Hugh is there to help, but at times she has him "as distracted as herself." Writing, working for her family, and gardening consume much energy, and it is not surprising that Vera eventually collapses while working in her garden. Father Hugh carries her into the house, where she dies four hours later, recalling the day Robert died. It is necessary for Vera to die and natural that she would remember Robert's last day. A finality to that relationship opens new doors for Mary Lavin through which she and Father Michael Scott can pass. "Happiness," more autobiographical than fictive, is the story of an insecure, emotionally fragile woman dealt some cruel blows.

IN A CAFÉ

The final book Mary Lavin saw through publication was *In a Café*, which included reprints of such stories as "In the Middle of the Fields" and "In a

Café"; revised versions of such stories as "The Convert" and "The Will"; and one story, "The Girders," which had never been published before. According to Elizabeth Lavin, one of her three daughters, who was responsible for selecting the stories, Lavin had been revising a number of stories for a collected edition of her short fiction; this shorter selection was published when she broke her hip and had to halt the revision process.

The new story in the collection was found by Lavin's daughter quite by accident. According to those who knew her, Lavin was quite sensitive about the stories she sent under contract to *The New Yorker* which were rejected. She reportedly had a big heap of such stories under a bed. Her daughter has said that she is sure she will discover many more unpublished Lavin stories, which will probably see print in the near future.

It is not known whether "The Girders" is a *New Yorker* reject or a story Lavin had not gotten around to submitting for publication. However, it is a typical Lavin story, straightforward and unadorned—an example of what William Trevor has referred to as her ability to be subtle "without making a palaver about it." The story reflects a typical Irish conflict between nostalgia for the country and pride in progress and work in the city. The central character is a man who works on large construction sites in Dublin as part of the economic boom in Ireland in the last decade of the century. Life in the city for the man seems crazed and giddy, but he knows that outside was a world "still as sane and sweet as ever." Thus, he longs to make enough money to return to the country.

When the man has an accident that cripples his feet and necessitates that he return to his mother's house in the country, he is not so sure that this is what he wants. The story ends with him looking out the hospital window at the construction girders and thinking he will never see them again. Instead, he would be looking at the trees and fields for the rest of his life. As he thinks of them, the fields seem a monotonous green and the trees clumsy and stupidly twisted. Now the girders of the great buildings do not look so cruel at all, and "the cranes looked as frail as the silk wings of a dragonfly that wouldn't harm a thing."

OTHER MAJOR WORKS

LONG FICTION: *The House in Clewe Street*, 1945; *Mary O'Grady*, 1950, 1986.

CHILDREN'S LITERATURE: *A Likely Story*, 1957; *The Second-Best Children in the World*, 1972.

BIBLIOGRAPHY

Bowen, Zack. *Mary Lavin*. Lewisburg, Pa.: Bucknell University Press, 1975. A concise introduction in the Irish Writers series to Lavin's life and work. Bowen touches on the social background of the fiction and a few themes. Nearly half the book is a discussion of Lavin's novels *The House in Clewe Street* and *Mary O'Grady*.

Caswell, Robert W. "Political Reality and Mary Lavin's *Tales from Bective Bridge*." *Eire-Ireland* 3 (Spring, 1968): 48-60. Caswell argues that Lavin's stories lack the "political reality" found in the works of Frank O'Connor and Seán O'Faoláin. He also states that she does not show nationalism as a driving force of her characters. Yet Caswell still feels that Lavin captures a distinctly Irish identity.

Deane, Séamus. "Mary Lavin." In *The Irish Short Story*, edited by Patrick Rafroidi. Atlantic Highlands, N.J.: Humanities Press, 1979. A general introduction to Lavin's short stories, focusing on her central theme of the nature of love. Argues that the power of the stories is related to the social and psychological habits of social suppression and secrecy in Irish life. Discusses her classical style and her communal ethic, commenting on several of her major stories.

Gottwald, Maria. "Narrative Strategies." In *Irish Literature*, edited by Birgit Bramsback and Martin Croghan. Uppsala: Sweden, 1988. Discusses the relationship of narrative techniques to character, theme, and value system in Lavin's stories. Argues that Lavin's most common approach is a figural narrative situation with an internal perspective.

Hawthorne, Mark D. "Words That Do Not Speak Themselves: Mary Lavin's 'Happiness.'" *Studies in Short Fiction* 31 (Fall, 1994): 683-688. Claims that in this well-known Lavin story the narrator's attempt to understand and account for her mother's enigmatic use of the word "happiness" illustrates the futility of trying to understand verbal constructs; the inability to communicate is a major theme in the story.

Kelly, A. A. *Mary Lavin: A Study.* New York: Barnes & Noble Books, 1980. The best critical book available on Lavin. Kelly discusses Lavin's use of the social hierarchy in her fiction. There are also excellent chapters on the themes of the family and religion found in Lavin's work.

Murray, Thomas J. "Mary Lavin's World: Lovers and Strangers." *Eire-Ireland* 7 (Summer, 1973): 122-131. Murray finds much "sterility" in the characters and situations in Lavin's fiction. The role of women in many of the stories, Murray argues, is to destroy the life-affirming fantasies of men.

Neary, Michael. "Flora's Answer to the Irish Question: A Study of Mary Lavin's 'The Becker Wives.'" *Twentieth Century Literature* 42 (Winter, 1996): 516-525. Discusses the protagonist of the story as a passive projection of a national Irish ideal; shows how the story deals with the Irish struggle to establish an identity from within.

Peterson, Richard F. *Mary Lavin.* Boston: Twayne, 1980. This book offers a brief biography of Lavin and then examines specific examples of the stories and novels. A useful introduction to the writer.

Shumaker, Jeanette Roberts. "Sacrificial Women in Short Stories by Mary Lavin and Edna O'Brien." *Studies in Short Fiction* 32 (Spring, 1995): 185-197. Examines sacrificial women in two stories by Lavin and two by O'Brien; claims that in the stories, female martyrdom (en)gendered by the Madonna myth has different forms, from becoming a nun to becoming a wife, mother, or "fallen woman."

Vertreace, Martha. "The Goddess Resurrected in Mary Lavin's Short Fiction." In *The Anna Book: Searching for Anna in Literary History*, edited by Mickey Perlman. Westport, Conn.: Greenwood Press, 1992. Argues that Lavin creates a number of mother figures in her stories based on pre-Christian goddesses worshiped in ancient Ireland. Suggests that characters who interact with this figure are redeemed through her by relinquishing other forms of creativity, such as artistic expression.

Eileen A. Sullivan, updated by James Sullivan and Charles E. May

---

D. H. LAWRENCE

Born: Eastwood, Nottinghamshire, England; September 11, 1885
Died: Vence, France; March 2, 1930

PRINCIPAL SHORT FICTION

The Prussian Officer and Other Stories, 1914
England, My England, 1922
The Ladybird, the Fox, the Captain's Doll, 1923
St. Mawr: Together with the Princess, 1925
Rawdon's Roof, 1928
The Woman Who Rode Away and Other Stories, 1928
The Escaped Cock, 1929 (best known as *The Man Who Died*)
Love Among the Haystacks and Other Stories, 1930
The Lovely Lady and Other Stories, 1933
A Modern Lover, 1934
The Complete Short Stories of D. H. Lawrence, 1961

OTHER LITERARY FORMS

D. H. Lawrence is one of the most prolific writers in English literary history. His major works include ten volumes of poetry, a collection of critical essays, four books of travel writings, several translations, and plays, in addition to the four novels (among others) for which he is popularly known. His most famous novel, *Lady Chatterley's Lover* (1928), brought him notoriety and further assured that he would be remembered as a novelist rather than a poet and short-story writer. After his novels, his most widely read and anthologized works are short stories and poems. In many of his works, Lawrence uses identical situations, plots, images, and themes.

ACHIEVEMENTS

The subject and style of Lawrence's works, of whatever kind, are so distinct and consistent that his name has given birth to an adjective, "Lawrentian," to describe a way of looking at the world and a method for presenting it. The bold originality and powerful style of his early novels attracted the attention of upper-class British writers and intellectuals such as the philosopher Bertrand Russell and even the prime minister Herbert Asquith. Lawrence's values, however, were not the same as theirs, and he spent most of his life as a nomad, searching for amenable landscapes and cultures. All of his works record that search and reveal its remarkable unity of purpose.

After Lawrence's death, his critical reputation eventually declined, though his works continued to sell. Then, in 1955, the influential modern English critic F. R. Leavis published a study of the novels and declared Lawrence to be the most important writer of his generation and as good as Charles Dickens. He praised *Sons and Lovers* (1913) as the first honest treatment of the British working class. Also in 1955 the American critic Harry T. Moore published the first authoritative biography, *The Intelligent Heart*, introducing Lawrence to a public as fascinated by his life as by his work. His reputation is worldwide; in 1982, there were nearly three hundred titles pertaining to Lawrence translated into thirty languages.

BIOGRAPHY

David Herbert Lawrence's life went through four distinct stages. The first may be indicated as the Nottingham or Eastwood years, the formative years before March, 1912. Lawrence's father, Arthur, was a miner and his mother, a teacher. Married beneath her status, Lydia Beardsall Lawrence detested the commonness of her husband and vowed that her sons

D. H. Lawrence (D. C. Public Library)

would never work the pits. She therefore doggedly saw Lawrence through a teacher-training program at Nottingham University College. The class struggle at home mirrored the larger class struggle, of which Lawrence was acutely aware.

Within the grim industrial village life there remained a lyrical beauty in intimate relations. In Eastwood, Lawrence was romantically involved with two women who represented the contradictory nature of love. Jessie Chambers (Muriel in *Sons and Lovers*), his mother's choice, was too spiritual and possessive for Lawrence. He was physically attracted to another, Louie Burrows, but the oedipal bonds were too strong to break. When Lydia Lawrence died in December, 1910, Lawrence drifted aimlessly and over the next few months severed all romantic attachments. Then, in March, 1912, he met Frieda Weekley, the wife of his modern languages professor. They were married in May.

The next period lasted until the end of World War I and his subsequent departure from England.

Lawrence published poems that treat his marriage to Frieda as at once physical and spiritual. He was at work on a long novel, *The Sisters*, which he split into two and published the first part, *The Rainbow*, in 1915. The work was suppressed by British censors because of its frank portrayal of sexual relations, and Lawrence was unable to find an American publisher. In 1917, he and Frieda applied for passports, which they were denied, ostensibly because Frieda's family was German and some of her relatives (notably, the infamous Red Baron) served prominently in the German army. For the next two years, the Lawrences lived in dire poverty, in cottages and on funds lent by friends.

Years of wandering characterize the third period. After relatively short residencies in various Italian towns, Lawrence visited Ceylon (now Sri Lanka) and Australia, and then from September, 1922, until September, 1925, lived in Taos, New Mexico, and Chapala and Oaxaca in Mexico, interspersed with a short return to England in late 1924. He traveled to the United States at the invitation of Mabel Dodge Luhan, who had read *Sea and Sardinia* (1921) and was convinced that only Lawrence could describe the "soul" of the Southwest landscape and Native Americans. His American works lyrically reveal the landscape but show little empathy for the people and their history.

In November, 1925, the Lawrences moved to Spotorno, Italy. In June, 1926, Lawrence declared that he no longer wanted to write fiction and began a series of watercolors and large oil paintings. From a villa near Florence in 1927, Lawrence wrote his last novel and *succès de scandale, Lady Chatterley's Lover*, and collected his lyrical accounts of travels in Mexico and the American Southwest. His last works, just before he moved to Bandol and then Vence in the French Provence, included his studies of the Etruscan tombs at Tarquinia; a short novel, *The Escaped Cock*, which is an idiosyncratic account of Christ's death and resurrection; *Apocalypse* (1931), a study of the Book of Revelation; and *Last Poems* (1932), which deals with the experience of dying. All of them reflect Lawrence's preparation for his own death, from tuberculosis, in March, 1930.

ANALYSIS

D. H. Lawrence's early stories are set, except for "The Prussian Officer," in the English Midlands; their plot and characters are a thinly veiled autobiography and are built on incidents that Lawrence would develop at length in other forms, notably the novels and plays that he was writing concurrently. Some readers prefer the stories over Lawrence's longer forms, which they regard as too insistent and repetitious; his stories, like his poems, are more structured, their images more intense. Like the longer works, however, the stories reveal Lawrence's central belief in a "fatal change" in the early twentieth century: "The collapse from the psychology of the free human individual into the psychology of the social being." Lawrence tried always to see unity in the behavior of human beings and the historical changes through which ages lived. In the longer works and in many essays, he developed a didactic style appropriate to his sweeping interpretation of human history and types of personality. In the stories, he lyrically and more intimately explores how the quality of individuals' lives is affected by their human relationships.

"ODOUR OF CHRYSANTHEMUMS"

A majority of the stories more frequently treat the failure of human relationships. "Odour of Chrysanthemums" is one of five accounts of such a discovery of lost human possibilities; other versions appear in three novels and a play, *The Widowing of Mrs. Holroyd* (1914), from this period. A proud miner's wife, Elizabeth Bates, waits with her two children for her husband, who is late coming from the pits. At first, she angrily surmises that he has gone to a pub; as time passes, the anger changes to fear. The husband has been killed in a mining accident, and his fellow colliers bring his body home. The climax of the story is one of Lawrence's best scenes, as the miner's mother and wife wash the corpse. In early versions of the story, from 1911, Lawrence treated the mother's and wife's whimperings and reveries equally; in the collected version in 1914, however, he added the powerful dramatic epiphany of Mrs. Bates's feeling of shame for having denied her husband's body. "She had denied him what he was . . . refused him as himself." The discovery is also liberating: "She was grateful to death, which restored the truth. And she knew she was not dead." The symbol of flowers is a derivative, almost gratuitous device. Their fragrance equates to memory, as the wife recalls the events of her married life: birth, defeat and reconciliation, and death.

Before Lawrence's own fulfillment with Frieda Weekley, it is problematic whether he could have known, or treated so honestly, the complex nature of human sexuality or the separateness of lovers. Without the revisions, the story is successful only as an account of lost love and patent realizations, much like others in *The Prussian Officer and Other Stories*. "The Shadow in the Rose Garden" and "The Shades of Spring" are stories about return and realization, but they lack dramatic climaxes. In "The Shadow in the Rose Garden," an unnamed woman returns on her honeymoon to the town where she first fell in love. There, she discovers that her first lover, whom she believed a Boer War casualty, is alive but confined to an insane asylum. In an unresolved ending, her husband learns that she is still attached to the soldier and concludes that it "would be violation to each of them to be brought into contact with the other." In "The Shades of Spring," Hilda Millership—rejected by a cultured suitor, John Syson—gives herself to her gamekeeper, Arthur Pilbury, on Syson's wedding night. Later, still foppishly attached to Hilda, Syson returns to her farm, learns about Hilda's affair, and is taunted by the gamekeeper for not having seduced her.

Both stories lack the dramatic structure of "Odour of Chrysanthemums." They exemplify a style that Lawrence told his literary agent in 1914 he wanted to outgrow: a method of "accumulating objects in the light of a powerful emotion, and making a scene of them." Nevertheless, these early stories use situations, characters, and symbols that one finds in all Lawrence's work. At the end of "The Shades of Spring," for example, a bee stings Pilbury, and Hilda sucks the wound and smears his mouth with bloody kisses. This gesture is one of the first symbolic statements of a Lawrentian paradigm: Blood symbolizes natural, unconscious life, in contrast to the mechanically intellectual and socially correct existence of Syson.

"THE BLIND MAN"

These two ways of living are also represented in a contrast between *feeling* and *seeing*, between intuitive knowledge and acquired, social knowledge. "The Blind Man" is Lawrence's most powerful treatment of both the necessity and the consequence of intimate physical contact. Isabel Pervin is married to Maurice, who was blinded and scarred in World War I and is completely dependent on her. The focus of the story is not their love but Maurice's sudden passion for his wife's cousin and former admirer, Bertie Reid. Maurice asks Isabel's to invite Bertie for a visit, hoping that he can become his closest friend. Isabel's ambivalent feelings about Bertie, fond yet contemptuous, derive from her knowledge of his lifestyle. "He had his friends among the fair sex—not lovers, friends." She knew that he was "unable to enter into close contact of any sort." This failure at relationships, Lawrence bitingly asserts, made him a "brilliant and successful barrister, also a litterateur of high repute, a rich man, and a great social success"—in short, the epitome of the aristocratic Englishman. The story, however, is more serious than it is satirical. At the electrifying climax, Maurice first runs his hand over Bertie's face and body, and then, to Bertie's horror, puts Bertie's hand over his scars and into his eye sockets. Maurice tells Isabel of the experience, which he regards as a ritual of undying friendship, but she sees Bertie's revulsion and his urge to flee such intimacy.

In his own life, Lawrence was attracted to the ritual of *Blutbruderschaft*, in which two male friends mix their blood from self-imposed cuts, and he used that ritual, along with a nude wrestling scene, in *Women in Love* (1920). The equivalent contact in "The Blind Man," heightened by Maurice's disfigurement, shows the failure of male relationships as a corollary of failed sexual love. Lawrence had been reading Carl Jung's "Psychology of the Unconscious" and "found much truth" in the oedipal "mother-incest idea." At times, Frieda could become for Lawrence the devouring mother: A man "casts himself as it were into her womb, and . . . the Magna Mater receives him with gratification. . . . It is awfully hard, once the sex relation has gone this way, to recover. If we don't recover we die." Lawrence professed to "believe tremendously in friendship between man and man, a pledging of men to each other inviolably."

"THE PRUSSIAN OFFICER"

While male friendship remained for all Lawrence's life an ideal, he was never able to produce an account of successful male relations, whether the bonds were sexual or not. "The Blind Man" symbolically rejects male friendship as a way out of an unavoidable sexual regression, despite what Lawrence professed to believe. In an earlier story, "The Prussian Officer," Lawrence had not yet acquired the skill of using symbolic gestures. He thus treats more directly the destructive nature of suppressed desires—in this case, for an overtly sexual male relationship. Originally entitled "Honour and Arms," the story's title was changed by an editor, much to Lawrence's dismay. While the revised title focuses on the dominant character and necessarily minimizes another, it removes the pun and limits Lawrence's intent to show how repressed or unconscious desires can erupt in sadistic violence in any relationship. The Prussian captain, attracted to his young orderly, Anton Schoner, vents his forbidden attraction, first in sadistic assaults and then by refusing to let the orderly see his sweetheart. The orderly's "normal" heterosexuality eventually yields to unconscious responses toward the captain, which drive Schoner to murder him. Lawrence treats the murder like a rape: "It pleased him . . . to feel the hard twitchings of the prostrate body jerking his own whole frame. . . ." The theme common to both "The Prussian Officer" and "The Blind Man" lies in the similarity between otherwise dissimilar characters. Anyone who has avoided his feelings, or acknowledged but repressed them, on being forced to recognize them, destroys himself—or, more usually, as in Bertie's case, flees to avoid entrapment in any permanent sexual relationship.

"THE HORSE DEALER'S DAUGHTER"

In contemporaneous stories of heterosexual love, physical contact has the opposite effect. A woman is, like Sleeping Beauty, awakened by physical touch to know and accept, usually gradually, her unconscious desires. In "The Horse Dealer's Daughter," a doctor rescues a drowning girl, takes her to his home, and strips off her wet clothes. When she awakens, she embraces him and stirs him into love for her. (Lawrence develops the same plot in a longer version in *The Virgin and the Gipsy*, 1930.)

"YOU TOUCHED ME"

"You Touched Me" also explores the theme of touch, complicated by an additional motive of inherited wealth. The lower-class male, ironically named Hadrian, has been adopted from a charity house. After wartime service, he returns to his adoptive father, Ted Rockley, a dying invalid cared for by his two natural spinster daughters, Emmie and Matilda. One night, Matilda goes into Hadrian's room, genuinely mistaking it as her father's, and caresses his face before discovering who he is. The touch stirs Hadrian's desire and determines him to conquer the proud Matilda. Ted Rockley approves Hadrian's offer to marry and threatens to leave his estate to Hadrian if Matilda refuses. Matilda's reason for agreeing to marriage is not the point, though it adds a realistic, common touch. The point is that her touching Hadrian validates his desire and gives him rights.

"You Touched Me" shares its plot with a longer work of this period, *The Fox*. In both narratives, a young man returns to England from Canada and falls in love with an older woman. In *The Fox*, the plot complication is not inheritance but a romantic and economic liaison of the loved one, Nellie March, with another woman, Jill Banford. As he does with other homosexual characters, Lawrence simply kills Jill: The young man, Henry Grenfel, cuts down a tree so that it falls where Jill is standing. Henry's repeated warnings to Jill to move and her refusal to do so leave vague whether the act was suicide or murder.

Homoeroticism in stories such as *The Fox* and the subject of sexual awakenings in all his works elicited the popular view of Lawrence's works as being pornographic. It was a charge against which Lawrence vigorously defended himself. His narratives were erotic, designed to awaken readers to their sexuality when they identified with his characters, but they were not pornographic, designed for genital arousal. Pornography offered a life-denying and self-consuming masturbatory release; the erotic stimulated the need for fulfillment with another. According to Lawrence, the British public was not accustomed to the open treatment of sexual relations as healthy. Instead, earlier writers had denied normal sexuality and reduced virile male characters to enervated victims of accidents or war. Nineteenth century readers could accept such vital characters as Rochester in Charlotte Brontë's *Jane Eyre* (1847) only when they were physically ruined or subjugated to a feminine domesticity. The impotent characters, Lawrence believed, that recur so often are both cause and effect of the decline of modern British civilization. In 1917, hoping to flee to the United States, Lawrence wrote to Bertrand Russell, "I cannot do any more work for this country . . . there is no future for England: only a decline and fall. That is the dreadful and unbearable part of it: to have been born into a decadent era, a decline of life, a collapsing civilization."

"THE CROWN"

Even a dying civilization has its beauty, Lawrence decided, but it was a demonic and apocalyptic one. In the most important essay for understanding his credo, "The Crown," Lawrence characterized modern society as the end of a civilization. It was self-indulgent, self-destructive, sensuous, power-seeking, monotheistic, and light-denying. A new and balanced society would eventually follow. Meanwhile, for generations caught at the end of such epochs, the only way out of a narcissistic egoism was to indulge demonically in sex or bloodlust. Destruction, like creation, required vitality. Lawrence hoped that demonic vitality, spent at last, would lead to a new civilization. Even if it made things worse, it was preferable to apathy.

Lawrence always saw correspondences between individuals, the kinds of societies that they fostered, and the religious myths that they created. The most cogent interpretation that Lawrence gives of the Christian myth is an oedipal one recorded in an unpublished foreword to *Sons and Lovers:*

> The Father was flesh—and the Son, who in himself was finite and had form, became Word. For form is the uttered Word, and the Son is the Flesh as it utters the word, but the unutterable Flesh is the Father.
>
> And God the Father, the Inscrutable, the Unknowable, we know in the Flesh, in woman. She is the door for our ingoing and our out-coming. In her we go back to the Father.

Much of this echoes Jung's "Psychological Approach to the Trinity." For both Lawrence and Jung, father and son constitute polarities in the male psyche. At the personal level, Lawrence has been separated from his father by the mother's interventions. The only way back to the father was to reject the mother and replace her with another female object of desire. The wife replaces mother and restores the son to the father.

Like civilization, Christianity had hardened into meaningless dogma. Lawrence's travels were undertaken not only to avoid a dying British culture but also to discover the nature of other, pre-Christian religions. In the Native American culture, Lawrence found, for a while, what he was seeking: the "oldest religion," when "everything was alive, not supernaturally but naturally alive." The Native Americans' "whole life effort" was to "come into immediate *felt* contact and, so derive energy, power, and a dark sort of joy." Their efforts to become one with the cosmos, without intermediation, was the "root meaning" of religion. Such rapturous description suggests an equivalence to Lawrence's "blood-consciousness" as an attempt to revive a vital religion. The stories and short novels set in the American Southwest and Mexico blend religious vitality and demonic indulgence. Many readers, unaware of Lawrence's metaphysical framework, disparage the stories for what they see as his approval of brute, male force against women. At the naturalistic level, the stories are gratuitously violent, but in the context of Lawrence's credo, they become fabulistic, not realistic. Character and action should be interpreted as symbolic. The presentation of a scene does not necessarily indicate the author's approval.

The juxtaposition of characters in three stories of the Southwest—"The Princess," "The Woman Who Rode Away," and the short novel *St. Mawr*—recalls the structure of earlier stories. Egotistical, haughty, coddled but unfulfilled American and European women come under the sway of dark-skinned heroes who embody Lawrence's ideal. Lawrence's male Native Americans are distinguished from even the most intuitive British men, like Maurice in "The Blind Man" or Henry in *The Fox:* They have rejected a white culture, including religion, which threatens to demean and confine them. Having escaped the coming Christian apocalypse, they are neither self-indulgent nor spiritual but living embodiments of a phallic mystery, the "only mystery" that the female characters have not unraveled. Their attempts to "know" that mystery leads to their alienation or destruction.

"THE PRINCESS"

In "The Princess," Dollie Urquhart travels, after her aristocratic father's death, to a dude ranch in New Mexico. There, she is drawn ineluctably to Domingo Romero, a guide at the ranch and the last of a line of great Native American landholders. Romero is himself unfulfilled and waits for one of two Lawrentian fates: to die or to be "aroused in passion and hope." One day, Dollie arranges a trip, with a female companion and Romero as guide, over the Rockies to a spot where animals can be observed in their "wild unconsciousness." Even though the companion's horse is injured, Dollie and Romero continue the trip. The cold mountains both terrify and seduce Dollie, as Lawrence makes the mountains represent what she is seeking, in perhaps his most successful use of settings as symbols. The guide and his charge spend the night in a miner's shack. Frightened by dreams of snow, a symbol of spiritual death, Dollie goes to Romero for "warmth, protection" and to be "taken away from herself," and Romero obliges. The next day, when Dollie tells him that she does not like "that sort of thing," Romero is broken and angry. Like Hadrian in "You Touched Me," he argues that Dollie's coming to him has given him the right to marry her. When she refuses, he strips her and violates her repeatedly, but she refuses to relent. Romero had successfully reached some "unrealised part" of her that she had never wanted to feel. Soon, rangers rescue Dollie and kill Romero. Unable to find her old self, "a virgin intact," she goes "slightly crazy."

"THE WOMAN WHO RODE AWAY"

In "The Woman Who Rode Away," the knowledge sought by the unnamed woman is much more profound. She wants to visit a remote tribe of Chilchuis and "to know their gods." She does not know that for years the Chilchui have waited for a female sacrificial victim to appease their gods. The woman uses the ploys that society has taught her to engage the Chilchuis, but they remain indifferent. They "were not human to her, and they did not see her as a beautiful white woman . . . no woman at all." Instead, she sees in the dark eyes of her guard a "fine spark" of derision. In a masterful confusion of object and metaphor, Lawrence has the Chilchui ask if the woman will "bring her heart to the Chilchui." Her affirmative response convinces the Chilchuis that she was sent in fulfillment of the prophecy. An aged Chilchui appears, drugs her, cuts away her clothes, and touches her body with his fingertips, which he has moistened at his mouth. At the dawn of the winter solstice, four Chilchuis lay her on a stone and hold her legs and arms. At her head, with knife poised and one eye on the sky, the old priest figure waits for the moment to strike.

ST. MAWR

In *St. Mawr*, Lawrence uses not a Native American or even a human figure but a red stallion to symbolize ideal maleness. Lou Witt's husband, typically for Lawrence, has lost his sense of what it means to be a man. The other two male characters, the grooms Phoenix and Lewis, a Navajo and a Welshman respectively, retain some of their fierce male separateness. None of them, however, measures up to the horse, who "stands where one can't get at him" and "burns with life." When *St. Mawr* throws Rico, an event full of symbolic suggestion, Lou plans to sell the horse. Then she discovers that the new female owner plans to geld him. To avoid that fate Lou moves with the horse to New Mexico. St. Mawr thrives in the new, stark, mountain landscape, but Lou feels thwarted and diminished. As in "The Woman Who Rode Away," Lawrence ritualizes Lou's quest and transforms her into another mythic sacrificial figure. "She understood now the meaning of the Vestal Virgins. . . . They were symbolic of herself, of woman weary of the embrace of incompetent men." So she turns to "the unseen gods, the unseen spirits, the hidden fire" and devotes herself "to that, and that alone."

THE MAN WHO DIED

In Lawrence's last major story, Lou's character and function as the waiting Vestal Virgin are transformed into the mythological figure of Isis, although with a peculiarly Lawrentian twist. *The Man Who Died* is Lawrence's ultimate revision of Christianity's emphasis on the Crucifixion. The work is divided in two parts. The first, published with the title that Lawrence wanted for all editions, "The Escaped Cock," follows the traditional story of Christ's rising and healing. He perceives intellectually the life around him but laments, "The body of my desire has died and I am not in touch anywhere." In 1927, when Lawrence wrote "The Escaped Cock," he may have seen the ending as incomplete, but he did not return to create a second part for two years.

In part 2, Lawrence recasts Christ as the dismembered Osiris whose parts are reassembled by Isis. Reborn in part 1, Christ can function only as a pagan male seasonal deity, dying in winter, while the eternal feminine, symbolized in Isis, waits for his rebirth in spring to reanimate her. Lawrence thus effectively unites two themes that obsess all his works: the renewal of the sexes and the concomitant discovery of a revitalized religion. At one level, Christ and Isis are merely man and woman, but as both deity and human, this new Christ integrates the physical and the spiritual. Lawrence is not advocating a return to paganism, as a facile reading might conclude, but a return of Christianity to its archetypal origins. The new Christ says, "On this rock I built my life," the rock of the living woman. It is not the rock of Saint Peter, of masculine control, but of phallic marriage.

OTHER MAJOR WORKS

LONG FICTION: *The White Peacock*, 1911; *The Trespasser*, 1912; *Sons and Lovers*, 1913; *The Rainbow*, 1915; *Women in Love*, 1920; *The Lost Girl*, 1920; *Aaron's Rod*, 1922; *Kangaroo*, 1923; *The Boy in the Bush*, 1924 (with M. L. Skinner); *The Plumed Serpent*, 1926; *Lady Chatterley's Lover*, 1928; *The Virgin and the Gipsy*, 1930; *Mr. Noon*, 1984 (wr. 1920-1922).

PLAYS: *The Widowing of Mrs. Holroyd*, pb. 1914; *Touch and Go*, pb. 1920; *David*, pb. 1926; *A Collier's Friday Night*, pb. 1934; *The Complete Plays of D. H. Lawrence*, pb. 1965.

POETRY: *Love Poems and Others*, 1913; *Amores*,

1916; *Look! We Have Come Through*, 1917; *New Poems*, 1918; *Bay*, 1919; *Tortoises*, 1921; *Birds, Beasts, and Flowers*, 1923; *The Collected Poems of D. H. Lawrence*, 1928; *Pansies*, 1929; *Nettles*, 1930; *The Triumph of the Machine*, 1931; *Last Poems*, 1932; *Fire and Other Poems*, 1940; *Phoenix Edition of Complete Poems*, 1957; *The Complete Poems of D. H. Lawrence*, 1964 (Vivian de Sola Pinto and Warren Roberts, editors).

NONFICTION: *Twilight in Italy*, 1916; *Movements in European History*, 1921; *Psychoanalysis and the Unconscious*, 1921; *Sea and Sardinia*, 1921; *Fantasia of the Unconscious*, 1922; *Studies in Classic American Literature*, 1923; *Reflections on the Death of a Porcupine and Other Essays*, 1925; *Mornings in Mexico*, 1927; *Pornography and Obscenity*, 1929; *Agrave; Propos of Lady Chatterley's Lover*, 1930; *Assorted Articles*, 1930; *Apocalypse*, 1931; *Etruscan Places*, 1932; *The Letters of D. H. Lawrence*, 1932 (Aldous Huxley, editor); *Phoenix: The Posthumous Papers of D. H. Lawrence*, 1936 (Edward McDonald, editor); *The Collected Letters of D. H. Lawrence*, 1962 (Harry T. Moore, editor, 2 volumes); *Phoenix II*, 1968 (Harry T. Moore and Warren Roberts, editors).

TRANSLATIONS: *Maestro-Don Gesualdo*, 1923; *Little Novels of Sicily*, 1925; *Cavalleria Rusticana*, 1928.

BIBLIOGRAPHY

Balbert, Peter. *D. H. Lawrence and the Phallic Imagination*. New York: St. Martin's Press, 1989. This book is a well-reasoned response to feminist critics, who, especially since the 1970's, have accused Lawrence of misogyny. For "The Woman Who Rode Away," Balbert gives a revisionist study that shows the causes for misreadings in other works.

Bell, Michael. *D. H. Lawrence: Language and Being*. Cambridge, England: Cambridge University Press, 1992. Discusses the development of Lawrence's metaphysics not only in terms of his emotional life but also in terms of Martin Heidegger's metaphysics. Although this study focuses primarily on Lawrence's novels, its comments on his thought are relevant to his short fiction as well.

Black, Michael. *D. H. Lawrence: The Early Fiction.* New York: Cambridge University Press, 1986. In this sensitive study, Black discovers new layers of meaning in five of the eight stories that he examines. He rejects earlier psychoanalytic readings as too reductionist. As soon as critics characterized Lawrence's works as oedipal, they went no further.

Ellis, David. *D. H. Lawrence: Dying Game, 1922-1930.* New York: Cambridge University Press, 1997. The third volume of the Cambridge biography of Lawrence links his writings with the incidents of his life; argues that more than most authors, Lawrence's fiction was associated with his daily living. Discusses his fiction and revisions during the 1920's, including his work on *Lady Chatterley's Lover* and "The Rocking-Horse Winner."

Flora, Joseph M. *The English Short Story, 1880-1945: A Critical History.* Boston: Twayne, 1985. Lawrence's stories are placed in a historical literary context with their contemporaries. Though Flora offers no interpretations, he does effectively show Lawrence's influences, how Lawrence absorbed and rejected early forms, and how his works both belong to and surpass their time.

Harris, Janice Hubbard. *The Short Fiction of D. H. Lawrence.* New Brunswick, N.J.: Rutgers University Press, 1984. Harris's book is the first to treat chronologically all Lawrence's short fiction. Weak discussions of some works (for example "England, My England") are more than compensated for by enlightening readings of others (such as *The Man Who Died*).

Kinkead-Weekes, Mark. *D. H. Lawrence: Triumph to Exile, 1912-1922.* New York: Cambridge University Press, 1996. Volume 2 of this three-part biography covers Lawrence's life from his elopement with Frieda von Richthofen and the publication of *Sons and Lovers* up through World War I. Highly detailed account based on newly available Lawrence letters; discusses Lawrence's relationship with Ezra Pound, T. S. Eliot, Wyndham Lewis, Ford Madox Ford, and others.

Moore, Harry T. *The Priest of Love: A Life of D. H. Lawrence.* Rev. ed. New York: Farrar, Straus & Giroux, 1974. In preparing this first objective biography, Moore lived for several years at Lawrence sites and interviewed Lawrence's family and friends. Moore's work remains the standard source for accuracy and completeness.

Schneider, Daniel J. *The Consciousness of D. H. Lawrence: An Intellectual Biography.* Lawrence: University Press of Kansas, 1986. Tracing all the major works chronologically, Schneider treats Lawrence's religious nature at all stages of his life. Nineteen stories, both early and late, are briefly analyzed to show how Lawrence shaped, over the years, his credo about kinds of consciousness and knowledge.

Thornton, Weldon. *D. H. Lawrence: A Study of the Short Fiction.* New York: Twayne, 1993. Makes a case for the technical skill, psychological depth, and thematic subtlety of Lawrence's short fiction by focusing on his most important short stories. Argues that Lawrence's work is always exploratory, a means of working through his own tentative ideas.

Widmer, Kingsley. *The Art of Perversity: The Shorter Fiction of D. H. Lawrence.* Seattle: University of Washington Press, 1962. Widmer focuses on the satirical and demonic forces at work in the stories. While his conclusions have been weakened by later studies of Lawrence's use of myth and psychology, the book remains a useful survey of many stories.

Alvin Sullivan

HENRY LAWSON

Born: Grenfell, Australia; June 17, 1867
Died: Sydney, Australia; September 2, 1922

PRINCIPAL SHORT FICTION
Short Stories in Prose and Verse, 1894
While the Billy Boils, 1896
On the Track, 1900
Over the Sliprails, 1900
Joe Wilson and His Mates, 1901
The Rising of the Court, 1910
Mateship: A Discursive Yarn, 1911
Triangles of Life and Other Stories, 1913
*Henry Lawson: The Bush Undertaker and Other
    Stories*, 1971
Henry Lawson: Selected Stories, 1971
Henry Lawson: Short Stories and Sketches, 1888-
    1922, 1972

OTHER LITERARY FORMS
While Henry Lawson is known primarily for his
short stories and prose sketches, he also wrote a substantial amount of verse. Collections of his poetry include *In the Days When the World Was Wide and
Other Verses* (1896), *Verses, Popular and Humorous*
(1900), and *When I Was King and Other Verses*
(1905). *Henry Lawson's Collected Verse* is published
in three volumes (edited by Colin Roderick, 1967-
1969).

ACHIEVEMENTS
Henry Lawson, while at the height of his career in
the 1890's, was a truly popular writer: He wrote for
and about the common people of Australia, and he
was read by those people. Fortune, however, did not
follow fame for him, and though his work was published, read, and admired, he lived most of his life in
penury and often misery. Even so, he was the first
Australian writer ever to receive a state funeral, and
his portrait was put on the ten-dollar note in 1965.
His reputation, then, has always been high in Australia, though with different people for different reasons
at different times; he has yet, however, to receive the

recognition he no doubt deserves among readers of
fiction in the rest of the world. By any acceptable
standard, Lawson, at his best, is a masterful short-
story writer.

BIOGRAPHY
Born on the goldfields of New South Wales at
Grenfell in 1867, Henry Lawson was the eldest of the
five children of Peter Larsen, a former Norwegian
sailor, and Louisa Albury, his Australian wife.
Henry's name was registered as Lawson and that became the family name. His childhood was not a
happy one: From the age of nine he had difficulties
with deafness; the family was poor and moved frequently; the parents disliked each other and fought
bitterly. Peter and Louisa finally separated by mutual
consent in 1883, Louisa taking the younger children
to Sydney; Henry remained briefly with his father before joining his mother to help support the family—
he was fifteen at the time. Lawson seems to have
been fond of his ne'er-do-well father, while he found
Louisa overbearing and lacking in human warmth. A
number of stories, presumably autobiographical,
touch upon this period of his life, especially "A Child
in the Dark, and a Foreign Father."

Lawson worked in Sydney as a coach painter and,
for a while, went to night school. His mother was ambitious for him and encouraged his intellectual endeavors, for by this time she was herself a considerable figure in feminist and republican circles in
Australia. Idealistic in nature, Lawson soon became
imbued with lifelong radical and socialist convictions. As a young writer, Lawson's first break came
in 1887, when he published a ballad, "The Song of
the Republic," in the prominent magazine *The Bulletin*, which also published his first story, "His Father's
Mate," in 1880, a few days before his father died. In
1890, Lawson traveled to Western Australia and
worked as a journalist, and in 1891, he moved to
Brisbane to write for the radical newspaper *Boomer-
ang*. Before the end of the year, however, he was back
in Sydney.

At this point in his career, Lawson began to develop his mastery of the short story; indeed, he was then known more for his poetry than his prose. In 1892, he wrote his first important story sequence, the Arvie Aspinall series, and a number of his most important stories, including "The Drover's Wife" and "The Bush Undertaker." During that same year, he took what became a crucial trip to Bourke, in the Outback, and farther, to "back of beyond." There, on the frontier, the virtues of "mateship" and solidarity, and the terrible realities of Bush life, were impressed on him and became important thematic features of his subsequent work. Returning to Sydney, Lawson worked at a number of jobs and published his first book, *Short Stories in Prose and Verse*, in 1894. His reputation growing, he brought out *While the Billy Boils* in 1896, perhaps his best collection of stories, and a volume of verse. That year, he fell in love with, and married, Bertha Bredt. In the midst of the Depression of the 1890's, they went to New Zealand and ran a Maori school until 1896, when again Lawson returned to Sydney. Lawson, by this time, had developed serious alcoholism, which was exacerbated by his frequenting the bohemian Dawn and Dusk Club. Nevertheless, he was able to bring out two more collections of prose in 1900, *On the Track* and *Over the Sliprails*, as well as another book of verse.

Having become dissatisfied with pursuing a writing career in Australia, Lawson took his wife and children to Great Britain, where he hoped to gain recognition. He met with some limited success there, and wrote a number of important stories, particularly the Joe Wilson series. Yet he was not happy; there was still poverty, illness, and drunkenness with which to contend, and, increasingly, he and his wife were becoming estranged. In fact, it appears that Lawson had fallen in love with another woman, Hannah Thornburn, before leaving for Great Britain, and his return in 1902 may well have been motivated by his desire to be with Thornburn. Upon arrival in Sydney, Lawson learned that Thornburn had died several days before. Lawson separated from his wife and the children, and his life thereafter steadily disintegrated. Not only were there the twin personal tragedies of death and estrangement, but also there was an artistic

Henry Lawson (Library of Congress)

crisis as well: His creative faculties were clearly in decline. Added to this was the painful recognition that the socialist political values he had so long espoused were permanently in eclipse. Whatever relationship each difficulty bore to the other, taken together they were a severe blow, and the remaining twenty years of Lawson's life saw him periodically in prison for indebtedness and drunkenness (out of which comes the famous ballad "One-Hundred-and-Three"), in convalescent or mental hospitals, and simply on the streets. Lawson's friends, particularly his landlady, were generous to him, and often helped him; even his political friends assisted with some government support. Lawson continued to write and publish, and his following continued to grow. Yet his best work was mostly retrospective and autobiographical. In 1921, Lawson had a partially disabling cerebral hemorrhage, though he still wrote, and in 1922, he died at home. He was accorded a state funeral by the government of New South Wales, and a statue was erected in commemoration.

ANALYSIS

Henry Lawson is a popular writer, both with the reading public at large and with professional critics, and for not dissimilar reasons: His limpid and engaging prose style seems a marvel of easy craftsmanship, and his sardonic wit, lively humor, and compassion render his stories attractive. He had a gift for realism that seemed to capture the authentic experience of people, his characters are believable and memorable, and his presentation of the harshness of life in the Bush, with its melancholy overtones of pessimism, has entered into the mythic structures of the Australian consciousness. Lawson mastered the difficult craft of artlessness, allowing the reader to enter into the world of his stories as one might enter a familiar room.

"THE UNION BURIES ITS DEAD"

From his earliest collections come many of Lawson's best stories, such as "The Bush Undertaker," "The Drover's Wife," "Rats," and "The Union Buries Its Dead," a frequently anthologized story. In the last story, Lawson describes the funeral procession in the Outback for a young man who, though a stranger in town, is nevertheless given a funeral because he was a fellow union laborer. This mateship or union solidarity is an ideal that underwrites much of Lawson's thinking, but it is rarely embodied in the world he presents. Most of the gathered crowd are too drunk to follow once the procession begins; the horseman who leaves to join his friend at the bar is an emblem of how good intentions get undermined in the Bush. The tone of the story wavers between an ironic and minimal affirmation of mateship and an almost nihilistic portrayal of the grimness of life on the margins. The comic touches are like gallows humor, and the respects paid to the corpse are the conditioned responses of human indifference. The confusion over the man's identity and name becomes significant: He is a stranger; then he is called James Tyson, according to his union papers; that proves to be a pseudonym. Later his real name is learned but is unfortunately forgotten by everyone. Identity becomes unimportant in the face of the absoluteness of death; it does not matter what his name is. The speaker, both involved participant and distant narrator, refuses the comforts of stock responses and conventions and leaves the reader with a bittersweet regard for the isolation of men striving to survive. The light he casts over the scene is harsh because it is real. As he says, "I have left out the 'sad Australian sunset' because the sun was not going down at the time. The burial took place exactly at mid-day."

"THE DROVER'S WIFE"

In "The Drover's Wife," Lawson delineates the drab and yet dangerous conditions of life for a woman alone in the Bush with her young children while her husband is away for long periods of time. The story is often taken as a tribute to the strength and stoicism of the pioneer woman, but Lawson is less concerned with her character (in certain respects she is a stereotype) than he is with the pattern of life in the Bush. As the drover's wife stands guard against a snake all night, the reader learns about her in a series of flashbacks or reminiscences that reveal the pitiable elements of her lonely life as well as the physical courage and resourcefulness on which she draws. Whether it is fighting a brush fire, trying to stem a flood, or protecting herself from animals and men (the difference is not always clear), the woman does what she must, what she can, because she has slowly adjusted to her existence. There is, however, a cost involved: Though she loves her children, she seems harsh to them. As Lawson puts it, "Her surroundings are not favourable to the development of the 'womanly' or sentimental side of nature." Lawson indicates that her fight with the snake is a symbol of her condition when he writes that the dog, helping her, "shakes the snake as though he felt the original curse in common with mankind." The monotonous Bush, with its "everlasting, maddening sameness of . . . stunted trees," is a false and fallen Eden, and she struggles not with the desire for a forbidden consciousness but with the consequences of male sexuality, with her confinement in isolation and "her worn-out breast."

Lawson never wrote a novel, but his stories often fall into sequences, which, though written in a haphazard order, suggest the outlines of a fragmented novel. Such stories tend to revolve around fictional characters that some critics regard as aspects of Lawson's personality and others see as composite figures from his past. There is Steelman, the clever trickster; his dim-witted sidekick, Smith (whom Lawson spoke of as "my conception of the weaker side of my own nature"); Jack Mitchell, who figures in almost forty pieces, often as an engaging and laconic narrator; Dave Regan, an amusing practical joker who is sometimes his own victim; and Joe Wilson, perhaps Lawson's most complex and developed character. The Joe Wilson series is the closest Lawson came to the expansive connectedness of long fiction; it was written at the height of his career (actually completed during his stay in London), just before his precipitous decline. There are four stories closely interconnected: "Joe Wilson's Courtship," "Brighten's Sister-in-law," "'Water Them Geraniums,'" and "A Double Buggy at Lahey's Creek." The central story in the sequence, "'Water Them Geraniums,'" is often regarded as Lawson's finest achievement as a short-story writer.

"'WATER THEM GERANIUMS'"

Like "The Drover's Wife," "'Water Them Geraniums'" is primarily a story of women in the Bush. Yet it is a deeper, more psychological analysis of what the Bush does to a person than the earlier story. Ostensibly, it is about the narrator, Joe Wilson, and his wife, Mary, and their move to a new home in the Outback. The central portrait, however, is of Mrs. Spicer, a woman in her forties who lives nearby with her children. Like the drover's wife, Mrs. Spicer is often left alone while her husband is away working, but unlike that capable woman, Mrs. Spicer is "haggard," pathetic and even slightly mad, the vitality of her spirit having been eroded by the appalling life she leads. As such, she represents for Mary, Joe's wife, a frightful example of what could become of her; indeed, she and Joe are already experiencing a breakdown in communication with each other, which seems exacerbated by the alienating, dehumanizing force of the Bush itself. More than once, Mary cries out to Joe that this life is killing her; "Oh, Joe! you must take me away from the Bush." The process is one of disintegration, and Mrs. Spicer has succumbed to it. Though she clings to the remnants of respectability, she has been brutalized by the coarseness of her desperate existence. Her death at the end is as

pitiful as it is inevitable. Lawson gives his readers a compassionate but dismal rendering of these people, whose lives are not quite redeemed by infrequent touches of tenderness. The fear of madness that constantly surfaces in the story is the fear of losing one's tenuous connection to humanity, of falling into an inward isolation that mirrors the outer circumstances of loneliness. This powerful and affecting story is one of Lawson's most detailed studies of character, and it is impossible not to sense behind it some of his own melancholic desperation with failure.

Lawson's stories are not always grim; his ironic sensibility often carries him into humor, at which he can be extremely successful. Some of his finest stories are his most amusing, in particular "The Loaded Dog," "The Ironbark Chip," and "Bill, the Ventriloquial Rooster." Even when he is comic, however, there is a sense that contact between people is at best precarious and often unsatisfying. For Lawson, the need for camaraderie, for a warmth of relations, is crucial, but it is constantly undercut by the overwhelming difficulties of life. At times, his stories seem to fall into self-pity and sentimentality, but at his best, he maintains a fine balance between an unflinching realism and a compassionate idealism. His easy, colloquial style, with its sardonic self-consciousness, has subsequently become a characteristic and abiding voice in Australian literature and culture.

OTHER MAJOR WORKS

POETRY: *In the Days When the World Was Wide and Other Verses*, 1896; *Verses, Popular and Humorous*, 1900; *When I Was King and Other Verses*, 1905; *The Skyline Riders and Other Verses*, 1910; *For Australia and Other Poems*, 1913; *My Army! O My Army! and Other Songs*, 1915; *Selected Poems of Henry Lawson*, 1918; *Poetical Works of Henry Lawson*, 1925 (3 volumes); *Henry Lawson's Collected Verse*, 1967-1969 (3 volumes).

NONFICTION: *The Romance of the Swag*, 1942; *Henry Lawson: Letters*, 1890-1922, 1970; *Henry Lawson: Autobiographical and Other Writings*, 1972.

MISCELLANEOUS: *Children of the Bush*, 1902.

BIBLIOGRAPHY

Clark, C. M. H. *Henry Lawson: The Man and the Legend*. Melbourne: Melbourne University Press, 1995. A good, updated biography of Lawson.

Matthews, Brian. "Eve Exonerated: Henry Lawson's Unfinished Love Stories." In *Who Is She?*, edited by Shirley Walker. New York: St. Martin's Press, 1983. Matthews examines the role of women in Lawson's fiction and finds them to be idealized creatures whose contact with the masculine world of reality inevitably scars them. There is little communication between men and women, who are seen essentially as victims.

Phillips, A. A. *Henry Lawson*. New York: Twayne, 1970. After identifying Australian cultural nationalism ("mateship," "common man," "socialism"), Phillips provides a biographical chapter as well as chapters on Lawson's folk art, his "personal views" (including guilt and melancholy), and his craft. Contains several fairly lengthy readings of short stories, as well as a chronology and an annotated bibliography.

Prout, Denton. *Henry Lawson: The Grey Dreamer*. Adelaide, Australia: Rigby Limited, 1963. The only full-length biography of Lawson, Prout's book is essential reading. It contains information, not criticism, about Lawson's fiction and approximately twenty illustrations, mostly photographs. The well-researched volume also contains numerous lengthy quotations from Lawson's work and from his contemporaries and places Lawson within the context of his time.

Roderick, Colin. *Henry Lawson: A Life*. North Ryde, Australia, 1991. A fine biography by a Lawson scholar.

_____. *Henry Lawson: Poet and Short Story Writer*. Sydney, Australia: Angus and Robertson, 1966. A sympathetic evaluation of Lawson's poetry and short stories. Roderick's monograph-length study examines the "modernity" of the stories, the literary influences on Lawson's work, and the role Lawson played in establishing the "Australian" short story. Roderick is especially helpful in placing Lawson within an Australian context and in discussing his use of Australian idioms and speech rhythms.

Stuewe, Paul. "In the Land of Oz: A Master of the Laconic Phrase and the Illuminating Incident." *The Toronto Star*, October 1, 1988, p. M6. Discusses Lawson's collection of "classic yarns," *While the Billy Boils*; claims that Lawson's style parallels that of Joseph Conrad and Stephen Crane; notes that Lawson is a consummate realist, with a marvelous sense of climactic epiphanies.

Wilding, Michael. "Henry Lawson's Radical Vision." In *The Rise of Socialist Fiction, 1880-1914*, edited by H. Gustav Klaus. New York: St. Martin's Press, 1987. Wilding examines Lawson's short stories in terms of their socialist philosophy. He discusses the Arvie Aspinall and Joe Wilson stories, and he devotes several pages to "The Drover's Wife," which he reads as an Australian Edenic story with Oedipal overtones.

Paul Kane, updated by
Thomas L. Erskine

DAVID LEAVITT

Born: Pittsburgh, Pennsylvania; June 23, 1961

PRINCIPAL SHORT FICTION

Family Dancing, 1984
A Place I've Never Been, 1990
Arkansas: Three Novellas, 1997

OTHER LITERARY FORMS

In addition to his short-story collections, David Leavitt writes novels: *The Lost Language of Cranes* was published in 1986, *Equal Affections* in 1989, *While England Sleeps* in 1993 and revised in 1995, *The Page Turner* in 1998, and *Martin Bauman: Or, A Sure Thing* in 2000. He also wrote a teleplay, *The Lost Language of Cranes* (1992), and he edited *Pages Passed from Hand to Hand: The Hidden Tradition of Homosexual Literature in English from 1748 to 1914* (1997; with Mark Mitchell).

ACHIEVEMENTS

While still a student at Yale University, David Leavitt won the Willets Prize for fiction in 1982 for his story "Territory," and a subsequent story, "Counting Months," won the 1984 O. Henry Award. His first published collection of short fiction, *Family Dancing*, was nominated for best fiction from the National Book Critics Circle in 1984, and in 1985 it was a finalist for the PEN/Faulkner Award for Fiction. Leavitt received National Endowment for the Arts grant in 1985 and a John Simon Guggenheim Foundation Fellowship in 1989; he was also foreign writer-in-residence at the Institute of Catalan Letters in Barcelona, Spain.

BIOGRAPHY

David Leavitt was born June 23, 1961, in Pittsburgh, Pennsylvania. His father, Harold Jack, was a professor, and his mother, Gloria Leavitt, a housewife who fought a battle with cancer for many years. This struggle is reflected in many of Leavitt's stories and particularly in one novel, *Equal Affections*, which deals with cancer and its impact on family life.

The young Leavitt grew up in Palo Alto, California, and some elements of his adolescence are found in a 1985 *Esquire* magazine article, "The New Lost Generation," where Leavitt discusses and compares the late 1960's and early 1970's generation of youth to his own of the late 1970's and early 1980's. Leavitt attended Yale University, where he published, at age twenty-one and while still a student, his first short story in *The New Yorker*. He received his B.A. from Yale University in 1983 and worked for a time as a reader and editorial assistant at Viking Penguin in New York, where he was, he said in interviews, a reader of the "slush" manuscripts.

Leavitt's first collection of short fiction was published by Alfred A. Knopf and received considerable literary acclaim in 1984. That volume, *Family Dancing*, did, however, generate some negative criticism for its limited choice of themes. Nevertheless, Leavitt was soon considered to be among the more promising group of young American writers first appearing in the 1980's. In addition to two stories in *The New Yorker*, he published short fiction in *Harper's*. His first novel, *The Lost Language of Cranes*, appeared in 1986 and generated controversy over its straightforward depiction of a homosexual youth's lifestyle compared to the closeted sexuality of the boy's father, who also had homosexual yearnings in secret. His second novel, *Equal Affections*, appeared in 1989 and centers on a family in which a dominant mother figure fights a long battle with cancer. One child in the family is homosexual and living with his lover in the East, while a daughter is a lesbian folk singer caught up in the world of concerts, travel, and performing. A second collection of short fiction, which picks up many themes from the first collection and also some of its characters in later stages of their lives (much as the southern writer Ellen Gilchrist has done with her fictional characters in several short-story collections), was published in 1990 under the title *A Place I've Never Been*. Leavitt continued to write full time, settling in East Hampton, New York.

David Leavitt ((Marion Ettlinger)

ANALYSIS

David Leavitt is one of a number of openly homosexual young writers whose work began to appear in the 1970's and 1980's but who, in spite of their declared homosexuality, have achieved a far wider audience than that normally restricted to "gay writers." While Leavitt (and other writers) may deal in their fiction with the topic of homosexuality and the difficulties posed by heterosexual society for those who are gay or are so perceived, that theme is not the entire focus of his fiction, and his handling of the homosexual experience is not of some isolated, hidden world (as gay and lesbian writing tended to be in the decades of the 1940's and 1950's). Instead, the homosexual experience in Leavitt's work is directly related to the family experience of which parents, brothers, sisters, and relatives are an integral everyday part. Thus, there is little homosexual eroticism present and no homosexual exoticism; homosexuals are present, everyday, and all around, rather as earlier homosexual activists liked to say: "We are everywhere." To that generalization, Leavitt's characters add the generalization, "and we are just like you, for the most part." To this homosexual theme which is found in Leavitt's fiction can be added two other areas that are sometimes linked (but sometimes unrelated) to ho-

mosexuality. One is the recurring fragility of human life and the threat to it by terminal illness such as cancer, acquired immunodeficiency syndrome (AIDS), or even a sudden fatal allergy. Another discernible theme is the fragility of the American family and the pressures on it in contemporary life, particularly the fragmenting effect of divorce.

Leavitt's systematic return to certain themes—homosexuality, sexual infidelity, the family, terminal illness—in his short fiction certainly is a vivid portrayal of contemporary American social mores, rendered all the more acute by the author's ability to select situations and details that become metaphors for his stories' issues. Leavitt, in a discussion of other contemporary fiction writers whom he admires, has suggested that a number of contemporary fiction writers are concerned with the shattering of the familial, or parental, edifice. Many today write of a world "where very little can be taken for granted or counted on, where potentially dangerous change looms around every corner, and where marriages and families, rather than providing havens, are themselves the fulcrum of the most sweeping upheavals." His comment about the works of a number of other contemporary fiction writers could, quite easily, be applied to his own work.

"DEDICATED"

Several stories in Leavitt's collections deal with the complications resulting from the confrontations of heterosexual and homosexual lives. This difficult relationship is seen particularly in a group of stories involving the characters of Celia, Nathan, and Andrew from their initial encounters as college students to their later lives, as their sexual relationships change, new ones are developed, and the later loves affect their friendships.

In "Dedicated," the final story in the *Family Dancing* collection, the trio of Nathan (dark and Jewish, from a wealthy family), Andrew (blond and the definitive WASP), and Celia (attracted to and friends with both Nathan and Andrew) is introduced at the residence of Nathan's parents while they are spending a leisurely weekend away from their Manhattan jobs. In a story seen primarily from Celia's point of view, the contentious sexual relationship between

Nathan and Andrew is explored in the present-time setting of the story and also in flashbacks to college, to scenes in New York, and to scenes recalled from a European trip, when Nathan and Andrew became lovers in Florence. The story centers on Celia's somewhat frustrated attempts to comprehend her attraction to homosexual men, which she sees not as an accident but as what she terms "a career."

Celia is a confidant to both Andrew, who professes not to love Nathan, and Nathan, who likes talking endlessly and analytically with her. While Nathan and Andrew constantly attempt to define for her their conflicting affair, Celia tries to determine why she is attracted only to men who, ultimately, can be attracted only to one another. Additionally, there are discussions among the trio in which issues such as whether one should be a gay activist or whether to discuss one's homosexuality with one's parents are argued. The complexities of Nathan's and Andrew's lives are further explored in scenes in which both Nathan and Andrew tell Celia of their first night of love together, and she becomes aware of the discrepancy of their points of view while experiencing her own ongoing sense of isolation from the men and their lives. She finally realizes that her happiness with each results in part from their unhappiness with each other. She also notices how much of her awareness comes from her repeated partings with the two young men.

"A PLACE I'VE NEVER BEEN"

In Leavitt's second collection, *A Place I've Never Been*, he again deals with the trio in several stories. In the book's title story, Nathan returns from a lengthy trip to Europe to find his apartment in shambles and immediately calls upon Celia, who continues to be for him a dependable prop in his life. Nathan's former lover, Martin, has tested positive for HIV, and Nathan has vowed to give up sex entirely. In Nathan's absence, Celia has discovered her own sense of being and has come to understand her own beauty and appeal. She also knows that as long as she is the only solace in Nathan's life, she cannot have a life of her own, and Nathan now is paralyzed by his fear of getting AIDS—or worse, giving AIDS to someone he loves.

"WHEN YOU GROW TO ADULTERY"

In "When You Grow to Adultery," Andrew resurfaces, having long been separated from Nathan and Celia, the friends of his college years. Andrew momentarily is suspended between his relationship with his established lover, Allen, and his new attraction to an architect named Jack Seldon. Andrew thus is torn between his love for Allen (who needs Andrew) and his need for Jack, a need that is underscored by the story's final scene, where, as he and Allen make love at the house of Allen's parents, Andrew traces Jack's name on Allen's back.

"I SEE LONDON, I SEE FRANCE"

In the story "I See London, I See France," Celia goes to Europe with Seth, a man she has met through a telephone dating service, and she discovers on their first date that they share a love of Italy. At the heart of Celia's life is an essential unhappiness about what her life is and has been and the impossibility of ever making it anything truly different. That realization comes to her vividly as she and Seth visit a "beautiful" couple—Alex and Sylvie Foster and their two daughters, Adriana and Francesca, at the Foster's Italian farmhouse, Il Mestolo. Yet, after an idyllic afternoon at the Italian house, Celia Hoberman, who grew up with her mother, Rose, and her grandmother, Lena, in an apartment in Queens, also comes to know that she, too, can change her life and live in Italy, but she will never break the umbilical cord that life uses to attach everyone to his or her undeniable past.

"TERRITORY" AND "AYOR"

Other problems associated with homosexuals appear in stories such as "Ayor," "Houses," and "My Marriage to Vengeance" in *A Place I've Never Been*, and in the story "Territory" in *Family Dancing*. In "Territory," a young man, Neil, whose mother supports liberal causes, brings his male lover, Wayne, home to visit. The confrontation with his lover brings about a subtle epiphany of suppressed feelings of guilt and responsibility between mother and son. The same kind of shared responsibility of one friend for another's life is seen too in "Ayor," where an unnamed narrator (Nathan, possibly?) tells of his sexual longing for a college friend, Craig Rosen, who later becomes the narrator's guide to the seedy underside of New York's homosexual life. After a trip to France—where he has an affair with a young Frenchman named Laurent, the narrator again meets Craig, who tells him that he has been raped by a man in Spain, a revelation that conjures up for the narrator a complex of feelings questioning the extent to which human beings all are, indeed, somewhat responsible for the lives upon which they impinge.

"MY MARRIAGE TO VENGEANCE"

In yet another story, "My Marriage to Vengeance," Ellen Britchkey is invited to the wedding of her former lesbian lover, Diane Helaine Winters. In this story, Leavitt fully explores both the ironies and the humor inherent in this situation: Ellen's being a lesbian is just how things are, while with Diana, it is merely the exploration of one of several options in life, which leads the narrator (Ellen) to comment, "Rich people are like that, I have noticed. They think a love affair is like a shared real estate venture they can just buy out of when they get tired of it." In actuality, Ellen comes to see, after witnessing Diane cry in desperation about her own wedding, that Diane simply has made a life of compromise for herself, but Ellen also knows that for many like Diane, dishonest compromise in life is easier than difficult honesty.

"HOUSES"

A similar theme is explored in "Houses," in which Paul, a real estate broker married to Susan, suddenly and impetuously enters into a sexual relationship with a local dog groomer, Ted, who cares for the couple's dog, Charlotte. Paul and Ted meet on their first "date" at a local restaurant frequented by homosexuals, the Dunes, and begin a three-month affair. Eventually, however, Paul decides to return to his wife, only to find that she views their marriage as something false and questions whether he ever truly loved her and if he really was not thinking of men as he made love to her. Paul's business occupation with houses is also a personal one, since he professes to "love" houses. After his second departure from his wife, he lives hit-or-miss in a succession of empty houses, a poignant symbol of his sexual life. As he states his condition at one point, it is possible in one's heart to love two different people in differing ways, but it is not possible to do so in life.

"THE LOST COTTAGE"

As Leavitt examines subtly the many ways in which homosexuality alters perceptions of family relationships and values, so too does he look regularly at how divorce can suddenly create a major shift in family values and alliances. In "The Lost Cottage," a story in *Family Dancing*, Leavitt presents the Dempson family, where the parents, Lydia and Alex, six months earlier have announced to their children that they are divorcing. Yet, in spite of the changed nature of the parents' relationship to each other, the family—at the mother Lydia's insistence—still assembles, as they have for twenty-six years, at their summer cottage on Cape Cod.

The Dempsons' three children are Mark, a homosexual who lives in Manhattan doing odd jobs; his sister Ellen, an unmarried lawyer; and Douglas, who, with his girlfriend of the past five years, conducts oceanographic research in Hawaii. All assemble at the family cottage, "Under the Weather," where Lydia, their mother, attempts to continue the same family gathering they long have observed each summer. Yet, this summer's reunion soon disintegrates as Lydia is unable to bear her husband's new relationship, an anxiety that is heightened to crisis proportions for the family when Alex's new girlfriend, Marian Hollister, shows up in the New England village to be near him as he spends time with his family and former wife. Amid the growing tensions set off by Marian's presence, Lydia reveals the blunt fact of her own—and her family's—problem: She still loves her husband, Alex, and always has, and, even if he has left her, he cannot escape the simple fact of that love.

The situation among the family, however, is one that cannot be resolved by any family member; the complexities set in motion by the parents' divorce are such that they are as insurmountable as Mark's trying to comprehend his brother's heterosexual indulgence of his girlfriend's demands. It is a confusion also mirrored in Mark's sister, who cannot understand Mark's ability to go to bed with someone he has just met. The shifts that occur in human relationships—such as homosexual and heterosexual desire—may simply be, ultimately, inexplicable and irreconcilable despite the good intentions of all involved. The tragedy is, as

Ellen tells her family at one point, not that they do not care but that they *do*.

Sexual complications and divorce's ramifications are two principal themes in Leavitt's short fiction. The impact of terminal illness forms a third major topic. In the stories "Counting Months" and "Radiation" (in *Family Dancing*), the manifestations of family problems surrounding the last days of cancer patients and their medical treatment are explored. In "Gravity" (in Leavitt's second collection), a mother's reaction to her son's fatal AIDS is seen. This invocation of fatal illness (especially that of cancer) is one to which the author frequently returns, and it is again treated in his novel *Equal Affections*, where the mother, Louise Cooper, has been involved in a twenty-year struggle with cancer.

"SPOUSE NIGHT"

Another story, "Spouse Night," also presents a group of characters whose lives have all been suddenly altered by the loss of a mate. The title refers to a postdeath support meeting, where persons attempt to come to grips with their individual losses. Arthur has lost his wife, Claire, to a sudden but quickly fatal skin disease, while his new companion, Mrs. Eve Theodorous, recently has lost her husband, Spiro. The survivors have begun a tentative sexual affair and even have acquired a new "child," a puppy that Mrs. Theodorous envies for its ability to forget its family connections and for being spared the sense of loss that humans must accept. Arthur's hesitancy in committing himself to his new relationship with Mrs. Theodorous is emphasized in his passionate scene of grief, when he attempts to scatter his wife's ashes from a boat in the harbor. This scene suggests in vivid detail (which Leavitt is so good at selecting) the anguish encountered in transitional moments in life from one form of commitment to another.

ARKANSAS

Leavitt chose to give his third collection of short fiction the idiosyncratic title *Arkansas: Three Novellas*. The only connection with that state is explained in a quotation he attributes to Victorian writer Oscar Wilde: "I should like to flee like a wounded hart into Arkansas." Ostracized and financially ruined by imprisonment for "gross indecency" (sodomy),

Wilde wanted to hide in some remote wilderness. Leavitt's own embarrassment was far less serious but apparently had a comparable effect.

When Leavitt published the novel *While England Sleeps* he created a furor gleefully reported on both sides of the Atlantic. Stephen Spender, once a prominent English poet, accused Leavitt of plagiarism and sued for libel, charging the young American with borrowing too freely from his autobiography *World Within World* (1948), which includes an account of an intimate relationship with a young man who served as a volunteer in the Spanish Civil War of the 1930's. Leavitt felt disgraced when his publishers pulled his novel out of bookstores. Instead of flying like a wounded hart to Arkansas, he fled Manhattan for the remote wilderness of Los Angeles, California.

"THE TERM PAPER ARTIST"

Leavitt briefly describes his humiliation in "The Term Paper Artist," then gives a hilarious account of being propositioned by a student at a major Southern California university. Eric offers sex in exchange for a ghostwritten term paper comparing and contrasting E. M. Forster's *A Room with a View* (1908) and Henry James's *Daisy Miller* (1878). Leavitt, paralyzed by writer's block, seizes this win-win opportunity. He would enjoy the sexual adventure with a raunchy but virginal young male and the challenge of writing about two homosexual authors with whom he is thoroughly familiar. Rereading their famous novels reminds him of the love for literature that inspired him to make it his career.

Word gets around that a prominent professional writer can be talked into exchanging high-quality papers for sex. He finds himself in a wonderland instead of a wasteland. Though shocked by the callous attitude of his rowdy young "clients" toward both homosexuality and turning in ghostwritten papers, he finds their coarse amorality arousing and adopts their sardonic attitude as a way of coping with the Spender debacle. Instead of corrupting these rowdy young men, they are corrupting him. Then he meets Ben, a confused, sensitive virgin. Their relationship transforms Ben's life when he realizes he has always been a latent homosexual and comes out of the closet with relief and gratitude.

"Saturn Street" and "The Wooden Anniversary"

"Saturn Street" recounts a tragic love affair with an actor the narrator encountered when he volunteered to deliver meals to housebound AIDS victims. Here again Leavitt demonstrates a talent for capturing the sunstruck anomie of sprawling Los Angeles. "The Wooden Anniversary," about dissolute homosexual expatriates in Italy, seems included to pad this slender volume. All three novellas show Leavitt's growing maturity and self-confidence in a confusing but infinitely varied and amusing world, his severance of emotional dependence on family, his abandonment of guilt and self-flagellation, his willingness to face the loneliness and stigma of homosexuality, and, especially, his power to recover from any set back through the healing magic of creative writing.

Other major works

LONG FICTION: *The Lost Language of Cranes*, 1986; *Equal Affections*, 1989; *While England Sleeps*, 1993, rev. 1995; *The Page Turner*, 1998; *Martin Bauman: Or, A Sure Thing*, 2000.

TELEPLAY: *The Lost Language of Cranes*, 1992.

NONFICTION: *Italian Pleasures*, 1996 (with Mark Mitchell).

EDITED TEXTS: *The Penguin Book of Gay Short Stories*, 1994; *Pages Passed from Hand to Hand: The Hidden Tradition of Homosexual Literature in English from 1748 to 1914*, 1997 (with Mitchell).

Bibliography

Bohlen, Celestine. "Writer on the Rebound: This Time, He Takes Liberties with His Own Life." *The New York Times*, February 25, 1997, p. C11. Notes that while Leavitt's book *While England Sleeps* was pulled from the presses after the English poet Stephen Spender filed a plagiarism suit because of sexual suggestions concerning his autobiography, Leavitt's story "The Term Paper Artist" features a character called David Leavitt who has gone home to his father's house to brood over a vengeful English poet's accusation of plagiarism.

Iannone, Carol. "Post Counter-Culture Tristesse." *Commentary* 84 (February, 1987): 57-61. Iannone's article discusses representative themes of Leavitt's work, including his short stories and his first novel, *The Lost Language of Cranes*.

Klarer, Mario. "David Leavitt's 'Territory': René Girard's Homoerotic 'Trigonometry' and Julia Kristeva's 'Semiotic Chora.'" *Studies in Short Fiction* 28 (Winter, 1991): 63-76. Argues that the mother-son-lover triangle in the story "Territory" calls for two different theoretical frames for analysis: René Girard's "erotic triangle" in his 1965 book *Deceit, Desire, and the Novel*, and Julia Kristeva's theory of a "semiotic territory" in her 1984 book *Revolution in Poetic Language*.

Leavitt, David. "Interview with David Leavitt." Interview by Jean Ross. In *Contemporary Authors*, vol. 122, edited by Hal May and Susan M. Trosky. Detroit: Gale Research, 1988. Leavitt, in a telephone interview transcript, discusses his writing habits, his training in creative writing at Yale University, the *Family Dancing* collection, and his novel *The Lost Language of Cranes*. Also reflects on his brief editorial assistant's position at a New York publishing house.

_____. "Interview with David Leavitt." Interview by Sam Staggs. *Publishers Weekly* 237 (August 24, 1990): 47-49. In this interview, Leavitt refers to his collection of stories *A Place I've Never Been* as the first book of "the middle years" of his career; Staggs claims the stories in Leavitt's collection reveal the maturity that his earlier work hinted at, with several excellent stories exploiting the theme of Americans in Europe.

_____. "The New Lost Generation." *Esquire* 103 (May, 1985): 85-88. In an autobiographical remembrance of adolescence in California, Leavitt compares the activist, socially conscious late 1960's generation with that of his own "Yuppie" era.

_____. "New Voices and Old Values." *The New York Times Book Review*, May 12, 1985, 1, 26-27. In a lengthy review of several books by contemporary authors, including Marian Thurm, Peter Cameron, Meg Wolitzer, Elizabeth Tallent, and Amy Hempel, Leavitt cites similarity of themes in their handling of crises in the traditional family and reveals as well elements of his own work and concerns.

_____. "The Way I Live Now." *The New York Times Magazine*, July 9, 1989, 28-29, 32, 80-82. Leavitt, in a personal revelation about his homosexuality, discusses the way in which AIDS has affected his life. He also discusses his involvement with ACT UP, the radical AIDS activist organization, and his views of that organization's necessity and positive influence.

Lo, Mun-Hou. "David Leavitt and the Etiological Maternal Body." *Modern Fiction Studies* 41 (Fall/Winter, 1995): 439-465. Discusses the figure of the mother in some stories from David Leavitt's

debut collection, *Family Dancing*; comments on Leavitt's obsessive interest in the specter of the strong mother, even as this interest can take the form only of looking everywhere except directly at the relationship between maternity and homosexuality.

White, Edmund. "Out of the Closet, onto the Bookshelf." *The New York Times Magazine*, June 16, 1991, 22-24. White writes about the 1980's generation of openly homosexual writers and how the AIDS epidemic has both decimated their ranks and at the same time created a maturity of creative writing as writers react to the disease and its threat.

Jere Real, updated by Bill Delaney

JOSEPH SHERIDAN LE FANU

Born: Dublin, Ireland; August 28, 1814
Died: Dublin, Ireland; February 7, 1873

PRINCIPAL SHORT FICTION

Ghost Stories and Tales of Mystery, 1851
Chronicles of Golden Friars, 1871
In a Glass Darkly, 1872
The Purcell Papers, 1880
The Watcher and Other Weird Stories, 1894
A Chronicle of Golden Friars, 1896
Madam Crowl's Ghost and Other Tales of Mystery, 1923 (M. R. James, editor)
Green Tea and Other Ghost Stories, 1945
Best Ghost Stories of J. S. Le Fanu, 1964
Ghost Stories and Mysteries, 1975

OTHER LITERARY FORMS

Joseph Sheridan Le Fanu is most famous for such horror and mystery novels as *Uncle Silas* (1864) and *Wylder's Hand* (1864), but he also wrote historical novels (*The Cock and Anchor*, 1845; *The House by the Churchyard*, 1863) which depict the social, politi-

cal, and religious conflicts that were surfacing in the Ireland of his day. Although not a prolific or generally important poet, his verse does contain two popular and memorable "Irish Ballads," "Shamus O'Brien" and "Phaudhrig Crochoore." Since, in the course of his literary career, he owned and edited a number of Irish periodicals, Le Fanu wrote numerous articles and essays which have not, as yet, been republished. Late in the nineteenth century his novel *Uncle Silas* was successfully adapted to the stage, and in 1971 his most famous short story, "Carmilla," was filmed as *The Vampire Lovers*.

ACHIEVEMENTS

Like many Anglo-Irish writers, Le Fanu's achievements are of two kinds. On the one hand, because he possessed the advantages of education, culture, and leisure, he was equipped to participate in, and contribute to, contemporary developments in fiction. In this regard, his role in the evolution of the English gothic novel has been widely noted. The modulation from merely sensationalist effects to psychological verisimilitude in Le Fanu's works is an ex-

Joseph Sheridan Le Fanu (CORBIS/Hulton-Deutsch Collection)

ample of a more general development in nineteenth century fiction.

In an Irish context, however, this modulation has a particular resonance. Its emphasis on withdrawal and duress, with failed fortunes and alienated circumstances, may be regarded as an unnervingly accurate representation of the declining importance of the Anglo-Irish as a culture-creating, and value-bearing, class. Le Fanu's artistic interests also led him toward the adaptation of Irish folklore material, a development which also presages, like much of his career, important shifts of emphasis in the cultural history of modern Ireland.

BIOGRAPHY

Descended from an upper-class Irish Protestant family on his father's side and a vitally artistic one on his mother's (his forebears included the playwright Richard Brinsley Sheridan and the actor Thomas Sheridan), Joseph Sheridan Le Fanu was well equipped by inheritance and upbringing for a suc-

cessful writing career. Although he studied law at Trinity College, Dublin, and was admitted to the Irish bar, he never practiced law, going immediately into literature and journalism after graduation. When his first historical novels were dismissed by the critics in the 1840's, he turned almost exclusively to journalism and editing for fifteen years. Le Fanu's journalistic commitments culminated in 1861 in his purchasing the leading Irish intellectual organ of the day, the *Dublin University Magazine*. He continued to own and edit this journal, in which most of his work had been and continued to have its initial publication, until 1869, some four years before his death. It was in this period of public engagement and cultural commitment that Le Fanu's major fiction was produced. In 1844, he married Susan Bennett, daughter of a prominent Dublin attorney; they had four children. This idyllic marriage ended prematurely, however, with her death in 1858. Le Fanu thereupon became a recluse, and it was during these last solitary years that he produced the bulk of his most memorable fiction.

ANALYSIS

Joseph Sheridan Le Fanu's method for writing horror fiction was unusual. After drinking copious amounts of tea for stimulation, he would retire around midnight to his dismal bedroom, where he would nap for approximately two hours, having, if possible, a few provocative nightmares. Upon awakening about two o'clock in the morning, he would begin to write and continue until daylight. He would then sleep again until noon. Unlikely and bizarre as this routine sounds, it was the ritual that Le Fanu followed during the last fifteen years of his life. This was the period in which he produced his best work, a body of fiction that entitles him to rank with Edgar Allan Poe as an innovator in the development of the modern horror and mystery genres.

Le Fanu began these curious compositional procedures following the premature death of his wife. The grief and shock of her passing were instrumental in turning him gradually from a socially active, convivial editor-journalist-writer to a recluse. This progressively increasing self-absorption, isolation, and preoccupation with the dark side of human experience found objective expression in the supernatural stories of his last years, as well as in such outstanding novels as *Uncle Silas* and *Wylder's Hand*. This is not to say, however, that his concentration on the morbid and supernatural represented an abrupt shift in Le Fanu's work. Although his earliest stories and novels focused more on Irish history and society, the macabre was an important ingredient in virtually everything he wrote, especially his shorter fiction. During his fifteen-year "dry spell" (1848-1863), the only book of fiction he published was *Ghost Stories and Tales of Mystery* in 1851.

"SCHALKEN THE PAINTER"

"Schalken the Painter" is vintage early Le Fanu, although in a brief summary it probably sounds as overblown and chaotic as the worst examples of Le Fanu's gothic predecessors. Schalken, a promising Flemish artist, is in love with Rose Velderkaust, the ward of his painting master, Gerard Douw. Because he is poor, Schalken's proposal of marriage to Rose is rejected by Douw in favor of a suit pressed by a rich, mysterious old man, "Minheer Wilken Vanderhausen of Rotterdam." When the principals finally get a good look at Vanderhausen, however, they are horrified: He looks to be a walking corpse. His face has a "bluish leaden hue," his eyes "an undue proportion of muddy white . . . a certain indefinable character of insanity," his lips "nearly black," and "the entire character of the face was sensual, malignant, and even satanic." Nevertheless, the marriage is contracted and takes place.

Some months later, after the couple has vanished and Vanderhausen has been exposed as a fraud, Rose suddenly comes to Schalken and Douw, dressed in a strange white garment, and babbling hysterically that "the dead and the living never can be one"; she eats ravenously and begs for protection. They attempt to guard her but fail, and she vanishes from behind a locked door, never to reappear in the flesh. Years later while in Rotterdam for his father's funeral, Schalken sees her in a dream. Dressed in her white costume, she leads him to a small apartment containing a curtained four-poster bed. She spreads the curtain apart, and Vanderhausen sits up. Schalken faints and is found unconscious the next day in the burial vaults, stretched out beside a coffin.

This narrative clearly leaves more questions than it answers; the reader who expects everything to be neatly tidied up and explained in the end will be disappointed. The *experience* it offers, however, is both unified and potent. Three factors enable Le Fanu to order the chaos in the story quite effectively: the precision with which he controls the structure and point of view; the careful balance in his language between graphic realism and suggestive abstraction; and strong suggestions of an underlying worldview in which such horrible events really do not seem out of place. The title notwithstanding, the main action of the story does not focus on Schalken but on the bizarre fate of the innocent Rose Velderkaust. The painter simply provides the eyes through which these strange events are viewed in bits and pieces. Since most of the action happens offstage, the reader is forced to share the rejected lover's anxiety and puzzlement. Like Schalken, the reader must guess at the awful details of her marriage, and, in the end, the reader is left with the same unanswered questions. As is typical of the best modern practitioners in this genre, Le Fanu stimulates fear and horror as much by what he omits as by what he includes, leaving it to the reader's imagination to make concrete horror out of his many dark hints.

When Le Fanu is specific, however, he is very precise, visual, and visceral. Vanderhausen is no wispy, floating ghost of the sort that haunted old gothic mansions. He is a physically solid—if rotting—corpse, who acts directly and purposefully. The reader cannot avoid identification with the distraught bride as she contemplates intimacy with such a creature. Later, when she makes her sudden appearance dressed in white, her agitation and hysteria are described with powerful visual images and telling details; and lastly, the dream sequence, although brief, ends with the sharp picture of Vanderhausen sitting up in his bedcoffin and grinning at Schalken, a striking final image of perverse sexuality and death.

"Schalken the Painter" bridges the gap between the old gothic and the modern horror story. The plotting probably belongs to the realm of the old—innocent girl sold to the highest bidder, walking corpses, kidnapping, violence behind locked doors, and necrophilia—but the manner of the telling—the carefully controlled structure, point of view, language, and imagery—is definitely new. In the later stories, the transition is complete; both form and content are modern. The best examples of the mature Le Fanu style can be found in his last and finest collection of short stories, *In a Glass Darkly*. All the horror stories in this anthology—,"The Familiar," "Mr. Justice Harbottle," "Carmilla," "Green Tea"—are fully realized, with the last two generally acknowledged as his masterpieces.

IN A GLASS DARKLY

The *In a Glass Darkly* stories all ostensibly come from the papers of the late "Dr. Martin Hesselius, the German Physician," as edited by his secretary. Le Fanu had used this kind of framing device in his first collection in a relatively superficial way. In this anthology, however, the technique is handled in a more sophisticated manner. In addition to gathering the stories, Hesselius personally "analyzes" each "case" and in one story, "Green Tea," plays a major role. If Hesselius, himself, is unconvincing as a personality and "psychic detective," the character type he represents was to become prominent in modern literature; he is, in fact, the first practicing (meddling?) psychiatrist in English fiction.

Hesselius is a mixed blessing. The concept of the psychic detective is a provocative one, and Hesselius's comments give the anthology some overall unity. On the other hand he is such a long-winded bore, with arrogant claims of infallibility that contrast sharply with his inept handling of the situations at hand, that he becomes an irritation. More annoying yet is the ambiguity regarding his ultimate function in these stories. Is he Le Fanu's spokesman or is he simply a pedantic fool? Or, which is more likely, might he be both? Is it possible that beneath the pompous rhetoric of his philosophical diatribes are the clues to Le Fanu's own worldview?

"CARMILLA"

Hesselius, however, has almost no role in the best-known of Le Fanu's short stories, "Carmilla." The secretary, in a short prologue, simply records that the doctor had much to say about the narrative and goes no further. "Carmilla" is probably the only pre-Drac-ula vampire story that can still be read for pleasure as well as historical interest. The vampire in this tale is no distant, forbidding male shrouded in a black cape and hovering in the shadows of a decaying castle but is, rather, Carmilla, a pretty, bright—if "langorous"—young girl who, after ingratiating herself with the family, wins the trust and affections of the story's heroine.

The reader is prepared for her entrance by two ominous events; in the first, at about age six, Laura, the narrator, has a dream in which she is accosted in bed by a beautiful young girl and experiences two needle-like pains in her breast; in the second, an expected visit from a potential girlfriend is canceled by the girl's mysterious death, caused, her guardian reports, by "the fiend who betrayed our infatuated hospitality." Then Carmilla appears suddenly when her carriage has an accident in front of the heroine's family chateau. Claiming she cannot wait for her daughter's recovery, Carmilla's "mother" manipulates Laura's father into accepting the young girl as a house guest.

Shortly after Carmilla is ensconced in the household, a mysterious illness begins to ravage the countryside, which kills only young peasant girls; an "oumpire" is suspected. The reader learns of these depredations, however, only in an indirect, fragmentary fashion. Life in the household is largely unaffected. Thus, the horror in "Carmilla" is much more psychological and less visceral than it was in "Schalken." As Le Fanu carefully reveals clues about Carmilla's demonic nature and sinister purposes, he also intensifies the emotional tie between the two girls. Carmilla woos Laura with the ardor of a lover. Le Fanu is most contemporary in the way he makes explicit (although restrained) use of the sexual connotations of the vampire myth. The lesbian implications in "Carmilla" have been strongly emphasized by some critics and, while there is some distortion evident in this approach, these elements are too overt to ignore. There is more here, however, than sexuality; the eroticism is linked to thoughts of death: Eros meets Thanatos. This association is central to the long, powerful appeal of the vampire myth and few writers since have treated it so directly and provocatively.

Paradoxically, however, this female-female relationship also creates Le Fanu's most serious artistic problem. Having created a villainess who, if not actually sympathetic, is at least very real and deeply involved with her victim, how can be mete out the just but gory punishment that Carmilla deserves without destroying the mood and direction of the story? His solution is to shift the focus completely away from Laura to a new set of characters. It is they who trap and destroy Carmilla in her coffin. Although this tactic does resolve Le Fanu's plotting problem, it also damages the momentum of the story; the ending of "Carmilla" is logically sound, but emotionally unsatisfying.

If "Carmilla," however, is a flawed masterpiece of the macabre, Le Fanu's shorter and more subtle "Green Tea" has no such defects; it is supreme example of the modern horror story. The simplicity of this tale contrasts with the gothic complexity of "Schalken the Painter" or even "Carmilla." Dr. Hesselius meets a pleasant middle-aged cleric, the Reverend Mr. Jennings, at a dinner party. Upon learning the doctor's identity, the clergyman seeks him out and requests treatment. Hesselius thus learns of his strange and frightening condition. Jennings has been plagued for nearly three years by a small black spectral monkey, which has harassed, abused, mocked, and threatened him with increasing fury. Although the clergyman has managed to maintain a calm demeanor, he is desperate, almost suicidal, when he finally contacts Hesselius. The German doctor, however, can offer only a little ineffective advice. Shortly thereafter, Hesselius goes into isolation, causing him to receive the cleric's last frantic communication a day too late; they find Jennings with his throat cut, a suicide.

Again, it is Le Fanu's skill in telling the story that separates "Green Tea" from the work of his contemporaries. Because the narration is indirect, the reader is drawn slowly and carefully into the story, thus allowing the horror to manifest itself gradually and muting the potentially comic effect of a monkey as specter. This subtlety in presentation is one of the important qualitative differences between even the best early Le Fanu stories, such as "Schalken the Painter," and his mature works. Jennings does not actually reveal his problem to Hesselius until the story is almost

half over; and, as the reader learns the facts in this case, he also comes to understand the personalities of the two principal characters. The arrogance and insensitivity of Hesselius contrasts sharply with the intelligence, sensitivity, and muted desperation of Jennings. In only a few pages the reader comes to like the doomed cleric; and although his final act comes as no surprise, it is a shock.

During Hesselius's first casual conversations with Jennings, he is surprised to hear of the cleric's interest in "Metaphysical Medicine," Swedenborgian philosophy, and pre-Christian religions. From others the doctor learns some additional facts about Jennings's life and background: that his father had conversed with a ghost; that he was addicted to strong green tea; that, despite his apparently vital appearance, his health always failed him whenever he attempted to assume his pastoral duties; and that he had the odd habit of staring into space as though actually seeing something. These bits of information, coupled with the sense of dread and desperation that increasingly shows beneath Jennings's controlled behavior, prepare the reader for the revelation of the troubled cleric's secret.

Jennings's red-eyed monkey is certainly one of the most memorable fiends in literature, a far cry from the disembodied, innocuous ghosts typical of Le Fanu's predecessors. Le Fanu chronicles the course of the relationship between cleric and creature with a meticulousness of detail and imagery that makes it vividly real. This relationship is described in three distinct stages: the initial meeting on an omnibus and Jennings's reactions to it; the protracted conflict between the clergyman and his specter; and the creature's intensified assault on his victim, which finally pushes Jennings to suicide. The monkey is a solid physical presence to Jennings, although he touches nothing when he attempts to run his umbrella through the thing. The focal point of the beast is its "smokey red eyes," which are never off of Jennings. Although black as pitch, the creature remains visible in the dark "in a halo that resembles a glow of red embers"; even with his eyes closed, Jennings sees the malevolent beast. Its absences, sometimes up to three months in duration, add to Jennings's torment, since he knows that the monkey will return with intensified malice when least expected. It also talks to him constantly, becoming most vociferous whenever the clergyman attempts to worship or carry out his pastoral duties; in the midst of sermons, it squats on the minister's text, forcing him to flee the lectern. As the clergyman becomes increasingly debilitated, the monkey becomes correspondingly more active, as though it were draining off his energies for its own use, until Jennings has no way out but suicide.

Dr. Hesselius never sees the specter himself, nor does Jennings do more than paraphrase the monkey's words. Thus, Le Fanu follows the dictum later articulated by his successor M. R. James to "leave a loophole for a natural explanation, but . . . let the loophole be so narrow as not to be quite practicable." Is it all a figment of Jennings's imagination or is the fiend truly a being from another order of reality? Or could it somehow be both?

Critics have used this "loophole" to develop a variety of interpretations of "Green Tea." To one critic, Jennings, a bachelor, is a classic schizophrenic having a breakdown and the monkey represents repressed sexuality surfacing. To an analyst of the Christian persuasion, the monkey is a demonic punishment for hidden sins or perhaps an embodiment of original sin. More mundane critics have simply cited the effects of green tea on the nervous system and have left it at that. All such views, which unduly narrow the story to a case history of one sort or another, miss the point of James's "loophole" theory. An inadequate or incomplete "rational" explanation in a supernatural fiction actually reinforces the sense of horror by heightening the ambiguity that underlies it. Certainly Jennings is made vulnerable to the unseen by virtue of his heredity, his addiction to green tea, his metaphysical bent, and his taste for primitive religion, but none of these things explains his fate, and nothing he does that the reader knows of—his religious views, his social behavior, or his sex life— indicates that he deserves it.

Perhaps the key lies in the Swedenborgian references as interpreted (and distorted) by Hesselius. Although the doctor is too much of a bore to be taken with complete seriousness, his ideas do seem to point toward Le Fanu's own vision, a vision that is both conceptually powerful and artistically convenient for the writer of horror fiction who would go beyond the conventional heaven/hell, black magic/white magic, good/evil dichotomies. In this view, there exists all about us a world of the unseen of which only a few, by design or accident, get a glimpse, and those who do are in great peril. Evil is not accidental; neither is it gratuitous or external, but it is everywhere, all the time, within as well as without. It is this sense of the pervasiveness of evil that separates Le Fanu's best work from that of his predecessors and contemporaries; the demonic exists just at the edge of our existence, just out of sight, and can force itself into vision at any time through almost any opening, even one created by so trivial a substance as green tea.

OTHER MAJOR WORKS

LONG FICTION: *The Cock and Anchor*, 1845; *The Fortunes of Colonel Torlogh O'Brien*, 1847; *The House by the Churchyard*, 1863; *Wylder's Hand*, 1864; *Uncle Silas*, 1864; *Guy Deverell*, 1865; *All in the Dark*, 1866; *The Tenants of Malory: A Novel*, 1867 (3 volumes); *A Lost Name*, 1868; *The Wyvern Mystery*, 1869; *Checkmate*, 1871; *The Rose and the Key*, 1871; *Morley Court*, 1873; *Willing to Die*, 1873 (3 volumes).

POETRY: *The Poems of Joseph Sheridan Le Fanu*, 1896.

BIBLIOGRAPHY

Begnal, Michael H. *Joseph Sheridan Le Fanu*. Lewisburg, Pa.: Bucknell University Press, 1971. Although this volume is only an essay-length discussion of Le Fanu's works, it is valuable in providing general commentary about Le Fanu's intellectual and artistic interests, especially his sensitive understanding of women.

Browne, Nelson. *Sheridan Le Fanu*. London: Arthur Barker, 1951. This short critical exposition places emphasis on Le Fanu's "essentially Gothick quality." The author believes Le Fanu to be at his beat in his short fiction, advancing familiar objections to his novels' prolixity. Old-fashioned in tone and attitude, but a pioneering study.

Crawford, Gary William. *J. Sheridan Le Fanu: A Bio-Bibliography*. Westport, Conn.: Greenwood Press, 1995. Part 1 discusses Le Fanu's biography; part 2 is a primary, annotated bibliography of magazines, books, anthologies, and manuscripts; part 3 is an annotated secondary bibliography. The beginning student of Le Fanu will find this book an indispensable tool, which includes an appendix on films and plays based on Le Fanu's work. Also contains two useful indexes.

McCormack, W. J. *Dissolute Characters: Irish Literary History Through Balzac, Sheridan Le Fanu, Yeats, and Bowen*. Manchester: Manchester University Press, 1993. The section on Le Fanu discusses his relationship to the English novel, the development of his fiction, his treatment of characters, and his drawing on history. Includes notes but no bibliography.

_____. *Sheridan Le Fanu and Victorian Ireland*. Oxford, England: Clarendon Press, 1980. The standard work on Le Fanu. The author's approach is twofold. First, this study is a detailed biography of Le Fanu. Second, it locates, with much intellectual sophistication, Le Fanu's life in his times, giving to what might remain mere biographical data the stamp of historical significance. A second, enlarged edition of this important work was issued in 1991.

Melada, Ivan. *Sheridan Le Fanu*. Boston: Twayne, 1987. Melada's approach is chronological, proceeding from Le Fanu's early short fiction to the major novels with which his career ends. The critical emphasis sees Le Fanu as a writer of popular fiction, the quality of which entitles him to serious academic consideration. Contains a chronology and a bibliography.

Orel, Harold. *The Victorian Short Story*. New York: Cambridge University Press, 1986. In his chapter on Le Fanu, Orel discusses Le Fanu's contributions to the development of the horror tale in the nineteenth century. Discusses the most important stories in *In a Glass Darkly*, including "Mr. Justice Harbottle," "Green Tea," and "Carmilla."

Signorotti, Elizabeth. "Repossessing the Body: Transgressive Desire in 'Carmilla' and *Dracula*." *Criticism* 38 (Fall, 1996): 607-632. Argues that in contrast to Bram Stoker's work, the female characters in Le Fanu's story are allowed to usurp male authority; claims that Dracula attempts to repossess the female body for the purposes of male pleasure and exchange and to rectify the reckless unleashing of female desire that occurs in Carmilla.

Sullivan, Jack. *Elegant Nightmares: The English Ghost Story from Le Fanu to Blackwood*. Athens: Ohio University Press, 1978. A detailed discussion of "Green Tea" as the archetypal ghost story in the nineteenth century. Argues that the story is an intentionally fuzzy narrative, much like many of the stories of Ambrose Bierce.

Sullivan, Kevin. "*The House by the Churchyard*: James Joyce and Sheridan Le Fanu." In *Modern Irish Literature: Essays in Honour of William York Tindall*, edited by Raymond J. Porter and James D. Brophy. New Rochelle, N.Y.: Iona College Press, 1972. Le Fanu's novel *The House by the Churchyard* has some of its significant scenes set in the village of Chapelizod, a few miles west of Dublin and at the western end of the Phoenix Park. James Joyce's *Finnegans Wake* (1939) contains numerous important allusions to both these Dublin settings. This essay traces the presence of the earlier work in the later. The undertaking is both an academic rehabilitation of Le Fanu's novel and an illustrative instance of Joyce's method in *Finnegans Wake*.

Towheed, Shafquat. "A Chasm in the Narrative of J. Sheridan Le Fanu's 'Green Tea.'" *Notes and Queries* 46 (March, 1999): 67. Accounts for a chronological inconsistency in the story by arguing the author of this serial fiction inadvertently confused real time and fictional time.

Veeder, William. "'Carmilla': The Arts of Repression." *Texas Studies in Literature and Language* 22 (1980): 197-223. A highly detailed discussion of the psychological dynamics of the story as a story of sexual repression. Discusses the dualities that dominate the story.

Keith Neilson, updated by George O'Brien

URSULA K. LE GUIN

Born: Berkeley, California; October 21, 1929

PRINCIPAL SHORT FICTION

The Word for World Is Forest, 1972
The Wind's Twelve Quarters, 1975
Orsinian Tales, 1976
The Water Is Wide, 1976
Gwilan's Harp, 1981
The Compass Rose, 1982
The Visionary: The Life Story of Flicker of the Serpentine, with Wonders Hidden, 1984
Buffalo Gals and Other Animal Presences, 1987
Fish Soup, 1992
A Fisherman of the Inland Sea: Science Fiction Stories, 1994
Solitude, 1994 (novella)
Unlocking the Air and Other Stories, 1996

OTHER LITERARY FORMS

Ursula K. Le Guin is best known for her novels, especially the Earthsea books, which include *A Wizard of Earthsea* (1968), *The Tombs of Atuan* (1971), *The Farthest Shore* (1972), and *Tehanu: The Last Book of Earthsea* (1990). Other well-known novels include *The Left Hand of Darkness* (1969), *The Lathe of Heaven* (1971), *The Dispossessed: An Ambiguous Utopia* (1974), *Always Coming Home* (1985), and the four linked novellas *Four Ways to Forgiveness* (1995). She also published poetry, including *Wild Angels* (1975), *Hard Words and Other Poems* (1981), and *Going Out with Peacocks and Other Poems* (1994). *The Language of the Night: Essays on Fantasy and Science Fiction* (1979) and *Dancing at the Edge of the World: Thoughts on Words, Women, and Places* (1988) are important collections of her critical writing. Le Guin edited *The Norton Book of Science Fiction: North American Science Fiction, 1960-1990* (1993) and *Steering the Craft: Exercises and Discussions on Story Writing for the Lone Navigator or the Mutinous Crew* (1998) and translated *Tao Te Ching: A Book About the Way and the Power of the Way* (1997).

ACHIEVEMENTS

Ursula K. Le Guin is recognized as a leading American writer of science fiction and fantasy. Her short stories, especially "The Ones Who Walk Away from Omelas," winner of a 1974 Hugo Award, often appear in college literature anthologies. Le Guin has received many awards and honors for her work. *The Left Hand of Darkness* and *The Dispossessed* received both the Nebula and Hugo Awards. Volumes of the Earthsea books earned awards for adolescent literature, including the *Boston Globe*/Horn Book Award for *A Wizard of Earthsea*, a Newbery Honor Book Citation for *The Tombs of Atuan*, and the National Book Award for Children's Literature for *The Farthest Shore*. Her other awards include a Hugo for *The Word for World Is Forest*, a Nebula and Jupiter Award in 1975 for "The Day Before the Revolution," and Jupiters for *The Dispossessed* and "The Diary of the Rose." She was given a Gandalf Award in 1979, an American Book Award nomination and the Janet Heidinger Kafka Prize for Fiction for *Always Home* in 1986, and Nebula Awards for *Tehanu* in 1991 and for *Solitude* in 1995.

BIOGRAPHY

Ursula Kroeber was born on October 21, 1929, in Berkeley, California, the daughter of anthropologist Alfred L. Kroeber and author Theodora Kroeber. She received her B.A. from Radcliffe College in 1951 and her M.A. from Columbia University in 1952. While on a Fulbright Fellowship in Paris in 1953, she married Charles A. Le Guin. They had three children: daughters Elisabeth and Caroline and a son, Theodore. She taught French at Mercer University and the University of Idaho before settling in Portland, Oregon, in 1959. In 1962, she began publishing fantasy and science fiction. In addition to writing, she was active in the Democratic Party, in writing workshops, and in Tai Chi Chuan, a Chinese form of exercise.

ANALYSIS

As literary scholars and critics give more attention

to fantasy and science fiction, Ursula K. Le Guin attracts a large share of their interest because she creates possible worlds that cast an informative light on perennial human problems, she explores gender issues that make her fiction popular among feminist readers, and she is precise and powerful in her use of language.

When Le Guin writes about her craft and her works, she often refers to Jungian psychology and Daoist philosophy as major components of her worldview. In her 1975 essay "The Child and the Shadow," Le Guin uses Jungian psychology to support her contention that fantasy is "the language of the night," an important means by which the collective unconscious speaks to the growing individual. In Le Guin's understanding of Jungian thought, consciousness, the part of the self that can be expressed in everyday language, emerges from the unconscious as a child matures. The individual's unconscious is shared in its essentials with all other humans and so is called the collective unconscious.

To become an adult, an individual must find ways of realizing the greatest potential of the unconscious. For Le Guin, these are summed up in the recognition by the individual that on unconscious levels, he or she is identical with all other humans. This recognition releases the irrational forces of social binding, such as compassion, love, creativity, and the sense of belonging to the human community. A major problem in achieving this recognition is learning to deal with "the shadow." Choosing to be one person involves choosing not to be other persons that one could be. Both the positive and the negative choices must be maintained to sustain an identity; the negative choices become one's shadow. The process of achieving adulthood is blocked by the shadow, an unconscious antiself with which one must deal in order to take possession of the rest of the unconscious.

For Le Guin, a child becomes an adult when he or she is able to cease projecting evil impulses onto others and to recognize that these impulses are part of the self. This process, she believes, is symbolically represented in the many fairy tales and fantasies in which an animal helps the protagonist to discover and attain his true identity. Such stories speak to the un-

Ursula K. Le Guin (Margaret Chodos)

conscious, telling the child by means of myth and symbol how to achieve wholeness of self.

Le Guin's writings tend to equate Daoism, a Chinese philosophy expressed about two thousand years ago in the *Dao De Jing*, with Jungian psychology. This goal of wholeness, as expressed in the Circle of Life, or yin and yang symbol of Daoist philosophy, is a recurrent theme in her fiction. The Circle of Life is a diagram of the dynamic relationship between being and nonbeing in the universe. Le Guin celebrates the balancing of such oppositions.

This metaphysic leads to an ethic of passive activity. All acts in the world of being imply their opposites, the assertion of being activating the potential for nonbeing of the end one seeks. Acts of coercion aimed at controlling human behavior are especially prone to produce equal and opposite reactions. Therefore, Le Guin's more successful characters do not try to influence people's actions by direct persuasion or by force but rather by being models of the desired activity.

Le Guin's science fiction differs from her fantasy and psychomyths in that the distinguishing feature of the story's world is technology rather than magic. Her best science-fiction stories accept the unique technology as a given and center on fully realized characters coming to terms with the problems or implications of that technology. "The Eye Altering" recounts the struggle of colonists trying to adjust to a new planet that does not quite mesh with their metabolism, especially the difficulties they encounter when they discover that they are bearing children who, in fact, are better suited to this new planet than to Earth. In "The Diary of the Rose," the psychoscope, a therapeutic tool, allows a form of mind reading. An apprentice analyst confronts the problem of how to treat a patient who seems perfectly sane but who is accused of political deviation. Several of Le Guin's best science-fiction stories became the seeds of later novels or developed in relation to her novels. "Winter's King" led to *The Left Hand of Darkness*. Written after *The Dispossessed*, "The Day Before the Revolution" is about the death of Odo, the woman who founded Odonianism, the anarchist philosophy of Anarres society in *The Dispossessed*. In "The New Atlantis," Le Guin combines psychomyth and science fiction. While a future America sinks into the sea under the weight of political tyranny and ecological sin, a mythical new world awakens and rises from the sea. In each of these stories, the fates of fully realized characters are more central than the science-fiction settings and technology.

Though Le Guin's stories nearly always contain multiple layers of meaning that repay rereading, they are usually also engaging and entertaining on first reading. She interests the reader in her characters or she sets up her problems in images and symbols that stimulate the imagination and lead to speculation. Many of her stories are also witty. Sometimes the wit is broad, as in "The Author of the Acacia Seeds," which tells of efforts to translate the writings of ants. Sometimes, her wit is more subtle, as in "Sur," an account of the "real" first expedition to the South Pole, made by a group of women who kept their feat a secret to avoid embarrassing Roald Amundsen.

This brief account cannot deal with many of Le Guin's themes. She has shown significant interest in feminism and other political and social themes. Her family background in anthropology contributed to her interest in imagining cultures and contact between alien cultures. Over the span of her career, she has tended to move from more traditional forms of fantasy and science fiction toward imagining alternative cultures and their interactions.

"DARKNESS BOX"

Several of these aspects of Le Guin's worldview appear in "Darkness Box," one of her earliest publications. "Darkness Box" is a fairy tale/allegory that takes place in a world of cycles. In this world, time does not pass. There is no source of light, though it is always midmorning. Certain events repeat themselves exactly and perpetually. A young prince rides with his army to the seashore to repel an invasion by his rebel brother. The brother always comes from the sea; he is always defeated and killed. At the same time that he leaves, the prince returns to the palace of his father, who exiled the brother. The prince always rides out again with his army to meet the restored and returning invaders. Into this cycle intrudes what appears to be a unique set of events that are sequential rather than cyclical. The son of a witch finds a box on the shore and gives it to the prince. The king recognizes it as a box he cast into the sea and warns the prince not to open it. The prince's longing for music that ends, for wholeness, leads him to knock the box open and restrains him from closing it. Darkness spills out, the darkness of shadows and their opposite, the sun. He begins to experience conflict, death, and the passing of time. Having achieved a shadow, he has entered into time and being.

Read as a Jungian myth of maturation, the tale represents the collective unconscious as a place of unrealized potentials for identity. The prince is a potential ego, his exiled brother a potential shadow, their endless battle a portent of the struggle consciousness must undergo to create a mature personality. Opening the box that lets out darkness becomes a symbolic representation of the birth of the ego, the entrance into time, and self-creation with real consequences for the self, such as the creation of a shadow and the acceptance of mortality.

Read as a Daoist allegory, the tale represents non-being, the dark half of the Circle of Life, as a place of unrealized potential for being. Nonbeing is timeless and changeless yet full of possibilities. In this reading, opening the box realizes some of the potentials for being. A real world begins, a world of cause and effect in time, a world bounded by nonbeing as reflected in the introduction of true death. Though not all of Le Guin's stories so directly communicate the Jungian and Daoist aspects of her worldview, many become richer and deeper when viewed in this context.

Le Guin defines fantasy as the manipulation of myths and symbols to communicate with the unconscious. Some of her fantasies she called psychomyths: "more or less surrealistic tales, which share with fantasy the quality of taking place outside any history, outside of time, in that region of the living mind which . . . seems to be without spatial or temporal limits at all."

"THE ONES WHO WALK AWAY FROM OMELAS"

"The Ones Who Walk Away from Omelas" is probably Le Guin's best-known psychomyth. This story combines fiction and essay in an unusual way. The narrator describes the beautiful and happy city of Omelas beginning its summer festival. Gradually, she reveals that this is an imagined city. The narrator cautions the reader against doubting that a utopian city filled with joy might also be a place of dynamic and meaningful life. The reader is encouraged to follow his own fancy in imagining a truly happy city. She suggests attitudes toward technology, sexual pleasure, and drug use that would foster happiness, then returns to a description of the festival.

Guessing that the reader will be skeptical even after helping to imagine this wonderful city, she then reveals two more facts. First, the happiness of Omelas depends upon one small child being locked forever in a dark room, deprived of all comfort and affection. Any effort to provide care and justice for that child would destroy the happiness of Omelas. Second, there are people who cannot bear to accept their happiness under this condition. These are the ones who walk away.

Structured as a mutually imagined myth, this story seems designed to provoke examination of the tendencies of human imagination. Why must people find

a dark side of beauty in order to believe in it? Why is happiness unimaginable without suffering? How do people manage to find ways of accepting life under these terms? Why are some people unable to accept that living inevitably entails gaining from the suffering of others? While this story is somewhat different in form from her more typical fantasies, it seems to share with them the central aim of fantasy Le Guin described in "The Child and the Shadow": to reduce the reader's inclination "to give up in despair or to deny what he sees, when he must face the evil that is done in the world, and the injustices and grief and suffering that we must all bear, and the final shadow at the end of all."

A FISHERMAN OF THE INLAND SEA

The importance of imagination in achieving balance continues in *A Fisherman of the Inland Sea*. The volume begins with an eleven-page introduction in which Le Guin dichotomizes readers into "us"—science-fiction readers—and people who cannot or will not program their VCRs, which is how she characterizes those who spurn the genre. She also explains thematic aspects of the eight stories in the collection, the last three of which are space-exploration fantasies that involve imagined cultures and technologies she has previously developed, namely the Hanish world and the ansible. She adds to these a time-space device called a "churten" drive, which allows instantaneous transmission of matter across any points in space.

"The First Contact with the Gorgonids" is a straightforward "justice served" narrative that explains how the much-abused housewife, Annie Laurie Debree, became the hero of Grong Crossing, at the expense of her difficult husband, Jerry. The second story, "Newton's Sleep," explores the psychological impact of an earthwide holocaust on the surviving escapees. "Ascent of the North Face" is predicated on the language pun of the title and rolls out in journal-entry style. "The Rock That Changed Things" depicts the evolutionary dynamic of an oppressed race as it attains autonomy, reminiscent of *The Word for World Is Forest*. The fifth story, "The Kerastion," describes a coherent set of cultural behaviors that involve the production of a musical instrument from human flesh. Taken together, these five stories show Le Guin to be varied in approach and treatment and interested in different subjects.

The trilogy of space stories begins with "The Shobies' Story." The Hanish-Gethenian-Human crew of ten take a test flight using a new "churten" drive. Their noninterval "transilence" to a distant location becomes problematic as they seek to interpret their separate realities. They are able to reintegrate into a unified story of their travel only out of a willingness to achieve group harmony. The next test, described in "Dancing to Ganam," involves a smaller crew of Cetians and Hanish that included Dalzul, a charismatic leader. Their arrival in another world, where they are treated as gods, ends in Dalzul's sacrifice, apparently as a willed conclusion from the collective group. The collection's title story, "Another Story: Or, A Fisherman of the Inland Sea," continues the "churten" theme. The narrator, Hideo, begins with the fable of a fisherman who catches the attention of the sea king's daughter, agrees to stay with her for a night, then finds that more than one hundred years have passed in the short time of his absence. Hideo leaves home and a nascent love interest, Isidri, in order to study temporal physics. Eventually, he becomes disjunct in time, when experimenting with the churten drive, and arrives back at home fifteen years earlier, just after he had decided to leave. Instead, he chooses to stay and follow a different path. Hideo then accepts the love of Isidri but wonders what has happened in the temporal paradox of his future.

OTHER MAJOR WORKS

LONG FICTION: *Rocannon's World*, 1966; *Planet of Exile*, 1966; *City of Illusions*, 1967; *A Wizard of Earthsea*, 1968; *The Left Hand of Darkness*, 1969; *The Tombs of Atuan*, 1971; *The Lathe of Heaven*, 1971; *The Farthest Shore*, 1972; *The Dispossessed: An Ambiguous Utopia*, 1974; *Very Far Away from Anywhere Else*, 1976; *The Eye of the Heron*, 1978; *Leese Webster*, 1979; *Malafrena*, 1979; *The Beginning Place*, 1980; *Always Coming Home*, 1985; *Tehanu: The Last Book of Earthsea*, 1990; *Searoad: Chronicles of Klatsand*, 1991; *Four Ways to Forgiveness*, 1995 (four linked novellas); *The Telling*, 2000.

POETRY: *Wild Angels*, 1975; *Hard Words and Other Poems*, 1981; *In the Red Zone*, 1983; *Wild Oats and Fireweed: New Poems*, 1988; *Blue Moon over Thurman Street*, 1993; *Going Out with Peacocks and Other Poems*, 1994; *Sixty Odd: New Poems*, 1999.

NONFICTION: *From Elfland to Poughkeepsie*, 1973; *The Language of the Night: Essays on Fantasy and Science Fiction*, 1979 (Susan Wood, editor); *Dancing at the Edge of the World: Thoughts on Words, Women, and Places*, 1988; *Napa: The Roots and Springs of the Valley*, 1989; *Steering the Craft: Exercises and Discussions on Story Writing for the Lone Navigator or the Mutinous Crew*, 1998.

CHILDREN'S LITERATURE: *The Adventure of Cobbler's Rune*, 1982; *The Visionary*, 1984; *Solomon Leviathan's 931st Trip Around the World*, 1988; *A Visit from Dr. Katz*, 1988; *Catwings*, 1988; *Catwings Return*, 1989; *Fire and Stone*, 1989; *A Ride on the Red Mare's Back*, 1992; *Tom Mouse and Ms. Howe*, 1998; *Jane on Her Own: A Catwings Tale*, 1999.

TRANSLATION: *Tao Te Ching: A Book About the Way and the Power of the Way*, 1997 (of Laozi).

EDITED TEXTS: *The Norton Book of Science Fiction: North American Science Fiction, 1960-1990*, 1993; *Steering the Craft: Exercises and Discussions on Story Writing for the Lone Navigator or the Mutinous Crew*, 1998.

BIBLIOGRAPHY

Bittner, James W. *Approaches to the Fiction of Ursula K. Le Guin*. Ann Arbor: UMI Research Press, 1984. This author discusses both Le Guin's short stories and novels, making connections among her works to show how certain themes are apparent in all of them.

Bucknall, Barbara J. *Ursula K. Le Guin*. New York: Frederick Ungar, 1981. The main emphasis in this book is a discussion of Le Guin's novels, mainly in chronological order. It does include one chapter devoted to her short fiction.

Collins, Jerre. "Leaving Omelas: Questions of Faith and Understanding." *Studies in Short Fiction* 27 (Fall, 1990): 525-535. Argues that "The Ones Who Walk Away from Omelas" can be read either as a religious allegory of the "suffering servant" or as an allegory of Western capitalism; however, rejection of the capitalist exploitation story undermines the redemption story. Thus, Le Guin indirectly supports the scapegoat theodicy she tries to undermine.

Cummins, Elizabeth. *Understanding Ursula K. Le Guin.* Columbia: University of South Carolina Press, 1990. An analysis of Le Guin's work emphasizing the different worlds she has created (Earthsea, the Hannish World, Orsinia, and the West Coast) and how they provide the structure for all of her fiction.

De Bolt, Joe, ed. *Ursula K. Le Guin: Voyager to Inner Lands and to Outer Space.* Port Washington, N.Y.: Kennikat Press, 1979. This volume is a collection of critical essays that discusses Le Guin's work from a variety of perspectives, including anthropology, sociology, science, and Daoist philosophy.

Kaler, Anne K. "'Carving in Water': Journey/Journals and the Images of Women's Writings in Ursula Le Guin's 'Sur.'" *Literature, Interpretation, Theory* 7 (1997): 51-62. Claims that Le Guin's story "Sur" provides a cleverly coded map for women striving to be professional writers; to illustrate the paths that women writers must take into the tundras ruled by male writers, she uses the devices of disorder, dislocation, and reversal in the journey/journal.

Reid, Suzanne Elizabeth. *Presenting Ursula K. Le Guin.* New York: Twayne, 1997. This critical biography helps young readers to understand how her childhood, family, and life have helped to shape Le Guin's work.

Spivack, Charlotte. *Ursula K. Le Guin.* Boston: Twayne, 1984. Begins with a brief chronology of important personal and professional milestones in Le Guin's life up to 1981, and then examines her background and her literary contributions. Includes annotated references, primary and secondary bibliographies, and an index.

Walsh, William. "I Am a Woman Writer; I Am a Western Writer: An Interview with Ursula Le Guin." *The Kenyon Review,* n.s. 17 (Summer/Fall, 1995): 192-205. Le Guin discusses such topics as the genre of science fiction, her readership, the feminist movement, women writers, and the Nobel Prize.

White, Donna R. *Dancing with Dragons: Ursula K. Le Guin and the Critics.* Columbia, S.C.: Camden House, 1999. Part of the Studies in English and American Literature, Linguistics, and Culture series, this volume examines Le Guin's works and critical reaction to them.

Terry Heller, updated by Eunice Pedersen Johnston and Scott Vander Ploeg

STANISŁAW LEM

Born: Lvov, Poland; September 12, 1921

PRINCIPAL SHORT FICTION

Sezam i inne opowiadania, 1954

Dzienniki gwiazdowe, 1957, 1971 (*The Star Diaries,* 1976, and *Memoirs of a Space Traveler: Further Reminiscences of Ijon Tichy,* 1982)

Inwazja z Aldebarana, 1959 (partial translation, *Tales of Pirx the Pilot,* 1979)

Księga robotów, 1961

Bajki robotów, 1964 (partial translation, *Mortal Engines,* 1977)

Cyberiada, 1965 (*The Cyberiad: Fables for the Cybernetic Age,* 1974)

Ratujmy kosmos i inne opowiadania, 1966

Opowieści o pilocie Pirxie, 1968 (*Tales of Pirx the Pilot,* 1979; *More Tales of Pirx the Pilot,* 1982)

Doskonała próżnia, 1971 (*A Perfect Vacuum,* 1979)

Wielkość urojona, 1973 (*Imaginary Magnitude,* 1984)

Maska, 1976 (partial translation, *Mortal Engines*, 1977)

Suplement, 1976

Mortal Engines, 1977

Powtórka, 1979

Golem XIV, 1981

The Cosmic Carnival of Stanisław Lem: An Anthology of Entertaining Stories by the Modern Master of Science Fiction, 1981

Prowokacja, 1984 (partial translation, *One Human Minute*, 1986)

Ciemność i pleśń, 1988

Apokryfy, 1998

Stanislaw Lem (Franz Rottensteiner)

Other literary forms

Stanisław Lem may well be the best-known Continental European science-fiction writer. He has written teleplays (produced in his native country), but his short stories and particularly his many novels have brought him an even wider circulation. In whatever form, he has concentrated on speculative fictions in which he frequently describes the future of society, combining philosophical argument with imaginative technological fantasies. He has also published book-length studies and collections of essays on technology, general literature, and science fiction. A valuable selection of those essays is available in English translation in *Microworlds: Writings on Science Fiction and Fantasy* (1984), which also includes the autobiographical essay "Reflections on My Life." An extensive account of Lem's early life has been translated as *Highcastle: A Remembrance* (1995).

Achievements

Several critics have stated that Lem is the only science-fiction writer worthy of the Nobel Prize in Literature. He is the widely recognized master of this genre in Eastern Europe and one of the best-known and highly respected science-fiction writers in the world. His books have been translated into more than forty languages and have sold over twenty-five million copies. He is the most widely translated Polish writer since Henryk Sienkiewicz. Through his achievements as a philosophical novelist, short-story writer, and essayist who has probed the social, psy-

chological, and intellectual ramifications of the human-machine interface, he has elevated science fiction from a denigrated genre to respected literature. He helped found the Polish Astronautical Society and was an influential member of the Polish Cybernetic Association until he canceled his membership in both organizations when he came to doubt the capacity of such institutions to foster creativity. In Poland, the Ministry of Culture honored Lem's work in 1965 and presented him with the 1973 Polish State Literary Award. He also received the Polish State Prize for Literature in 1976. In France, Andrei Tarkovsky's film version of Lem's novel *Solaris* (1961; English translation, 1970) won the Special Jury Prize at the 1972 Cannes Film Festival. In recognition of the important body of work he had created he was given the Great Austrian State Award for European Literature in 1986. His works have also earned him a special Nebula Award. The Science Fiction Writers of America made Lem their second honorary member (their first was J. R. R. Tolkien), but his scathing criticisms of American science-fiction writers led to the withdrawal of his honorary membership.

BIOGRAPHY

Stanisław Lem was born in Lvov, Poland, on September 12, 1921, the son of a successful laryngologist. As a young boy he was fascinated by the science books in his father's library. Based on his reading he began to invent fantastic machines and imaginary worlds. Called by his friends "the most intelligent child in southern Poland," he was an outstandingly good student, but his medical studies were interrupted by the Nazi invasion of Poland in 1939. Because of their Jewish heritage, the Lems assumed Gentile identities to survive the occupation. While working as a garage mechanic and welder, Stanislaw also helped resistance fighters and Jews living in the ghetto.

At war's end the family moved to Cracow, where Lem received his M.D. degree and where he began writing poems and novels. His first science-fiction stories, published in the 1950's, were naïvely utopian, though they also dealt with such themes as the threat of global annihilation. The success of his writings in Poland and the Soviet Union allowed him to pursue a literary career. He married his wife Barbara, a roent-genologist, in 1953 (their son Tomek was born in 1968).

After 1956 and extending through the 1960's, Lem's writing entered what many critics have called his "golden" period, during which he wrote his most popular and critically acclaimed works. Through many novels and short stories he was able to extend the range and plumb the depths of the science-fiction and mystery genres. In 1961 he published *Solaris*, his best-known novel, in which astronauts from Earth investigate the planet Solaris, whose ocean, sentient and intelligent, uses the crew's subconscious memories to construct lifelike forms. Lem also probed the effects of radically different alien intelligences on human psychology in many of his short stories.

Lem has described himself as an ideological loner and has eschewed any official connection to either the Communist Party or the Solidarity Movement. Although he occasionally participated in ideological discussions (he once debated theological issues with Karol Wojtyła, who later became Pope John Paul II), he generally dealt with social, cultural, and political questions through his writings. During the turbulent period of the 1980's and 1990's, Lem spent time in Germany, Austria, and Italy, where his ironic reflections on the future of the human species were presented in the guise of imaginary publications, reviews of nonexistent books, and philosophical fables. He gave up writing fiction after 1988, following his return home to Poland from Austria, though he still writes articles "from the domain of the philosophy of the future." Lem continued to be scornful of writers who think of science fiction as mere entertainment rather than a valid means of speculating on such serious issues as the ultimate fate of humanity.

ANALYSIS

Readers fond of the short story will find much both conventional and unconventional in the works of Stanisław Lem. He has published several collections of short stories of the familiar kind; he has also contributed to a form perhaps peculiar to the twentieth century, one that contains all the same elements as a short-story or novel—characters, setting, theme, and plot—but which adds an additional fiction that removes the author one step further from his creation. In this form, Lem pretends that the author of the work is someone else; instead of telling the story, Lem summarizes and reviews it.

A Perfect Vacuum and *Prowokacja* (partially translated as *One Human Minute*) consist of just such reviews of nonexistent books, and *Imaginary Magnitude* plays slight variations on the theme, being composed of an introduction to the work, three introductions to nonexistent works, an advertisement for a nonexistent encyclopedia, and a final set of six pieces bearing the general title "Golem XIV." Golem XIV is a reasoning, self-programming supercomputer that has composed several "lectures"; the pieces in this section consist of an introduction and a foreword to those lectures, instructions for consulting the computer, and an afterword. For perfect consistency, Lem should have left the lectures themselves unwritten, but (perhaps unable to resist) he supplies two of them.

A PERFECT VACUUM

Although these forms are unusual, Lem did not create them: He cites the Argentine writer Jorge Luis Borges as his predecessor at the labor of reviewing nonexistent books and suggests that the practice pre-dates even Borges. Lem, however, consistently attempts to add further levels of complication. For example, the introduction to *A Perfect Vacuum* is a brief essay by the same title. "A Perfect Vacuum" (the introduction) functions like the usual preface or fore-word, but it is itself also a review and—like the rest of the essays in the book—in part a critique of a work that does not exist. The essay that the reader sees presupposes that the collection *A Perfect Vacuum* begins with an introduction by Stanisław Lem, a fictitious introduction titled "Auto-Momus." What the reader sees, therefore, is at the same time an introduction to the real book in hand and a critique of the nonexistent introduction to that book. Reading "A Perfect Vacuum" is an excellent way to begin one's experience of these unusual forms because it discusses at some length why a writer would choose to write them. A writer, says "S. Lem," may simply be producing parodies or satires, may be producing drafts or outlines, or may be expressing "unsatisfied longings." Yet a final reason is suggested as well:

> Books that the author does not write, that he will cer-tainly never undertake, come what may, and that can be attributed to fictitious authors—are not such books, by virtue of their nonexistence, remarkably like sci-ence? Could one place oneself at any safer distance from heterodox thoughts?

It should be added, however, that in keeping with the convolutions of the form, this opinion is immediately contradicted in the next sentence.

It is tempting to believe that the reviews of ficti-tious books imply Lem's dissatisfaction with conven-tional forms; this belief is buttressed by what the author has called "Lem's Law": "No one reads; if someone does read, he doesn't understand; if he un-derstands, he immediately forgets." Lem's Law not-withstanding, it is far safer to resist attributing a mo-tive to so subtle and comic a writer, especially since Lem has also written (and become famous for) the kind of fiction that he here claims no one reads.

In those more conventional short fictions, Stanisław Lem has shown a fondness for stories of two general kinds: those with human space voyagers as the cen-tral characters, and those set in a world of robots. There is no hard-and-fast separation; almost all the stories show some kind of human-machine interac-tion or confrontation. Both types demonstrate that one of Lem's especially noteworthy abilities is his talent for the comic in a field—science fiction—that is not on the whole rich in humor. A second simple preliminary division of Lem's short fiction, in fact, can be made by separating the comic adventures of Ijon Tichy from the serious tales of Pirx the Pilot; both heroes are space travelers of the future, but they inhabit stories quite different in tone and language, although the stories are often similar in the themes they examine.

Lem worked on the stories with Ijon Tichy as a hero for well over a decade, and the publishing his-tory of the work is complicated enough to warrant a word of explanation. There are two Polish versions of the work originally titled *Dzienniki gwiazdowe*: the first was published in 1957, was translated in 1976, and carries the English title *The Star Diaries*. The second Polish edition, that of 1971, contains a num-ber of stories not included in the 1957 collection. These later stories were translated into English and published in 1982 under the title *Memoirs of a Space Traveler*. The two collections in English, *The Star Di-aries* and *Memoirs of a Space Traveler* together with the short novel *Bezsenność* (1971; partial translation, *The Futurological Congress*, 1974), make up the complete adventures of Ijon Tichy available in En-glish.

MEMOIRS OF A SPACE TRAVELER

Tichy, the comic side of Lem's vision, is described by the anonymous narrator not only as the discoverer of 83,003 new stars but also as someone to rank with Baron Münchhausen and Lemuel Gulliver. The liter-ary allusions warn the reader that Tichy's truthfulness is not guaranteed, but since his creator employed him as a character for fifteen years, Tichy must provide a useful vehicle for his author's statements. In fact, many readers may find Tichy the best introduction to Lem: The comedy of the stories is easy to appreciate regardless of the nationality of the reader. The stories are comic not only in their exaggerated space-opera action and in the wildness of their plots but also in their often pointed satire: In these works, Lem parodies an astonishing range of targets. Critics have noted that the author makes fun of his own early attempts at science fiction, and he burlesques many of the more shopworn themes and plots of the genre—for example, time travel. In "Ze wspomnień Ijona Ticheyo IV" ("Further Reminiscences of Ijon Tichy: IV"), in *Memoirs of a Space Traveler*, Tichy is approached by the inventor of a working time machine for capital to continue his research. Greatly impressed, the explorer agrees to approach potential investors, but both to save time and to provide a demonstration of the machine, the inventor offers to go thirty years into the future, find out who the investors were historically, and return with the information on exactly which backers to approach. Unfortunately, the inventor forgets that thirty years in the future he will be thirty years older. He steps into his machine, turns it on, and as he fades from sight before Tichy's eyes in the present, dies of old age. Tichy concludes by observing that everyone travels in time, and if we age when we travel together at the same rate, why not expect that if the speed of travel is accelerated, the speed of aging will also increase? Readers of science fiction will recognize some subtle thrusts at the genre in Tichy's complaint that science fiction, like the inventor, forgets this problem.

Lem satirizes not just science fiction; in fact, critics' most frequent applause is reserved for Lem's linguistic inventiveness as a tool for his satire: His coinage of new words, his skill with names, and especially his fluent parodies of different styles of writing (scientific reports, political speeches) provide commentary on the whole spectrum of the ways in which people communicate (or fail to communicate). In questions of the style of the author, the reader is entirely dependent on the skill of the translator, but even without considering style, the humor of the stories is abundant and genuine.

Two larger targets of the satire of the Tichy stories are human imperfection and human philosophy. The way in which systems of thought have explained or failed to explain human flaws is one of Lem's constant themes. Lem does not hesitate to explore large questions: the purpose of an imperfect creature in a puzzling universe, why evil exists, the possibility of perfection of the human or another species, the utopias for which the human race strives—all these are among the themes that Lem examines in both the comic and the serious stories.

TALES OF PIRX THE PILOT

Tichy's serious counterpart is Pirx, a spaceman whose career the reader follows (in *Tales of Pirx the Pilot* and *More Tales of Pirx the Pilot*, both translated from *Opowieści o pilocie Pirxie*) from cadet to commander. Pirx in many ways seems absolutely ordinary as a human being, if not as a literary character. Although in excellent physical condition, he is no superman like Edgar Rice Burroughs's John Carter, but rather a rounded character who changes as he matures. Through the tales, Pirx is subjected to a series of challenges of increasing difficulty, ones that bring all of his abilities into play. He has courage, skill, and training, but he often confronts as adversaries machines with powers far superior to his. Tichy, by contrast, is frequently only a bystander or an observer of such a machine. In the first tale of Pirx, "Test" ("The Test"), for example, the malevolent machine is the cadet's own ship. Through a series of mechanical failures, it seems to threaten to end his maiden flight by splattering him across the surface of the Moon. Yet Pirx always survives, through intuition when systematic thought is fruitless, through indecision when action fails, or simply through being more adaptable than his adversaries or his competitors.

Pirx is called a dreamer in that first story, but his dreams are sometimes nightmares. In "Patrol" ("The Patrol") two space pilots disappear while routinely surveying an uninhabited region of space. Their disappearance is a mystery until Pirx himself almost falls prey to a mental aberration caused by yet another ship malfunction. The breakdown produces the illusion of a light outside the ship, a will-o'-the-wisp that the two earlier pilots followed to their destruction. Only by using pain to bring himself back to reality is Pirx able to regain control and survive. Here the emphasis is on the fragility of the human endeavor in space: The vulnerable humans inside the ships are totally dependent on the machines that enclose and guard them. They are at the mercy of the machines that make it possible for them to exist. If the machines fail, the humans die. "Albatros" ("The Albatross") drives home this message; in it, the line between safety and disaster is even thinner, because Pirx witnesses a suspenseful but unsuccessful rescue attempt from a luxury passenger liner complete with swimming pools and motion-picture theaters.

Such brief descriptions may make the stories sound pessimistic, but students of Lem have traced in these tales the seemingly contradictory theme that humanity's weakness, its very vulnerability, defines its strength. One might point out that in "The Test," Pirx succeeds when a cadet whom he considers far better qualified fails. The other cadet, Boerst, is handsome and brilliant. Boerst always has the right answers in class and always knows the accepted procedures. Yet the final examination for the cadets aims to test their capacity for innovation and imagination: No procedure covers what to do when a cover falls off a control panel at the same time that a fly has stowed away. No procedure covers what to do when the fly crawls into the open panel and shorts out an electric circuit. In a crisis for which the standard operating procedures are not enough, even perfect knowledge of those procedures is useless. Boerst fails in just such a crisis.

Pirx, by contrast, makes mistakes and—even more important—knows that he makes mistakes. He will not, therefore, stick with a procedure if it does not yield immediate results; rather, since he has failed before, he will assume he is failing again and try something else. With enough tries, he is bound to hit on something that works. The method may seem irrational, but it simply takes into account that humans cannot plan for every eventuality and must therefore leave open an avenue for new solutions. The situation of the electrocuted fly might not occur in a thousand years, but someone in charge of the examination has realized that some unforeseen circumstance is bound to occur, and probably sooner rather than later. One must therefore keep one's mind open. This openness, as Pirx himself comments, results from the fact that we are "the sum of our faults and defects." Pirx's own success in the test can be explained in these terms. Since he lacks superior or outstanding ability in any

one dimension, he cannot afford to become one-dimensional; he cannot become a specialist like the humans who fail before him or like the machines that failed them. He must remain open to possibilities from every direction. In short, he must be adaptable. In the final analysis, Pirx is not simply a sympathetic yet bungling hero, as one commentator has called him, nor is his success merely good luck; he is simply human in the best sense—adaptable.

In a third set of stories, Lem asks the question, "What does *simply human* mean?" As Bullpen, one of the instructors at cadet school, likes to remind his pupils, "A computer is only human." Even in the tales of Pirx or of Ijon Tichy, machines sometimes take on human attributes and characteristics. In "Further Reminiscences of Ijon Tichy: V," competing washing-machine manufacturers escalate their competition by building models that seem more and more human: They converse, they instruct, they even make love. By the end of the story, their original purpose has been so submerged that they have room to wash only a handkerchief or two, but they look like Jayne Mansfield.

THE CYBERIAD *and* MORTAL ENGINES
The stories in *The Cyberiad* (*Cyberiada*) and *Mortal Engines* carry this development into the far future, when computers and other machines have become only too human. In that distant setting, humans are no longer the central figures in the drama of civilization. Robots occupy the center stage, but the play seems familiar. Although the robots disparage and scorn humans, the robots' fairy tales have the forms and plots of human ones. Endow robots with consciousness and freedom of action, the stories seem to argue, and the meaning of "human" is called into question. The robot societies even show the same weaknesses as earlier human ones. They have their own villains and heroes, who show the same vices and virtues that humans do. There is not much difference between the men and the machines.

If there is an overarching vision in Lem's motley of novels, stories, fables, monographs, essays, reviews, prophecies, and other literary experiments, it is his view that the symbiotic relationship between humanity and technology has significant ethical consequences. Although Leszek Kolakowski called him a "leading ideologist of scientific technocracy," Lem insists that he is essentially a humanist who believes that no machine, known or imagined, can create human happiness. His favorite people are not scientists or technicians but writers (William Shakespeare), musicians (Frédéric Chopin), and artists (Hieronymus Bosch). Like them, he is deeply concerned with freedom, communication, and creativity. He believes that his work in science fiction can help humans to develop clever responses to those new technologies that have the potential to destabilize societies in unpredictable ways. Seeing human nature as flawed (because the brain is the consequence of innumerable evolutionary accidents), Lem can be pessimistic about the possibilities of future human improvement, but his pessimism is often tempered with an infectious sense of fun, and in his humor there is truth. Humans may be unable to create perfect societies, but through their inventiveness and determination they can take the stumbling steps that lead to a better and fuller life.

OTHER MAJOR WORKS

LONG FICTION: *Astronauci*, 1951; *Obłok Magellana*, 1955; *Czas nieutracony*, 1955 (includes *Szpital przemienienia* [*Hospital of the Transfiguration*, 1988], *Wśród umarłych*, and *Powrót*); *Eden*, 1959 (English translation, 1989); *Śledztwo*, 1959 (*The Investigation*, 1974); *Pamiętnik znaleziony w wannie*, 1961 (*Memoirs Found in a Bathtub*, 1973); *Powrót z gwiazd*, 1961 (*Return from the Stars*, 1980); *Solaris*, 1961 (English translation, 1970); *Niezwyciężony i inne opowiadania*, 1964 (*The Invincible*, 1973); *Polowanie*, 1965 (*The Hunt*, in *Mortal Engines*, 1977); *Głos pana*, 1968 (*His Master's Voice*, 1983); *Bezsenność*, 1971 (partial translation, *The Futurological Congress*, 1974); *Ze wspomnień Ijona Tichego: Kongres futurologiczny*, 1971 (*The Futurological Congress [from the Memoirs of Ijon Tichy]*, 1974); *Katar*, 1976 (*The Chain of Chance*, 1978); *Wizja lokalna*, 1982; *Fiasko*, 1986 (*Fiasco*, 1987); *Pokój na Ziemi*, 1987 (*Peace on Earth*, 1994).

PLAY: *Jacht Paradise*, pb. 1951 (with Roman Hussarski).

POETRY: *Wiersze młozieńcze*, 1966.

NONFICTION: *Dialogi*, 1957, 1984; *Wejście na orbitę*, 1962; *Summa technologiae*, 1964; *Wysoki Zamek*, 1966 (*Highcastle: A Remembrance*, 1995); *Filozofia przypadku*, 1968; *Fantastyka i futurologia*, 1970; *Rozprawy i szkice*, 1975; *Microworlds: Writings on Science Fiction and Fantasy*, 1984 (essays); *A Stanisław Lem Reader*, 1997 (with Peter Swirski); *Bomba megabitorva*, 1999.

miscellaneous: *Noc księżycowa*, 1963; *Powtórka*, 1979.

BIBLIOGRAPHY

Barnouw, Dagman. "Science Fiction as a Model for Probablistic Worlds: Stanisław Lem's Fantastic Empiricism." *Science-Fiction Studies* 6 (1979): 153-163. Examines Lem's concept of science fiction as a cognitive aesthetic model whereby he focuses on contemporary social and psychological behavior.

Davis, J. Madison. *Stanisław Lem*. Mercer Island, Wash.: Starmont House, 1990. Though Davis does not discuss all Lem's works in detail, he does provide thorough discussions of his major novels and many of his short stories, showing the development of Lem's thought as reflected in his fiction. Includes a chronology, a biographical sketch, and extensive annotated primary and secondary bibliographies.

Macdonald, Gina. "Lem, Stanisław." In *Twentieth-Century Science-Fiction Writers*, edited by Curtis C. Smith. 2d ed. Chicago: St. James Press, 1986. Macdonald offers a brief biographical sketch and overview discussion of Lem's work.

Malmgren, Carl D. "Self and Other in SF: Alien Encounters." *Science-Fiction Studies* 20 (March, 1993): 15-33. Argues that Lem uses alien encounters to probe the limits of human understanding and knowledge; claims that for Lem communication with aliens is problematic, conducted through a veil of incomprehensible signs, for communication with aliens is beyond words.

Mullen, R. D., and Darko Suvin, eds. *Science Fiction Studies: Selected Articles on Science Fiction, 1973-1975*. Boston: Gregg Press, 1976. This volume contains essays on Lem by one of his best translators, Michael V. Kandel, and by Jerzy Jarzebski. Kandel's short "review" is a witty introduction to some of Lem's themes. Jarzebski's "Stanislaw Lem, Rationalist and Visionary," is an overview of Lem's career that provides a good introduction to his major themes and techniques, as well as to phases of his development during his career.

Science-Fiction Studies 19 (July, 1992). A special issue on Lem, with essays on most all facets of his work and discussions of his major novels and short-story collections. Includes essays on Lem's story "The Mask," the concept of gender, psychoanalysis, and *Solaris*.

Slusser, George E., George R. Guffey, and Mark Rose, eds. *Bridges to Science Fiction*. Carbondale: Southern Illinois University Press, 1980. This volume contains essays on Lem by Gregory Benford and Stephen Potts. Benford deals mainly with *Solaris*, discussing Lem's use of the unknowable alien being. Potts discusses Lem's major theme of the limits of human knowledge and human ability to understand the unknown, comparing him to other authors, such as Franz Kafka.

Solataroff, Theodore. "A History of Science Fiction and More." *The New York Times Book Review*, August 29, 1976, 1, 14-18. This appreciative review of a few of Lem's books, including *The Cyberiad*, is a helpful introduction to Lem's themes and works.

Warrick, Patricia S. "Stanisław Lem's Robot Fables and Ironic Tales." In *The Cybernetic Imagination in Science Fiction*. Cambridge, Mass.: MIT Press, 1980. Discusses Lem's use of irony to parody cybernetic fiction in both the utopian and dystopian modes; includes a brief discussion of the tone and content of the typical Lem short story.

Swirski, Peter. *A Stanislaw Lem Reader*. Evanston, Ill.: Northwestern University Press, 1997. In this book Swirski has collected various writings by and about Lem. It includes an introductory essay by Swirski, two lengthy interviews of Lem, and an essay by Lem, and it concludes with a complete bibliography of Lem's books in English and Polish, a list of Lem's essays and articles in English, and an extensive bibliography of critical sources on Lem in English.

Ziegfeld, Richard E. *Stanisław Lem*. New York: Frederick Ungar, 1985. This introduction to Lem surveys his translated works and his themes. It includes a biographical sketch, two substantial chapters on the short fiction, an annotated primary bibliography, and a select secondary bibliography.

Walter E. Meyers, updated by Terry Heller

NIKOLAI LESKOV

Born: Gorokhovo, Oryol, Russia; February 16, 1831
Died: St. Petersburg, Russia; March 9, 1895

PRINCIPAL SHORT FICTION

Povesti, ocherki i rassakazy, 1867
Rasskazy, 1869
Sbornik melkikh belletristicheskikh proizvedenii, 1873
Tri pravednika i odin Shermaur, 1880
Russkie bogonostsy: Religiozno-bytovye kartiny, 1880

Russkaia rozn', 1881
Sviatochnye rasskazy, 1886
Rasskazy kstati, 1887
Povesti i rasskazy, 1887
The Sentry and Other Stories, 1922
The Musk-Ox and Other Tales, 1944
The Encanted Pilgrim and Other Stories, 1946
The Amazon and Other Stories, 1949
Selected Tales, 1961
Satirical Stories, 1968
The Sealed Angel and Other Stories, 1984

OTHER LITERARY FORMS

Although Nikolai Leskov's most memorable work was in the shorter forms of fiction, he also attempted to meet the characteristic nineteenth century demand for "major works" with two full-length novels, *Nekuda* (1864; no way out) and *Na nozhakh* (1870-1871; at daggers drawn). Recognizing that novels were not his forte, he also tried to develop a different long form, the "chronicle," the major result of this effort being *Soboriane* (1872; *The Cathedral Folk*, 1924). Leskov also wrote one play, *Rastochitel'* (1867; the spendthrift), and a large body of journalistic nonfiction.

ACHIEVEMENTS

Despite the continued output over more than thirty years of much high-quality fiction and despite his popularity among Russian readers, Nikolai Leskov's immense narrative talent went largely unrecognized by the critics of his time. He was to some extent eclipsed by his great contemporaries: Ivan Turgenev, Fyodor Dostoevski, and Leo Tolstoy. He was also adversely affected by the view that only big novels really "counted." Finally, he was caught in political cross fire and early in his career was virtually read out of literature by certain radical critics for his supposed retrograde views. Nevertheless, the first twelve-volume edition of his collected works (1889-1896) was a symbolic acknowledgment of his status as a classic, and that status has been more and more widely recognized in the decades since his death. New Russian editions of his works are frequent, and there is a substantial body of scholarship dealing with him. His reputation has also spread abroad, and many volumes of translations and of books about him have been published in English, French, German, Italian, Dutch, Swedish, and other languages. He is regarded as a major narrative artist and a thoughtful critic and moralist, a keen and often caustic observer of Russian society, and an especially penetrating and well-informed commentator on Russian religious life.

BIOGRAPHY

Nikolai Semyonovich Leskov was born on February 16, 1831, in Gorokhovo, a village in Oryol Province. His class background was varied and unusual.

Nikolai Leskov (Library of Congress)

His father, a priest's son, had become a government official, receiving technical membership in the hereditary gentry when he attained the required rank. His mother was the daughter of an impoverished gentleman married to a merchant's daughter. Leskov grew up partly in the country, where his father had bought a tiny estate, and partly in the town of Oryol, where he attended the *gymnasium*. He did not complete the course, however, dropping out to take a lowly civil service job, first in Oryol and later in Kiev, where an uncle was a university professor. Though in later years by wide and incessant reading he educated himself enough for several university degrees, the lack of a formal one remained a sore point for Leskov. In Kiev, he worked in an army recruiting bureau, a position that obliged him to witness and take part in some of the gross injustices and cruelties of Nicholas I's regime. In 1857, Leskov took leave from the service and entered private business, working as a factotum for an uncle by marriage, a Russified Scotsman who managed the estates of some wealthy grandees. This work necessitated much travel within Russia, and Leskov drew heavily on these experiences in his later writings, which exhibit a connoisseur's knowledge of colorful nooks and crannies of Russian provincial life. The success of a few early experiments with writing convinced Leskov to move to St. Petersburg with the intention of becoming a professional journalist.

Leskov obtained a position as editorial writer for a leading newspaper, but in 1862 he fell afoul of the radicals. At issue was an article in which he suggested that a recent series of fires in the capital might actually have been set by revolutionary arsonists, as had been rumored; he urged the police to make public its list of suspects so that popular anger would be deflected from the general body of university students. The threats and attacks on him infuriated Leskov, and he retaliated with an antiradical *roman à clef, Nekuda*, which incensed the radicals against him even more. He struck again with a second novel, *Na nozhakh*, and there are also antiradical sallies in *The Cathedral Folk*. In fact, however, despite all the anger and name-calling, Leskov's views on society and politics were consistently progressive. He called himself a "gradualist." He hailed the reforms of Alexander II, especially the abolition of serfdom, and he favored equality of all citizens before the law, freedom of speech and of the press, and an independent judiciary. Yet he was often discouraged, as were many others, by the enormity of the country's problems and the inadequacy of the resources, human and material, it could bring to bear on them. The age-old demons of hunger and cold still haunted the lives of all too many Russians, making other problems seem trivial luxuries.

As early as 1862, Leskov began to publish short stories, and he soon became convinced that fiction was his true calling. Some of his most famous stories date from this early period; he went through no phase of literary maturation. In the 1870's, after the termination of his long war with the radicals, Leskov produced another series of classic stories. Many were published in the organ of the right-wing ideologue Mikhail Katkov, and for some time Leskov was considered an established member of the Katkov camp. In 1874, Leskov broke with Katkov, ostensibly because of high-handed editing of one of his stories; in fact, their political differences would eventually have led to rupture anyway.

Because of *The Cathedral Folk* and other works with clerical heroes, Leskov had been typed as Russian literature's chief expert on the clergy and its most ardent proponent of orthodoxy, but actually, by 1875 his own religious development had led him to break with that church. Meditation, rereading of the Gospels, and contacts with Protestants during an extended trip to Western Europe in 1875 brought about this major reorientation. "I no longer burn incense to many of my old gods," Leskov wrote to a friend. His alienation from Orthodoxy only deepened during the remainder of his life. Eventually he went so far as to assert categorically that Orthodoxy was "*not* Christianity." By that time, his ideas had "coincided," as he put it, with those of Tolstoy. Though he acknowledged the brighter light cast by Tolstoy's "enormous torch," Leskov had valid reason to claim that in many respects he became a Tolstoyan even before Tolstoy did. Leskov had suffered from heart disease for several years; he died suddenly on March 9, 1895.

ANALYSIS

Nikolai Leskov, early in his career, developed a characteristic form for his short stories: the "memoir"—half fiction, half fact—with a narrating "I" who regales the reader with tales of the colorful personalities and unusual events that he has experienced in his adventurous life. The border between "fiction" and "fact" is left intentionally blurred—an adroit illusionistic stratagem in an age that claimed the label "realism." In "Ovtsebyk" ("The Musk-Ox"), for example, the narrator is presumably to be equated, at least by unsophisticated readers, with the actual author. Indeed, the story contains, in a lengthy digression, a lyrical account of what are believed to be the actual pilgrimages to monasteries on which the real Leskov as a boy accompanied his grandmother. The main focus of the story, however, is on the mature narrator's encounters with a character who illustrates Leskov's conviction of the futility of the radical intellectuals' efforts to stir the peasantry to revolt.

"THE STINGER"

"Iazvitel'nyi" ("The Stinger") evokes a theme Leskov touched on many times later, the difficulties encountered by the foreigner in Russia. An Englishman working as an estate manager in Russia comes to grief and brings disaster on his peasant charges through his inability to understand their mentality. The story avoids the impression of chauvinism, however, by the narrator's clear recognition that the downfall of the humane Englishman is caused not by any Russian superiority of soul but by the peasants' stubborn barbarism and backwardness.

"THE AMAZON"

"Voitel'nitsa" ("The Amazon") remains one of the classic examples of what the Russians call *skaz*, in which a frame narrator, more or less identifiable with the author, hears and records an inner, oral narrative, which is related in picturesque, "marked" language by a folk character. In this case, the inner narrator is one of Leskov's most colorful literary offspring, a Petersburg procuress. Catering to the secret sexual needs of the capital, she has entrée into all levels of society, and her language is a mixture of correspondingly disparate layers, the substratum of local dialect being overlaid with upper-class words, often of Western origin, but not always perfectly understood or accurately reproduced. Her motley language is in perfect harmony with her personality: vulgar, down-to-earth, cynical, yet endlessly vital.

"LADY MACBETH OF THE MTSENSK DISTRICT"

"Ledi Makbet Mtsenskogo uezda" ("Lady Macbeth of the Mtsensk District"), though somewhat atypical in technique, remains one of Leskov's most famous stories; it was the basis for the libretto of Dmitry Shostakovich's opera. Like Turgenev's earlier "Gamlet Shchigrovskogo uezda" ("Hamlet of the Shchigrovsky District"), the title oxymoronically situates a regal Shakespearean archetype in a maximally unromantic, provincial Russian setting; the story itself demonstrates that such human universals know no boundaries of place, time, or class. Presented in a more conventional omniscient-author format than the pseudo-memoirs, "Lady Macbeth of the Mtsensk District" is a lurid tale of adultery and murder in a provincial merchant milieu.

In 1866, Leskov began the most ambitious literary enterprise of his career: to encapsulate in a single artistic work, class by class, the provincial Russia he knew so well. The life of a single town would serve

as its microcosm. The huge project was never completed, but the section dealing with the clergy eventually emerged in 1872 as a full-length book, the celebrated novel *The Cathedral Folk*. This volume opened up for Russian literature a hitherto unexplored social territory, the provincial clergy, presented in a highly attractive form, with a winning mixture of sentiment and humor. Leskov insisted that *The Cathedral Folk* was not a novel, a genre he considered hackneyed in form and limited in content to man-woman "romance," but rather a "chronicle," a genre already made classic in Russian literature by Sergei Aksakov. The chronicle had the advantage for Leskov of legitimizing almost unlimited structural looseness, since its only explicit guiding principle is the sequence of events in time.

Leskov sustained a high level of narrative art through his works of the early 1870's.

"THE SEALED ANGEL"

"Zapechatlennyi angel" ("The Sealed Angel") is one of his most virtuoso performances in the art of *skaz*. Its narrator is a former Old Believer whose speech combines two highly marked linguistic stocks: the religious jargon of the "ancient piety" and the technical language of icon-painting. In this picturesque language, he relates a stirring, skillfully paced tale of his comrades' struggle to recapture a confiscated icon. "Ocharovannyi strannik" ("The Enchanted Pilgrim") is the life story of a monk purportedly encountered by the "author" on a steamer plying Lake Ladoga. This character, Ivan Severyanovich Flyagin, a former serf whose life has been a kaleidoscopic series of extraordinary adventures, is made to epitomize some of the essential qualities of the Russian national character as Leskov perceived it. These generalizations, however, are incarnated in a vivid sequential narrative that grips the reader from beginning to end.

"AT THE EDGE OF THE WORLD"

In "Na kraiu sveta" ("At the Edge of the World"), Leskov explored in fictional form an issue concerning which he had strong personal opinions: the missionary activities of the Orthodox Church among primitive tribes in Siberia. It was a risky subject, but Leskov cleverly camouflaged his subversive message by having his tale told by a sympathetic and unimpeachably Orthodox bishop. Intense experiences in Siberia convince the bishop that there is more natural Christianity among the heathen tribesmen than among all the lazy clerics and rapacious, hard-drinking officials then engaged in bringing "civiliza-tion" to Siberia. The bishop's tale includes one of the most powerful blizzard stories in Russian literature.

"IRON WILL"

Religious subjects did not occupy Leskov exclu-sively. "Zheleznaia volia" ("Iron Will") again takes up the theme of the difficulties of the foreigner work-ing in Russia. This time, a German engineer who car-ries Teutonic discipline and self-control to the point of absurdity is vanquished by the "doughy" formless-ness of Russian life. Again, Leskov avoids any im-pression of chauvinism by showing that it is Russian weaknesses—insouciance, irresponsibility, and hedo-nism—that bring the German to his doom.

"RIGHTEOUS" PEOPLE

Even when not dealing directly with religious themes, Leskov took very seriously his responsibility to teach morality through literary art. He produced a whole cycle of portraits of *pravedniki* or "righteous ones," people who demonstrate that moral beauty and even sainthood are still possible in the tainted modern world. For all their differences of form and style, these stories are intended to function much like medi-eval hagiography: While entertaining the reader, they inculcate ideas of virtue. Among the most successful are "Odnodum" ("Singlethought"), "Nesmertel'nyi Golovan" ("Deathless Golovan"), and "Chelovek na chasakh" ("The Sentry"). Leskov took pugnacious pride in his ability to depict virtuous characters. "Show me another writer who has such an abundance of positive Russian types," he demanded. In some of these latter-day moralities, to be sure, artistic perfor-mance far overshadows morality. The left-handed hero of the famous "Levsha (Skaz o tul'skom kosom lefshe i o stal'noy blokhe)" ("Lefty: Being the Tale of the Cross-eyed Lefty of Tula and the Steel Flea") is indeed a "righteous one"—not only a craftsman of extraordinary skill but also an (unappreciated) pa-triot. Yet the principal impact of this classic *skaz* comes from its manner, not its message—its marvel-ous display of verbal acrobatics. "The Sentry," on the

other hand, is cast in a more somber key. There, an omniscient author, moving through a series of terse chapters, builds up extraordinary tension by focusing on the hour-by-hour movement of the clock.

THE MEMOIR FORM

The memoir form employed in many of his stories had many advantages for Leskov. It at least ostensibly transposed a "story" from the realm of fiction to that of history or fact, thus not only enhancing the illusion of reality but also avoiding the charge of deception and even lying that troubled such creators of imagi-nary realities as Tolstoy. Furthermore, reminiscences of the past provide both philosophical perspective and didactic impetus. The memories Leskov resur-rects are drawn mainly from the period of his youth, the reign of Nicholas I. It was not only enlightening to show Russians how far their country had evolved since those dark days, largely through the reforms of Czar Alexander II, but also disturbing to reveal how dangerously reminiscent of the tyrannies of Nicho-las's time were the reactionary tendencies prevalent under Alexander III. Finally, the ultimate paradox of the memoir form lies in the nature of art: Concrete images, even explicitly dated memories of a vanished past, may be a vehicle for universal, timeless truths about human nature and fate.

"THE TOUPEE ARTIST"

From Leskov's memoir tales of the era of Nicho-las I, one could construct a comprehensive sociology of Russia as it was then. Its most egregious evil was serfdom, and in "Tupeinyi khudozhnik" ("The Tou-pee Artist") Leskov created one of the most searing evocations in Russian literature of the horrors of that institution, especially its corrupting effect on both master and slave. For all his abhorrence of serfdom, however, Leskov never succumbed to the populist tendency to idealize the "people." From the begin-ning of his career to the end, he demonstrated again and again the "darkness" of the peasant world. Char-acteristically, the terrible famine of 1891-1892 in-spired Leskov to recollect, in "Iudol" ("Vale of Tears"), the equally terrible famine of 1840. The comparison revealed that society had measurably ad-vanced in that interval: Relief measures were now open, energetic, and public. Yet the peasants were as benighted as ever, superstitious, and prone to sense-less violence. By no means all of Leskov's memoir pieces, however, are so somber. One of the most humorous is "Grabezh" ("A Robbery"), another superb example of *skaz*, which evokes the atmosphere of the prereform provincial merchant class as a setting for comedy.

DIDACTICISM

After his "conversion" to Tolstoyanism, Leskov placed even greater stress on the didactic function of literature. He plumbed a medieval Russian translation of the ancient Greek text *Synaxarion* for materials for an entire cycle of moralistic stories, slyly doctoring their plots to fit Tolstoyan specifications. The most substantial of these stories is "Gora" ("The Mountain"). In another *Synaxarion*-based fable, "Povest' o Fedore-khristianine i o druge ego Abrame zhidovine" (the story of Theodore the Christian and his friend Abraham the Hebrew), Leskov preached a much-needed sermon of tolerance and fraternity between Christians and Jews, thus demonstratively reversing the anti-Semitic tendency of some earlier stories.

SATIRE

Perhaps the most memorable and artistically most successful works of Leskov's late years were his satires of contemporary Russian society, which he viewed with deep pessimism, seeing little but corruption and folly among the elite and savagery in the masses. "Polunoshchniki" ("Night Owls") ridicules as a fraud (though without naming him) the highly touted Orthodox thaumaturge, Father Ioann of Kronstadt; the contrasting figure is a saintly Tolstoyan girl. In "Zimnii den'" ("A Winter's Day"), Leskov depicts another pure-hearted Tolstoyan girl alone in a degenerate milieu of police informers, extortionists, and sexual delinquents. Perhaps the greatest of these satires, Leskov's swan song, is "Zaiachii remiz" ("The March Hare"). Here, beneath a humorous camouflage—the narrator is a lovable Ukrainian lunatic who relates muddled memories of his adventurous youth—Leskov ridicules the "police paranoia" so pervasive in Russia (and elsewhere) at that time and later, the mentality that sees a subversive plotter lurking behind every bush. The camouflage, however, proved insufficient; no magazine editor could be found brave enough even to submit the story to the censors.

In his depiction of nineteenth century Russian life, Leskov's sociological range is broader than that of any other writer before Anton Chekhov. For those who can read him in Russian, his verbal pyrotechnics are simply dazzling, and his *skaz* technique has inspired many twentieth century imitators, notably Aleksei Remizov, Yevgeny Zamyatin, and Mikhail Zoshchenko. For non-Russians, such as Walter Benjamin, Leskov remains the storyteller *par excellence*, a practitioner of pure, uncontaminated narrative art. This description would doubtless have surprised and perhaps annoyed Leskov, who set greater store by his efforts as a moralist, but it seems to be the verdict of history.

OTHER MAJOR WORKS

LONG FICTION: *Nekuda*, 1864; *Oboidennye*, 1865; *Ostrovitiane*, 1866; *Na nozhakh*, 1870-1871; *Soboriane*, 1872 (*The Cathedral Folk*, 1924).

PLAY: *Rastochitel'*, pb. 1867.

NONFICTION: *Velikosvetskii raskol*, 1876-1877; *Evrei v Rossii: Neskol'ko zamechanii po evreiskomu*, 1884.

MISCELLANEOUS: *Sobranie sochinenii*, 1889-1896; *Polnoe sobranie sochinenii*, 1902-1903 (thirty-six volumes); *Sobranie sochinenii*, 1956-1958 (eleven volumes).

BIBLIOGRAPHY

Andrews, Larry R. "Hugo's Gilliatt and Leskov's Golovan." *Comparative Literature* 46 (Winter, 1994): 65-83. Compares the two heroes; suggests that Leskov was influenced by native experience in creating his hero; discusses the hybrid genre that Leskov develops in which his hero represents a specifically Russian virtue.

Benjamin, Walter. "The Storyteller: Reflection on the Works of Nikolay Leskov." In *Illuminations*. New York: Harcourt, Brace & World, 1968. In this general study of the short story as an oral and written genre, Benjamin discusses Leskov and the technique of *skaz* by linking it to the oral transmittance of stories either by foreign travelers or by natives familiar with their own oral tradition.

Eekman, Thomas A. "The Genesis of Leskov's *Soborjane.*" *California Slavic Studies* 2 (1963): 121-140. Eekman traces the genesis of *Soboriane,* the first great novel about the life of the Russian clergy, and examines its relationship to some of Leskov's stories that may have been planned for future volumes of the novel.

Howe, Irving. "Justice for Leskov." *The New York Review of Books* 34 (April 23, 1987): 32-36. Points out that Leskov has never been widely received outside Russia because he defies the rigid expectations that Westerners impose on Russian literature; argues that in Leskov's work the faith of the rationalist and the faith of the pietist are parallel, and both faiths are secularized as part of national culture.

Lantz, K. A. *Nikolay Leskov.* Boston: Twayne, 1979. A brief biography and a general study of Leskov's works. A useful book for quick reference.

Lottridge, Stephen S. "Nikolaj Leskov and the Russian *Prolog* as a Literary Source." *Russian Literature* 3 (1972): 16-39. A detailed discussion of Leskov's *Prolog* tales of 1886-1891, which he patterned after Russian religious legends from various sources, and how they influenced him in writing these tales and in his overall development. Lottridge also touches upon culture and literature in the second half of nineteenth century Russia.

_____. "Solzhenitsyn and Leskov." *Russian Literature TriQuarterly* 6 (1973): 478-489. Although Lottridge deals here primarily with Solzhenitsyn, by commenting on Leskov's short stories he provides valuable insights into Leskov, whom he considers Russia's greatest pure storyteller.

McLean, Hugh. *Nikolai Leskov: The Man and His Art.* Cambridge, Mass.: Harvard University Press, 1977. The standard work in English on Leskov, satisfactory in every respect. McLean presents Leskov in both scholarly and interesting fashion, making Leskov less foreign to the English-speaking reader. The first book on Leskov to be recommended to those interested in him.

Hugh McLean, updated by Vasa D. Mihailovich

DORIS LESSING

Born: Kermanshah, Persia; October 22, 1919

PRINCIPAL SHORT FICTION

This Was the Old Chief's Country, 1951
Five: Short Novels, 1953
No Witchcraft for Sale: Stories and Short Novels, 1956
The Habit of Loving, 1957
A Man and Two Women, 1963
African Stories, 1964
Winter in July, 1966
The Black Madonna, 1966
Nine African Stories, 1968
The Temptation of Jack Orkney and Other Stories, 1972 (also known as *The Story of a Non-Marrying Man and Other Stories*)
This Was the Old Chief's Country: Volume 1 of Doris Lessing's Collected African Stories, 1973
The Sun Between Their Feet: Volume 2 of Doris Lessing's Collected African Stories, 1973
Sunrise on the Veld, 1975
A Mild Attack of Locusts, 1977
To Room Nineteen/Her Collected Stories, 1978
The Temptation of Jack Orkney/Her Collected Stories, 1978
Stories, 1978
London Observed: Stories and Sketches, 1991 (pb. in U.S. as *The Real Thing: Stories and Sketches,* 1992)
Spies I Have Known and Other Stories, 1995

OTHER LITERARY FORMS

Doris Lessing's many books include poetry, memoirs, reportage, plays, essays, and reviews. She is best known, however, for her novels, particularly *The Golden Notebook* (1962), and the five-volume Children of Violence series, which includes *Martha Quest* (1952), *A Proper Marriage* (1954), *A Ripple from the Storm* (1958), *Landlocked* (1965), and *The Four-Gated City* (1969). She explored the genre she terms "space fiction" in the volumes *Shikasta* (1979), *The Marriages Between Zones Three, Four, and Five* (1980), *The Sirian Experiments* (1981), *The Making of the Representative for Planet 8* (1982), and *Documents Relating to the Sentimental Agents in the Volyen Empire* (1983), as well as "inner space fiction" in novels such as *Briefing for a Descent into Hell* (1971) and *The Memoirs of a Survivor* (1974). In the mid-1980's, she returned to more realistic fiction, publishing, among others, two novels under the pseudonym Jane Somers. In the 1990's Lessing published the novels *Playing the Game* (1995), *Love, Again* (1996), and *Mara and Dann* (1999), as well as the dramatic *Play with a Tiger, and Other Plays* (pb. 1996) and the autobiographical *Walking in the Shade* (1997).

ACHIEVEMENTS

Doris Lessing was a finalist for the Booker McConnell Prize for *Briefing for a Descent into Hell*, *The Sirian Experiments*, and *The Good Terrorist* (1985). She was nominated for the Australian Science-Fiction Achievement Award in 1982 for *The Sirian Experiments*. *The Good Terrorist* won her the W. H. Smith and Son Literary Award, the Palermo Prize, and the Premio Internazionale Mondello. In 1995 the nonfiction *Under My Skin* (1994) earned the James Tait Black Memorial Prize and the *Los Angeles Times* Book Prize. *Walking in the Shade* received a nomination for the 1997 National Book Critics Award in the biography/autobiography category. Lessing has been a nominee for the Nobel Prize in Literature.

BIOGRAPHY

Born to British parents in Persia, where her father, Alfred Cook Tayler, worked in a bank, Doris May Lessing moved to southern Rhodesia (now Zimba-

Doris Lessing (Ingrid Von Kruse)

bwe) in 1925, when she was five. There she lived on a remote farm, south of Zambezi. "Our neighbors were four, five, seven miles off. In front of the house . . . no neighbors, nothing; no farms, just wild bush with two rivers but no fences to the mountains seven miles away." In her teens, she moved to a "very small town that had about ten thousand white persons in it. The black population did not count, though it was fairly large." This was the Africa of apartheid; Lessing would later chronicle its horrors.

While still in her teens, Lessing married and had two children. She later married again and, in 1949, left her second husband to go to England, bringing her son with her. The emptiness of the African veld and the life of small African towns are the themes of much of her earlier work, including the early volumes of the Children of Violence series. The scene then shifts in her fiction, as it did in her life, to England, and particularly London.

Lessing was a member of communist groups in both Africa and England. In Africa, she describes the group as "having no contact with any kind of reality. . . . I found this when I came to England and had a short association with the British Communist party." Lessing's disillusionment with the difference between the official Communist Party and the "beautiful purity" of the ideas which lie behind communism is an extremely important theme in her fiction. For many of her characters, disillusionment with the possibility of a political solution to the inequities and horror of modern life, leads them first to madness, suicide, or acquiescence. Later, beginning with *The Four-Gated City*, it leads them to visionary solutions. Once her characters give up politics as a solution, they come more and more to accept the mystic resolutions of the Eastern traditions, especially those of Sufism, an ancient form of Islamic human-centered mysticism. In *Prisons We Choose to Live Inside* (1987), a series of lectures she gave for the Canadian Broadcasting Corporation, she reaffirms her view that the survival of the human race depends on its recognizing its connection to all nature rather than stressing a sense of separation.

In 1995 Lessing returned to South Africa to visit her daughter and grandchildren. It was her first trip to the country since being forcibly removed in 1956 for her political views. The same year she also received an honorary degree from Harvard University and collaborated with illustrator Charlie Adlard to publish the novel *Playing the Game*. In 1996 she published *Love, Again*, her first novel in seven years. In 1997 *Walking in the Shade*, the second volume of her autobiography, was issued.

ANALYSIS

Doris Lessing engaged in a lifelong process of self-education, becoming involved with all the important intellectual and political movements of the twentieth century: Freudian and Jungian psychology, Marxism, feminism, existentialism, mysticism, sociobiology, and speculative scientific theory. All these interests appear in her fiction, which consequently serves as a record of the changing climate of the times. She has also displayed in her writing an increasing anxiety about humanity's ability to survive.

In Doris Lessing's short fiction, the reader meets characters remarkable for their intelligence, their unceasing analysis of their emotions, and their essential blindness to their true motivations. The people who move through her stories, while very vividly placid in the details of their lives, are in essence types. As Lessing says in her preface to *The Golden Notebook*, they are "so general and representative of the time that they are anonymous, you could put names to them like those in the old Morality Plays." Those whom the reader meets most frequently in the short fiction are Mr. I-am-free-because-I-belong-nowhere, Miss I-must-have-love-and-happiness, Mrs. I-have-to-be-good-at-everything-I-do, Mr. Where-is-a-real-woman, and Ms. Where-is-a-real-man; and there is one final type Lessing names, Mrs. If-we-deal-very-well-with-this-small-problem-then-perhaps-we-can-forget-we-daren't-look-at-the-big-ones. This last type is the character so often met at the beginning of Lessing's stories, the character who has become uneasily aware of a discrepancy between intention and action, between the word and the deed, but who would prefer not to take the analysis too far. Lessing is inexorable, however, and in story after story characters are driven to new, usually unpleasant knowledge about themselves and their motivations. Typically, the stories end with the situation unresolved. The reader sees the awakening but not the translation of new knowledge into action. For Lessing, the jump from dealing very well with small problems to looking at the big ones is the jump from History to Vision and lies beyond the scope of short fiction.

The great obstacle facing Lessing's characters in their movement toward self-knowledge, toward vision, is emotion—particularly romantic love. Lessing sees romantic love as essentially egocentric; people love what they wish to see in the beloved, not what is really there. They love so that they will feel loved in return. They love, in the terms of the title story of one of her collections, from "the habit of loving." This, Lessing insists, is nothing but masochistic self-indulgence. Love robs people of their ability to reason clearly, diverts their energy into useless and potentially harmful channels, causes them to agonize over choices which make, in the end, very little real difference.

Worse, in terms of her visionary philosophy, romantic love, by keeping people focused on the particular, prohibits their making the necessary connections between the individual and the collective consciousness. In story after story, readers watch people live out the same patterns, search for love at all costs, focus on the small problems, the matter at hand: Does he love me? Readers watch them try to believe that this is fundamentally what matters, that there is meaning in the small patterns of their lives. Lessing would deny that this is so. There is meaning, she seems to say, but it lies beyond these insignificant details. One must break through them, destroy them, in order to find it.

Some of her characters, although by no means all, do so. Anna Wulf, the writer-heroine of *The Golden Notebook*, succeeds in first dismantling the old patterns and then in synthesizing new ones, as does the anonymous narrator of "How I Finally Lost My Heart."

"How I Finally Lost My Heart"

An uncharacteristic story in its resemblance to fable, "How I Finally Lost My Heart" is fascinating in its diagrammatic exposition of Lessing's views on romantic love. The story opens as the unnamed "I," a woman, is awaiting the arrival of her escort for the evening, a man designated only as C. The narrator explains that C is the third "serious" love of her life, the first two being A and B. Earlier in the day, the speaker has had lunch with A and tea with B and is pleased that she has been able to enjoy their company with equanimity; she is, finally, "out of love" with them. Recognizing her sensation at this discovery as one of relief, the speaker begins to question her exhilaration at the thought of spending the evening with C, "because there was no doubt that both A and B had caused me unbelievable pain. Why, therefore, was I looking forward to C? I should rather be running away as fast as I could."

Her questioning leads her to a new recognition of what lies behind the human desire to be "in love." It is not, she concludes, that "one needs a person who, like a saucer of water, allows one to float off on him/her, like a transfer." It is not, then, that one needs to "lose one's heart" by blending with another. Rather, "one carries with one a sort of burning spear stuck in one's side, that one waits for someone else to pull out; it is something painful, like a sore or a wound, that one cannot wait to share with someone else." One needs to "lose one's heart" literally, to get rid of

it by giving it to someone else. The catch is that we are expected to take their heart in return. Lessing envisages a grotesque sort of barter, two people demanding of each other, "take my wound."

Moving to the telephone to call C and suggest that they agree to keep their hearts to themselves, the speaker is forced to hang up the phone:

> For I felt the fingers of my left hand push outwards around something rather large, light and slippery— hard to describe this sensation, really. My hand is not large, and my heart was in a state of inflation after having had lunch with A, tea with B, and then looking forward to C. . . . Anyway, my fingers were stretching out rather desperately to encompass an unknown, largish, lightish object, and I said: Excuse me a minute to C, looked down, and there was my heart, in my hand.

There her heart stays, attached to her hand, for four days, growing to the flesh of her palm. She cannot remove it by any "act of will or intention of desire," but when, distracted by events outside her window, she temporarily forgets herself, she feels it begin to loosen. One can "lose one's heart" only by forgetting about it' but it is still attached, and who is one to give it to?

She has previously covered the heart with aluminum foil, in part because it is messy and in part because, unaccustomed to the air, "it smarts." Now wrapping a scarf around her hand, heart and all, she walks about London, finally taking a train on the underground. In the train, she sits across from a woman maddened by love, who ceaselessly, jerkily, accuses her lover or husband of giving his mistress a gold cigarette case. The woman is on the verge of total breakdown, of lapsing into total immobility and, watching her, the narrator forgets herself. She feels the heart loosen from her hand, plucks it off and gives it to the mad woman:

> For a moment she did not react, then with a groan or a mutter of relieved and entirely theatrical grief, she leaned forward, picked up the glittering heart, and clutched it in her arms.

The woman has "taken heart"; she now has the energy of the heart and the "theatrical" grief it brings with it. She can once again play love as a game, insisting that her husband or lover "take her wound." The narrator, finally, is free. "No heart. No heart at all. What bliss. What freedom."

"How I Finally Lost My Heart," although uncharacteristic in its style, can serve as a paradigm for most of Lessing's stories on the relations between men and women. It is valuable because it points out so clearly her vision that the important choice is not among A and B and C, but it is rather the choice of freedom or bondage. If people choose freedom and break out of the patterns of romantic love, they are then able to see clearly and can move on to new ways of loving. This will necessitate new forms of the family, which Lessing sees, in its traditional structure, as the institutionalized destruction of its individual members. If, however, they remain convinced that the important choice is that of who to love, not how to love, they remain in delusion.

"A MAN AND TWO WOMEN"

This same lesson is exemplified in the more traditional story "A Man and Two Women," one of Lessing's many explorations of the strains and restrictions of marriage. The plot is simple: Two couples, good friends, arrange to spend some time together in a country cottage. The couple who owns the cottage, Dorothy and Jack, have recently had a baby. Of the visiting couple, Stella and Paul, only Stella is actually able to come. The story is impressing in its precise delineation of the relationships among the members of the quartet and in its explorations of Dorothy's languor and withdrawal after childbirth. The real excitement, however, lies in Stella's slow examination of her own marriage in light of the situation she finds between Jack and Dorothy. Both marriages are perceived by the couples to be extraordinary in their strength and exuberance, yet both are strained. The connection between Jack and Dorothy is threatened by the strength of Dorothy's attachment to her new son. Also, Stella realizes that her connection with Paul has been more strained by their occasional infidelities than she has realized.

In the final scene, Jack begins to make love to Stella, something Dorothy has goaded him into, declaring that she does not care what he does; he has become insignificant to her. At first, Stella responds:

She thought: What is going to happen now will blow Dorothy and Jack and that baby sky-high; it's the end of my marriage. I'm going to blow everything to bits. There was almost uncontrollable pleasure in it.

Remembering the baby, however, she pulls back and waits for Jack to drive her to the station, making the final comment "It really was a lovely night"—a mundane comment for a return to the usual.

Using the paradigm of "How I Finally Lost My Heart," readers see that the story ends with Stella's struggle over choosing A or B, Jack or Paul, and with her desire to abandon herself to love. "There was almost uncontrollable pleasure in it." She agonizes only over whom she will ask to "take my wound." Although she perceives that both her marriage and Jack's marriage are failures, she leaves with her heart in her hand, carrying it back to Paul. She sees more clearly than she did at the opening of the story, but she is not yet able to act on her perceptions. She has not yet lost her heart.

"A Man and Two Women" ends, then, in ambiguity but not in pessimism. Stella may not yet be able to act on her perceptions, but she is admirable in her willingness to reexamine her life. Readers should consider emulating her. They are left not with a blueprint for action but with feelings and emotions that must be examined. It is typical of Lessing's short fiction that they, like Stella, are awakened to reality and then are left to take their own directions.

"THE NEW CAFÉ"

In her collection *The Real Thing: Stories and Sketches*, Lessing offers glimpses of life in her hometown of London in the 1980's, played out in a series of everyday human experiences. As usual, Lessing's stories on a surface level are simple enough, common to even the most detached observer of urban life. However, her aim is much deeper, as demonstrated in "The New Café," the story of a woman entranced by the conduct of a fellow customer who appears at once distant and interested in his flirtatious banter with female acquaintances, but whose charms suddenly disappear during a mysterious encounter with a young mother and her child on a London street. In recalling the story, Lessing's narrator notes:

here, as in all good cafés, may be observed real-life soap operas, to be defined as series of emotional events that are certainly not unfamiliar, since you are bound to have seen something like them before, but to which you lack the key that will make them not trite, but shockingly individual.

"SPARROWS"

With "Sparrows," set again in a café, the trite once more becomes the profound, as a series of diners react to a family of sparrows who persist in feeding off scraps of food thrown by guests or left at tables. The seemingly innocuous behavior of the birds elicits reactions ranging from outright indifference to the intrigue expressed by members of one family who see in the sparrows' actions a lesson that applies to their own personal situations.

"CASUALTY"

In "Casualty" matters of life and death are clearly distinguished, as Lessing relates the tale of a group of hospital emergency room patients and their reactions not only to their own plights but also to the hysterics of an elderly woman who feels her condition warrants immediate attention, despite being deemed minor by the head nurse. Only when a critically injured young workman is rushed into the room do the others give pause to their situations, and then only temporarily in the case of the older woman, who appears to the reader to be a casualty of another kind.

"STORMS"

Lessing's love of London comes through clearly in "Storms," the story of a woman's encounter with a cranky old taxi driver with whom she is paired upon her return from a visit to Frankfurt. Adding to the driver's dim disposition is the debris covering the streets through which he is attempting to maneuver following an overnight storm. With each compliment the woman expresses for her hometown on the drive back, the driver immediately counters with an invective. By journey's end the woman comes to the realization that the litany of complaints she was hearing was born of sorrow, not of age.

"TWO OLD WOMEN AND A YOUNG ONE"

"Two Old Women and a Young One" explores the seemingly unlimited capacity of people to deal in delusional thoughts, particularly when engaged in social intercourse with the opposite sex. Beginning with the two women of the title who grossly misinterpret the charms of their young male host at a business luncheon, to the host himself, who later mistakes the attentions of an attractive young woman at the same affair, there is little but empty rhetoric. The conversations reflect neither the personal needs nor the identities necessary to building a human connection. It is a rampant self-absorption that inflicts many of Lessing's characters throughout her work, no matter the setting.

OTHER MAJOR WORKS

LONG FICTION: *The Grass Is Singing*, 1950; *Martha Quest*, 1952; *A Proper Marriage*, 1954; *Retreat to Innocence*, 1956; *A Ripple from the Storm*, 1958; *The Golden Notebook*, 1962; *Landlocked*, 1965; *The Four-Gated City*, 1969; *Briefing for a Descent into Hell*, 1971; *The Summer Before the Dark*, 1973; *The Memoirs of a Survivor*, 1974; *Shikasta*, 1979; *The Marriages Between Zones Three, Four, and Five*, 1980; *The Sirian Experiments*, 1981; *The Making of the Representative for Planet 8*, 1982; *Documents Relating to the Sentimental Agents in the Volyen Empire*, 1983; *The Diary of a Good Neighbour*, 1983 (as Jane Somers); *If the Old Could . . .*, 1984 (as Jane Somers); *The Diaries of Jane Somers*, 1984 (includes *The Diary of a Good Neighbour* and *If the Old Could . . .*); *The Good Terrorist*, 1985; *The Fifth Child*, 1988; *Playing the Game*, 1995; *Love, Again*, 1996; *Mara and Dann*, 1999; *Ben, in the World*, 2000.

PLAYS: *Each His Own Wilderness*, pr. 1958; *Play with a Tiger*, pr., pb. 1962; *Making of the Representative for Planet 8*, pr. 1988 (libretto); *Play with a Tiger, and Other Plays*, pb. 1996.

POETRY: *Fourteen Poems*, 1959.

NONFICTION: *Going Home*, 1957; *In Pursuit of the English: A Documentary*, 1960; *Particularly Cats*, 1967; *A Small Personal Voice*, 1974; *Prisons We Choose to Live Inside*, 1987; *The Wind Blows Away Our Words*, 1987; *African Laughter: Four Visits to Zimbabwe*, 1992; *Under My Skin*, 1994; *A Small Personal Voice: Essays, Reviews, Interviews*, 1994;

Doris Lessing: Conversations, 1994 (pb. in England as *Putting the Questions Differently*); *Shadows on the Wall of the Cave*, 1994; *Walking in the Shade*, 1997.

MISCELLANEOUS: *The Doris Lessing Reader*, 1988 (selections).

BIBLIOGRAPHY

Brewster, Dorothy. *Doris Lessing*. New York: Twayne, 1965. The first book-length study of the fiction. Provides a good general overview of Lessing's work up to the fourth novel in the Children of Violence series, *Landlocked*. Includes a brief biography and a discussion of the early novels, including *The Golden Notebook*, a chapter on the short fiction, which analyzes stories published up to 1964, and a concluding chapter on attitudes and influences. Select bibliography, index, and chronology.

Butcher, Margaret. "'Two Forks of a Road': Divergence and Convergence in the Short Stories of Doris Lessing." *Modern Fiction Studies* 26 (1980): 55-61. Asserts that "Homage to Isaac Babel" provides a rebuttal that Lessing's later stories move away from her earlier larger concerns with moral and political issues and retreat into a feminine world of social satire. In her appreciation of Babel's detachment and control, Lessing has at last learned that mannerism and a directness in writing are neither mutually exclusive nor antithetical.

Halisky, Linda H. "Redeeming the Irrational: The Inexplicable Heroines of 'A Sorrowful Woman' and 'To Room Nineteen.'" *Studies in Short Fiction* 27 (Winter, 1990): 45-54. Discusses the inexplicable behavior of the protagonist of Lessing's story by comparing it to Gail Godwin's "A Sorrowful Woman." Argues that the heroine of "To Room Nineteen" is inexplicable only if one is locked into a belief that reason is the only integrating, sense-making force. Discusses the redemptive force of mythic truth in the story.

Harris, Jocelyn. "Doris Lessing's Beautiful Impossible Blueprints." In *The British and Irish Novel Since 1960*, edited by James Acheson. New York: St. Martin's Press, 1991. A discussion of Lessing's discarding of political and social blueprints such as Marxism and sentimental idealism about the brotherhood of man and her moving in her later fiction to mystical solutions and interventions.

Lessing, Doris. *A Small Personal Voice*. New York: Alfred A. Knopf, 1974. This collection of interviews and essays by Lessing gives the reader an insight into the novelist's constantly expanding consciousness and agenda.

Pickering, Jean. *Understanding Doris Lessing*. Columbia: University of South Carolina Press, 1990. A brief, clear overview of Lessing's work. Begins with a chapter providing a biographical and analytical look at Lessing's career, then continues with a short but sharp analysis of her fiction through *The Fifth Child* (1988). Includes an index and an annotated bibliography of books and articles about Lessing.

Taylor, Jenny, ed. *Notebooks/Memoirs/Archives: Reading and Rereading Doris Lessing*. London: Routledge & Kegan Paul, 1982. A collection of essays by British women, mostly from a political standpoint defined in the introduction, which looks at Lessing and Sufism, mysticism, and comparison with Simone de Beauvoir. Supplemented by a select bibliography of Lessing criticism and a complete index.

Thorpe, Michael. *Doris Lessing*. Essex, England: Longman, 1973. A good general introduction that is very thorough, including a select bibliography, with an emphasis on the short fiction. Although only thirty-five pages in length, this volume includes a biography, discussion of Lessing's life and attitudes, and a sociopolitical analysis.

Tyler, Lisa. "Our Mothers' Gardens: Doris Lessing's 'Among the Roses.'" *Studies in Short Fiction* 31 (Spring, 1994): 163-173. Examines the mother-daughter relationship in Lessing's short story "Among the Roses"; argues that the breach between mother and daughter suggests a division between two worlds—one of female community and another of heterosexuality.

Whittaker, Ruth. *Doris Lessing*. New York: St. Martin's Press, 1988. A short but excellent overview of the fiction through *The Good Terrorist*. Ideal for a first reader of Lessing or to clarify points for those familiar with her work. Includes background and influences, the colonial legacy, in-depth analysis, an index, and a select bibliography that lists all Lessing's work and the major books, articles, and interviews published to 1988. Also includes reference to the *Doris Lessing Newsletter*, published by the Brooklyn College Press.

Mary Baron, updated by Mary LeDonne Cassidy and William Hoffman

WYNDHAM LEWIS

Born: Amherst, Canada; November 18, 1882
Died: London, England; March 7, 1957

PRINCIPAL SHORT FICTION

The Wild Body, 1927
Rotting Hill, 1951
Unlucky for Pringle, 1973

OTHER LITERARY FORMS

In addition to his short fiction, Wyndham Lewis published more than forty books in his lifetime, including a number of novels. He wrote some poetry and plays, two autobiographies, a considerable amount of art criticism and literary criticism, a volume of letters, and a mass of materials published posthumously. His "Human Age" trilogy was successfully performed as British Broadcasting Corporation (BBC) radio drama, and his novels partake of a number of genres: Nietzschean novel, fantasy, political thriller, travelogue, murder mystery, detective thriller, and country house weekend novel. Lewis's canon is diverse and his productivity stunning. Lewis was interested in the political, cultural, and philosophical repercussions of art and literature; he enjoyed polemic. His subjects included Adolf Hitler (whom he initially praised and later condemned), James Joyce, D. H. Lawrence, all Bergsonian advocates of stream of consciousness (of which he disapproved on artistic grounds), the Bloomsbury Group, and Gertrude Stein. His best-known critical work is *Time and Western Man* (1927).

ACHIEVEMENTS

A man of multiple talents—poet, novelist, essayist, satirist, critic, editor, philosopher, political thinker, journalist, revolutionary, and painter—Wyndham Lewis was one of the major controversial intellectual figures of his age. He originated the British neoclassic, vorticist movement in the arts, together with Ezra Pound founded the journal *Blast* to further vorticism, and was a longtime contributor to such periodicals as *The Egoist*, *Athenaeum*, *The Little Review*, and *The Listener*. Although Lewis never won a large readership, the literary greats of his age admired his work. T. S. Eliot called him "the most fascinating personality of our time" as well as "the greatest prose master of style" of their generation; William Butler Yeats praised his philosophical work, and Pound believed that Lewis should have won the Nobel Prize for his novel *Self Condemned* (1954). If Lewis had been less irascible, dogmatic, and self-destructive, if he had not tainted his public image with anti-Semitic and fascist political tracts, he might be better received. Yet, in spite of everything, as Marvin Lachman notes in his *Dictionary of Literary Biography* article on Lewis, he was "an independent, courageous artist and brilliant social observer," a gadfly for contemporaries and well deserving of modern consideration.

BIOGRAPHY

Percy Wyndham Lewis was born on November 18, 1882, on his father's yacht moored near Amherst, Nova Scotia, Canada. Lewis was the son of an American army officer who had fought in the Civil War, Charles Lewis, and a British woman, Anne Prickett. He kept the Canadian nationality all of his life. When he was eleven, Lewis's parents separated, and he lived for some years in genteel poverty with his mother in the London suburbs. At Rugby, Lewis ranked at the bottom of his class, but at the Slade School of Art he began to write poetry and make friends with poets such as Thomas Sturge Moore and Lawrence Binyon. In the early 1900's, Lewis resided mainly in Paris (in Montparnasse, the artists' quarter) but also visited Spain, Holland, and Germany and spent summers in Normandy and Brittany. During this time, he studied painting and lived a profligate life of garrets and mistresses (by several of whom he had illegitimate children); as a consequence, he suffered several bouts of illness and venereal disease. His first novel, *Tarr* (1918, 1928), was set amid the Parisian student and café life.

When he returned to England in 1909, he began publishing his first stories and became associated with various art movements. Together with Pound he publicized the vorticist revolution. He met Henri Gaudier-Brzeska, Richard Aldington, Rebecca West, and Ford Madox Ford, among others, but, arrogantly brash, argumentative, and egotistical, he made more enemies than friends. In 1913, when he led an active opposition against Roger Fry, he lost his former friends among the Bloomsbury Group and began a critical exchange that led eventually to his satiric novel *The Apes of God* (1930). In 1914, he and Pound founded *Blast*, "Review of the Great English Vortex," a publication edited and largely written by Lewis but with later contributions by T. S. Eliot. It advocated abstract art, hard geometrical lines, African and Polynesian motifs, classical detachment but an underlying explosiveness that would capture urban life and its machinery. In 1916, he joined the military to battle "German barbarism," trained as a gunner and bombardier, received a commission in the Royal Artillery, and was sent to France. He describes his war experiences in *Blasting and Bombardiering* (1937). Demoralized by the war, he returned to London to pursue his interests in architecture and art, producing drawings and editing the art review *The Tyro*.

For Lewis, the 1920's were a productive period of literature and criticism. Calling himself "The Enemy," he blasted those whose ideas or style offended him. In 1929, Lewis married Gladys Anne Hoskyns. He visited Germany and traveled in North Africa in 1930. After a period of illness and controversy in the early 1930's, particularly about his profascist, anticommunist stance, several of Lewis's books were withdrawn from publication. Ernest Hemingway, stung by Lewis's criticism of his novels in "The Dumb Ox," retaliated much later with a vicious portrait of Lewis in *A Moveable Feast* (1964). In 1938, his portrait of Eliot was refused by the Royal Academy, and, when Sir Winston Churchill defended the academy's action, Lewis attacked him for his "passionate advocacy of platitude." Condemned in England for his association with the British Union of Fascists, for his right-wing tracts, and his book praising Hitler as a true democrat and a "Man of Peace," Lewis went to the United States (Buffalo, New York City, and Long Island) in 1939 and moved to Canada in 1940 (Toronto and Windsor), where he lectured for a year at Assumption College in Windsor, Ontario. When faced with the true nature of Hitler's fascism,

Wyndham Lewis (Library of Congress)

Lewis recanted his previous stance but was permanently tainted by it. His novel *Self Condemned* is a subjective analysis of his own self-destructive patterns.

In 1945, Lewis returned to London to Notting Hill Gate and became art critic for *The Listener* until his eyesight failed in 1951. At that time, he was granted a small government pension, and a friend, Agnes Bedford, came to help his wife care for him and to help him continue to write. In 1952, the University of Leeds awarded him a doctorate of literature. In 1953, Lewis went totally blind. The Tate Gallery put on a Retrospective Exhibition in 1956: "Wyndham Lewis and Vorticism." Lewis died March 7, 1957, after a lifetime of controversy and criticism, his final words being "Mind your own business."

ANALYSIS

A staunch elitist whose barbed wit won for him many enemies, Wyndham Lewis began his literary career writing the first literary form with which he had become familiar: the short story. Later, he claimed that the short story was "the crystallization of what I had to keep out of my consciousness while painting." Despite this seemingly negative attitude toward a form in which he continued to write throughout most of his lifetime, Lewis's stories reflect the diversity, values, and creative concerns of his other artistic endeavors. In fact, literary critic E. W. F. Tomlin says of *The Wild Body* that it contains "almost the whole of Lewis." Lewis himself is occasionally a character in his stories, and even when he is not there personally, many of the figures reflect his experiences as a student, a lover, a soldier, and an artist, as if the fictive and the nonfictive merge. His lifelong belief was that art should be about something, that politics, theology, philosophy—all human beings' intellectual concerns—are implicit in any serious work of art. Most of his short stories are satires that focus on the divided person: the split between mind and body, between good intentions and negative results, between the creative spirit and commercial needs, between surface appearances and hidden realities. The imagery reinforces these ideas: in them, clean and hard is good; soft and mushy is bad.

Lewis's prose style is unforgettable; characterized by structural clarity, vivid visual descriptions, striking metaphors, a range of diction, and a sense of discord, all with a biting edge. Stories such as "Some Innkeepers and Bestre" and "The Cornac and His Wife" are small gems, beautifully conceived. In keeping with his artistic theories of the vortex, continually in motion round a fixed and motionless center, his short fiction shifts perspective and attention but maintains a still, unchanging artistic center. His is the eye of a painter, who, in a few words, can capture the essence of "a slut of a room, dribbling at the sink, full of unsavoury pails, garishly dirty" ("Unlucky for Pringle") or of an athletic Frenchwoman on a cold day ("Some Innkeepers and Bestre"):

> The crocket-like floral postiches on the ridges of her head-gear looked crisped down in a threatening way: her nodular pink veil was an apoplectic gristle round her stormy brow; steam came out of her lips upon the harsh white atmosphere. Her eyes were dark, and the Contiguous color of her cheeks of a redness quasi-venetian, with something like the feminine colouring of battle.

The Frenchman in the hotel window of "A Soldier of Humour" and Carl in *The Wild Body* are sketched in black and white with "dazzling skin and black patches of hair alternating"; many of the early stories describe the small things (such as a fishing boat, an athletic interest, an arrested conversation) that become the focus of human obsessions.

THE WILD BODY

Lewis's first collection of short stories, *The Wild Body*, began as a travelogue, a sociological documentary characterized by realistic detail and a fragmentary vision, but developed into a far more complex dramatization of modern human beings. "Inferior Religions" and "The Meaning of the Wild Body" comment on the stories' meaning and construction and emphasize Lewis's vision of human absurdity, echoing Henri Bergson's idea of humanity as "a thing behaving like a person" and therefore comic. A Lewis character is often driven by obsessions beyond his control and mechanically repeats patterns that create both comedy and pathos. In *The Wild Body* the inhabitants of the Pension Beau Séjour, Francis the wandering musician, Bestre, and Cornac and his wife (poverty-stricken traveling entertainers savagely at odds with their village audiences) are just such creatures, while the Soldier of Humour, Ker-Orr, Lewis's projected persona, is self-described as a "barbarian clown . . . large, white and savage" and as a "forked, strange-scented, blond-skinned gut-bag, with its two bright rolling marbles with which it sees, bull's-eyes full of mockery and madness." The innkeeper in "A Breton Innkeeper" is a study of a domineering personality, a bullying, bellowing menace, a murderous "buffoon" characterized by empty and mechanical behavior patterns. Patient Eldred in "The Room Without a Telephone" is at times a "clown" whose mind was "blotted out by his frantic vanity" and his "spiteful animal" self. Lewis's detached narrator provides a surreal edge to even his most realistic tales.

Lewis's metaphors provide clues to his themes. He describes many of his characters as animals, a bestiary of modern people: horses, camels, walruses, sea lions, ferrets, dogs, placid cows, silly goats, sharp sheep, or even "some strenuous amoeba." John Leslie in "Junior" declares "We are a beastly race"; the head of Misrow in "The War Baby" reminds one of a "snake's sling-like extremity," and diners at a popular restaurant are "a lot of glum-looking cattle" who need stirring up. One character has "clam" eyes. *The Wild Body*, in particular, focuses on humans as primitive, like "big, obsessed, sun-drunk insects." Lewis as anthropologist scrutinizes strange new species of human beings and categorizes them according to their animal parallels, from the French or Spanish settings of *The Wild Body* stories or the English settings of his later tales. The French landlord in "Unlucky for Pringle" has an "animal-like selfishness and self-absorption," while Pringle's portmanteau lets loose its squashed contents "like a flock of birds and pack of dogs." "Cantleman's Spring-Mate" describes humans as "the most ugly and offensive of the brutes because of the confusion caused by their consciousness" and Cantleman as "an animal disguised as an officer and gentleman"; it advocates a return to raw animal nature. Eldred in "The Room Without a Telephone" is "like a sea beast—but blowing blood."

Lewis was particularly disturbed by the modern movement toward standardization and mechanization. His stories repeatedly attack human beings for "herd" behavior and "herd" philosophies. Similar to his herd images is his description of humanity as "a pea disguising itself from a million other peas . . . soft, subtle, clever, insolent." His other images focus on machines: The sun appears "bitterly and mechanically." Many of his characters seem little more than robots or automatic machines, endlessly repeating the same dull tasks, the same inescapable patterns, the same windup dialogue. For Lewis, stupidity, primitive behavior, and mechanical patterns are interrelated and sum up the absurdity of all mankind. Bestre, Brocatnaz, and various other inhabitants of the Breton Coast (*The Wild Body*) are elemental figures, seemingly rugged individualists who give rein to their "wild bodies" but in fact are cogs, "bobbins," "puppets," and mere "shadows of energy" caught up in "the complexity of the rhythmic scheme," "a pattern as circumscribed and complete as a theorem of Euclid" ("The Soldier of Humour"). The Frenchman in "Bestre" fixes Ker-Orr "with the blankness of two metal discs"—his eyes; at a trapeze performance the clown is "a cheerful automaton" and his barker, inspired by him, springs back and forth "as though engaged in a boxing match" as the audience howls with delight. Mr. Patrick, a shopkeeper in *Rotting Hill* is like "a wound-up toy," while the socialist parson, Rymer, is at times "an infuriated animal"; "X" in "Tyronic Dialogues" defines himself as an "animal" and his friends as "automata"; Arghol yawns in "mechanical spasms," "Father" François is described as "automata," the face of a woman reclined in bed is "a flat disc . . . sideways on the pillow," and a young boy's face might physically change as he imagines himself "a steamroller" or a "sightless Juggernaut" (all in *The Wild Body*). The pugilists in "The Man Who Was Unlucky with Women" spring left and right like mechanical toys or batter away like "a compact, seemingly heavily-loaded machine."

Related to his emphasis on the animalistic and the mechanistic is Lewis's interest in sudden, unpredictable violence, the meaningless events that will have a country parson scuffling with an angry opponent in the local pub and ignominiously kicked in the genitals ("The Bishop's Fool") or the cuckold husband of "The Man Who Was Unlucky with Women" frustratedly picking vicious fights with strangers at every opportunity and being unexpectedly killed by an enraged wolfhound that takes his warlike exhibitionism as a direct challenge. All the early stories in *The Wild Body* include violence, brutality, and callousness. Brobdingnag dispels the bruises left on his wife by an unknown rival by adding his own, while Brotcotnaz believes that he can kill an invalid woman with impunity. The patterns are behavioristic: cause-effect patterns of stimulus-response. "The French Poodle" connects the motives that would cause an animal lover to kill his own pet with the horrible death that the pet owner is doomed to face in the trenches.

In contrast to the mechanistic and animalistic are a few characters who have learned to control mind and body, ones Lewis sometimes calls puppet-masters. For example, Ker-Orr in "A Soldier of Humour" operates with detachment as he uses his body as "a stalking horse." Cantleman is another such figure, for he imitates the murderous callousness of nature to assert his own superiority amid a world of trench warfare and inescapable horror.

Lewis's sense of place is directly related to his sense of humanity. The distant foreign settings of *The Wild Body*—the hotels and boardinghouses, cafés and bars—emphasize the narrator's alienation, while the insufferable restrictions of domestic hells in other tales contrast with the lonely but open spaces of homeless vagabonds. Frequently Lewis depicts rooms and flats as microcosms reflecting the world of their owners, their personality and essence. "Unlucky for Pringle," for example, traces the rootless Pringle's search, from Morocco to Canada to Chelsea, for the perfect accommodations, ones harmonious with his sense of self and with his need to extract sensations from his environment while imposing his own personality on it. With a gusto for common things, he might pass "like a ghost . . . through a hundred unruffled households," whose peaceful landladies he enjoys; yet Pringle awakens such hostility in observant landlords that his lodging houses "vomit him forth" unassimilated. "The Rot" in *Rotting Hill* in turn de-

scribes the narrator and his wife's encounters with both the dry rot of his own apartments and the dry rot of the new socialism as a stream of lazy, unmotivated repairmen make them feel like bruised grapes "in a basketful of glass marbles"; they dream of workers accusingly declaring that the couple themselves are the dry rot that infects the heart of their home and country. "The Room Without a Telephone" attacks socialized medicine as a diseased system that turns the individual into a guinea pig, promotes monumental waste, and endangers human life, accusations summed up in the treatment of patient Paul Eldred, whose confinement in a room without a telephone spells near doom.

ROTTING HILL

Rotting Hill sketches the bedraggled people and patterns of post-World War II London, a place that Lewis describes as rotting, both physically from the wartime bombing and the dry rot produced by neglect and metaphorically from the political and social decay. Basically a political treatise, it captures a period of shortages, rationing, and depressing poverty. In "Time the Tiger," Lewis describes a London morning as "a constipated mass, yellowed by the fog, suspended over a city awaiting the Deluge" and city streets "like Pompeii with Vesuvius in catastrophic eruption, a dull glare, saffronish in colour, providing an unearthly uniformity." As is frequent in Lewis's books, many of the stories depend on a conflict or disagreement between two characters representing totally opposite points of view, morality, politics, or social conditions, with Lewis's literary persona sometimes appearing as the representative of one side of an argument. In "The Bishop's Fool," for example, Lewis describes a chance meeting with a village rector, whose admirable but foolish views sum up what Lewis saw going wrong all over England: a Christian-influenced movement toward socialism, the dominance of the Labour Party, and the potential for England to perpetuate the abuses of a godless communism—socialism without Christian restraint. In "Time the Tiger," two old friends, a Tory and a socialist, exchange views and insults in a friendly fashion until an opinionated woman turns the disagreement into a permanent separation and the predatory "tiger," time, consumes the last of the world that they once knew. In "My Disciple," the Lewis persona is accosted by an advocate of spontaneous, undisciplined child art, in "My Fellow Traveler to Oxford" by a leftist undergraduate with firm opinions, and throughout the *Rotting Hill* stories by plumbers, carpenters, and other assorted repairmen halfheartedly trying to shore up the decay that threatens to engulf him, while Britannia herself (in "The Rot Camp") begs alms and sings "Land of Hope and Glory" in "a cracked wheeze."

Some of Lewis's stories focus on the artist, his life and vision. A bitter central theme is the hostile treatment of artists and the fate of the artist in modern society—beset by poverty, fearful of failure, tempted to compromise his talent for short-term financial gain. "Doppelganger" argues through its portrait of Thaddeus Trunk, an aging and purposefully eccentric artist, that "a man's publicity is a caricature of himself." Beset by adoring students, Trunk has chosen to play "the Dispenser of Culture" and in doing so has submerged his creative and spiritual self for the applause of "a horde of anonymous beings." His *Doppelgänger*, in the guise of a distant cousin, calls attention to Trunk's concern with his reputation and his betrayal of his art simply by being what Trunk should be but is not, a quiet, private artist, true to his artistic vision, a gadfly showing up the limitations of Trunk's admirers. As such, the *Doppelgänger* wins the heart of Trunk's wife, who sees in the double the real "Thaddeus," and the two leave the publicity-seeking Trunk "a shadow, a shell" of whom "the vulgar" would have the last word about "what his actions signified." "The Cornac and His Wife" portrays a melancholy showman who is a victim of his own audiences; as he manipulates them, they demand and elicit the kind of humor that they prefer, so that instead of puppet-master he becomes in part puppet, contorted to conform to the desires of his audience.

Related to his concern with artists is Lewis's Nietzschean belief that women are traps set for the creative man. In "The Code of a Herdsman," he voices his contention that "women, and the processes for which they exist, are the arch conjuring trick." He calls women "chocolate-cream traps" or "lush red sex-fruit" and finds situations such as those in "The

War Baby" and "Junior" all too typical. The women in such stories are overweight, indolent, soft, and determined. "Junior" describes mankind as "walking factories for procreation" and women as walking "time-bombs" whose "delight-producing machinery" will inevitably produce a child to trap a man in marriage and domesticity. The hero of "Junior" flees his mewling son, his wife, and a home transformed by marriage into a woman's club; forced by bad publicity to return home, he renounces them all, only to be taunted that the child was not his anyway and that he does not have "the guts to have a child." The young man in "The War Baby," desperate to find just the right kind of woman to seduce before going off to war, is reminded of another more subtle battle, the battle of the sexes: "All women seemed to feel that they should have their luxurious battles too; only they were playing at dying, and their war was fruitful." In this case, a woman chosen to affirm life before frontline confrontations pursues the young man with letters and after her death leaves him obliged to support their child, a dull, homely daughter, "a blast of God's irony." "Children of the Great" focuses on a similar irony, the child of a famous historian, totally lacking his father's arrestingly handsome looks, his sharp intelligence, and his interest in the world of the mind yet courted and pursued by women who adored his father, until captured by a rich, clever girl who sees him as the holder of valuable genes and a potential breeder of remarkable children, throwbacks to their grandfather, and uses him as such. Cantleman, the main character in "Cantleman's Spring-Mate," treats women with the same animalistic power that makes him a successful soldier. Assuming that "all women were contaminated with Nature's hostile power" and might be dealt with as secret agents or enemies, he craftily plans to outwit Nature by paving the way for the sexual "devouring of his mate" with the courtship niceties that women demand but then committing the sexual act with "the same impartial malignity" that he displayed "when he beat a German's brains out." The brutality of some of Lewis's male characters is directly linked to their sexual drive and their fear of the power it might give women over them.

Lewis effectively depicts neurotic compulsives. For example, he details the lunatic behavior of Captain Polderdick, in "The King of the Trenches," who races about pretending to be a "flying pig" (a nickname for a World War I British bomb) and who sends fusillades into the enemy camp, precipitates retaliatory attacks, and then heads for the safety of the back lines. The busybody Lionel Letheridge (nicknamed "Pish-Tush") rushes about spraying dichloro-diphenyl-trichloroethane (DDT) to drive out a supposedly ghostly inhabitant of a neighbor's apartment, while the beach bum (a comic Cuchulainn) who finds a yachting cap (in "The Yachting Cap") is convinced that it has overpowered his consciousness and led him to challenge the sea to battle and that he can escape the sea's clutches only by giving the cap back to the sea. Some of Lewis's stories follow traditional genre lines, made slightly offbeat, such as the ghost story in "Pish-Tush" or the bank robbery and con game in "The Two Captains."

Lewis believed that "true satire must be vicious," and his stories reflect this viciousness in their attack on mechanistic behavior, scheming women, brutish men, dull heads, compromising artists, wrongheaded liberals, and general social and political corruption and decay. Lewis's fiction seems modern, and indeed his avant-garde stance anticipated the self-conscious, surrealistic fiction of later generations.

OTHER MAJOR WORKS

LONG FICTION: *Tarr*, 1918, 1928; *The Childermass*, 1928; *The Apes of God*, 1930; *Snooty Baronet*, 1932; *The Revenge for Love*, 1937; *The Vulgar Streak*, 1941; *Self Condemned*, 1954; *The Human Age: Monstre Gai and Malign Fiesta*, 1955; *The Red Priest*, 1956; *The Roaring Queen*, 1973 (wr. 1936); *Mrs. Dukes' Million*, 1977.

PLAYS: *Enemy of the Stars*, pb. 1914, 1932; *The Ideal Giant*, pb. 1917.

POETRY: *One-Way Song*, 1933.

NONFICTION: *The Caliph's Design: Architects! Where Is Your Vortex?*, 1919; *Harold Gilman*, 1919; *The Art of Being Ruled*, 1926; *The Lion and the Fox: The Role of the Hero in Shakespeare's Plays*, 1927; *The Enemy: A Review of Art and Literature*, 1927, 1929; *Time and Western Man*, 1927; *Paleface: The Philosophy of the Melting Pot*, 1929; *Satire and Fiction*, 1930; *Hitler*, 1931; *The Diabolical Principle and the Dithyrambic Spectator*, 1931; *The Doom of Youth*, 1932; *Filibusters in Barbary*, 1932; *The Old Gang and the New Gang*, 1933; *Men Without Art*, 1934; *Left Wings over Europe*, 1936; *Blasting and Bombardiering*, 1937; *Count Your Dead, They Are Alive*, 1937; *The Jews, Are They Human?*, 1939; *Wyndham Lewis: The Artist from "Blast" to Burlington House*, 1939; *The Hitler Cult*, 1939; *America, I Presume*, 1940; *Anglosaxony: A League That Works*, 1941; *America and Cosmic Man*, 1948; *Rude Assignment: A Narrative of My Career Up-to-Date*, 1950; *The Writer and the Absolute*, 1952; *The Demon of Progress in the Arts*, 1954; *Letters of Wyndham Lewis*, 1963 (W. K. Rose, editor); *Wyndham Lewis on Art*, 1969; *Wyndham Lewis: An Anthology of His Prose*, 1969 (E. W. F. Tomlin, editor); *Hitler, the Germans, and the Jews*, 1973 (5 volumes); *Enemy Salvoes: Selected Literary Criticism*, 1976; *Creatures of Habit, Creatures of Change*, 1989.

MISCELLANEOUS: *Collected Poems and Plays*, 1979.

BIBLIOGRAPHY

Ayers, David. *Wyndham Lewis and Western Man.* New York: St. Martin's Press, 1992. See especially Ayers's chapter on Lewis and Bergson. Ayers is particularly concerned with Lewis's concept of self. Includes detailed notes and bibliography.

Edwards, Paul. "Wyndham Lewis's Narrative of Origins: 'The Death of the Ankou.'" *The Modern Language Review* 92 (January, 1997): 22-35. Traces Lewis's modernist style, satire, and primitivism; compares his misleading autobiographical account of writing the original story and the story as published; argues that the series of displacements that take place in the story indicate an artist in a relationship with a tragic reality.

Foshay, Toby Avard. *Wyndham Lewis and the Avant-Garde: The Politics of Intellect.* Montreal: McGill-Queens University Press, 1992. Foshay explores the reasons for Lewis's "perverse" opposition to modernism. Includes detailed notes and excellent bibliography.

Grigson, Geoffrey. *A Master of Our Time: A Study of Wyndham Lewis*. London: Methuen, 1951. Grigson, a strong admirer of Lewis, argues that "all Lewis's work is one work" and that, whether he was right or wrong about life and politics, one can profit from his intellectual passion and his "crystalline" understanding of art. Grigson also praises Lewis's prose as "Nashe-like," a prose that "demands reading" and that "cannot be absorbed effortlessly like air."

Head, Dominic. *The Modernist Short Story: A Study in Theory and Practice*. Cambridge, England: Cambridge University Press, 1992. Head devotes a chapter to Lewis's development of the Vorticist short story. Argues that his collection *The Wild Body* represents a systematic application of the Vorticist program to the short story. Claims that the fluid representation of personality in modernist literature, a challenge to the limitations of short-story form, was anathema to Lewis; the result is that his characters are isolated.

Jameson, Fredric. *Fables of Aggression*. Berkeley: University of California Press, 1979. Jameson, ironically, applies Marxist criticism and psychoanalysis to a staunch anticommunist to argue that Lewis's explosive language practice was a symbolic political act. He explores in Lewis's canon his aggressiveness, sexism, flirtation with Fascism, and polemics against the countercultural trends of his age. He finds Lewis contemplating a sham world filled with unreal puppets, "a paper world of falsefaces and hollow effigies, walking caricatures, split-men, scarecrows and automata," and ultimately denouncing himself for the innocence that led him to misread the political trends of his age.

Kenner, Hugh. *Wyndham Lewis*. Norfolk, Conn.: New Directions, 1954. This critical estimate of the importance of Lewis's writings is reliable and convincing, though its style might be daunting for students. Lewis himself called it a "splendid study." It places each work in the progression of Lewis's career to argue that "Lewis reveals the time's nature" and that "this tough-minded failure . . . was right . . . about Western Man" though wrong about himself as an antithesis. He calls Lewis's harangues "electrifying" and traces themes and concerns throughout his fiction as a whole: his interest in the unreal and in gradations of unreality, in the disharmony of reason and power and the mechanistic nature of human behavior.

Meyers, Jeffrey, ed. *Wyndham Lewis: A Revaluation*. London: Athlone Press, 1980. Describing Lewis as "the most neglected and underrated major author of this century," Meyers hopes to "stimulate critical appreciation of the depth and diversity of Lewis's fifty years of creative life" by providing essays on his prose style and imagery, his philosophical influences, and representative works in a variety of genres (autobiography, short story, mystery, play, Nietzschean novel, fantasy, satire, political tract, travelogue, and literary criticism). Along with Saul Bellow, he praises Lewis as "a brilliant, thoughtful and original observer" of contemporary society.

Pritchard, William. *Wyndham Lewis*. New York: Twayne, 1968. Pritchard examines Lewis's canon by exploring his various roles: as satiric humorist, sage and mocker, dystopic social critic, literary critic, vulgarian, and self-appraiser. He calls *Rotting Hill* Lewis's "greyist and least artistic" fictive work.

Sherry, Vincent. *Ezra Pound, Wyndham Lewis, and Radical Modernism*. New York: Oxford University Press, 1993. Examines Pound's and Lewis's claim that aesthetic principles could apply to politics; traces the source of this claim in European history.

Stockton, Sharon. "Aesthetics, Politics, and the Staging of the World: Wyndham Lewis and the Renaissance." *Twentieth Century Literature* 42 (Winter, 1996): 494-515. Discovers the origin of Lewis's combination of aesthetics with politics in an obscure work Lewis did on the English Renaissance; claims that in his work on William Shakespeare, Lewis constructs a way to validate a binary model of oppression and opposition that extends other modernist binary models to their full political potential.

Wagner, Geoffrey. *Wyndham Lewis: A Portrait of the Artist as Enemy*. London: Routledge & Kegan Paul, 1957. Wagner discusses Lewis's interest in group rhythms and herd instinct, his elitism, and his attack on "time." He labels his antagonism toward women partly French and partly antiromanticism. Wagner is puzzled "that a man so sensitive to words could use them so wildly and irresponsibly" in his political writings, finds his satire lacking in universality and his later works indicative of artistic decline, but he praises *The Apes of God* as Lewis's best book: its ideas honest, its every page functional. This study contains a large bibliography but its mine of information about Lewis itself overwhelms the critique.

Gina Macdonald

JOHN L'HEUREUX

Born: South Hadley, Massachusetts; October 26, 1934

PRINCIPAL SHORT FICTION

Family Affairs, 1974
Desires, 1981
Comedians, 1990

OTHER LITERARY FORMS

John L'Heureux began his literary career by publishing four volumes of poetry, written while he was a Jesuit. His autobiographical memoir, *Picnic in Babylon: A Jesuit Priest's Journal, 1963-67* (1967), chronicles and analyzes the years of theological study leading to his ordination as a priest. Since leaving the Jesuits in 1971, he has written several novels. The first two, *Tight White Collar* (1972) and *The Clang Birds* (1972), grew out of his experiences in religious life, whereas his later novels, especially *An Honorable Profession* (1991) and *The Handmaid of Desire* (1996), spring from his career in teaching.

ACHIEVEMENTS

Editors of *The Best American Short Stories* and *Prize Stories: The O. Henry Awards* have selected several of John L'Heureux's stories for inclusion in their annuals. He received creative writing fellowships from the National Endowment for the Arts in 1981 and 1986. At Stanford University he won the Dean's Award for Excellence in Teaching in 1983 and again in 1998.

BIOGRAPHY

John Clarke L'Heureux was born in South Hadley, Massachusetts, on October 26, 1934, the second son of Wilfred Joseph L'Heureux, a civil engineer, and his wife Mildred (Clarke) L'Heureux. While attending local schools, he began to write, mainly poetry. Upon graduating from high school, he spent a summer at the National Academy of Theatre Arts before entering Holy Cross College. In 1954, at the end of his sophomore year, he decided "on the grounds of coldest reason" to enter the Society of Jesus because it was "the best and most generous thing" he could do with his life. He began his ascetical training at Shadowbrook, the Jesuit novitiate, in Lenox, Massachusetts, but when it burned down, he was sent to Wernersville, Pennsylvania, where he took his perpetual vows of poverty, chastity, and obedience in July of 1956.

In the course of his Jesuit training he earned a licentiate in philosophy from Weston College in Massachusetts in 1959 and a licentiate in theology from Woodstock College in Maryland in 1967. He was ordained "a priest forever" on June 11, 1966. By this time his collections of poetry had begun to be published, starting with *Quick as Dandelions* in 1964. After the completion of his theological studies he began work for a doctorate in English at Harvard University, but, seeing himself as primarily a creative writer, he left with his master's degree in 1968. While working as an editor for *The Atlantic Monthly*, he decided to leave the Society of Jesus, essentially because of difficulties with his vow of obedience (he wanted to be "his own man"). After being laicized in 1971, he married Joan Polston, a writer, on June 26. In the early 1970's, while he was a visiting professor at Tufts College and Harvard University, he alchemized his Jesuit experiences into two novels and into several short stories that were published in such magazines as *The Atlantic Monthly* and *The New Yorker*.

In 1973, he began what would become a long and fruitful academic career at Stanford University. He expeditiously passed through the ranks of assistant professor (1973-79) and associate professor (1979-81) to full professor (beginning in 1981), while also serving as the Director of the Creative Writing Program (1976-1994). He also led workshops for the Wallace Stegner Fellows, a program to nourish promising talent, through which he has influenced such writers as Ron Hansen, David Henry Hwang, Kathryn Harrison, Tobias Wolff, and many others. He has continued to write novels, including *The Shrine at Altamira* (1992) and *The Handmaid of Desire* (1996), both of which received mostly favorable critical response. Characteristically, he has taken care of life after L'Heureux by composing his own obituary and completing a "posthumous" novel, "Lies."

ANALYSIS

In an analysis of John L'Heureux's short fiction John Gardner compared him to Anton Chekhov, the stodgy old doctor who enjoyed clinically dissecting his characters' desperate desires and destructive loves. On initially encountering L'Heureux's characters, with their mind-forged manacles and emotional cages, imprisoned in a muddled world of hopeless disillusion, a reader might sympathize with Gardner's assessment, but a deeper reading reveals that above this surface of disorder and despair dwells a transcendent God who may or may not be enjoying the human comedy. For L'Heureux, the cord between the mean-

ingless absurdity of life and the meaningfulness of religious faith is weak and easily frayed, but God is still able to write straight with crooked lines. L'Heureux seems to enjoy making his characters' lives as tortuous as possible, the better to bring out the irony of God (one of his favorite themes). Humans seem to make messes of their lives, and yet his characters, even though they may have lost the sense that anything transcends their troubled existences, somehow muddle through to an encounter with something (someone?) larger and more meaningful than themselves.

L'Heureux's stories, with their caustic insights and wicked wit, have been compared to the works of Iris Murdoch and Muriel Spark, two writers he admires. Despite the bleakness of life detailed in many of his stories, L'Heureux has said that he still believes in God, and he believes even more deeply in the amazing grace that can save the wretches about whom he writes. As a Jesuit priest, he was duty-bound to save the world, to do everything "for the greater glory of God" (St. Ignatius of Loyola's motto for the Society of Jesus, which he founded), but as a man of the world L'Heureux has said that he writes for his own salvation, not the world's. He sees his stories as "a pack of lies intended to entertain and illumine and dismay." Nevertheless, he does try to probe the mystery underlying or overarching the few truths he knows for certain, for example, that people carry within themselves the means of their own destruction—or salvation. In his stories he tries to create something good that will help people "appreciate the wonders of another person, or of being alive."

In several of his best-known and most successful stories L'Heureux portrays priests and former priests, whose crises often arise from the conflicts between their sacred and secular lives. His fictional creations often discover an ineradicable egocentricity that lies at the core of even their most spiritual activities. For some critics, L'Heureux's stories about the religious life are a lament for the world he lost when he left the Jesuits. For others, particularly those who have remained in the religious life, his depictions of priests and nuns who are more avid about sex than salvation, more eager for alcoholic spirits than the Holy Spirit, are demeaning and untrue to the lives they have experienced in their service of God. While the priests and nuns of L'Heureux's stories share little common ground with their fictional predecessors in the novels of Georges Bernanos and Graham Greene, or with the movie incarnations played by Bing Crosby and Julie Andrews, their lives are not as totally lacking in redeeming spiritual value as some of his detractors contend. In his own defense L'Heureux emphasizes that his duty as a writer is to create people as they really are—on the way to redemption but not there yet.

"FOX AND SWAN"

Judging from interviews and several of his short stories, L'Heureux's break with the Jesuit Order after sixteen years of service occasioned much soul-searching, and it is understandable that he dealt with the feelings generated by this wrenching event, albeit in a transformed way, in some of his stories. Indeed, several of the stories in his first collection, *Family Affairs*, have the religious life as their subject, and for some critics his stories about priests and nuns are more convincing than those with secular protagonists. Martha Foley selected "Fox and Swan" to appear in *The Best American Short Stories 1972*. The story focuses on Francis Xavier Madden, a Jesuit working for his doctorate at Harvard University, who is agonizing over his vocation (he is called "fox" by a girl who finds his beard "groovy"). He develops an intimate relationship with Caryl Henderson, a fellow doctoral student who is a devout Catholic. While waiting to be dispensed from his vows, Francis feels guilty about their sexual activities, whereas she sees their lovemaking as "the most beautiful thing in the world." Using humor and irony, L'Heureux deals with their carnalities compassionately, particularly in contrasting how a theologian and a red-blooded human being view sexual desires. Another conflict in the story is the decision facing Francis about whether to pursue his doctorate or a career as a creative writer. He is fascinated by an image of swans whose legs are frozen in ice, making them easy prey for voracious foxes, and he writes a story about it. This story resolves one of his problems, because he decides to become a writer (but how many swans will this fox devour in order to survive?).

"THE PRIEST'S WIFE"

This story, subtitled "Thirteen Ways of Looking at a Blackbird," has been anthologized several times and appears in 1980's *Prize Stories: The O. Henry Awards*. It also was an important part of *Desires*, L'Heureux's second collection of short fiction, whose stories continue his attempt to reconcile the best ideas and feelings he absorbed as a Jesuit and his new insights into the modern world, in which he chose to live and work. L'Heureux treats this story of the marriage of a former nun and a former priest with a tone of methodical detachment. He not only constructs the story in thirteen brief scenes but also uses lists within some of these scenes. For example, after the priest meets the woman who will become his wife, he is "of three minds what he ought to do": be a poet and write perfect love songs to God; be a professional writer for publication; or be an incorruptible creator of good things.

The marriage of the former priest and the former nun seems doomed from the start (it was "like having a buzzard sitting . . . square on your tombstone"). Unhappy in his job as a high school teacher and despondent over his avocation as a poet, he heaps abuse onto his wife, who responds, "Why didn't you stay a priest and drink yourself to death?" After eleven endless months the couple separates, and she pursues a career as a writer while he works in an advertizing agency. They eventually resume their relationship, and on their anniversary his wife writes that "the river carrying them out of control at least carried them together."

"DEPARTURES"

An appearance in *The New Yorker* has traditionally indicated a high level of success for a short-story writer. This widely anthologized story, which appeared in *The New Yorker* in 1980, occupies a special place in L'Heureux's oeuvre, because he views its central character as closer to who he really is than any of his other creations. The story centers on a young seminarian, who decides to become a priest because it will allow him to live an ordered life securely isolated from the chaos of the secular world. After several years of Jesuit training, he travels home to visit his parents. During his trip, he feels ill at ease in public. Instead of seeing people through the eyes of Christian charity, as fellow children of God, he is repelled by the vulgarities of the hoi polloi. They put him into such a sour mood that he refuses to let his mother embrace him when his train arrives (the pain in her eyes will haunt him for the rest of his life).

Though his parents live to see their son ordained, his priesthood is neither fulfilling nor joyful. He is bored with his life and drinks too much. Even in his priestly functions, the symbols of transcendence fail to work their magic in sanctifying his soul. After his father quickly dies of a heart attack and his mother dies slowly of Parkinson's disease, his spiritual aridity becomes pandemic, infecting all aspects of his life. The story ends at an Easter vigil service, during which the priest puts out the holy fire. When critics in religious publications complained that L'Heureux was too hard on the priests he so acidly depicts, he responded that he was not easy on himself as a Jesuit, but "if kindness means treating people a lot better than they deserve," then he feels that he has been "extraordinarily kind" to his characters, who happen to be priests.

"THE COMEDIAN"

In a famous poem, Robert Frost asked God to forgive his little jokes, and he in turn would forgive the great big joke of God's creating humanity. In L'Heureux's third collection of short fiction, *Comedians*, he often presents human life as just such a cosmic prank. In a pivotal story of this collection, "The Comedian," which William Abrahams chose for *Prize Stories: The O. Henry Awards* in 1986, L'Heureux's protagonist is not a priest but a stand-up comic named Corinne, who wants only two things from life: a lot of laughs and a successful career. When a doctor discovers her unexpected pregnancy, he suggests abortion, but she is not sure. She had been a Catholic "until the end of her first marriage," and she needs some time to think about her decision, which is made more complicated when she hears her fetus singing. Her husband thinks that this is a joke for her act, but L'Heureux seems to be using Corinne's singing fetus as a vehicle for her spiritual redemption.

Corinne continues to perform, but her boss tells her that her routine provokes laughter from the head

not the heart. It is true that she is having difficulty finding things to joke about, as she hates jokes that put down women, ridicule husbands, or make fun of people's looks, and she certainly cannot make a good joke about abortion (can anyone?).

When amniocentesis reveals that her fetus is deformed, Corinne decides to abort it, whereupon it promptly stops singing. On the abortion table, just before the doctor is to inject the fatal salt solution, she stops him, saying that she wants the baby, who begins to sing again. Even though her baby is born dumb (an ironic God getting the last laugh), she accepts her baby, who has become her way to transcend the profane chaos of her life.

OTHER MAJOR WORKS

LONG FICTION: *The Clang Birds*, 1972; *Tight White Collar*, 1972; *Jessica Fayer*, 1976; *A Woman Run Mad*, 1988; *An Honorable Profession*, 1991; *The Shrine at Altamira*, 1992; *The Handmaid of Desire*, 1996; *Having Everything*, 1999.

POETRY: *Quick as Dandelions*, 1964; *Rubrics for a Revolution*, 1967; *One Eye and a Measuring Rod*, 1968; *No Place for Hiding*, 1971.

NONFICTION: *Picnic in Babylon: A Jesuit Priest's Journal, 1963-67*, 1967.

BIBLIOGRAPHY

Colby, Vineta, ed. *World Authors, 1985-1990*. New York: H. W. Wilson, 1995. The article on L'Heureux begins with a helpful interview with the writer, who reflects on his life and writings, and includes a short biography and a long analysis of his poetry, short fiction, and novels. Also included are a list of his principal publications and a selection of articles about him.

Farrell, Michael J. "L'Heureux's People Perplexed by Ironic God." *National Catholic Reporter* 27 (May 11, 1990): 21, 30. Using the publication of *Comedians* as a pretext to explore the author's fiction about priests, Farrell analyzes L'Heureux's Catholic background and the effect that this has had on his short stories and novels. The article is also enlivened by material gathered in an interview with L'Heureux.

Johnson, Greg. "Jokers Are Wild." *The Georgia Review* 44 (Winter, 1990): 713-722. In this essay review Johnson discusses five American writers who have linked humor with hostility in their critiques of modern life. He sees Flannery O'Connor and Iris Murdoch as influencing L'Heureux's fictional methods, which he incisively uses to probe the spiritual realities behind his characters' moral dilemmas.

Stefano, Frances. "*Comedians* by John L'Heureux." *Theology Today* 47 (Fall, 1990): 319-324. Stefano analyzes the stories in L'Heureux's last collection from a theological perspective. She sees them as being ultimately about the light of God's grace becoming visible in a dark world of apparent randomness and waste. Though she finds L'Heureux's stories contrived and not as convincing as those of Flannery O'Connor, she is nonetheless enthralled by his overdrawn characters, whose actions are "comically, sometimes terrifyingly, true to the strangeness of life."

Robert J. Paradowski

JAKOV LIND
Heinz Landwirth

Born: Vienna, Austria; February 10, 1927

PRINCIPAL SHORT FICTION

Eine Seele aus Holz, 1962 (*Soul of Wood, and Other Stories*, 1964)

Der Ofen: Eine Erzählung und sieben Legenden, 1973 (*The Stove: Short Stories*, 1983)

Travels to Enu: Story of a Shipwreck, 1982 (novella)

OTHER LITERARY FORMS

As important as his collection of stories *Soul of Wood, and Other Stories*, which deals with the atrocities associated with Nazi persecution during World War II, is Jakov Lind's novel *Landschaft in beton* (1963; *Landscape in Concrete*, 1966) about the terrible effects of German nationalism in the 1930's and 1940's. Lind is also the author of several plays, a book of nonfiction entitled *The Trip to Jerusalem* (1973), and several autobiographical works.

ACHIEVEMENTS

Jakov Lind was highly praised by American critics in 1964 on the publication of his collection of short stories *Soul of Wood, and Other Stories*. Noted critic Maxwell Geismar called him the most noted short-story writer to appear in the last two decades, saying the long title novella was utterly unlike any story he had ever read. Other reviewers compared Lind to Nikolai Gogol, Franz Kafka, Günter Grass, and Sholem Aleichem. However, Lind's subsequent books have not been received with as much acclaim as was *Soul of Wood, and Other Stories*, either in Germany or in America.

BIOGRAPHY

Jakov Lind was born Heinz Landwirth in Vienna, Austria, in 1927. In 1938, when the Nazis occupied Austria, he was sent to Holland, while his parents were taken to a concentration camp, where they died. After the Nazis invaded Holland, Lind escaped once more, this time into the countryside, where he worked on a collective farm. When Jews were forced by the Nazis to live in Amsterdam, Lind obtained forged papers, identifying him as a Dutch farmer with another name; thus he was able to live in Germany and work as a deckhand on a barge on the Rhine.

After the war, Lind moved to Israel, where he lived from 1945 to 1950. Since then he has lived in England and the United States. In his autobiographical work *Counting My Steps*, Lind has written that fear is the stuff his life was made of: "My roots are fear and fear is the marrow of my bones."

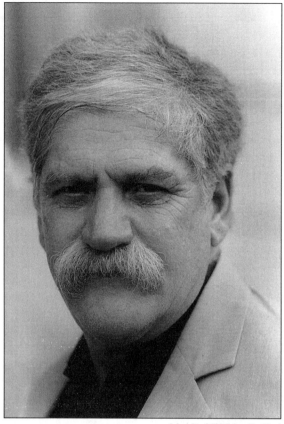

Jakov Lind (©Miriam Berkley)

ANALYSIS

Jakov Lind's short stories fall within the European tradition of the hallucinatory and the tragicomic grotesque brilliantly initiated by Gogol, pushed to paranoid extremes by Kafka, and horrifyingly popularized by Jerzy Kosinski. Characteristic of this tradition, Lind focuses on gruesome acts of evil so extreme that the result is a kind of macabre comedy that puzzled a number of American reviewers. As one said about the title story of *Soul of Wood, and Other Stories*, "in a story so inherently sad, how can one laugh with such pleasure?" One admires the writer's skill, but is baffled by his intentions. Lind's intention, like Gogol and Kafka's, is to push the reader's awareness of humankind's inhumanity to such appalling lengths that he or she must react; the fact that the reader laughs at such things magnifies the sense of horror.

"SOUL OF WOOD"

In "Eine Seele aus Holz" ("Soul of Wood"), the novella-length title story of Lind's most highly praised collection, a Viennese man named Hermann Wohlbrecht, a one-legged veteran of World War I, has been given the responsibility of caring for a paralytic boy named Anton Barth after the boy's Jewish parents have been cremated by the Nazis. However, Wohlbrecht, a man with a "soul of wood"—his wooden leg—takes the boy to the country and leaves him alone on a mountain top; then returns to town to take over the Barth family apartment, which he tries to sell to a Nazi district leader.

Wohlbrecht is put in a sanatorium, which, in its absolute overall lunacy, represents the madness of the Nazi persecution. The story ends when Anton Barth, having been magically transformed into a deer, is found and Wohlbrecht is executed in the woods. The final image is of Wohlbrecht's one-legged skeleton still lying there on the mountaintop, the wooden leg propped beside him against a tree, "waiting patiently for the resurrection of its master, which will surely happen some day. Any day." Lind blends hallucination, fairy tale, realism, and nightmarish fantasy so thoroughly in this story that even as the characters and events seem to be abstract embodiments of satire, they convince the reader of their terrifying actuality.

"HURRAH FOR FREEDOM"

In this brief, hallucinatory story, "Es lebe die Freiheit" ("Hurrah for Freedom"), a medical student from Vienna named Leonard meets a three-hundred-pound Lithuanian man named Balthasar who has fled the Russians for refuge in Sweden, where he and his family have become (comically) nudists and (horrifyingly) cannibals. Invited to spend the night, the medical student is appalled by his host's overweight, nude sisters and mother and shocked by the carcass of a horse hanging from the ceiling and by the fact that he is offered hog's blood to drink. The family explain that they drink hog's blood in memory of a shepherd who drank his children's blood because he could not stand to see them starve; they say that they keep the dead horse in memory of the old country, believing that when only the skeleton is left, Lithuania will be free and the Russians will be gone. The stink, they say, reminds them that the Russian occupation stinks to heaven of corruption and slavery; "a dead horse in the house is the least we can do for our country."

Because he is a medical student, the guest tries not to let anything upset him; however, when he realizes that he and his hosts are eating the bodies of children, he gets sick and tries to leave. The old mother justifies their cannibalism by saying they are just poor refugees who are reduced to eating their own children since they have been so deprived of food. The student, feeling like a well-dressed hunter on safari sympathetic to the savages he meets, thinks he is seeing for the first time real victims. However, when he leaves, he thinks, "that's what insanity is like," realizing that none of his friends, all medical men, will believe him. In this nightmarish, Kafkaesque satire, Lind reduces to absurdity the extreme dehumanization of people deprived of freedom and simple needs.

"JOURNEY THROUGH THE NIGHT"

In this brief story, "Reise durch die Nacht" ("Journey Through the Night") Lind's most frequently anthologized piece of fiction, a man shares a compartment on the Nice-Paris express train with a madman who has threatened to dismember and eat him as soon as he falls asleep. Unlike the cannibals in "Hurrah for Freedom," who are evoked to satirize the absurd results of deprivation and political suppression, the cannibal in this story, with his small black bag of tools, is an embodiment of the natural order, the law of the jungle in which animals eat other animals in order to stay alive.

Although the threatened narrator tries desperately not to fall asleep, he begins philosophically to consider that since everyone dies one way or another, "why not be eaten by a madman in the Nice-Paris express?" A feeling of warmth comes over him, for he knows the madman, unlike himself, at least has a purpose. However, the madman, who seems to know his intended victim's thoughts, says that now he does have a purpose, thanks to him.

At just this crucial point in the story, when the madman opens his bag and takes out a mallet, the narrator pulls the train cord, making it stop. With disgust the cannibal packs his bag and leaves the train,

chiding the narrator that his foolishness will cost him a ten-thousand-franc fine. "Look, who wants to live?" he shouts back as he leaves, vanishing into the darkness "like a country doctor on his way to deliver a baby."

"Journey Through the Night" is Lind's most frequently reprinted story not only because it is his most economical Kafkaesque parable but also because its philosophical implications transcend the limits of a particular historical time and place. Although the train travels between Paris and Nice, it is a metaphor for the basic human journey toward the inevitability of death as the only abiding human destiny.

THE STOVE

Originally published in German as *Der Ofen* in 1973, this collection, when translated into English and published by a small press in 1983, did not receive the powerful reviews of Lind's first collection *Soul of Wood, and Other Stories*. Primarily an assortment of Kafkaesque fables and fairy tales, the collection lacks the hallucinatory horror of the Holocaust that powered the earlier stories.

With the exception of the title story, an absurdist satire composed of letters between two men, the remaining seven stories begin with the traditional "Once upon a time" introduction associated with German fairy tales. Some of the tales are versions of Jewish legends, such as "Beinahe Mord" ("A Near-Murder"), which retells the story of Abraham almost sacrificing his son Isaac, and ("Die Geschichte von Lilith und Eva" ("The Story of Lilith and Eve") which recounts how Eve enters the body of Lilith in order to experience Adam's passion. Others, such as "Die Lüge" ("The Theft") and "Der Diebstahl" ("The Lie"), are moral and literary parables about peace of mind and truth.

The title story, "The Stove," begins with one man's proposition to a cousin that they go into the business of selling stoves, stating both economic and philosophical justifications for the advisability and viability of the arrangement. As the two men exchange letters, the mundane business matter becomes the center of extended philosophical ruminations about stoves representing warmth, about mystical experiences and wondrous fairy tales, about the evil of attaining riches, and about seeing things in terms of eternity as opposed to focusing on everyday reality. The story ends with the failure of the business venture and the original letter-writer saying he is going back to being an author. A philosophical dialogue based on an everyday metaphor, "The Stove" lacks the seriousness and horror of Lind's best-known stories. The basis of the metaphor is too limited and the philosophical discussions are too predictable and ordinary to elevate the story above the level of a satiric set piece.

OTHER MAJOR WORKS

LONG FICTION: *Landschaft in Beton*, 1963 (*Landscape in Concrete*, 1966); *Eine bessere Eelt: In fünfzehn Kapiteln*, 1966 (*Ergo*, 1967); *The Inventor*, 1987.

PLAYS: *Das Sterben der Silberfüchse*, pb. 1965 (*The Silver Foxes Are Dead*, 1968); *Ergo: A Comedy*, pr., pb. 1968; *The Silver Foxes Are Dead, and Other Plays*, pb. 1968.

NONFICTION: *Counting My Steps: An Autobiography*, 1969; *Numbers: A Further Autobiography*, 1972; *The Trip to Jerusalem*, 1973; *Crossing: The Discovery of Two Islands*, 1991.

BIBLIOGRAPHY

Geismar, Maxwell. "A Universe of Utter Evil." *The New York Times Book Review*, January 24, 1965, 4, 34. Calling Lind the most notable short-story writer to appear since World War II, Geismar says that "Soul of Wood," the title story of Lind's best-known collection, is so complex that it is hard to convey its quality. Calls Lind a Viennese blend of Charles Addams and Roald Dahl, but more serious and more talented.

Karpowitz, Stephen. "Conscience and Cannibals: An Essay on Two Exemplary Tales—'Soul of Wood' and 'The Pawnbroker.'" *Psychoanalytic Review* 64 (1977): 41-62. Argues that Anton Barth in "Soul of Wood" is the development of a metaphor of a totem Jew rescued from oblivion, a symbol of the modern cannibal's victim. Says he is an instrument used to create the illusions people need to make their brutal motives palatable to the world.

Klein, Roger. "Punching Away at Our Stomachs." *The New York Herald Tribune Book Week*, February 21, 1965, 4-12. Argues that what characterizes "Soul of Wood" is its total dependance on grotesque and macabre comedy. Claims that Lind's stories have no compassion and thus become a series of freak shows with no moral impact. Says they bring the reader no closer to the truth of the Holocaust.

"A Monstrous Complicity." *Time* 85 (March 19, 1965): 116, 118. This anonymous review of *Soul of Wood, and Other Stories* argues that the guilt suggested by Lind's stories is not merely German, but the result of a monstrous complicity produced by the sleep of reason in the twentieth century.

Rosenfeld, Stella P. "*Crossings: The Discovery of Two Islands.*" *World Literature in Review* 66 (Summer, 1992): 523. A review of the third volume of Lind's autobiography, which deals with his life after moving to London in 1950. Discusses Lind's perception of self as a permanent alien, driven from his native Austria and robbed of his language. Argues that the flaws of the memoir are outweighed by its merits as a document of alienation.

_____. "Jakov Lind: Writer at the Crossroads." *Modern Austrian Literature* 14 (1971): 42-47. Discusses the reaction of American reviewers to *Soul of Wood, and Other Stories* in 1964, Lind's relationship to Vienna, and the autobiographical elements in "Soul of Wood." Claims that the central figure in the story is symbolic of Lind's own transformation in order to survive. Discusses Lind's place in modern European literature.

Charles E. May

CLARICE LISPECTOR

Born: Chechelnik, Ukraine, U.S.S.R.; December 10, 1925
Died: Rio de Janeiro, Brazil; December 9, 1977

PRINCIPAL SHORT FICTION

Alguns contos, 1952
Laços de família, 1960 (*Family Ties*, 1972)
A legião estrangeira, 1964 (*The Foreign Legion*, 1986)
Felicidade clandestina: Contos, 1971
A imitação da rosa, 1973
Onde estivestes de noite, 1974
A via crucis do corpo, 1974
A bela e a fera, 1979
Soulstorm, 1989 (includes stories from *Onde estivestes de noite* and *A via crucis do corpo*)

OTHER LITERARY FORMS

Clarice Lispector achieved almost equal success in the short story and the novel. Her novels include *Perto do coração selvagem* (1944; *Near to the Wild Heart*, 1990), *O lustre* (1946; the chandelier), *A cidade sitiada* (1949; the besieged city), *A maçã no escuro* (1961; *The Apple in the Dark*, 1967), *Água viva* (1973; *The Stream of Life*, 1989), and *A hora da estrela* (1977; *The Hour of the Star*, 1986). Lispector also wrote a limited number of works for children, the most famous of these being *O mistério do coelho pensante* (1967; the mystery of the thinking rabbit) and *A mulher que matou os peixes* (1968; the woman who killed the fish). She also wrote nonfiction prose pieces.

ACHIEVEMENTS

It is no exaggeration to suggest that Clarice Lispector was one of the most original and singular voices to be found in twentieth century Western literature. In a career that spanned more than thirty years, Lispector produced a series of novels and short stories that not only helped lead a generation of Brazilian writers away from the limitations of literary regionalism but also gave Western literature a unique body of narrative work characterized by a highly personal lyrical style, an intense focus on the subconscious, and an almost desperate concern for the individual's need to achieve self-awareness. Though her works earned for her numerous literary awards during her lifetime (including an award she received in 1976 from the Tenth National Literary Competition for her contributions to Brazilian literature), Lispector is only beginning to receive the attention she deserves from critics and readers alike as her spellbinding narratives attract a growing international audience.

BIOGRAPHY

Clarice Lispector was born in the tiny Ukrainian village of Chechelnik on December 10, 1925, while her family was emigrating from the Soviet Union to Brazil. The family settled in the city of Recife in northeastern Brazil before moving to Rio de Janeiro, when Lispector was twelve years old. A precocious child, Lispector began composing stories as early as age six, even attempting to have them published in a local newspaper. A voracious reader in general and a devotee of writers such as Hermann Hesse and Katherine Mansfield in particular, it was a well-read Clarice Lispector who enter the National Faculty of Law in 1940, from which she was graduated in 1944. While in law school, she first took a job on the editorial staff of the Agência Nacional (a news agency) and then as a reporter for the newspaper *A noite*. It was while working for the newspaper that Lispector began writing her first novel, *Near to the Wild Heart*. It was during this period that she met Lúcio Cardoso, an innovative novelist who would serve as her mentor.

Lispector married Mauri Gurgel Valente in 1943 and after being graduated from law school accompanied him to his diplomatic post in Naples, Italy. She followed her husband to Berne, Switzerland, and to Washington, D.C., before separating from him in 1959 and returning with the couple's two children, Pedro and Paulo, to Rio de Janeiro, where she lived and wrote until she died of inoperable cancer only one day before her fifty-second birthday, in 1977.

Clarice Lispector (Courtesy of New Directions Publishing)

ANALYSIS

Although Clarice Lispector achieved fame as a novelist as well as a writer of short stories, most critics agree that it is the shorter genre to which the author's storytelling talents, writing style, and thematic concerns are more suited. The bulk of Lispector's stories (particularly those published before 1970, for which the author is most famous) are intense and sharply focused narratives in which a single character (almost always female) is suddenly and dramatically forced to deal with a question concerning an integral part of her existence, and, by extension, on a thematic level, human existence itself. Save for a single act that prompts the character to look inward, there is little action in Lispector's stories, as the author seeks not to develop a plot but instead to capture a moment in her character's life. The central event of each story is not nearly so significant as the character's reaction to it, as he or she is shocked out of complacency and forced into a situation that will lead to self-examination and, in most cases, self-discovery.

Because Lispector's stories focus on the rarefied world of her characters' subconscious, many of the short narratives possess a dreamlike quality. Adding to this quality is the lyrical prose in which the stories are written, a prose in which not only every word but also the syntax seems to have been very carefully selected, frequently making the reading of the pieces more like reading poetry than prose.

In spite of the emphasis on the inner world of her characters and the subjective and highly metaphorical language, Lispector's stories still maintain contact with the world that exists beyond the confines of her characters' minds. While the characters' reaction to a given situation is intensely personal, the theme dealt with in that reaction is always a universal one, such as frustration, isolation, guilt, insecurity, uncertainty, or the coming of age; in other words, fundamental questions of human existence. Also, the events that trigger these questions in the characters' minds are everyday events of modern society. In this way, Lispector manages to examine both private and universal human concerns while still keeping her stories grounded firmly in reality.

ALGUNS CONTOS

Lispector's first collection of short stories, *Alguns contos* (some stories), appeared in 1952 and was immediately praised by critics. In fact, this one collection not only placed the author among the elite of Brazil's writers of short fiction of the time, but also it showcased her as a leader among the new generation of writers in this genre.

Alguns contos contains six stories: "Mistério em São Cristóvão" ("Mystery in São Cristoóvão"), "Os laços de família" ("Family Ties"), "Começos de uma fortuna" ("The Beginnings of a Fortune"), "Amor" ("Love"), "A galinha" ("The Chicken"), and "O jantar" ("The Dinner"). All six narratives are lyrical pieces that focus on the act of epiphany—that is, a single moment of crisis or introspection from which the character emerges transformed. The story most representative not only of this collection but also of all Lispector's short fiction is "Love." Its central character, Ana, is a basically satisfied, middle-class wife whose world is stable, controlled, predictable. Taking the tram home from shopping one afternoon, however, she spots a blind man chewing gum. For some reason, Ana's world is totally and inexplicably shaken by the sight of him. Disoriented, she gets off the tram well past her stop and finds herself in the relatively primitive and hostile setting of a botanical garden. Feeling out of place and even threatened, she makes her way home and attempts to resume her normal patterns, but while she is happy to be back in the security of her predictable domestic lifestyle, she has been profoundly affected by her brief and confusing excursion into a world foreign to her own, and she wonders if she can ever be as happy in her world as she was before.

This story is a Lispector classic, both because it presents a single character whose normal existence is shaken by a seemingly insignificant event, an event that destroys the stable lifestyle of the character and takes him or her to a new level of awareness concerning life, and because, in large part a result of its language, the story takes on a dreamlike quality that reflects the disoriented state of the protagonist. This story, however, is not unique; it is simply the best of a collection of six similar tales.

FAMILY TIES

As good as *Alguns contos* is, Lispector's next collection, *Family Ties*, surpasses it. In fact, this collection, the high point of Lispector's work in short fiction, is truly one of the masterpieces of Brazilian literature, regardless of period or genre.

Family Ties is composed of thirteen enigmatic stories, six of which had already appeared in *Alguns contos*, and once again the stories focus on the act of epiphany. For example, in "Preciosidade" ("Preciousness"), a girl going through puberty experiences both fear and confusion after an ambiguous encounter with some boys. This story is particularly interesting in that the event that triggers the protagonist's reaction is never fully described to the reader. The reader sees the character's reaction to the event, however, and it is that reaction, full of anxiety and uncertainty, that constitutes the story, demonstrating that Lispector is not so concerned with the central event of her stories as she is with her characters' reactions to the event. By not providing details concerning the event in this particular story, she assumes that her reader's

concerns are the same as her own. Another interesting story included in this collection is "O crime do professor de matemática" ("The Crime of the Mathematics Professor"), which recounts the story of a man who buries a stray dog he has found dead in a desperate attempt to relieve himself of the guilt he feels for having once abandoned his own dog. Finally, there is "Feliz aniversário" ("Happy Birthday"), the story of an old woman surrounded by her family on her eighty-ninth birthday. Rather than celebrate, she observes with disdain the offspring she has produced and, much to the shock of those in attendance, spits on the floor to show her lack of respect. All the stories in this collection present individual characters in turmoil and how each deals with this turmoil from the inside out.

THE FOREIGN LEGION

Lispector's preoccupation with personal growth through epiphany continues in her third collection of stories, *The Foreign Legion*. Here again, Lispector's protagonists grow as a result of some sort of circumstance in which they find themselves. There is a difference in this collection, however, as the author appears more overtly interested in an existentialist angle concerning her characters' reactions to the situations they confront. For example, in one story, "Viagem a Petrópolis" ("Journey to Petrópolis"), an old woman, told to leave the house in which she has been living, realizes that she is no longer of any use to the world and that she is not only alone but also unwanted. Her "growth," her manner of dealing with the truth surrounding her existence, is quite fatalistic, existentialist in nature: She dies. In stories in previous collections, the character might well have emerged with some sort of new insight that would have made life more interesting if not better. Here, however, the character merely dies, reflective perhaps of Lispector's growing interest in existentialist thought.

FELICIDADE CLANDESTINA

Lispector's fourth collection of stories, *Felicidade clandestina* (clandestine happiness), follows much the same track as her previous collections. The style is still lyrical, the focus is internal, and the thematic concerns are self-awareness and self-discovery. Yet there are some differences between this collection and the earlier ones. In this work, for example, Lispector is more sharply ironic, at times bordering on an almost cruel humor. Also new, or at least intensified, is the author's criticism concerning the condition of both women and the elderly in modern society, concerns that are present in earlier works but never brought before the reader in such an obvious manner.

A LIMITAÇÃO DA ROSA

After publishing *A limitação da rosa* (the imitation of the rose), a collection of some of her best previously published stories, Lispector published *Onde estivestes de noite* (where were you last night?). While a number of the pieces included in this collection are indeed stories, fictions in the truest sense, several pieces are personal commentaries or reflections by the author, while still others seem to be a mixture of both fiction and commentary. In the pieces that are in fact stories, it is easy to see that Lispector has abandoned neither her thematic concerns nor her interior perspective. This is best seen in the story entitled "A procura de uma dignidade" (the search for dignity), which focuses on a nearly sixty-year-old woman who becomes lost in the maze of halls and tunnels that run beneath the mammoth soccer stadium of Maracanã. While wandering the halls in search of an escape route, she comes to the realization that she is not only physically lost but also psychologically lost, that it is indeed possible that her life up to this point, a life lived in large part through her husband, may have been a wasted, empty existence. By the end of the story, she is seeking an escape route from both her physical and her psychological confinements.

A VIA CRUCIS DO CORPO

A via crucis do corpo (the via crucis of the body) is somewhat of a departure from the stories previously published by Lispector—so much so, in fact, that it has confounded critics, most of whom admire it for its quality but nevertheless are left uncertain as to how to interpret it since it does not fit neatly into the Lispector mold. The two main differences between this collection and the others before it is that the stories in this collection contain not only eroticism but also open sexuality, as well as an ample dose of sardonic humor, neither of which is found, at least

not to such a degree, in her earlier stories. There is, for example, the story "Miss Ruth Algrave," in which the protagonist is visited by an alien being from Saturn named IXTLAN. He makes love to her and in so doing raises Miss Algrave to a new level of existence. She quits her job and becomes a prostitute while awaiting her extraterrestrial lover's return. Then there is the story "O corpo" (the body), about a bigamist who is murdered by his two wives. Rather than going to the trouble of arresting the two women, the police tell them to leave the country, which they do. This collection is nothing if not entertaining.

A BELA E A FERA

Published after her death, *A bela e a fera* (the beauty and the beast) is a collection of Lispector stories put together by her friend Olga Borelli. Some of the stories included in this collection were written when the author was a teenager and had never been published. Given the time they were written, these stories and the collection in which they appear are potentially revealing for those interested in the evolution of Lispector the short-story writer. Unlike other collections, however, such as *Alguns contos, Family Ties*, and *The Foreign Legion, A bela e a fera* is not considered a major collection of the author's stories but rather a literary curiosity piece.

Between 1952 and 1977, Clarice Lispector produced a consistent body of short narratives characterized by a sharpness of focus, a lyrical presentation, and a deep and sincere interest in the psychological growth of the individual human being. These three qualities, which pervade all the author's short stories, are the same ones which form her individual literary voice and which will guarantee that the popularity of her short fiction not only endures but also increases as more readers gain access to it.

OTHER MAJOR WORKS

LONG FICTION: *Perto do coração selvagem*, 1944 (*Near to the Wild Heart*, 1990); *O lustre*, 1946; *A cidade sitiada*, 1949; *A maçã no escuro*, 1961 (*The Apple in the Dark*, 1967); *A paixão segundo G. H.*, 1964 (*The Passion According to G. H.*, 1988); *Uma aprendizagem: Ou, O livro dos prazeres*, 1969 (*An Apprenticeship: Or, The Book of Delights*, 1986);

Água viva, 1973 (*The Stream of Life*, 1989); *A hora da estrela*, 1977 (*The Hour of the Star*, 1986); *Um sopro de vida: Pulsa cões*, 1978.

NONFICTION: *Para não esquecer*, 1978.

CHILDREN'S LITERATURE: *O mistério do coelho pensante*, 1967; *A mulher que matou os peixes*, 1968.

MISCELLANEOUS: *Selecto de Clarice Lispector*, 1975.

BIBLIOGRAPHY

Cixous, Hélène. *Reading with Clarice Lispector*. Edited and translated by Verena Andermatt Conley. Minneapolis: University of Minnesota Press, 1990. A playfully profound deconstructionist reading of a number of Lispector's works, including the stories "Sunday Before Falling Asleep" and "The Egg and the Chicken." Argues that Lispector's texts, like Franz Kafka's, contain a secret that cannot be understood on a first reading.

Fitz, Earl E. *Clarice Lispector*. New York: Twayne, 1985. An excellent, book-length study of Lispector's writings. Chapters include "Biography and Background," "The Place of Clarice Lispector in the History of Brazilian Literature," "Some Intrinsic Considerations: Style, Structure, and Point of View," "Novels and Stories," and "The Nonfiction Work." Both descriptive and analytical. This insightful and extremely readable book is written by the foremost authority on Lispector's works. A must-read for serious readers of the Brazilian writer's fiction or for anyone seeking a deeper understanding of both Lispector and her works.

Lindstrom, Naomi. "Clarice Lispector: Articulating Woman's Experience." *Chasqui* 8 (November, 1978): 43-52. Lindstrom examines the narrative voice employed in the short story "Love" (from *Family Ties*) and said voice's relationship to the emerging (and then fading) self-awareness of the protagonist, Ana. Lindstrom shows how the narrator first dominates the story, then allows Ana to speak more, before retaking the narrative in the end as the protagonist "finds no supportive response." An interesting slant on an important story in Lispector's body of work.

Marting, Diane E. "Clarice Lispector's (Post)modernity and the Adolescence of the Girl-Colt." *MLN* 113 (March, 1998): 433-444. Examines the story "Seco estudo de cavalos" in terms of post-structuralist theories; argues that Lispector configures the unrepresentable as the Feminine and valorizes words as an approach to the object more than as a designation.

Moisés, Massaud. "Clarice Lispector: Fiction and Cosmic Vision," translated by Sara M. McCabe. *Studies in Short Fiction* 8 (Winter, 1971): 268-281. A study of how the thematics of Lispector's short fiction reflect and support the author's "cosmic vision." Moisés discusses, for example, "the privileged moment," in which "the 'I' and the universe meet as if for the first time, framed in a halo of original 'purity,' causing the mutual discovery to become suspended in time, a vision of the most intimate part of reality, without deformation of thought or prejudice." An excellent article on the themes in Lispector's short fiction.

Nunes, Maria Luisa. "Narrative Modes in Clarice Lispector's *Laços de família*: The Rendering of Consciousness." *Luso-Brazilian Review* 14 (Winter, 1977): 174-184. Citing several stories in *Family Ties*, Nunes examines how Lispector renders the consciousness of her protagonists, stating that the Brazilian writer employs "*style indirect libre* or narrated monologue, interior monologue, internal analysis including sensory impressions, direct discourse in the form of 'asides,' and the mixture of many of the above techniques." Nunes explains each technique and demonstrates how each is used by Lispector to reveal the inner workings of her characters. Insightful and very readable.

Peixoto, Marta. "*Family Ties*: Female Development in Clarice Lispector." In *The Voyage In: Fictions of Female Development*, edited by Elizabeth Abel, Marianne Hirsch, and Elizabeth Langland. Hanover, N.H.: University Press of New England, 1983. Peixoto focuses on the protagonists of the stories in *Family Ties*, stories that the critic believes "can be read as versions of a single developmental tale that provides patterns of female possibilities, vulnerability, and power in Lispector's world." Peixoto examines the epiphanies experienced by the female protagonists of several stories, epiphanies that allow the characters, although only momentarily, to break out of their "metaphoric prisons formed by their eager compliance with conforming social roles." An excellent piece.

_____. *Passionate Fictions: Gender, Narrative, and Violence in Clarice Lispector*. Minneapolis: University of Minnesota Press, 1994. Written with a decidedly feminist bias, *Passionate Fictions* analyzes Lispector's frequently violent subject matter, juxtaposing it with her strange and original use of language. Special attention is paid to the nexus with Helene Cixous and to the autobiographical elements of *The Stream of Life* and *A via crucis do corpo*.

_____. "Rape and Textual Violence in Clarice Lispector." In *Rape and Representation*, edited by Lynn A. Higgins and Brenda R. Silver. New York: Columbia University Press, 1991. An analysis of three short narratives in terms of how Lispector distances and naturalizes violence against women. The three short narratives move in a progression from a mild symbolic representation to a literal and farcical plot event, yet all three minimize violence.

Rosenberg, Judith. "Taking Her Measurements: Clarice Lispector and 'The Smallest Woman in the World.'" *Critique* 30 (Winter, 1989): 71-76. Claims that the core of "The Smallest Woman in the World" is sexual politics, a female fantasy of autonomy in competition with the male fantasy of domination. In the story, Little Flower is the object of male desire, the pure essence of femininity as refined, rare, valuable, and potent.

Keith H. Brower

JACK LONDON

Born: San Francisco, California; January 12, 1876
Died: Glen Ellen, California; November 22, 1916

PRINCIPAL SHORT FICTION
The Son of the Wolf, 1900
The God of His Fathers and Other Stories, 1901
Children of the Frost, 1902
The Faith of Men and Other Stories, 1904
Tales of the Fish Patrol, 1905
Moon-Face and Other Stories, 1906
Love of Life and Other Stories, 1906
Lost Face, 1910
When God Laughs and Other Stories, 1911
South Sea Tales, 1911
The House of Pride and Other Tales of Hawaii, 1912
A Son of the Sun, 1912
Smoke Bellew Tales, 1912
The Night-Born, 1913

The Strength of the Strong, 1914
The Turtles of Tasman, 1916
The Human Drift, 1917
The Red One, 1918
On the Makaloa Mat, 1919
Dutch Courage and Other Stories, 1922

OTHER LITERARY FORMS
Jack London's more than fifty published books include plays, children's fiction, novels, sociological studies, essays, and short stories. Although generally known as a writer of short fiction, London is remembered also for two novels, *The Call of the Wild* (1903) and *The Sea-Wolf* (1904), both of which have been made into motion pictures several times. London is also credited with pioneering work in the development of tramp fiction (*The Road*, 1907) and science fiction (*The Star Rover*, 1915).

ACHIEVEMENTS

Jack London's numerous stories and his many novels capture with a bold and sometimes brutal reality the confrontation between humans and nature, which by some writers may easily have been portrayed romantically. Instead, London was at the forefront of the move toward naturalistic fiction and realism. He was influenced by social Darwinism, and his stories often reflect the idea that human beings, to survive, must adapt to nature yet are themselves creatures of nature, subject to forces they do not really understand. London was also interested in Marxism, and his work often employs a working-class hero.

London's realistic stories were very popular in the United States when they were first published and continue to be so. He has also achieved wide popularity abroad, with his work being translated into more than fifty languages. His stories in the naturalistic mode continue to influence writers.

BIOGRAPHY

Largely self-educated, Jack London was the product of California ranches and the working-class neighborhoods of Oakland. London's rise to fame came as a result of the Klondike Gold Rush. Unsuccessful in his attempt to break into the magazine market, he joined the flood of men rushing to make instant riches in the Yukon. Although he found little gold, he returned after the winter of 1897 with a wealth of memories and notes of the Northland, the gold rush, and the hardships of the trail. London married Elizabeth May Maddern in 1900, and the couple settled in Oakland, soon adding two daughters to the family. The marriage, however, was not successful, and London divorced his wife in 1905 and married Charmian Kittredge the same year. With Charmian, he sailed across the Pacific aboard a small yacht, intending to continue around the world on a seven-year voyage. The trip ended in Australia, however, when ill health forced London to abandon the voyage after only two years. London's last years were spent in the construction of a scientifically run ranch complex in Glen Ellen, Sonoma County, California. It was there that he died at age forty, on November 22, 1916. His death still has not been satisfactorily explained.

Jack London (Library of Congress)

ANALYSIS

Jack London's fame as a writer came about largely through his ability to interpret realistically humans' struggle in a hostile environment. Early in his career, London realized that he had no talent for invention and that in his writing he would have to be an interpreter of the things that are rather than a creator of the things that might be. Accordingly, he turned to the Canadian Northland, the locale where he had gained experience, for his settings and characters. Later on he would move his setting to the primitive South Seas, after his travels had also made him familiar with that region. By turning to harsh, frontier environment for his setting and themes, London soon came to be a strong voice heard over the genteel tradition of nineteenth century parlor-fiction writers. His stories became like the men and women about whom he wrote—bold, violent, sometimes primitive. London was able to give his stories greater depth by using his extraordinary powers of narrative and language, and by infusing them with a remarkable sense of irony.

"TO BUILD A FIRE"

"To Build a Fire" has often been called London's masterpiece. It is a story which contrasts the intelligence of human beings with the intuition of the animal and suggests that humans alone cannot successfully face the harsh realities of nature. The story begins at dawn as a man and his dog walk along a trail which eventually could lead them, thirty-two miles away, to a companion's cabin and safety. The air is colder than the man has ever experienced before, and although the man does not know about the cold, the dog does. While the animal instinctively realizes that it is time to curl up in the snow and wait for warmer weather, the man lacks the imagination which would give him a grasp of the laws of nature. Such perception would have enabled him to see the absurdity of attempting to combat the unknown, especially since an old-timer had warned him about the dangers of the cold to inexperienced men. With his warm mittens, thick clothes, and heavy coat, the man feels prepared for the cold and protected while the dog longs for the warmth of a fire. As the man walks along the trail, he looks carefully for hidden traps of nature, springs under the snow beneath which pools of water lie, since to step into one of these pools would mean calamity. Once he forces the dog to act as a trail breaker for him, and, when the dog breaks through and ice immediately forms on its extremities, the man helps the dog remove the ice.

At midday the man stops, builds a fire, and eats his lunch. The dog, without knowing why, feels relieved; he is safe. The man, however, does not stay beside the fire; he continues on the trail and forces the dog onward too. Finally, inevitably, the man's feet become wet. Although he builds a fire to dry out, snow puts out the fire, and before he can build another fire, the cold envelops him, and he freezes to death. The dog senses the man's death and continues on the trail toward the cabin, wherein lies food and the warmth of a fire.

The irony of the story is that the man, even with the benefit of all the tools with which civilization has provided him, fails in his attempt to conquer nature and instead falls victim to it, while the dog, equipped only with the instinct which nature has provided, survives. The story, representing London's most mature expression of pessimism, stresses the inability of human beings to shape their environment and conquer the unknown. Unlike the dog, they cannot draw from instinct since civilization has deprived them of it. They are therefore unfit and totally unequipped to face the unknown and conquer the cosmic power.

"LAW OF LIFE"

"Law of Life" exhibits another recurring theme in London's work, the inability of humans to assert positive values. It tells the story of the last moments of life for an old Native American. As the tale begins, the old man, son of the chief of the tribe, sits by a small fire with a bundle of wood nearby. The tribesmen are busy breaking camp in preparation for departure since they must go to new hunting grounds in order to survive. The old man, too old to benefit the tribe further, represents only a burden to the rest of his society and must therefore stay behind. As the man sits beside the fire, he remembers the days of his youth and an incident when he tracked an old moose. The animal had become separated from the rest of the herd and was being trailed by wolves. Twice the young Native American had come across the scene of a struggle between the moose and the wolves, and twice the moose had survived. Finally, the Native American witnessed the kill, the old moose dying so that the wolves might live. The moose-wolf analogy to the old Native American's situation is obvious, and as the story closes, the old Native American feels the muzzle of a wolf upon his cheek. At first he picks up a burning ember in preparation for battle, but then resigns himself to the inevitability of fate and extinguishes it.

London uses several vehicles to express his pessimism. Like the protagonist in "To Build a Fire," the old Native American is a man of limited vision. Encircled by an everconstricting set of circumstances, he waits by a dying fire for his own death. Finally, as the moose-wolf analogy has foretold, the inevitability of nature dominates. As the story ends, the fire goes out, the wolves are no longer kept at bay, and the reader is left repulsed by the knowledge of the Native

American's horrible death. London employs a number of symbols in this story as well. The fire gives light which symbolizes life, as does the white snow which falls gently at the beginning of the story. As the fire ebbs, the man remembers the grey wolves, and at the end of the moose-wolf analogy, London writes of the dark point in the midst of the stamped snow, foretelling the end of the fire, and thus of life.

Although London's earlier stories embody a pessimism which reflects humans' helplessness in challenging the unknown, his later ones mark a dramatic changeover. Following an intensive study of Carl Jung and Sigmund Freud, London began writing stories in the last years of his life which reflected his discovery of some unique human quality that enabled humans to challenge successfully the cosmos and withstand the crushing forces of nature. One of London's last stories, also with a Northland setting, reflects this change of philosophy and contrasts markedly with the earlier "To Build a Fire" and "Law of Life."

"LIKE ARGUS OF ANCIENT TIMES"

"Like Argus of Ancient Times" begins as a largely autobiographical account of London's trek to Dawson City with a man known as "Old Man" or "John" Tarwater. Unlike the unnamed protagonist of "To Build a Fire," Tarwater is totally unequipped to face the rigors and challenges of the north. He is old and weak; furthermore, he arrives on the trail without money, camping gear, food, and proper clothing. Somehow he manages to join a group of miners, serve as their cook, and earn his passage to Dawson. Although the winter snows force the group to make camp until spring, Tarwater (who is also called "Old Hero" and "Father Christmas") is driven by gold fever. He strikes out on his own, gets lost in a snowstorm, and falls to the ground, drifting off into a dreamlike world between consciousness and unconsciousness. Unlike London's earlier characters, Tarwater survives this confrontation with nature, awakens from his dream, turns toward the "rebirthing east," and discovers a treasure of gold in the ground. Couched in Jungian terms, the story is directly analogous to the Jungian concepts of the wandering hero who, undertaking a dangerous night journey in search

of treasure difficult to attain, faces death, reaches the highest pinnacle of life, and emerges in the East, reborn. "Like Argus of Ancient Times" marks London's return to the many stories he wrote in which the hero feels the call of adventure, encounters difficulties and confronts nature, battles with death, and finally achieves dignity.

Often called the successor to Edgar Allan Poe, an imitator of Rudyard Kipling, or a leader of writers emerging from the nineteenth century, London wrote stories which mark the conflict between the primitive and the modern, between optimism and pessimism. He created fiction which combined actuality and ideals, realism and romance, and rational versus subjective responses to life. More than a new Poe, imitator of Kipling, or new genre writer, however, London is a legitimate folk hero whose greatness stems from his primordial vision and ability to center upon the fundamental human struggles for salvation and fears of damnation.

OTHER MAJOR WORKS

LONG FICTION: *A Daughter of the Snows*, 1902; *The Call of the Wild*, 1903; *The Sea-Wolf*, 1904; *The Game*, 1905; *White Fang*, 1906; *Before Adam*, 1906; *The Iron Heel*, 1907; *Martin Eden*, 1908; *Burning Daylight*, 1910; *Adventure*, 1911; *The Abysmal Brute*, 1913; *The Valley of the Moon*, 1913; *The Mutiny of the Elsinore*, 1914; *The Scarlet Plague*, 1915; *The Star Rover*, 1915; *The Little Lady of the Big House*, 1916; *Jerry of the Islands*, 1917; *Michael, Brother of Jerry*, 1917; *Hearts of Three*, 1920; *The Assassination Bureau, Ltd.*, 1963 (completed by Robert L. Fish).

PLAYS: *Scorn of Women*, pb. 1906; *Theft*, pb. 1910; *The Acorn-Planter*, pb. 1916.

NONFICTION: *The Kempton-Wace Letters*, 1903 (with Anna Strunsky); *The People of the Abyss*, 1903; *The War of the Classes*, 1905; *The Road*, 1907; *Revolution and Other Essays*, 1910; *The Cruise of the Snark*, 1911; *John Barleycorn*, 1913; *Letters from Jack London*, 1965 (King Hendricks and Irving Shepard, editors).

CHILDREN'S LITERATURE: *The Cruise of the Dazzler*, 1902.

BIBLIOGRAPHY

Auerbach, Jonathan. *Male Call: Becoming Jack London*. Durham: Duke University Press, 1996. Auerbach reverses the trend of earlier London studies, emphasizing how London used his writing to reinvent himself. Above all, Auerbach argues, London wanted to become a successful author, and in that respect he shaped his life to suit his art. Includes detailed notes but no bibliography.

Cassuto, Leonard, and Jeanne Campbell Reesman, eds. *Rereading Jack London*. Stanford, Calif.: Stanford University Press, 1996. Essays on London as "representative man," his commitment to authorship, his portrayal of American imperialism, his handling of power, gender, and ideological discourse, his relationship to social Darwinism, and his status as writer/hero. Includes end notes, but no bibliography.

Freund, Charles Paul. "Call of the Whites." *Reason* 28 (April, 1997): 52-53. Discusses London as a racist and a propagandist for the overthrow of capitalism; notes how London influenced some of the Weimar Germany's pulp racists.

Furer, Andrew J. "Jack London's New Women: A Little Lady with a Big Stick." *Studies in American Fiction* 22 (Autumn, 1994): 185-214. Discusses London's representation of "new womanhood" that emphasizes physical power and capability and an economic and intellectual independence, but is nonetheless feminine and heterosexual.

Hedrick, Joan D. *Solitary Comrade: Jack London and His Work*. Chapel Hill: University of North Carolina Press, 1982. Hedrick interweaves a discussion of London's stories and novels with details of his life in an attempt to see behind London's self-created myth. She does some close reading of the stories and includes a useful bibliography and an index.

Kershaw, Alex. *Jack London: A Life*. New York: St. Martin's Press, 1997. Concentrates on the "powerful drama" of London's life. Includes notes, illustrations, bibliography, and several helpful maps.

Labor, Earle, and Jeanne Campbell Reesman. *Jack London*. Rev. ed. New York: Twayne, 1994. This clear introduction, first published in 1974, takes into account the twenty years of scholarship after the volume first appeared. This volume also takes issue with the widespread belief that the quality of London's work declined in the last decade of his life. Includes chronology, notes, and an annotated bibliography.

London, Jack. *The Letters of Jack London*. Edited by Earle Labor, Robert C. Leitz III, and I. Milo Shepard. 3 vols. Stanford, Calif.: Stanford University Press, 1988. Includes the most significant letters of the thousands London wrote during his lifetime. The editors have thoroughly annotated each letter, explaining references and identifying people. The letters include love letters, letters to editors and publishers, and to fellow writers on London's ideas and methods, as well as to friends and family.

McClintock, James I. *White Logic: Jack London's Short Stories*. Grand Rapids, Mich.: Wolf House Books, 1975. McClintock's work is the only one to focus solely on London's short stories. He provides a detailed analysis of the stories in a clear and useful way.

Reesman, Jeanne Campbell. "'Never Travel Alone': Naturalism, Jack London, and the White Silence." *American Literary Realism* 29 (Winter, 1997): 33-49. Argues that even in London's most naturalistic stories, readers find the search for spirit, the desire for community, and the need to address the Other. Provides a detailed analysis of "To Build a Fire" to illustrate these concepts.

Sinclair, Andrew. *Jack: A Biography of Jack London*. London: Weidenfeld & Nicolson, 1978. A well-researched, extensively documented biography that focuses on London's life rather than his work. Includes a bibliography and many photographs.

*David Mike Hamilton, updated by
Karen M. Cleveland Marwick*

AUGUSTUS BALDWIN LONGSTREET

Born: Augusta, Georgia; September 22, 1790
Died: Oxford, Mississippi; July 9, 1870

PRINCIPAL SHORT FICTION

*Georgia Scenes, Characters, Incidents, Etc. in the
First Half Century of the Republic*, 1835

OTHER LITERARY FORMS

Although Augustus Baldwin Longstreet's unquestioned masterpiece is *Georgia Scenes*, he also published a variety of books, pamphlets, letters, and other materials, most of which deal with politics, religion, or the South, and often with the intersection of the three. Perhaps the most significant is *Letters on the Epistle of Paul to Philemon: Or, The Connection of Apostolic Christianity with Slavery* (1845), a closely reasoned defense of slavery on biblical grounds. *A Voice from the South, Comprising Letters from Georgia to Massachusetts* (1847) vehemently sets forth antebellum southern political positions. Late in life he published a long-contemplated didactic novel on the folly of indulging youth, *Master William Mitten: Or, A Youth of Brilliant Talents Who Was Ruined by Bad Luck* (1864).

ACHIEVEMENTS

Augustus Baldwin Longstreet is best known for his collection of humorous tales, *Georgia Scenes*. His use of the tall-tale form, vernacular speech, and the setting of the Georgia frontier (then considered part of the "southwest") marks him as foremost among the Southwest humorists. In a form known for its combination of oral folklore with more traditional forms such as the sketch, Longstreet's contributions are marked for their polished, literary quality. Like the border region that comprises his settings, Longstreet's stories reveal a literary territory that combines genteel prose with raucous renderings of local scenes and characters. He often uses an Addisonian-type gentleman narrator who describes the less civilized, more outrageous behavior of the "locals." Later writers such as Mark Twain and Wil-

liam Faulkner make similar use of the contrast between exaggerated storytelling and vivid, even cynical, realism. Longstreet's renderings of unique Georgia characters, who speak in uncensored and often hilarious voices, place him firmly within the tradition of southern literature.

BIOGRAPHY

Augustus Baldwin Longstreet was born in Augusta, Georgia, on September 22, 1790. He was graduated from Yale and from the Litchfield Law School, then widely considered the finest in America, and returned to Augusta in 1814. He became a successful lawyer and subsequently a judge. He left the bench, became a farmer, and, a little later, a newspaper editor. It was during this period that he published, first periodically and then in book form, his *Georgia Scenes* (1835). In 1838, Longstreet became a professing Christian and a most active Methodist minister; the next year he was appointed the first president of Emory College, a Methodist institution, and in following years he served as president of Centenary College in Louisiana, the University of Mississippi, and the University of South Carolina. Longstreet died July 9, 1870, and was buried in Oxford, Mississippi.

ANALYSIS

Augustus Baldwin Longstreet's *Georgia Scenes* covers such a remarkably wide variety of behavior that he largely succeeds in his ambition to be a social historian. He vividly pictures men involved in such noble occupations as "The Horse-Swap," "The Fight," "The Militia Company Drill," and "The Foxhunt." He portrays women as charming their beaux with an impromptu concert in "The Song," engaging in polite battles of status and manipulation in "The Ball," or simply gossiping into the wee hours in "A Sage Conversation." Longstreet structures some "scenes," less typical but often more interesting, around elaborate practical jokes: "The Character of a Native Georgian" follows Ned Brace through an involved series of capers that bewilder dozens of

Augustus Baldwin Longstreet (Library of Congress)

people; in "The Debating Society," two young men confound their peers by putting up for discussion a completely incomprehensible question; and in "The Wax-Works," a group of touring rowdies try to swindle enough for their tavern bill by masquerading as wax figures at an exhibition.

"GEORGIA THEATRICS"

Longstreet combines many of these elements in the book's brief opening sketch, "Georgia Theatrics." The narrator begins in uncharacteristically precise fashion: "If my memory fail me not, the 10th of June, 1809, found me, at about eleven o'clock in the forenoon, ascending a long and gentle slope in what was called 'The Dark Corner' of Lincoln [County]." In a kind of thematic prelude to the volume as a whole, he explains that the corner was "Dark" from a "moral darkness" which, he avers, by "wonderful transitions," has been dispelled in the past quarter century. The narrator takes care, however, to distinguish the area's former "*moral* condition" from its "*natural* condition." The latter, in terms of physical contours, trees, streams, birds, flowers, he characterizes as idyllic. Early in the sketch, as the narrator mounts a slope, the aura of Edenic grace shatters with a concat-

enation of "loud, profane, and boisterous voices," the source hidden in the undergrowth. Violent oaths give way to sounds of muffled blows and terrific thrashings; the narrator watches the largely obscured back of one man rise briefly, then plunge heavily, "and at the same instant I heard a cry in the accent of keenest torture, 'Enough! My eye's out!'" The victor rises bragging until he sees the narrator, then looks "excessively embarrassed." The narrator orders the swaggering bully to help him aid the horribly maimed victim, but the young victor defiantly replies that there has been no one else involved: "I was jist seein' how I could 'a' *fout*." He then bounds over to a plough that he had left in a fence corner several yards off. The narrator surveys the battlefield; in the soft dirt, he sees two thumbprints, about as far apart as a man's eyes;

> . . . would you believe it, gentle reader? his report was true. All that I had heard and seen was nothing more nor less than a Lincoln rehearsal, in which the youth who had just left me had played all the parts of all the characters in a court-house fight.

The brief sketch effectively introduces several of the book's dominant motifs: violence, crude humor, cultural conflict, close attention to physical detail, and a style that abruptly alternates between the narrator's polite affection and the powerful dialect of the lower classes.

"THE GANDER-PULLING"

Many of these elements reach a sort of climax in "The Gander-Pulling," a sketch which none of the others can top for sheer crudity and high spirits. Longstreet sets the scene in 1798, just beyond the outskirts of Augusta proper and not far from three very close satellite "towns." He opens reprinting an "advurtysement" for the gander-pulling, a notice every bit as enthusiastically unconventional in its phrasing as in its spelling. After elaborately describing the general area and petty rivalries of the neighboring towns, he details the immediate scene of action. The locals have outlined a circular path about forty yards in diameter around which the entrants will ride their horses. At one point on each side of the path, about ten feet apart, stands a post; between the posts a rope is slung loosely enough that a gander attached can vibrate in an arc of four or five feet. The gander-pull impresario, Ned Prator, first passes a hat into which each contestant tosses twenty-five cents, the sum to be the victor's prize. He next proceeds to bind the gander's feet and then to coat the bird's neck liberally with goose grease—inspiring in the narrator an ironic paean to the gander's former mate. Finally Prator attaches the gander to the rope directly over the path, stations men at the posts to whip any horse inclined to dawdle, arranges in a rough line the contestants mounted on their increasingly spooked horses, and sets them off.

The riders make three raucous but uneventful rounds until one man, riding a horse aptly named Miss Sally Spitfire, finally makes a solid grab, jerks the gander's neck close to his startled horse's head, while at the same instant each of the two lashers lays on with all his might. The crazed horse gives one look at the gander, feels both lashes, and bolts through the crowd carrying along a circus worth of bawling dogs, alarmed and belled cattle, and three tobacco-rollers, hauling over all in her path until she arrives at not just one airborne gander but a whole flock immediately at her feet. She stops suddenly enough to convert her rider into an unguided projectile. Gridiron, a second and rather more coolly rational horse, ignores his rider's whoops, kicks, and lashings, while he pauses to examine and consider Miss Sally Spitfire's experience, and then heaves a deep sigh.

> It was plain that his mind was now made up; but, to satisfy the world that he would do nothing rashly, he took another view, and then wheeled and went for Harrisburg as if he had set in for a year's running. Nobody whooped at Gridiron, for all saw that his running was purely the result of philosophic deduction.

One of two of the remaining contestants seems most certain to win on each succeeding round, especially after one breaks the neck, but finally a third jerks away the head to win the prize. He brags and struts outrageously, but, as he and his audience are all aware since he triumphed through luck rather than skill, his vaunting puts the whole crowd in a high good humor—except for one little man who lost his

bet of six quarts of huckleberries: "*He* could not be reconciled until he fretted himself into a pretty little *piny*-woods fight, in which he got whipped, and then he went home perfectly satisfied."

Much of the piece's charm derives from the relaxed focus which easily shifts from the advertisement to the area's history to the field of competition to the organizer to the gander to the competitors to the horses to the victor and on to the end, no one element taking precedence over another. Longstreet focuses where and how he pleases to gain maximum local effect from each element of his sketch—which is precisely the sum of its parts. What the sketch does not have is a controlling fictional perspective that can compel the piece to do more than merely sum up its parts, more than exploit a fascinating, bizarre, and self-sufficient surface. Longstreet vividly represents the gander-pulling but merely represents it rather than significantly developing a meaningful experience arising out of that activity; consequently, he produces here one of his typical sketches rather than a story.

"THE SHOOTING-MATCH"

In the final section of *Georgia Scenes*, "The Shooting-Match," Longstreet does produce a genuine short story, although—compared to earlier pieces in the book—in some ways a rather bland one. About a year ago, the narrator tells the reader, traveling on business in Northeastern Georgia, he encountered a small man carrying a massive old rifle and bound for a shooting-Match. The native, Billy Curlew, learns that this well-dressed stranger (the narrator) is the same person who, years ago as a child barely large enough to hold a shotgun, had earned a lasting reputation in a shooting-match—and incidentally a fine silk handkerchief for Billy's father who had bet on the boy. The narrator admits that the shot years before had been pure luck, but Billy talks him into coming along to see the fun.

When they arrive, Billy, unreservedly a partisan of the man who won his father's bet so long ago, startles the narrator by arranging for him to have a shot in the match, but none of the locals fear much from the strange dude. The narrator then vividly details the rules, target, prizes, contestants, and finally the shifting fortunes of all in the match. Hoping to delay his humiliation as long as possible, the narrator insists on shooting last. The dreaded time arrives, his arms cannot hold the ponderous rifle without trembling, and he paradoxically begins bragging (quite unconvincingly) to relieve somehow his own acute embarrassment. Finally, on impulse he halfheartedly fires and amazes absolutely everyone—except Billy—by making the second best shot of the day, missing first prize (won by Billy) by only fractions of an inch. Except for a handful of agnostics, the narrator converts the whole crowd, who promise to vote for him no matter what office he is seeking. When he objects that he is seeking no office, they insist he let them know when he does, for they would all back him to the death. "If you ever come out for anything," Billy vows, "jist let the boys of Upper Hogthief know it, and they'll go for you to the hilt, against creation, tit or no tit, that's the *tatur.*"

The story capitalizes on some nice ironies: Generous backwoods Billy seems fated to share in the narrator's humiliation but has judged better than anyone else. The narrator's nervous bragging during his ludicrous preliminaries ironically helps him to carry the day once he fires his shot. The narrator deserves a rich load of backwoods contempt for his lack of manliness but winds up with a whole region ready to back him to a man. Here Longstreet uses a fine rhetorical sensitivity to prepare, develop, and capitalize on his climactic surprise. Unlike a typical Georgia "scene," this story has no extraneous characters, no long descriptions or discussions of purely local interest, and no digressions to include bizarre comic incidents. Longstreet focuses not, as usual, on broadly representing typical scenes, characters, or actions, but more narrowly on re-creating the narrator's experience, an experience which encompasses his sympathy for the sympathetic Billy Curlew. Here Longstreet has created a genuine story by concentrating, uncharacteristically, on form at the expense of content. Later frontier humorists and local-color writers learned techniques which allowed them the best of both dimensions, but they could hardly have written as well as or as intelligently without the pioneering example of *Georgia Scenes*.

OTHER MAJOR WORKS

LONG FICTION: *Master William Mitten: Or, A Youth of Brilliant Talents Who Was Ruined by Bad Luck*, 1864.

NONFICTION: *Letters on the Epistle of Paul to Philemon: Or, The Connection of Apostolic Christianity with Slavery*, 1845; *A Voice from the South, Comprising Letters from Georgia to Massachusetts*, 1847; *Letters from President Longstreet to the Know-Nothing Preachers of the Methodist Church South*, 1855.

BIBLIOGRAPHY

Blair, Walter. *Native American Humor, 1800-1900*. New York: American Book, 1931. This classic in American humor studies provides a general discussion of nineteenth century humorists, an extensive bibliography (which is outdated but useful in its listing of "Individual Writers of Native American Humor"), and more than one hundred selections from a wide range of authors. The chapter on "Humor of the Old Southwest" discusses Longstreet among his contemporaries.

Brown, Carolyn S. *The Tall Tale in American Folklore and Literature*. Knoxville: University of Tennessee Press, 1987. Brown traces the origins of the popular tale in both folklore and literature. Chapter 3, "Flush Times: Varieties of Written Tales," has an extended analysis of Longstreet's *Georgia Scenes*. Brown does not oversimplify in her discussion of Longstreet's sketches but rather explores the complexity of his work within the tall-tale tradition.

Fitzgerald, Oscar Penn. *Judge Longstreet: A Life Sketch*. Nashville: Methodist Episcopal Church, 1891. Bishop Fitzgerald's biography covers Longstreet's life and work in eloquent terms—and at times does little to dispel some of the reigning legends surrounding Longstreet. Exaggerations aside, this biography distinguishes itself by the inclusion of many letters to and from Longstreet, allowing a more personal glimpse into the life of a complex and talented man.

King, Kimball. *Augustus Baldwin Longstreet*. Boston: Twayne, 1984. King's study provides an excellent general discussion of Longstreet's life and work. Much of the book discusses *Georgia Scenes*, Longstreet's major work of short fiction, and gives a wealth of background material on both the writing and subject matter of *Georgia Scenes*. The annotated list of secondary sources is a very useful component of this book.

Rachels, David. "Oliver Hillhouse Prince, Augustus Baldwin Longstreet, and the Birth of American Literary Realism." *The Mississippi Quarterly* 51 (Fall, 1998): 603-619. Shows that Longstreet published "The Militia Company Drill," a work by Prince, as his own; claims that because Prince did not receive recognition for the work, his role in the founding of American literary realism has been ignored.

Romine, Scott. "Negotiating Community in Augustus Baldwin Longstreet's *Georgia Scenes*." *Style* 30 (Spring, 1996): 1-27. Argues that rather than simply asserting and justifying class privilege, Longstreet undertakes a complex negotiation of class roles. Lyman Hall, the primary narrator, initially demonstrates a socio-narrative style—that is, a social style reflected in narrative stylistics—that keeps the lower class at a social and moral distance; by the end of the text he is able to nego-

tiate with the lower class a mutual perception of class roles.

Wade, John Donald. *Augustus Baldwin Longstreet: A Study of the Development of Culture in the South.* New York: Macmillan, 1924. This engaging biography of Longstreet, the result of Wade's extensive research, tells about the life of a literary man whose interests and activities ranged far beyond that of writing humorous sketches. Wade refers not only to the *Georgia Scenes* but also to Longstreet's career as a lawyer and judge, his religious and political interests, and his terms as president of several leading universities in the South.

Wegmann, Jessica. "'Playing in the Dark' with Longstreet's *Georgia Scenes*: Critical Reception and Reader Response to Treatments of Race and Gender." *The Southern Literary Journal* 30 (Fall, 1997): 13-26. Claims that *Georgia Scenes* advocates theories of a paternalistic, God-ordained slavery. In many of the stories in the text, an African American or a white woman attempts to exert authority and, using humor as a vehicle to trivialize, Longstreet subdues them, bringing them back under white patriarchal rule.

Walter Evans, updated by Ann A. Merrill

BETH LORDAN

Born: Perkin, Illinois; December 1, 1948

PRINCIPAL SHORT FICTION
And Both Shall Row, 1998

OTHER LITERARY FORMS
Beth Lordan is the author of the novel *August Heat* (1989), which has been highly praised for its Magical Realist evocation of American small-town life.

ACHIEVEMENTS
Beth Lordan received a National Endowment for

the Humanities Fellowship in 1993, and her short fiction has won prizes from the New York State Council on the Arts and the Illinois Arts Council. *And Both Shall Row* was named one of *The New York Times* notable books for 1998.

BIOGRAPHY
Ellenora Beth Lordan was born in Perkin, Illinois, on December 1, 1948. She has said that when she went to the University of Missouri just after graduation from a small and poor high school, she failed everything but Western civilization. She took a job as a secretary in the entomology department at Cornell

University, editing, copywriting, and typing professors' manuscripts. Taking advantage of the employee degree program there, she began work toward a B.A. in creative writing, which she finished in 1983, after nine years.

After graduation, she entered the M.F.A. program at Syracuse University, but pregnant and tired of the seventy-mile commute she decided to enter the graduate creative writing program at Cornell, closer to home, where she received her M.F.A. in 1987. Her first short story, "Running Out," appeared in *The Atlantic* in 1986. Her first novel, *August Heat*, was published in 1987. Since 1991, she has been teaching creative writing at Southern Illinois University at Carbondale, where she was named director of the creative writing program in 1992.

ANALYSIS

Beth Lordan's first collection of short stories focuses on a small number of people who live in the midwestern town of Clayborne. Often in her stories, Lordan's characters get a rare opportunity to see, behind the routines and everyday demands of life, a glimpse of the special and the beautiful. In "Running Out," a carpenter who is out of work and down on his luck experiences a single day in which everything goes right. In "The Snake," a woman strikes back symbolically at her husband's betrayal by heroically attacking a snake that has invaded her house. In "The Cow Story," two lonely people almost, but not quite, break out of their loneliness and make a gesture toward each other. In "The Widow," an elderly woman discovers magic in the midst of the ordinary.

Lordan makes use of a familiar short-story tradition pioneered by Ivan Turgenev, Anton Chekhov, James Joyce, and Sherwood Anderson—the exploration of the complex secret lives of small-town people—creating a world that, even though it seems ordinary and real, becomes extraordinary and magical. Like all great writers, Lordan creates a world that, even though it seems common and familiar, is at the same time strange and wonderful.

"THE WIDOW"

"The Widow" is a hauntingly magical story about the ultimate mystery of the other. The story begins cryptically with the sentence "The morning Warren Boyd dropped dead in his kitchen, he was the only living person on the farm." The sentence echoes poignantly in readers' minds when they discover that the other person in the house at the time is the spirit of Boyd's wife Ann, who has been hovering about him since her death three years earlier.

In addition to the supernatural suggestion of the wife, who, after having devoted her attentions to her husband for forty-two years, now devotes herself to studying him as a spirit, there is also the matter of Warren's periodic transformations. The first time this occurred was after they had been married about a year and she saw him out of the upstairs window, walking as if under water, slowly and gracefully. In the folds of his clothes and on the hair of his head and the stubble on his cheeks she saw "tiny air bubbles, gleaming like glass pearls." When Ann witnesses the mystery again, Warren, glowing in the darkness, does a series of somersaults across the lawn. The third event takes place after the death of their daughter, when Ann sees a soft brilliance rising from him, like mist off a barn roof; as he turns around and around in a circle, a bright color trails about him like veils in the rain.

Ann watches her husband for the rest of their lives together, and although he transforms again and again, it is never enough to completely offset the ordinary routine of their everyday experience. When she knows she is dying, she makes three wishes, the first of which is to remain with him until his death, hoping to see by then the meaning of his splendor. When Warren dies, the story ends with her making her second wish—for tears. It is understood that the third wish is that she will join him. No matter how long one may have known someone, Lordan's story suggests, at the very core of that person is an elusive magical mystery that too often one is unable to see.

"THE COW STORY"

The cow in this whimsical story chooses the afternoon of the only tornado in the history of the small village of Clayborne to escape her pasture and wander through the town. Lordan uses the cow running through the mysterious silence just before the tornado to introduce a magical setting for a restrained romantic encounter between Byron Doatze, the cow's owner, and Maude Nash, a fifty-three-year-old librarian.

When Maude invites Byron into her house out of the driving rain, their conversation is inconsequential but mildly flirtatious as they wait out the storm. Both know that something is happening, that they have moved from friendly joking to another level of possible intimacy, but neither has the nerve to make that intimacy actual. When the clock strikes midnight, both know that it is a moment when a decision must be made. They sit with their hands on the table looking at each other, knowing it would be hard to get from where they are into bed together: "They saw that this, after all, was coffee and cookies and a warm dry house in a rainstorm, in spite of the tornado and the cow."

Byron takes his cow home, smiling and saying to himself, "You damned jerk," while at the same time Maude smiles and says to herself, "You damn fool." The story ends with the reassertion of the everyday routine world when the cow sighs and goes back to sleep. "The Cow Story" is a delicately done piece in which ordinary natural and domestic events—a storm, an escaped cow, and a casual conversation between two lonely people—take on an otherworldly beauty and mystery; it is a classic example of how story transforms the actual into the purely imaginary.

"AND BOTH SHALL ROW"

The long title story of Lordan's collection focuses on Margaret and May, sisters, who in their seventies live together on the farm where they were born and raised. After May has a stroke and is unable to communicate, Margaret cares for her. This is about all that happens in the story in terms of plot, but lyrical revelation of the relationship of the two, rather than simple event, is what moves the story compellingly along. The ultimate end of the novella is the fulfillment of the implications of the title, which is from the last lines of a song May was humming before her stroke: "Give me a boat that can carry two, and both shall row, my love and I."

The story is made up largely of May's memories and Margaret's talk, both of which focus primarily on the lifelong relationship of the two sisters. An important symbolic past event May remembers is a time when they were children and wore identical dresses, looking like ecstatic twin conspirators when they clipped their mother's roses for a game they never played. Another significant memory involves the two going to a dance during adolescence and Margaret purposely breaking the strap of her shoe to provide an excuse for leaving the dance early because of May. However, the most important event that both May and Margaret recall is Margaret's husband's divorcing her to marry May, something that Margaret then accepted with seeming equanimity but which, fifty years later, still rankles her.

The most important story that Margaret recalls and tells is about her grown son Nick trying to shoot his wife and then turning the gun on himself. May recalls that the state trooper came to her house first with news of the death, thinking she was the mother. The blurring of identities and simultaneous separation of the two sisters is the central motif throughout the story, for even as Margaret accuses May of not comforting her after Nick's death, May recalls a vision of Margaret on that night when her eyes said that there was nothing she could do.

The lyrical confluence of the memories of Margaret and May culminates in Margaret's daughter's insisting that May be placed in a home for the elderly. In the last section of the story, May feels events come together like the end of a mystery story as she realizes that the way Margaret is going to escape her daughter's plan is to kill May and then herself; May tries to shout to Margaret, "I don't belong to you, you can't decide that for me." However, as the story comes to an end, the two women become so blended into one entity that it is difficult to separate them; even their memories are inextricably entwined.

In the final scene, May shows Margaret the pills she has been saving, and Margaret adds to them what is left in the bottle. In a reenactment of tea parties she used to have for her dolls, Margaret divides the pills into six each and goes to get a glass of water before telling one last story about a little doll she had that used to fit in her pocket—a doll called May Flower which she identified with her sister.

Because of its dependence on memory and the gradual convergence of two characters into one entity, "And Both Shall Row" is not an easy story to read unless readers allow themselves to be engulfed and engaged in the closed-in subjective world of the two sisters. It is a highly lyrical story of reverie as reality, a story in which language creates a seductive spell that draws the reader more and more into a world that mixes memory and desire in an irresistible way.

OTHER MAJOR WORKS

LONG FICTION: *August Heat*, 1989.

BIBLIOGRAPHY

Cameron, Julia. "Weaving a Picture of a Small Town." *Los Angeles Times Book Review*, September 10, 1989, p. 13. Says that *August Heat* uses a form of literary pointillism to create a picture of a sour, dyspeptic town. Calls Lordan a fine writer who is perhaps sometimes too fine, too writerly; says her story could use some plot to thicken it.

Glover, Charlotte L. "*And Both Shall Row.*" Review of *And Both Shall Row*, by Beth Lordan. *Library Journal*, 123 (July, 1998): 39. A review that argues that storytelling does not get any better than this collection. Compares Lordan's characters to those of Garrison Keillor; says each story illuminates a different aspect of a community, providing a rich collage of experiences and emotions.

Hand, Elizabeth. "The Village Fairy Tale." Review of *August Heat*, by Beth Lordan. *The Washington Post*, August 22, 1989, p. E3. A review of Lordan's novel *August Heat* that says the book creates a vision of postwar small-town America so fully realized yet so strange to a modern sensibility that it seems like an American Brigadoon. Says Lordan's prose style recalls that of Eudora Welty and Carson McCullers.

Houston, Robert. "Luminous Husbands and Geriatric Cows." *The New York Times*, August 30, 1998, p. 19. Calls Lordan's *And Both Shall Row* a strong collection and praises Lordan's voice as "utterly assured and utterly distinctive." Says Lordan focuses on the kinds of experience that go beyond words and the kinds of understanding that cannot be named but only described.

Kirkus Review. Review of *And Both Shall Row*, by Beth Lordan. 66 (June 15, 1998): 834. Claims that the title novella is the best of its kind since Tillie Olsen's *Tell Me a Riddle* (1961). Says the collection explores the buried visionary dimensions of rustic midwesterners. Compares the collection to Sherwood Anderson's *Winesburg, Ohio* (1919).

Publishers Weekly. Review of *And Both Shall Row*, by Beth Lordan. 245 (June 22, 1998): 83. Says that Lordan can weave a "dense tapestry out of the most mundane detail." Says her precise prose and subtle wisdom heighten an ominous tone in the stories. Claims that small, understated epiphanies bring the characters comfort in struggles over disappointment.

Wanner, Irene. "Collection Tells Tales of Emotion." Review of *And Both Shall Row*, by Beth Lordan. *The Seattle Times*, October 11, 1998, p. M10. This review suggests that whereas "The Snake" has the clearest conflict and the strongest ending, the title story creates the most memorable and fascinating character study.

Charles E. May

H. P. LOVECRAFT

Born: Providence, Rhode Island; August 20, 1890
Died: Providence, Rhode Island; March 15, 1937

PRINCIPAL SHORT FICTION

The Dunwich Horror and Others, 1963
Dagon, and Other Macabre Tales, 1965
The Horror in the Museum, and Other Revisions,
    1970

OTHER LITERARY FORMS

Except for his personal correspondence, H. P. Lovecraft's total output was quite modest, even considering his relatively short life. Like that of his illustrious predecessor, Edgar Allan Poe, almost all of Lovecraft's narratives are in the shorter forms, with at most three works qualifying as novelettes. Other than fiction, his writings consist of some poetry, a few essays on literature and science, and a voluminous amount of personal correspondence, much of which has been published. In addition to his own work, Lovecraft revised, rewrote, and "ghosted" a large number of works for other authors, including one short story for Harry Houdini. Although a number of his stories have served as the basis for films, the products have seldom resembled the originals. Indicative of this is the ironical fact that probably the most successful adaptation of Lovecraftian material was released under the title "Edgar Allan Poe's *Haunted Palace*."

ACHIEVEMENTS

H. P. Lovecraft brought an intimate knowledge of the short story to his horror-story creations. Beginning as a ghost writer and pulp-fiction hack, Lovecraft produced a body of tales that is still viewed as important by those who write fantasies on the dark side: Robert Bloch and Stephen King, to name only two who cite Lovecraft as an important influence on their own work. Of equal importance is Lovecraft's study of horror literature, *Supernatural Horror in Literature* (1945), in which he outlines the structure of the tale of terror. This work is still cited as an impor-

tant study in the narrative structure of the horror story.

BIOGRAPHY

Except for a few trips with friends in the last years of his life and residence in New York City during part of his brief marriage to Sonia Greene, Howard Phillips Lovecraft spent almost all of his life in Providence, Rhode Island, living with aunts in genteel poverty on the diminishing family capital. Most of the money he made as a writer came from collaborative efforts and ghostwriting. As a pulp-fiction author he wrote too little to make much money and was too reticent to sell much of what he did produce. By far, the bulk of his writing was done for nonpaying amateur publications and in personal correspondence. Lovecraft died at age forty-six of intestinal cancer.

ANALYSIS

The critical acceptance of H. P. Lovecraft as an important American writer, and as the finest exponent of dark fantasy since Poe, has not come quickly or easily. Much of this neglect was due to a blanket rejection of the "pulp writer," reinforced by the fact that Lovecraft published nothing in book form during his own lifetime. The primary outlet for his stories was *Weird Tales*, a pulp magazine whose circulation barely reached twenty thousand a month although its influence on horror fiction has been enormous. Moreover, Lovecraft's entire oeuvre was modest in size and, for reasons both personal and commercial, a considerable portion of it never saw print during his lifetime.

There are, perhaps, even more obvious reasons for this general critical dismissal: In many ways Lovecraft was a poor writer. The prose is often vague, ornate, and studded with overblown adjectives such as "eldrich," "uncanny," "hellish," and "weird." At a time when even the pulps featured the hard, lean prose of a Dashiell Hammett or James M. Cain, Lovecraft's purple verbosity sounded like a relic from the mid-nineteenth century. His characterization tends to be flat and undifferentiated. His plots sometimes collapse in the middle or disintegrate altogether, and his strain for sensational effect occasionally becomes painful. Lovecraft's characteristically italicized last-line climaxes—"*and the Monster was Real!!!*"—sometimes evoke more laughter than dread.

How then can the reader take this author seriously, let alone grant him status as an important writer? The answer lies in the two unique contributions Lovecraft made to the supernatural horror genre in particular and to modern literature in general: His original approach to dark fantasy revitalized the genre and has influenced every important new writer in the field, and the vision that animates his fictions transcended the limits of the popular genre to offer a provocative and significant view of modern human beings' predicament.

"THE OUTSIDER"

Because it has been so frequently anthologized, Lovecraft's best-known work is probably the somewhat uncharacteristic short story "The Outsider." An unnamed narrator laments his unhappy, bizarre youth. Having grown up bereft of human contact in a dismal, decaying castle, filled with damp "crumbling corriders" that smell like "piled-up corpses of dead generations," he resolves to escape by ascending a partly ruined black tower whose top "reaches above the trees into the unknown outer sky." After a difficult, perilous climb the narrator reaches a trapdoor, which he pushes open. To his amazement, he finds that he is not, as expected, on some "lofty eminence," but is, instead, "on *the solid ground*." Wandering about, he then comes upon a castle where a party is in full progress. As he enters, the guests run screaming. He assumes that there is a horrible presence lurking near him and becomes frightened. Sighting the beast, he overcomes his fears and approaches it, finally touching the thing's "*rotting outstretched paw*." Terrified, he flees back to the trapdoor but finds it blocked. Thus, he is forced to linger on the fringes of the world of the living, alienated from all contact with its inhabitants. In the last sentence of the story, the speaker reveals what he touched that so frightened him: "*a cold and unyielding surface of polished glass*."

The effect of this story on the reader is chilling—even if the story, when analyzed, is a bit absurd. Lovecraft succeeds in gaining the reader's sympathetic identification with the narrator so the revelation of its monstrous being is a shock; and the experience itself is almost archetypal. One ingenious critic has offered five separate and different interpretations of the tale: autobiographical, psychological (Jungian), metaphysical, philosophical, and political. Although none of these readings is completely satisfying, they all have some merit and illustrate the important point: "The Outsider" evokes emotional responses that are not fully explained by critical exegesis.

At the same time, the story turns essentially on a clever deception: The reader is tricked into identifying with a creature who turns out to be a corpse or zombie or ghoul or something of that sort, a fact that is not revealed until the punch line. So the sensitive reader is likely to be moved and irritated by a story that seems both profound and trivial. This mixed reaction is characteristic of many of Lovecraft's stories, and any attempt to assess his importance must somehow take it into consideration.

Despite its popularity, "The Outsider" does not suggest the full range of the author's powers. At best it is a story with more resonance than substance, a very clever exercise in imitating Poe. To truly appreciate Lovecraft one must examine his central vision—the somewhat misnamed "Cthulhu Mythos." (The term was coined by August Derleth, but Cthulhu is not really the major figure in the hierarchy. Contemporary Lovecraftians prefer to call it the "Lovecraft Mythos.")

The Mythos did not spring full blown from Lovecraft's head but emerged in bits and pieces. In "Nyarlathotep," a fragment, Lovecraft presented the first important figure in his pantheon. "The Nameless City" introduced the "mad Arab, Abdul Alhazrad," author of the *Necronomicon*, a fictive text of magical spells and arcane knowledge which became the bible of the Mythos. The book itself was brought into "The Hound" and "The Festival," the latter story being the first set in the "Arkham, Massachusetts" region, site of most Mythos tales. It was not until 1926, however, that Lovecraft really consolidated his ideas and presented them in a single story, "The Call of Cthulhu."

The artistic assumption behind the Mythos is that by the 1920's the usual menaces of horror fiction—such as Satan, demons, werewolves, and vampires—had become overworked and obsolete. A new set of menaces, he felt, one more in keeping with contemporary views of humans and their place in the universe, was needed to breathe life into the genre.

The metaphysical assumption behind the Mythos is stated in the famous first paragraph of "The Call of Cthulhu":

> The most merciful thing in the world, I think, is the inability of the human mind to correlate all its contents. We live on a placid island of ignorance in the midst of black seas of infinity, and it was not meant that we should voyage far. The sciences, each straining in its own direction, have hitherto harmed us little; but some day the piecing together of dissociated knowledge will open up such terrifying vistas of reality, and of our frightful position therein, that we shall either go mad from the revelation or flee from the deadly light into the peace and safety of a new dark age.

In the Cthulhu Mythos, that "terrifying reality" consists of an order of beings, vast, powerful, and immortal, who hover at the edges of humans' consciousness, poised to enter their world and sweep them away like so much useless debris. These creatures—the "Great Old Ones" or "Ancient Ones," with exotic forbidding names and titles such as "Cthulhu," "the messenger Nyarlathotep," "the blind, idiot god Azathoth," "the key to the gate Yog-Sothoth"—had dominated the earth long before human beings but lost the power eons ago for reasons that vary from story to story (in early tales, they tended to be supernatural creatures from another dimension; in later ones, they were usually powerful extraterrestrials).

The Old Ones remain on the periphery of human beings' reach in outer space or lie dormant in vast submerged cities, and they strive to reenter the human domain or to awaken from their enforced sleep. Since this reentry is barred to them without human assistance, the Old Ones have established contact with various degenerate groups, families, or individuals, who attempt to utilize the occult knowledge found in forbidden books such as the *Necronomicon* to summon their "masters."

Thus, the typical Mythos story pits the degenerate servants of the Old Ones against the harried but valiant human defenders (most often professors from Miskatonic University). In a few stories the Old Ones can be banished by various magical defenses, but, for the most part, once they are reanimated, they are invulnerable; only accident, luck, or whim saves humanity. Perhaps the most frightening thing about the Old Ones, however, is that, despite their horrendous appearances and destructive capacities, they are not truly evil or consciously malevolent. They simply regard humankind with total indifference and would destroy it for mere convenience without concern or rancor, as a human would step on a pesky insect.

"THE CALL OF CTHULHU"

The narrator of "The Call of Cthulhu" states that "he has had a glimpse" of that awful reality, which "like all dread glimpses of truth, flashed out from an accidental piecing together of separated things—in this case an old newspaper item and the notes of a dead professor." Lovecraft wisely maintains this fragmentary approach in narrating his tale. Instead of a simple chronology, the reader has isolated events and revelations which slowly form into a pattern. This indirect, quasi-journalistic approach also enables Lovecraft to mix real historical events, places, characters, and references with the fictional ones, and to insert newspaper clippings and interviews into the text along with straight narrative; the effect is to give the story a strong feeling of authenticity that not only underscores the horrors described but also implies that horrors even more profound lurk just beyond the limits of perception.

"The Call of Cthulhu" is presented in three self-contained sections, which are brought together in the narrator's final conclusions. In the first section, "The Horror in Clay," he describes a set of notes left to him by his granduncle, George Gammell Angell, a Brown University Professor Emeritus of Semitic Languages, who has recently died mysteriously after being jostled by a "nautical looking negro."

Angell's package contains a number of interesting items: a strange bas-relief covered with odd hieroglyphics, including a symbol suggesting "an octopus, a dragon, and a human caricature"; a document headed "Cthulhu Cult"; a number of notes on queer dreams, as well as references to secret cults; and occult, mythological, and anthropological texts. As the narrator examines these fragments, a frightening picture gradually coalesces, from dreams and hints, to accounts of the sinister machinations of the Cthulhu cults and the lore surrounding the creature, to a final confrontation with the thing itself. This semidocumentary approach works brilliantly. The dreams of a young sculptor, as relayed to Angell and reinforced by a series of weird events around the world, give the reader a feeling of pervasive cosmic evil on the brink of erupting.

That evil is made more concrete in the second part, "The Tale of Inspector Legrasse," which chronicles the apprehension of a mysterious, bestial swamp cult in the midst of human sacrificial rituals. From the cultists and an old mestizo named Castro, the officers hear the story of the Great Old Ones, the first articulation of the Mythos in Lovecraft's stories.

In the third part, "The Madness from the Sea," the reader meets the dreaded Cthulhu itself in the grotesque experiences of Gustaf Johansen, a Norwegian sailor. Although Johansen has apparently been killed by the cultists, the narrator obtains his journal which describes the encounter. After meeting and subduing a boatload of bizarre, savage sailors, Johansen and his comrades discover a mysterious island and inadvertently release Cthulhu from his slumber. All but Johansen and one other are killed; chased by Cthulhu they flee and survive by ramming the monster head-on. The actual meeting with the beast is the least satisfying moment in the story. It is unlikely that any other writer, and certainly one not given to Lovecraft's extravagant use of language, could depict a creature as awful as the one suggested in the story prior to the actual meeting. Even the reader's disappointment in the monster, however, does not seriously undermine the power of Lovecraft's conception; the meeting with the creature is brief and sketchy, leaving the momentum of the story largely undamaged. Neither Lovecraft nor his successors ever made the mistake of bringing Cthulhu back to the surface again.

With "The Call of Cthulhu" Lovecraft established his Mythos, but the story is uncharacteristically expansive and fragmentary. It lacks one element that was typical of most of his best fiction, a solidly realized setting. The hierarchy of supernatural beings was only one side of Lovecraft's coin; the other was the very real, believable New England world into which they usually intruded, "Arkham, Massachusetts," and environs. As the elements of his cosmic design grew and became more subtle and intricate, so, too, the world of Arkham became more concrete and familiar. Like William Faulkner's Yoknapatawpha County, the real area it was modeled after (Salem and vicinity) can easily be identified, but the fictional region takes on a separate identity of its own.

"THE DUNWICH HORROR"

The importance of this milieu is nowhere better illustrated than in "The Dunwich Horror," as underscored by the fact that Lovecraft devotes the first five pages to convincing the reader that the township of Dunwich, located in Northern Arkham County, is a particularly desolate, foreboding, and degenerate area. Only after thoroughly establishing this realistic environment and eerie atmosphere does he introduce the diabolical and perverse Whateley family, the subjects of the narrative.

Once an important, aristocratic family, the Whateley clan has split into two factions, one that clings to normality and some sense of respectability, the other that has thoroughly degenerated into bestiality, viciousness, and black magic. The story proper begins with the birth of Wilbur Whateley to Lavinia, "a somewhat deformed albino woman of about 35"; the father is unknown. Lavinia's aged, half-mad, "wizard" father publicly rejoices and tells the villagers that *some day yew folks'll hear a child o' Lavinny's a-callin' its father's name on the top o' Sentinel Hill!* The child grows rapidly and strangely. At a year and a half he is as big as a four-year-old; at ten he is fully grown; at thirteen he assumes the role of an adult—and a height of more than seven feet. Other odd events occur around the Whateley household: Extra rooms are built for no apparent reason; whippoorwills crowd about the house and sing constantly; cattle mysteriously disappear—as does Lavinia; and finally the old man dies, mumbling incoherently about "Yog-Sothoth" and "the old ones as wants to come back."

Shortly thereafter Wilbur attempts to secure the Miskatonic University Library copy of the *Necronomicon*. He fails but excites the curiosity of the librarian, Henry Armitage. Some time later Wilbur is killed by a guard dog while attempting to steal the forbidden text during the night. When young Whateley's clothing is ripped off, he is revealed to be a monster whose torso is covered with black fur, tentacles, unformed eyes, feelers, and the legs of a lizard; instead of blood a greenish-yellow ichor flows out. As people watch, the dead creature dissolves into a putrid mess.

With Wilbur dead, something in the house breaks loose and begins to terrorize the countryside. Armitage recruits two colleagues, and they study the dangerous, arcane books in hopes of finding a defense against the invisible creature, who leaves only huge footprints at the scenes of its carnage. At last they encounter the thing, make it momentarily visible with a powder spray, and deliver the magical chants. As it dissolves, it cries for help to "FATHER. YOG-SOTHOTH!" thus fulfilling old Whateley's prediction, but not in the manner he had desired. As usual, Lovecraft gives us the final explanation of things in the last line: "You needn't ask how Wilbur called it out of the air. He didn't call it out. *It was his twin brother, but it looked more like the father than he did.*"

"The Dunwich Horror" is probably the most direct and visceral of Lovecraft's major horror stories. If it lacks some of the subtlety and complexity of other masterworks such as "The Colour Out of Space," *At the Mountains of Madness* (1964), and "The Shadow Out of Time," it is a potent, memorable narrative that perhaps conveys the essence of the Mythos more clearly than any other single story.

OTHER MYTHOS TALES

Lovecraft continued to flesh out his Mythos for the rest of his life, producing a number of impressive stories, notably "Pickman's Model," "The Whisperer in Darkness," "The Shadow over Innsmouth," *At the Mountains of Madness*, "The Dreams in the Witch-House," and "The Shadow Out of Time." At the same time it should be remembered that at least half of Lovecraft's fictional output had little or nothing to do with the Cthulhu group. Even if there had been no Mythos, Lovecraft's place as America's foremost master of the macabre after Poe would have been assured by non-Cthulhuian works such as "The Outsider," "The Rats in the Walls," "Cool Air" (after Poe's "The Facts in the Case of M. Valdemar"), the eerie science-fiction story "The Colour Out of Space," the Salem witchcraft novelette *The Case of Charles Dexter Ward* (1943), and his most enigmatic nightmare/heroic fantasy, *The Dream-Quest of Unknown Kadath* (1943).

The thing that sets the Mythos narratives apart from Lovecraft's other fiction, however, is their collective power and the fact that the Mythos has continued to grow and prosper many years after its originator's death. Fortunately, however, the power of the original concept, at least in Lovecraft's own stories, comes through safely; and, in the end, it is that cosmic vision which gives primary stature to Lovecraft among modern horror writers. Lovercraft was a materialist in belief and attitude who viewed all supernatural ideas, whether conventionally religious or occult, as make-believe. The previously quoted opening paragraph from "The Call of Cthulhu" is a succinct summary of its author's own thinking. Thus, his Old Ones, with their indifferent cruelty and overwhelming powers, were, to Lovecraft, metaphors for a cruelly indifferent universe that provides a fragile, temporary refuge for the most ephemeral and insignificant of creatures—humans.

In essence, Lovercraft's cosmic view resembles that of many modern writers, including artists as different as Thomas Hardy and Robinson Jeffers. Like them, Lovecraft's art was an attempt to find a set of metaphors and images with which to express that worldview. The power of the Cthulhu Mythos lies in the fact that, despite the clumsiness, turgidity, and triteness of much of the writing, it presents a powerful metaphorical construct of the modern world and the extremely precarious place of human beings in it.

OTHER MAJOR WORKS

LONG FICTION: *The Case of Charles Dexter Ward*, 1943; *The Dream-Quest of Unknown Kadath*, 1943; *At the Mountains of Madness and Other Novels*, 1964.

POETRY: *Collected Poems*, 1963; *A Winter Wish*, 1977.

NONFICTION: *Supernatural Horror in Literature*, 1945; *Selected Letters*, 1965-1976 (edited by August Derleth and Donald Wandrei); *Lovecraft at Last*, 1975 (with Willis Conover).

MISCELLANEOUS: *The Outsider and Others*, 1939; *Beyond the Wall of Sleep*, 1943; *Marginalia*, 1944; *The Something About Cats*, 1949; *The Shuttered Room, and Other Pieces*, 1959; *The Dark Brotherhood, and Other Pieces*, 1966; *To Quebec and the Stars*, 1976.

BIBLIOGRAPHY

Airaksinen, Timo. *The Philosophy of H. P. Lovecraft: The Route to Horror*. New York: Peter Lang, 1999. A good study of Lovecraft's themes and execution. Includes bibliographical references and an index.

Burleson, Donald R. *H. P. Lovecraft: A Critical Study*. Westport, Conn.: Greenwood Press, 1983. A very helpful consideration of Lovecraft's fiction, nonfiction, and poetry. Provides a good overview of his work as well as placing him among other writers in the genre.

_____. "Lovecraft's 'The Colour Out of Space.'" *The Explicator* 52 (Fall, 1993): 48-50. A discussion of the story "The Colour Out of Space," focusing on the craft and intricacy of this masterful piece.

Cannon, Peter, ed. *Lovecraft Remembered*. Sauk City, Wis.: Arkham House, 1998. A look at Lovecraft's life and works.

Carter, Lin. *Lovecraft: A Look Behind the "Cthulhu Mythos."* New York: Ballantine, 1972. An extended examination of Lovecraft's mythic horror pantheon. Useful for following the development of his fictive world of demons and altered "realities."

Clements, Nicholaus. "Lovecraft's 'The Haunter of the Dark.'" *The Explicator* 57 (Winter, 1999): 98-100. Argues that the lightning in the story is not ordinary light, but upward lightning, a dark light not ordinarily found in our universe but that comes from other dimensions of space.

Joshi, S. T. *H. P. Lovecraft: A Life*. West Warwick, R.I.: Necronomicon Press, 1996. A good biography of Lovecraft by a scholar.

_____. *H. P. Lovecraft and Lovecraft Criticism: An Annotated Bibliography*. Kent, Ohio: Kent State University Press, 1981. A thorough presentation of Lovecraft scholarship. Including both primary and secondary works.

_____, ed. *H. P. Lovecraft: Four Decades of Criticism*. Athens: Ohio University Press, 1980. Contains essays by Barton Levi St. Armand, J. Vernon Shea, and Dirk W. Mosig, as well as a survey of Lovecraft criticism by Joshi.

Joshi, S. T., and L. D. Blackmore. *Lovecraft and Lovecraft Criticism: An Annotated Bibliography: Supplement*. West Warwick, R.I.: Necronomicon Press, 1985. Supplement to the 1981 Joshi bibliography, covering materials published between 1981 and 1985.

Lévy, Maurice. *Lovecraft: A Study in the Fantastic*, translated by S. T. Joshi. Detroit: Wayne State University Press, 1988. A useful consideration of Lovecraft's fiction as examples of the fantastic in literature. Helpful to those interested in genre study and critical theory.

Nelson, Victoria. "H. P. Lovecraft and the Great Heresies." *Raritan* 15 (Winter, 1996): 92-121. Compares the imaginative universe of Lovecraft to that of Daniel Paul Schreber; claims that, obsessed by themes whose full dimension he was unable or unwilling to grasp consciously, Lovecraft used his intense sensitivity to his own unconscious to give modern readers a unique body of work and a new variation on some very old religious and philosophical traditions of Western culture.

Schultz, David E., and S. T. Joshi. *An Epicure in the Terrible: A Centennial Anthology of Essays in Honor of H. P. Lovecraft*. London: Associated University Presses, 1991. Includes essays on

Lovecraft's themes, the uses of isolation in his works of fiction, his cosmic vision, his unique mythology, his modernism, his use of the pulp magazine tradition, and his relationship to Jorge Luis Borges.

Keith Neilson, updated by Melissa E. Barth

LU XUN
Zhou Shuren

Born: Shaoxing, China; September 25, 1881
Died: Shanghai, China; October 19, 1936

PRINCIPAL SHORT FICTION

Ah Q zheng zhuan, 1921 (serial), 1923 (book; in
    Nahan: *The True Story of Ah Q*, 1927)
Nahan, 1923 (*Call to Arms*, 1981)
Panghuang, 1926 (*Wandering*, 1981)
Gushi xinbian, 1935 (*Old Tales Retold*, 1961)
Ah Q and Others: Selected Stories of Lusin, 1941
Selected Stories of Lu Hsün, 1960, 1963
The Complete Stories of Lu Xun, 1981

OTHER LITERARY FORMS

Lu Xun wrote prolifically throughout his life, producing essays, verses, reminiscences, and translations of other writers as well as the short fiction for which he is known in the West. The bulk of Lu Xun's writing consists of polemical essays, written between 1907 and 1936, directed against aspects of Chinese culture and politics of which he disapproved. These writings have been collected from time to time and make up more than twenty volumes. Varying in style, these essays were published in newspapers and magazines and are journalistic in design compared to the sensitive, imaginative, and carefully constructed short stories.

Much of Lu Xun's writing as a whole consists of the translations of foreign authors, a practice he continued during his entire career. His translations were rendered from Japanese or German, the only foreign languages he knew. As early as 1903, he translated the science fiction of Jules Verne. In 1909, he and his brother, Zhou Zuoren, collaborated in publishing *Yuwai xiaoshuo ji* (collection of foreign stories). In two volumes, it included works by Anton Chekhov, Leonid Andreyev, Vsevolod Mikhaylovich Garshin, Henryk Sienkiewicz, Guy de Maupassant, Oscar Wilde, and Edgar Allan Poe. In the 1930's, Lu Xun translated works by many other Russian authors. He and his brother also issued an anthology of Japanese authors titled *Xiandai riben xiaoshuo ji* (1934; a collection of modern Japanese short stories), which included works by Mushakoji Saneatsu, Kunikida Doppo, Mori Ōgai, and Natsume Sōseki.

Lu Xun also produced autobiographical sketches in *Zhaohua xishi* (1928; *Dawn Blossoms Plucked at Dusk*, 1976) and prose poems and reminiscences in *Ye cao* (1927; *Wild Grass*, 1974). He composed verses in *wenyan* (classical Chinese) as well as in the vernacular, *baihua*. According to the late scholar and critic, Zian Xia, Lu Xun's classical verses are superior to those in the vernacular and are at least equal to his best *pai-hua* prose. Lu Xun also kept copious diaries, which have been published in facsimile in twenty-four volumes.

Lu Xun maintained a lifelong interest in graphic art. In 1929, he published a volume of British wood engravings and another which featured the work of Japanese, Russian, French, and American artists. In 1934, he published selected works of young Chinese artists in *Muke jicheng* (the woodcut record). He also published, in collaboration with Zheng Zhenduo, two collections of traditional-style stationery by the seventeenth century artist Wu Zhengyan. He developed a strong interest in the wood engravings of socialist artists in Western Europe and the Soviet Union, and he published books on the form.

Lu Xun (Library of Congress)

ACHIEVEMENTS

Lu Xun is generally regarded as one of the most important of modern Chinese writers. His short story "Kuangren riji" ("The Diary of a Madman"), modeled on Nikolai Gogol's story of the same title, was the first Chinese story written in the style of Western fiction and Lu Xun's first story written in the modern vernacular. His reputation as a short-fiction writer rests primarily on two volumes of stories written between 1918 and 1925, *Call to Arms* and *Wandering*. After these, Lu Xun wrote little fiction. His best-known story is the novella *The True Story of Ah Q*.

Lu Xun developed a narrative style of pointing without commentary, allowing silence to generate meaning within the form of the short story, a method reminiscent of Poe, who may have influenced Lu Xun's sense of structure. Like many Chinese writers of short fiction, Lu Xun was influenced by Western masters of the form, especially those whom he translated. It was Lu Xun, however, who pioneered the

movement in short fiction that helped launch a new literary era in China, and his assimilation of Western ideas became the new reality in Chinese fiction.

Lu Xun's tales often tend toward satire, and his sense of irony is masterful and pervasive. Reminiscent of the traditional Chinese painter, Lu Xun renders a whole person from a few deft strokes and evokes atmosphere without elaborate detail. Considered a pioneer of modern Chinese realism, he has been translated more than any other modern Chinese writer. Because he believed that the literature of a nation reflected its character or spirit, he also believed that in order for his country to emerge from centuries of torpor there must be a reawakening in its literature. The prevailing view of Lu Xun has been that he was a writer who considered literature to be propaganda for social ends; Mao Zedong called him "not only a great writer but also a great thinker and a great revolutionist." It is true that Lu Xun was fervently committed to his nation's future and the development of Chinese society, but his fiction is redeemed from didacticism by his humanism and the high quality of his art.

The communists attacked Lu Xun at first as a bourgeois writer but later accepted him as a proletarian. After they established the Chinese People's Republic in Peking, they considered him to be the Maxim Gorky of China. Mao Zedong referred to him as a "national hero." In 1939, the Communists established the Lu Xun Academy of Arts in Yen'an. Following the fall of Shanghai to the Japanese in 1937, the magazine *Lu Zun Feng* (*Lu Xun's Style*) was started by a group of Communist writers. After Communist troops shattered the Chinese Nationalist defenses of Shanghai in 1949 and occupied the city, the Lu Xun Museum was established in Beijing. Lu Xun's tomb is located in northeast Shanghai.

Many books and articles have been written about Lu Xun. For his pioneering efforts in restructuring the Chinese short story and in developing vernacular speech into a new form of written prose, Lu Xun deserves to be considered the leader of the Chinese Literary Renaissance of 1917-1937. As a writer of short stories, however, he has formidable contenders in such colleagues as Chang Tianyi, Shen Congwen, and Mao Dun.

BIOGRAPHY

Lu Xun (the pen name of Zhou Shuren) was born on September 25, 1881, into an upper-middle-class family in the village of Shaoxing, Zhejiang Province, China. He was the eldest of the four sons of Zhou Fengyi (or Zhou Boyi), an old-style Chinese scholar, and Lu Rui, the daughter of a minor government official. Of Lu Xun's three younger brothers, Zhou Zuoren became a writer, Zhou Jianren became a scientist, and the youngest died of pneumonia at the age of five.

The Zhou family was prosperous until 1893, when Lu Xun's grandfather, Zhou Fuqing, a *jinshi* (entered scholar), was convicted of attempting to bribe a provincial examination official and sentenced to be beheaded. His execution, however, was postponed until he was fortunate enough to be released from prison under a general amnesty. This scandal and the prolonged illness and death of Lu Xun's father in 1896 brought the family to the brink of poverty.

Lu Xun's formal education began at the age of five under the tutelage of his granduncle Chao-lan, who taught him to love books. Grandfather Fuqing, always unorthodox, required him to read history but encouraged him to read popular novels as well. At the age of eleven, Lu Xun was enrolled in a private school supported by the Zhou clan, where he was obliged to study the Confucian classics known as the Four Books.

Although as late as 1898 Lu Xun was still practicing the writing of the *baguwen*, or the eight-legged essay, and the poetry required for the civil service examinations, he decided to pursue an unorthodox path to social advancement. He enrolled in the Kiangnan Naval Academy at Nanjing. Dissatisfied with the poor quality of education offered there, however, at the end of the year he returned to Shaoxing.

Deciding now to attempt the orthodox route, he presented himself at the Kuanji District examination for the *xiucai* (flowering talent) degree. Although he passed this examination, he never sat for the prefectural examination. Instead, he returned to Nanjing and transferred from the Naval Academy to the School of Mines and Railroads attached to the Kiangnan Army Academy. He was graduated in 1901.

Lu Xun obtained a government scholarship to study medicine in Japan. Arriving in Tokyo in 1902, he entered the Kōbun Institute to study the Japanese language. After being graduated from Kōbun in 1904, he enrolled in the medical school at Sendai, Honshū. In 1906, however, he received a severe shock. In viewing a newsslide of the Russo-Japanese War, he witnessed a bound Chinese man awaiting execution as a spy for the Russians while a crowd of Chinese stated indifferently at him. As a result, Lu Xun was convinced that the soul and not the body of China needed curing. Withdrawing from medical school, he returned to Shaoxing. There, he submitted to an arranged marriage to a woman he never afterward regarded as his wife. Then, in company with his brother, Zhou Zuoren, he returned to Japan, this time resolved to devote himself to literature.

The brothers spent their time reading, writing, and translating foreign literature. Although able to read German and Japanese, Lu Xun used these languages mainly to gain access to the cultures of the "oppressed peoples" of Russia, Eastern Europe, and the Balkans. He also composed essays in classical Chinese on a variety of cultural topics. Near the end of his stay in Japan, the brothers published their *Yuwai xiaoshuo ji* (collection of foreign stories), rendered in classical Chinese. Succeeding in obtaining a teaching position at the Zhejiang Normal School at Hangzhou, he returned to China in 1909.

Lu Xun quit teaching at Hangzhou in 1910 to return to Shaoxing to serve as the school principal. On October 10, 1911, the Republican Revolution, led by Sun Yat-sen, burst forth, throwing the country into turmoil. With the overthrow of the monarchy in 1911, Lu Xun composed his first short story—in classical Chinese—which was entitled "Huaijiu" ("Remembrances of the Past") when published in 1913.

When Sun Yat-sen resigned the presidency of China in favor of Yuan Shikai, Lu Xun was called to Beijing to serve in the ministry of education. Soon disgusted with reform party politics, he buried himself in the study of ancient Chinese texts and inscriptions and developed a strong interest in the history of Chinese literature. This latter interest resulted in his famous volume *Zhongguo xiaoshuo shilue* (1923-

1930; *A Brief History of Chinese Fiction*, 1959).

Awakened to creative activity by the Literary Revolution of 1917, the following year Lu Xun wrote his first short story in *baihua*, or colloquial Chinese, "The Diary of a Madman," employing Western technique. From this time until 1926, he would write twenty-five such stories that would appear in two collections—fourteen stories in *Call to Arms* and eleven in *Wandering*. His novella *The True Story of Ah Q* brought him national recognition. After 1926, however, Lu Xun wrote only brief satirical tales, collected in *Old Tales Retold*, devoting himself mostly to writing polemical essays.

Following the massacre of demonstrating students in Beijing on March 18, 1926, by the Duan Qirui government, Lu Xun was looked upon as a dangerous radical and was forced into hiding. Leaving Beijing, he joined the faculty of Amoy University. In 1927, he moved to Sun Yat-sen University in Canton, where he taught and served as academic dean. Resigning in the spring, Lu Xun and Xu Guangping, a former student who had become his common-law wife, left Guangzhou for Shanghai.

In 1930, Lu Xun, having studied Marxism-Leninism, lent his name to the founding of the League of Left Wing Writers. He joined the International Union of Revolutionary Writers. In 1933, he became associated with the Far Eastern Conference against Imperialist War. A close friend of Chu Qiubai, former general secretary of the Communist Party, Lu Xun provided him with a safe haven from arrest and acted as a courier for the Communists. He himself lived in constant fear of arrest and possible execution.

Although by 1930 Lu Xun had apparently concluded that the Chinese Communist Party rather than the Guomindang was the only viable force to reform China, he neither accepted Marxist-Leninist dogma fully nor became a member of the Communist Party. Although from 1927 until his death from tuberculosis on October 19, 1936, Lu Xun produced no original creative work, he has continued to be viewed by many Chinese as China's leading writer of short fiction in the twentieth century.

ANALYSIS

Nearly all Lu Xun's short stories were written between 1918 and 1925. The time they deal with is from the eve of the Republican Revolution of 1911 until the May Fourth movement of 1919. The characters they present are mostly women whom Lu Xun considers victims of traditional Chinese society—he calls them "unfortunates"—whether a failed *litteratus*, a *maudit révolté* (cursed rebel), an unlucky ricksha puller, or a young village woman plagued by widowhood. Although Lu Xun seems more comfortable as a writer when he deals with the downtrodden, he also sometimes concerns himself with certain members of the ruling class, the scholar-gentry either in or out of office, who are opportunists, compromisers, or oppressors of the common people. Although the stories usually focus on a single protagonist and expose either his or her misery or hypocrisy and cruelty, sometimes they also condemn the entire Chinese populace. This view is developed in "The Diary of a Madman," in which the protagonist goes beyond tradition and sees the people as cannibals— the weak devouring the strong. Lu Xun was a moralist who viewed contemporaneous China as a sick and degenerate society badly in need of treatment. Ironically, the young man's concern for the health of China gains for him the diagnosis of "mad."

Lu Xun is usually termed a "realist" as a writer of short fiction. Communist critics call him a "critical realist," a "militant realist," and even a Socialist Realist. Although Lu Xun sought to make his stories conform to reality as he had experienced it and wanted his readers to credit them as based on the truth, he was not realistic in the sense of the fiction of the great European exponents of nineteenth century realism and naturalism, such as Ivan Turgenev, Gustave Flaubert, and Émile Zola, in whom he never showed any interest. His realism was very personal and highly subjective. He was not interested in the material but in the spiritual. In his short stories, he probes into the human spirit as that has been affected by environment and tradition. If one considers the men he took for his intellectual mentors, T. H. Huxley, Max Stirner, Søren Kierkegaard, Henrik Ibsen, Friedrich Nietzsche, Georg Brandes, Lord Byron, Gogol, and

Andreyev, one sees a curious thing: The majority are associated with the anti-Romantic spirit of individualism, and only two of them, Huxley and Brandes, with the anti-Romantic spirit of positivism. Lu Xun had an ironic view of reality that was highly subjective and tempered by strong Romantic elements. It was this view that attracted him to writers such as Gogol and Andreyev, both of whom attempted the fusion of Romanticism and realism and then the fusion of realism and symbolism, and Lu Xun adopted similar practices. Therefore, as a writer, Lu Xun might be more usefully termed a subjective realist or an expressionist rather than a social realist. He was surely not a Socialist Realist. One wonders how he would have taken Mao's Yen'an Forum Talks of 1942. A satirist must exaggerate, draw sharp contrasts between good and evil. Although he exposed the faults of Chinese society, Lu Xun never offered any remedy except that it should honor the individual and free the spirit.

Lu Xun's short stories, for the most part, grew out of his personal experience. He enhanced this subjectivity by the power of his imagination and taut artistic skill. His stories are characterized by their brevity but above all by their compactness of structure and their pithy, sharp style, in which each word is needed and apposite. His prose is strongly imagistic, especially in its visual appeal. Lu Xun seldom employs the figures of metaphor or simile; when he does use such a figure, however, it is usually highly effective. He makes use of historical and literary allusion, and one or more such allusions are to be found in the vast majority of his stories. He sometimes resorts to symbolism. Dialogue is usually kept to a minimum. Irony is a pervasive element in nearly all Lu Xun's stories, with satire a frequent weapon used in defense of individual freedom. He shows unusual skill in fusing an action with its scene. Although description is suppressed, atmosphere emerges strongly.

Lu Xun was a highly sensitive man with a strong sense of justice. He was not content to endure evil with passive indifference. A sedentary literary man (a *wenren*), he admired action more than anything else but had no heart for it himself. An acute observer of human nature, but one with a limited range, he had a special knack for sketching what he saw with deft,

swift strokes of his pen and with a minimum of words. He was a very gifted writer of short fiction but a mediocre thinker. His thinking fell short of complete clarity. A "wanderer" in the wasteland of hopes and broken dreams, he was at first inspired by Charles Darwin and Friedrich Nietzsche but misunderstood both. His later excursions into Karl Marx and Vladimir Ilich Lenin curtailed his imagination, aroused in him resentment and prejudice, and ran counter to his natural instinct for freedom, independence, and appreciation of individual worth. It was unfortunate that as a creative writer he thought that changing the face of China was more important than painting its portrait. As an individual, he could do little about the former but could have done much about the latter. He never realized this truth until the last year of his life.

Perhaps Lu Xun's major weakness as a writer of fiction is his fondness for nostalgia, his lapses into sentimentality, and his inability always to deal fairly with persons other than the downtrodden. If in his short fiction Lu Xun had depicted humanity as he found it in all its richness, splendor, and nobility together with its poverty, stupidity, and moral degeneracy—in a spirit that extended charity to all and with a sense of the kinship of all human beings that included tolerance and a readiness on his part to pardon, leaving moral lessons for others to proclaim and class distinctions for others to condemn—he might have been a great writer rather than simply a gifted one whose full potential as a creative artist was never realized.

"THE DIARY OF A MADMAN"

Of Lu Xun's stories collected in *Call to Arms*, "The Diary of a Madman," although it made its author prominent, is not one of his best. The first story to be written in the Western manner, it is more clever in conception than effective as a well-constructed tale. As C. T. Hsia, a judicious critic, has pointed out, the story's weakness lies in the author's failure to provide a realistic setting for the madman's fantasies.

"KONG YIJI"

The story "Kong yiji," about a failed scholar who has become a wine bibber at a village tavern, where he is the butt of jokes, is a much stronger story than "The Diary of a Madman." Kong yiji has studied the classics, but he has failed to pass even the lowest official examination. With no means of earning a living, he would have been reduced to beggary except for his skill in calligraphy, which enabled him to support himself by copying. He loved wine too much, however, and he was lazy. When he needed money, he took to stealing books from the libraries of the gentry. For such actions he was frequently strung up and beaten. After being absent from the tavern for a long time, he reappears, dirty and disheveled, his legs broken. Partaking of warm wine, he is the butt of the jokes and taunts of the tavern yokels. He departs from the tavern, but he is never seen again. It is presumed that he has died. As a commentary on the Chinese social order, the story presents a man who is a part of the detritus left by the examination system. At the same time, he must take responsibility for his own weaknesses of character. In addition, the story shows how cruel and unfeeling people can be to those who are less fortunate than they.

"Mᴇᴅɪᴄɪɴᴇ"

"Yao" ("Medicine") is another powerful story. It shows especially careful construction and makes effective use of symbolism. The story concerns two boys who are unknown to each other but whose lives follow equally disastrous courses to become linked after their deaths. Hua Xiaozhuan is the tubercular son of a tea-shop owner and his wife. The boy is dying. Anxious to save his life, the parents are persuaded to pay a packet of money for a *mantou* (steamed bread-roll) soaked with the blood of an executed man, which is alleged by tradition to be a sure cure for tuberculosis. The beheaded man is young Xia You, the son of the widow Xia. A revolutionary seeking the overthrow of the Manchu or Qing Dynasty, he was betrayed to the authorities by his conservative Third Uncle, who collected a reward for his treason. Thus, the blood of a martyr and hero, a representative of the new order, is used in the service of a superstitious and useless medical cure. If the parents are ignorant and superstitious, they also truly love their son and try by all the means they know to save him, but he dies, regardless. Nobody has sought to save Xia You from execution; indeed, all the customers at the tea shop highly approve of his arrest

and beheading. His widowed mother, who loved him dearly, was powerless to help her son.

Influenced by his admiration for the Russian writer Andreyev, Lu Xun sought to emphasize the story's purport through the use of symbolism. Since the two boys in the story are linked in the action purely by accident, Lu Xun reinforces the connection through their surnames, "Hua" and "Xia," which as "Huaxia" literally means "glorious and extensive"; this compound is also an ancient name for China. It is a story of the opposition between the old China—the China of darkness, superstition, and lethargy under foreign rulers—and the new China—the China trying to emerge into the light, the China of the awakened, of the revolutionary. The symbolism is especially dense at the conclusion of the story, when the two mothers meet at the graves of their sons, who are buried opposite each other. Natural flowers are growing on the grave of the Hua boy, but on Hsia Yu's grave has been placed a wreath of red and white flowers. When Xia You's mother perceives the wreath, she cannot understand its presence. She believes that her son has wrought a miracle as a sign of the wrong done to him, that he desires that his death be avenged. Perplexed, she looks around her but sees only a crow perched on a leafless bough. She tells her son that heaven will surely see that a day of reckoning will come. Uncertain of his presence, though, she requests him to make the crow fly onto his grave as a sign to her that he is really there. The crow remains still perched on its bough, as if made of iron. Mrs. Xia and Mrs. Hua have, in their mutual grief, formed a bond of sympathy. Mrs. Hua now suggests that the two of them might as well leave for home. As they depart, they hear a loud caw behind them. Startled, they turn their heads to look behind them. They see the crow stretch its wings and fly off toward the horizon.

Tʜᴇ Tʀᴜᴇ Sᴛᴏʀʏ ᴏғ Aʜ Q

The True Story of Ah Q is Lu Xun's longest and most important story. It originally appeared serially on a weekly basis in the Beijing *Chenbao* (weekly post) in its Sunday supplement; these circumstances may have been responsible for its rambling, episodic plot and other literary defects. The story made a powerful impact, however, on its Chinese audience. It saw in the protagonist, Ah Q, what Lu Xun wanted it to see: the embodiment of all the weaknesses of the Chinese national character, which just prior to the fall of the Qing Dynasty had constituted a national disease. Ah Q is a homeless peasant who lives in the temple of the tutelary god of Wei village. Since no one knows his true surname, the narrator calls him simply "Ah Q" because the foreign letter "Q" resembles a man's head with a queue, or pigtail, hanging down. Thus, "Q" is a pictograph of every Chinese man during the rule of the Manchus, since the conquerors required Chinese men to shave their heads and wear queues. Ah Q is a Chinese Everyman.

Ah Q is a dunce whose foolish actions result in repeated humiliating defeats. He just as repeatedly glosses over these defeats by convincing himself that, if he has been physically overcome, he has nevertheless won a "spiritual victory." Ah Q is a perfect antihero, but he is an unusual one in that he is, as William A. Lyell, Jr., has pointed out, "victimizer as well as victim." He is bullied and mistreated by those stronger than he, but he, in turn, bullies and mistreats those who are weaker. Like the other inhabitants of Wei village, he follows the Chinese social principle: *Pa chang qiruo* (fear the strong, bully the weak). He is opposed to revolutionaries until he learns that the village power elite is terrified of them. He tries to join them, but they arrest him for thievery. He is condemned to death, not by the sword but by the rifles of a firing squad. He tries to be brave, but, his soul ripped, he is about to utter, "Help." Yet, as Lu Xun writes, "Ah Q never said that. Blackness had already covered his eyes. He heard the shots ring out and felt his body scatter like a heap of dust."

Ah Q may personify the Chinese social sickness of his time. According to the perceptive scholar, Lee Oufan Lee, Ah Q's life revolves around subsistence in a world that he does not understand. He is only a face in the crowd without spirit, interior self, or self-consciousness. His negative qualities combine to depict a slave mentality. He may suggest how the people of Wei village responded to the Republican Revolution of 1911. He suggests as well why the revolution eventually failed.

WANDERING

On the whole, the stories collected in Lu Xun's second volume *Wandering* are superior to those of his first. He himself favored them and pointed out the reasons for their superiority: his having outgrown his foreign influences; his more mature technique; his more incisive delineation of reality; and his having cooled his personal anger and sorrow. Of the eleven stories included in *Wandering*, three of them are particularly noteworthy: "Zhufu" ("The New Year's Sacrifice"), "Zai jiulou shang" ("Upstairs in a Wineshop"), and "Lihun" ("Divorce").

"THE NEW YEAR'S SACRIFICE"

"The New Year's Sacrifice" is the story of the tragic lot and cruel treatment accorded a peasant woman, Xiang Linsao, who, widowed at twenty-six, is forced to remarry against her will, is then widowed a second time, has her infant son carried off by a wolf, and is hired as a servant by a scholar-gentry family named Lu. The head of the Lu family, Hanlin, the neo-Confucian scholar Fourth Uncle Lu, thinks that Xiang Linsao, as a twice-married widow, is impure and unfit to touch any food or implement connected with the family ancestral sacrifices. Despite her religious efforts to atone for her "sin," she is rejected by the Lus and turned into a beggar. She dies in poverty just as the Lus are about to invoke a New Year's blessing. The news of her death annoys Fourth Uncle Lu. In anger, he berates her for dying at such an unpropitious time. He remarks to his wife, "You can tell from that alone what a rotten type she is." Thus, this renowned neo-Confucian scholar and rationalist reveals himself to be an inhumane, unfeeling, superstitious, rigid traditionalist whose narrow and inflexible morality is the executioner of a good, simple-hearted peasant woman. The twice-widowed woman is the victim of tradition and superstition. Being a widow, she must bear the stigma of carrying the ghosts of her two husbands; in fact, it may even be believed that she caused their deaths. When she asks the noncommittal narrator if he believes a person's soul goes on after death, she seems to be clutching for meaning in a realm of existence beyond the world she has known, where she can be reunited with her child who was eaten by wolves.

"Upstairs in a Wineshop"

"Upstairs in a Wineshop" is the story of the chance reunion one winter evening of two former friends and colleagues upstairs in a village wine shop, back home after a ten-year interval. The story is obviously autobiographical and the unnamed narrator a mask for Lu Xun himself. The narrator arrives at the wine shop alone. He goes upstairs, orders wine and some dishes, and sits drinking and eating while looking out over the snow-covered courtyard outside. The atmosphere here is beautifully evoked by Lu Xun—inside warm wine and food, outside snow. The snow introduced at the beginning, the symbolism of the crimson camellias blossoming in the snow (suggesting the homeliness of the south as opposed to the strangeness of the north), and the snow and wind at the end that wash away the bittersweet taste of the remembrances of the past give to this story a special pictorial quality in respect to its text—reminiscent of those scholar-painters who did *Wenrenhua* (literary men's painting), harmonizing text with picture. When the narrator's old friend and colleague Lü Weifu appears by chance, each is surprised at meeting the other, and they greet each other warmly. Both recollect their younger days when they were avid reformers who had rejected the Old Learning in favor of the New. Now they are both middle-aged. To his dismay and disappointment, the narrator learns that his friend is changed, has lost his nerve and rejoined the Confucian establishment. He lives with his mother in a northern province where he tutors the children of a prosperous family in the Confucian classics. He also deceives his mother by making up white lies in order to shield her from a painful reality. Lü Weifu has given up "pulling the beards of the gods."

Perhaps the most remarkable feature of "Upstairs in a Wineshop" is Lu Xun's seeming ambivalence of his anti-Confucian position. As C. T. Xia has observed, although Lu Xun undoubtedly intended to present Lü Weifu as a weak-kneed, broken man, "the kindness and piety of Lü Weifu, however pathetic, also demonstrate the positive strength of the traditional mode of life, toward which the author must have been nostalgically attracted in spite of his contrary intellectual conviction." Xia concludes that the story, then, with an irony contrary to its author's intention, "is a lyrical confession of his own uncertainty and hesitation."

"Divorce"

"Divorce" provides a vivid portrait of a tough, uncouth, rebellious country girl as well as a picture of how the power structure of traditional Chinese society works in a rural setting to cow such a female rebel. As the story opens, a family feud has been going on for three years between the Xhuangs and the Shis. The girl, Aigu, born a Chuang, married young Mr. Shi. After a time, however, she and her husband did not get along and his parents disliked her. Soon, her husband took up with a young widow and informed his wife that he no longer wanted her. Since that time, she has been living with her father, Zhuang Musan, and her six brothers. For the past three years, the two feuding families have entered into negotiations several times without any settlement being reached. Preferring to be an unloved wife with honor rather than a dishonored divorcée, Aigu has insisted each time that her husband take her back despite an offer of money by the Shis to effect a separation, and until now her father has supported her position. Father and daughter are now traveling by boat to the village of Pang, where another meeting between the Shis and the Zhuangs has been arranged by Old Gentleman Wei in a final effort to produce a settlement of the family feud. When they arrive, Wei announces that Seventh Master, a prestigious urban relative of the Weis, visiting him for the New Year's celebration, has agreed to preside over Aigu's case and will attempt to persuade the Zhuangs to accept the terms of divorce proposed, with which he, Wei, already agrees. To make the settlement more agreeable, Seventh Master has persuaded the Shis to add ten dollars to the sum of money already offered to the Zhuangs. Although Aigu is confident that her father will again reject the divorce proposal, she becomes alarmed when he remains silent. In desperation, she speaks out in her own defense.

Seventh Master reminds her, however, that a young person ought to be more compliant in adjusting to reality, for "compliance produces riches." Furthermore, he informs her, since her in-laws have already dismissed her from their presence, she will have to suffer a divorce, regardless of whether there is a money settlement. At this point, Young Shi takes the opportunity to remind Seventh Master that if Aigu acts in this manner here, she must have acted much worse in his father's home. He complains that at home she always referred to his father and to himself as "beasts." Indeed, she even called him a *sishengzi* (bastard). Aigu breaks in to deny this charge and counters that he called her a *pinchuan* (bitch).

At Aigu's response, Seventh Master cries out a command: "Come in!" Silence immediately follows. Aigu is thunderstruck. A servant enters and hurries up to the dignitary, who whispers some order to him which nobody can understand. The man replies: "Yes, venerable sir," and departs. Fearfully, Aigu blurts out to Seventh Master that she always meant to accept his decision. Wei is delighted. The families exchange wedding certificates and money. The servant enters and gives something to Seventh Master, who puts his hand to his nose and then sneezes; the whispered order was for snuff. Zhuang Musan and Aigu leave after refusing to take a cup of New Year's wine.

OTHER MAJOR WORKS

POETRY: *Yecao*, 1927 (*Wild Grass*, 1974).

NONFICTION: *Zhongguo xiaoshuo shilue*, 1923-1930 (*A Brief History of Chinese Fiction*, 1959); *Refeng*, 1925; *Huagai ji*, 1926; *Fen*, 1927; *Huagai ji xubian*, 1927; *Eryi ji*, 1928; *Zhaohua xishi*, 1928 (*Dawn Blossoms Plucked at Dusk*, 1976); *Sanxian ji*, 1932; *Erxin ji*, 1932; *Wei ziyou shu*, 1933; *Jiwai ji*, 1934; *Nan quiang beidiao ji*, 1934; *Zhun fengyue tan*, 1934; *Huabian wenxue*, 1936; *Qiejieting zawen*, 1937; *Qiejieting zawen er ji*, 1937; *Qiejieting zawen mobian*, 1937; *Lu Xun riji*, 1951.

TRANSLATIONS: *Yuwai xiaoshuo ji*, 1909 (with Zhou Shuren; of works by Anton Chekhov, Leonid Andreyev, Vsevolod Mikhaylovich Garshin, Henryk Sienkiewicz, Guy de Maupassant, Oscar Wilde, and Edgar Allan Poe); *Xiandai riben xiaoshuo ji*, 1934 (of short stories by Mushakoji Saneatsu, Kunikida Doppo, Mori Ōgai, and Natsume Sōseki).

ANTHOLOGY: *Muke jicheng*, 1934 (2 volumes).

MISCELLANEOUS: *Selected Works of Lu Hsün*, 1946-1960 (4 volumes); *Silent China: Selected Writings of Lu Xun*, 1973.

BIBLIOGRAPHY

Chang, Lung-hsi. "Revolutionary as Christ: The Unrecognized Savior in Lu Xun's Works." *Christianity and Literature* 45 (Autumn, 1995): 81-93. Discusses Lu Xun's fascination with the Christ figure, particularly as recorded in the Gospel of Matthew. Argues that by rereading his works and carefully considering the neglected aspects of those works, such as his use of the Christ figure, we may begin to really understand Lu Xun and his significance for modern China.

Chen, Pearl Hsia. *The Social Thought of Lu Hsün, 1881-1936*. New York: Vantage Press, 1976. Chronicles the development of Lu Xun's thought against his cultural background, including his encounter with Western ideas, his belief in women's rights, his involvement with liberal socialism, and his reevaluation of traditional Chinese culture. The preface, by Franklin S. C. Chen, is an essay on traditional China's economic structure as it related to social thought.

Hanan, Patrick. "The Techniques of Lu Hsün's Fiction." *Harvard Journal of Asiatic Studies* 34 (1974) 53-96. Using a broad definition of "technique," Hanan discusses possible influences of writers such as Nikolai Gogol, Vsevolod Mikhaylovich Garshin, and Leonid Andreyev, as well as Lu Xun's use of symbols and different types of irony.

Kowallis, Jon Eugene. *The Lyrical Lu Xun: A Study of His Classical-Style Verse*. Honolulu: University of Hawai'i Press, 1996. Examines the verse but offers insight into Lu Xun's style.

Lee, Lee Ou-fan, ed. *Lu Xun and His Legacy*. Berkeley: University of California Press, 1985. This collection of essays by various scholars discusses Lu Xun's perception of traditional and modern literature, his development of form, and his intellectual and political views.

_____. *Voices from the Iron House*. Bloomington: Indiana University Press, 1987. The stated purpose here is to "demythify" Lu Xun with the aim of evaluating his literary accomplishments on their own ground. Good discussions include biographical information but emphasize analysis.

Lyell, William A., Jr. *Lu Hsün's Vision of Reality.* Berkeley: University of California Press, 1976. The first third of this book provides a biography, and the remainder is devoted to good basic discussions of Lu Xun's fiction.

Pusey, James Reeve. *Lu Xun and Evolution.* Albany: State University of New York Press, 1998. Explores the theme of evolution in the works.

Seminov, V. I. *Lu Hsün and His Predecessors.* White Plains, N.Y.: M. E. Sharpe, 1980. Describes Lu Xun's role as innovator in Chinese fiction from a moderate Soviet perspective.

Shiqing, Wang. *Lu Xun: A Biography.* Beijing: Foreign Languages Press, 1984. Traces Lu Xun's life, particularly his political and intellectual development. Includes several photographs.

Tang, Xiaobing. "Lu Xun's 'Diary of a Madman' and a Chinese Modernism." *PMLA* 107 (October, 1992): 1222-1234. A reading of Lu Xun's short story as a modernist text, particularly in the modernist time-consciousness it introduces; argues the story can be read as a manifesto of the birth of modern subjectivity as well as the birth of modernist politics in twentieth century China. Discusses the nature of the madness of the madman, the story as a search for meaning, and the modernism of the story as one that displaces the myth of a homogeneous nature culture.

Yn, Xiaoling. "The Paralyzed and the Dead: A Comparative Reading of 'The Dead' and 'In a Tavern.'" *Comparative Literature Studies* 29 (1992): 276-295. Shows how both stories rely on opposing the themes of paralysis and death; claims that in both the theme of death undermines the theme of paralysis by making the protagonists ironic.

Richard P. Benton, updated by

Mary Rohrberger

M

MARY McCARTHY

Born: Seattle, Washington; June 21, 1912
Died: New York, New York; October 25, 1989

PRINCIPAL SHORT FICTION

The Company She Keeps, 1942
Cast a Cold Eye, 1950
The Hounds of Summer and Other Stories, 1981

OTHER LITERARY FORMS

Mary McCarthy began writing as a drama critic for the *Partisan Review*. She wrote six novels. *The Group* (1963), the most widely read of these, was subsequently made into a film in Hollywood. She also wrote two autobiographies as well as numerous articles and books on art and politics. Most groundbreaking among her nonfiction is the autobiography *Memories of a Catholic Girlhood* (1957), an idiosyncratic combination of fiction and nonfiction. In italicized bridges between each essay/story, McCarthy comments on the proportions of fact and fantasy in each selection. In her second autobiography, *How I Grew* (1987), she presents her life as an artist. Reviewers responded quite well to the second autobiography but typically noted the superiority of the first. McCarthy's literary criticism for *The New Republic* and *The Nation* earned her an important place in American literature.

ACHIEVEMENTS

Mary McCarthy's exceptional skill as a writer won her immediate recognition. An essay she wrote for the College Entrance Examination Board (CEEB) was published anonymously in a CEEB journal of the early 1930's as an example of a high-scoring essay. Recognition for her excellence includes the 1949 *Horizon* literary prize for *The Oasis* (1949), an O. Henry short-story prize in 1957 for "Yellowstone Park," and

in 1984 both the National Medal of Literature and the Edward MacDowell Medal for outstanding contributions to literature. McCarthy, a Guggenheim Fellow in both 1949 and 1959, was a member of the American Institute of Arts and Letters from 1960 until her death. Recognized for her astute observation of literary works, she was a judge for a number of fiction awards, including the Prix Formentor, the Booker Prize, and the National Book Award.

McCarthy's own writing style is classic: her sentences, architectural structures of balance and cadence; her rebellious point of view, a rainbow prism of satiric wit. The typical McCarthy story is realistic and satirical, revealing the self-deception of the supposedly intelligent and well educated. Her fiction is peopled with veiled portraits of those whom she knew well. Critical opinion tends to cast each of McCarthy's husbands, except James Raymond West, as the model for one or more of her male "antagonists": Harold Johnsrud for Harald Peterson in *The Group* and the husband in "Cruel and Barbarous Treatment"; Edmund Wilson for Miles Murphy in *A Charmed Life* (1955) and a legion of short-story husbands; and Bowden Broadwater for John Sinnot in *A Charmed Life* and a young American in "The Cicerone." Generally, McCarthy's characters are viewed ironically from a vantage point of cool detachment.

BIOGRAPHY

Mary Therese McCarthy's biography is unusually significant for understanding her fiction, since various clusters of biographical details seem to generate all her stories and characters. McCarthy's childhood began in Seattle with a doting, extravagant mother and a romantic, imaginative father. Her early life was an eden of picnics, parties, and stories that ended abruptly in 1918, when the flu killed both her parents

Mary McCarthy (©Jerry Bauer)

within the same week. McCarthy was then remanded to the harsh and punitive custody of her Aunt Margaret and Uncle Myers, but she survived in this new environment, which included beatings and deprivation, by excelling in school. These early triumphs led her to Vassar College, the crucible of her imaginative life and scene of her most popular work, *The Group*. All these details can be variously found in the lives of her fictional heroines, principally in that of Meg Sargent, the recurring figure in *The Company She Keeps* (indeed, Sargent was her great-grandmother's maiden name).

On her graduation from Vassar College, McCarthy married an actor, Harold Johnsrud, and at the same time she became drama critic for the *Partisan Review*; the marriage lasted three years, her career ten. By 1938, she had branched out into fiction and had a new marriage with Edmund Wilson. After six cataclysmic years and one son, Reuel, McCarthy divorced Wilson and married Bowden Broadwater, from whom she was divorced in early 1961. Later in that year, McCarthy married James Raymond West, a State Department official, in Paris. She and West spent half of each year in their Paris home and half in Maine. Dur-

ing the last few years of her life, McCarthy had several operations for hydrocephalus but continued to work on her memoirs, plan a study of gothic architecture, teach literature at Bard College, study German, and write literary criticism and commentary. She died in New York City on October 25, 1989, of cancer.

ANALYSIS

Mary McCarthy's stories are, on the whole, about errors endemic to intellectuals, which lead them to indignity, despair, and sterility. McCarthy's typical intellectuals are political radicals or artists who fail to comprehend that their analytical acumen or talent does not raise them sufficiently from the common dilemma to empower them either to save the rest or to live more beautifully than do others. Meg Sargent, who, like Ernest Hemingway's Nick Adams, reappears continually in a series of short stories, is McCarthy's Every-intellectual, her voyage the purgatory of those with pretensions to education. "Cruel and Barbarous Treatment" is a good example of McCarthy's literary universe, and Meg's.

"CRUEL AND BARBAROUS TREATMENT"

In this story, Meg is going through a divorce, orchestrating the breakup of her marriage with the self-image of a diva in her greatest role. Meg considers herself to be a member of the intelligentsia, but McCarthy etches her as a grandiose fraud whose view of her situation is riddled with tired clichés. McCarthy comments on Meg economically by simply capitalizing strategically to turn Meg's thoughts into a series of buzz words. Meg is anxious to hear "What People Would Say" and "How Her Husband Would Take It." Finally, even the heroine realizes what she is doing. She will go ahead with her divorce, but she understands that The Young Man whom she thought she had waiting in the wings has been her factotum, not her passion. She will not be fool enough to fly into his arms. Unfortunately, her insight does not last, and on the train to Reno, she fabricates a new opera for her fellow passengers, deciding what to answer to queries concerning her destination. Neither will she be vulgar enough to blurt out "Reno" nor will she equivocate and reply "San Francisco." At first, she will say "'West,' with an air of vagueness and hesitation. Then, when pressed, she might go as far as to say 'Nevada.' But no farther."

"The Man in the Brooks Brothers Shirt"

The most pointed and, some might say, best treatment of McCarthy's theme, is "The Man in the Brooks Brothers Shirt," her most widely anthologized story. In this story, Meg is traveling West to tell her aunt in Portland that she is to be married again. As a result of her trip, she realizes that she will never marry her new intended. The source of Meg's revelation is her encounter with Mr. Breen, a mid-level corporate executive in the steel business, whose wife Leonie and three children live comfortably in the Gate Hills section of Cleveland. Meg begins the trip flashing an advance copy of a very unimportant novel with which she intends to impress her suitor with her cultural superiority.

A political radical, Meg patronizes Breen's position in the corporate structure. Along with Meg's self-dramatized contempt for the man, however, McCarthy explores attitudes of which Meg is not aware. Meg is a poseur, and she envelops others in mythological poses. Despite her initial characterization of Breen as a "middle-aged baby, like a young pig, something in a seed catalogue . . . plainly Out of the Question," when Breen reveals that beneath his Brooks Brothers shirt beats a heart that wants to vote for Norman Thomas, Meg immediately romanticizes him as the last of the old breed of real American men. Stringing along behind her fantasy, she allows herself to get drunk in Breen's private compartment; the predictable revelry and sex follow in short order.

The next morning Meg is filled with shame, but Breen is wildly in love with her and wants to divorce Leonie and throw himself into an unconventional life with his Bohemian Girl. For Meg, sudden realization follows her drunken, sensual orgy; she begins to feel that she is not so much a free spirit, as she has always prided herself, but a sort of misfit. All the men in her life have suited her because they, like her, were in some way "handicapped" for American life. Although Breen seems to break the pattern, he does not. He is fifty, she thinks, over-the-hill. Would he, she wonders, have been in such hot pursuit if he were ten years younger?

What is clear, at least to the reader, is that each character is ambivalent about the characteristic of the other that holds the most attraction. Meg is contemptuous of Breen's conventionality, and Breen is critical of Meg's individualism. He tells her to shape up, because, if she does not, "In a few years you'll become one of those Bohemian horrors with oily hair and long earrings." The liberation that each affords the other does not mitigate these streaks of aversion. Meg and Breen do not run off together, but Meg also knows that she cannot marry her intended, and Breen manages to tryst with Meg several times before disappearing from her life. Meg has gained, through Breen, some humility about her elite self-image, but only temporarily; ultimately, she writes Breen off. Her last contact with him is a telegram she receives from him after the death of her father: "SINCEREST CONDOLENCES. YOU HAVE LOST THE BEST FRIEND YOU WILL EVER HAVE." Meg disposes of the missive, disgusted and embarrassed by Breen's middle-class sentimentality.

The portraits of Meg's individualism and Breen's conventionalism are ironic, but, although both characters are supremely flawed, the story nevertheless treats Breen's limitations more charitably than Meg's. If Breen is corny, at least he fulfills the obligations of social convention to be nurturing, even if he is a bit obtuse. The nature of the intellect is to enlighten society, and Meg is too cliché-ridden to fulfill her obligations; all one sees are her limitations. In the end, her bohemian lifestyle is merely another form of convention. She shreds Breen's telegram at the end of the story because "It would have been dreadful if anyone had seen it." No bourgeoise could have better phrased the sentiment. McCarthy is a mistress of such deft, deflating touches. In the final ten words of the story she irretrievably nails Meg to the wall, just as she did at the end of "Cruel and Barbarous Treatment." She frequently uses a parting shot to devastate her protagonists.

McCarthy also grants her characters an occasional victory. When she does, the victory is hard-won and painfully small, but it can be lyrically affecting, as in "Ghostly Father, I Confess." In this story, Meg is now the wife of Frederick (perhaps based on Edmund Wilson) and is in analysis with Dr. James. Through numerous digressions, much is learned about other people in Meg's life, but the story takes place almost entirely during a session with her analyst. The beginning of the session is awash with stereotype; Meg stereotypes Dr. James, and he counters with the routine Freudian castration theory and dream interpretation. They move past this initial standoff, however, and begin to examine the effect of Meg's childhood on her terrible marriages. The details are all recognizable from McCarthy's own biography.

Meg explains how her marriage to Frederick shows that she is in a downward spiral initiated by the cruelty of her childhood guardians. James comes forward with a surprising inversion of Meg's rather obvious, although painfully arrived at, analysis, suggesting that "This marriage took more daring on your part than anything you have done since you left your father's house." He goes on to say that, with the marriage to Frederick, Meg has stopped denying the trauma of her childhood because she is now strong enough to face it and work through it. James quiets Meg's doubts by referring to her brains and beauty, which he tells her will overcome her problems. The session comes to a sudden close as James snaps shut his notebook, as though clicking the interview off. He is transformed, now uninvolved. Meg is upset by the abruptness but somewhat intoxicated by her discovery that James has given her five extra minutes and by his parting remark about her brains and beauty.

Once in the street, Meg is suddenly struck by the meaning of the dream for which James had given her an unsatisfying, conventional interpretation during the session. In her dream, she had seen herself loved by a Byronic figure who slowly metamorphosed into a Nazi war prisoner. She understands that the changing figure is her own mind revealing its true identity, not truly Byronic, after all, but a victim of rigidity and cruelty. As in the other stories, Meg has an insight into her fraudulent self-images, but this time the self-awareness seems to take hold. The story closes with the image of Meg in front of a window full of hot water bottles begging God to let her hold onto her uncomfortable revelation. McCarthy cryptically ends her narrative with the statement, "It was certainly a very small favor she was asking, but . . . she could not be too demanding, for, unfortunately, she did not believe in God."

McCarthy's sly portrait explores the enormity of trying to think at all. The mind tends to fall in love with its own creations and perpetrate frauds on itself. There is the fraud of the analyst who can turn his involvement on and off; the vanity of Meg's greed for five more minutes; the possible disingenuousness of James's remark about brains and beauty; the war between flesh and spirit, one of which desires the vulgar comfort of the hot water bottle, the other the irritant of enlightenment; and James's inordinate pleasure about his various interpretations, although we do not know if they are true or false. Finally, there is the magnitude of the universe for which we desire the comfort of a caretaker, whom McCarthy would deny as a vulgarity equal to the hot water bottle. The mind is surely nine-tenths dissembler, but Meg, by intuiting profoundly her own shabby role-playing has made an inroad on that great disabler of the intellect, its own narcissism. Such an inroad is the outer limit of McCarthy's concept of human achievement.

OTHER MAJOR WORKS

LONG FICTION: *The Oasis*, 1949; *The Groves of Academe*, 1952; *A Charmed Life*, 1955; *The Group*, 1963; *Birds of America*, 1971; *Cannibals and Missionaries*, 1979.

NONFICTION: *Sights and Spectacles: 1937-1956*, 1956; *Venice Observed*, 1956; *Memories of a Catholic Girlhood*, 1957; *The Stones of Florence*, 1959; *On the Contrary: Articles of Belief*, 1961; *Mary McCarthy's Theatre Chronicles, 1937-1962*, 1963; *Vietnam*, 1967; *Hanoi*, 1968; *The Writing on the Wall and Other Literary Essays*, 1970; *Medina*, 1972; *The Seventeenth Degree*, 1974; *The Mask of State*, 1974; *Ideas and the Novel*, 1980; *Occasional Prose*, 1985; *How I Grew*, 1987.

BIBLIOGRAPHY

Brightman, Carol. *Writing Dangerously: Mary McCarthy and Her World*. New York: Clarkson Potter, 1992. Supplements but does not supersede Carol W. Gelderman's earlier biography. Like

Gelderman, Brightman was able to interview her subject, and her book reflects not only inside knowledge but also (as its subtitle suggests) a strong grasp of the period in which McCarthy published. Includes a biographical glossary and notes.

Epstein, Joseph. "Mary McCarthy in Retrospect." *Commentary* 95 (May, 1993): 41-47. Provides a summary of McCarthy's work; comments on her role in intellectual life in America; discusses the relationship of her life to her fiction.

Gelderman, Carol W. *Mary McCarthy: A Life.* New York: St. Martin's Press, 1988. Gelderman offers an objective biography of McCarthy. Although much of the narrative is familiar, the book is well written and amply documented. The photographs provide important perspective on McCarthy's childhood and a satisfying glimpse into her adult life. This biography makes good reading for a general audience as well as for a student of McCarthy.

Gelderman, Carol W., ed. *Conversations with Mary McCarthy.* Jackson: University Press of Mississippi, 1991. A series of interviews with the author, dating from 1962 to 1989.

Goldman, Sherli Evens. *Mary McCarthy: A Bibliography.* New York: Harcourt, Brace & World, 1968. Goldman explains that Mary McCarthy was "more collaborator than subject" in this work. The book is divided into five categories: books, contributions to books, contributions to periodicals, translations into foreign languages, and appendix of miscellanea. The appendix lists interviews, McCarthy;s own translations of French works, and Braille and recorded editions of books by McCarthy.

Kufrin, Joan. *Uncommon Women.* Piscataway, N.J.: New Century, 1981. In a book that examines women who have succeeded within several different fields, McCarthy is "The Novelist" for the chapter so named. The portrayal of the writer is friendly and informal, largely the transcription of an interview in McCarthy's home in Maine. McCarthy comments on her writing process of extensive revision. The two photographs capture a sense of fun and humor in McCarthy. A light and readable piece.

McKenzie, Barbara. *Mary McCarthy.* New York: Twayne, 1966. McKenzie offers a one-page chronology of McCarthy's life as well as an opening chapter titled "The Fact in Biography." The fourth chapter, titled "The Key That Works the Person," concerns the short stories in *The Company She Keeps* and *Cast a Cold Eye*. The final chapter assesses McCarthy's overall contribution to literature. McKenzie's book, with notes, a bibliography, and an index, would benefit the serious student of McCarthy's work.

Stock, Irvin. *Mary McCarthy.* Minneapolis: University of Minnesota Press, 1968. Stock's forty-seven-page essay includes overall critical comment on McCarthy's work, noting the moral concerns evident in her fiction. Stock also provides a brief biography. He summarizes and then provides analysis of *The Company She Keeps, Cast a Cold Eye, The Oasis, The Groves of Academe*, and *The Group*. Stock's character studies are particularly good.

Stwertka, Eve, and Margo Viscusi, eds. *Twenty-four Ways of Looking at Mary McCarthy: The Writer and Her Work.* Westport, Conn.: Greenwood Press, 1996. Part of the Contributions to the Study of World Literature series, this volume is based on essays presented at a conference on the author at Bard College in 1993.

Wilford, Hugh. "An Oasis: The New York Intellectuals in the Late 1940's." *Journal of American Studies* 28 (August, 1994): 209-223. In this discussion, Wilford analyzes Mary McCarthy's fictional portrayal of Europe-America Groups, a political organization created by New York intellectuals.

Martha Nochimson, updated by Janet T. Palmer

CARSON McCULLERS

Born: Columbus, Georgia; February 19, 1917
Died: Nyack, New York; September 29, 1967

Principal short fiction

The Ballad of the Sad Café: The Novels and Stories of Carson McCullers, 1951
The Ballad of the Sad Café and Collected Short Stories, 1952
The Shorter Novels and Stories of Carson McCullers, 1972

Other literary forms

Carson McCullers's remarkable first novel, *The Heart Is a Lonely Hunter* (1940), establishes the themes that were to concern her in all her other writing: the spiritual isolation of individuals and their attempt to transcend loneliness through love. Thereafter, she wrote short stories, some poetry (mostly for children), three other novels, and two plays. The most popular of the novels, *The Member of the Wedding* (1946), she adapted for the stage; the play was a great success on Broadway and was also made into an award-winning film. *The Heart Is a Lonely Hunter* and her somber Freudian novel, *Reflections in a Golden Eye* (1941), were also adapted for film. McCullers also wrote a number of significant essays, which are collected in *The Mortgaged Heart* (1971). The essays that are most important to understanding the method and content of her fiction, especially her use of the grotesque, are "The Russian Realists and Southern Literature" and "The Flowering Dream: Notes on Writing."

Achievements

Carson McCullers was the winner of a number of literary awards during her lifetime, including membership in the National Institute of Arts and Letters, two John Simon Guggenheim Memorial Foundation Fellowships, and an Arts and Letters Grant. She also won the New York Drama Critics Circle Award, a Gold Medal, and the Donaldson Award (all for the play version of *The Member of the Wedding*). Her fiction and nonfiction works were published in a number of reputable magazines, including *The New Yorker, Harper's Bazaar, Esquire*, and *Mademoiselle*. For her story "A Tree. A Rock. A Cloud," she was nominated for an O. Henry Award.

A praiseworthy writer of short fiction, McCullers succeeds with objective narration, the theme of loneliness, and her lyric compression. While McCullers is perhaps not as great a writer of short stories as her peers Flannery O'Connor, Eudora Welty, and Katherine Anne Porter, she is nevertheless successful at affecting her readers' emotions. The brevity and compression of stories such as "The Jockey" and "The Sojourner" are remarkable based on any standards. Although her techniques are not as innovative as those of many other postmodern fiction writers, she influenced, among others, Truman Capote, Flannery O'Connor, and Anne Tyler, particularly with the expert use of the grotesque and the freakish, and the portrayal of human alienation. Her knowledge of human psychology also makes her a great spokesperson for the complexity of human experience.

Biography

Carson McCullers, born Lula Carson Smith, was reared in a small southern town, a milieu that she used in much of her fiction. Exhibiting early talent in both writing and music, she intended to become a concert pianist but lost her tuition money for the Juilliard School of Music when she went to New York in 1935. This loss led her to get part-time jobs while studying writing at Columbia University. She earned early acclaim for her first novel, *The Heart Is a Lonely Hunter*, written when she was only twenty-two. Her friends included many prominent writers, including Tennessee Williams, W. H. Auden, Louis MacNeice, and Richard Wright. Her health was always delicate; she suffered early paralyzing strokes, breast cancer, and pneumonia. She stayed remarkably active in literature and drama, however, even when confined to bed and wheelchair. She died of a stroke at the age of fifty.

ANALYSIS

Carson McCullers's short stories (ruling out for the moment the novella *The Ballad of the Sad Café*, 1943, serial; 1951, book) often explore the intense emotional content of seemingly undramatic situations. Plot is minimal, although there is often at least one unusual or grotesque element. "Wunderkind," for example, deals with the confused feelings of a gifted fifteen-year-old girl at a piano lesson. Her social development has been sacrificed to her musical talent; now her mastery of the keyboard is faltering and she is profoundly humiliated. The reader realizes that part of her difficulty is the awakening of sexual feelings for her teacher, Mister Bilderbach. Neither the teacher, who thinks of her as a child prodigy, nor the young girl herself understands her tension and clumsiness.

"THE JOCKEY"

"The Jockey" describes an even more ordinary situation—a brief encounter in a restaurant between a jockey and three other men identified as a trainer, a bookie, and a rich man whose horse the jockey has ridden. The dwarflike jockey, called Bitsy Barlow, is one of those grotesque figures who seem an embarrassing mistake in nature. The point of the story is the ironic contrast between the three "normal" men's callous pretense of sympathy for a rider's crippling accident on the track and the jockey's bitter grief for that rider, who is his closest friend. Although the jockey, because of his physical deformity, seems a caricature of humanity, the intensity of his sorrow makes the other men's callousness seem the more monstrous.

"MADAME ZILENSKY AND THE KING OF FINLAND"

"Madame Zilensky and the King of Finland" is, on the most obvious level, at least, a revelation of the emotional price of artistic excellence. Like "Wunderkind" and "The Jockey," the story concerns the subjective significance of seemingly minor events. Mr. Brook, head of a college music department, hires Madame Zilensky, a famous composer and teacher, for his faculty. He is tolerant of her several eccentricities, her tales of adventures in exotic places, and even her somewhat shocking assertion that her three sons are the offspring of three different

Carson McCullers (Library of Congress)

lovers. When she claims to have seen the King of Finland, however, Mr. Brook realizes that she is a pathological liar, since Finland has no king. Mr. Brook is sensitive enough to intuit the motive for her prevarications: the terrible constriction of her actual experience. "Through her lies, she lived vicariously. The lies doubled the little of her existence that was left over from work and augmented the little rag end of her personal life."

Point of view is vital in this story. The pathetic emotional dependence of Madame Zilensky on fantasy is the explicit and obvious content, but the story's real focus is on the growing perception of Mr. Brook, who has himself led a somewhat dull, repetitive life in academia. It is his character which receives the more subtle delineation. He represents those countless ordinary people whose individuality has been subdued, but not utterly extinguished, by professional duties. When Mr. Brook, in his official capacity, feels he must reprimand Madame Zilensky for propagating lies about herself, he comes face to face with stark tragedy. The terrible emotional deprivation he is about to expose echoes in his own solitary soul. Compassion for her loneliness and his own makes him realize that truth is not the highest virtue.

This terrified retreat from reality into the most banal of polite conversation ironically combines tragedy and sardonic humor. To use the name of love in this context is surprising, at once accurate and absurd. A final symbolic image captures the grotesque irrationality embedded in the most familiar landscape. As Mr. Brook looks out of his office window later, he sees, perhaps for the hundredth time, a faculty member's old Airedale terrier waddling down the street. This time, however, something is strange: The dog is walking backward. He watches "with a kind of cold surprise" until the dog is out of sight, then returns to the pile of student papers on his desk.

This story is thematically typical of McCullers's fiction. Love, which has little or nothing to do with sexuality, is the only way to bridge the terrible isolation which separates individuals. Too many other factors in the situation, however—habit, social custom, human perversity, the demands of artistic creativity, or simply devotion to duty—conspire against the goal of giving love and comfort to one another. Each person is trapped, incommunicado, in the little cage he or she has chosen.

"A Domestic Dilemma"

The irrational persistence of love and its inadequacy to solve the everyday problems of existence are also apparent in "A Domestic Dilemma." Here, too, the story is told from the point of view of a patient, kindly man whose attitude toward his alcoholic wife is a curious blend of compassion, love, and angry exasperation. He fears for the welfare of his two children. He comes home to the suburbs from his New York office to find his children unattended, playing with Christmas tree lights, a supper of cinnamon toast on the kitchen table, untouched except for one bite. The little boy complains, "It hurt. The toast was hot." His wife, Emily, had mistaken cayenne pepper for cinnamon.

The bewildered children do not understand the painful scene between mother and father, in which Emily vacillates drunkenly between belligerent defense of her behavior and tearful shame. Martin finally persuades her to go to bed and let him feed the children, bathe them, and put them to bed. He successfully reestablishes an atmosphere of tender solicitude, hoping the children will not remember their mother's puzzling behavior. How long will it be, he wonders, before they understand and despise her? There are moments when Martin hates his wife, imagining "a future of degradation and slow ruin" for himself and his children. When he finally lies down beside Emily and watches her sleeping, however, his anger gradually dissipates. "His hand sought the adjacent flesh and sorrow paralleled desire in the immense complexity of love."

One interpretation offered for "A Domestic Dilemma" points to the stresses of an urban lifestyle on a woman reared in an emotionally supportive small southern town. In suburbia, Emily is isolated from everyone she ever knew, while Martin commutes long distances into the inner city. Thus, it is social isolation that is destroying her. This interpretation has considerable validity, although the cause of her alcoholism is not really central to the story; isolation and loneliness occur in all kinds of social situations in McCullers's fiction, and small southern towns are as deadly as urban suburbs in that regard. Isolation is a metaphysical affliction more than a cultural one. Emily's social isolation is analogous to Bitsy Barlow's physical deformity or even Madame Zilensky's enslaving musical genius—one of the many accidents of nature or situation over which people have little control. As Mr. Brook's empathy for Madame Zilensky cannot alleviate her isolation, Martin's love for his wife will not necessarily save her from her unhappiness. In McCullers's fiction it is usually the act of love, not the comfort of being loved, that has power to transform the lover.

"A Tree. A Rock. A Cloud"

One of the most anthologized of McCullers's stories is "A Tree. A Rock. A Cloud," which was chosen for the 1942 *Prize Stories: The O. Henry Awards*, even though it may be inferior, in some ways, to "A Domestic Dilemma," "Wunderkind," and "Madame Zilensky and the King of Finland." It deals more philosophically and perhaps more ironically with the art of loving. The lover, in this case, is an old, boozy wanderer who waylays a newspaper delivery boy in a café. He is compulsively dedicated to explaining how he learned to love "all things both great and small." The quotation comes not from the story but from *The Rime of the Ancient Mariner* (1798), which is quite possibly its inspiration. The irony of Samuel Taylor Coleridge's Ancient Mariner waylaying an impatient wedding guest with his story of salvation through love is translated here into a somewhat different context.

Three persons, rather than two, are involved. Although the tale is addressed to the naïve newspaper delivery boy, it is overheard by Leo, the proprietor of the café, who is early characterized as bitter and stingy. When the wanderer accosts the boy and says distinctly, "I love you," the initial laughter of the men in the café and their immediate return to their own beer or breakfasts suggest both a widespread cynicism and an utter indifference concerning the welfare of the boy. Although Leo is also cynical and often vulgar, he listens to the conversation carefully. When the old man orders a beer for the boy, Leo brings coffee instead, reminding the other man, "He is a minor."

Although Leo soon understands that the old man's intention is not to proposition the boy, he continues to interject insulting remarks into the wanderer's sad tale of love for a wife who deserted him for another man. The old man struggles to explain the unifying effect of love on the fragmented psyche. Before his marriage, he says, "when I had enjoyed anything there was a peculiar sensation as though it was laying around loose in me. Nothing seemed to finish itself up or fit in with other things." His wife, however, transformed his experience of himself—"this woman was something like an assembly line for my soul. I run these little pieces of myself through her and I come out complete." Yet, after years of frantic search for the lost wife, the man realizes with horror that he cannot even remember distinctly what she looked like. It was then that he began his "science" of love.

At this point, Leo explodes in exasperation:

Leo's mouth jerked with a pale, quick grin. "Well none of we boys are getting any younger," he said. Then with sudden anger he balled up a dishcloth he was holding and threw it down hard on the floor. "You draggle-tailed old Romeo!"

The wanderer solemnly explains that one must practice the art of loving by starting with small or inanimate things—a tree, a rock, a cloud—and graduate from one thing to another. He learned to love a goldfish next. Now he has so perfected the science of loving that he can love anything and everyone. By this time, Leo is screaming at him to shut up.

As an explanation of Platonic love, this, to be sure, may be feeble. The reactions of Leo and the boy do, however, provide depth to the story. The newsboy is puzzled and confused—presumably because he has yet to pass through adolescence, when the importance and complexity of love will become clearer to him. After the old man leaves, the boy appeals to Leo for answers. Was the man drunk? Was he a dope fiend? Was he crazy? To the first two questions Leo says, shortly, "No." To the last he is grimly silent. Probably Leo responds so emotionally to the old man's tale because it makes him too keenly aware of his own barren lovelessness. His role is somewhat analogous to that of Mr. Brook in this respect. He recognizes, perhaps, that the old man, unlike himself, has found a way to transcend his wretchedness. Can it be "crazy" to be at peace with oneself, in spite of outwardly miserable circumstances? If so, it is a craziness a sane man might covet. The boy, thinking of nothing else to say, comments that the man "sure has done a lot of traveling." As the story ends, McCullers emphasizes therefore that the story is about adolescent versus adult perceptions of love.

Autobiographical Elements

McCullers's short fiction, like her most popular novel, *The Member of the Wedding*, has many autobiographical elements. Her own absorption in music and early aspirations to be a concert pianist are reflected in "Wunderkind" and "Madame Zilensky and the King of Finland." The particular mode of Madame Zilensky's escape from a narrowly focused existence is even more pertinent to McCullers's short, intense life. She escaped the limitations of her frail body through fantasy, transforming it into fiction and drama.

Even the situation in "A Domestic Dilemma" echoes her own life curiously altered. She lived both the Emily role, that is, the maimed personality who desperately needs love and companionship, and the Martin role, the hopeless lover of the psychologically crippled person. McCullers's husband, whom she divorced and later remarried, was an alcoholic whose drinking was aggravated by the fact that, although he fancied himself a writer, she was so much more successful than he. She has disguised the personal element in the situation by changing the presumed cause of the alcoholism (although she, too, knew the effect of migrating from a small southern town to New York) and by projecting her role more on the husband than the wife.

Both Martin and Mr. Brook exhibit qualities ordinarily ascribed to women—intuition, gentleness, patience, and unselfish love. McCullers's blurring of gender roles (Miss Amelia in "The Ballad of the Sad Café" is strikingly masculine) was probably not motivated by a feminist revolt against stereotyped sex roles; she was not a polemicist but a lyrical writer, projecting her own personality, feelings, dreams, and fears. If her men act like women or vice versa, it is because she was herself decidedly androgynous. She loved both men and women and somehow contained them both. Some of her most ardent attractions were for women who repudiated her attentions (or at least did not remain in her vicinity), which may account for the wistful need for love in some of her fictional characters.

In spite of her personal sorrows and her emotional isolation and loneliness, McCullers was beloved by many friends and generous in her own affections. Even the odd triangular love affairs that appear in *The Member of the Wedding* and *Reflections in a Golden Eye* have some autobiographical parallels. Both Carson and her husband, according to McCullers's biographer, Virginia Spencer Carr, were intimately involved with Jack Diamond, a concert musician. It is not an accident that McCullers was one of the first American writers to deal openly (in *Reflections in a Golden Eye*) with repressed homosexuality. In the case of her husband, at least, his homosexual orientation was not always repressed; whether she was an active bisexual is more ambiguous.

Her personal life and her fiction both seem marked by a curious combination of sophisticated intuition into human motives and an odd childlike quality that sometimes verges on immaturity. Most writers, for example, would not write of Mr. Brook that he could not speak until "this agitation in his insides quieted down"; nor would many writers try to express the blurred Platonic idealism of "A Tree. A Rock. A Cloud." Although the situational irony of that story saves it from being naïvely expressed philosophy, one has a lingering impression that the writer is mocking a sentiment that she really wants to advocate.

"THE BALLAD OF THE SAD CAFÉ"

"The Ballad of the Sad Café," sometimes grouped with novellas, sometimes with short stories, is the most successful of McCullers's ventures into the grotesque. The melancholy mood suggested by the title is appropriate; like many a folk ballad, it tells a mournful tale touched with sardonic humor. The story celebrates the love of a cross-eyed, mannish woman for a conceited, hunchbacked dwarf. It also involves a curious love triangle, for the climax is a grotesque battle between the protagonist, Miss Amelia, and her former husband for the affection of the dwarf.

True love, paradoxically, is both a cruel joke and the means of redemption, not only for the lover, Miss Amelia, but also for the whole ingrown, backwoods community, which otherwise dies of emotional starvation. The inhabitants of this stifling southern village, like a somber chorus in a Greek tragedy, observe and reflect the fortunes of Miss Amelia, their leading citizen. Cousin Lymon, the hunchback, appears out of nowhere at the door of Miss Amelia, who runs the town store and the best distillery for miles around. To everyone's amazement, instead of throwing him out, as she has done to others who claimed kinship, Miss Amelia takes in the wretched wanderer and even falls in love with him. Cousin Lymon becomes a pompous little king of the castle, although not, apparently, her bed partner. Love transforms the mean, hard, sexless Miss Amelia into a reasonable facsimile of a warmhearted woman. She opens a café in her store because Cousin Lymon likes company, and her place becomes the social center of the community. Miss Amelia blossoms; the community blooms with goodwill, until the arrival of another person who is to destroy this interlude of happiness and peace.

Miss Amelia had once married the town bad boy, who had unaccountably fallen in love with her. Her motivation had apparently been solely commercial, the hope of acquiring a strong helper in her business; when the bridegroom expected sexual favors, Miss Amelia had indignantly refused. After ten stormy days, she threw him out entirely, earning his undying hatred for causing him such frustration and humiliation; he turned to a life of crime and landed in the penitentiary. Now he is out of jail and returns with malevolent thoughts of revenge. Poor Miss Amelia, now vulnerable in a new and surprising way, accepts his unwelcome presence in her café because Cousin Lymon is fascinated with him, and Miss Amelia and her former spouse become rivals for the affection of the dwarf.

This rivalry culminates in a ludicrous variation of the western showdown, solemnly witnessed by the whole community, when Miss Amelia and her former husband have a battle of fisticuffs in the café. Moreover, Miss Amelia, who has been quietly working out with a punching bag in preparation for the event, is winning. At the last moment, however, the traitorous Cousin Lymon leaps onto her back, and the two men together beat her senseless. Afterward, they vandalize her store and her still in the woods and flee. Miss Amelia thereafter closes her business and becomes a permanent recluse in a town now desolate and deserted.

OTHER MAJOR WORKS

LONG FICTION: *The Heart Is a Lonely Hunter*, 1940; *Reflections in a Golden Eye*, 1941; *The Member of the Wedding*, 1946; *The Ballad of the Sad Café*, 1943 (serial), 1951 (book); *Clock Without Hands*, 1961.

PLAYS: *The Member of the Wedding*, pr. 1950; *The Square Root of Wonderful*, pr. 1957.

CHILDREN'S LITERATURE: *Sweet as a Pickle and Clean as a Pig*, 1964.

MISCELLANEOUS: *The Mortgaged Heart*, 1971 (short fiction, poetry, and essays; Margarita G. Smith, editor).

BIBLIOGRAPHY

Carr, Virginia Spencer. *The Lonely Hunter: A Biography of Carson McCullers*. Garden City, N.J.: Anchor Press, 1975. This definitive biography offers an interesting read and provides significant biographical elements that are related to McCullers's works. The complexity, pain, and loneliness of McCullers's characters are matched by their creator's. Includes an extensive chronology of McCullers's life, a primary bibliography, and many endnotes.

_____. *Understanding Carson McCullers*. Columbia: University of South Carolina Press, 1990. A thoughtful guide to McCullers's works. Includes bibliographical references.

Clark, Beverly Lyon, and Melvin J. Friedman, eds. *Critical Essays on Carson McCullers*. New York: G. K. Hall, 1996. A collection of essays ranging from reviews of McCullers's major works to tributes by such writers as Tennessee Williams and Kay Boyle, to critical analyses from a variety of perspectives. Most helpful to a study of the short story is Robert Philips's "Freaking Out: The Short Stories of Carson McCullers."

Cook, Richard M. *Carson McCullers*. New York: Frederick Ungar, 1975. A good general introduction to McCullers's novels, short stories, and plays. Cook's analyses of the short stories and *The Ballad of the Sad Café* are especially good, though the book includes chapters on each of the novels, McCullers's life, and her achievements as well. Cook, while admiring McCullers, recognizes her limitations but nevertheless praises her success with portraying human suffering and isolation and enabling readers to relate to the most grotesque of characters. The book's endnotes and primary and secondary bibliographies may be useful in finding other sources.

Graver, Lawrence. *Carson McCullers*. Minneapolis:

University of Minnesota Press, 1969. An early, though still useful, extended essay in the University of Minnesota pamphlet series. Offers a chronological overview of McCullers's life and career. Particularly good are the brief analyses of the novels and *The Ballad of the Sad Café*, but some of Graver's comments, especially some psychoanalytical observations, are outdated. Graver's admiration of McCullers is questionable since at times he does not admit her fiction's power at the psychological and mythical level and instead praises male authors' superiority, reducing McCullers to a mere lyricist. Complemented by a brief bibliography of primary and secondary sources.

James, Judith Giblin. *Wunderkind: The Reputation of Carson McCullers, 1940-1990*. Columbia, S.C.: Camden House, 1995. Examines McCullers's place in literature as a southern female author. Bibliographical references and an index are provided.

McDowell, Margaret B. *Carson McCullers*. Boston: Twayne, 1980. A good general introduction to McCullers's fiction, with a chapter on each of the novels, the short stories, and *The Ballad of the Sad Café*. Also included are a chronology, endnotes, and a select bibliography. Stressing McCullers's versatility, McDowell emphasizes the lyri-

cism, the musicality, and the rich symbolism of McCullers's fiction as well as McCullers's sympathy for lonely individuals.

Westling, Louise. *Sacred Groves and Ravaged Gardens: The Fiction of Eudora Welty, Carson McCullers, and Flannery O'Connor*. Athens: University of Georgia Press, 1985. In this study, important comparisons are made between these three major southern writers of short fiction and novels. While Westling is not the first to use a feminist approach with McCullers, the book offers useful insight concerning the portrayal of the female characters and the issue of androgyny in McCullers's fiction. Her analysis of *The Ballad of the Sad Café* is particularly good. Supplemented by useful endnotes and a bibliography of secondary material.

Whitt, Margaret. "From Eros to Agape: Reconsidering the Chain Gang's Song in McCullers's *Ballad of the Sad Café*." *Studies in Short Fiction* 33 (Winter, 1996): 119-122. Argues that the chain gang was a rare visual example of integration in an otherwise segregated South; notes the irony suggested through the song—that the men must be chained together to find harmony.

Katherine Snipes, updated by D. Dean Shackelford

IAN McEWAN

Born: Aldershott, England; June 21, 1948

Pʀɪɴᴄɪᴘᴀʟ sʜᴏʀᴛ ꜰɪᴄᴛɪᴏɴ
First Love, Last Rites, 1975
In Between the Sheets, 1978

Oᴛʜᴇʀ ʟɪᴛᴇʀᴀʀʏ ꜰᴏʀᴍs
Ian McEwan turned to longer forms after beginning his career as a writer of short fiction, publishing his first novel, *The Cement Garden*, in 1978; a play, *The Imitation Game*, in 1981; a screenplay for the

film *The Ploughman's Lunch* (1983); and subsequent novels, including *The Child in Time* (1987), *Enduring Love* (1997), and the Booker McConnell Prize-winning *Amsterdam* (1998). He also wrote the children's literature work *The Daydreamer* (1994).

Aᴄʜɪᴇᴠᴇᴍᴇɴᴛs
Ian McEwan's first collection of short fiction, *First Love, Last Rites*, won the Somerset Maugham Award in 1976, and many of his other works have been recognized for their excellence. *The Comfort of*

Ian McEwan (©Miriam Berkley)

Strangers (1981) and *Black Dogs* (1992) were finalists for the prestigious Booker McConnell Prize, which was awarded to *Amsterdam* (1998). *The Child in Time* won the 1987 Whitbread Novel of the Year award, and *The Ploughman's Lunch* won the *Evening Standard* Award for best screenplay. McEwan was also awarded an honorary doctorate in literature from the University of Sussex in 1989.

Bɪᴏɢʀᴀᴘʜʏ

Ian Russel McEwan was born in Aldershot, England, on June 21, 1948, where his father, David McEwan, a career military man, was stationed. His mother, Rose Moore McEwan, the widow of a soldier killed in World War II, had two older children, and McEwan considered himself "psychologically, an only child." He spent his childhood at military bases in Singapore and Libya before returning to England in 1959 to attend a state-run boarding school and then enter the University of Sussex, from which he gradu-

ated with a B.A. honors degree in English in 1970.

During his third year at Sussex, he had begun to write fiction, and he decided to enter the M.A. program at the University of East Anglia because he could "submit a little fiction instead of writing a thesis." After graduating in 1971, he spent a year traveling before placing a story, "Homemade," with *New American Review*. His first book, *First Love, Last Rites*, which developed out of his graduate thesis, was published in 1975. Explaining that he sometimes felt confined by fiction, McEwan began to write screenplays for television and films, and composed an oratorio, *Or Shall We Die?* (1983), about nuclear annihilation, which was performed by the London Symphony Orchestra. His primary area of work, however, is the novel, and, after being shortlisted twice for the increasingly prestigious Booker McConnell Prize, his novel *Amsterdam* won the award in 1998. Some critics felt that *Enduring Love*, which was the best-selling work of fiction in the United Kingdom for months, was an even stronger effort, although it was (unaccountably) left off the Booker shortlist.

Aɴᴀʟʏsɪs

Ian McEwan's short fiction was a significant element in the transformation of British literature during the 1970's from the gritty realism of the Angry Young Men and the still genteel social explorations of more traditional authors toward the anarchic, dystopic, neo-gothic postmodern writing of a generation responding to the fragmentation, fracture, and aggression of a postcolonial society in convulsive transition. Following the temporary euphoria of the "swinging London" of the 1960's, McEwan and contemporaries like Martin Amis, Angela Carter, J. G. Ballard, and Will Self completely removed and discarded a veneer of semirespectability to reveal and examine what they regarded as the essence of life in the British Isles. While some critics accused McEwan of dwelling in depravity, he has insisted that he is illuminating some of the most fundamental aspects of the human condition and that the base impulses to which his characters respond reveal essential aspects of human nature usually unacknowledged.

Like Ballard, McEwan has envisioned a late twentieth century world in which technological innovations have undermined human interaction; like Carter, he has explored the darkest regions of the human psyche in a style that recalls the almost delicious horror of the classic gothic genre; like Amis, he has looked with scathing contempt at the stupidity and opacity of people at their most selfish and narcissistic; and like Self, he has described with apparent relish the fullest range of the physical, examining the Body with curiosity and an almost obsessive fascination. Nonetheless, McEwan has maintained, "I can't locate myself inside any shared, any sort of community taste, aesthetic ambition or critical position or anything else."

Aside from an understandable preference for avoiding categorization or superficial grouping, McEwan's expression of singularity is an attempt to provoke a discussion of his work that is not reduced to a reiteration of subjects like incest, sexual violence, and murder, which make his short fiction troubling for some readers. The shocking or macabre features of many stories are disturbing, attracting the initial attention a young writer might require, but the most successful stories use sensational detail and situation as a way to introduce questions about the societal norms that permit or encourage such behavior. McEwan, in his short fiction, seeks to understand without endorsing the characters he depicts and to convey the entropic turmoil that has resulted in the disintegration of the structure that supported relationships between people in earlier times.

FIRST LOVE, LAST RITES

A summary catalog of the central subjects of McEwan's first collection, *First Love, Last Rites*, suggests the sources of discomfort that produced uneasy responses from some commentators. The stories concern calculated, passionless incest ("Homemade"), compassionless control ("Solid Geometry"), exploitation and humiliation ("Disguises"), affectless murder ("Butterfly"), blatant sexual exhibitionism ("Cocker"), and a hideous rat as a symbol of pregnancy ("First Love, Last Rites"). The protagonists—frequently the narrators—of these stories range from the not particularly appealing to the pa-

thetic and repulsive. McEwan explained his choices in 1979 by saying that he needed the tension of "what is bad and difficult and unsettling . . . to start me writing." His interest in the actions of his characters leads to an intense probing of the psychological basis for their motivation and derives from his desire to identify, describe, and, at least implicitly, condemn the social forces that have resulted in their isolation. McEwan's characters are outcasts or outsiders, marginal figures effectively beyond the reach of what social support might still be available, and only in the title story is there a suggestion of a personal relationship that might sustain and support a degree of hope for the future.

"IN BETWEEN THE SHEETS"

Many of the protagonists of *First Love, Last Rites* are adolescents, in accordance with McEwan's feeling that this cohort is an

> extraordinary, special case of people; they're close to childhood, and yet they are constantly baffled and irritated by the initiations into what's on the other side.

He goes on to say that "short stories, and especially first-person narratives—can thrive on a point of view which is somehow dislocated, removed." One of the limitations of this position, however, is an almost total enclosure within the mind of the narrator, a factor which McEwan addressed in the title story of his next collection where a single father, Stephen Cooke, arranges a visit from his fourteen-year-old daughter Miranda and her strange close friend, the diminutive Charmian. The third-person narrative enables McEwan to remain slightly beyond the central characters while evoking their thoughts and feelings, especially Stephen's, through a persistent probing of their responses and reactions. The awkwardness that Stephen feels in his daughter's presence, an uncertainty growing out of separation and compounded by her growth toward young womanhood (and sexual echoes of Stephen's estranged wife) and by the mystery of Miranda's friendship with Charmian, is complicated but also ameliorated by his rediscovery of a deep care and concern for her. The title, taken from a popular rock song, is obviously designed to emphasize the sexual component of many of the stories, but the prior line "Don'cha think there's a place for you" is equally important as an indication of the need for a comfortable or safe place in any relationship.

"Dead as They Come"

"Dead as They Come" joins some of McEwan's prevalent concerns in a very compact, consistently intense narrative delivered by a wealthy middle-aged man who relates his obsessive fascination with a store-window mannequin. The story evolves as a kind of continuing present-tense confession that is clearly a record of progressive mental deterioration but which reads like a completely rational account of understandable behavior. The erudition, self-rationalization, sexual absorption, increasingly violent responses to frustration when will and desire are thwarted, and vividly graphic and explicit description of action are features of McEwan's writing at its most effective. The narrator is, characteristically, completely removed from any social constraint and is bereft of any human relationship which might alleviate his rage. The story almost functions as an allegory because the figure of desire has no mind or soul of her own and is seen only through the consciousness of a person who does not care about another's inner life. The fact that she is literally a model of a woman rather than a woman as supermodel is part of McEwan's point.

"Psychopolis"

"Psychopolis" reaches beyond the limits of the short story toward the broader social and personal explorations that have marked McEwan's novels. His narrator is a young Englishman, probably closer to McEwan's own sensibility than any other character in the short fiction. The story developed from McEwan's brief visit to Los Angeles, a city he uses as the template for the chaotic energy of a contemporary Western city in the last decades of the twentieth century. Adrift but exalted by the pulse of life in a strange land, open to experience, friendly with other self-absorbed but not unpleasant young people, the narrator is alternately bemused and fascinated by what seems like the inexplicable but compelling behavior of his friends, or more accurately, social associates in what he calls "a city of narcissists." The bizarre situations, sexual latency, and lurking semi-violence that is common to McEwan's fiction is present in "Psychopolis," but instead of a feeling of dread, despair—or, even worse—benumbed indifference, the unnamed narrator generally regards his own confusion and his friends' peculiarities with a degree of humor that widens the field of the story beyond the circumscribed lives that are effectively prisons in other stories. There are more distinct characters in this story than in any other one; their vehement if somewhat incoherent arguments indicate a degree of complexity to their lives, and the narrator shares a few moments of exuberance and even temporary joy with the others, which suggests his wayward quest for "something difficult and free" is not automatically doomed to failure.

Other major works

LONG FICTION: *The Cement Garden*, 1978; *The Comfort of Strangers*, 1981; *The Child in Time*, 1987; *The Innocent*, 1990; *Black Dogs*, 1992; *Enduring Love*, 1997; *Amsterdam*, 1998.

PLAYS: *The Imitation Game and Other Plays*, pb. 1981; *Or Shall We Die?*, pr., pb. 1983 (oratorio; music by Michael Berkeley).

SCREENPLAYS: *The Ploughman's Lunch*, 1983.

CHILDREN'S LITERATURE: *The Daydreamer*, 1994.

Bibliography

Broughton, Lynda, "Portrait of the Subject as a Young Man: The Construction of Masculinity Ironized in 'Male' Fiction." *Subjectivity and Literature from the Romantics to the Present Day*. New York: Pinter, 1991. After a general discussion of "feminist critical practice," Broughton presents an intellectually powerful and provocative discussion of the male narrator in "Homemade" as an exemplar of contemporary masculine concerns.

Hanson, Claire. *Short Stories and Short Fictions, 1880-1980*. New York: St. Martin's Press, 1985. Examines several of McEwan's short stories in terms of their explorations of the creative process, especially McEwan's innovative uses of form and structure.

Ricks, Christopher. "Adolesence and After: An Interview with Ian McEwan," *Listener* (April 12,

1979): 527. A characteristically candid and revealing conversation, with McEwan touching on
many important aspects of his short fiction.

Slay, Jack. *Ian McEwan*. New York: Twayne, 1996.
An excellent overview of McEwan's writing life,
with detailed, incisive discussions of the short fiction.

Vannatta, Dennis. *The English Short Story, 1945-
1980: A Critical History*. New York: Twayne,

1985. Identifies and explains the aesthetic strategies underlying McEwan's use of unconventional
situations, which Vannatta claims are ultimately
connected to concerns that are "determinedly traditional, unrelentingly moral," focusing on
"Homemade," "Butterflies," "Disguises," "Dead
as They Come," and "In Between the Sheets."

Leon Lewis

JOHN McGAHERN

Born: Dublin, Ireland; November 12, 1934

PRINCIPAL SHORT FICTION
Nightlines, 1970
Getting Through, 1978
High Ground, 1985
The Collected Stories, 1992

OTHER LITERARY FORMS

After the publication of his first novel, *The Barracks* (1963), John McGahern encountered trouble
with the Catholic Church and the Irish Censorship
Board because of his second novel, *The Dark* (1965);
as a result of these experiences, McGahern decided to
fictionalize the loss of his teaching job in *The
Leavetaking* (1974, revised 1984) and parody the
problems of writing about sex in *The Pornographer*
(1979). *Amongst Women* (1990) is his most highly
praised novel.

ACHIEVEMENTS

John McGahern's first novel, *The Barracks*, was
the first prose work to win the A. A. Memorial Award
in Ireland, and he was awarded the Arts Council
Macauley Fellowship for the work as well. *Amongst
Women*, an international success, won the Aer Lingus
Prize, was a finalist for the Booker McConnell Prize
in 1990, was a best-seller in Ireland, and brought him
wide recognition.

BIOGRAPHY

John McGahern was born in Dublin in 1934, the
son of a police officer. He was raised in County
Roscommon, in the west of Ireland. He received his
education at Presentation College, Carrick-on-Shan-
non, St. Patrick's Training College in Drumcondra,
and University College, Dublin. For a brief time after
receiving his degree, he worked as a laborer in London but soon returned to teach at St. John the Baptist
Boys' National School in Clontarf. After seven years
of teaching, he published *The Barracks* in 1963,
which was well received and highly honored.

McGahern took a year's leave from teaching after
the publication of *The Barracks* to go to London and
write his second novel, *The Dark*. When the book
was banned by the Irish Censorship Board because of
its treatment of sexuality and child abuse, McGahern
lost his teaching job. After appeals and legal action
failed to reverse the Board's decision, McGahern began a career as a visiting lecturer in the United States,
England, and Europe. He later returned to settle in
Ireland.

ANALYSIS

John McGahern's writing career has been plagued
by controversy due to his challenging many of Ireland's past religious, social, and sexual values. Although such abstract social issues are not at the center
of his stories, there are no sentimental images of Ire-

land in them either; many are darkly pessimistic. Nor is there a garrulous, Irish storyteller voice, for his stories are concise, controlled, and clipped—much more characteristic of Chekhovian writing than a folklorish oral style. It is not the speaking voice of Frank O'Connor that dominates these stories but the stylized tone of so-called modern minimalism.

Because of the self-conscious control of McGahern's narrative technique, his short stories have received as much critical analysis as those of Mary Lavin and Edna O'Brien. These writers are both realistic and lyrical at once, as is typical of the modern Joycean tradition, pushing mere description of the material world to unobtrusive symbolic significance. McGahern is also typical of that tradition; although his stories have a recognizable social context, he is not interested in confronting his characters with the abstractions of social limitations. More often in his short stories, his characters face the universal challenges of responsibility, guilt, commitment, and death.

"KOREA"

"Korea" is a deceptively simple story with a seemingly misleading title. Although the story is quite brief, it contains within it another story, which a father tell, about being captured just after the revolution in 1919, when the British were shooting prisoners. The father describes a young man of sixteen or seventeen who, after being shot, plucked at the tunic over his heart as if to tear out the bullets, his buttons flying into the air. The father says that years later, while he was on his honeymoon, he saw bursting furze pods, which reminded him of the young man's buttons.

After the father urges his son to go to America, the boy overhears him excitedly telling a man that American soldiers' lives are insured for $10,000 and that, for the duration of a soldier's service, his parents receive $250 a month. Later when the boy tells his father he has decided he will not go to America, the father says it will be his own funeral if he refuses this chance and comes to nothing in "this fool of a country." Although this seems to be a story about a calculating father willing to sacrifice his own son for money, the boy does not see it that way, feeling closer to the father than ever before.

"PEACHES"

Both in terms of the clipped, repetitive syntax and the basic situation of a couple living in Spain, "Peaches" is McGahern's most Hemingwayesque story. It begins with a prevailing metaphor, also reminiscent of Ernest Hemingway, of a dead shark that lies stinking on the beach beneath a couple's house. The couple, referred to simply as "the man" and "the woman," have come to Spain, where they can live cheaply and where he can write and she can paint; however, the two do little more than quarrel, have sex, and talk about why they are unhappy, much as Hemingway's couples do.

The title metaphor of peaches brings the couple's lethargic and unproductive lifestyle to a head when the magistrate of the area invites them to his house to try his peaches, making it clear that it is the woman in whom he is interested by stuffing peaches into the breast pockets of her dress. When he urges them to come again so they can swim naked in his pool, the couple feel both shocked and bewildered. The story ends with the woman feeling somewhat responsible for what has happened, although she blames the man for not doing anything when the magistrate stuffed the peaches in her pockets. At the end, she says that the incident is no more than what she deserved.

"THE COUNTRY FUNERAL"

Described by several reviewers as McGahern's short-fiction masterpiece, this story has been compared to Joyce's "The Dead" (1914). The surface similarities are clear enough; the story approaches novella length, and it focuses on a social ritual, albeit a funeral instead of a dinner party, that ultimately leads to a kind of communal affirmation. The story centers on three brothers, who go to the funeral of an uncle they never really liked. The focus is both on the discrepancy between their view of the uncle and others' views of him and on the relationship of the past to the present.

As in "The Dead," nothing much happens in this story except a routine, ritual meeting, common to Irish wakes, in which friends and relatives tell stories about the dead person. One of the brothers, Philly, who has come back home from the oil fields, is the most affected by the death, impressed by the respect everyone shows to his uncle's memory; Fonsie, who is confined to a wheelchair, is the most acerbic and sarcastic, sneering that everyone is respected for a short time after he or she dies because he or she does not have to be lived with anymore. Philly, who says he cannot work in the oil fields forever, wants to buy his uncle's farm, where his mother was raised, and the story ends as undramatically as it has proceeded throughout.

"THE BEGINNING OF AN IDEA"

As the title suggests, this story actually begins with the idea that dominates it: the first sentences of Eva Lindberg's notebook, which describe how on a hot day the corpse of Anton Chekhov was carried home to Moscow on an ice wagon with the word "Oysters" chalked on the side of it. McGahern's story then describes, almost word for word, a brief Chekhov story, entitled "Oysters," about a young boy and his father who, begging on the street, are given oysters to eat by prosperous diners, who laugh when the boy also tries to eat the shells.

Eva Lindberg gives up her work as a theater director and her affair with a married man to go to Spain to write an imaginary biography of Chekhov beginning with the oyster story and ending with the story of the oyster wagon. The lines in her journal haunt her and are repeated several times throughout the story. However, when she arrives at the isolated house where she will be staying, she cannot write, taking on routine translation jobs instead. The only person she sees is a local police officer named Manolo, who visits her daily. When she agrees to get him some contraceptives, which are illegal in Spain, Manolo and the police chief tell her she will go to jail unless she has sex with them. Repeating the Chekhov sentences in her mind like a mantra, she gives in and afterward packs up and leaves, feeling rage about her own foolishness. On the train she has the bitter taste of oysters in her mouth, and when a wagon passes she has a sudden desire to see if the word "Oysters" is chalked on it.

"ALL SORTS OF IMPOSSIBLE THINGS"

The central metaphor of this story is a brown hat, which has been worn by a teacher, James Sharkey, for the past twenty years. The central event is his friend Tom Lennon's facing exams to determine whether he is eligible to become a permanent instructor; Lennon's anxiety about the exams is complicated by the fact that he is frail and has a weak heart.

As is frequently the case in McGahern's short fiction, the story has a story within it: Twenty years previously, when Sharkey's hair began to fall out, he felt his life slipping away and was desperate to moor it to a woman; however, from the day the woman rejected him, he has never taken off his brown hat. When he is warned that he must take off his hat in church, he tells the priest that his encroaching baldness has the effect on him of *timor mortis*, the fear of death, so he has decided to cover it up.

However, the more serious sign of mortality in the story is Lennon's weak heart, for when he goes to take his exams, he falls dead. Sharkey feels a certain amazement that it is Lennon lying there and not he. He keeps Lennon's dog and after the funeral feels the same rush of feelings that occurred when his hair started to fall out. Now, however, he has a wild longing to throw away his hat, find a woman, and enter the dog in a race to win the silver cup. The story ends with his mind racing with a desire for "all sorts of impossible things."

OTHER MAJOR WORKS

LONG FICTION: *The Barracks*, 1963; *The Dark*, 1965; *The Leavetaking*, 1974, revised 1984; *The Pornographer*, 1979; *Amongst Women*, 1990.

PLAY: *The Power of Darkness*, pb. 1991.

BIBLIOGRAPHY

Banville, John. "Big News from Small Worlds." *The New York Review of Books* 40 (April 8, 1993): 22-24. In this extended review of McGahern's *The Collected Stories*, fellow novelist Banville discusses a characteristic often criticized in the stories—their floating quality, resulting from the fact that they take place in no discernible place or time period.

Bradbury, Nicola. "High Ground." In *Re-reading the Short Story*, edited by Clare Hanson. New York: Macmillan, 1989. Discusses "Parachutes" and "High Ground" as works that embody the short story's technique of being both involved and objectively distant at once; briefly discusses the historical and geographical contexts of McGahern's stories.

Brown, Terence. "John McGahern's *Nightlines:* Tone, Technique, and Symbol." In *The Irish Short Story*, edited by Patrick Rafroidi and Terence Brown. London: Colin, Smythe, 1979. Discusses McGahern's use of the Irish storytelling mode; argues that he tries to exploit symbolist possibilities in physical properties without resorting to the traditional symbols of church and religion.

_____. "Redeeming the Time: The Novels of John McGahern and John Banville." In *The British and Irish Novel Since 1960*, edited by James Acheson. New York: St. Martin's Press, 1991. Discusses McGahern's literary realism, which has allowed him to treat subjects that have always been taboo in Irish fiction; argues that in his novels the protagonist's world is explored with such obsessiveness that it reminds the reader of the short story.

Cahalan, James M. "Female and Male Perspectives on Growing Up Irish in Edna O'Brien, John McGahern and Brian Moore." *Colby Quarterly* 31 (March, 1995): 55-73. Focusing primarily on *The Dark* but providing a context for McGahern's short stories, Cahalan discusses McGahern's treatment of father-son relationships and the difficulty of trying to come of age in Ireland in the 1940's

Quinn, Antoinette. "Varieties of Disenchantment: Narrative Technique in John McGahern's Short Stories." *Journal of the Short Story in English* 13 (Autumn, 1989): 77-89. Describes McGahern's characters as obsessed with death but ill prepared for the infinite; says they are disappointed with the everyday, disillusioned by love, and in retreat from life.

Sampson, Denis. *Outstaring Nature's Eye: The Fiction of John McGahern.* Washington, D.C.: Catholic University of America Press, 1993.

Charles E. May

JOAQUIM MARIA MACHADO DE ASSIS

Born: Rio de Janeiro, Brazil; June 21, 1839
Died: Rio de Janeiro, Brazil; September 29, 1908

PRINCIPAL SHORT FICTION

Contos fluminenses, 1870
Histórias da meia-noite, 1873
Papéis avulsos, 1882
Histórias sem data, 1884
Várias histórias, 1896
Histórias românticas, 1937
The Psychiatrist and Other Stories, 1963
What Went on at the Baroness', 1963
The Devil's Church and Other Stories, 1977

OTHER LITERARY FORMS

Joaquim Maria Machado de Assis' first published works were poems and literary criticism, including

two frequently cited studies on Brazilian literature. He wrote comedies for the theater, was master of a journalistic genre known as the *crônica* (literally, "chronicle"), and carried on an extensive correspondence, since published. He is best known for his novels, especially the last five, for which *Memórias póstumas de Brás Cubas*, 1881 (*The Posthumous Memoirs of Brás Cubas*, 1951; better known as *Epitaph of a Small Winner*, 1952) and *Dom Casmurro*, 1899 (English translation, 1953) are probably the best known outside Brazil.

ACHIEVEMENTS

At the time of his death, in 1908, Joaquim Maria Machado de Assis was revered as Brazil's most important and influential man of letters, a distinction many critics feel he deserves. An innovator in such areas as the use of irony and of self-conscious but un-reliable narrator/protagonists, Machado de Assis was instrumental in leading Brazilian literature toward an appreciation of both technical sophistication and authenticity of expression. Although he did outstanding work in all the literary genres, including poetry, drama, translation, and critical theory, it was in narrative—the novel and short-story forms especially—that he achieved his greatest successes. His extraordinary work *Memórias póstumas de Brás Cubas* (1881; *The Posthumous Memoirs of Brás Cubas*, 1951; better known as *Epitaph of a Small Winner*, 1952) can, for example, be regarded as the first modern novel of either North or South America, while the text widely held to be his supreme achievement, *Dom Casmurro* (1900; English translation, 1953), ranks as one of the outstanding novels of its time. Perhaps even more brilliant as a writer of short fiction, however, Machado de Assis is credited with having originated the modern short-story form in Brazil, where tales such as "The Psychiatrist," "Midnight Mass," "A Singular Event," "The Companion," and "Dona Paula" are still judged to be masterpieces of his laconic, metaphoric art.

BIOGRAPHY

A lifelong resident of Rio de Janeiro, Joaquim Maria Machado de Assis was the son of a Portuguese mother and a mulatto father. Despite humble origins, epilepsy, and a speech defect, this self-taught intellectual not only attained the highest civil service position open to him but also founded the Brazilian Academy of Letters and served as its president until his death in 1908. While still living, Machado de Assis saw himself acknowledged as Brazil's greatest writer.

ANALYSIS

To some modern readers it may appear lamentable that Joaquim Maria Machado de Assis' works bear neither overt references to his racial heritage nor arguably even oblique ones. In this regard the Brazilian mulatto will be seen to be fully integrated with the concerns and priorities of the European-leaning dominant bourgeois society in late nineteenth century

Brazil. Nevertheless, Machado de Assis wrote on the fringes of "polite" society in a way that did not specifically derive from race, although a sense of social inferiority may well have contributed to his development of a cynical and biting stance toward the higher spiritual aspirations of the socially dominant Brazilian of his day. Specifically, this stance can be seen in his critical analyses of the ambiguities of the human soul (his "Jamesian" quality) and in his dissection of the pious self-sufficiency of the ignorant bourgeoisie (his "Flaubertian" and "Tolstoian" qualities). Like many of the great realists, Machado de Assis lends himself to a Lukacsian or Marxist analysis. His works bespeak, beneath the surface of the comings and goings of polite, ordered society, the tremendous conflicts, passions, and irreconcilable tensions of a society that fragments human experience and strives to metaphorize, in terms of a myth of spiritual transcendence, humans' carnal and materialistic nature. The patterned texture of an ordered society remains permanently at odds with fundamental aspects of the human soul which it chooses to ignore or metaphorize.

"A SINGULAR EVENT"

In this regard, Machado de Assis' story "Singular occurrência" ("A Singular Event") may be considered a metatext not only of the Brazilian's concern with ambiguities of the human experience that polite society cannot account for in terms of its own ideological construction of the world but also of his typically nineteenth century rhetorical strategies for the framing of ambiguous narrative. The story concerns the "singular event" in the amorous relations between a young married lawyer and a woman of unspecified occupation ("she was not a dressmaker, nor a landlady, nor a governess; eliminate the professions and you will get the idea") who becomes not only his devoted lover but also his "pupil" as well. The relationship described between the two goes beyond simply the sexual bond between a gentleman and his extramarital companion (a Latin American sociocultural cliché). The lawyer undertakes to form the woman, teaching her to read and to appreciate the "finer" things in life in the form of the high cultural artifacts of the period. Then one night the woman undertakes a sordid adventure with another man in such a way that it appears she is flaunting her perfidy. The idolizing lawyer is possessed with despair; yet she remains silent as to the reasons for her infidelity or at least for the "dramatization" of an apparent flagrant infidelity. The lovers are reconciled, she bears him a child who soon dies, he subsequently dies while out of town, and she spends the rest of her days conducting herself as a proper widow: When the story opens she is seen going to church clad in somber black.

The semantic contrasts put forth by the narrator's story of the beautiful "widow" and the singular event that colors it are the overt markers of the ambiguities of human nature involved: the intensely correct and well-bred man versus the woman of questionable occupation; her natural goodness versus his cultural refinement; her acquisition of ennobling culture versus subjugation to an all-consuming passion willing to accept even her putative fall from grace; the predictable patterns of behavior that characterize their socially acceptable liaison versus the traumatic and inexplicable flouting of the propriety that the woman seems to have gone to such lengths to accomplish; her refusal to give an accounting of her actions versus his need to reimpose the security of a proper relationship; and her past—particularly the singular event—versus her insistence on assuming the role of a dutiful widow.

There are many ways in which the foregoing semantic contrasts may be interpreted as they are given narrative form in the story. First, the woman's dramatic rebellion may be seen as a gesture of class differences: The socially inferior courtesan must affirm her status by reminding her lover of her sordid origin. Second, the singular event may be seen as a dramatic farce in a game of sexual politics: The woman ensures her dominance of her lover by threatening to deceive him with other men. Third, the relationship may be seen in feminist terms: the unstable and degrading situation of a woman who, despite the social acceptance of the man's extramarital affairs, is a social outcast, treated as an adoring child by the man-father who educates her to his own sociocultural norms. Fourth, in larger social terms, the story concerns exploitation, with sex in the guise of ennobling love the instrument of

dominance on both sides. Which of these interpretations is the "true meaning" of Machado de Assis' story is less important than the reader's understanding of the text's narrative strategies for arranging semantic contrasts and for underscoring the fundamental ambiguities of the human relations these ambiguities signal. "A Singular Event" is a metatext of Machado de Assis' fiction not so much because it typifies a prominent thematic preoccupation in the Brazilian's works but because it is paradigmatic of the narration of an event that is strikingly ambiguous and lacking in any reductionary meaning that will make either it or the narrative about it a transparent explanation of human experience.

The narrative framing of "A Singular Event" is the direct correlative, in terms of literary *écriture*, of the paradox of ambiguity: how to explain what has no coherent explanation. The reader reads a formal literary text (with all the external trappings of literature, from title to the inclusion in a self-identified literary work, to the complete graphic array of grammatological texts) which is ostensibly the verbatim transcription of a natural narrative. By natural narrative the reader understands a tale or a story told in an oral register that does not purport to be written literary narrative. (The classic examples are natural narrative introduced by the marker "That reminds me of the story about . . ."; a parallel marker that has been extensively literaturized is "Once upon a time. . . .") It is significant in this regard that Machado de Assis' interlocutors situate themselves in the street (a "natural" setting), that their narrative is triggered by the chance passing of the black-dressed mistress, and by the fact that only the "natural" interlocutors speak—that is, there is no extra-natural narrative commentary by Machado de Assis as either literary author or omniscient literary narrator. Moreover, the natural narrator narrates the "singular event" not as he saw or experienced it but as it was told to him by the distraught lawyer in his desperate attempt to understand the occurrence and to know how to handle it. All these layers are a sort of interpretational deferral of meaning of the event being related, to the extent that each can and does give the particulars but none can explain them—not the lawyer, not his confidant-turned-narrator, not the silent author. The narrator can say only, "I have invented nothing. It's the pure truth."

By contrast, the one person who _can_ explain things, the woman, not only refuses to do so in the real-life world posited by the story but also fails to have any direct or indirect speaking role in the natural narrative transmitted by the literary text (her lover does, as he is paraphrased repeatedly by the narrator). From the point of verisimilitude, one can say this silence derives from the narrator's opportunity to interview the woman. In terms of the semiological strategies of the literary text, however, her lack of voice in the story, like Machado de Assis' failure to exercise the authorial prerogative he uses elsewhere in his fiction to comment on events or others' natural narratives about those events, can be seen only to reinforce the image in the story of ambiguous, enigmatic events that are in a certain sense semantic voids. One can talk about them, with extensive reference to concrete particulars, but one can never explain them in a way that will satisfy the driving need to understand complex human experience.

OTHER MAJOR WORKS

LONG FICTION: _Resurreicão_, 1872; _A mão e a luva_, 1874 (_The Hand and the Glove_, 1970); _Helena_, 1876; _Yayá Garcia_, 1878 (English translation, 1976); _Memórias póstumas de Brás Cubas_, 1881 (_The Posthumous Memoirs of Brás Cubas_, 1951; better known as _Epitaph of a Small Winner_, 1952); _Quincas Borba_, 1891 (_Philosopher or Dog?_, 1954; also translated as _The Heritage of Quincas Borba_, 1954); _Dom Casmurro_, 1899 (English translation, 1953); _Esaú e Jacob_, 1904 (_Esau and Jacob_, 1965); _Memorial de Ayres_, 1908 (_Counselor Ayres' Memorial_, 1972).

PLAYS: _Desencantos_, pb. 1861; _Quase ministro_, pb. 1864; _Os deuses de casaca_, pb. 1866; _Tu só, tu, puro amor_, pb. 1880; _Teatro_, pb. 1910.

POETRY: _Crisálidas_, 1864; _Falenas_, 1870; _Americanas_, 1875; _Poesias completas_, 1901.

NONFICTION: _Páginas recolhidas (contos ensaios, crônicas)_, 1899; _Relíquias de Casa Velha (contos crônicas, comédias)_, 1906; _Crítica_, 1910; _A semana_, 1910; _Crítica por Machado de Assis_, 1924; _Crítica

literária, 1937; _Crítica teatral_, 1937; _Correspondência_, 1938.

MISCELLANEOUS: _Outras relíquias_, 1908; _Obra completa_, 1959.

BIBLIOGRAPHY

Caldwell, Helen. _The Brazilian Othello of Machado de Assis_. Berkeley: University of California Press, 1960. The first book-length study in English to deal with Machado de Assis. Focuses on his masterpiece _Dom Casmurro_ and shows how Machado apparently utilized a modified version of _Othello_'s plot structure. Also discusses numerous other examples of the influence William Shakespeare had on Machado de Assis' work. Caldwell was the first critic to argue that the novel's heroine, Capitu, was not necessarily guilty of adultery, as generations of readers had assumed.

_____. _Machado de Assis: The Brazilian Master and His Novels_. Berkeley: University of California Press, 1970. A concise survey of Machado de Assis' nine novels and his various narrative techniques. Also includes good discussions of his primary themes, a useful bibliography, and some comments on his plays, poems, and short stories.

Dixon, Paul. _Retired Dreams: Dom Casmurro, Myth and Modernity_. West Lafayette, Ind.: Purdue University Press, 1989. Though he limits his critical discussion to _Dom Casmurro_, Dixon leads his reader to see Machado de Assis as cultivating a radically new style of writing, one that featured ambiguity as the most "realistic" aspect of language and that conceived of language as a system of tropes only arbitrarily connected to physical reality. Dixon also suggests that Machado de Assis was critical of his society's patriarchal codes and that, as evidenced in the relationship between the novel's two major characters (Bento and Capitu), he implies the virtues inherent in a more matriarchal approach to sociopolitical organization.

Douglas, Ellen H. "Machado de Assis' 'A Cartomante': Modern Parody and the Making of a 'Brazilian' Text." _MLN_ 113 (December, 1998): 1036-1055. Discusses the story's introduction of an act of modern parody; argues that this act of parody occurs in its intertextual opening, which features a reference to William Shakespeare's *Hamlet*.

Fischer, Sibylle Maria. "Geography and Representation in Machado de Assis." *Modern Language Quarterly* 55 (June, 1994): 191-213. Discusses geography and representation in the fiction of Machado de Assis. Argues that his narratives respond to the interplay of three factors: a postcolonial nationalism with a strong desire for self-representation, a displaced "high culture" maintained through continuous transfer of literary and cultural products from Europe to Brazil, and social and economic structures unlike those of any relevant European country.

Fitz, Earl E. *Machado de Assis*. Boston: Twayne, 1989. The first English-language book to examine all aspects of Machado de Assis' literary life (his novels, short stories, poetry, theater, critical theory, translations, and nonfiction work). Also includes sections on his life, his place in Brazilian and world literature, his style, and his themes. Features an annotated bibliography and argues that Machado de Assis—largely because of his ideas about the connection between language, meaning, and reality—is best appreciated as a modernist.

Gledson, John. *The Deceptive Realism of Machado de Assis: A Dissenting Interpretation of "Dom Casmurro."* Liverpool: Francis Cairns, 1984. Focusing on what the majority of critics have judged to be Machado de Assis' greatest novel, *Dom Casmurro*, Gledson argues against interpreting the author either as a modernist or as a precursor of the New Novel in Latin America and in favor of regarding him as a master (if unique) realist. Sees him as a subtle and artful stylist whose work accurately reflects the prevailing social and political tensions of his time.

Graham, Richard, ed. *Machado de Assis: Reflections on a Brazilian Master Writer*. Austin: University of Texas Press, 1999. Part of the Critical Reflections on Latin America series, this volume has essays by John Gledson, Daphne Patai, and Sidney Chalhoub.

Jackson, K. David. "The Brazilian Short Story." In *The Cambridge History of Latin American Literature*. Vol. 3, edited by Robert González Echevarria and Enrique Pupo-Walker. Cambridge, England: Cambridge University Press, 1996. Discusses Machado de Assis' technique of suggestions and implication within an ironic frame of reference. Suggests that Machado de Assis' humor and irony underline the futility of human conflict in a world in which the nature of reality is illusory. Points out that he eschews naturalist explanations and uses complex narrative strategies.

Neto, José Raimundo Maia. *Machado de Assis, the Brazilian Pyrrhonian*. West Lafayette, Ind.: Purdue University Press, 1994. Part 1 explores Machado de Assis' first phase (1861-1878)—from writing essays to stories to his first novels. Part 2 concentrates on his second phase (1879-1908), with separate chapters on *The Posthumous Memoirs of Brás Cubas*, *Dom Casmurro*, and later fiction. Includes detailed notes and bibliography.

Nist, John. "The Short Stories of Machado de Assis." *Arizona Quarterly* 24 (Spring, 1968): 5-22. Nist hails Machado de Assis as not only a great novelist but also perhaps the outstanding prose fiction writer of either North or South America during the late nineteenth and early twentieth centuries. Surveys a number of his most celebrated stories, including "The Psychiatrist," "A Woman's Arms," and "Midnight Mass." Nist also notes the economy of means that marks the author's style, the ironic and philosophic base of his fiction, his alleged "pessimism," and the modernist ethos inherent in his ambiguous vision of human reality.

Nunes, Maria Luisa. *The Craft of an Absolute Winner: Characterization and Naratology in the Novels of Machado de Assis*. Westport, Conn.: Greenwood Press, 1983. An excellent study of Machado de Assis' novelistic techniques, his skill at characterization, and his primary themes. Offers good summaries of his novels and shows both how they compare to one another and how their author grew in sophistication and skill. Argues that the essence of Machado de Assis' genius, like that of all truly great writers, lies in his singular ability to create powerful and compelling characters.

Schwarz, Roberto. "The Historical Meaning of Cruelty in Machado de Assis," translated by S. E. Wilson. *Modern Language Quarterly* 57 (June, 1996): 165-179. Discusses the historical meaning of cruelty as represented in Machado de Assis' *Memórias Póstumas de Brás Cubas.*

David W. Foster, updated by Earl E. Fitz

ARTHUR MACHEN

Arthur Llewellyn Jones
Born: Caerleon-on-Usk, Wales; March 3, 1863
Died: Beaconsfield, Buckinghamshire, England; December 15, 1947

PRINCIPAL SHORT FICTION

The Chronicle of Clemendy: Or, The History of the IX Joyous Journeys, 1888
The Great God Pan, 1890 (novella)
"The Great God Pan" and "The Inmost Light," 1894 (novellas)
The Three Impostors: Or, The Transmutations, 1895
The House of Souls, 1906
The Angels of Mons, The Bowmen, and Other Legends of the War, 1915
The Children of the Pool and Other Stories, 1936
The Cosy Room and Other Stories, 1936
Holy Terrors, 1946
Tales of Horror and the Supernatural, 1948
Ritual and Other Stories, 1992

OTHER LITERARY FORMS

Early in his career Arthur Machen translated several works from French, including *The Memoirs of Jacques Casanova* (1894). His major novel is *The Hill of Dreams* (1907). Autobiographical volumes include *Far Off Things* (1922) and *Things Near and Far* (1923). Machen's highly readable essays are collected in such volumes as *Dog and Duck* (1924).

ACHIEVEMENTS

In recognition of his literary accomplishments, Arthur Machen received a civil-list pension from King George V in 1933. Over the years several societies of enthusiastic readers have been formed to reprint Machen's works and advance his reputation.

BIOGRAPHY

Arthur Llewellyn Jones was born on the border between England and Wales in the village of Caerleon-on-Usk on March 3, 1863, the son of an Anglican clergyman, John Edward Jones. "Machen," Jones's mother's name, was legally taken by his father a few years later to fulfill the requirements of an inheritance. The childhood he spent in this remote countryside, which still bore the traces of ancient Roman occupation, would remain with him all his life.

Having foiled his parents' plans for a formal education, Machen moved to London at the age of eighteen, earning a bare subsistence as a journalist and translator. His first important literary effort was *The Great God Pan* (1890), a controversial novella of supernatural horror that was to be followed by many more works in the same vein. Machen wrote his most important novel, *The Hill of Dreams*, during the mid-1890's but was not able to find a publisher until about ten years later. Referring to Daniel Defoe's famous novel, Machen described his own effort as "a *Robinson Crusoe* of the soul," and in it he described the agonizing experiences of a sensitive writer much like him in the vast, impersonal metropolis of London.

Machen had made a name for himself as a novelist and short-story writer, but his income was negligible. Although he never quite gave up fiction, he made a living as an actor, journalist, and essayist during the latter part of his life. Machen died in Beaconsfield, Buckinghamshire, on December 15, 1947.

ANALYSIS

Almost all of Arthur Machen's works—fiction and nonfiction alike—are touched by his sense of the marvelous, his belief that another, more meaningful world lies behind the facade of routine, everyday sense experience. Sometimes this other world is one of horror—as in the nightmarish events described in "The White People"—and sometimes it is a world of wonder and joy. As a character in his story "The Red Hand" puts it, "There are sacraments of evil as well as of good about us, and we live and move to my belief in an unknown world, a place where there are caves and shadows and dwellers in twilights."

In many cases Machen's protagonists use drugs or other medical means to pierce the veil of so-called reality. A theory that Machen dramatized in many of his works—that the folklore of elves and fairies has its origin in the survival of a primitive dwarf race driven underground by the invading Celts—represents an extension of this belief. His interests and subject matter place Machen outside the realistic tradition of British fiction but mark him as an important and highly influential figure in the development of modern fantasy.

Machen's writings defy easy classification. His best fictional writings inhabit a middle ground between the short story and the novel; his works in the former category are often developed with the indirection and leisurely pace readers associate with the latter. One important volume, *The Three Impostors*, incorporates several stories into a larger and more complex framework. In addition, many of Machen's apparently fictional works have the expository tone of nonfiction, and a number of the shorter pieces he wrote toward the end of his career can be read as either stories or essays.

THE GREAT GOD PAN

Although critics have pointed out its crudity, this early novella is the work most modern readers associate with Machen's name. It introduced many of its author's themes and methods, and despite its wayward approach and its reliance on the most outlandish coincidences, it remains a gripping if disquieting reading experience. The story is told from several points of view but deals essentially with an unortho-

dox brain operation that will allow a young woman to "see" the Great God Pan. Although Pan is ostensibly the Greek god of pastures and flocks, in this case he represents the hideous reality that lies behind our day-to-day world. The patient—Mary Vaughan—ultimately dies, but not before giving birth to a daughter. It is this daughter who, years later, is the cause of a series of suicides in London society. It turns out that she is the daughter of Mary Vaughan and Pan and, when confronted, commits suicide herself and regresses through a series of devolutionary steps to a kind of primeval slime.

THE THREE IMPOSTORS

Machen's 1895 collection works several stories into a larger framework that defies logical summary but that clearly conveys his belief in a reality underlying the everyday. The stories involve or are told to one or the other of two friends, Dyson and Phillipps, the former a romantic dreamer and unpublished writer and the latter a pragmatic scientist, the two having met in a London tobacco shop. Aside from the work's obvious horror, it is also surprisingly humorous.

In "Adventure of the Gold Tiberius" Dyson recovers an extraordinarily rare coin after observing a violent pursuit. A young woman tells Phillipps the "Novel of the Black Seal," in which famous scientist Dr. Gregg pursues the "little people," much to his subsequent regret. In "Novel of the Iron Maid," an acquaintance describes to Dyson how a third party is beset by his own instrument of torture. "Novel of the White Powder" is related to Dyson by a young woman (who seems somehow familiar to the reader) and concerns a medical prescription that has unluckily degenerated into a potion that witches once took at their Sabbaths. Through all these strange adventures passes an enigmatic figure, a "young man with spectacles," who is somehow the key to the entire series of events.

The Everyman edition of this intriguing work (Rutland, Vt.: Tuttle, 1995) contains an introduction by critic David Trotter as well as other valuable supplementary material. Two of the embedded stories, "Novel of the Black Seal" and "Novel of the White Powder," are regarded as classics of fantasy and are often reprinted individually under shortened titles.

"THE WHITE PEOPLE"

Originally published in 1899, "The White People" is regarded not only as a high point in Machen's writing career but also as one of the best supernatural stories ever written. The heart of the story, "The Green Book," is framed by a discussion between two characters about the nature of evil. One of the two, Ambrose, announces a central belief of Machen's, that "Sorcery and sanctity . . . are the only realities. Each is an ecstasy, a withdrawal from the common life."

"The Green Book" itself is the diary of a young girl and recounts in naïve, largely unpunctuated fashion the girl's "ecstasy," her initiation into Satanism by her nurse. Machen incorporated both authentic and imaginary folklore into the girl's account and wrote it in a run-on "stream-of-consciousness" style that would later be identified with novelist James Joyce. Looking far beyond the logical (and thus inadequate) utterances of Ambrose and his friend, this fragment illustrates literature's ability to create a viable world outside the confines of realism.

"THE BOWMEN"

"The Bowmen" became Machen's most famous story during World War I. It originally appeared in the London newspaper *The Evening News* for September 29, 1914, and professed—in an age-old fictional ploy—to be a true account of extraordinary events. During the recent Battle of Mons, Machen said, an inadvertent reference to St. George had resulted in the appearance of phantom bowmen in shining armor who had attacked the Germans. The implication was that the British patron saint of soldiers had summoned the archers from the Battle of Agincourt (1415), where they had saved the day for the British, to fight once again for their descendants. Almost immediately, "witnesses" stepped forward to testify to the reality of these and similar events. Although Machen made it clear after the fact that his brief tale was fiction, he was inspired to write further works on the same theme. These were collected as *The Angel of Mons, The Bowmen, and Other Legends of the War*. The material of these stories subsequently became part of the folklore of Britain's wartime experience.

"N"

"N" is Machen's most important later story, a leisurely and elegiacal variation on one of his favorite themes. It originally appeared in *The Cosy Room and Other Stories*, a collection of what were otherwise reprints. The story is set in the London suburb of Stoke Newington and concerns a small group of friends who discover through their idle talk that an interpenetration of two worlds has taken place. This phenomenon results in stories of an unusually pleasant if confoundingly elusive garden somewhere in the area. Machen even coined a term, "perichoresis," to describe the phenomenon. "N" has been criticized as somewhat diffuse, but it is hard to imagine that a more tightly developed story could have conveyed the fragile wonder that Machen produces in this work. Another of Machen's works, his novel *The Green Round* (1933), develops some of the same material, although not so memorably.

OTHER MAJOR WORKS

LONG FICTION: *The Hill of Dreams*, 1907; *The Great Return*, 1915; *The Terror*, 1917; *The Secret Glory*, 1922 (complete edition 1998); *The Shining Pyramid*, 1923; *A Fragment of Life*, 1928; *The Green Round*, 1933.

NONFICTION: *The Anatomy of Tobacco*, 1884; *Strange Roads*, 1923; *The Canning Wonder*, 1925; *Notes and Queries*, 1926; *Hieroglyphics: A Note upon Ecstasy in Literature*, 1902; *Far Off Things*, 1922; *Things Near and Far*, 1923; *Dog and Duck*, 1924; *The London Adventure*, 1924; *Dreads and Drolls*, 1926; *The Secret of the Sangraal*, 1995.

TRANSLATIONS: *The Heptameron: Or, Tales and Novels of Marguerite, Queen of Navarre*, 1886; *The Memoirs of Jacques Casanova*, 1894.

BIBLIOGRAPHY

Cavaliero, Glen. "Watchers on the Threshold." In *The Supernatural and English Fiction*. Oxford: Oxford University Press, 1995. Cavaliero stresses the importance of landscape and cityscape in Machen's works as well as the sexual content of his stories. Like most commentators, he praises "The White People" in particular.

Joshi, S. T. "Arthur Machen: The Mystery of the Universe." In *The Weird Tale*. Austin: University of Texas Press, 1990. Taking a largely negative view of Machen's work, Joshi dismisses the author's philosophy and his narrative skill. He observes that, with few exceptions, Machen's best works were written during the decade 1889-1899.

Nash, Berta. "Arthur Machen Among the Arthurians." In *Minor British Novelists*, edited by Charles Alva Hoyt. Carbondale: Southern Illinois University Press, 1967. Examines Machen's use of the Matter of Arthur, particularly the Holy Grail, which Nash believes functioned for Machen as a symbol of humankind. Despite the title of the volume, Machen's short as well as his long works are considered.

Reynolds, Aidan, and William Charlton. *Arthur Machen: A Short Account of His Life and Work*. Oxford: Caermaen, 1988. As the standard biography of Machen, this volume is not likely to be surpassed. Originally published in 1963, it includes illustrations, notes, brief bibliographies, and an index.

Sweetser, Wesley D. *Arthur Machen*. Boston: Twayne, 1964. Sweetser's study remains the most complete book on Machen, summarizing his life and discussing almost all his vast production. Includes useful (although now dated) primary and secondary bibliographies.

Valentine, Mark. *Arthur Machen*. Bridgend, Mid Glamorgan, Wales: Seren, 1995. A sympathetic introduction to Machen, briefer than Sweetser's but taking advantage of more recent scholarship and taking issue with Joshi on several points. Includes illustrations and a select bibliography but no index.

Wagenknecht, Edward. "Arthur Machen." In *Seven Masters of Supernatural Fiction*. New York: Greenwood Press, 1991. This survey by an objective critic gives fair consideration to Machen's later, lesser-known stories and novels as well as his more familiar works.

Grove Koger

REGINALD McKNIGHT

Born: Fürstenfeldbruck, Germany; 1956

PRINCIPAL SHORT FICTION
Uncle Moustapha's Eclipse, 1988
The Kind of Light That Shines on Texas, 1992
White Boys, 1998

OTHER LITERARY FORMS

Reginald McKnight has written one novel, *I Get on the Bus* (1990). He has also edited two collections of folk wisdom, *African American Wisdom* (1994) and *Wisdom of the African World* (1996).

ACHIEVEMENTS

Reginald McKnight is the recipient of a National Endowment for the Arts fellowship, an O. Henry Award, the Kenyon Review Award for excellence (twice), a PEN/Hemingway Special Citation, a Pushcart prize, the Drue Heinz Literature Prize, the Watson Foundation Fellowship, the Whiting Writers' Award, and the Bernice M. Slote Award.

BIOGRAPHY

Reginald McKnight was born in Fürstenfeldbruck, Germany, to military parents in 1956. His father Frank was a U.S. Air Force noncommissioned officer, and his mother Pearl was a dietician. Because of his military background, McKnight has lived all over the world, moving a total of forty-three times. After a brief stint in the U.S. Marine Corps, McKnight earned an associate degree in anthropology (1978) from Pike Peak Community College and a B.A. in African literature (1981) from Colorado College. He received the Thomas J. Watson Fellowship to study folklore and literature in West Africa, so he spent a year teaching and writing in Senegal. In 1987, he earned an M.A. in English with an emphasis in creative writing from the University of Denver. McKnight has taught at Arapahoe Community College, the University of Denver, and the University of Maryland at College Park. He married Michele Davis in 1985 and had two daughters.

ANALYSIS

Reginald McKnight's work is a refreshing change from much of the black protest literature of the 1970's and 1980's. While white people are often presented as unpleasant, annoying, and mean-spirited, they are seldom presented as outrightly diabolical. McKnight deliberately refrains from political statement in his fiction, believing that art has the higher purpose of bringing a sense of joy to the reader, the type of joy that makes one think that "life is deep, limitless, and meaningful." Yet he does not believe that art should be harmless. "It should get under your skin," he says. McKnight refuses to accept or to promote any singular concept of black identity; instead, he respects the diversity of black experience found in the United States and elsewhere.

Like many writers, McKnight draws heavily on personal experience to find subject matter for his stories. For example, several stories found in his collections are set in West Africa with an anthropologist as the narrator. Other stories include the painful experience of being one of a handful of black children in a school. His experience in the military is also woven into several stories. His stories, however, are no mere transcription of personal experience. He is equally successful in portraying the experiences of black working-class males.

Many of McKnight's stories are boldly experimental in point of view, tone, style, and concept. His stories set in West Africa are particularly notable for their non-western philosophical views and the incorporation of the fantastic. For example, in "The Homunculus: A Novel in One Chapter" (found in *The Kind of Light That Shines on Texas*), the protagonist is a young writer in a fairy-tale-like place who becomes so consumed with his writing that it becomes a

Reginald McKnight (©Miriam Berkley)

flesh and blood likeness of himself. McKnight's work is characterized by his successful, convincing use of multiple voices.

"UNCLE MOUSTAPHA'S ECLIPSE"

"Uncle Moustapha's Eclipse," the title story of McKnight's first collection, is narrated in the broken English of a Senegalese interpreter working for an American anthropologist living in Africa. This story has the feel of a folktale; that is, it is clearly meant to teach a lesson. Uncle Moustapha is a successful peanut farmer, who lives in a small African village with his three wives and seven children. His only problem is that he constantly thinks of death; he would not have this problem if he had not adopted the white man's tradition of celebrating his birthday. On the eve of his sixtieth birthday (or at least what he has designated as his birthday), he goes to bed anticipating an eclipse of the sun, which has been predicted for the next day. On the following morning, a white scientist arrives to set up his viewing equipment on Uncle Moustapha's land.

The scientist warns Moustapha not to view the eclipse directly with naked eyes. At first, Moustapha complies and views the eclipse properly through the scientific equipment. However, he quickly becomes overjoyed with the eclipse, believing that it was sent to him as a gift from Allah and his ancestors. Moustapha runs to fetch his favorite wife, Fatima. They rush together to the baobab tree, which is believed to house the spirits of their ancestors. After a brief prayer, Moustapha experiences a rush of heightened sensory perceptions. He turns to stare at the eclipse with his eyes wide open, so that he can see "it all in supreme detail." As he returns home, the world seems more beautiful to him than ever before, except for a black shape that begins to flicker on and off in his left eye. The ending of the story is ambiguous. It is not clear whether he goes blind or it is death that is finally coming to Uncle Moustapha. However, he has no regrets because he has seen "what no other living soul has seen today." Clearly, he does not believe that going blind or even dying is too great a price to pay for such a magnificent experience.

"THE KIND OF LIGHT THAT SHINES ON TEXAS"

In this O. Henry Award-winning story, McKnight explores the ambivalence of friendship, not just between blacks and whites but also between blacks and blacks. Clinton Oates, the narrator, is one of three black children in his sixth-grade class in Waco, Texas. Oates, who is eager to prove himself inoffensive to whites, feels embarrassed by the presence of Marvin Pruitt, a black boy who fulfills most negative black stereotypes. Pruitt "smelled bad, was at least two grades behind, was hostile, dark skinned, homely, close-mouthed." Pruitt sleeps away most of the school day; the other black child is a large, passive girl who refuses to speak. This class is full of older children, including a sixteen-year-old white bully, Kevin Oakley, who is just looking for a reason to fight with Oates. One day, their coach (who probably wants to see Oates get hurt) singles out the two boys for a game of "murder ball," using two hard-pumped volley balls instead of the usual red rubber balls. Completely in fair play, Oates hits Oakley square in the face, causing a nosebleed and the boy's humiliation. Shortly afterward, in the locker room,

Oakley threatens to attack Oates after school. Oates sees Marvin Pruitt, an innocent bystander, and asks, "How come you after me and not him?" Oates escapes from Oakley that afternoon by getting on the bus early, but he cannot escape the implications of what he had said in the locker room. Clearly, Oates meant that Pruitt deserved to be picked on or beaten up because he so neatly fit all the negative stereotypes of blacks. The next morning, Oakley predictably picks a fight with Oates. Surprisingly, Pruitt intervenes on Oates's behalf, with a disdainful "git out of my way, boy." This action shows that Pruitt is, without a doubt, morally superior to Oates, the nice young black who is only too eager to do his "tomthing." The reader is left to believe that Pruitt knows exactly what Oates had meant in the locker room, but he still rises above this black-on-black racial insult. While never exactly friends, the black boys' relationship proves that blood is, indeed, thicker than water.

"QUITTING SMOKING"

This story, also found in *The Kind of Light That Shines on Texas*, is narrated by a working-class black man, Scott Winters, who lives with his white lover Anna. Their relationship does not work, partly because Scott cannot stop smoking, partly because race becomes a barrier, and partly because Scott cannot bring himself to share his deepest secret with her. Scott began smoking in his late teens to hide the smell of reefer from his parents. He discovers that he likes the buzz from cigarettes better than any other "high." When he meets Anna—a vegetarian, health nut, and feminist—he naturally and easily loses his desire to smoke and to eat meat. One night, Anna confides to him an incident of acquaintance rape. This confidence immediately reminds him of a time in his teens that he and three other males witnessed the abduction of a woman into a car. The woman struggled and screamed for help, but none of the young men intervened on her behalf. Nagged by this memory, Scott goes out and buys a pack of cigarettes. What follows is a story of cigarette addiction that anyone who has ever smoked will find familiar. He continues to sneak out for smokes in the middle of the night. He begins to keep an arsenal of cover-up supplies in his truck—gum, toothpaste, mouthwash, deodorant, and air freshener. Cigarettes become his secret infidelity. When Anna confronts him with a cigarette she has found, Scott vows to quit but does not. Scott's deeper problem is that he cannot bring himself to confess to Anna what he had allowed to happen to the woman who had been abducted and perhaps raped or killed. One night, he makes elaborate preparations for this confession; he cleans the house, makes dinner, and buys wine and flowers. Scott tentatively approaches the subject by saying, "I wouldn't be surprised if you hated men." Anna, who has grown distant for other reasons, counters, "I'm surprised I don't hate black men. The guy who raped me was black." Scott, who feels this racial insult as an almost physical injury, immediately packs his bags and walks out the door. Both partners are guilty of erecting barriers that destroy the relationship, but only Anna chose to use race as a weapon.

"THE WHITE BOYS"

This story opens with yet another move for a black military family. The Oates are, in many ways, a typical black middle-class family. Both parents are strict, even to the point of violence. Two particularly nasty beatings of the young protagonist Derrick are recounted in this narrative. His two siblings Dean and Alva are spared similar beatings, mostly because they are less conspicuous or odd than Derrick. Both parents greatly fear that one of their children will bring shame or trouble to their home. They know, only too well, that white people will conjure up the worst possible racial stereotypes at the slightest provocation. The day after they move in, Derrick provides this type of provocation by innocently scooping snow off of his neighbor's car. The neighbor, Sergeant Hooker, vehemently hates blacks, following his childhood experience of growing up in a predominantly black neighborhood in Baltimore. His mother, with whom he no longer communicates, even married a black man. Ironically, Hooker's best friend from childhood was also black. Furious over the Oates's moving next door, Hooker sets out to instill racial hatred equal to his own in his three sons. The youngest son Garrett is determined to hate Derrick, but a friendship begins to grow between the two boys. When Hooker discovers

this friendship, he devises a diabolical scheme to scare Derrick away permanently. He plans to take Derrick and his three sons on a fishing trip, during which time the four whites will stage a mock lynching of Derrick. Garrett, unable to confront his father or to warn Derrick, comes up with his own scheme to save his friend. On the Friday before this fateful weekend, he calls Derrick a nigger, not just once but repeatedly. His act destroys their friendship (exactly what his father wanted) but saves Derrick from a far more horrific experience.

In an interview, McKnight has said that the stories in *White Boys* should produce this response: "It's too bad that blacks and whites don't get along very well today." This response is exactly what this story produces. There is every reason except race that the Hookers and Oateses should have been good friends and neighbors.

OTHER MAJOR WORKS

LONG FICTION: *I Get on the Bus*, 1990.

EDITED TEXTS: *African American Wisdom*, 1994; *Wisdom of the African World*, 1996.

BIBLIOGRAPHY

McKnight, Reginald. "An Interview with Reginald McKnight." Interview by Renée Olander. *The Writer's Chronicle* 3 (February, 2000): 5-14. McKnight discusses literary influences, his writing philosophies, the use of the word "nigger," and two of his works: *I Get on the Bus* and *White Boys*.

_____. "We Are, in Fact, a Civilization." Interview by William Walsh. *Kenyon Review* 16, no. 2 (Spring, 1994): 27-42. McKnight discusses his background, writing style, and use of first- and third-person narrative.

Megan, Carolyn. "New Perceptions on Rhythm in Reginald McKnight's Fiction." *Kenyon Review* 16, no. 2 (Spring, 1994): 56-62. Megan discusses the importance of sound and rhythm in McKnight's writing process. Her discussion includes the emotional responses evoked by this rhythm.

Nancy Sherrod

JAMES ALAN McPHERSON

Born: Savannah, Georgia; September 16, 1943

PRINCIPAL SHORT FICTION

Hue and Cry, 1969

Elbow Room, 1977

OTHER LITERARY FORMS

With Miller Williams, James Alan McPherson has edited and contributed essays and a short story to a volume of essays, stories, poems, and pictures entitled *Railroad: Trains and Train People in American Culture* (1976). After 1969, McPherson also contributed several essays to *The Atlantic Monthly* and to *Reader's Digest*. *Crabcakes* (1998), a volume of meditations on many topics, was McPherson's first book after the short-story collection *Elbow Room*. *Fathering Daughters: Reflections by Men* (1998), edited by McPherson and DeWitt Henry, is a collection of essays on the father-daughter bond.

ACHIEVEMENTS

Even though James Alan McPherson has not published many collections of short fiction, his adroit characterizations and his strong sense of place have attracted many readers and influenced a number of writers. His work has been anthologized and has appeared in *The Atlantic Monthly, Playboy, The New York Times Magazine, The Harvard Advocate, Reader's Digest, The Iowa Review, The Massachusetts Review*, and *Ploughshares*. His association with the Writer's Workshop at the University of Iowa and his teaching of courses in fiction writing have given him a forum from which he influences beginning writers across the United States. Though earlier critics noted similarities between McPherson and other African American writers such as James Baldwin and Ralph Ellison, critical attention was later placed on his unique use of language and his ability to create a mythical dimension to his stories. Because of this, his fiction has begun to be examined in a much wider context than previously.

The story "Gold Coast" won the prize for fiction awarded by *The Atlantic Monthly* in 1968. McPherson won the literature award of the National Institute of Arts and Letters in 1970, and he was the recipient of a John Simon Guggenheim Memorial Foundation Fellowship in 1972. *Elbow Room* won the 1978 Pulitzer Prize for fiction and was nominated for the National Book Award. In 1981, his writing achievements earned him a MacArthur Fellowship.

BIOGRAPHY

James Alan McPherson earned degrees from Morris Brown College (B.A., 1965), Harvard Law School (LL.B., 1968), and the Iowa Writers' Workshop (M.F.A., 1971). He has taught at the University of Iowa, the University of California, Harvard University, Morgan State University, and the University of Virginia. Besides being a contributing editor of *The Atlantic Monthly*, he held jobs ranging from stock clerk to newspaper reporter. In the early 1980's, McPherson began teaching fiction writing in the Writers' Workshop at the University of Iowa in Iowa City. After writing *Elbow Room*, McPherson primarily focused on nonfiction essays that center on the need for African Americans to help define the cultural realities of contemporary American life. His first book in twenty years, *Crabcakes* (1998), focuses on his ultimate understanding of what makes people human.

ANALYSIS

James Alan McPherson is one of the writers of fiction who form the second major phase of modern writing about the African American experience. Indebted, like all of his generation, to the groundbreaking and theme-setting work of Richard Wright, Ellison, and Baldwin, McPherson shies away from doctrinaire argumentation about racial issues. Rather, he uses these issues to give his work a firmly American aura, which includes a preoccupation not only with what it means to be a black person in modern America but also with how the individual responds to a culture that often is plagued by subtle and not-so-subtle racial discriminations. Hence, there are times when blackness becomes for McPherson a metaphor for the alienation experienced by the individual in contemporary society.

This comprehensive concern with American culture informs all of McPherson's work, including those pieces that are included in the prose and poetry collection compiled by McPherson and Miller Williams entitled *Railroad: Trains and Train People in American Culture*. A celebration, a lament, and a plea, this volume deals with the passing of the great era of passenger railcar service in the United States. To McPherson, the liberating motion integral to the railroad is important, but so is the sense of place and time that builds for his characters much of their sense of self. McPherson's characters are often confined by the conventions of locale, yet McPherson is not a regional writer in the usual sense of the word; he can bring to life stories set in Tennessee, Virginia, Boston, Chicago, or London.

Because of the tension in this body of work between the individual and the community, McPherson's people often feel alienated, lonely, and unable fully to reach or to maintain contact with acquaintances, friends, families, or lovers. Yet, such isolation may lead to a character's growth to near-tragic stature. The integrity of the individual is thus asserted even while a narrator may worry over the deep inability of any person to penetrate into the heart and mind of another. Such recognitions contribute to the sympathetic portrayal even of unpromising characters. It should be noted that the reader is not given solutions in McPherson's fiction, only access to degrees of awareness of the mysteries of race, sexuality, identity, and love. Reading McPherson, a reader may be reminded of Baldwin's presentation of agonizingly complex racial and sexual problems, of Saul Bellow's portrayal of characters battling absurdity and despair, and of the struggle of characters, both in Baldwin and in Bellow, toward the ameliorating but no less mysterious experience of love.

"Gold Coast"

McPherson's first volume of short fiction, *Hue and Cry*, is an often-grim affair, containing stories of loneliness, destitution, defeat, sexual alienation, and racial tension. A prime example of this early work is "Gold Coast." The narrator of this story is an "apprentice janitor" in a hotel near Harvard Square in Boston, a hotel that has seen better days and is now populated with aging singles or couples who are almost as disengaged from the mainstream of Boston life as is the superintendent of the building, James Sullivan. Listening to Sullivan and observing the people in the apartments, the narrator, Robert, seeks to gather information for the stories and books he hopes to write. For Robert, being a janitor is in some ways a whim; in addition to gleaning experiential details from rubbish bins, he is constructing his life along romantic lines. Hence, Robert notes that, almost nightly,

I drifted off to sleep lulled by sweet anticipation of that time when my potential would suddenly be realized and there would be capsule biographies of my life on dust jackets of many books, all proclaiming: "He knew life on many levels. From shoeshine boy, free-lance waiter, 3rd cook, janitor, he rose to. . . ."

Naïve but witty, the narrator humors Sullivan, putting up patiently with the Irishman's redundant reminiscing and opinionated ramblings on society and politics. Sullivan, however, comes to rely on Robert's company; he turns from the horrors of life in the filthy apartment he shares with his obscene, insane wife to interminable conversations with Robert.

Robert's sympathetic tolerance of Sullivan emanates from his sense of the pathetic isolation of Sullivan from human contact and from Robert's recognition for the first time of the terrors of aging. Robert is the archetypal youth coming to awareness of old age as a time of foreshortened expectations and straitened lifestyles, of possible despair and near dehumanization. The apprentice janitor can tolerate Sullivan and his new knowledge while his relationship with the rich, lovely Jean goes well, but Jean and he are soon torn apart by social forces. In fact, they play a game called "Social Forces," in which they try to determine which of them will break first under social disapproval of their interracial relationship. When the game defeats them, Robert first is comforted by and then pulls back from his friendship with the dejected Sullivan, who is especially upset over the loss of his dog.

When Robert finally leaves his briefly held janitorial position, he does so with both relief and guilt over his abandonment of Sullivan. He knows, however, that he is "still young" and not yet doomed to the utter loneliness of the old man. McPherson suggests that the young, nevertheless, will inevitably come to such bleak isolation and that even the temporary freedom of youth is sometimes maintained at the expense of sympathy and kindness. There are dangers in being free, not the least of which are the burden of knowledge, the hardening of the self, and the aching realization of basic, but often unmet, human needs. This theme of loss is picked up in the volume's title story, "Hue and Cry," which includes this interchange between two characters:

"Between my eyes I see three people and they are all unhappy. Why?"

"Perhaps it is because they are alive. Perhaps it is because they once were. Perhaps it is because they have to be. I do not know."

These voices cannot make sense of the losses to which life dooms McPherson's characters, nor does Robert. He simply moves away from the hotel to enjoy, while he can, youth and his sense of potential.

"A SOLO SONG: FOR DOC"

The theme of old age and its defeats is further developed in McPherson's well-received "A Solo Song: For Doc," a story which displays well the author's rhythmic and precise control of narration conceived of as speech. McPherson resolves to initiate readers of all races into a facet of their culture that is quickly passing out of sight. The narrator, an aging waiter on a railroad line, tells a young listener about the good old days in the service and about their embodiment, a waiter called Doc Craft. "So do you want to know this business, youngblood?" begins the teller of the tale, and he goes on, "So you want to be a Waiter's Waiter? The Commissary gives you a book with all the rules and tells you to learn them. And you do, and think that is all there is to it." This "Waiter's Waiter" then proceeds to disillusion the "youngblood" by describing the difficult waiter's craft—the finesse,

grace, care, and creativity required to make the job into an art and to make that art pay. The grace and dedication displayed by men of Doc Craft's generation is shown to be losing ground to the contemporary world of business in which men such as "Jerry Ewald, the Unexpected Inspector," lie in wait to trap heroes like Doc Craft and to remove them from the service that keeps them alive. The narrator specifies what kept Doc on the road: having power over his car and his customers, hustling tips, enjoying women without being married to them, getting drunk without having to worry about getting home. The shift from passenger to freight service on the railroad, however, begins the company's attempt to fire Doc and also initiates Doc's rise to heroic stature. Older ways of work and life yield to new technology, and, like the old-time railroad, Doc Craft is doomed; Ewald catches Doc on a technicality about iced tea service, and the waiter is fired.

Clearly, McPherson's thematic preoccupations and love of the railroad have coalesced in this story. He captures the complexity, richness, and hardships of the lives of African American traveling men, as well as the initiative and kinship developed by black workers. Movement, adventure, freedom, self-expression, craftsmanship, commitment, exuberance, and endurance—these qualities mark both Doc Craft and the railroad as valuable American entities. Yet the passing of Doc carries McPherson's sense of the epic loss suffered by an America that has allowed the railroad, the metaphoric counterpart of imaginative integration of all kinds, to decay.

"WHY I LIKE COUNTRY MUSIC"

Even while remaining faithful to McPherson's characteristic themes, *Elbow Room*, his second volume, includes stories which reach a kind of comic perfection. One example is "Why I Like Country Music." The narrator, a southern-born black, addresses to his northern-born wife an explanation of his love of square-dance music. His wife will not believe or accept this preference, but the narrator quietly insists on it. In one sense, this insistence and the narration that justifies it may be viewed as evidence of the eternal and invincible isolation of the human heart from sympathetic understanding even by loved ones. The forces of memory and of individual development work to isolate human beings from one another. Further, the narrator's insistence that the South Carolina traditions of his youth have given to him preferences and ideas alien to those of the New York-born tends to strengthen this theme of the coherence but separateness of the self.

Such thematic reverberations, however, do not form the main concern of this story. Rather, the narrator tells us of a comic case of childhood puppy love; he explains that he loves country music because it is permanently associated in his mind with a girl in his fourth-grade class whose name was Gweneth Larson. Born in Brooklyn and redolent of lemons, Gweneth is for the narrator an object of first love. The moments when he square danced with her in a school May Day celebration were etched in his mind as moments of surpassing joy and love. Far from exploring alienation, the story celebrates the endurance of such affection.

McPherson's comedy is never heavy-handed, always a matter of a light tone or a moment of incongruity. An example occurs when the narrator describes the calling of the Maypole teams to the playground for their performance:

> "Maypole teams *up!*" called Mr. Henry Lucas, our principal, from his platform by the swings. Beside him stood the white Superintendent of Schools (who said later of the square dance, it was reported to all the classes, "Lord, y'all square dance so *good* it makes me plumb *ashamed* us white folks ain't takin' better care of our art stuff").

"A LOAF OF BREAD"

A more somber story in *Elbow Room*, "A Loaf of Bread," addresses important issues associated with racism and assimilation by depicting the isolation of the African American middle class. As in many of his other stories, McPherson expresses hope for the evolution of a model of American identity toward which all Americans can proudly gravitate. In "A Loaf of Bread," he explores the difference between exploitation and participation of African Americans in American society.

Store owner Harold Green charges higher prices

for goods in his store in an African American neighborhood than in the stores he owns in white neighborhoods. Consequently, as an act of restitution for exploiting the black community, Green decides that the best solution is to open his store and give away his merchandise free of charge to members of the exploited black community. The ensuing frenzy leaves Green's store in complete disarray, totally depleted of merchandise.

Nelson Reed, the leader of the community protest against Green, returns to the store later in the day to pay Green one dollar for the loaf of bread that his wife had taken from the store that morning. Reed is evidently seeking the status of a participating consumer versus an exploited one. Characteristic of McPherson's writing, characters in difficult situations struggle for some measure of success. However, Reed's attempt to receive equitable treatment as an American citizen is nullified by Green's response.

Similar to other fiction written by McPherson, the overall plot of "A Loaf of Bread" appears to argue for an American citizenship that eradicates racial boundaries and produces a coherent, color-blind American society. However, McPherson believes that racial exclusion continues to exist like an undeviated line from decades past and that acts of racial prejudice continue to demonstrate the pervasiveness of racial chauvinism. Furthermore, pointing fingers and using the "we/they" phrase in reference to other races only proliferates prejudice and isolation.

In "A Loaf of Bread," the hope for the black community to achieve unified American citizenship seems to be superseded by the lure of participating as a consumer in the marketplace. McPherson suggests that the African American middle class has abandoned the process of discarding some of the traditions of their fathers and embracing a sense of commonality with the white world. Consequently, the African American middle class becomes further isolated from the mainstream of American society. It is notable that in both his comedy "Why I Like Country Music" and his very somber "A Loaf of Bread," McPherson remains firmly focused on the human personality, which is for him the incentive for narration and the core of his art.

OTHER MAJOR WORKS

NONFICTION: *Why I Like Country Music*, 1982; *Crabcakes*, 1998; *A Region Not Home: Reflections from Exile*, 2000.

EDITED TEXTS: *Railroad: Trains and Train People in American Culture*, 1976 (with Miller Williams); *Fathering Daughters: Reflections by Men*, 1998 (with DeWitt Henry).

BIBLIOGRAPHY

Beavers, Herman. "I Yam What You Is and You Is What I Yam: Rhetorical Invisibility in James Alan McPherson's 'The Story of a Dead Man.'" *Callaloo* 9 (1986): 565-577. Beavers discusses the linguistic and rhetorical characteristics of McPherson's dialogue and how language shapes perceptions, specifically in "The Story of a Dead Man."

_____. *Wrestling Angels into Song: The Fictions of Ernest J. Gaines and James Alan McPherson.* Philadelphia: University of Pennsylvania Press, 1995. Provides criticism and interpretation of Gaines's and McPherson's works of fiction.

Cox, Joseph T. "James Alan McPherson." In *Contemporary Fiction Writers of the South*, edited by Joseph M. Flora and Robert Bain. Westport, Conn.: Greenwood Press, 1993. A brief introduction to McPherson's art, including a short biographical sketch, a summary and critique of the criticism of his work, and a short discussion of his short-story themes of intolerance and general absence of grace and love in modern society.

Laughlin, Rosemary M. "Attention, American Folklore: Doc Craft Comes Marching In." *Studies in American Fiction* 1 (1973): 221-227. Laughlin discusses McPherson's use of myth and folklore, as well as his ability to create new kinds of folklore in the pages of his story based on his aesthetic use of language and his unique mythical style.

"McPherson, James Alan." *Current Biography* 57 (September, 1996): 34-38. A biographical sketch of McPherson; claims that he sees the United States as a land populated by diverse peoples who are connected by a larger heritage; asserts that his major theme in both fiction and nonfiction has been the common humanity that transcends race.

McPherson, James Alan. "Interview with James Alan McPherson." Interview by Bob Shacochis. *Iowa Journal of Literary Studies* 4 (1983): 6-33. Shacochis focuses on questions relating to McPherson's vision of his literary role and on specific works in his collections. Contains also some discussion of McPherson's obligations as a "black-American" author.

Reid, Calvin. "James Alan McPherson: A Theater of Memory." *Publishers Weekly* 244 (December 15, 1997): 36-37. A biographical profile of McPherson; contends McPherson presents a wonderfully accurate social tableau full of vivid characters and lively, true dialogue, which is delivered within narratives so universal and directly meaningful that the stories aspire to the mythic realm of folklore and legend.

Wallace, Jon. *The Politics of Style: Language as Theme in the Fiction of Berger, McGuane, and McPherson.* Durango, Colo.: Hollowbrook, 1992. A study of the importance of language in the fiction of several authors, including McPherson.

_____. "The Politics of Style in Three Stories by James Alan McPherson." *Modern Fiction Studies* 34 (Spring, 1988): 17-26. Wallace argues that, in three stories by McPherson, "The Story of a Dead Man," "The Story of a Scar," and "Just Enough for the City," characters use language to construct for themselves a defense against human involvement and human communities which often threaten to weaken their sense of self.

_____. "The Story Behind the Story in James Alan McPherson's *Elbow Room*." *Studies in Short Fiction* 25 (Fall, 1988): 447-452. Wallace argues that McPherson's stories are often attempts to create a new kind of mythology, or mythological space, in which to place the experiences of his characters in the larger context of American society. Because of this, Wallace argues that in McPherson's work it is narrative form that matters much more than either the particulars of the story or the characters.

Cheryl Herr, updated by Edward Huffstetler and Alvin K. Benson

NAGUIB MAHFOUZ

Born: Cairo, Egypt; December 11, 1911

PRINCIPAL SHORT FICTION

Hams al-junūn, c. 1948

Dunyā Allāh, 1963 (partial trans. *God's World*, 1973)

Bayt sayyi' al-sumʿa, 1965

Taḥta al-miẓalla, 1967

Khammārat al-qiṭṭ al-aswad, 1968 (*The Tavern of the Black Cat*, 1976)

Hikaya bila bidaya wala nihaya, 1971

Al-Jarima, 1973

God's World, 1973

Al-Ḥubb fawqa haḍabat al-haram, 1979

Al-Shaytan Yaʿiz, 1979

Ra'aytu fimā yarā al-nāʿim, 1982

Al-Tanẓīm al-sirri, 1984

Al-Fajr al-kāadhib, 1989

The Time and the Place and Other Stories, 1991

OTHER LITERARY FORMS

Despite his lifelong dedication to the short story, Naguib Mahfouz's reputation stems chiefly from the many novels he has produced over his lengthy career, notably the Cairo Trilogy (1956-1957). He has also been an important influence in the Egyptian cinema, having written the screenplays for many films drawn from Arabic novels, including some of his own works. He is the author of several short plays, some of which have been performed on stage. He has also written the nonfiction work *Asda' al-sirah al-dhatiyah* (1995; *Echoes of an Autobiography*, 1997).

ACHIEVEMENTS

By the late 1950's, Naguib Mahfouz had earned recognition throughout the Arab world as one of the most sophisticated authors of the Arabic novel. While earlier Arab novelists had initiated this literary form, Mahfouz demonstrated a gift for presenting characters and situations that intimately captured the spirit of his native Egypt. His generally tragic works often center their interest on individuals in crisis and examine issues relating to class, ambition, and morality in government. They illustrate the personal faults or the incidents of fate that can bring tragedy to humankind; though didactic, they are usually nonjudgmental. Contemporary political and social issues, both of the Middle East and of the world at large, are central to his writing. The recipient of many honorary doctoral degrees from foreign universities and prestigious awards from the Egyptian government, Mahfouz received in 1988 the Nobel Prize in Literature.

BIOGRAPHY

Though gregarious and accessible, Naguib Mahfouz has disclosed little about his personal life or background. His father was apparently a shopkeeper (or perhaps a minor civil servant), and Mahfouz was the youngest of seven children. At the time of his birth, the family resided in Gamaliya, an area named after a street traversing an ancient quarter of Cairo. It is this colorful, conservative environment that provides the locale for many of his works. In his pre-teens, the family moved to the wealthier and more European neighborhood of Abbasiya. His early education was in public schools, and he earned a B.A. in philosophy from Cairo University in 1934. He continued studies there for an M.A. in philosophy but withdrew for undisclosed reasons to take employment in the university's administration; shortly thereafter, he joined the bureaucracy, first working in the ministry of religious endowments. In 1971, he retired and became director of the government-controlled board of film censorship, while continuing to devote himself to his writing. He married in his early forties and has two daughters.

Mahfouz was awarded the Nobel Prize in Literature in 1988. After this recognition, he became more widely translated and read outside the Arab world. Within the Arab world, he continues to be controversial, because he advocates peace with Israel. In 1994, he was stabbed in the neck outside his Cairo home, in an assassination attempt by Muslim ultraconservative extremists.

ANALYSIS

In his fiction, Naguib Mahfouz has assumed the role of chronicler and conscience of Egypt in the twentieth century. Since, however, many of his works examine issues that are common to all humanity, they are timeless and of universal interest. Mahfouz's works have consistently expressed his interest in the role of women in society. His fiction suggests that he has generally been supportive of women exerting their personal choice. Even women who become prostitutes are viewed with equanimity and understanding, if not admiration.

Mahfouz is perhaps the best-known Arab fiction writer in the Anglophone world. Over a period of half a century he has given voice to the hopes and frustrations of his nation. Through his fiction, Egyptian and Arab-Islamic cultural heritage has become accessible to Westerners. His works illustrate the position of women in his culture, and clarify the changes and disruptions that Western ideas and culture have brought to individuals and society as a whole in Egypt.

HAMS AL-JUNŪN

Mahfouz is said to have published his first short story in an obscure Cairo journal, *Al-Siyasa*, in July, 1932. This was followed by a regular production in several Egyptian journals, both literary and popular. These early stories number approximately eighty, of which over twenty have been republished in a collection entitled *Hams al-junūn*. They frequently present situations in which sadness results from faults of character and immorality or from ill fortune. The situations are often domestic and the problems prosaic, such as marital infidelity or a family's descent into poverty through unemployment or the death of the wage earner.

These stories are generally didactic and sentimental and reflect the influence of the works of the then hugely popular Sheikh Mustafa Lutfi al-Manfaluti; this author's genius for archaic, sonorous, and rhythmic prose Mahfouz was, however, unable to match. Other early stories present flat and static character sketches of the lives and personalities of curious characters; these are reminiscent of the fiction of Mahmud Taymur, a prominent Egyptian writer who was himself a devotee of Guy de Maupassant. Often

Naguib Mahfouz, Nobel Laureate for Literature in 1988 (©The Nobel Foundation)

with characters and situations that are unconvincing and lack development, these works nevertheless suggest the pessimism and high seriousness that have characterized Mahfouz's literary production.

"GOD'S WORLD"

The short stories of the late 1930's and 1940's, like the novels, still largely concern themselves with the issues and dilemmas that affect the poor, the bureaucracy, and the petit bourgeois. They emphasize the negative aspects of Egypt's class structure and demonstrate how the struggle for survival and advancement entails loss of mortality and personal happiness. They suggest a general compassion for the underprivileged and a disapproval of the values of his compatriots who enjoy wealth and power.

The whimsical "Dunyā Allāh" ("God's World"), in the collection *Dunyā Allāh*, and available in various English translations, centers sympathetically on an aging man, an impoverished messenger in a department of the bureaucracy, who, having stolen the salaries of his colleagues, absconds to Alexandria with a young woman. Though his idyllic vacation ends with her rejection of him and his capture by the police, the thief has no cause for regret since he has achieved one brief period of happiness in an otherwise dismal life.

Mahfouz's writings of the 1950's and 1960's became increasingly complex in their structure and style and more political and obscure in their themes. As was the case with other Egyptian writers, such as Yusuf Idris, and Ihsan 'Abd al-Quddus, his works now contained subtle expressions of discontent at the repressive nature of the rule of the country's dictator, Gamal Abdel Nasser, who had led an army coup in 1952 that had overthrown the monarchy. While viewed as generally benevolent and reformist, the regime brooked no criticism from its citizenry, and brief jail sentences were served by many intellectuals whose loyalty became suspect. Caution and obfuscation were clearly necessary to escape notice or defy interpretation by the "defenders of the revolution." The stories are therefore metaphorical and the criticisms oblique, though some do lend themselves to easy equational interpretation.

"SA'IQ AL-QITAR"

For example, his "Sa'iq al-qitar" (in the collection *Bayt sayyi' al-sum'a*) presents passengers in a train; one man, reminiscent of a bear, standing for the Soviet Union, constantly challenges another, reminiscent of an "eagle," representing the United States, over the future of a woman who presumably stands for Egypt. The passengers realize that their train is rushing headlong into certain disaster. The train driver—clearly Nasser—locked in the engine compartment refuses all advice to slow down and seems crazed and suicidal. It is implied that the nation is helpless and headed for tragedy under his leadership.

"ZAABALAWI"

Other short stories of the period reflect the malaise and confusion widely shared by Egyptian intellectuals. While they applauded the new international attention and prestige that the regime had won for Egypt as a leader of the neutralist Third World and were pleased at the downfall of the landowning aristocracy, they suffered from involvement in a debilitating war in Yemen, a stagnant economy, and restric-

tions on travel. They also chafed at the abolition of the country's political parties and freedoms of expression, while they disdained the Nasser worship of the powerful state-controlled media. Stories such as "Zaabalawi" (in the collection *Dunyā Allāh*) clearly suggest this malaise; it involves a sick man's search for a revered healer, a holy man who embodied inherited rather than imported values and procedures of contemporary "doctors." The dissatisfaction at the root of this story is viewed by some critics as similar in its message to that of Mahfouz's extremely controversial novel *Children of Gebelawi*, which chronicles the failures of both the religions and the governmental structures to satisfy people's needs for security and justice.

"BENEATH THE SHELTER"

In the several months following the disastrous war of June, 1967, between Israel and the Arabs, Mahfouz wrote a variety of curious and disturbing short stories and five one-act plays, which were collected and published in 1967 in the volume *Tahta al-mizalla*. These works present characters and situations that show Egyptians to be living in a Kafkaesque and chaotic world where individuals live in distress and terror. The story reflects the trauma then affecting Egyptians from two sources—the fear of death from sporadic Israeli air attacks and the repressive policies being pursued by the Nasser regime.

While the internal message in these works is constrained and camouflaged by symbolism, their intent to reveal despair and to suggest criticism is clear. While not lending themselves to full equational interpretation, unlike some of his earlier stories, they contain enough "clues" to suggest the author's purpose, which at times extended beyond the prosaic criticism of the country's leadership into the metaphysical.

For example, the story "Tahta al-mizalla" ("Beneath the Shelter") could obviously be interpreted as an expression of the tragedy and absurdity of the human experience stemming from failure to replace brutality and chaos with an order based on morality and compassion. In this story, dramatic and tragic events unfold in the street before onlookers awaiting the arrival of a bus. These incidents, occurring in an atmosphere of unrelieved gloom and downpourings of rain in increasing intensity, suggest the progression of the recent history of the Middle East as seen from an Egyptian perspective. The onlookers are reluctant to accept as reality the strange and bloody events that they witness. To justify their own fear of involvement, they convince themselves that the changing scene is merely the action of a motion picture being shot. A final horrific event, however, convinces them that they are witnessing a reality too horrible to ignore; a head gushing blood—presumably during the 1967 war—rolls down the street before them. Belatedly seeking involvement, they call out to a "policeman" who has also been an uninvolved observer of the scenes. His response, however, is to question their identity and loyalty and to shoot them all dead. While the general intent of the story is evident, its specific symbols may be variously interpreted. It is not clear, for example, whether the uninvolved spectators are Egyptian or foreign, or whether the brutal and callous policeman is Nasser or an abstraction, such as time or fate.

Such stories, for all the interest they arouse in Arabic and the speed and frequency with which they have been published in translation, have received little interpretation. Clearly, commentators have realized that it would be an act of betrayal to reveal the purposes of an author who has taken such pains to present his ideas in so obscure and circumspect a manner.

TAḤTA AL-MIẒALLA

The issue of commitment against injustice is clearly a major theme of Mahfouz's oeuvre, and, in works written before 1978, this theme often finds expression in relation to the Arab-Israeli conflict. In several works—for example "Fijian Shayy" (in the collection *Taḥta al-miẓalla*) and the one-act play "Death and Resurrection" (from the collection *Taḥta al-miẓalla*, in English in the 1989 collection *One-Act Plays*)—Mahfouz insists on the need to redress the wrongs done to the Palestinians and to continue the Arab struggle against Israel. These works all appeared before Egypt's 1978-1979 rapprochement with Israel, following which Mahfouz has been an outspoken advocate of peace and cooperation between Arabs and Israelis.

The chaotic and fast-changing nature of contemporary Egyptian society and its values and the resultant sense of disorientation and bewilderment has been the subject of several stories. In "False Dawn" (in the collection *Al-Fajr al-kādhib*), the reader follows a young man's apparently logical search for an enemy only to discover that he has been suffering from paranoid schizophrenia caused by the confusion of change in modern society.

"THE ANSWER IS NO" AND "MIN TAHT ILA FAWQ"

Several of the short stories similarly center on strong-willed women; indeed, it could be maintained that Mahfouz, like many prominent Arab authors, has his female characters exemplify virtues lacking in his male figures. Mahfouz's advocacy of the right to choose or reject marriage clearly contradicts traditional male mainstream opinion in his society. For example, in the story "The Answer Is No" (from the collection *Al-Fajr al-kādhib*), a young girl who is seduced by a teacher refuses to marry him despite his dutiful proposal to her as soon as she reaches the legal age for marriage. Years later, when he becomes the principal of the school where she teaches and inquires after her marital status, she expresses no regret at her unmarried state. Similarly, in "Min taht ila Fawq" (also in *Al-Fajr al-kādhib*), an unmarried young woman, orphaned as a child and exploited by her family for whom she acts as an unpaid cook and housekeeper, decides to take employment as a servant in luxury Cairo apartments. Formerly sickly and depressed at home, she becomes happy and earns a fine salary. When her health, morale, and dress improve, she marries an electrician, whom she proudly introduces to her family; she has married by choice, and as an equal.

OTHER MAJOR WORKS

LONG FICTION: *'Abath al-Aqdār*, 1939; *Khān al-Khalīli*, 1945; *Zuqāq al-Midaqq*, 1947 (*Midaq Alley*, 1966, revised 1975); *Bidāya wa-nihāya*, 1949 (*The Beginning and the End*, 1951); *Bayn al-qaṣrayn*, 1956 (*Palace Walk*, 1990); *Qaṣr al-shawq*, 1957 (*Palace of Desire*, 1991); *Al-Sukkariya*, 1957 (*Sugar Street*, 1992; previous 3 titles collectively known as

Al-Thulāthiya [*The Trilogy*]); *Awlād Ḥāratinā,* 1959 (serial), 1967 (book; *Children of Gebelawi,* 1981, also known as *Children of the Alley,* 1996); *Al-Liṣ wa-al-kilāb,* 1961 (*The Thief and the Dogs,* 1984); *Al-Summān wa-al-kharīf,* 1962 (*Autumn Quail,* 1985); *Al-Ṭarīq,* 1964 (*The Search,* 1987); *Al-Shaḥḥādh,* 1965 (*The Beggar,* 1986); *Tharthara fawq al-Nīl,* 1966 (*Adrift on the Nile,* 1993); *Mirāmār,* 1967 (*Miramar,* 1978); *Al-Marāya,* 1972 (*Mirrors,* 1977); *Al-Karnak,* 1974 (*Karnak,* 1979); *Ḥikāyāt Ḥāratinā,* 1975 (*The Fountain and the Tomb,* 1988); *Ḥaḍrat al-muḥtaram,* 1975 (*Respected Sir,* 1986); *Malḥamat al-ḥarāfish,* 1977 (*The Harafish,* 1994); *Afrāḥ al-qubbah,* 1981 (*Wedding Song,* 1984); *Layāāī alf Laylah,* 1982 (*Arabian Nights and Days,* 1995); *Yawm Qutila al-Za ʿīm,* 1985 (*The Day the Leader Was Killed,* 1989); *Al-āʾish fī al-ḥaqīqah,* 1985 (*Akhenaten: Dweller in Truth,* 2000).

PLAYS: *One-Act Plays,* pb. 1989.

NONFICTION: *Asda' al-sirah al-dhatiyah,* 1995 (*Echoes of an Autobiography,* 1997).

TRANSLATION: *Miṣr al-Qadīmah,* 1931 (of James Baikie's *Ancient Egypt*).

MISCELLANEOUS: *Taḥta al-miẓallah,* 1967.

BIBLIOGRAPHY

Abadir, Akef, and Roger Allen. Introduction to *God's World.* Minneapolis, Minn.: Bibliotheca Islamica, 1973. This introduction by Abadir and Allen is followed by twenty translations selected from Mahfouz's short stories.

Beard, Michael, and Adnan Haydar, eds. *Naguib Mahfouz: From Regional Fame to Global Recognition.* Syracuse, N.Y.: Syracuse University Press, 1993. A collection of essays derived from a symposium recognizing Naguib Mahfouz's 1988 Nobel Prize. Includes essays on Mahfouz's image of woman, on dreams, on the sublime, and on his critics. An essay on existential themes focuses specifically on Mahfouz's short stories.

Coetzee, J. M. "Fabulous Fabulist." *The New York Review of Books* 41 (September 22, 1994): 30-33. Argues that it was Mahfouz's example that spurred interest in the novel in Arabic in the 1950's and 1960's. Briefly discusses Mahfouz's fiction, describing the world of Cairo as he depicts it.

Hesse, Reinhard. "Egypt's Intelligentsia Fights Back." *World Press Review* 42 (February, 1995): 50. Argues that the galvanizing moment of the culture wars being waged to deny Egypt its rich heritage occurred when Mahfouz was stabbed. Notes that Mahfouz's novel *Children of Gebelaawi* had been banned by fundamentalists as a disrespectful allegory of the life of the Prophet.

Johnson-Davies, Denys. Introduction to *The Time and the Place and Other Stories.* Garden City, N.Y.: Doubleday, 1991. Consists of twenty of Mahfouz's short stories selected and translated, following an introduction by Denys Johnson-Davies.

Kilpatrick, Hilary. *The Modern Egyptian Novel: A Study in Social Criticism.* London: Ithaca Press, 1974. This academic study examines Mahfouz's novels in the context of contemporary Egyptian fiction. Contains appropriate literary and critical evaluations, notes, and bibliographies.

Le Gassick, Trevor, ed. *Critical Perspectives on Naguib Mahfouz.* Washington, D.C.: Three Continents Press, 1991. Eleven articles by authorities on Mahfouz, following an introduction by the editor. The articles, four of which are in translation from Arabic, range widely over Mahfouz's contributions to the short story, the novel, and the Egyptian cinema. Complemented by bibliographies of materials in English.

Somekh, Sasson. *The Changing Rhythm.* Leiden, The Netherlands: E. J. Brill, 1973. A careful, comprehensive study of Mahfouz's major novels. Academically sound and with good bibliographies, it addresses the general reader as well as the student of Near Eastern literatures.

Viorst, Milton. "Man of Gamaliya." *The New Yorker* 66 (July 2, 1990): 32-38. In this brief biographical sketch, Viorst discusses Mahfouz's denunciation by Muslim authorities and the death threats made against him for defending Salman Rushdie; also comments on his later view that Rushdie should stand trial for slander.

Weaver, Mary Anne. "The Novelist and the Sheikh."

The New Yorker 70 (January 30, 1995): 52-58. In this brief biographical sketch, the author notes that the stabbing of Mahfouz underscores the battle between the Egyptian government and Islamic militants. Discusses how Mahfouz's characters

debate issues of justice and injustice, expectation and disillusionment, and belief in God.

Trevor Le Gassick, updated by
Susan Butterworth

CLARENCE MAJOR

Born: Atlanta, Georgia; December 31, 1936

PRINCIPAL SHORT FICTION
Fun and Games, 1990

OTHER LITERARY FORMS

Clarence Major is the author of a number of novels and books of poetry, including *Parking Lots: A Poem* (1992) and *Configurations: New and Selected Poems 1958-1998* (1999). He has also edited a number of collections, like *The New Black Poetry* (1969) and *Calling the Wind: Twentieth-Century African-American Short Stories* (1993). In addition, he has written several critical studies, including *The Dark and Feeling: Black American Writers and Their Work* (1974), and *Dictionary of Afro-American Slang* (1970, reprinted in 1994 as *Juba to Jive: A Dictionary of African-American Slang*).

ACHIEVEMENTS

Clarence Major has won numerous awards and grants in his career, including a Pushcart Prize for poetry in 1976 and a Fulbright-Hays Exchange Award in 1981-1983. His novel *My Amputations* (1986) won the Western States Book Award, *Such Was the Season* (1987) was a Literary Guild Selection, *Painted Turtle: Woman with Guitar* (1988) was a *New York Times* notable book, *Fun and Games* was a finalist for the *Los Angeles Times* Book Critics Award, and his collection *Calling the Wind: Twentieth-Century African-American Short Stories* (1993) was a Book-of-the-Month Club selection.

BIOGRAPHY

Clarence Major was born in Atlanta, Georgia, grew up on the South Side of Chicago, and served in the U.S. Air Force from 1955 to 1957. He studied at the Chicago Art Institute, graduated from the State University of New York at Albany, and earned a Ph.D. from the Union of Experimenting Colleges and Universities. Major taught at a number of universities, both in the United States and abroad, and after 1989 at the University of California at Davis. In addition to his fiction and poetry, Major has exhibited and published paintings and photographs. He has also been an editor and columnist and has lectured widely. He has been married twice and has lived in various parts of the United States and for extended periods in France and Italy.

ANALYSIS

Clarence Major's short fiction has attracted much less critical attention than his novels, and yet, as Doug Bolling has noted, "his short fiction is valuable in its own right and deserves wide reading and critical discussion." Among other strengths, Major is capable of a range of fictional styles, from the conventional to the experimental. Nearly all of his fiction is marked by lyricism and a fascination with language, but even his most realistic short stories (like "My Mother and Mitch" and "Ten Pecan Pies") tend to challenge readers. His antimimetic, experimental fiction, as Bolling argues,

helps us to see that fiction created within an aesthetic of fluidity and denial of 'closure' and verbal freedom can generate an excitement and awareness of great value; that the rigidities of plot, characterization, and illusioned depth can be softened and, finally, dropped in favor of new and valid rhythms.

Jerome Klinkowitz has written that the central achievement of Major's career

> has been to show just how concretely we live within the imagination—how our lives are shaped by language and how by a simple act of self-awareness we can seize control of the world and reshape it to our liking and benefit.

FUN AND GAMES

Clarence Major's short-story collection *Fun and Games* was nominated for the *Los Angeles Times* Book Critics Award in 1990. While the volume represents Major's short fiction through the 1980's, it is a good barometer of his continuing fictional interests and forms. The sixteen stories in the volume are divided into five parts: Section 1 contains three stories

Clarence Major (©Layle Silbert)

(including the realistic "My Mother and Mitch" and "Ten Pecan Pies"), section 2 also has three shorter and more surreal stories, section 3 contains six stories, section 4 has three, and section 5 comprises "Mobile Axis: A Triptych," three interconnected short fictions. While Major is capable of one form of social realism (as in "Letters"), he more regularly leans toward a staccato, fragmentary prose fiction in which the links are missing among characters and incidents ("The Horror" and the title story). "The Exchange," for example is a fairly realistic, even comic story about a faculty exchange gone horribly wrong. When the narrator and his wife arrive on the opposite coast to begin the year-long exchange, they find a dilapidated house. Worse, when they return to their own home at the end of the year, their exchangees have turned the house into a replica of their own—down to the moldy contents of the refrigerator. Likewise, the collection's title story is a first-person narration about a man's three or four girlfriends, who keep leaving him and returning. The story is comic and at the same an oblique commentary on transience and commitment in contemporary society. More common in *Fun and Games*, however, is "Mother Visiting," a short, three-page story that violates most of the conventions of fictional verisimilitude. While the story touches upon a number of contemporary issues (notably sex and violence), its postmodernist style emphasizes the play of language over sense. Likewise in the short story "Virginia," the dazzling use of language and image have replaced the demands of plot.

"MY MOTHER AND MITCH"

This story won the Pushcart Prize for fiction in 1989 and leads off the *Fun and Games* collection. In some ways it does not resemble Major's other short fiction, being a leaner and less experimental coming-of-age story. "My Mother and Mitch" centers on the date that Tommy Anderson's mother had with Mitch Kibbs when Tommy was a teenager in Chicago in 1951. Mitch had dialed a wrong number and then kept calling to talk with Tommy's mother, even after he discovered that she was black. The climax of the story comes when Mitch asks her to meet him in a restaurant, and Tommy watches the white man and his mother talking at the counter of a predominantly black eatery. The story is barely about interracial dating, for the couple never meet again after that night. What is more important is what the young Mitch discovers about his single mother: "I learned for the first time that she did not always know what she was doing. It struck me that she was as helpless as I sometimes felt." That knowledge makes the adolescent Tommy feel closer to his mother: "there she was, just finding her way, step by step, like me. It was something wonderful anyway." The story may remind readers of Sherwood Anderson's "Death in the Woods," for Tommy is retelling the tale many years later and still trying to get it right and discover its meaning through the retelling. In its lean re-creation of the spare events here, the story may also remind readers of Raymond Carver and other minimalist short-story writers of the late twentieth century, who forsake long exposition and elaborate descriptions for the psychological revelations of a single voice.

"TEN PECAN PIES"

"Ten Pecan Pies" uses still another fictional style, here a third-person, more traditional narration. The story was first published in *Seattle Review*, is reprinted in the first section of *Fun and Games*, and may remind readers of William Faulkner or Truman Capote in its rural southern setting and voices. "Ten Pecan Pies" concerns one Christmas in the Flower household, when the patriarch Grady Flower has kept two bags of pecans to himself and will not let his wife make her annual Christmas pies. The other preparations for Christmas—finding and decorating a tree, for example—go on, but Grady hoards the pecans in his room until Christmas Eve, when Thursday finally shames her husband and then, when he gives in, "suddenly kisse[s] the side of his face. The first time in years." The story has other tensions—the drunken son Slick John killing the rabbits in front of his niece, Gal, for example—but the overwhelming feeling of the story is lyrical and nostalgic. Thursday douses the fire in the stove, the story concludes, "Yet the warmth stayed."

"SCAT"

"Scat" was the only story of his own that Clarence Major selected for *Calling the Wind*, the collection of twentieth century African American fiction he edited in 1990, so readers can assume he thinks the story is important, but it is also representative of a certain comic-surreal style Major mastered. The story covers a nightmare cab ride the narrator and his white girlfriend take into New York City with a cabdriver who subjects them to a monologue about the dangers of Manhattan, where the couple want to go, and the relative safety of Brooklyn, where the cabdriver lives. In his frustration at the cabdriver's tales of the "superstitious practices" and "voodoo rites" in Manhattan, the narrator counters with his own stories of body snatching in Brooklyn. Readers conclude the story still not knowing who is crazier: the cabdriver, who talks knowingly of the "evil art of capnomancy," or the narrator, who speaks of "the Plot, I mean the Sacrifice" and seems equally deranged. Perhaps, if one pursues the definition of the tale's title, the story is the fictional equivalent of jazz singing with nonsense syllables, each voice trying to outdo the other.

"AN AREA IN THE CEREBRAL HEMISPHERE"

This story has been collected in Gloria Naylor's *Children of the Night: The Best Short Stories by Black Writers, 1967 to the Present* (1995) and is the best example of Major's postmodernist style, fragmentary and barely coherent but with a powerful edge to it. The story centers on a young African American woman, a visit by a friend, and the young woman's thoughts about her father and her own life. These events are parceled out in a style that dispels meaning: "The friend lit a cigarette and sat on the sounds of her own voice. Motion. And made a blowing sound," Major writes early in this story, and, a little later on, "And mother's couch was eaten by what might easily have been taxicabs with hooks on them. Anything can happen. (In any case, swift traffic was known to move through her living room.)" This metaphor of motion runs through the story, but it hardly ties together the various fragmented incidents and scraps of dialogue. What readers are left with is Major's brilliant and poetic use of language. Naylor titled the section containing this story "Breaking New Ground," which Major does with his experimental and poetic fictions.

OTHER MAJOR WORKS

LONG FICTION: *All-Night Visitors*, 1969; *NO*, 1973; *Reflex and Bone Structure*, 1975; *Emergency Exit*, 1979; *My Amputations*, 1986; *Such Was the Season*, 1987; *Painted Turtle: Woman with Guitar*, 1988; *Dirty Bird Blues*, 1996.

POETRY: *The Fires That Burn in Heaven*, 1954; *Love Poems of a Black Man*, 1965; *Human Juices*, 1966; *Swallow the Lake*, 1970; *Symptoms and Madness*, 1971; *Private Line*, 1971; *The Cotton Club*, 1972; *The Syncopated Cakewalk*, 1974; *Inside Diameter: The France Poems*, 1985; *Surfaces and Masks: A Poem*, 1988; *Some Observations of a Stranger at Zuni in the Latter Part of the Century*, 1989; *Parking Lots: A Poem*, 1992; *Configurations: New and Selected Poems 1958-1998*, 1999.

NONFICTION: *Dictionary of Afro-American Slang*, 1970 (also known as *Juba to Jive: A Dictionary of African-American Slang*, 1994); *The Dark and Feeling: Black American Writers and Their Work*, 1974.

EDITED TEXTS: *Writers Workshop Anthology*, 1967; *Man Is Like a Child*, 1968; *The New Black Poetry*, 1969; *Calling the Wind: Twentieth-Century African-American Short Stories*, 1993; *The Garden Thrives: Twentieth-Century African-American Poetry*, 1996.

BIBLIOGRAPHY

Bell, Bernard W. "Introduction: Clarence Major's Double Consciousness as a Black Postmodernist Artist." *African American Review* 28 (Spring, 1994): 5-10. Bell introduces this special issue of the journal, which includes eight "Writings by Clarence Major," a section of his artwork, as well as critical analyses of his poetry and fiction.

Bolling, Doug. "A Reading of Clarence Major's Short Fiction." *Black American Literature Forum* 13 (1979): 51-56. This early study of Major's short stories recognizes that the artist "works with 'process,' with open forms, with the inconclusive, and with the interplay of formal and informal tensions." One of the best analyses of Major's short fiction, the essay includes discussions of "Ten Pecan Pies," "Fun and Games," and "An Area in the Cerebral Hemisphere."

Klinkowitz, Jerome. "Clarence Major's Innovative Fiction." *African American Review* 28 (Spring 1994): 57-63. While dealing primarily with Major's novels, Klinkowitz recognizes the "anti-realistic (and even anti-mimetic)" strain to much of Major's fiction.

_____. *The Life of Fiction*. Urbana: University of Illinois Press, 1977. Chapter 8 of Klinkowitz's early study of a dozen postmodernist American writers focuses on Major and recognizes both the lyricism and the anticonventional strains of Major's fiction.

O'Brien, John. "Clarence Major." In *Interviews with Black Writers*. New York: Liveright, 1973. This fourteen-page interview with Major sheds light on the writer's life and work.

Weixlmann, Joe. "Clarence Major: A Checklist of Criticism." *Obsidian* 4, no. 2 (1978): 101-113. This checklist brings together some of the most important works of literary criticism written about Major's fiction.

David Peck

BERNARD MALAMUD

Born: Brooklyn, New York; April 26, 1914
Died: New York, New York; March 18, 1986

PRINCIPAL SHORT FICTION

The Magic Barrel, 1958
Idiots First, 1963
Pictures of Fidelman: An Exhibition, 1969
Rembrandt's Hat, 1973
The Stories of Bernard Malamud, 1983
The People and Uncollected Stories, 1989

OTHER LITERARY FORMS

Bernard Malamud devoted his writing career to fiction. In addition to his highly praised short stories, he wrote seven well-received novels: *The Natural* (1952), *The Assistant* (1957), *A New Life* (1961), *The Fixer* (1966), *The Tenants* (1971), *Dubin's Lives* (1979), and *God's Grace* (1982). He is also the author of many literary essays and reviews.

ACHIEVEMENTS

Of the last half of the twentieth century, Bernard Malamud is one of the best American writers. In his seven novels and numerous short stories, he transcends the Jewish experience so ably chronicled by the so-called Jewish literary renaissance writers (such as Saul Bellow and Philip Roth) by using Jewish life as a metaphor for universal experience. Critic Robert Alter has proclaimed that short stories such as "The First Seven Years," "The Magic Barrel," "The Last Mohican," "Idiots First," and "Angel Levine" will be read "as long as anyone continues to care about American fiction written in the 20th century."

Both a traditionalist and an experimenter in his fiction, Malamud won rave reviews, literary plaudits, and many awards. *The Magic Barrel* brought a National Book Award in 1959. In 1967, *The Fixer* won for him a second National Book Award as well as a Pulitzer Prize. In addition, he was president of the International Association of Poets, Playwrights, Editors, Essayists, and Novelists (PEN Club) from 1979 to 1981.

BIOGRAPHY

Born on April 26, 1914, Bernard Malamud was the eldest of two sons of Max and Bertha Malamud. His parents, who had emigrated from Russia, ran a grocery store. Both Yiddish and English were spoken in the Malamud household, where much emphasis was placed on the cultural aspects of Judaism.

This milieu as well as his father's tales of life in czarist Russia provided much fodder for Malamud's fiction. He was also influenced by many trips to the Yiddish theater on Manhattan's Second Avenue, and by novels such as his favorite Horatio Alger stories and a multivolume *Book of Knowledge* that his father gave him when he was nine.

Throughout his boyhood in the back room of the family store, where he wrote stories, and his high school days at Erasmus Hall in Brooklyn, where he was an editor of the literary magazine, he was devoted to storytelling. In 1936, he was graduated from City College of New York. He had written a few stories in college and continued to write during a series of odd jobs. While working on an M.A. at Columbia University, he taught at Erasmus Hall Evening High School and wrote. In 1945, he married a Gentile, Ann de Chiara.

During the 1940's, Malamud's stories appeared in some noncommercial magazines. Then, in 1949, he sold the appropriately titled "The Cost of Living" to *Harper's Bazaar*. That same year, he moved with his family to Corvallis, Oregon, where he worked at Oregon State University. Finally adjusting from the urban to the rural lifestyle, Malamud developed a new perspective and a weekly routine that allowed him much quality time for writing: He taught three days a week and wrote four. Without a Ph.D., he was forced to teach composition, not literature, so his favorite course was a compromise—a night workshop in short-story writing for townspeople. His stories began to appear in such noted magazines as *Partisan Review, Commentary*, and *Harper's Bazaar*.

The Natural, his first novel, appeared in 1952 to mixed reviews. Some critics were put off by what they saw as an obscure symbolism, while others applauded the masterful use of fable and its art of ancient storytelling in a modern voice. In 1956, the *Partisan Review* made him a fellow in fiction and recommended him for a Rockefeller grant, which made it possible for Malamud to spend a year in Europe. In 1957, his next novel, *The Assistant*, was published, winning for him many awards and establishing him as a major Jewish American writer. The short-story collection *The Magic Barrel* came out in 1958, followed by his third novel, *A New Life*. In 1961, he moved to Bennington College, where he taught for more than twenty years. *Idiots First* was followed by *The Fixer*, which was researched during a trip to Russia.

From 1969 until his death in 1986, Malamud continued to publish both novels and short stories. His works include *Pictures of Fidelman: An Exhibition*, a collection of stories about one character; *The Tenants*, a novel; *Rembrandt's Hat*, another short-story collection; *Dubin's Lives*, a novel; *God's Grace*, a novel; and *The Stories of Bernard Malamud*, still another collection.

Bernard Malamud (©Jerry Bauer)

ANALYSIS

All Bernard Malamud's fiction seems based on a single affirmation: Despite its disappointments, horror, pain, and suffering, life is truly worth living. His work may be best understood in the context of mid-twentieth century American literature. When Malamud arrived upon the literary scene, he disagreed with the period's twin pillars of negativism and nihilism, and his work is a reaction to this prevailing trend. "The purpose of the writer," contends Malamud, "is to keep civilization from destroying itself." Therefore, his characters, no matter how bad their lot, push toward a better life, a new life. "My premise," notes the author, "is that we will not destroy each other. My premise is that we will live on. We will seek a better life. We may not become better, but at least we will seek betterment."

In this respect, for Malamud the most important element of fiction is form, a belief that appropriately reinforces his thematic beliefs. Literary form as "ultimate necessity" is the basis of literature. The writer's

duty, he argues "is to create the architecture, the form." This element of structure, so prevalent in both his short and long fiction, runs counter to the practice of many of his contemporaries, who preferred the inherent formlessness of the so-called New Novel. The essence of this form, says Malamud, is "story, story, story. Writers who can't invent stories often pursue other strategies, even substituting style for narrative. I feel that story is the basic element of fiction."

This belief, however, raises the question of what for Malamud constitutes a good story. Here Malamud is likewise a traditionalist, returning to such nineteenth century influences as Fyodor Dostoevski, Leo Tolstoy, and Gustave Flaubert. Malamud's stories grow out of character. More often than not, the typical protagonist is the schlemiel (usually Jewish, though sometimes Italian). According to the author himself, "A Malamud character is someone who fears his fate, is caught up in it, yet manages to outrun it. He's the subject and object of laughter and pity." When Malamud began publishing his stories, the emphasis was often on case studies rather than elaborate personality development, a trend that irritated Malamud:

> The sell-out of personality is just tremendous. Our most important natural resource is Man. The times cry out for men of imagination and hope. Instead, our fiction is loaded with sickness, homosexuality, fragmented man, "other-directed" man. It should be filled with love and beauty and hope. We are underselling Man. And American fiction is at its weakest when we go in for journalistic case studies instead of rich personality development.

A typical Malamud story, then, is an initiation story, the classic American pattern. Malamud admits that his American literary roots lie in Stephen Crane, Ernest Hemingway, and Sherwood Anderson. The story usually begins with a youth—or an older man with arrested personality development—who has led an unfulfilled life because of undeveloped emotions, failed relationships, and questionable morality. This protagonist then encounters a father figure—similar to the Hemingway tutor-tyro technique—who guides him through his odyssey by prodding him to ask the right questions, teaching him the meaning of suffering and spirituality, and ultimately coaxing him to accept the responsibility for his own life.

Because Malamud is Jewish, his protagonists are, more often than not, Jewish as well. Given Malamud's background—his father was a Jewish immigrant and passed on his knowledge of the Yiddish tradition of storytelling—this is to be expected. Malamud himself admits, "I write about Jews because I know them. But more important, I write about them because Jews are absolutely the very *stuff* of drama." By itself, this assertion is misleading, for unlike his fellow members of the Jewish literary renaissance, Malamud is not preoccupied with the uniqueness of the Jewish experience. The Jew for Malamud is a metaphor for all human beings. "Jewishness is important to me," Malamud asserts, "but I don't consider myself only a Jewish writer. I have interests beyond that, and I feel I am writing for all men." Malamud's method, then, is synecdochic—by detailing the plight of his Jews, he reveals human's common humanity.

Throughout his career Malamud alternated writing novels with short stories. Of the two forms, he confesses to "having been longer in love with short fiction." One aspect of the short story that Malamud especially enjoys is "the fast payoff. Whatever happens happens quickly." A related matter is compression. Short fiction, Malamud argues, "packs a self in a few pages predicating a lifetime. . . . In a few pages a good story portrays the complexity of a life while producing the surprise and effect of knowledge—not a bad payoff."

Ironically, this fastness and compression are part of the ultimate illusion of Malamud's art. For him the writing of a short story is a long task that demands constant revision. "I would write a book, or a short story," Malamud admits, "at least three times—once to understand it, the second time to improve the prose, and a third to compel it to say what it still must say."

"THE FIRST SEVEN YEARS"

"The First Seven Years," which first appeared in the *Partisan Review* in 1950 and later in *The Magic Barrel*, is a straightforward tale set in the favorite Malamudian milieu, the New York Jewish ghetto. Feld, the shoemaker, decides to play matchmaker for his nineteen-year-old daughter, Miriam, whom he desires to attend college. Feld's choice is Max, a college boy, but the shoemaker is disappointed to learn that Max is a materialist (he wants to be an accountant), and for this reason his daughter rejects the chosen suitor. Simultaneously, Sobel, Feld's assistant, quits his job, and Feld has a heart attack.

The story turns on a typical Malamud irony. What Feld has failed to realize is that he, like Max, is a materialist and that his dreams of his daughter's having "a better life" are wrapped up in money, her marrying well. Malamud here also reverses the typical older-man-equals-tutor, younger-man-equals-tyro pattern. Apparently, Feld is teaching Sobel the shoemaker's trade, but in truth, Sobel is the instructor: He admits that he has worked cheaply and lived poorly for the past five years only to be around the woman whom he truly loves, Miriam. As Malamud might have punned, the assistant teaches the master the difference between soles and souls. Finally, Sobel agrees to remain an assistant for two more years before asking Miriam to marry him.

Malamud's symbolism is both simple and mythic. Feld suffers literally from a damaged heart and metaphorically from an organ that is too materialistic. The rebirth pattern is inherent in the story's time frame, which moves from winter toward spring. The seven-year cycle of fertility—Sobel's wait—suggests that he is in tune with larger forces in the universe. Interestingly, the story is also an early version of the tale on which Malamud would elaborate in *The Assistant*.

"THE MAGIC BARREL"

"The Magic Barrel" utilizes another familiar Malamud pattern, the fantasy. Here, he blends elements of the traditional fairy tale with Jewish folklore. The story in fact begins like a fairy tale, with the line "Not long ago there lived. . . ." In the story, Leo Finkle, a rabbinical student searching for a wife, is the prince; Salzman, the marriage broker with the "magic" barrel and his sudden appearances, is the supernatural agent; and Stella, Salzman's prostitute daughter, is the princess of the tale. The plot is likewise reminiscent of a fairy tale as the prince finally meets the princess and through the intervention of the supernatural agent has a chance at a happy ending.

Malamud's fairy tale borrows elements from Jewish folklore. The characters are certainly stereotypical: the marriage broker, the schlemiel, and the poor daughter. The setting is the usual lower-class milieu. With Leo helping Salzman at the end (each man plays both tutor and tyro), the plot has the familiar reversal, and the story is based on the age-old subject of parent as matchmaker. Even the theme is familiar: Love is a redemptive force earned through suffering and self-knowledge. Malamud also infuses his story with humor. Aside from the stock characters and stock situations, he utilizes puns (for example "Lily wilted"), hyperbole, and comic juxtaposition (prospective brides are described in the jargon of used-car salesmen). Finally, the story contains social criticism directed at the Jews. Leo Finkle, the would-be rabbi, has learned the Jewish law but not his own feelings. He takes refuge in his self-pity (a frequent Malamud criticism), he wants a wife not for love but for social prestige, and he uses his religion to hide from life.

"ANGEL LEVINE"

"Angel Levine" is part fable, part fantasy, and an example of the typical Malamud theme, the brotherhood of all people. Manischevitz, a Malamudian Job-victim, seeks relief from his suffering and aid for his sick wife, Fanny. In the Malamudian world, help comes from human rather than divine sources; here, the aide is a Jewish Negro angel, Angel Levine. In his narrow religious pride and prejudice, Manischevitz can only wonder why God has failed to send him help in the form of a white person. The tailor's subsequent refusal of aid, an act saturated with egotistical pride, fails to lead to relief.

Eventually, Manischevitz, in pursuit of aid, roams into Harlem, where, finding Angel Levine in Bella's bar, he overhears the essential Malamudian lesson about the divine spark in all persons: "It de speerit," said the old man. "On de face of de water moved de speerit. An' dat was good. It say so in de Book. From de speerit ariz de man. . . ." God put the spirit in all things.

Socially color-blind at last, Manischevitz can now believe that the same spirit dwells within every human, uniting them all. In a scene reminiscent of Felicity's vision at the end of Flaubert's "Un Cœur simple," Manischevitz is rewarded by the sight of a dark figure flying with dark wings. The final meaning of his experience he conveys to Fanny when he admits, "Believe me, there are Jews everywhere." Here, he is Malamud's rationalizer, mouthing the familiar theme of brotherhood.

"THE LAST MOHICAN"

"The Last Mohican" introduces the recurring Everyman character Arthur Fidelman (the stories about him were collected in *Pictures of Fidelman: An Exhibition*) and reveals Malamud's growth and artistry in enlarging the scope of his essentially Jewish materials. Although the setting is not New York City but Rome, the protagonist is familiar. Fidelman, "a self-confessed failure as a painter," is also a failure as a human being, a self-deluded egotist who knows little about his self. His teacher is the familiar aged Jew—this time called Shimon Susskind in typical Malamudian gentle irony, "a Jewish refugee from Israel."

The essential lesson is again brotherhood. As

Susskind persists in asking for help on his own terms, Fidelman inquires, "Am I responsible for you, Susskind?" The elderly Jew replies, "Who else . . . you are responsible. Because you are a man. Because you are a Jew, aren't you?" Like Dante descending into the depths of Hell, Fidelman must enter the personal hell of his own ego to learn the powerful lesson. Fearing that Susskind has stolen his manuscript-laden briefcase, Fidelman discovers the refugee in the Jewish ghetto of Rome, "a pitch black freezing cave." Susskind admits to burning the Giotto manuscript inside the case because "the spirit was missing."

This "rebirth of the spirit" story reads less like a Jewish parable than do many of Malamud's stories. Malamud has set the tale in Rome, and he has obviously undergirded it with mythic dimensions by using *Inferno* motifs (using, for example, "Virgilio" Susskind and a street named Dante). Some critics even contend this is the best of the stories in *The Magic Barrel*. Perhaps this story is more believable than others, for rather than merely learning an abstract lesson, Fidelman actually begins to care about Susskind, even forgiving him.

"IDIOTS FIRST"

"Idiots First," the title story of his second collection, reveals Malamud's willingness to experiment. The story is a strange combination of fantasy and fable. Although set at night in his familiar territory, this New York is more of a dreamscape, a nightmare, than a realistic environment. No character motivation is provided, key information is omitted, and one Jewish character, Ginzburg, matter-of-factly introduced à la the fairy godmother in "Cinderella," follows an elderly Jew named Mendel, has the ability to freeze people, and seems to represent God/death. Malamud has either invented a new dramatic form or reverted to an old, nineteenth century American mode known as the romance.

Mendel, convinced that he will die that night, desperately seeks thirty-five dollars in order to send his retarded son to Uncle Leo in California. What is not made clear is that Mendel seems to have made a pact with Ginzburg—he will go willingly to his death if he is given time to take care of his son. Mendel is helped not by the rich (a pawnbroker or the supposedly philanthropic Mr. Fishbein), but by the poor, a dying rabbi who gives him a coat, and by death (or Ginzburg) himself, who gives him extra time.

Whereas earlier Malamud stories usually had contrivances such as obvious symbols or preachy *raisonneurs*, "Idiots First" offers no such aid. On one level, the story seems almost metaphysical, a questioning of God/death for being so detached ("What will happen happens. This isn't my responsibility") and wrathful (Ginzburg sees wrath mirrored in Mendel's eyes) that He no longer understands what it means to be human. In any case, this open-endedness and general ambiguity represent a new development.

"BLACK IS MY FAVORITE COLOR"

"Black Is My Favorite Color," first appearing in *The Reporter* in 1963, is representative of another of Malamud's frequent concerns, the relationship among the races. Like "Angel Levine" before it and the novel *The Tenants* after it, this story explores the fragile love-hate bonds between Jews and African Americans.

Nat Lime, a white Jew who operates a liquor store in Harlem, professes to be color-blind ("there's only one human color and that's the color of blood"). Throughout his life, Lime has befriended "colored" people, but they all seem to resent his attempts. Buster Wilson, his would-be childhood buddy, Ornita Harris, the black woman to whom he proposes marriage, and Charity Sweetness, his current maid, all reject his overtures of friendship and more.

This story is difficult to understand. Both Lime's words and his actions indicate that he is free of prejudice. He operates a business in black Harlem, and he hires black workers. In return, he is rejected by the three black people he truly likes and helps; twice, he is beaten and robbed by blacks, once obviously for dating a black woman. Yet, through it all, Lime retains his good sense as well as his good humor, and he pursues his cleaning lady everywhere ("Charity Sweetness—you hear me?—come out of that goddamn toilet!"). Malamud appears to be indicating that prejudice and divisiveness can reside in black people as well as white.

"THE GERMAN REFUGEE"

"The German Refugee," one of the few first-person stories in the Malamud canon, also illustrates the theme of brotherhood. The narrator, Martin Goldberg, relates his attempts to teach English to a German refugee, Oskar Gassner, who is scheduled to give a lecture in English about Walt Whitman's relationship to certain German poets.

Two distinct stories emerge: Oskar's anguish over his failure to comprehend English and the irony of Goldberg's failure to understand why. Thus, once again, each man is both tutor and tyro. While Martin teaches Oskar English, the German army begins its summer push of 1939. What the narrator fails to grasp is his pupil's deep involvement in his former country's fate and that of his non-Jewish wife, whom he left there.

To emphasize the irony, Malamud uses references to Whitman. Oskar ends up teaching his teacher the important lesson when he declares about the poet that "it wasn't the love of death they [German poets] had got from Whitman . . . but it was most of all his feeling for Brudermensch, his humanity." When Oskar successfully delivers his speech, the narrator feels only a sense of pride at what he taught the refugee, not the bonds of *Brudermensch* that have developed between them. When Oskar commits suicide, the narrator never sees that he is partially responsible.

"THE JEWBIRD"

"The Jewbird" is a modern, urban version of "The Raven." Just as the raven flew through the open window of Edgar Allan Poe's narrator and stayed to haunt his conscience, so Schwartz, this black jewbird, which looks "like a dissipated crow," flaps through the window of Harry Cohen's top-floor apartment and lingers to bedevil him. "Bird or devil," demands Poe's narrator; "How do I know you're a bird and not some kind of a goddman devil?" asks Cohen.

Malamud's beast fable, however, is concerned with more than nebulous guilt over a lost love. On one hand, the tale is lighthearted with a considerable amount of hyperbole, sarcasm, and comic banter; on the other, "The Jewbird" focuses on a heavier theme, prejudice. When Schwartz first enters the Cohen apartment, the bird announces that it is running from

"anti-Semeets." At the conclusion of the story, young Maurie Cohen goes in search of the bird, which had been driven from the apartment by his father. Finding the damaged jewbird by the river, the boy asks his mother who so hurt Schwartz, and his mother replies, "Anti-Semeets." In other words, Harry Cohen is anti-Semitic.

Malamud's story, however, is still more than a parable of anti-Semitism. Harry Cohen is a cruel man and an inherently selfish father who has little to do with his son. When Schwartz begins to help Maurie with his reading, math, violin lessons, and even games, the narrator notes that the bird "took on full responsibility for Maurie's performance in school." Harry Cohen is so self-absorbed that he has been unable to function successfully as a parent.

"REMBRANDT'S HAT"

Nathaniel Hawthorne once admitted that a few of his tales suffered from an inveterate love of allegory. The same diagnosis might apply to some of Malamud's stories. "Rembrandt's Hat," the title story from the collection that was published in 1973, is typical of the essentially two-person psychological dramas that Malamud does so well. Often in such stories, two people who apparently work closely together never grasp what is truly going on in each other. As a result, painful misunderstandings occur, with a major one and its subsequent suffering leading to self-knowledge as well as a greater understanding between the two. Feld and Sobel, Finkle and Salzman, Manischevitz and Levine, Goldberg and Gassner, Fidelman and Susskind—the names change, but the pattern remains.

In "Rembrandt's Hat," Rubin, a sculptor, and Arkin, an art historian, are colleagues at a New York art school, and they run into each other occasionally and utter polite, meaningless words. One day, Arkin makes a chance remark to Rubin that the latter's white headwear resembles a hat that Rembrandt wears in one of his self-portraits. From this point on, Rubin grows silent and starts shunning his colleague. Then, each wearing a different hat, the two art teachers go to great lengths to avoid each other. Ultimately, Arkin apologizes, Rubin weeps, and the two men resume their tenuous friendship.

The story turns on another prominent Malamud motif; like Henry James before him, Malamud uses art as a touchstone of character. For example, Fidelman's success as a human being is mirrored in his self-appraisal as an artist. Arkin, like some other Malamud characters, uses art to hide from life; it occurs to him that "he found it easier to judge paintings than to judge people." Rubin's self-portrait is sculpted in a single welded piece, a dwarf tree in the midst of an iron jungle. Thus, when Arkin makes the innocent comment, Rubin's inferiority complex interprets it as a comparison of the sculptor to the old master, Rembrandt, with the sculptor much less prominent. Finally, all the hats, from Arkin's white Stetson to Rubin's railroad engineer's cap, become self-Rorschach tests of the story's participants.

"NOTES FROM A LADY AT A DINNER PARTY"

"Notes from a Lady at a Dinner Party," appearing in *Rembrandt's Hat*, is a typical Malamud tale about the relationship between the sexes. In the Malamudian world, men and women desperately seek out each other, reach the verge of true commitment, but find it difficult to communicate, often to commit. Thus, Sobel silently pursues Miriam for seven years without revealing his true feelings, and Fidelman in "Naked Nude" finds it necessary to forge paintings in a whorehouse.

At a dinner party, Max Adler finds himself attracted to Karla Harris, the young wife of his former professor who is more than twice her age. Adler and Harris develop an alluring intimacy by secretly passing notes back and forth. An artist mired in the traditional role of wife-mother, Karla flirts with Adler, who, though previously daring only in his architecture, kisses her. After planning a late-night rendezvous at a nearby motel, they both get cold feet, part, and return to their separate lives of quiet desperation.

Both Karla and Adler are different versions of Malamud's self-limiting human beings. For the most part, Adler can only express his desires in architecture, while Karla's inner self comes out only in the relative safety of watercolors and romantic notes. In Malamud's twentieth century America, then, would-be lovers still cling to the courtly love tradition. Art is a medium not solely to express one's feelings but a

place to hide and sublimate. Love rarely blossoms. Adler is divorced. Karla is content to write enticing notes to strange men and keep getting pregnant by her aging husband. Other Malamud men never marry. Oskar Gassner and his wife live in two different countries and are separated by war. Mendel's wife has died. Feld claims his wife does not understand man-woman relationships. Fidelman ultimately becomes bisexual.

"GOD'S WRATH"

"God's Wrath" is another story about parent-child relationships. As with the sexes and the races, Malamud indicates that there is very little communication between parents and children. Glasser, a retired sexton, is a Lear-like figure with three daughters (by two wives) who have all been disappointments. His hope for one's having a better life are pinned on his youngest daughter, Luci, who quits college, leaves her job, and moves out of his apartment. After a long search, Glasser finally locates Luci, learning that she has become a prostitute. "God's Wrath" offers little explanation for the reason things are the way they are, except that God occasionally winks an eye. The story's conclusion is once again open-ended. Unable to dissuade his daughter from a life of prostitution, Glasser stations himself at her haunts and calls down God's wrath on her. Interestingly, at this point, Malamud switches from the past to the present tense, which indicates a sort of never-ending tension between parent and child, a perpetual inability to communicate, and the ultimate ignorance about how a parent affects a child. In the midst of a pessimistic, naturalistic universe, Malamud suggests that certain conflicts are eternal.

Malamud is an acclaimed twentieth century master of the short story. Often writing realistic fantasy, he is able to imbue his initiating Jews with a mythic dimension, while simultaneously depicting social and spiritual squalor in a realistic manner. His tales contain a great depth of feeling that is occasionally marred by obvious moralizing and transparent mythology. He evinces a deep concern for his fellow human beings. His major flaw has been called the narrowness of his subject matter, the plight of the lower-class Jew, but this problem is only a misunderstanding when one realizes that the Jew is a symbol for people everywhere.

OTHER MAJOR WORKS

LONG FICTION: *The Natural*, 1952; *The Assistant*, 1957; *A New Life*, 1961; *The Fixer*, 1966; *The Tenants*, 1971; *Dubin's Lives*, 1979; *God's Grace*, 1982.

BIBLIOGRAPHY

Abramson, Edward A. *Bernard Malamud Revisited*. New York: Twayne, 1993. Abramson's chapter on the short stories is a brief, general introduction, divided into such categories as fantasies, Italian stories, father-son stories, and sociopolitical stories. Echoes a familiar judgment that in his stories Malamud is a moralist in the tradition of Nathaniel Hawthorne and Henry James, but that he writes with the rhythms of Yiddish and the contours of the folktale.

Field, Leslie A., and Joyce W. Field, eds. *Bernard Malamud and the Critics*. New York: New York University Press, 1970. The Fields present a collection of critical essays that are separated into sections on the Jewish tradition; myth, ritual, and folklore; varied approaches; and specific novels and stories. Although the material is somewhat dated, this book is a valuable guide for scholars trying to review early Malamud criticism. Contains a select bibliography and an index.

Giroux, Robert. "On Bernard Malamud." *Partisan Review* 64 (Summer, 1997): 409-413. A brief general discussion of the life and work of Malamud, commenting on his major novels and short-story collections, his reception of the Pulitzer Prize, and the National Book Award.

Malamud, Bernard. Introduction to *The Stories of Bernard Malamud*. New York: Farrar, Straus & Giroux, 1983. This untitled introduction by Malamud offers an invaluable insight into the mind and theories of the writer himself. After a short literary autobiography, Malamud details his belief in form, his assessment of creative writing classes, and the reasons he loves the short story.

_____. "Reflections of a Writer: Long Work, Short Life." *The New York Times Book Review* 93, no. 20 (March, 1988): 15-16. This essay, originally a lecture at Bennington College, offers numerous anecdotes and details about Malamud's life as a writer. He elaborates upon his influences, his various professions, his friends, and some of his theories.

Ochshorn, Kathleen. *The Heart's Essential Landscape: Bernard Malamud's Hero*. New York: Peter Lang, 1990. Chapters on each of Malamud's novels and his short-story collections. Seeks to continue a trend in Malamud criticism that views his heroes as tending toward the *mensch* and away from the *schlemiel*. Includes a bibliography but no notes.

Richman, Sidney. *Bernard Malamud*. Boston: Twayne, 1966. In the first book-length study of Malamud, Richman systematically appraises each of Malamud's works through *A New Life*. Richman also provides a chapter on Malamud's Jewishness, a select bibliography, and some personal correspondence with the writer. A must for students getting started on Malamud.

Sío-Castiñeira, Begoña. *The Short Stories of Bernard Malamud: In Search of Jewish Post-immigrant Identity*. New York: Peter Lang, 1998. A good study of the short fiction and its major themes.

Sloan, Gary. "Malamud's Unmagic Barrel." *Studies in Short Fiction* 32 (Winter, 1995): 51-57. Argues that everything that Pinye Salzman does in "The Magic Barrel" can be accounted for in naturalistic terms; claims that the story is more dramatic and ingenious as a naturalistic story than as a supernatural fable.

Watts, Eileen H. "Jewish Self-Hatred in Malamud's 'The Jewbird.'" *MELUS* 21 (Summer, 1996): 157-163. Argues that the interaction of assimilated Jew and the Jewbird in the story reveals the political, social, and psychological fallout of assimilated Jew as good tenant, unassimilated Jew as bad, and Gentile as landlord.

Hal Charles

SIR THOMAS MALORY

Born: Warwickshire(?), England; early fifteenth century

Died: London(?), England; March 14, 1471

PRINCIPAL SHORT FICTION

Le Morte d'Arthur, 1485; the Winchester manuscript, 1934 (discovered by W. F. Oakeshott)

OTHER LITERARY FORMS

Le Morte d'Arthur, published in 1485, is the only work that has been attributed to Sir Thomas Malory.

ACHIEVEMENTS

Although a vast body of Arthurian legend, fable, and romance existed (in works such as the Latin *Historia Regum Britanniae* by Geoffrey of Monmouth, the French verse romances of Chrétien de Troyes, and the English Layamon's *Brut*) before Malory's *Le Morte d'Arthur*, Malory was the first writer to give unity and coherence to this mass of material. Popular for centuries after its publication by William Caxton in 1485, Malory's collection of Arthurian tales served as inspiration to many later writers such as Alfred, Lord Tennyson (*Idylls of the King*, 1859-1885) and T. H. White (*The Once and Future King*, 1958). In addition, Malory is credited with being the first English writer to use prose with a sensitivity and expressiveness that had hitherto been reserved to poetry.

BIOGRAPHY

Controversy surrounds the precise identity of the Sir Thomas Malory who wrote *Le Morte d'Arthur*. Long identified as a knight born in Newbold Revell, Warwickshire, who wrote his work in prison, and died in 1471, modern scholars have identified several other contenders. Opinion seems divided concerning whether he supported the York or the Lancastrian side in the Wars of the Roses which ravaged England in the fifteenth century.

ANALYSIS

Although in 1570 Roger Ascham attributed the popularity of Sir Thomas Malory's work to an unhealthy interest in "open manslaughter and bold bawdy," the continuing popularity of *Le Morte d'Arthur* is itself evidence of this medieval author's remarkable grasp of narrative technique. The aesthetic principles governing Malory's art have been a matter of debate since the discovery of the Winchester manuscript in 1934. Eugène Vinaver, who edited the modern standard edition, *The Works of Sir Thomas Malory* (1947), has argued that Malory unraveled the complicated *entrelacement* of his French sources, focusing on narrative units which approach the unity readers expect in modern short stories. Since the appearance of his edition, critics have argued that whatever Malory's intentions, *Le Morte d'Arthur* is one work with a cumulative effect. This controversy seems to have subsided, with most scholars agreeing that Malory wrote eight separate tales rather than one unified narrative and that each of the tales exists within a well-defined cycle. Malory's work thus represents an important transition from the medieval romance to the modern narrative or short story.

"THE TALE OF KING ARTHUR"

"The Tale of King Arthur," Malory's first treatment of Arthur, describes Arthur's battles to consolidate England as one kingdom. Within this one large unit, there are a number of tales which, although linked to the overall theme of Arthur's conquests, illustrate Malory's narrative techniques. "The Tale of Balin," for example, is a self-contained story in which one learns all that is needed to know about Balin; on the other hand, Malory includes inscriptions on tombs, puzzling prophecies by Merlin, and other interpolations which allude to incidents in the stories of Galahad, Lancelot, and Tristram. These vestiges of the medieval *entrelacement* supply information which is not necessary to an understanding of Balin's adventures; their existence makes it impossible to claim "The Tale of Balin" an absolute unity of effect. Nevertheless, the presence of this unnecessary information does not make the story of Balin any less a self-contained and independent narrative unit. This story affords a particularly interesting example of Malory's characteristic style and use of techniques which were to find their greatest themes in "The Quest of the Holy Grail" and "The Death of King Arthur."

"THE TALE OF BALIN"

"The Tale of Balin" begins when a mysterious damsel appears at Arthur's court, wearing a sword that can only be drawn out of its sheath by a virtuous knight. All of Arthur's knights try and fail to unsheathe the sword. Balin, however, draws out the sword only to be told by the damsel that if he keeps it, he will destroy his best friend and the man whom he most loves. It is then that the Lady of the Lake appears, demanding that Arthur give her the heads of Balin and the sword-damsel. Hearing this, Balin claims that the sword-damsel caused his mother's death and cuts off her head. By this action Balin violates Arthur's safe conduct and loses his favor.

In the incidents which follow, Balin tries to regain Arthur's favor by conquering his enemies; however, in adventure after adventure Balin's success as a knight, the greatest in the world, is juxtaposed with prophecies of disaster and tragedy. He unintentionally causes the suicides of two sets of lovers and strikes a "dolorous stroke" in self-defense which lays waste three kingdoms. Finally, he meets his brother Balan, his best friend and the person he most loves. Disguised with unfamiliar shields, they fail to recognize each other and fight to the death. Just before they die, they recognize each other and ask to be buried in the same tomb.

While readers accept the supernatural prophecies as tragic foreshadowings, Balin refuses to believe them. Reluctant as he is to accept the validity of the prophetic warnings, he accepts the disasters themselves with a simple fortitude. At three different points in the narrative, he says: "I shall take the aventure that God woll ordayne me." This courageous acceptance of a tragic fate becomes a compelling secondary theme in the tale.

Of the foreshadowings, the most significant occurs just before the final episode in which Balin and his brother engage in fatal battle. Balin hears a horn blow "as it had ben the dethe of a best. . . . 'That blast,' said Balyn, 'is blowen for me, for I am the pryse, and yet am I not dede.'" After causing the death of innocent lovers and the waste of three kingdoms, Balin says with stark but effective simplicity that he is the prize or victim of the hunt, but he is not yet dead. At this point, he realizes that he is being pursued by supernatural forces.

In fact, this image of fate as the hunter and Balin as the prize or victim epitomizes the irony and pathos of Balin's fortunes. Through the use of tragic foreshadowing, Malory contrasts Balin's success as a knight, his demonstration of faith and virtue by winning the sword, with his human vulnerability to fate.

"THE QUEST OF THE HOLY GRAIL"

"The Quest of the Holy Grail" is linked somewhat loosely to "The Tale of Balin" by allusions to the failure of all knights, even Lancelot, to draw out Balin's sword, but it is principally concerned with parallelism between Galahad and his father Lancelot. Malory emphasizes Lancelot's supremacy over all earthly knights, but it is Galahad who serves as model for the followers of Christ and becomes the spiritual ideal.

Traditionally, the Grail is the name of the cup Jesus used at the Last Supper. Later, Joseph of Arimethea was supposed to have caught Christ's blood in it during the Crucifixion. A vision of the Grail was seen by a nun, the sister of one of the Knights of the Round Table, but only three knights achieve the quest—Galahad, Percival, and Bors. At the conclusion of the tale, a multitude of angels appear and bear Galahad's soul to heaven; a hand descends to take the Grail and the sacred spear which pierced Christ's body into heaven.

At the very outset of the quest for the Grail, Arthur laments that however worthy this quest may be, it will destroy the solidarity of the Round Table. Lancelot insists that the quest will bring great honor to the knights. It is a tribute to Malory's success as a storyteller that he does justice both to the spiritual ideal of the quest and the earthly, but splendid, fellowship of the Round Table.

"THE DEATH OF KING ARTHUR"

Malory's "The Death of King Arthur" is both his greatest work and the one in which he demonstrates most independence from his sources. With profound psychological understanding, he dramatizes the conflict between two loyalties: the chivalric code with its emphasis upon comradeship and devotion to one's lord, epitomized in the Round Table, and the service of the knight-lover for his lady, the romantic theme of courtly chronicles. In rescuing Queen Guinevere whom he loves and serves as knight, Lancelot is forced to kill Sir Gareth, the brother of Gawain and the knight who loves Lancelot more than all other men. This incident is Malory's own invention; his sources describe only vaguely the death of Gawain's brothers.

Faced with the prospect of battle against Lancelot, Arthur realizes that this battle will indeed result in the destruction of the fellowship of the Round Table. His lament emphasizes the tragedy of the loss: "I am soryar for my good knyghtes losse than for the losse of my fayre queen; for quenys I myght have inow, but such felyship of good knyghtes shall never be togydirs in no company." Eugène Vinaver has commented:

> . . . it is not through sin or weakness of heart that the end comes about, but through the devotion of the truest friend and the truest lover, though a tragic greatness which fixes forever the complex and delicate meaning of Arthur's epic.

Confronted with accusations by Agravain and Mordred, his bastard son and nephew, that Lancelot has traitorously loved the queen, Arthur is reluctant to take action. When he agrees to test Lancelot, it is with misgivings because, as he acknowledges, "sir Launcelot had done so much for hym and for the quene so many tymes." After Lancelot is discovered in the queen's chamber, Guinevere is sentenced to burning. Lancelot rescues her, and in the process of saving her from the flames, slays Gareth. The war which follows destroys everything.

Even after Lancelot returns the queen to Arthur, Lancelot is exiled and then attacked in France by Arthur and Gawain. While Arthur is gone, Mordred seizes the kingdom and Guinevere, whom he plans to marry. In the first battle with Mordred, Arthur wins, although Gawain receives his death wound and writes repentantly to Lancelot, begging him to come to Arthur's assistance. Arthur dies on the plains of Salisbury and with him pass the ideals of the Round Table.

When Lancelot returns to avenge the king and queen, he finds that Guinevere has entered a convent. As she explains to Lancelot, she has renounced the world because she feels that their love has caused the wars and the death of Arthur. Although she urges Lancelot to marry and to find his own happiness, he insists that he will become a hermit for her sake: "And therefore, lady, sithen you have taken you to perfection I must needs take me to perfection of right."

Finally, in an episode that seems to be Malory's invention, Lancelot learns of Guinevere's death in a dream and is told to bury her near Arthur. During her burial he swoons in sorrow. When he dies shortly afterward, consumed by grief for the king and queen, the bishop hermit relates a vision in which he sees angels raising Lancelot to heaven. At his burial his brother Ector delivers a eulogy which represents Malory's definitive statement on the chivalric ideal:

> Thou were never matched of erthely knyghtes hande. . . . And thou were the truest frende to thy lovar that ever bestrade hors, and thou were the trewest lover of a synful man that ever loved woman, and thou were the kyndest man that ever strake wyth swerde. And thou were the godelyest persone that ever cam emonge prees of knyghtes, and thou was the mekest man and the jentyllest that ever ete in halle emonge ladyes, and thou were the sternest knyght to thy mortal foo that ever put spere in reeste.

It is because of Malory's handling of the Arthurian materials that the stories of King Arthur became part of English literary tradition. From the complexity of his French sources he produced narratives which remain vital and appealing to the modern reader. Perhaps, however, the best critical summary of Malory's achievement was offered by William Caxton, Malory's first editor and critic, who tells readers that in *Le Morte d'Arthur* they will find "many joyous and playsaunt hystoryes and noble and renomed actes of humanyte, gentylnesse, and chyvalryes."

BIBLIOGRAPHY

Archibald, Elizabeth, and A. S. G. Edwards, eds. *A Companion to Malory*. Woodbridge, England, 1996. Part of the Arthurian Studies series, this volume examines the Arthurian legend in Malory's seminal work. Includes bibliographical references and an index.

Bennet, J. A. W., ed. *Essays on Malory*. Oxford, England: Clarendon Press, 1963. A collection of seven essays by such outstanding Middle English scholars as C. S. Lewis, Derek Stanley Brewer, and W. F. Oakeshott. Included is an essay on art and nature by Eugène Vinaver, one of the most prominent Malory scholars of his day, written in the form of an open letter to C. S. Lewis, which responds to many of the points made by Lewis in his own essay in this collection ("The English Prose *Morte*"). A lengthy examination of chivalry in *Le Morte d'Arthur* is also included.

Benson, Larry D. *Malory's "Morte Darthur."* Cambridge, Mass.: Harvard University Press, 1976. Four aspects of Malory's work are examined in a work concerned chiefly with the context in which Malory wrote: a discussion of the relationship of the genre of *Le Morte d'Arthur* to Arthurian legend and traditional romances; the structure of Malory's work particularly as it relates to the English romance; a historical perspective on chivalric traditions and chivalry in Malory; and a detailed literary and historical interpretation of the tale of the Sancgreal, the book of Sir Lancelot and Guinevere, and the death of Arthur.

Falcetta, Jennie-Rebecca. "The Enduring Sacred Strain: The Place of the Tale of the Sankgreal Within Sir Thomas Malory's *Le Morte d'Arthur*." *Christianity and Literature* 47 (Autumn, 1997): 21-34. Discusses the Grail's effects on three levels: its association with sensuous trappings, its effect on the main characters of the Arthuriad, and its impact on the conclusion of *Le Morte d'Arthur*.

Field, P. J. C. *The Life and Times of Sir Thomas Malory*. Cambridge: D. S. Brewer, 1993. A very detailed, scholarly retelling of Malory's life. Recommended for advanced students and scholars.

_____. *Malory: Texts and Sources*. Cambridge, England: D. S. Brewer, 1998. An examination of the sources for Malory and Arthurian tales.

Kennedy, Beverly. *Knighthood in the Morte Darthur*. Cambridge, England: D. S. Brewer, 1985. A comprehensive, detailed examination of knighthood and chivalry and a meticulous discussion of *Le Morte d'Arthur* in this light. Kennedy considers different facets of knighthood, such as "The High Order of Knighthood," "Worshipful Knighthood," and "True Knighthood."

McCarthy, Terence. *Reading the "Morte d'Arthur."* Wolfeboro, N.H.: Boydell and Brewer, 1988. An excellent introduction to *Le Morte d'Arthur*. McCarthy outlines the structure of the work, book by book, with plenty of background and analysis, then offers more in-depth discussions of chivalric tradition, historical background, Malory's style, and his method of storytelling. He also suggests a selection of passages for closer study to give the newcomer to Malory a representative and manageable introduction to an occasionally difficult text.

Parry, Joseph D. "Following Malory out of Arthur's World." *Modern Philology* 95 (November, 1997): 147-169. Argues that the final resting place of King Arthur at Avalon is fitting in terms of the narrative's focus on two types of location that correspond to two concurrent but contradictory narratives of the dissolution of the Arthurian society.

Takamiya, Toshiyuki, and Derek Brewer, eds. *Aspects of Malory*. Totowa, N.J.: Rowman & Littlefield, 1981. Eleven essays on Malory. Examines topics such as sources of Malory, the structure of Malory's tales, and the Malory manuscript. Eugène Vinaver discusses Malory's prose style, and Richard R. Griffiths offers a new theory on the author's identity.

J. R. Brink, updated by Catherine Swanson

THOMAS MANN

Born: Lübeck, Germany; June 6, 1875
Died: Zurich, Switzerland; August 12, 1955

PRINCIPAL SHORT FICTION

Der Kleine Herr Friedemann, 1898

Tristan, 1903

Tonio Kröger, 1903 (novella; English translation, 1914)

Der Tod in Venedig, 1912 (novella; *Death in Venice*, 1925)

Das Wunderkind, 1914

Herr und Hund, 1919 (novella; *Bashan and I*, 1923; also known as *A Man and His Dog*, 1930)

Erzählung, 1922

Children and Fools, 1928

Mario und der Zauberer, 1930 (novella; *Mario and the Magician*, 1930)

Stories of Three Decades, 1936

Die vertauschten Köpfe: Eine indische Legend, 1940 (novella; *The Transposed Heads: A Legend of India*, 1941)

Ausgewahlte Erzählungen, 1945

Die Betrogene, 1953 (novella; *The Black Swan*, 1954)

Death in Venice and Seven Other Stories, 1954

Stories of a Lifetime, 1961

OTHER LITERARY FORMS

In addition to his short fiction, Thomas Mann wrote novels, essays, and some poetry. When he received the Nobel Prize in Literature in 1929, his novel *Buddenbrooks* (1901; English translation, 1924) was cited specifically, though many of his later novels have received wide acclaim. Especially widely read and written about are the novel *Der Zauberberg* (1924; *The Magic Mountain*, 1927), a philosophical exploration of post-World War I dilemmas, and the four volumes of *Joseph und seine Brüder* (1933-1943; *Joseph and His Brothers*, 1934-1944, 1948), a modern mythology based on biblical tales. Mann's essays, collected in *Adel des Geistes* (1945; *Essays of*

Three Decades, 1947), cover a broad range of political and literary issues.

ACHIEVEMENTS

During more than half a century of writing and publishing both fiction and nonfiction, the German writer Mann received at least a dozen honorary doctoral degrees from universities in Europe and the United States. Though Mann lost both his honorary doctorate from the Rheinische Friedrich Wilhelm Universität in Bonn and his German citizenship in 1936, when he was accused of "subversive attacks on, and the gravest insults to, the Reich," he was reinstated as an honorary doctor at Bonn in 1947. Among his other honorary doctorates, two stand out in particular: One was his honorary doctorate from Harvard University, which he received together with Albert Einstein in 1935; the other was an honorary doctorate of natural sciences from the Eidgenössische Technische Hochschule of Zurich in 1955, a degree that especially pleased Mann because it was so unusual.

Mann received the Nobel Prize in Literature in 1929, and he received numerous other honors throughout his writing career, including the Herder-Prize of Czechoslovakia for exiled writers in 1937. During his international travels, both before and during his exile, Mann received many personal honors. In 1935, he was the guest of former American president Franklin D. Roosevelt and his wife at a private dinner at the White House. From 1938 to 1941, he was a visiting professor at Princeton University, and in 1953, two years before his death, Mann saw Pope Pius XII in private audience.

Mann's fiction is diverse, sometimes reflecting conventions of the nineteenth century, as in Mann's early novel *Buddenbrooks*, sometimes exploring philosophical dilemmas, as in his novel *The Magic Mountain*, sometimes experimenting with stream-of-consciousness writing, as in the final chapter of his novel *Lotte in Weimar* (1939; *The Beloved Returns*, 1940), and sometimes rewriting mythology, as in the tetralogy *Joseph and His Brothers*, based on a bibli-

Thomas Mann, Nobel Laureate for Literature in 1929
(©The Nobel Foundation)

cal story, and the novella *The Transposed Heads*, adapted from a Hindu legend. Always, however, Mann infused a new irony into his fiction. He is a key figure in Western literature.

BIOGRAPHY

Thomas Mann was born on June 6, 1875, in Lübeck, Germany. He was the son of Johann Heinrich Mann, a minor politician and grain merchant, and Julia Mann (née da Silva-Bruhn), an accomplished musician, born and reared in Brazil. The dichotomy between the burgher and the artist, embodied in Mann's parents, is one of the themes of Mann's fiction, appearing in such works as the novella *Tonio Kröger*. One of five children, Mann was especially close to his older brother Heinrich, who traveled through Italy with him. The philosophical and political conflicts between the brothers fueled some of the

debates in Mann's fiction, particularly in *The Magic Mountain*.

Though Mann worked briefly as an editor and an insurance agent, he was primarily a writer. When he was nineteen years old, the prestigious journal *Die Gesellschaft* published his first short story, "Gefallen"; after this first publication, Mann continued to write and publish until his death.

In 1905, Mann married Katya Pringsheim, whose father was a mathematics professor at the University of Munich. The Manns had six children: three girls and three boys. Their oldest son, Klaus, who was a writer, took his own life in 1949 at the age of forty-three.

In addition to the influence of Mann's family on his writing, there were two other sources of influence: the political climate of Europe and the social environment of the artist. It was the political climate of Europe that brought about Mann's exile. According to André von Gronicka's account of Mann's life, the "immediate cause of Mann's exile" from Germany was Mann's reading of the essay on Richard Wagner ("Leiden und Grösse Richard Wagner," "The Suffering and Greatness of Richard Wagner") at the University of Munich in 1933. Shortly after the reading, the Manns went to Holland, where they received a call from their children, warning them not to return. As a result, the Manns went into self-imposed exile, spending a brief time in Holland, Switzerland, and the south of France. In 1934, Mann made his first visit to the United States at the invitation of the publisher Alfred A. Knopf. In 1936, when Mann lost his German citizenship, he and his wife became citizens of Czechoslovakia. In 1938, they returned to the United States, and in 1944, they became American citizens. Though Mann's writing has an international flavor, as is evident in the wide range of settings in his fiction, Mann was acutely aware of his German roots. Only briefly between 1933 and his death was he able to return to his homeland.

Mann's social environment as an artist was especially diverse. Because he published from the age of nineteen, in 1894, until his death, in 1955, he had lifelong friendships with such artists as Bruno Walter and Hermann Hesse, and he often visited other friends and acquaintances, such as Hugo von Hofmannsthal, André Gide, Sigmund Freud, and Gustav Mahler.

In 1953, the Manns returned to Europe and went to Kilchberg, Switzerland, where they bought their last home. Though Mann had begun to show signs of ill health as early as 1945, his death was fairly sudden. On August 12, 1955, he suffered a sudden collapse. By eight o'clock that evening, he was dead.

ANALYSIS

Thomas Mann's early stories are set in late nineteenth century and early twentieth century Europe, primarily in Germany and Italy. The protagonists are artists, disillusioned romantics with an ironic view of the cost of their art, which is an isolation from others. They are often burghers turned artist, often physically deformed, further isolating them from life around them and traditional courtship. To avoid the pain and disappointment of love, these protagonists retreat to art and nature, but in midlife, usually when they reach thirty years of age, they are suddenly overwhelmed by passion, usually for an unworthy and superficial beloved. Simultaneously, the disillusioned romantic usually comes face to face with his own superfluity, as does Mann's dilettante, in the story "Der Bajazzo" ("The Dilettante"), when he recognizes himself as "a perfectly useless human being." Though the sense of superfluity is quite often triggered by unrequited love, the object of the love, the beloved, is treated only superficially.

Such is the case, for example, with Amra in "Luischen" ("Little Lizzy"), who obliviously orchestrates her husband's destruction and stares vacantly at him while he dies of grief over her mistreatment of him. Mann says of Amra that she is not "sensitive enough to betray herself because of a guilty conscience." The disillusionment, in fact, has little to do with the beloved. Rather, the disillusionment is a device to trigger the protagonist's introspection, his moment of awareness brought on by the experience. The moment of awareness for Amra's husband, Christian Jacoby, kills him. Other protagonists live on, lacking the will even to kill themselves, such as the narrator in Mann's story "Enttäuschung" ("Disillusionment"),

who says of his disillusionment that it has left him "alone, unhappy, and a little queer."

Mann's protagonists yearn for experience, for connection with the day-to-day living of those around them, and for a synthesis between body and spirit, discipline and impulse, reason and passion, involvement and withdrawal, action and inaction. They are fascinated by grief, death, and disease. In Mann's story "Der Kleiderschrank" ("The Wardrobe"), for example, the dying man is drawn to the boardinghouse of a woman who has a "repulsive eruption, a sort of fungus growth, on her brow." Again, in Mann's story "Tobias Mindernickel," Tobias is fascinated by a child's bleeding injury and by his dog Esau's injury. He is so fascinated by Esau's injury that, after it has healed, he tries to reinjure the dog and, in the process, kills it.

Two works typical of Mann's early short fiction are "Der kleine Herr Friedemann" ("Little Herr Friedemann") and *Tonio Kröger*. In these works, Mann develops the Symbolist theme of the artist's solitude, the theme of the burgher turned artist, and the themes involved in the battles between body and mind, passion and intellect, action and inaction.

"LITTLE HERR FRIEDEMANN"

In "Little Herr Friedemann," the title story from Mann's 1898 collection of stories, Mann explores the themes of obsession with beauty and disillusionment with romanticism. Johannes Friedemann, a hunchback because he was dropped by his drunken nurse when he was an infant, seeks a life of fulfillment through art and nature. This pursuit is encouraged by his ailing mother, who, after fourteen years of a lingering illness, dies, leaving Friedemann with his three unmarried sisters. Like other protagonists in Mann's short fiction, Friedemann "cherishes" his grief over his mother's death and moves further into his solitary existence. To the extent that he thinks of his own death, he envisions it like his mother's death, a "mild twilight radiance gently declining into dark." At the age of thirty, after constructing a rigorously disciplined life, Friedemann becomes obsessed with a beautiful woman, Frau Gerda von Rinnlingen. Battling between passion and reason, between action and inaction, Friedemann finally summons his courage to go to Frau Rinnlingen and confess his love. He hopes that she will feel pity for him. She instead dismisses him with a "short, scornful laugh" as she clutches his arm and flings him sideways to the ground. The rejection leaves Friedemann "stunned and unmanned" and shuddering. In this moment of awareness, he directs his anger against himself. He is filled with "a thirst to destroy himself, to tear himself to pieces, to blot himself utterly out." He drags himself to the river and, with a faint splash, drowns himself. The final image is a "faint sound of laughter" in the distance. Friedemann is among Mann's disillusioned romantics who do not survive their moment of awareness.

Friedemann, often considered a prototype of Gustave von Aschenbach in the novella *Death in Venice*, illuminates the struggle between passion and intellect, a leitmotif linking the various stories in the first volume together. It is the disillusioned romanticism embodied in Friedemann that moves Mann, in his second volume of stories, *Tristan*, toward what critics have called a "new artistic intellectualism."

TONIO KRÖGER

In the novella *Tonio Kröger*, Mann again develops the burgher-artist theme, evident in the title name itself. The name "Tonio," for Mann, symbolizes the artistic heritage of Italy, and "Kröger" symbolizes the disciplined intellectualism of his German father. The protagonist, Tonio Kröger, is a sort of synthesis of the artist and intellectual. An outsider in his youth, Tonio later considers isolating himself from society, but he rejects the impulse, thus allowing himself to find a sort of consolation.

The novella begins as Tonio waits for his childhood friend Hans Hansen, so that they can go for a walk, something Hans has almost forgotten while Tonio has "looked forward to it with almost incessant joy." Though Tonio does not want to be like Hans, he loves Hans, not only because he is handsome but also because he is "in every respect his [Tonio's] own opposite and foil." Tonio is brooding, sensitive, and introspective, while Hans is lively, insensitive, and superficial.

Hans and Tonio are separated, years pass, and when Tonio is sixteen years old, his passion for Hans turns to Ingeborg Holm, who makes his heart throb

with ecstasy. Tonio, like Friedemann in "Little Herr Friedemann," is aware that his beloved is "remote and estranged," but still he prefers her company to that of Magdalena Vermehren, who understands him and laughs or is serious in the right places. Tonio, realizing the implications of his unrequited love for Hans and later for Inge, speaks of being flung to and fro forever "between two crass extremes: between icy intellect and scorching sense."

In contrast to Hans and Inge is Lisabeta Ivanova, Tonio's close and candid artist-friend of approximately his own age. Though she offers Tonio consolation during his turmoil, she also calls him bourgeois, because he is drawn to the superficial Hans and Inge and because he wants to be ordinary. Lisabeta and Tonio explore in dialogue the implications of the artist's existence. Lisabeta, unlike Tonio, is reconciled to her role as an artist.

After thirteen years, Hans returns, and Tonio comes upon him with Inge; Hans and Inge, two of a type, get along well together. Nevertheless, when Tonio, Hans, Magdalena, and Inge all end up at a dance, Tonio tries to make Inge jealous by dancing with Magdalena. Like many of Mann's disillusioned romantics, Tonio hopes that his beloved will suddenly return the passion that he feels for her. Inge, however, is incapable of feeling passion for Tonio. She is, in fact, oblivious to his anguish and remains at the dance with Hans. Dejectedly, Tonio returns to his room.

The novella ends with a letter that Tonio writes to Lisabeta from his room at Aalsgard. In the letter, Tonio concludes that he can be happy with the unrequited love of his ideal beauty. He says to Lisabeta of his unrequited love that it is "good and fruitful." He relishes the "longing" in it and the "gentle envy." He concludes that, through the love, he experiences a "touch of contempt and no little innocent bliss." Unlike the unrequited love of Johannes Friedemann that leads to Friedemann's self-loathing and death, the unrequited love of Tonio Kröger somehow consoles and sustains him.

A significant change in Mann's later short fiction appears in his treatment of aging. In the earlier works, the protagonists tend to be thirty-year-old disillusioned romantics, characters drawn to youth as much as beauty. The culminating point of this fascination with youth is in the story "Das Wunderkind" ("The Infant Prodigy"), in which the protagonist is eight, looks nine, and is given out for seven. The child, dressed in white silk, has dark circles around his eyes and is already bored, isolated, and somewhat cynical. Nevertheless, the audience is spellbound by the prodigy's youth.

In Mann's later works, the protagonists develop a fear of aging. For example, Gustave von Aschenbach in the novella *Death in Venice* and Frau Rosalie von Tümmler in the novella *The Black Swan*, upon reaching their early fifties, fall passionately in love as they are dying, Aschenbach of cholera and Tümmler of cancer. As in Mann's early works, the beloved ones are young. In the later works, however, the protagonists dread their own aging, eventually creating young-old death masks for themselves, masks that, ironically, turn out to be their death masks. In addition to exploring the fear of aging, Mann begins to explore new ideas, such as the effects of evil on passive people, as in *Mario and the Magician*, and the implications of mythologies, as in *The Transposed Heads*.

DEATH IN VENICE

Death in Venice has received high critical acclaim; it is often called Mann's finest novella and one of the finest novellas of Western literature. Mann explores several themes in the novella: the conflict between discipline and impulse, the fear of aging, the draw to beauty that destroys, the death wish, the draw to homoerotic love, and the battle between passion and reason.

Death in Venice is set in the early twentieth century in Munich, Germany, and Venice. The central character, Gustave von Aschenbach, is a well-known German author in his early fifties. At the beginning of the novella, Aschenbach, suffering from insomnia, takes a walk near his home in Munich. On the walk, he encounters a man near the burying ground. The man, who later appears in Venice, awakes in Aschenbach an irresistible longing to travel. This longing eventually puts him on board a ship bound for Venice, where he encounters a repulsive "young-old

man," masquerading as one of the youths and trying to keep pace with them. The man, "pitiably drunk," approaches Aschenbach, and as the young-old man drools and stutters nonsense, the upper plate of his false teeth falls loose. Clearly disgusted by the young-old man, Aschenbach escapes. This encounter foreshadows Aschenbach's later battle against his own aging.

In Venice, Aschenbach becomes obsessed with the beautiful Tadzio, a Polish youth about fourteen years old. Mixed with Aschenbach's passion for Tadzio's beauty is a conscious fascination with Tadzio's mortality. For example, as Aschenbach watches Tadzio play, he realizes that it is not Tadzio he sees, "but Hyacinthus, doomed to die because two gods were rivals for his love." When Aschenbach recognizes Tadzio's ill health, he thinks that Tadzio will "most likely not live to grow old." This idea gives Aschenbach pleasure, but Aschenbach refuses to analyze his response. Later, upon the same realization, "compassion" struggles with "reckless exultation" in Aschenbach's heart. Though Aschenbach chooses not to explore this exultation, clearly one part of his joy lies in what critics have called "the seduction of the individual by disease and death" and the other part in Tadzio's avoidance of the aging that disgusts and frightens Aschenbach. Aschenbach feels exultation not because Tadzio will die but because Tadzio will not live to grow old.

As Venice becomes plague-ridden with Asiatic cholera, Aschenbach himself begins to look haggard. He is plagued by the odor of carbolic acid from the man from the burying ground, an odor that Aschenbach suspects others may not detect. He is repulsed by the pervasive stench of germicide and by the "odour of the sickened city." At this point, in his own battle against the physical effects of his declining health and his aging, Aschenbach dyes his hair black and "freshens up" his skin, making himself into a ghoulish "young-old man."

Aschenbach, nearing his end, has a terrifying dream about the "bestial degradation of his fall." In the dream, he realizes that he has lost the battle between passion and reason. Tadzio has smiled at Aschenbach and has, in that small gesture, left Aschenbach feeling "quite unmanned." Aschenbach, still made up into a young-old man, dies in Venice of the cholera. Aschenbach's death reinforces Mann's theme that in the battle between spirit and body, there are no winners. In death, Aschenbach satisfies his need to be free of the yearning that is opposed to his art, the "lure, for the unorganized, the immeasurable, the eternal—in short, for nothingness."

Finally, in *Death in Venice*, Mann explores again, as he does in "Little Herr Friedemann," the theme of the artist being drawn to "beauty that breaks the heart." Even while Aschenbach recognizes the superficiality of the physical attraction, even of his beloved, as he comes to the subtle realization that the lover is "nearer the divine than the beloved," he finds that beauty compelling. He concludes, as does Tonio Kröger, that "in almost every artist is inborn a wanton and treacherous proneness to side with the beauty that breaks the heart, to single out aristocratic pretentions and pay them homage." It is this homage to beauty that makes Aschenbach incapable of action and holds him in Venice to meet his death.

MARIO AND THE MAGICIAN

A novella in a different vein is *Mario and the Magician*, published between World War I and World War II. It is generally considered an attack on fascism. The story begins with a German family visiting Italy and experiencing a series of minor humiliations. The family later becomes part of the audience of an evil hypnotist, Cipolla, who humiliates the members of his passive audience, one at a time, until one of them, Mario, shoots him, an act that leaves the audience liberated.

Early in the novella, Mann introduces the theme of peace. He says, "We all know how the world at once seeks peace and puts her to flight—rushing upon her in the fond idea that they two will wed, and where she is, there it can be at home." Peace, however, is treated ironically, in that the desire for peace keeps the passive audience from acting, even as they become the humpbacked magician's victims. Mann's narrator soon begins to realize that in "yielding to another person's will—there may lie too small a space for the idea of freedom to squeeze into." In contrast to Johannes Friedemann, who is destroyed when he

acts, the audience in *Mario and the Magician* is saved only through action.

Among Mann's last short fiction, first published between 1940 and 1955, are *The Transposed Heads* and *The Black Swan*. Significant in these last major works of short fiction are two characteristics of Mann's work. The first is one of adapting mythology in new contexts, as he does in the novella *The Transposed Heads*, an adaptation of a Hindu legend about seeking harmony between the inner and outer self. The second characteristic is one represented in the novella *The Black Swan*, in which Mann's earlier theme of the conflict between youth and age, life and death, occurs.

THE TRANSPOSED HEADS

In *The Transposed Heads*, Mann creates his most abstract and mythic characters. Shridaman, a merchant and the son of a merchant, represents spirit and intellect, while Nanda, a smith and a cowherd, represents body and intuition. The girl represents beauty. Though Mann called this work "a metaphysical farce," it offers an integral vision of a new humanity. It is in this tale that Mann includes his clearest synthesis of the unity between "Shridaman" and "Nanda":

> This world is not so made that spirit is fated to love only spirit, and beauty only beauty. Indeed the very contrast between the two points out, with a clarity at once intellectual and beautiful, that the world's goal is union between spirit and beauty, a bliss no longer divided, but whole and consummate.

Following this vision, Mann returns to the farce, concluding, "This tale . . . is but an illustration of the failures and false starts attending the effort to reach the goal."

THE BLACK SWAN

In *The Black Swan*, Mann retells the story of Gustave von Aschenbach of *Death in Venice* but with a new twist. The novella, set in Düsseldorf in the 1920's, tells the story of Frau Rosalie von Tümmler, a fifty-year-old widow, who is caught up in passion for her son Eduard's youthful tutor, Ken Keaton, an American expatriate. Once again, the lover is closer to the divine than the beloved. Ken Keaton is variously described by critics as insipid, mediocre, and commonplace, an amiable nonentity. Like Aschenbach, Rosalie, as she becomes increasingly obsessed with her beloved, dyes her hair and applies cosmetics to conceal her age. Like Aschenbach, she does active battle against physical aging.

Rosalie von Tümmler's daughter Anna, born with a clubfoot, paints abstract art and tries to purge all feeling from her work. It is she, recognizing her mother's unhealthy passion, who urges her mother to establish a more socially acceptable relationship with Keaton. Still, Rosalie ignores her daughter's advice.

In an ironic twist, Mann has Rosalie develop cancer of the womb before she can go to Keaton's room to consummate their relationship. The cause of the cancer is, again ironically, the agitation that she experiences during menopause, her passion for Keaton thus leading to her own death in a matter of weeks. A further irony is evident in that the rejuvenation that Rosalie feels in her passion for Keaton is, in fact, a symptom of her physical decay.

Unlike Aschenbach, however, Rosalie regains her dignity during the final weeks of her life. She yearns for the aristocratic black swans, a death symbol. The German title, *Die Betrogene*, means "the deceived," and Rosalie von Tümmler is indeed deceived, by both her passion and her body, which has sent her messages of a new vitality even while she was mortally ill. Still, unlike Aschenbach, whose passion remains unresolved, Rosalie dies a "gentle death, regretted by all who knew her."

Throughout Mann's lengthy writing career, from 1894 to 1955, the bulk of critical opinion of his work was consistently favorable. It has remained so after his death. Nevertheless, significant changes occur between his early and late short fiction. To some extent, Mann's protagonists do achieve, if not a synthesis of polarities, at least a complex worldview in which they find consolation. The shift in worldview is particularly evident in Mann's treatment of the conflicts between self-destruction and survival, between passion and discipline, and between action and inaction.

First, in the conflict between self-destruction and survival, Mann's early protagonists cannot survive their disillusionment. Johannes Friedemann in "Little

Herr Friedemann" is filled with self-loathing and drowns himself. Christian Jacoby in "Little Lizzy" becomes suddenly aware of his wife's infidelity and dies instantly from shock and grief. With Mann's development of Tonio Kröger in *Tonio Kröger*, however, the disillusioned romantic finds a new, though not fully gratifying, illusion that can permit him to survive. Some critics have referred to this new worldview as Mann's artistic intellectualism. This artistic intellectualism is based on a sort of ironic realization that perhaps the wanting is superior to the having, an idea that acknowledges both the passion and the intellect. Mann explores another sort of synthesis of the conflict between self-destruction and survival in Frau Rosalie von Tümmler in *The Black Swan*. Though Frau Tümmler's passion triggers the cancer that kills her, she clearly comes to terms with her self-destructive passion. Her death is not a suicide but rather a "gentle" death, the sort envisioned by Johannes Friedemann before his disillusionment.

Second, in the conflict between passion and discipline, Mann's early protagonists are undone by their passion. Johannes Friedemann and Christian Jacoby illustrate Mann's early theme that in conflicts between passion and discipline, body and intellect, there are no winners. Though Tonio Kröger provides a respite from the conflict, as he learns to live with unrequited love, Mann explores this conflict in a new light with Gustave von Aschenbach in *Death in Venice*. Aschenbach does not act on his passion, except insofar as he does not leave the plague-ridden Venice, an inaction that, in fact, becomes a self-destructive action. Unlike Johannes Friedemann and Christian Jacoby, however, Aschenbach does not confess his love to his beloved; to that extent, he displays discipline. Nevertheless, the inaction caused by his passion leads as clearly to his destruction as if he had taken his own life, and though he dies with his self-loathing at what he calls his "bestial degradation," he has not destroyed his reputation as a novelist. Mann does a final exploration of the battle between passion and discipline in the character of Rosalie von Tümmler. Frau Tümmler, fully prepared to act on her passion despite her daughter's advice, collapses on her way to meet her beloved and consummate their passion. To that point, Frau Tümmler has lost her battle between passion and discipline, but through the remainder of her mortal illness, she has a second chance to retrieve her dignity, and she does so with grace.

Finally, in the conflict between action and inaction, Mann's protagonists become increasingly complex. In the early stories, characters who act, especially on their passion, destroy themselves. For example, when Johannes Friedemann in "Little Herr Friedemann" acts on his passion for Frau Rinnlingen, the action leads to his death. When Christian Jacoby in "Little Lizzy" acts on his wife's wishes and against his better judgment, he faces a moment of awareness that destroys him. Later, Mann's Tonio Kröger in *Tonio Kröger* opts for inaction with his beloved Inge. That inaction saves him. Mann's treatment of Gustave von Aschenbach in *Death in Venice* is among Mann's most complex explorations of the conflict between action and inaction. Had Aschenbach not acted on the yearning to travel, triggered by the stranger at the burying ground in Munich, he might not have been in Venice during the cholera epidemic. Aschenbach's failure to act by leaving Venice when he had the opportunity, however, results in his death of cholera. Mann introduces another new complexity into the conflict between action and inaction in *Mario and the Magician*. The audience sits by passively while the magician victimizes them, one after another. When Mario acts, killing the magician, his action liberates the audience. In Mann's final exploration of the conflict between action and inaction, Rosalie von Tümmler, in her decision to act on her passion, loses her option for further action on her passion, but in her final weeks of illness, she acts again, this time to reclaim her dignity. Her final action leads to her self-respect and to a gentle death.

Part of the resolution of conflicts in Mann's later short fiction undoubtedly comes from his use of his own experience in the creation of his protagonists. In fact, in 1936, when *Stories of Three Decades* was published, Mann, then officially in exile, referred to the collection as "an autobiography in the guise of a fable." In Mann's work during his years of exile, he moved increasingly toward exploring syntheses of the conflicts in his earlier protagonists. As a result, his later protagonists, as they expand their worldviews, begin to synthesize humanism, culture, and philosophy, and through these protagonists, one sees, always, Mann's ironic observations of the world.

OTHER MAJOR WORK

LONG FICTION: *Buddenbrooks: Verfall einer Familie*, 1901 (English translation, 1924); *Tristan*, 1903 (English translation, 1925); *Königliche Hoheit*, 1909 (*Royal Highness*, 1916); *Der Zauberberg*, 1924 (*The Magic Mountain*, 1927); *Unordnung und frühes Leid*, 1926 (novella; *Disorder and Early Sorrow*, 1929); *Joseph und seine Brüder*, 1933-1943 (*Joseph and His Brothers*, 1934-1944, 1948; includes *Die Geschichten Jaakobs*, 1933 [*Joseph and His Brothers*, 1934; also as *The Tales of Jacob*, 1934]; *Der junge Joseph*, 1934 [*The Young Joseph*, 1935]; *Joseph in Ägypten*, 1936 [*Joseph in Egypt*, 1938]; *Joseph, der Ernährer*, 1943 [*Joseph the Provider*, 1944]); *Lotte in Weimar*, 1939 (*The Beloved Returns*, 1940); *Doktor Faustus: Das Leben des deutschen Tonsetzers Adrian Leverkühn, erzählt von einem Freunde*, 1947 (*Doctor Faustus: The Life of the German Composer Adrian Leverkühn as Told by a Friend*, 1948); *Der Erwählte*, 1951 (*The Holy Sinner*, 1951); *Bekenntnisse des Hochstaplers Felix Krull: Der Memoiren erster Teil*, 1954 (*Confessions of Felix Krull, Confidence Man: The Early Years*, 1955).

PLAY: *Fiorenza*, pb. 1906.

POETRY: "Gesang vom Kindchen," 1919.

NONFICTION: "Friedrich und die grosse Koalition," 1915 ("Fredrick and the Great Coalition," 1929); *Betrachtungen eines Unpolitischen*, 1918 (*Reflections of a Nonpolitical Man*, 1983); *Rede und Antwort*, 1922; *Bemühungen*, 1925; *Die Forderung des Tages*, 1930; *Lebensabriss*, 1930 (*A Sketch of My Life*, 1960); *Three Essays*, 1932; *Past Masters and Other Papers*, 1933; *Leiden und Grösse der Meister*, 1935; *Freud, Goethe, Wagner*, 1937; *Achtung, Europa!*, 1938; *Dieser Friede*, 1938 (*This Peace*, 1938); *Vom künftigen Sieg der Demokratie*, 1938 (*The Coming of Victory of Democracy*, 1938); *Deutsche Hörer!*, 1942 (*Listen, Germany!*, 1943); *Order of the Day: Political Essays and Speeches of Two Decades*, 1942; *Adel des Geistes: Sechzehn Versuche zum Problem der Humanität*, 1945 (*Essays of Three Decades*, 1947); *Neue Studien*, 1948; *Die Entstehung des "Doktor Faustus": Roman eines Romans*, 1949 (*The Story of a Novel: The Genesis of "Doctor Faustus,"* 1961); *Altes und Neues: Kleine Prosa aus fünf Jahrzehnten*, 1953; *Versuch über Schiller*, 1955; *Nachlese: Prosa, 1951-1955*, 1956; *Last Essays*, 1958; *Briefe*, 1961-1965 (3 volumes; partial translation, *Letters of Thomas Mann, 1889-1955*, 1970); *Addresses Delivered at the Library of Congress*, 1963; *Wagner und unsere Zeit*, 1963 (*Pro and Contra Wagner*, 1985); *Reden und Aufsätze*, 1965 (2 volumes); *Essays*, 1977-1978 (3 volumes); *Tagebücher*, 1977-1986 (6 volumes; partial translation, *Diaries 1918-1939*, 1982); *Goethes Laufbahn als Schriftsteller: Zwölf Essays und Reden zu Goethe*, 1982.

MISCELLANEOUS: *Gesammelte Werke*, 1956 (12 volumes; includes critical writings in volumes 10-11); *Gesammelte Werke*, 1960-1974 (13 volumes; includes critical writings in volumes 9-11); *Werkausgabe*, 1980-1986 (20 volumes; includes 3 volumes of critical writings); *Frage und Antwort: Interviews mit Thomas Mann 1909-1955*, 1983; *Thomas Mann's "Goethe and Tolstoy": Notes and Sources*, 1984.

BIBLIOGRAPHY

Berlin, Jeffrey B., ed. *Approaches to Teaching Mann's "Death in Venice" and Other Short Fiction*. New York: The Modern Language Association, 1992. Part 1 (materials) focuses on general introductions, reference works, and critical studies. Part 2 (approaches) contains in-depth essays on Mann's handling of many themes and his approach to comedy, tradition, modernism, Sigmund Freud, and other thinkers and writers. Includes an extensive bibliography.

Cullander, Cecil C. H. "Why Thomas Mann Wrote." *The Virginia Quarterly Review* 75 (Winter, 1999): 31-48. Examines Mann's statements about his creativity, his fiction, and his journals and diaries; argues that his diaries helped him come to terms with his homosexuality and to know himself.

Feurlicht, Ignace. *Thomas Mann*. Boston: Twayne, 1968. A critical introduction to Mann that analyzes the plots, characters, ideas, and styles of his stories and novels against the background of his life. Notes that most of his early stories focus on a marked man, one who is weak, sick, or odd, an outsider who cannot endure everyday life.

Heilbut, Anthony. *Thomas Mann: Eros and Literature*. New York: Knopf, 1996. The most commanding biography of Mann in English, with a carefully detailed narrative of his life and work. Provides detailed useful notes and an extensive bibliography.

Heiney, Donald W. *Barron's Simplified Approach to Thomas Mann*. Woodbury, N.Y.: Barron's, 1966. A basic introduction to Mann's life and art. The chapter on the short stories and tales includes brief discussions of each of the important stories in *Stories of Three Decades*.

Heller, Erich. *The Ironic German: A Study of Thomas Mann*. Boston: Little, Brown, 1958. A study of Mann and his intellectual ancestry. Contains a chapter on "Mario and the Magician" and "Death in Venice." A stimulating and influential book on Mann.

Hollingdale, R. J. *Thomas Mann: A Critical Study*. Lewisburg: Bucknell UP, 1971. Rather than an analysis of individual novels and stories, this study discusses the basic philosophic assumptions, especially the philosophy of Friedrich Nietzsche, in Mann's works. Hollingdale focuses on such themes as crime, sickness, decadence, irony, and myth.

Lesér, Esther H. *Thomas Mann's Short Fiction: An Intellectual Biography*. Rutherford, N.J.: Fairleigh Dickinson University Press, 1989. Lesér states the purposes of her biography as twofold: "as a reference work in which each story may be read individually with its comprehensive study materials, and as an organic study of Thomas Mann's intellectual development." The chapters are arranged thematically, each integrating analyses of representative works.

Mann, Thomas. *Death in Venice*. Edited by Naomi Ritter. Boston: Bedford Books, 1998. A reprinting of a widely acclaimed translation of Mann's novella, along with the presentation of five critical essays that serve to familiarize students to the novella.

Nemerov, Howard. "Themes and Methods in the Early Stories of Thomas Mann." In *Poetry and Fiction: Essays*. New Brunswick, N.J.: Rutgers University Press, 1963. Discusses the types of characters in Mann's stories, such as disappointed lovers of life, those whose love has turned to hatred, and those whose love masquerades as indifference and superiority. Contends that "The Infant Prodigy" is the first appearance in Mann's work of some sinister qualities belonging to the underside of the artist's nature.

Reed, T. J. *Thomas Mann: The Uses of Tradition*. New York: Oxford University Press, 1996. A meticulously researched and well-documented study on Mann's thought and fiction. Includes bibliographical references and index.

Thomas, R. Hinton. *Thomas Mann: The Mediation of Art*. Oxford, England: The Clarendon Press, 1956. A discussion of selected works from the point of view of Mann's concern with art as a moral task of self-discipline. The short stories are discussed as Mann's apprenticeship to the central theme of the yearning for art as a escape from practical life into infinity.

Travers, Martin. *Thomas Mann*. New York: St. Martin's Press, 1992. An excellent, short introductory study, with chapters on Mann's life, the autobiographical elements of his first novels and early stories, and separate chapters on the novels. A concluding chapter assesses Mann as a modern novelist. With notes and very useful annotated bibliography.

Von Gronicka, André. *Thomas Mann: Profile and Perspectives*. New York: Random House, 1970. The author, in his biographical analysis of Mann and his works, hopes "to offer some new insights to the specialists while helping the general reader to orient himself in Thomas Mann's vast and complex world." The book also includes two previously unpublished letters and a chronological list of significant events in Mann's life.

Votteler, Thomas, ed. "Thomas Mann: 1875-1955." In *Short Story Criticism, Excerpts from Criticism of the Works of Short Fiction Writers*. Vol. 5. Detroit: Gale Research, 1990. The entry begins with a brief introduction to Mann, but it is primarily a series of excerpts of the criticism of Mann's short fiction.

White, Andrew. *Thomas Mann*. London: Oliver & Boyd, 1965. White uses a thematic approach to the life and works of Mann. He concludes with a review of six decades of criticism.

Winston, Richard. *Thomas Mann: The Making of an Artist, 1875-1911*. New York: Alfred A. Knopf, 1981. Winston arranges the biographical information chronologically, but he intersperses chapters of thematic analysis and explication. The book, aimed at readers of literary biography, covers Mann's early years.

Carol Franks

KATHERINE MANSFIELD

Born: Wellington, New Zealand; October 14, 1888
Died: Fontainebleau, France; January 9, 1923

PRINCIPAL SHORT FICTION

In a German Pension, 1911
Bliss and Other Stories, 1920
The Garden Party and Other Stories, 1922
The Doves' Nest and Other Stories, 1923
Something Childish and Other Stories, 1924 (also
    known as *The Little Girl and Other Stories*,
    1924)

OTHER LITERARY FORMS

Although Katherine Mansfield is best known as a
writer of short stories, she also wrote poems and
book reviews, which were collected and edited posthumously by her second husband, John Middleton
Murry. She once began a novel, and several fragments of plays have survived. She left a considerable
amount of personal documents; their bulk greatly exceeds that of her published work. Murry edited the
Journal of Katherine Mansfield (1927; "Definitive
Edition," 1954), *The Letters of Katherine Mansfield*
(1928), *The Scrapbook of Katherine Mansfield*
(1939), and *Katherine Mansfield's Letters to John
Middleton Murry*, 1913-1922 (1951).

ACHIEVEMENTS

Although extravagant claims have been made for
her, many critics insist that Mansfield's achievements
were modest. She completed no novel, and, although
she wrote about a hundred stories, her fame rests on
no more than a dozen. Yet, in any age, her stories
would be remarkable for their precise and evocative
descriptions, their convincing dialogue, their economy and wit, and their dazzling insights into the
shifting emotions of their characters.

In her own age, she was a pioneer. She and James
Joyce are often credited with creating the modern
short story. Though this claim may be an exaggeration, her stories did without the old-fashioned overbearing author-narrators, the elaborate settings of

scenes, and the obvious explanations of motives and
themes of earlier fiction. Instead, she provided images and metaphors, dialogues and monologues with
little in between. Like T. S. Eliot's *The Waste Land*
(1922), her stories seem to have had their nonpoetic
dross deleted.

Her stories have influenced such writers as Elizabeth Bowen, Katherine Anne Porter, and Christopher
Isherwood; the standard "*New Yorker* story" owes
much to her. Most important, many decades after her
death, her stories are read with pleasure.

BIOGRAPHY

Almost everything Katherine Mansfield wrote
was autobiographical in some way. It helps a reader
to know about Mansfield's life because she often
does not identify her stories' locations. For example,
readers may be puzzled by her combining English
manners and exotic flora in her New Zealand stories.

The author was born Kathleen Mansfield Beauchamp in Wellington, New Zealand, on October 14,
1888. (In her lifetime, she used many names. Her
family called her "Kass." She took "Katherine
Mansfield" as her name in 1910.) Her father, Harold
Beauchamp, was an importer who became chairman
of the Bank of New Zealand and was knighted in
1923. In 1903, the Beauchamps sailed for London,
where Kass was enrolled at Queen's College, an institution for young women much like a university. She
remained at Queen's until 1906, reading advanced
authors such as Oscar Wilde and publishing stories in
the college magazine. Her parents brought her back
to Wellington in 1906, where she published her first
stories in a newspaper. She left New Zealand for London in 1908, never to return.

Her next decade was one of personal complexities
and artistic growth. She was sexually attracted to
both women and men. At Queen's College, she met
Ida Baker, her friend and companion for much of her
life. Back in London, she fell in love with a violinist
whom she had known in New Zealand. After she
learned that she was pregnant by him, she abruptly

married George C. Bowden on March 2, 1909, and as abruptly left him. At her mother's insistence, she traveled to Germany, where she had a miscarriage. The Bowdens were not divorced until April, 1918.

In Germany she met the Polish translator Floryan Sobieniowski, who, in the opinion of biographer Claire Tomalin, infected her with gonorrhea. Most of her medical problems may have come from this infection: the removal of a Fallopian tube, rheumatic symptoms, pleurisy, and eventually tuberculosis. Back in London, Mansfield met the future editor and critic John Middleton Murry. Their on-again, off-again relationship endured until her death. They were married on May 3, 1918; after she died, Murry edited her stories, letters, and journals. Meanwhile, she was strongly affected when her brother was killed in France in 1915. His death and her own worsening health were probably strong influences on her stories.

During these years, she and Murry knew many famous writers and artists, particularly those who frequented Lady Ottoline Morrell's famous salon at Garsington: Lytton Strachey, Dora Carrington, David Garnett, Aldous Huxley, Dorothy Brett, J. M. Keynes, T. S. Eliot. She and Virginia Woolf had an off-and-on friendship and professional association; she seriously flirted with Bertrand Russell. The Murrys' most notable friendship was with D. H. and Frieda Lawrence; "Gudrun" in D. H. Lawrence's *Women in Love* (1920) is said to be based on Mansfield. Both Woolf and Lawrence were influenced by Mansfield; both made nasty remarks about her in her last years.

Another result of meeting Sobieniowski in Germany may have been reading the works of Anton Chekhov; her story "The Child-Who-Was-Tired" is a free adaptation—perhaps a plagiarism—of a Chekhov story. During 1910 and 1911, she published a number of bitter stories with German settings, collected in *In a German Pension*. For the next seven years, Mansfield experimented with many styles and published stories in journals such as *New Age, Rhythm*, and *Blue Review* before she discovered a mature voice. Her first great story, "Prelude," was published as a booklet in July, 1918, by Virginia and Leonard Woolf's Hogarth Press.

Her health had not been good for several years; her gonorrhea remained undiagnosed until 1918. From the time she learned that she had tuberculosis in December, 1917, she spent most of each year out of England. Accompanied by Murry or Ida Baker, she traveled to France, Switzerland, and Italy, trying to fight off her disease. In 1922, her search led her to Georges Ivanovitch Gurdjieff's Institute of the Harmonious Development of Man near Paris, where she seems to have been moderately happy until she died.

During her last five years, she wrote most of the stories for which she is best known. They were often published in journals such as *Athenaeum, Arts and Letters, London Mercury*, and *Sphere*. Many were then collected in *Bliss and Other Stories* and *The Garden Party and Other Stories*.

ANALYSIS

Katherine Mansfield's themes are not hard to discover. In 1918, she set herself the tasks of communicating the exhilarating delicacy and peacefulness of the world's beauty and also of crying out against "corruption." A reader will soon make his or her own list of themes: the yearnings, complexities, and misunderstandings of love; loneliness, particularly of independent women; the superficiality of much of modern life; the erosions of time and forgetfulness; the beauty and indifferent power of the natural world, especially plant life and the sea. Her exact meanings are not so easily pinned down, for her tone is complex: She mixes witty satire and shattering emotional reversals. Moreover, she uses dialogue and indirect speech extensively, and she does not often seem to speak directly in her own voice; the reader is not sure exactly who is speaking. It is vital for readers to understand that Mansfield (like Chekhov, to whom she is often compared) does not conceal a hidden "message" in her stories. If a story appears to point in many directions, not all of which are logically consistent, that is the way Mansfield feels the whole truth is most honestly communicated. This essay suggests some of the ways these stories may be read.

The action of her stories (again, like Chekhov's) does not surge powerfully forward. Often her stories are designed, by means of quick changes in time and by surprise turns, to lead the reader to unexpected moments of illumination or epiphanies. Her stories are economical, edited so that there is usually not one unnecessary or insignificant word. She can be witty if she chooses, but more often her stories provide arresting descriptions and startling metaphors, which evoke shifting states of happiness, yearning, or despair.

"IN A CAFÉ"

Mansfield's stories often evoke the complexities of the conversational give-and-take between women and men and the unexpected courses that passion can take. An early story, "In a Café," portrays a youthful "new woman" and her male acquaintance, a musician. They flirt as they discuss life, art, and the future. Before he leaves, he asks the girl for her violets, but once outside he drops them because he must keep his hands warm for performing. The young woman is totally happy until she sees the violets on the sidewalk. The reader knows that her love has been crushed, but, new woman that she is, she kicks the flowers and goes her way laughing.

"EPILOGUE II"

"Epilogue II" (also known as "Violet") is more complex. At a pension in France, where the acidly worldly narrator is recovering from an attack of nerves, she reports a long conversation with an exasperating woman named Violet, who in turns tells of a conversation she has had with a man named Arthur. Violet says that, after a few dances, Arthur asked her if she believed in Pan and kissed her. It was her first adult kiss, and they immediately became engaged. The narrator can hardly believe what Violet tells her and is repelled by how easily the naïve Violet and Arthur have found each other. The story (a conversation within a conversation) ends with the narrator thinking that she herself might be too sophisticated. (In this story, Mansfield has imported a piece of conversation from real life. Sometime before she wrote "Epilogue II," she startled a man by asking him if he believed in Pan.)

"PSYCHOLOGY"

In "Psychology," Mansfield dissects the ebb and flow of attraction between two older artists, culminating in a moment of potential, a moment which, be-

cause of their agonizing self-consciousness, they miss. This story shows both minds, but readers are left with the woman and with another characteristically unexpected psychological twist. An older female acquaintance brings her flowers—violets again. This spontaneous gift revitalizes the woman, and with renewed hope she begins an intense letter to the man who has left her. Readers may guess that their next meeting will be no more satisfying than their last.

"JE NE PARLE PAS FRANÇAIS"

Mansfield often portrays more complex and ambiguous sexual and psychological relationships and, as usual, constructs her story to lead her reader in roundabout ways into unexpected territory. Though she often takes readers briefly into male minds, the story "Je Ne Parle Pas Français" has one of her rare male narrators. Raoul Duqette, a grubby Parisian writer, pimp, and gigolo, tells of an Englishman, Dick Harmon, and the woman nicknamed "Mouse," whom he brings to Paris. Not all critics agree on whom the story concerns. Although the reader learns much about the English couple's tortured relationship (Dick leaves Mouse because he cannot betray his mother, and Mouse knows she cannot return to England), many readers think that the story centers on the Frenchman. Incapable of deep emotion, Raoul spies on those with fuller lives than his own; he despises women, is sexually attracted to Dick, and is able to recognize only dimly the suffering that he has witnessed. At the end, he revels in Mouse's sorrow and imagines selling a girl like her to an old lecher.

"BLISS"

The triangle in "Bliss" is different, and again, Mansfield mixes her tones. Bertha seems childishly happy in her marriage, her home, her child, and her arty friends. She gives a marvelous party in which sophisticated guests make inane, decadent conversation. Meanwhile, Bertha finds herself physically attracted to one of her guests, the cool Miss Fulton, and thinks that she detects Miss Fulton giving her a signal. Together in the garden, they contemplate a lovely, flowering pear tree, and Bertha senses that they understand each other intuitively. Again Mansfield surprises the reader. Bertha transfers her feelings for Miss Fulton to her husband; for the first time, she really desires him. When she overhears him making an assignation with Miss Fulton, however, her life is shattered. In "Bliss," as elsewhere, Mansfield's brilliant and precise descriptions of the nonhuman world are always evocative. Although sometimes nature simply reveals an unsympathetic force, allied to human passions but beyond human control, some natural features demand to be interpreted as symbols, such as the phallic pear tree in this story. Phallic it is, but it may be feminine as well, for Bertha identifies with it. The story is read, however, and the pear tree cannot be explained simply. Neither can the reader's final reaction: Is Bertha trapped in an evil world? Is she a free adult at last?

"THE LOST BATTLE"

Mansfield also explores the problems of lonely women, often by showing the reader their inmost trains of thought. In "The Lost Battle," a woman traveling alone is escorted to her room in a French hotel by an overbearing man who makes demeaning and insinuating remarks: A bed in a small room will be enough for her, he implies. She asserts herself and demands a better room, one with a table on which to write. She wins her struggle and is happy with her new room—its size, the view from its windows, and its sturdy table. When she overtips the boy who delivers her bags, however, her joy somehow leaves her. In a convincing but mysterious moment typical of Mansfield's stories, the woman's bravery collapses in self-consciousness, memory, tears, and desire.

"MISS BRILL"

Perhaps Mansfield's best-known version of the lonely woman is the central character of "Miss Brill." The reader follows Miss Brill's thoughts as she arrives at the public gardens. The first faint chill of fall and the noise of the band signal that a new season has begun. Miss Brill's sympathetic interest extends to the various sorts of people in the park; the reader senses an older, precise woman who yearns that happiness and gentleness will come for herself and others. Even some unpleasantries fail to shake Miss Brill's enjoyment, as she rejoices that everyone there is performing in some wonderful, happy play. Her illusions, however, are shattered by two insensitive

young lovers who simply wish that the fussy old woman would move. Again the reader is taken into a lonely woman's mind as she undergoes a psychic shock.

"THE DAUGHTERS OF THE LATE COLONEL"

In "The Daughters of the Late Colonel," the shock is muffled, and the reader does not enter the two sisters' minds so deeply so soon. The story at first appears to center on the familiar Mansfield theme of male domination. The sisters seem to react alike to the death of their domineering father. They are still under his spell. Mansfield shows her dry wit as their hesitant and ineffectual efforts to assert themselves with the nurse and their maid are pathetic and hilarious at the same time. Even sisters, however, may be alone. Not only have they lost their father and are without prospects of marriage, but also they differ so much in temperament that they will never understand each other—the older sister is prosaic, the younger one dreamy. It is only at the end of the story that each sister shows small signs of vitality. The prosaic sister hears a cry from within, muses on lost chances, and feels a hint of hope. When Mansfield takes readers into the thoughts of the younger sister, they discover that all along she has been living in a secret and extravagant imaginary world of repressed desire: her real life. For a moment, each sister thinks that some action could be taken, but the moment passes without communication. Their lives will never bear fruit.

Mansfield's wit is sometimes closer to the center of a story. In "Bliss," many early pages show a devastating view of the world of artists that Mansfield knew so well at Garsington and elsewhere. "Marriage à la Mode" is more purely a social satire. A nice, plodding husband, William, supports his wife Isabel's ambitions. They move from a cozy little house to the suburbs and entertain her artistic friends. Mansfield's acute ear for conversation enables her to give the reader the wonderful remarks that pass for wit among the arty set. The reader cheers when William, in a dignified letter, asks for a divorce. Isabel's friends mock the letter. Isabel herself realizes how shallow they are, but she runs to them laughing. The story has a moral, but its chief impact is satirical. This is also true of "The Young Girl." The title character is the disgustingly spoiled and overdressed teenage daughter of a selfish mother who is mainly interested in gambling at a casino. By the end of the story, the girl has revealed her youth and vulnerability, but a reader probably remembers the story's vapid world most vividly.

"THE FLY"

Mansfield's modernist method seldom gives the reader straightforward statements of her themes; the reader needs to interpret them carefully. Her most deliberately ambiguous and hotly debated story is "The Fly." A businessman ("the boss") is reminded of his beloved son's death in World War I and how he has grieved. Now, however, the boss is troubled because he can no longer feel or cry. At this point, he rescues a fly caught in his inkwell; the fly carefully cleans itself. Then the Mansfield surprise: The boss drops another gob of ink on the fly, admires its courage as it cleans itself again, but then drops more ink. The fly is dead. The boss feels wretched and bullies an employee. The story may remind some readers of William Shakespeare's "As flies to wanton boys are we to the gods;/ They kill us for their sport."

Murry said that "The Fly" represents Mansfield's revulsion from the cruelty of war; other critics discover her antipathy to her own father. Whatever its biographical source, the reader must try to decide his or her reaction to the boss. Where are the readers' sympathies? At first they are with the aged employee who jogs the boss's memory and perhaps with the boss himself. When readers hear of the son's death, they do sympathize with the father. What do they make of his torturing—yet admiring—the fly? Do readers despise him as a sadistic bully? Do they sympathize with him? Is the fly simply another victim of society's brutality, the boss's brutality? Are readers to see Mansfield as the fly, unfairly stricken with tuberculosis? Does the boss refuse to admit his own mortality until he sees himself as a victim, like the fly? At the very end, is he repressing such thoughts again? Critics are divided about this story, but what is clear is that its ambiguities raise a host of issues for consideration.

"THE MAN WITHOUT A TEMPERAMENT"

Another story that poses problems is "The Man Without a Temperament." The reader has trouble establishing where the story is taking place and who are its characters. Gradually it can be determined that the story takes place at a continental hotel and that the central characters are, not the grotesque guests like The Two Topknots, but The Man (Robert Salesby) and his invalid wife (Jinnie—Mrs. Salesby). The Mansfield woman here is not only lonely but also sick—sick with something that resembles the author's own tuberculosis. The reader's difficulties are slightly compounded when Mansfield manipulates time; readers soon decide that the dislocations in the story are Robert's memories of happier days in England. This story's greatest problem, however, is what the reader is to think of Robert. At first glance, he seems without temperament; all his care is for his wife, her comfort, her health, and her whims. Soon, the tension that he is under becomes obvious. He is tortured by his memories. When his wife encourages him to take a walk by himself, he quickly agrees and almost forgets to return. The exquisite tact and humor that his wife loves so much ring hollow: Readers know that he suspects that she will not live much longer. Is he an icy, resentful, and disgusting hypocrite? Some readers may think so. Is he admirably patient and forbearing? Murry, who acknowledged that Robert was a portrait of himself, thought it was drawn with admiration.

NEW ZEALAND STORIES

Soon after her return to London, Mansfield wrote some stories based on her experiences among the common people of New Zealand. "The Woman at the Store" is a chilling and dramatic tale in which three travelers stop far from civilization at a dilapidated store run by a slatternly woman and her child. Although the travelers feel sympathy for the woman's hard life, they also laugh at the woman and child—laugh until the child's drawing makes clear that the woman has murdered her husband. The travelers leave quickly. "Ole Underwood," a character sketch based on a real Wellington character, lets readers see into the mind of a deranged former convict as he makes his way around town, driven by memories of his wife's infidelity. In both cases, Mansfield tries to get into the minds of lower-class people, people much different from those she usually depicts. Another story that deals sympathetically with the doomed struggles of a lower-class character is "The Life of Ma Parker."

When Mansfield returned in earnest to telling stories of the New Zealand life that she knew best, she produced her finest work. (The critic Rhoda B. Nathan thinks that the New Zealand stories, taken as a group, can be considered as a *Bildungsroman*, or story of an artist's growth.) The family drama of her childhood provided material for many of these stories. Her mother was attractive but delicate. Her father was forceful and successful. They lived in a substantial house in Wellington just on the edge of a poor district, then in a nearby village, and later at the edge of the sea in Wellington harbor. She was the third of five surviving children living among a number of aunts and cousins, an uncle and a grandmother.

"PRELUDE"

Her two longest works of fiction, "Prelude" and "At the Bay," are strikingly different from conventional short stories. Both take a slight narrative line and string on it a number of short episodes and intense renderings of the inner lives of members—mainly female—of an extended family. In both, readers are set down among these people without preparation; they must work out their relations for themselves. In both, readers must take time to discover the rich vision that Mansfield is giving them.

In "Prelude," the reader enters the consciousness of several members of the family as they adjust to a new house in the country. (The Beauchamps moved from Wellington to Karori in 1893.) The reader is led into the minds of the child Kezia (the character who resembles the author as a girl), her hearty father (Stanley), her pregnant mother (Linda), and her unfulfilled aunt (Beryl). Their relations are strained, and they reveal their hopes, loves, and anxieties. Gradually, Mansfield's emphasis becomes clear. She gives most weight to Linda and Beryl, whose inner worlds invite a range of analysis. Analysis begins with the aloe tree. Mansfield had earlier prepared readers for this huge, ugly, ominous growth, which flowers only once every hundred years. Readers sense that the tree is somehow symbolic. Linda is fascinated by it.

When she sees the tree by moonlight, its cruel thorns seem to embody the hate that she often feels, or do they embody the masculine force that she hates? Either way, the aloe tree brings out for the reader the secret that Linda keeps from everyone else: Alongside her other emotions (dislike for her children, love and concern for her husband) is pure hatred. She wonders what Stanley would think of that. Beryl too has her secret self. The story ends with her taking an inventory of her attractive qualities and wondering if she can ever get beyond her poses, her false life, to the warm authentic life that she thinks is still within her. Mansfield's apparently haphazard plot has in fact been drawing the reader to two striking female visions.

"AT THE BAY"

"At the Bay" tells about the same household perhaps a year later. Some characters, such as Kezia, appear to have changed. Mansfield's methods, however, are much the same, though the sea that frames this story does not insist on its symbolic force so obviously as did the aloe tree. Stanley forges off to work. The women he leaves are happy that he is gone, especially Linda, his strangely passive wife, who still loves him but dislikes their children, including a new baby boy. The children and their cousins play games. Kezia almost faces death when she pleads with her grandmother not to leave them. Linda's weak brother does face his failure. Beryl has a new friend, a vivid witchlike woman with an attractive younger husband. Though Linda briefly finds love with Stanley, this story, like "Prelude," ends with two dissimilar kinds of unfulfilled love. Linda loves her baby only for a moment. Beryl yearns for sexual contact but is terrified and revolted when she finds the real thing. Perhaps at the end, the sea (as a possible symbol of female fecundity, time, and destruction) sympathizes with human desires, perhaps not. Mansfield's way of presenting her incidents and structuring her story creates intense sympathy for her characters, yet simultaneously lets readers see them, without obviously judging them, from a distance.

"THE DOLL'S HOUSE"

Two shorter New Zealand stories probably show Mansfield at her finest, and they show most clearly how her narrative surprises and moments of brilliant revelation of character and motive can be concentrated in a single phrase, in what might be called a domestic epiphany: a small moment of great importance not easily summarized. In "The Doll's House," Kezia and her sisters are given a vulgar plaything. The house is despised by Aunt Beryl but loved by the girls (Kezia is particularly enthralled by a tiny lamp in the diminutive dining room) and much admired by their schoolmates. The story seems to be about adult cruelty and juvenile snobbery. All along, however, there appear to be two social outcasts, Lil Kelvey and her silent little sister, Else, both daughters of a washerwoman and (perhaps) a criminal. When Kezia impulsively invites them to look at the house, Aunt Beryl orders them away. Lil says nothing, but her silent, wretched little sister had got one glimpse of the beautiful doll's house and remembers, not her humiliation, but that she saw the house's tiny lamp. A small human spirit asserts itself.

"THE GARDEN PARTY"

"The Garden Party" is based on what happened at a real party that the Beauchamps gave in Wellington in 1907. Part of its meaning concerns the relations between two social classes. The central character is Laura, clearly a Mansfield-like character, an adolescent Kezia. Laura is thrilled by the promise of festivity, but in the middle of the expensive preparations—canna lilies, dainty sandwiches, a small band to play under the marquee—she learns of the death of a poor man who lived close by in a wretched house. Readers see the clash of generations when Laura demands that the party be canceled, but her worldly mother says no. The party is a grand success. As usual in Mansfield, important matters slip the mind; Laura enjoys herself immensely, especially because her large new hat is widely admired. After the guests have left, her mother sends Laura with a basket of party food to the house of the dead man. Her journey at dusk is phantasmagoric. Her sympathies, forgotten at the party, return. She is shocked by the somber house of death and by the grieving wife, and overwhelmed by the stillness, even the beauty, of the corpse. Laura feels that she must say something: "Forgive my hat." What she says is certainly inadequate, but it seems to signal

a moment of understanding and growth—or does it? Laura has found a moment of beauty in death. Is that evasive or profound? She accepts the sympathy of her brother at the very end. He understands—or does he?

OTHER MAJOR WORKS

POETRY: *Poems*, 1923 (edited by J. M. Murry).

NONFICTION: *Novels and Novelists*, 1930 (edited by J. M. Murry).

BIBLIOGRAPHY

Alpers, Antony. *The Life of Katherine Mansfield.* Rev. ed. New York: Viking Press, 1980. This volume is the standard biography, sensible, balanced, and detailed. Alpers draws on years of research and includes interviews with people who knew Mansfield, such as Murry and Ida Baker, and their comments on his earlier book, *Katherine Mansfield: A Biography* (1953). He offers some analyses, including passages on "At the Bay," "Prelude," and "Je Ne Parle Pas Français." Includes notes, illustrations, index, a detailed chronology, and a full bibliography.

Bateson, F. W. "The Fly." *Essays in Criticism* 12 (1962): 39-53. In these pages, two critics interpret "The Fly," giving it the kind of close reading usually reserved for lyric poetry. Other correspondents support and contest the original reading. Although they discuss the functions of characters and many details, they focus on the mind of the boss and a reader's reaction to him.

Berkman, Sylvia. *Katherine Mansfield: A Critical Study.* New Haven, Conn.: Yale University Press, 1951. This study has a chapter on how Mansfield used details of her family's life to write "The Aloe" and then to revise it as "Prelude." The final chapter compares Mansfield with Anton Chekhov and James Joyce.

Daly, Saralyn R. *Katherine Mansfield.* Rev. ed. New York: Twayne, 1994. A revision of Daly's earlier Twayne study of Mansfield, based on the availability of Mansfield manuscripts and letters. Interweaves biographical information with discussions of individual stories, focusing on method of composition and typical themes.

Darrohn, Christine. "'Blown to Bits': Katherine Mansfield's 'The Garden-Party' and the Great War." *Modern Fiction Studies* 44 (Fall, 1998): 514-539. Argues that in the story Mansfield tries to imagine a moment when class and gender do not matter; claims the story explores the conflicting demands of the postwar period, specifically, the painful task of mourning and recovery and the ways in which this task complicates the project of critiquing a society that is founded on the structures of exclusion, hierarchy, and dominance that foster wars.

Fulbrook, Kate. *Katherine Mansfield.* Bloomington: Indiana University Press, 1986. The chapters on the stories focus on Mansfield's continual attention to the distortions in social relations created by gender. Argues that Mansfield's stories are overtly feminist and demand to be read as critical accounts of social injustice grounded in the pretense of a natural psychological or biological order.

Hankin, C. A. *Katherine Mansfield and Her Confessional Stories.* New York: St. Martin's Press, 1983. Hankin's thesis is that Mansfield's stories are confessional, with the result that this book connects each story as precisely as possible to its sources in Mansfield's life. The detailed analyses of each of the major stories are more valuable than the thesis suggests. Hankin's readings are subtle and detailed, especially when they discuss the complexities of characters and symbols.

Mansfield, Katherine. *The Complete Stories of Katherine Mansfield,* edited by Antony Alpers. Auckland: Golden Press/Whitcombe & Tombs, 1974. Not the complete short stories but a full and comprehensive collection of almost all of them, scrupulously edited and arranged chronologically in natural and instructive groups. Alpers's notes provide basic facts about each story and much essential information about many of them. The notes also list all the stories not included in this collection, thus forming a complete catalog of Mansfield's short fiction.

Nathan, Rhoda B. *Critical Essays on Katherine Mansfield.* New York: G. K. Hall, 1993. Organizes previously published and new essays on Mansfield into three categories: "The New Zealand Experience," "The Craft of the Story," and "The Artist in Context." Essays represent a variety of approaches: feminist, postcolonial, historicist.

_____. *Katherine Mansfield.* New York: Continuum, 1988. A detailed and useful chapter on the New Zealand stories considered as a group. Includes comments on the "painterly" qualities of "Je Ne Parle Pas Français." The final two chapters discuss Mansfield's achievement with regard to other writers.

New, W. H. "Mansfield in the Act of Writing." *Journal of Modern Literature* 20 (Summer, 1996): 51-63. Argues that Mansfield's notebooks are an active guide to the process of reading her stories; discusses three categories of manuscript commentary and revision: those that emphasize figure and performance, those that change lexicon and syntax, and those that deal with agency and other larger strategies of arrangement.

Robinson, Roger, ed. *Katherine Mansfield: In from the Margin.* Baton Rouge: Louisiana State University Press, 1994. Reprints papers from two Mansfield centenary conferences. Features essays on Mansfield's feminine discourse, her interest in the cult of childhood, the narrative technique of her stories, and her position in the modernist tradition.

Tomalin, Claire. *Katherine Mansfield: A Secret Life.* New York: Alfred A. Knopf, 1987. A very readable biography, though without many critical comments, emphasizing the medical consequences of Mansfield's sexual freedom and treating the question of her plagiarizing "The Child Who-Was-Tired." An appendix gives *The Times Literary Supplement* correspondence on this topic.

George Soule

MARIE DE FRANCE

Born: Île de France, France; c. 1150
Died: England(?); c. 1215

PRINCIPAL SHORT FICTION

Lais, c. 1167 (English translation, 1911)

OTHER LITERARY FORMS

In addition to the *Lais*, Marie de France is also known for the *Ysopet* (after 1170; *Medieval Fables*, 1983), a translation of a Latin text by Aesop. Besides being a demonstration of Marie's poetic skill, the lively and witty *Medieval Fables* is historically important as the earliest existing collection in the vernacular of Western Europe of this material. She is also known for *Espurgatoire Saint Patriz* (1208-1215; the purgatory of St. Patrick), a translation of a Latin text attributed to a twelfth century Cisterian monk, to which she added a prologue and an epilogue.

ACHIEVEMENTS

Although her identity remains unclear, France's first woman poet, known as Marie de France, emerges from the twelfth century as an important literary figure. As a writer of vernacular literature, she ranks, along with Chrétien de Troyes, among the best-known medieval writers of the period. Her ability as a writer has been noted by critics, who cite her mastery of irony and understatement, her creation of suspense and description, and her use of material from folktales. A product of her times, her work is a reflection of medieval attitudes and society.

Her best-known and most representative work, the *Lais*, is characterized by a view of the problems of a love that finds itself in confrontation with social conventions. In form, they are brief works in rhymed octosyllabic couplets. The *Lais* have been much imitated, and there are several others attributed to Marie beyond the twelve that scholars are reasonably sure are her work.

BIOGRAPHY

Only two facts are certain about Marie: her name and her provenance. She names herself in each of her works, and in the *Medieval Fables* she says that she is "de France." Although there are several Maries mentioned in this period, notably Marie de Champagne, daughter of Eleanor of Aquitaine and patroness of Chrétien de Troyes, the most appealing identification of Marie de France is with Marie, abbess of Shaftesbury, the natural daughter of Geoffrey of Anjou and half sister of Henry II of England. The precise date of Marie's birth is unknown but a *floruit* of 1155-1215 seems reasonably firm. From the allusions in her works, she was obviously well educated (she mentions Priscian and Ovid), and she was aware of the conventions of "courtly" romance of her time, although her connections with and influence of and by her contemporaries are unclear.

ANALYSIS

Marie is best known for the twelve *Lais* that represent her earliest work and also present her narrative art in its fullest variety. The *Medieval Fables* and the *Espurgatoire Saint Patriz* are clearly derivative (more or less faithful translations of earlier works) and allow very little opportunity for the development of character, ironic situations, or the exploitation of supernatural elements that are hallmarks of Marie's work. It has been suggested that, in the *Lais*, Marie is the creator of a narrative form. Although this is a debatable point and one that is difficult to support, it is reasonable to say that the form Marie gave to the *lai* became normative in the centuries that followed.

LAIS

Marie states that she is writing down *lais* that she has heard from Breton *conteurs* or from other sources. The titles of some of her *Lais*, "Yonec," "Eliduc," or "Laüstic," for example, are of Celtic provenance, but it is impossible to determine precisely how much and in what ways Marie depended on her "Celtic sources." Even the etymology of the word *lai*—possibly the Celtic *laid*, Latin *leudas* (*laus* or *laudis?*), meaning a tale to be sung—is in dispute and can give little substance to theories of the origin of this genre. If there were Breton minstrels who composed and performed, possibly with musical accompaniment, the short adventures known as "Breton lays," there is very little evidence of connection between such performers and the courts of Norman England.

The general prologue to the *Lais* provides Marie's definition of the genre and her own statement of purpose in writing the *Lais*. A *lai* is composed to commemorate an adventure, generally an affair of love, that had first become current as a *conte*, a tale (prologue, vv. 33-42) which was then formulated in verse so that it could better be remembered. Marie desired to demonstrate her literary skills, which should not be hidden; she also saw in her writing a labor that would keep her from idleness and sorrow: "Who wishes to defend herself from wickedness should study and learn and undertake serious work."

Both the general prologue and the prologue to "Guigemar," her first *Lai*, show an artist at once confident in her skill and defensively aware that her learning makes of her an anomaly in her culture, the object of jealousy and scorn. In a strongly worded passage, she compares her detractors to "evil, cowardly, felonious dogs/ who bite people treacherously," but she will not allow such opposition to stop her from writing. Isolated by her talents and quite possibly also isolated in her personal circumstances since "de France" indicates that she is not writing in her native land, it is not surprising that many of her characters find themselves in some form of alienation created either by their own natures, or their societies, or by the love relationship that is the core of their adventure. This is not to suggest that the *Lais* are autobiographical; rather, the theme of isolation or alienation is one of the most effectively expressed elements in the *Lais* of Marie.

"LANVAL"

Most notable in this regard is "Lanval." The protagonist, Lanval, a young knight of Arthur's court, finds himself neglected and unrewarded by the king he serves and envied by his fellows because of his prowess. His own pride prevents him from seeking help in his impoverished state and, near despair, he leaves the court to seek the consolations of solitude. He is approached by the handmaidens of a princess of the fairy realm. The princess welcomes him as a lover and promises to free him from want and loneliness as long as he keeps their relationship a secret. When he returns to court, he finds himself both the possessor of miraculous wealth and also the lover of the lady. He keeps his lady's identity a secret until he is taunted by Arthur's queen, whose efforts at seduction he has repulsed, claiming that the least of his lady's maidens is more beautiful than the queen. His words earn him the king's displeasure and it is only at the last moment that he is rescued from the penalties of *lèse majesté* by the arrival of his lady, who makes good his boast.

The theme of isolation is the most consistently developed element of "Lanval." Although Marie alludes specifically to the plight of one who finds himself a stranger in a foreign land, her implicit references to alienation are more effective. Lanval is wretched in his neglected state, but part of his plight is the result of his own prideful refusal to seek aid. His eminence in knightly skill—which should alleviate his difficulties—ironically worsens them since he earns only the envy of his fellows. Even in the consolations of love he finds himself shut out from the knightly community since he must keep secret his lady's existence. This same necessity for secrecy opens the way for the vicious taunts of the queen (spurned, she accuses Lanval of unnatural vice) that lead to Lanval's breaking of his oath to his lady.

Marie's presentation of isolation in "Lanval" has a lyric force and intensity, yet Lanval is agent as well as victim; his own sexual pride is the cause of the betrayal that redoubles his isolation. The poignancy of his situation is balanced by the aesthetic distance that Marie provides in indicating that much of Lanval's distress can be attributed to his own nature. At the same time, she emphasizes the exclusivity of the love relationship, the effect of which is heightened by the use of the supernatural, since, in gaining the fulfillment of love, Lanval must leave behind the society that both nurtured and scorned him. Lanval's lady comes from the fairy realm, and it is to her land that Lanval is taken in the end. In this and in many others of the *Lais* of Marie, the denouement is ambiguous at best.

If Marie's lovers are isolated in and by their loves, they are also, initially, deprived of love. In "Guigemar," "Laüstic," "Yonec," "Les Deus Amanz" ("The Two Lovers"), and "Milon," the protagonists either spurn love initially ("Guigemar") or are the victims of jealous mates (as are the wives in "Guigemar," "Laüstic," "Yonec," and "Milon") or of too-possessive parents (the daughter in "The Two Lovers"). The jealous husband in "Laüstic" is Marie's most distinct portrayal of this character type. He is aware that his wife is in love with their neighbor and that, although the two never meet, they exchange gifts and glances from the windows of their towers. The wife dissembles, claiming only her joy in the song of a nightingale (*L'eostic*) as the reason for her frequent risings at night. Her husband then sets his whole entourage to trap the nightingale. He confronts his wife with the bird, and when she demands it, he kills it and flings the corpse at her so that her shift is bloodied. The lady entombs the bird in a gem-ornamented casket and sends it, as a sign that their affair must end, to her lover who treasures the casket as a relic.

"LAÜSTIC"

In "Laüstic," Marie maintains dramatic contrast and tension between the highly idealized passion of the lovers and the debasing jealousy of the husband; between the two codes—social and amatory; and between the fragility of the affair and the violence unleashed on it and its symbol, the nightingale, by the opposing passion of jealousy. The husband has "right" on his side as Marie attests in the words she chooses to conclude her description of the lover: "He loved his neighbor's wife." Nevertheless, the husband's rage is so exaggerated and his vengeance aimed at a bird is so incongruous, that there is little to relieve his negative portrait. Marie does not wholly exonerate the lovers, especially the lady, who dooms the affair by her lack of prudence and her transparent guile. However sincere the lovers' passion might seem to be, it is no more concrete than the song of the nightingale. Even if, as some critics maintain, the lovers are only playing at love, the husband is sin-

cere, and if the song of the bird corresponds to the love affair, the bird's corpse and, yet more graphically, the blood on the lady's garment correspond to the violence with which reality can destroy an ideal. Marie focuses the interplay of passions by means of the nightingale, a multiplex image whose song exemplifies unrestrained passion, destroyed nevertheless by the passions of which it becomes the focus.

The nightingale is one of several concrete focusing images that Marie uses in the *Lais*. Others are the lovers' knots in "Guigemar" which can only be untied when the lovers are reunited; the ring and coverlet in "Le Frêne" ("The Asa Tree"), signs of the heroine's noble birth; the sea in "Eliduc" with its complex referents of passion and isolation; and the double image of the interwoven honeysuckle (*chèvrefeuille*) and hazel in "Chèvrefeuille" ("The Honeysuckle"). In the latter tale, which recounts an episode from the legend of Tristan and Iseult, Tristan, banished from court, uses a carved hazel twig wreathed with honeysuckle to convey this message: "Fair friend, thus it is with us/ not you without me, nor I without you." This image functions both within the *lai* and between the *lai* and the reader, who receives the message in the same moment as does Iseult. The elegant simplicity of the verse, which English cannot convey, reinforces the image of interdependence of the hazel and the honeysuckle.

Not all of the *lais* deal with faithfulness in love. Two, "Equitan" and "Bisclayret," are tales of disloyalty and punishment. "Equitan" is as close to a *fabliau* as one can find among Marie's *Lais* a pleasure-loving king commits adultery with his seneschal's wife. The two conspire to murder the husband, but they are destroyed in the trap they set for him. "Bisclayret" is the tale of a werewolf who, betrayed by his wife, is forced to remain in wolf-form while his wife lives with her lover. He is befriended by his king, and when the guilty couple come to court, he avenges himself, and his wife is forced to allow him to return to his human form. In both instances, the penalties for disloyalty in love are harsh and swiftly dealt out. At the same time, vengeance is insufficient since the survivor in both cases had been truly in love. There is thus a double condemnation of disloyalty—the simple wish fulfillment of justice meted out and the more complex implicit condemnation presented in the fate of the regretful survivor.

"ELIDUC"

"Eliduc," the longest of Marie's *Lais*, is one of the most problematical. Based on the folk motif of the "man with two wives," this *lai* presents a seemingly unresolvable dilemma and a barely probable solution. The happily married Eliduc, unfairly exiled, falls in love with the daughter of the king whose service he has entered. When he is allowed to return home, he is welcomed by his king and his wife Guildeluec whom he still loves; but he yearns for Guilliadun, the princess. He returns to the land of his exile, ostensibly to aid Guilliadun's father, and she elopes with him. Their ship is caught in a storm, and the sailors blame Guilliadun's presence for their ill fortune. When she learns that Eliduc is married, she falls unconscious, and all believe her to be dead. Eliduc has her placed in a hidden chapel and visits her bier daily. Guildeluec learns of the visits, comes to the chapel, and finds Guilliadun. The princess is magically revived by an herb Guildeluec discovers by chance, and Guildeluec enters a convent to allow the lovers to marry. In their later years, Eliduc and Guilliadun also enter the religious life, and all spend their last years in holiness and charity.

The denouement of "Eliduc" is purest romantic wish fulfillment, although Guildeluec's abdication is not without overtones of much grimmer possibilities. Marie never suggests that the passionate affair is tarnished by any implicit contrast with the wife's sacrifice; Eliduc's new love is taken for granted. He can be considered an analogue to those other characters in Marie's *Lais* who are deprived of love. Although he is content in marriage, the new affair is the love of free consent, the romantic passion somewhat inaccurately called "courtly love." Guilliadun is exonerated by her innocence of Eliduc's obligations and, furthermore, she is quite similar to the lover of Lanval. Her role is analogous to that of a fairy princess: She lives in a realm apart, her lover is drawn or compelled to come to her, and her power is absolute. The element of conflict between "ideal" love and social reality is also present, but here a near-miraculous decision resolves the dilemma. The denouement moves the story from the secular context entirely, since it is only in the realm of *caritas*, Christian charity, that the complex loves of the "Eliduc" can exist.

No one *lai* of Marie can be selected as supremely characteristic of her work. All show the cool, ironic detachment that tempers the allegiances and responses of the readers as they observe her characters in their respective dilemmas of love. The "Eliduc," however, may be seen as a compendium of motifs, technique, and thematic emphasis. From the all-powerful princess, the isolation and deprivation of the protagonist, the celebration of free passion tempered by the ironic observation of its consequences, to the validation of faithfulness in loving even when the *context* of that love must be transposed to a higher realm, "Eliduc" shows Marie at her best.

MEDIEVAL FABLES

Perhaps the best evaluation of the *Medieval Fables* of Marie, her translation of a Latin text of Aesop, is that which, in one scholar's words, describes her work as a depiction not of "humanity" but of "feudalism." The moral application of a typically Aesopian tale, the lamb confronted by the wolf who chooses any imagined grudge as an excuse to devour his victim, is appropriate to twelfth century society. Marie's contribution to this genre was to bestow contemporary referents on these ancient tales and render them skillfully in the octosyllabic couplets popular with the readers and the listeners of her milieu.

ESPURGATOIRE SAINT PATRIZ

Marie's *Espurgatoire Saint Patriz* is also a translation, this time of a Latin text attributed to Henry of Saltrey, a twelfth century Cistercian monk. Marie followed her Latin text very closely, adding a prologue and an epilogue of her own and a very small number of lines not in the original for purposes of clarification. The work narrates the adventures of an Irish knight, Owein, who serves as interpreter for an English monk who is establishing a monastery in Ireland. He visits the entrance to Purgatory established by the second St. Patrick, is allowed to enter, witnesses the various torments inflicted on sinners, and is himself menaced by demons. Later he is shown the Terrestrial Paradise. He survives the ordeal and lives for twelve years more as a lay Brother at the monastery established by the Englishmen. Although Marie states that she is translating the story for the purpose of spiritual edification, the *Espurgatoire Saint Patriz* has attractive literary qualities as well. It is vividly descriptive of Owein's experiences, and scholars have noted its resemblance to a tale of knightly adventure. The established sequence of Marie's works (the *Lais*, the *Medieval Fables*, and *Espurgatoire Saint Patriz*) might suggest a turning away on her part from purely secular works, but thematic and stylistic similarities, such as the journey, elements of the supernatural, the concern with moral obligations, and the verse form, show a basic consistency in her works. Although it pleased her to instruct, Marie did not allow didacticism to overshadow her impulse to produce a well-wrought narrative.

OTHER MAJOR WORKS

TRANSLATIONS: *Ysopet*, after 1170 (*Medieval Fables*, 1983); *Espurgatoire Saint Patriz*, 1208-1215.

BIBLIOGRAPHY

Burgess, Glyn S. "The Fables of Marie de France: Some Recent Scholarship." *French Studies*, no. 61 (Winter, 1996): 8-13. Summarizes and critiques contemporary studies of Marie de France's fables; includes a bibliography of studies on the fables.

_____. *The "Lais" of Marie de France: Text and Context*. Athens: University of Georgia Press, 1987. A detailed study of the twelve *lais* contained in the British Library. The study notes thematic and textual parallels in the *lais*, with the author's hope that they will help scholars in future evaluations of the authorship of these works (given the possibility that the twelve *lais* were not all written by the same person). Burgess discusses the problem of internal chronology and focuses attention on key terms in Marie's use of language. Includes extensive notes for further study, a bibliography, and an index.

Donovan, Mortimer J. *The Breton Lay: A Guide to Varieties*. Notre Dame, Ind.: University of Notre Dame Press, 1969. A well-documented and readable general discussion of the Breton lay. Chapter 1 is devoted to Marie de France and the tradition of the Breton lay as it relates to her work.

Ferguson, Mary H. "Folklore in the *Lais* of Marie de France." *Romantic Review* 58 (1966): 3-24. A catalog of folklore motifs. This article can be a useful introduction to this aspect of the *Lais*.

Gertz, Sun Hee Kim. "Echoes and Reflections of Enigmatic Beauty in Ovid and Marie de France." *Speculum* 73 (April, 1998): 372-396. Examines Ovid's and Marie de France's fascination with the subject of beauty and its relation to love; compares Ovid's tale of Narcissus and Echo in the *Metamorphoses* with Marie's *Lai* "Guigemar."

McCash, June Hall. "The Swan and the Nightingale: Natural Unity in a Hostile World in the Lais of Marie de France." *French Studies* 49 (October, 1995): 385-396. Discusses Marie de France's symbolic and mimetic depiction of nature in her *Lais*. Notes that although she uses a wealth of symbolic associations of birds, she does not violate their natural functions.

Marie, de France. *Fables*. Edited and translated by Harriet Spiegel. Toronto: University of Toronto Press, 1987. Provides the text and English translation for the *Medieval Fables*. This book has an especially interesting introduction with informative notes, in which Spiegel suggests that Marie herself could have gathered and recorded these fables for the first time. Spiegel includes a discussion of Marie's role in adapting existing tales, and her comments on the meaning of "translation" in regard to the *Medieval Fables* are particularly thought-provoking.

Mickel, Emanuel J. *Marie de France*. New York: Twayne, 1974. A good, full-length study of Marie de France, her works, and the intellectual background of the twelfth century for the general reader as well as the student of medieval literature. Contains individual chapters on Marie's identity, the narrative *lai*, sources and plot summaries for the various *Lais*, an interpretation, and the structure and style of the *Lais*. Includes a chronology of the time period, useful notes and references for further study, a select bibliography (with many foreign language sources), and an index.

_____. "Marie de France's Use of Irony as a Stylistic and Narrative Device." *Studies in Philology* 71 (1974): 265-290. Mickel discusses Marie's gentle irony as an inherent element in several of the plots in the *Lais*; he also considers her use of irony as an important part of her skill as a writer. Detailed presentation of the question with examples.

_____. "A Reconsideration of the *Lais* of Marie de France." *Speculum* 46 (1971): 39-65. A careful consideration of the various *Lais* from the point of view of Marie's concept of love. Many of the same points are made in chapter 7 of Mickel's book, *Marie de France* (above).

Semple, Benjamin. "The Male Psyche and the Female Sacred Body in Marie de France and Christine de Pizan." *Yale French Studies*, no. 86 (1994): 164-186. Discusses the first of Marie de France's lais, "Guigemar," and Christine de Pizan's *Livre de la cité des dames*; argues that the image of humanity that emerges from the texts, like the mystical vision, invites us to contemplate the essential paradox of a body that is at once sexual, intellectual, and ethical.

Amelia A. Rutledge,
updated by Susan L. Piepke

ADAM MARS-JONES

Born: London, England; October 26, 1954

PRINCIPAL SHORT FICTION

Fabrications, 1981 (pb. in England as *Lantern Lecture and Other Stories*, 1981

The Darker Proof: Stories from a Crisis, 1987 (with Edmund White)

Monopolies of Loss, 1992

OTHER LITERARY FORMS

In 1997, Adam Mars-Jones published a selection of nonfiction writings on gay issues and other topics in a book entitled *Blind Bitter Happiness*. His 1993 novel *The Waters of Thirst* received critical praise on both sides of the Atlantic. He also edited *Mae West Is Dead: Recent Lesbian and Gay Fiction* (1983).

ACHIEVEMENTS

In 1982, Adam Mars-Jones received the Somerset Maugham Award for *Lantern Lecture and Other Stories*. He has received widespread critical praise for his fiction; Edmund White hailed him as England's most incisive and intelligent writer.

BIOGRAPHY

Adam Mars-Jones was born in London, England, on October 26, 1954. His early education, which included instruction in Greek and Latin, shows in his impeccable prose style. He became aware of being gay at an early age. His stern father, a High Court judge who "anathematized" homosexuals, created his most serious adolescent crisis. It was many years before he finally admitted he was gay to his father and much longer before his father accepted it.

Mars-Jones caught critical attention with the publication of *Lantern Lecture and Other Stories* in 1981, published in the United States as *Fabrications*. These stories were distinguished by the author's zany humor, imagination, and irreverence. When the acquired immunodeficiency syndrome (AIDS) epidemic hit England and began to decimate his gay friends, Mars-Jones realized that here was a subject worthy of his serious attention. In 1985 he discovered the work of the gay American writer Edmund White, and they became friends. They jointly published a collection of their stories dealing with the tragedies of lovers whose lives were destroyed by AIDS.

Mars-Jones has become a leading crusader for tolerance and better medical treatment for homosexuals. He earns part of his living by writing film and book reviews and is becoming increasingly popular as a fiction writer on both sides of the Atlantic.

Analysis

Most of Adam Mars-Jones's short stories deal with AIDS. The most striking feature about these stories is his humorous treatment of this tragic subject. In this respect he resembles the older American writer Edmund White, with whom he published an anthology of their stories about AIDS titled *The Darker Proof: Stories from a Crisis*. It is most helpful to read some of White's stories in order to appreciate the courage implicit in the lighthearted, campy tone both employ in telling about death and suffering.

One critic called Mars-Jones's fiction "discursive," another way of saying that he rambles, digresses, and never seems to be aiming at any particular point. The point, then, of a Mars-Jones story is often contained more in his tone and in what he decides *not* to say. The sensitive reader will recognize that his narrators deliberately avoid the painful truth and instead talk about everything else under the sun, as people sometimes do when distracted by grief. It is as if they are desperately searching for other things to talk about, including memories of brighter days, in order to avoid facing the horror haunting their lives. *The Times Literary Supplement* reviewer Peter Parker wrote of *Monopolies of Loss:* "Without in any way mitigating the catastrophe of AIDS, these grim, funny, touching, eloquent and brave stories demonstrate that it is possible to salvage something of lasting value from the wreckage."

Although Mars-Jones and White write about similar subjects, it should be noted that the characters in Mars-Jones's stories belong to a lower social class. His characters are forced to earn a living at semiskilled jobs and often lead rather precarious existences, whereas White's characters belong to an international gay society and are cultured, educated, and sophisticated.

The most comprehensive collection of Mars-Jones's short stories is *Monopolies of Loss*. This vol-

Adam Mars-Jones (©Miriam Berkley)

ume contains nine stories, including the four published in *The Darker Proof: Stories from a Crisis*. *Monopolies of Loss* also contains an illuminating introduction, in which Mars-Jones explains his purpose and rationale in writing about AIDS. He realized that the scourge killing his friends had ironically provided him with timely, internationally significant subject matter. "Aids is a theme that won't let go of me," he wrote, "or else I won't let go of it. It isn't really a question of social responsibility. How often does a writer not have to go looking for a subject, but more or less have to barricade his door against it?"

"Slim"

"Slim" is one of several stories written in the first person by a fictitious narrator, an approach with which Mars-Jones became comfortable. (His novel *The Waters of Thirst* is an unbroken monologue by an adopted persona.) This narrative device was popularized by the Victorian poet Robert Browning, well known for such dramatic monologues as "My Last Duchess," the device being very popular with contemporary fiction writers. "Slim" is a euphemism for "AIDS," a word Mars-Jones, like Edmund White and many other gay fiction writers, tends to avoid. "Slim" is the African word for AIDS; one common characteristic of victims is that they become emaciated because they cannot retain food. The narrator fantasizes that he has an unknown African family who were too poor to give him any other legacy but the disease that is decimating their unfortunate continent. Although the narrator is dying, he maintains a "gay," witty facade when visited by his friend Buddy so as not to distress him, as well as to avoid succumbing to the fear and hopelessness that lie just below the surface.

"An Executor"

"An Executor" is one of Mars-Jones's most technically complex stories. The protagonist has the unwelcome responsibility of disposing of the belongings of his recently deceased lover. He also has to hide some conspicuously "gay" articles of clothing from his deceased lover's parents, who are still unaware their son was a homosexual. He is forced to grapple with an aggressive acquaintance, who gives the story dramatic tension by claiming certain items with no proof he is entitled to them. Every personal item the dead man's executor handles brings back memories of the past, and there is a constant shifting from somber present to happy past and back again which displays the author's literary talent to advantage.

"A Small Spade"

A gay couple visit the English seaside resort town of Brighton. Like many of Mars-Jones's characters, they are working-class people with limited incomes. The title refers to a little spade-shaped splinter that Neil, a hairdresser, picks up under a fingernail. An incident that most people would consider trivial is a matter of extreme importance to the lovers because Neil, who is suffering from AIDS, is highly susceptible to infections. This story is notable for its recreation of the appearance and atmosphere of modern Brighton.

"Summer Lightning"

Only one of the nine stories, "Summer Lightning," does not deal with AIDS, but it blends in well with the others because it involves death and bereavement. "Summer Lightning," about the sudden death of a beloved aunt due to a stroke or heart attack which she suffers at a nude beach, also has Mars-Jones's characteristic humorous treatment of tragedy and is told in the first-person narrative style he favors. Both aunt and nephew have brought along books by P. G. Wodehouse containing his famous Jeeves stories. The reader senses that Wodehouse's characteristically humorous approach to all subjects and strict avoidance of anything sad or serious must have influenced Mars-Jones as well as other gay writers.

"Remission"

"Remission" is generally regarded as one of Mars-Jones's best short stories. As the title suggests, it concerns a man experiencing temporary relief from a serious disease. The narrator in this case is ostensibly dictating his random thoughts into a tape recorder, using his brief periods of freedom from suffering to collect "a hoard of positive moments" to which he can listen when his next attack occurs. This narrative device has the effect of conveying the terrible loneliness which so many AIDS victims endure because friends, relatives, even professionals in the health field are afraid to be near them. The narrator has two "lovers" who come to visit him, do his housecleaning, run his errands, and take turns sleeping with him, although he has never been physically intimate with either of them. As the story demonstrates, the AIDS epidemic has brought out the best in some individuals and the worst in others. It has created a subculture within the gay subculture, consisting of those gay males who are afflicted with the disease and those who stand by them to the inevitable end.

"Bears in Mourning"

"Bears in Mourning" deals with a group of men who are attracted to each other because of certain physical characteristics. "To be a Bear you need, let's see, two essential characteristics, a beard and a bit of flesh to spare, and preferably some body hair." This story contains one of the rare instances in which one of Mars-Jones's narrators refers to AIDS by name. "All of us were involved in the epidemic in some way, socially, politically, rattling collection buckets at benefit shows if nothing else. And of course we were all terrified of getting sick." The narrator introduces Victor, who was, "an absolute Bear" and the center of "the Bear community." When the fatherly Victor commits suicide, the community is dispersed. Throughout the story, the narrator maintains the campy, "discursive," fanciful, courageous, and ironically humorous tone that typifies Mars-Jones's fiction. The reader is frequently reminded of the wisdom William Shakespeare expressed in *King Lear* (pr. c. 1605-1606):

> The lowest and most dejected thing of fortune
> Stands still in esperance, lives not in fear:
> The lamentable change is from the best;
> The worst returns to laughter.

OTHER MAJOR WORKS

LONG FICTION: *The Waters of Thirst*, 1993.

NONFICTION: *Venus Envy*, 1990; *Blind Bitter Happiness*, 1997.

EDITED TEXT: *Mae West Is Dead: Recent Lesbian and Gay Fiction*, 1983.

BIBLIOGRAPHY

Canning, Richard. "Not Fade Away." *New Statesman and Society* 5 (September 25, 1992): 57. Discusses the stories in *Monopolies of Loss*, distinguishing between those previously published in *The Darker Proof* and those written since, finding that the newer pieces are distinguished by "subtler gradations of character."

McCann, Richard. "Writing AIDS." *Lambda Book Report* 3 (July/August, 1992): 10-11. An interview with Adam Mars-Jones, who discusses the peculiar problems involved in writing about AIDS. He asserts that an understated style, such as his own, encourages readers to avoid emotional judgments and to treat AIDS-related issues rationally while being sympathetic to victims and those who care for them.

Mars-Jones, Adam. "I Was a Teenage Homophobe." *New Statesman* 11 (June 19, 1998): 23-25. Mars-Jones, an openly gay man, admits that he was homophobic himself during his teens. Explores attitudes of "straights" towards gays and the homophobia of his own father, who was a judge noted for his harsh sentencing of homosexuals. Mars-Jones concludes that there is little difference between gays' fear of straights and straights' fear of gays. This short article contains much interesting biographical information.

Murphy, Timothy F., and Suzanne Poirier, eds. *Writing AIDS: Gay Literature, Language, and Analysis*. New York: Columbia University Press, 1993. This excellent volume contains essays by fifteen authors on every aspect of writing about AIDS for the purpose of informing the public and demystifying the disease. Contains discussions of Mars-Jones's short stories and those of his highly influential friend and mentor Edmund White.

Wine, Pamela. "Fiction in the Plague Years: Writing in the Shadow of AIDS." *JAMA* 271 (March 2, 1994): 717-718. Compares and contrasts Mars-Jones and Dale Peck, both gay fiction writers, from a medical perspective. Such works of fiction, Wine contends, can help medical students understand the special problems facing the AIDS patients they are likely to encounter as medical professionals.

Wood, Gaby. "Something Fresh and Citric." *The Times Literary Supplement* (March 7, 1997): 36. This insightful article uses the publication of Mars-Jones's *Blind Bitter Happiness* as a springboard for a discussion of the author's entire career.

Bill Delaney

PAULE MARSHALL

Born: Brooklyn, New York; April 9, 1929

PRINCIPAL SHORT FICTION

Soul Clap Hands and Sing, 1961
Reena and Other Stories, 1983
Merle: A Novella and Other Stories, 1985

OTHER LITERARY FORMS

Paule Marshall is best known for her 1959 novel *Brown Girl, Brownstones*, which tells the story of Barbadian immigrants striving to surmount poverty and racism in their new home, as seen through the eyes of the young heroine, Selina Boyce, daughter of a hardworking, ambitious mother and an easygoing, romantic father. Ten years later, *The Chosen Place, the Timeless People* (1969) was published, followed by *Praisesong for the Widow* (1983), *Daughters* (1991), and *The Fisher-King*, (2000). Marshall has also written a number of essays on African American woman writers and her own experience as an artist.

ACHIEVEMENTS

Paule Marshall was awarded a John Simon Guggenheim Memorial Foundation Fellowship in 1961, the Rosenthal Award from the National Institute of Arts and Letters in 1962 for *Soul Clap Hands and Sing*, a Ford Foundation grant for 1964-1965, a National Endowment for the Arts grant for 1967-1968, and the Before Columbus Foundation American Book Award in 1984 for *Praisesong for the Widow*. She also received the Langston Hughes Medallion Award (1986), the New York State Governor's Award for Literature (1987), the John Dos Passos Award for Literature (1989), and the John D. and Catherine T. MacArthur Fellowship (1992).

BIOGRAPHY

Paule Marshall was born in Brooklyn in 1929, the daughter of Samuel and Ada Burke, émigrés from Barbados who arrived in the United States shortly after World War I. She thus grew up in a culture with its roots in the Caribbean, which she visited for the first

time when she was nine years old, an experience that had a strong influence on her future writing. She wrote poetry as a child and listened to the talk of women, both preparing her for her career as a powerful and poetic writer. In the opening of *Reena and Other Stories*, she describes the influence of her mother, woman relatives, and other female friends on her experience in an essay called "From the Poets in the Kitchen":

> They taught me my first lesson in the narrative art. They trained my ear. They set a standard of excellence. This is why the best of my work must be attributed to them; it stands as testimony to the rich legacy of language and culture they so freely passed on to me in the workshop of the kitchen.

Marshall attended Brooklyn College, receiving a B.A. cum laude in 1953; she was also a member of Phi Beta Kappa. She wrote her first novel, *Brown Girl, Brownstones*, while a graduate student at Hunter College. She married Kenneth E. Marshall in 1950; they had a child, Evan, but the marriage ended in 1963. In the meantime, Marshall worked as a librarian for the New York Public Libraries and as a staff writer for *Our World* magazine in New York; she also published her first collection of short stories for Atheneum, *Soul Clap Hands and Sing*. With the help of grants from the Ford Foundation and the National Endowment for the Arts, she completed her second novel, *The Chosen Place, the Timeless People*, which, like her earlier work, was critically well received but commercially only marginally successful.

On July 30, 1970, Marshall married Nourry Menard, and that fall she took the position of lecturer on creative writing at Yale University. She also lectured on black literature at several colleges and universities, including the University of Oxford, Columbia University, Michigan State University, Lake Forest College, and Cornell University. In 1983, Marshall's third novel, *Praisesong for the Widow*, won the Before Columbus Foundation American Book Award. The Feminist Press published *Reena and*

Other Stories, which includes the novella *Merle*, excerpted from *The Chosen Place, the Timeless People*, and the short stories "Brooklyn" and "Barbados," which originally appeared in *Soul Clap Hands and Sing*. Other stories in *Reena and Other Stories* appeared in various periodicals. This collection was reprinted in 1985 by Virago Press under the title *Merle: A Novella and Other Stories*. In 1991, Marshall published the novel *Daughters*, which was also greeted with great critical acclaim.

ANALYSIS

Paule Marshall's first novel, *Brown Girl, Brownstones*, ushered in a whole new approach to the African American female protagonist; only Gwendolyn Brooks's *Maud Martha* (1953) and the earlier *Their Eyes Were Watching God* (1937) by Zora Neale Hurston had focused on an African American woman's search for identity within a black community and her own conscious, interior life. Marshall's work has been concerned from the beginning with a number of major themes: the experience of growing up African American in the United States; the clash of cultures between Westerners and African Americans, West Indians and inhabitants of the American mainland; and the relationships between men and women.

SOUL CLAP HANDS AND SING

Marshall's first collection of shorter works, *Soul Clap Hands and Sing*, contains four longer short stories, almost novellas. They are given the titles of the settings: "Barbados," "Brooklyn," "British Guiana," and "Brazil." In each, the main character is an older man, and the stories explore how that man has failed to live his life fully, for whatever reasons. This failure is indicated by the title of the collection, taken from the William Butler Yeats poem "Sailing to Byzantium," which includes the lines "An aged man is but a paltry thing/ A tattered coat upon a stick, unless/ Soul clap its hands and sing." In each case, the failure of the man to allow his soul to "clap hands" has led to the emptiness or aridity of his life. Thus, he is forced to realize his failure to live truly through the intervention of a woman who, in some way, exposes his inadequacies.

Paule Marshall in 1991 (AP/Wide World Photos)

"BARBADOS"

In "Barbados," Mr. Watford, who has returned to his native island after having worked single-mindedly throughout his adult life in the United States just so he can return for this purpose, lives like a white colonizer. He has built a house, bought plantation land, and planted coconut trees, which he tends faithfully, despite years of accumulated fatigue. He has never completely finished his house, however, and he lives in total isolation, proud of the fact that he needs no one and no one needs him. It takes a young native woman, foisted on him as a servant, to reveal the paucity of his life, the emptiness of his days. He recognizes that he has not been able to bear the responsibility for the meaninglessness of his life, but when he goes to confront the young woman with the hope of some renewal, he is capable only of attacking her verbally, to which she responds, "you ain't people, Mr. Watford, you ain't people." It is this that destroys him: He has not been able to be a part of the people who bore him, and has not found sustenance living the same way as those who oppressed him.

"BROOKLYN"

In "Brooklyn," an aging Jewish professor, who has been banned from teaching by the Red-baiters of the McCarthy era, attempts to coerce a young black woman who is taking his class to spend some time at his summer home. She refuses but in the end returns to his class for the final and takes him up on his invitation, only to express her outrage as well as the freedom that she now feels. She has also felt an outcast from her own people, while unable to trust whites. Now she has the courage to live not as her parents have taught her but as she chooses. Professor Max Berman, on the other hand, is forced to recognize that it is his failure to believe in or stand up for anything that has resulted in his loneliness and misery. Interestingly, in "Barbados" the female protagonist is not given a name, while here she is named only in dialogue as Miss Williams.

"BRITISH GUIANA"

"British Guiana" explores the present of Gerald Motley, a man who is indeed a motley collection of races; he could have been taken for white, because of the British army officer who was one of his ancestors, or black, for the slave woman that officer had been intimate with, or East Indian, from some Hindu who also had a part in his creation. He has achieved a certain amount of success as the head of a radio station, but he knows that he has failed to live his life fully. Although as a young man he had shown a great ability and had rejected his middle-class background to organize a strike, he had been bought off by a job in radio, which forces him to copy the whites who have colonized his country. When he attempts to penetrate the jungle, to prove his worth to himself, he is prevented by another motley person, Sybil, an African Chinese woman with whom he is involved. He is forever conscious of his betrayal of himself and also of Sybil's part in this, which results in a life of cynicism and taking the easy way. At the end of the story, when Sybil, whom he might have married, returns to visit, his last act is to bargain with her for a protégé who despises him but deserves a chance. In the conclu-

sion, he realizes that he is going to die a failure by his own doing.

"BRAZIL"

The final story in the book, "Brazil," reminds the reader of Carson McCullers's *The Ballad of the Sad Café* (1951) in that it is the story of what appears to be a strange love affair between a white woman of epic proportions and a black dwarf. In this story, the dwarf is a performer who goes by the name of O Grande Caliban and has teamed up with a blonde of Germanic appearance to perform a comic and athletic act. He has decided that it is time to retire, but his mistress does not wish to do so. One of the interesting things about the story is the breaking of the traditional white reader's expectations; it is the undersized black man who is trying to end a relationship with the Aryan-looking female. He has become so famous as Caliban, however, that no one, not even his wife, knows him as he had been. He has been living a lie so long that he cannot convince people of the truth anymore, and so he ends by destroying everything.

REENA AND OTHER STORIES

Reena and Other Stories is a collection of previously printed works gathered together for the first time in 1983 by Feminist Press. It begins with Marshall's autobiographical essay, "From the Poets in the Kitchen," which had originally been published in *The New York Times Book Review*'s series called "The Making of a Writer." This essay celebrates the women in Marshall's life who helped form her thought and shape her voice. The collection includes two of the stories discussed above, "Brooklyn" and "Barbados," previously published in *Soul Clap Hands and Sing*. Also included is a novella, *Merle*, which has been excerpted from her 1969 novel *The Chosen Place, the Timeless People* but was extensively reshaped and rewritten. Marshall wrote autobiographical headnotes to each story, which help to place them in the context of her experience and development as a writer.

"THE VALLEY BETWEEN"

The first story in the collection, "The Valley Between," was, as Marshall explained, "my very first published story, written when I could barely crawl, never mind stand up and walk as a writer." In it, the characters are white, a deliberate decision as Marshall herself was at the time married to Kenneth E. Marshall, a marriage she describes as "an early, unwise first marriage," and she wished to disguise the autobiographical elements in it. It is the story of a marriage falling apart because the wife (and mother of a small child) continues to grow, while the husband wishes her to remain the same, to be nothing more than a wife and mother. Published in August, 1954, it is a story well before its time in its depiction of the stifling expectations placed upon a woman of talent and energy.

"REENA"

The title story, "Reena," is unusual in that it was commissioned by *Harper's Magazine* for a special supplement on "The American Female," published in October of 1962. Intended by the editors to be an article on the African American woman, the story instead became a thinly disguised fiction concerning the women whom Marshall knew best: "those from an urban, working-class and lower middle-class, West Indian American background who, like [Marshall herself], had attended the free New York City colleges during the late forties and fifties."

A first-person narrator named Paulie recounts her meeting again after twenty years with a friend from her childhood, Reena, formally named Doreen, who—being a child who shapes her own life as best she can in a world that discriminates against women, African Americans, and particularly African Americans from the West Indies—had transformed herself into Reena, "with two ees!"

The meeting place is at the funeral of Aunt Vi, Reena's aunt, a woman who represents the strong, nurturing, enduring women "from the poets in the kitchen," and who will reappear in Marshall's fiction. Having been out of touch for so long, Reena and Paulie have much to discuss, and much of the story is Reena's recounting of what has been happening in her life: the struggle for meaningful work; her relationship with her family, particularly her mother; relationships with white men (usually unsuccessful) and with black men, who have to learn how to relate to and accept a strong, educated, ambitious black woman; childbearing; radical politics; and loneliness.

In almost essayistic form, this story provides an intimate glimpse into the struggle, suffering, and successes of this group of African American women.

"TO DA-DUH, IN MEMORIAM"

"To Da-duh, in Memoriam" is based on a visit that Marshall made to her maternal grandmother in Barbados when she was nine. Da-duh is another of the ancestor figures who populate Marshall's fiction, like Aunt Vi in the previous story and Merle in the story of that same name; as Marshall says, "Da-duh turns up everywhere."

MERLE

Another example of ancestor figures appears in the final selection in the collection, the novella *Merle*, from *Merle: A Novella and Other Stories*. Merle is "Part saint, part revolutionary, part obeah woman," a woman who, wherever she goes, exhorts people to resist oppression, while on a personal level she is "still trying to come to terms with her life and history as a black woman, still seeking to reconcile all the conflicting elements to form a viable self."

Merle is the woman whom Paule Marshall creates in various guises, calling into being a new character for twentieth century American literature. In her compelling portrayal of women in her works, she brings to life for her readers a vision of the direction in which the world should be going by showing readers the people whom the world desperately needs to listen to and perhaps emulate.

OTHER MAJOR WORKS

LONG FICTION: *Brown Girl, Brownstones*, 1959; *The Chosen Place, the Timeless People*, 1969; *Praisesong for the Widow*, 1983; *Daughters*, 1991; *The Fisher King*, 2000.

BIBLIOGRAPHY

Brown, Lloyd W. "The Rhythms of Power in Paule Marshall's Fiction." *Novel: A Forum on Fiction* 7, no. 2 (Winter, 1974): 159-167. This essay focuses on Marshall's short story "To Da-Duh, in Memoriam," tracing Marshall's concern with the problems of African American women, tied to her commitment to feminism and racial equality. Brown argues that Marshall sees power as both a political goal of ethnic and feminist movements and a social and psychological phenomenon that affects racial and sexual roles, shapes cultural traditions, and molds the individual psyche.

Collier, Eugenia. "The Closing of the Circle: Movement from Division to Wholeness in Paule Marshall's Fiction." In *Black Women Writers, 1950-1980*, edited by Mari Evans. Garden City, N.Y.: Anchor Press/Doubleday, 1984. Collier finds in Marshall's writing a movement from the separated, segmented self to a discovery of wholeness and completion; this healing and wholeness is found within the context of the community. Contains good discussions of the short fiction. The first of two essays on Marshall in Evans's collection, which should be required reading for anyone interested in African American woman writers. Contains a bibliography of criticism on Marshall and an index.

Coser, Stelamaris. *Bridging the Americas: The Literature of Paule Marshall, Toni Morrison, and Gayl Jones*. Philadelphia: Temple University Press, 1995. Compares and contrasts the fiction of the three authors, taking their cultural heritage into consideration.

Denniston, Dorothy Hamer. *The Fiction of Paule Marshall*. Knoxville: University of Tennessee Press, 1995. Examines the fiction of Marshall as an imaginative reconstruction of African history and culture; provides close readings of Marshall's work along with biographical information.

Kapai, Leela. "Dominant Themes and Technique in Paule Marshall's Fiction." *College Language Association Journal* 16 (September, 1972): 49-59. Examines Marshall's use of folk tradition in her novels through *The Chosen Place, the Timeless People* and also in the short story "Reena." Kapai claims that Marshall puts being a human being and the universal human experience before racial identity and states that Marshall is aware of her Western heritage, even as she writes out of her personal experience as an African American. Contains some good, close readings.

Lock, Helen. "'Building Up from Fragments': The Oral Memory Process in Some Recent African-American Written Narratives." *College Literature* 22 (October, 1995): 109-120. Discusses Marshall and others as representative of a generation of African American literary artists whose sensibilities do not exclude orally constituted modes of thought; claims she energizes the dialectic between oral and literate conceptions of memory by reasserting—through the medium of the written word—the value of an orally derived perception.

McClusky, John, Jr. "And Called Every Generation Blessed: Theme, Setting, and Ritual in the Works of Paule Marshall." In *Black Women Writers, 1950-1980*, edited by Mari Evans. Garden City, N.Y.: Anchor Press/Doubleday, 1984. This essay, the second on Marshall in Evans's book, gives an overview of Marshall's achievement, evolution, and her future directions in writing.

Macpherson, Heidi Slettedahl. "Perception of Place: Geopolitical and Cultural Positioning in Paule Marshall's Novels." In *Caribbean Women Writers*, edited by Mary Condé and Thorunn Lonsdale. New York: St. Martin's Press, 1999. Although the focus of this article is on Marshall's novels, it is a helpful discussion of her use of fictionalized island backdrops in her fiction generally; argues that while she acknowledges a geopolitical place, her representation of place moves beyond a specific locale.

Waxman, Barbara Frey. "Dancing out of Form, Dancing into Self: Genre and Metaphor in Marshall, Shange, and Walker." *MELUS* 19 (Fall, 1994): 91-106. Discusses how texts by Paule Marshall, Ntozake Shange, and Alice Walker articulate truths about the multiple selves of African American women by creating new mythopoetic genres and tropes that mediate between the word and the dance.

Mary LeDonne Cassidy, updated by
Theodore C. Humphrey

BOBBIE ANN MASON

Born: Mayfield, Kentucky; May 1, 1940

PRINCIPAL SHORT FICTION

Shiloh and Other Stories, 1982
Love Life, 1989
Midnight Magic: Selected Stories of Bobbie Ann Mason, 1998

OTHER LITERARY FORMS

Bobbie Ann Mason has written novels, including *Feather Crowns* (1993); literary criticism; a memoir, *Clear Springs: A Memoir* (1999); and popular-culture journalism. She has also been the subject of numerous interviews.

ACHIEVEMENTS

Bobbie Ann Mason has earned a place in American literature with her short stories. She won the Ernest Hemingway Foundation Award for first fiction in 1983 for her first collection of short stories, *Shiloh and Other Stories*. That collection also earned for Mason nomination for the National Book Critics Circle Award (1982), the American Book Award (1982), the PEN/Faulkner Award for Fiction, a National Endowment for the Arts Fellowship, and a Pennsylvania Arts Council grant (1983), a John Simon Guggenheim Memorial Foundation Fellowship and an American Academy of Arts and Letters award (1984). Mason received the Appalachian Medallion Award (1991), and her novel *Feather Crowns* was cowinner of the Southern Book Award for fiction and a finalist for the National Book Critics Circle Award (1994). Mason's writing for newspapers and magazines includes work as a society columnist for the *Mayfield Messenger* in Kentucky and as a writer of fan magazine stories for the Ideal Publishing Company in New York City. She has also written "Talk of the Town" columns and feature articles for *The New Yorker*.

Mason's novels have reinforced her reputation. The first of her novels, *In Country* (1985), was particularly well received, and a film (also titled *In Country*) based on the book was released by Warner Brothers in the fall of 1989. That year the Vietnam Veterans of America gave Mason its first President's Citation, which honors a nonveteran who promotes public understanding of the war and its residual effects.

BIOGRAPHY

Bobbie Ann Mason was born in rural Kentucky, and her southern background appears to have been a major force in shaping her fiction. She attended a country school through the eighth grade and then attended Mayfield High School. Her descriptions of country schools in "State Champions" certainly ring true, and apparently her novel *Spence + Lila* (1988) fictionalizes a part of her parents' experience. Another aspect of her high school life echoes in her fiction: her love of rock and roll.

Mason majored in English at the University of Kentucky in Lexington, where she wrote for the university paper, *The Kernel*. While in college, she also wrote the summer society column for the *Mayfield Messenger*. After graduating with a B.A. degree in 1962, she spent fifteen months in New York City working for the Ideal Publishing Company writing for fan magazines such as *Movie Life* and *TV Star Parade*. In addition to her undergraduate degree, Mason earned an M.A. degree in literature from the State University of New York at Binghamton in 1966, as well as a Ph.D. in literature from the University of Connecticut in 1972. In her doctoral dissertation, she analyzed the garden symbolism in *Ada or Ardor: A Family Chronicle* (1969), by Vladimir Nabokov. Nabokov's artistry in presenting the details of his characters' lives apparently touched a chord in Mason. While pursuing her Ph.D., she met Roger B. Rawlings at the University of Connecticut; they were married in 1969.

From 1972 to 1979, Mason was an assistant professor of English at Mansfield State College (which later became Mansfield University) in Pennsylvania, where she taught journalism as well as other English courses. She had been writing short stories during this period and had received encouraging responses

Bobby Ann Mason (AP/Wide World Photos)

from editors who, nevertheless, rejected her stories for publication. In 1979, Mason stopped teaching to write fiction. She settled in rural Pennsylvania, sometimes giving readings and sometimes writing for *The New Yorker.* In 1990, she and her husband moved back to Kentucky. Her life, with its movement from rural to urban and back to rural living, mirrors a typical concern of her fiction: the tension between rural and urban life. Apparently her own feelings match those of many of her protagonists.

ANALYSIS

Often compared with Ann Beattie, Raymond Carver, and Frederick Barthelme, Bobbie Ann Mason writes fiction that reads like life. Her characters struggle with jobs, family, and self-awareness, continually exuding a lively sense of being. Those who people her stories often transcend circumstance without losing their rootedness in place. Most often her characters struggle to live within a relationship, but

are frequently alone. In fiction that resonates with rock-and-roll music and family conflicts, her descriptions leave a reader sometimes feeling uncomfortably aware of a truth about families: Caring does not guarantee understanding or communication.

The short stories are for the most part set in small towns in Kentucky and explore the lives of lower-middle-class people from small towns or farms. Kentucky, a North/South border state, is emblematic of Mason's concerns with borders, separations, and irrevocable decisions. Mason's stories typically explore a conflict between the character's past and future, a conflict that is often exemplified in a split between rural and urban leanings and a modern as opposed to a traditional life. Most often, the point of view in Mason's short fiction is limited omniscient. She is, however, adept with first-person narration as well. Readers are most often left with a sense of her characters' need to transcend their life scripts through action, frequently a quest. Her stories typically lack resolution, making them uncomfortably true to life.

SHILOH AND OTHER STORIES

"Shiloh," the title story in Mason's first collection, is a story about love, loss, and history. A couple, Leroy and Norma Jean, have been married for sixteen years. They married when Norma Jean was pregnant with their son Randy, a child who died as an infant. Leroy is home recuperating from an accident he had in his truck. His leg is healing, but he is afraid to go back to driving a truck long distances. He takes on traditionally feminine activities in the story: He starts doing crafts, watches birds at the feeder, and remains the passenger in the car even after his leg has healed enough for him to drive.

The accident that forced Leroy to remain at home for months recuperating is the second crisis in the couple's marriage. The earlier crisis had been their baby's death. After the baby died, Leroy and Norma Jean remained married but emotionally isolated from each other:

They never speak about their memories of Randy, which have almost faded, but now that Leroy is home all the time, they sometimes feel awkward around each other, and Leroy wonders if one of them should mention the child. He has the feeling that they are waking up out of a dream together.

Now that Leroy is at home, he "sees things about Norma Jean that he never realized before." Leroy's staying at home so much leads to several important changes for Norma Jean: She begins to lift weights, takes a writing course, and curses in front of her mother. In response to the repeated suggestion of Norma Jean's mother, the couple drives to the Shiloh battleground for a second honeymoon trip. At Shiloh, Norma Jean tells Leroy that she wants to leave him. The history of Shiloh is significant to the story of this marriage. Shiloh, an early battle in the Civil War, proved that the Civil War would be a long and bloody one. The story concludes with Leroy merging family history with battleground history and Norma Jean literally flexing her muscles. Their civil war will be Leroy fighting for union and Norma Jean seeking her independent self.

A contemporary history lesson on the fear of polio and communists, "Detroit Skyline, 1949" narrates in first person the summer spent by a nine-year-old girl, Peggy Jo, and her mother as they visit the mother's sister and her family in Detroit. The story reveals the conflict between rural and city life through the perceptions and desires of Peggy Jo. Seeing her aunt's neighborhood for the first time, Peggy Jo immediately knows that she wants to live "in a place like this, with neighbors." When she plays with the neighbor child, however, Peggy Jo is made to feel incompetent because she does not know how to roller-skate, so she instead spends her time watching television and examining newspaper articles and pictures in her aunt's scrapbook.

Peggy Jo feels isolated that summer. She observes the smoothness with which her mother and aunt converse, how natural their communication is. When she attends a birthday party for the neighbor child, Peggy Jo notes:

> I did not know what to say to the children. They all knew each other, and their screams and giggles had a natural continuity, something like the way my mother talked with her sister, and like the splendid houses of the neighborhood, all set so close together.

For Peggy Jo there is little "natural continuity" of speech or gesture within her aunt's household that summer. Her own comments are most often cut short, silenced, or discredited by the others. By the end of the summer, Peggy Jo realizes that her "own life [is] a curiosity, an item for a scrapbook."

Another of Mason's stories concerning rural isolation is "Offerings," in which the isolation is redemptive for Sandra, who stays in the couple's country home instead of traveling with her husband, Jerry, to Louisville, "reluctant to spend her weekends with him watching go-go dancers in smoky bars." She instead spends her time growing vegetables and tending her cats, ducks, and dogs. Her cobweb-strewn house is not her focus; the outdoors is. The offerings that Sandra makes are many: to her mother, tacit agreement to avoid discussing the separation from Jerry; to her grandmother, the fiction of Jerry's presence; and to the forces of nature around her, her tamed and dependent ducks. Sandra finds grace through the natural world, exemplified within the final image of the story: dewy spiderwebs that, in the morning, are trampolines enabling her to "spring from web to web, all the way up the hill to the woods." She cannot be honest with her grandmother and avoids truth in conversation with her mother, but she feels at peace and at home with her yard, the woods, and the wildlife there.

In "Residents and Transients," Mason's narrator is also married to a man who has gone away to work in Louisville. Mary, the narrator, is finding her place within a relationship as well as a location. Several images in this story reinforce the theme of stability as opposed to movement. The cats Mary cares for on the farm represent her dilemma of moving to Louisville. To Stephen, her lover, she explains that she has read about two basic types of cats, residents and transients. She cites difference of opinion by researchers over which type is truly superior: those who establish territories and stay there or those who show the greatest curiosity by going from one place to another. Mary is drawn to the stability of her parents' old farmhouse, feeling the pull of traditional value of place. The single image that most succinctly and horrifically mirrors her dilemma is a rabbit, seen in the headlights as she is driving home. The rabbit at first appears to be running in place, but she realizes that its forelegs are still moving despite the fact that its haunches have been run over. Throughout the story, Mary has been literally running in place, running from her relationship with her husband by taking a lover and running from her life with her husband by remaining in her parents' old home.

Mary's position at the end of the story is mirrored by the image of the odd-eyed cat, whose eyes shine red and green. The narrator has been waiting for some signal to move. Her husband's words do not convince; Mary thinks of them as words that are processed, computerized renderings. She needs more than words; she needs an integrated part of her world to spur her to act. Because her husband is no longer an integral part of her world, she listens and looks for other cues. Apparently, the dying rabbit has spurred her to action. The story ends with Mary "waiting for the light to change."

LOVE LIFE

Within Mason's second collection of short fiction, *Love Life*, the reader sees continued the skillful treatment of people's decisions and perceptions. "State Champions" is a reminiscence of twenty years past, so it offers a perspective different from that of other works. "State Champions" further explores Mason's theme of rural versus urban experience by recounting the success of the Cuba Cubs, Kentucky state champions in basketball in 1952. The narrator, Peggy (who appeared earlier in "Detroit Skyline, 1949" but is three years older when this story begins), had seen the team as glamorous, certainly larger than life. As an adult in upstate New York, Peggy is surprised to hear the team referred to as "just a handful of country boys who could barely afford basketball shoes." Although Peggy had shared in the excitement of the championship season, "State Champions" presents her perceptions of being different from the rest even at that time. She rebelled against authority at school by talking back to the history teacher. She surprised her friend Willowdean with the assertion that she did not want to get pregnant and get married, a normal pattern for the girls at the high school. From her adult perspective, Peggy ascribes her own struggle for

words with Glenn, the boy she cared about in 1952, to her status as a "country kid":

> I couldn't say anything, for we weren't raised to say things that were heartfelt and gracious. Country kids didn't learn manners. Manners were too embarrassing. Learning not to run in the house was about the extent of what we knew about how to act. We didn't learn to congratulate people; we didn't wish people happy birthday. We didn't even address each other by name.

Ironically enough, what triggers Peggy's recollection of the state championship year is the comment by the New Yorker about the poor country boys' basketball team, certainly a comment not springing from a mannered upbringing.

In "Coyotes," Mason provides a third-person account from the perspective of a young man, Cobb, who embodies the ambivalence and sensitivity often seen in Mason's characters. He has asked Lynnette Johnson to marry him, and he continues to look for signs and indications that marriage is the right thing to do. Cobb sees a young clerk in a drugstore showing her wedding ring to a young couple. Their conversation is flat: no congratulations, no excitement. The matter-of-fact nature of the exchange haunts Cobb. He wants his marriage to be the subject of excitement, hugs, celebration. Marriage in general presents itself as a risk, leading him to look further for signs that his own marriage will work. He wonders if Lynnette will find more and more things about him that will offend her. For example, he fails to tell her about having hunted after she tells him that his sweatshirt, on which is written "Paducah, the Flat Squirrel Capital of the World," is in bad taste. He is reassured by their similarities—for example, the fact that they both pronounce "coyote" with an *e* sound at the end. Lynnette's past, with a mother who had attempted suicide, is something he recognizes to be significant to them, but he nevertheless speaks confidently with Lynnette about their future. Lynnette fears that her past will somehow intrude on their future, and so, in fact, does Cobb. Their relationship is, as is typical of Mason's fiction, freighted with all those tangled possibilities.

Past and future as conflicting forces also form a theme of "Private Lies," in which the male protagonist, Mickey, reestablishes his relationship with his former wife and decides to search for the child they gave up for adoption eighteen years earlier. Mickey's wife, Tina, has compartmentalized their lives with a regular television schedule and planned activities for their children. Tina has forbidden him to tell their children about his daughter. Mickey, however, cannot ignore the eighteenth birthday of his daughter given up to adoption. The story concludes with Mickey and his former wife, Donna, on the beach in Florida, the state in which they gave up their daughter for adoption. Donna insists that she does not want to find their daughter and that searching is a mistake. She nevertheless accompanies him to Florida, where Mickey seeks to stop telling lies (by silence) and where Donna still seeks to avoid the search, exemplified by her refusal to look inside shells for fear of what she may find in them. Mickey seeks the daughter who will be his bridge between past and future. He seeks to make a new present for himself, a present free of Tina's control.

MIDNIGHT MAGIC

All of the stories in *Midnight Magic* appeared earlier in either *Shiloh and Other Stories* or *Love Life*, but this collection provides a new arrangement and a new introduction by the author. The protagonist of the title story, Steve, is a young man whose personal power is no match for that of his showy "muscle" car. Like other Mason characters, he takes to the road in search of elusive secrets of life, but most of the time Steve merely drives in circles around his small hometown. When he finally heads for a specific destination (the Nashville airport to pick up his recently married friend), he is several hours late. His lateness for this appointment parallels his tardiness in maturing. After seeing a body lying beside the road, Steve tries to report it to a 911 emergency operator. Unfortunately, he cannot discover his specific geographic location just as he cannot define his place on the road of life. Steve's girlfriend, Karen, finds guidance in the spiritual teachings of Sardo, an ancient Native American now reincarnated in the body of a teenager. Steve also "wants something miraculous" but simply "can't be-

lieve in it." Thus, his persistent hope outstrips his fleeting faith.

Mason recalls that as a college student she associated late-night hours with a "mood of expectation"—"the sense that anything might happen." Thus, the title "Midnight Magic" suggests sympathy for a feckless but engaging misfit. In her introduction Mason describes Steve as a "guy who keeps imagining he'll get it together one day soon, who seeks transcendence and wants to believe in magic."

Another story with a confused male protagonist is "Big Bertha Stories." Written while Mason was working on *In Country*, this story also dramatizes the lingering effects of the war in Vietnam. Donald has come back from war physically, but he cannot make it all the way home emotionally. He operates a huge machine in a strip mine, and his destruction of the land recalls the horrors of war. Attempting to create some order in his life, Donald makes up stories about powerful superheroes. These stories begin with humor and high hopes but break off in chaos. Just as Donald cannot complete his journey home, he can never bring his fictions to a suitable conclusion. Having lost his youth in Vietnam, he becomes old prematurely and can no longer function as husband and father.

Still another story from *Midnight Magic* that tries to reconcile past with present is "Nancy Culpepper." Here the title character is apparently based on Mason herself, and she reappears in the story "Lying Doggo" and the novel *Spence + Lila*. The key symbols in "Nancy Culpepper" are photographs. Nancy recalls that the photographs from her wedding were fuzzy double exposures, just as the wedding itself was a superimposition of a strange new identity upon her southern rural past. Several years after the wedding she returns home to Kentucky to rescue old family pictures. She searches in particular for a likeness of her namesake, but this particular photograph is not found just as her own sense of identity remains elusive.

OTHER MAJOR WORKS

LONG FICTION: *In Country*, 1985; *Spence + Lila*, 1988; *Feather Crowns*, 1993.

NONFICTION: *Nabokov's Garden: A Guide to "Ada,"* 1974; *The Girl Sleuth: A Feminist Guide to the Bobbsey Twins, Nancy Drew, and Their Sisters,* 1975; *Clear Springs: A Memoir,* 1999.

BIBLIOGRAPHY

Blythe, Hal, and Charlie Sweet. "The Ambiguous Grail Quest in 'Shiloh.'" *Studies in Short Fiction* 32 (Spring, 1995): 223-226. Examines the use of the Grail myth in "Shiloh"; claims the story is a contemporary version of Jessie Weston's "Waste Land." Argues that the myth lends universal significance to the minutiae-laden lives of a twentieth century western Kentucky couple in a troubled marriage.

Brinkmeyer, Robert H., Jr. "Never Stop Rocking: Bobbie Ann Mason and Rock-and-Roll." *Mississippi Quarterly: The Journal of Southern Culture* 42, no. 1 (1988-1989): 5-17. Footnoted from seven other articles and interviews, this essay explores Mason's use of rock music as a significant expression of contemporary culture.

Giannone, Richard. "Bobbie Ann Mason and the Recovery of Mystery." *Studies in Short Fiction* 27 (Fall, 1990): 553-566. Claims that Mason's rural characters are caught between an incomprehensible otherworldly force and the loss of their this-worldly anguish; they are mystified by contemporary life while robbed of the mysteries of their lives. Discusses "Shiloh," "Retreat," and "Third Monday."

Morphew, G. O. "Downhome Feminists in *Shiloh and Other Stories.*" *The Southern Literary Journal* 21, no. 2 (1989): 41-49. In a considered treatment of Mason's down-home feminists, Morphew notes that the heroines want space within relationships, not equal pay for equal work. The essay notes differences between the actions of Mason's educated and uneducated heroines.

Pollack, Harriet. "From *Shiloh* to *In Country* to *Feather Crowns:* Bobbie Ann Mason, Women's History, and Southern Fiction." *The Southern Literary Journal* 28 (Spring, 1996): 95-116. Argues that Mason's fiction is representative of southern women authors who, without general recognition,

have been transforming southern literature's characteristic attention to official history.

Rothstein, Mervyn. "Homegrown Fiction: Bobbie Ann Mason Blends Springsteen and Nabokov." *The New York Times Biographical Service* 19 (May, 1988): 563-565. This essay reports Mason's love of rhythm and blues in high school and notes the semiautobiographical details of *Spence + Lila.*

Ryan, Maureen. "Stopping Places: Bobbie Ann Mason's Short Stories." In *Women Writers of the Contemporary South,* edited by Peggy W. Prenshaw. Jackson: University Press of Mississippi, 1984. An overview of Mason's themes and character portraits, this sampling provides a brief treatment of many different works.

Thompson, Terry. "Mason's 'Shiloh.'" *The Explicator* 54 (Fall, 1995): 54-58. Claims that subdivisions play an important role in the story for gaining a full appreciation of the two main characters; argues that the subdivision is a metaphor for the marriage of the couple.

Wilhelm, Albert E. *Bobbie Ann Mason: A Study of the Short Fiction.* New York: Twayne, 1998. This critical study of Mason's short fiction examines the influence of her femininity and her identity as a southerner on her writing. Includes such topics as the place that Kentucky plays in her work as well as a bibliography and index.

_____. "Bobbie Ann Mason: Searching for Home." In *Southern Writers at Century's End,* edited by Jeffrey J. Folks and James A. Perkins. Lexington: The University Press of Kentucky, 1997. Discusses the effect of American involvement in Vietnam in "Big Bertha Stories" and *In Country.* Argues that these two stories of soldiers' attempts to return home expand the theme of social dislocation to mythic proportions.

_____. "Private Rituals: Coping with Change in the Fiction of Bobbie Ann Mason." *Midwest Quarterly* 28, no. 2 (1987): 271-282. This article includes interview commentary from Mason as well as analysis of the rituals in several of the stories. Of the works he treats, Wilhelm examines "Shiloh" most closely.

Janet Taylor Palmer, updated by Albert Wilhelm

W. SOMERSET MAUGHAM

Born: Paris, France; January 25, 1874
Died: Saint-Jean-Cap-Ferrat, France; December 16, 1965

PRINCIPAL SHORT FICTION

Orientations, 1899
The Trembling of a Leaf: Little Stories of the South Sea Islands, 1921
The Casuarina Tree, 1926
Ashenden: Or, The British Agent, 1928
Six Stories Written in the First Person Singular, 1931
Ah King, 1933
East and West: The Collected Short Stories, 1934
Cosmopolitans, 1936
The Favorite Short Stories of W. Somerset Maugham, 1937
The Round Dozen, 1939
The Mixture as Before: Short Stories, 1940
Creatures of Circumstance: Short Stories, 1947
East of Suez: Great Stories of the Tropics, 1948
Here and There: Selected Short Stories, 1948
The Maugham Reader, 1950
The Complete Short Stories, 1951
The World Over, 1952
Seventeen Lost Stories, 1969

OTHER LITERARY FORMS

A dedicated professional, W. Somerset Maugham earned more than three million dollars from his writing, a phenomenal amount for his day. Between 1897 and 1962, a career spanning eight decades, Maugham published twenty novels, four travel books, more than twenty stage plays, an autobiography of ideas, and innumerable essays, *belles-lettres*, and introductions, in addition to more than one hundred short stories, of which about ninety are readily accessible in different editions. Much of his work has been adapted for use by television and cinema.

ACHIEVEMENTS

W. Somerset Maugham is best known for his ur-banity, his wit, his controlled sense of writing, and his ability to describe not only objectively but also so realistically that he has been accused of lifting stories directly from life. Many of his stories do spring from real incidents or actual people, but the perceptions and surprise plot twists are always Maugham-inspired. In fact, Maugham is expressly known as a master of the surprise or twist ending to an inextrica-bly woven plot in his short stories, many of which have been converted to film. His early work, under the influence of Oscar Wilde and his cult of aesthetes, shows a refined and civilized attitude toward life. Several of his novels illustrate the demanding sacri-fices that art necessitates of life or that life itself can become, in turn, an art form, thereby demonstrating the "art of living" (*The Razor's Edge*, 1944).

Maugham was curiously denied many conspicu-ous honors (such as knighthood) usually conferred on a man of letters of his distinction, but he was awarded by the Royal Society of Literature the title of Com-panion of Literature, an honor given to "authors who have brought exceptional distinction to English let-ters." Furthermore, the occasion of his eightieth birth-day was celebrated with a dinner at the Garrick Club, a distinction given to only three writers before him: Charles Dickens, William Makepeace Thackeray, and Anthony Trollope.

BIOGRAPHY

When William Somerset Maugham was eight, his mother died, and his father, a solicitor for the British Embassy in Paris, died two years later. Shy and speaking little English, Maugham was sent to Whitstable in Kent to live with an uncle, the Rever-end Henry MacDonald Maugham, and his German-born wife, and thence almost immediately to King's School, Canterbury. These wretched and unhappy years were later detailed in Maugham's first master-piece, the novel *Of Human Bondage* (1915). A stam-mer which stayed with him for life seems to have originated about this time. At seventeen, Maugham went to Heidelberg and attended lectures at the university. His first play, *Schiffbrüchig* (*Marriages Are Made in Heaven*), was written during this year abroad and first performed in Berlin in 1902.

Returning to London, he began the study of medicine at St. Thomas' Hospital, where the misery of the nearby Lambeth slums profoundly impressed him. He took his medical degree in 1897, the same year *Liza of Lambeth*, his first novel, was published, then abandoned medicine. By 1908, Maugham had an unprecedented four plays running simultaneously in London, and by 1911, he had become successful enough to buy a fashionable house in Mayfair.

In 1915, he married Syrie Barnardo Wellcome. Divorced in 1927, they had one daughter, Liza, who became Lady Glendevon. During World War I, Maugham served as a medical officer in France and as an agent for the British Secret Service in Switzerland and Russia, where he was to prevent, if possible, the Bolshevik Revolution. During and after the war, he traveled extensively in Hawaii, Samoa, Tahiti, China, Malaysia, Indochina, Australia, the West Indies, various Central and South American countries, and the United States. In 1928, Maugham settled on the French Riviera, buying Villa Mauresque. Maugham died in Nice, France, on December 16, 1965.

ANALYSIS

W. Somerset Maugham first claimed fame as a playwright and novelist, but he became best known in the 1920's and 1930's the world over as an international traveler and short-story writer. Appearing in popular magazines such as *Nash's, Collier's, Hearst's International, The Smart Set*, and *Cosmopolitan*, his stories reached hundreds of thousands of readers who had never attended a play and had seldom read a novel. This new public demanded simple, lucid, fast-moving prose, and Maugham's realistic, well-defined narratives, often set amid the exotic flora of Oceania or Indochina, were among the most popular of the day.

THE TREMBLING OF A LEAF

The Trembling of a Leaf: Little Stories of the South Sea Islands collected six of these first "exotic stories" and assured Maugham fame as a short-story

W. Somerset Maugham (Library of Congress)

writer on equal footing with his established renown as novelist and dramatist. It was actually his second collection, coming twenty years after *Orientations*, whose title clearly bespeaks its purposes. Apparently, Maugham had found no suitable possibilities for short fiction in the meantime until, recuperating from a lung infection between World War I assignments for the British Secret Service, he took a vacation to Samoa and Hawaii:

> I had always had a romantic notion of the South Seas. I had read of those magic islands in the books of Herman Melville, Pierre Loti, and Robert Louis Stevenson, but what I saw was very different from what I had read.

Although Maugham clearly differentiates life as he saw it in the South Seas from life as he had read about it in the writings of his "romantic" predecessors, his stories of British Colonials, of natives and half-castes in exotic environments, are reminiscent of these authors and also of Rudyard Kipling. Maugham's assessment of Kipling, the only British short-story writer he thought comparable to such greats as Guy de Maupassant and Anton Chekhov, neatly clarifies their similar subject, as well as their ultimate stylistic differences. Kipling, Maugham writes,

> opened a new and fruitful field to writers. This is the story, the scene of which is set in some country little known to the majority of readers, and which deals with the reactions upon the white man of his sojourn in an alien land and the effect which contact with peoples of another race has upon him. Subsequent writers have treated this subject in their different ways, but . . . no one has invested it with more romantic glamour, no one has made it more exciting and no one has presented it so vividly and with such a wealth of colour.

Maugham's first South Sea stories are essentially criticisms of the "romantic glamour" of Kipling and his predecessors, especially Stevenson, his most immediate literary forefather in terms of location. Rather than repeat their illusions, Maugham tries to see the "alien land" as it really is, without poetic frills. "Red," which Maugham once chose as his best story, is a clear example of this process.

"RED"

A worldly, gruff, and overweight skipper of a bedraggled seventy-ton schooner anchors off one of the Samoan Islands in order to trade with the local storekeeper. After rowing ashore to a small cove, the captain follows a tortuous path, eventually arriving at "a white man's house" where he meets Neilson. Neilson seems a typical character out of Robert Louis Stevenson, a life deserter unable either to return to his homeland or to accommodate himself completely to his present situation. Twenty-five years ago he came to the island with tuberculosis, expecting to live only a year, but the mild climate has arrested his disease. He has married a native woman called Sally and built a European bungalow on the beautiful spot where a grass hut once stood. His walls are lined with books, which makes the skipper nervous but to which Neilson constantly and condescendingly alludes. Offering him whiskey and a cigar, Neilson decides to tell the skipper the story of Red.

Red was Neilson's romantic predecessor, Sally's previous lover, an ingenuous Apollo whom Neilson likes to imagine "had no more soul than the creatures of the woods and forests who made pipes from reeds and bathed in the mountain streams when the world was young." It was Red who had lived with Sally in the native hut, "with its beehive roof and its pillars, overshadowed by a great tree with red flowers." Glamorizing the young couple and the lush habitat, Neilson imagines them living on "delicious messes from coconuts," by a sea "deep blue, wine-coloured at sundown, like the sea of Homeric Greece," where "the hurrying fish were like butterflies," and the "dawn crept in among the wooden pillars of the hut" so that the lovers woke each morning and "smiled to welcome another day."

After a year of bliss, Red was shanghaied by a British whaler while trying to trade green oranges for tobacco. Sally was crestfallen and mourned him for three years, but finally, somewhat reluctantly, she acceded to the amorous overtures of the newcomer Neilson:

> And so the little wooden house was built in which he had now lived for many years, and Sally became his wife. But after the first few weeks of rapture, during which he was satisfied with what she gave him, he had known little happiness. She had yielded to him, through weariness, but she had only yielded what she set no store on. The soul which he had dimly glimpsed escaped him. He knew that she cared nothing for him. She still loved Red. . . .

Neilson, admittedly "a sentimentalist," is imprisoned by history. His books, a source of anxiety to the skipper, are a symbol of what Maugham believes he must himself avoid: useless repetition of and bondage to his forebears. As creation, Neilson does repeat Stevenson, but as character, he shows the absolute futility of this repetition. The dead romance assumes priority from the living one, and priority is everything. For the sentimentalist Neilson, tropical paradise has become living hell and the greatest obstacle preventing his own present happiness, the fulfillment of his own history, is his creation of an insurmountable predecessor, one whose "romantic glamour" is purer and simpler than his own reality.

The final irony, that the skipper, now bloated and bleary-eyed, is in fact the magnificent Red of Neilson's imagination and that when Sally and he meet they do not even recognize each other, snaps something in Neilson. The moment he had dreaded for twenty-five years has come and gone. His illusions disintegrate like gossamer; the "father" is not insurmountable:

> He had been cheated. They had seen each other at last and had not known it. He began to laugh, mirthlessly, and his laughter grew till it become hysterical. The Gods had played him a cruel trick. And he was old now.

In "Red," Neilson's realization of failure and waste do prompt some action, possibly an escape from the cell of his past. Over dinner, he lies to Sally that his eldest brother is very ill and he must go home. "Will you be gone long?" she asks. His only answer is to shrug his shoulders.

In its natural manner, Maugham's prose in these stories never strains for effect; each could easily be retold over coffee or a drink. Like Maupassant, Maugham is a realist and a merciless ironist, but while his narrator observes and his readers chuckle, characters such as Neilson grapple in desperate roles against the onrushing determination of their lives. In the style of the best "magazine" stories, incidents in Maugham inevitably build one on top of the other, slowly constraining his protagonists until, like grill-work, these incidents all but completely bar the protagonists from realizing their individual potential and freedom. Maugham's predilection for the surprise ending helps some find a final success, but not all; most end as we have believed they would—like the cuckolded Scotsman Lawson in "The Pool" who, after losing job, friends' respect, wife, and self, is "set on making a good job of it" and commits suicide "with a great stone tied up in his coat and bound to his feet."

Lawson, another "great coward" in the Stevenson mold, has married a beautiful half-caste and, naïvely assuming human nature the same the world over, has treated her as he would a white woman. By providing primarily in terms of his own culture's expectations,

Lawson unwittingly shoulders "the white man's burden," that bequest of Kipling's, until he becomes himself a burden. Maugham implies, with great irony, that if Lawson had been less "a gentleman" and had taken the girl as a mistress, his tragedy might have been averted. As the reader must see the "alien land" for what it really is, so must they see its peoples.

"RAIN"

"Rain," Maugham's best-known short story, develops many of these same themes. Pago Pago is unforgettably described, but no one could confuse it with the romanticized "loveliness" of Neilson's island. When the rain is not falling in torrents, the sun is oppressive. Davidson, the missionary, and Sadie, the prostitute, act out their parts with the same furious intensity. Neither is banalized; Maugham neither approves nor condemns. Only the "mountains of Nebraska" dream foreshadows Davidson's lust. (With its overtones of sexual repression, this dream makes "Rain" a notable pioneer in Freudian fiction.) Other than that, however, Davidson's sincere religious fervor seems convincingly real, inspired though it is by his "mission," yet another example of "the white man's burden." In the ensuing struggle between spiritual and "heathen" sensuality, the ironic stroke is that the prostitute wins; up to the last few pages, the story's outcome looks otherwise. Finally, Davidson must admit that he cannot proscribe human nature, not even his own. Neither saint nor sinner, he is simply human. On a more universal level than either "The Pool" or "Red," "Rain" shows that of human nature, only its unaccountability is predictable.

Maugham's detachment and moral tolerance, as well as assuring Davidson's and Sadie's vitality as characters, benefits his handling of the tale. The restraint exercised in *not* portraying for the reader either of the two "big scenes," Sadie's rape or Davidson's suicide, gives Maugham's story "Rain" an astounding dramatic power. The "real life" genesis of "Rain" is well known. Maugham jotted down his impressions of a few passengers aboard ship traveling with him in the winter of 1916 from Honolulu to Pago Pago; four years later he created a story from these notes. Of his prototype for Sadie Thompson he wrote:

Plump, pretty in a coarse fashion perhaps not more than twenty-seven. She wore a white dress and a large white hat, long white boots from which the calves bulged in cotton stockings.

SIX STORIES WRITTEN IN THE FIRST PERSON SINGULAR

This practice of taking characters and situations directly from life is nowhere better elaborated in Maugham than in the volume entitled *Six Stories Written in the First Person Singular*. The personal touch—clear in the book's title—leaves a strong impression of reality. Whereas "Rain" seems a small classic in its theme, conflict, effective setting, and dramatic ending, it has one difficulty: The reader is unable to sympathize clearly with any one character, and this detracts from a greater, warmer effectiveness it might otherwise have. When the narrator-as-detached-observer is introduced as a character, however, there is no such problem with sympathy. This creation, the consistent and subsequently well-known cosmopolite, the story*teller* for his stories, is one of Maugham's finest achievements.

In "Virtue" the narrator—here differentiated as "Maugham"—browses at Sotheby's auction rooms, goes to the Haymarket, and dines at Ciro's when he has a free morning; he was once a medical student and is now a novelist. In "The Round Dozen," he is a well-known author whose portrait appears in the illustrated papers. He is at Elson, a tattered seaside resort "not very far from Brighton," recovering from influenza. There, "Maugham" coincidentally observes a well-known bigamist—whose portrait at one time had also graced the pages of the press—capture his twelfth victim. In "Jane," the versatile man-of-the-world is introduced as a writer of comedies, while in "The Alien Corn" he is a promising young novelist who has grown middle-aged, written books and plays, traveled and had experiences, fallen in and out of love. Throughout *Six Stories Written in the First Person Singular*, "Maugham" is intermittently away from London, "once more in the Far East." Such frank appeals to verisimilitude (in other words, that "Maugham" is in fact Maugham) succeed extremely well.

"THE HUMAN ELEMENT"

In "The Human Element," the narrator is a popular author who likes "a story to have a beginning, a middle, and an end." He meets Carruthers, whom he does not much like, one night at the Hotel Plaza in Rome during the late summer "dead season." Carruthers is inhumanly depressed and tells Maugham why: He has found his life's love, the woman he would make his wife, Betty Weldon-Burns, living in Rhodes "in domestic familiarity" with her chauffeur.

Carruthers, also a short-story writer, has been praised by critics for "his style, his sense of beauty and his atmosphere," but when "Maugham" suggests he make use of his experience for a story, Carruthers grows angry: "It would be monstrous. Betty was everything in the world to me. I couldn't do anything so caddish." Ironically, the story ends with Carruthers's excuse that "there's no story there." That "Maugham" has in fact just made a story of it suggests that life can and does provide limitless possibilities for art if we are only ready to accept them.

Maugham specifically delineates these dual creative principles, life and art, in his introduction to the six stories in the collection. Defending the practice of drawing fictional characters from personal experience, Maugham cites Henri Beyle (Stendhal), Gustave Flaubert, and Jules Renard. "I think indeed," he writes, "that most novelists and surely the best, have worked from life." The concern of Maugham's South Sea stories, to convey what he "saw" rather than what he "had read," is continued here on a higher plane. Maugham qualifies that there must also be art:

> A real person, however eminent, is for the most part too insignificant for the purposes of fiction. The complete character, the result of elaboration rather than of invention, is art, and life in the raw, as we know, is only its material.

Illustrating the unaccountability of human behavior (for how could he endeavor to account for it?), "Maugham" remains a detached observer of life. Critics have wished for more poetry, loftier flights of imagination, more sympathy for his characters, and even occasional indirection; the lack of these things constitutes the limitation of Maugham's style. Rejecting both the atmospheric romanticism of his predecessors and the exhaustive modernism of his contemporaries, Maugham's short stories do not seek to penetrate either landscape or life. His reader, like his narrator, may experience admiration, annoyance, disgust, or pity for the characters, but he does not share or become immersed in their emotions. This point of view of a calm, ordinary man, so unusual for the twentieth century, is instructive, teaching careful and clear consideration of life's possibilities, its casualties and successes, banalities, and gifts. In this way, objective understanding is increased by reading Maugham much as intersubjective facilities are by reading James Joyce, D. H. Lawrence, or the other moderns.

OTHER MAJOR WORKS

LONG FICTION: *Liza of Lambeth*, 1897; *The Making of a Saint*, 1898; *The Hero*, 1901; *Mrs. Craddock*, 1902; *The Merry-Go-Round*, 1904; *The Bishop's Apron*, 1906; *The Magician*, 1908; *Of Human Bondage*, 1915; *The Moon and Sixpence*, 1919; *The Painted Veil*, 1925; *Cakes and Ale*, 1930; *The Narrow Corner*, 1932; *Theatre*, 1937; *Christmas Holiday*, 1939; *Up at the Villa*, 1941; *The Hour Before Dawn*, 1942; *The Razor's Edge*, 1944; *Then and Now*, 1946; *Catalina*, 1948; *Selected Novels*, 1953.

PLAYS: *A Man of Honour*, wr. 1898-1899, pr., pb. 1903; *Schiffbrüchig*, pr. 1902 in German (pb. in English as *Marriages Are Made in Heaven*, 1903); *Loaves and Fishes*, wr. 1903, pr. 1911; *Lady Frederick*, pr. 1907; *The Explorer*, pr. 1908; *Jack Straw*, pr. 1908; *Mrs. Dot*, pr. 1908; *The Noble Spaniard*, pr. 1909; *Penelope*, pr. 1909; *Smith*, pr. 1909; *Grace*, pr. 1910 (better known as *Landed Gentry*, 1913); *The Tenth Man*, 1910; *The Land of Promise*, pr. 1913; *Caroline*, pr. 1916 (pb. as *The Unattainable*, 1923); *Our Betters*, pr. 1917; *Caesar's Wife*, pr. 1919; *Home and Beauty*, pr. 1919 (also as *Too Many Husbands*); *The Unknown*, pr., pb. 1920; *The Circle*, pr., pb. 1921; *East of Suez*, pr., pb. 1922; *The Constant Wife*, pr., pb. 1926; *The Letter*, pr., pb. 1927; *The Sacred Flame*, pr., pb. 1928; *The Breadwinner*, pr., pb. 1930; *Collected Plays of W. Somerset Maugham*, pb., 1931, 1952 (3 volumes, includes 18 plays); *For Services Rendered*, pr., pb. 1932; *Sheppey*, pr., pb. 1933.

SCREENPLAY: *Trio*, 1950 (with R. C. Sherriff and Noel Langley).

NONFICTION: *The Land of the Blessed Virgin: Sketches and Impressions in Andalusia*, 1905 (also known as *Andalusia*, 1920); *On a Chinese Screen*, 1922; *The Gentleman in the Parlour: A Record of a Journey from Rangoon to Haiphong*, 1930; *Don Fernando*, 1935; *The Summing Up*, 1938; *Books and You*, 1940; *France at War*, 1940; *Strictly Personal*, 1941; *Great Novelists and Their Novels*, 1948; *A Writer's Notebooks*, 1949; *The Writer's Point of View*, 1951; *The Vagrant Mood: Six Essays*, 1952; *The Partial View*, 1954 (includes *The Summing Up* and *A Writer's Notebook*); *Ten Novels and Their Authors*, 1954 (revision of *Great Novelists and Their Novels*); *The Travel Books*, 1955; *Points of View*, 1958; *Purely for My Pleasure*, 1962; *Selected Prefaces and Introductions*, 1963.

BIBLIOGRAPHY

Archer, Stanley. *W. Somerset Maugham: A Study of the Short Fiction*. New York: Twayne, 1993. An introductory survey of Maugham's short fiction, focusing on style and technique of the stories and the frequent themes of how virtue ironically can cause unhappiness, how colonial officials come in conflict with their social and physical environment, and how people are often unable to escape their own cultural background. Reprints some of Maugham's own comments on short fiction and three previously published critical excerpts.

Burt, Forrest D. *W. Somerset Maugham*. Boston: Twayne, 1985. This volume asserts that Maugham has long been an underestimated and neglected writer in terms of an assessment of his value and position in the literary canon and that there has been a more serious appraisal of his works since his death. Includes a chronology, a basic biography (in the early chapters), and a focus on the literary works from a critical standpoint.

Calder, Robert L. *W. Somerset Maugham and the Quest for Freedom*. London: Heinemann, 1972. This impressive study primarily emphasizes critical and thematic assessment of the novels, breaking them down into categories of genre ("Novels of Apprenticeship") or categories of thematic focus ("Artist-Hero Novels"; "Aspects of the Maugham *Persona*"). This work also exhaustively delineates several of the important issues with which Maugham was concerned—that is, the absolute importance of money, the nature of marriage and bondage, the interest in Native American mysticism (*The Razor's Edge*), and the nature of individual freedom. Also provided are four informative appendices, including material on Maugham's role in Allied espionage (1917) and a discussion of recurring images of bondage and freedom in his works.

Cordell, Richard A. *Somerset Maugham: A Writer for All Seasons*. 2d ed. Bloomington: Indiana University Press, 1969. Cordell, who was Maugham's friend and confidant, provides an in-depth examination of the writer's life and works. Cordell disputes the labeling of Maugham as "enigmatic" and "inscrutable," charging instead that Maugham was just the opposite. This volume includes a substantial section devoted to a discussion of Maugham's short stories along with chapters on three of the "autobiographical novels," plays, other fiction, and critical reception.

Curtis, Anthony. *Somerset Maugham*. Windsor, England: Profile Books, 1982. An excellent forty-seven page pamphlet-sized volume that provides both an intensive and lucid overview of the writer, his genres, his life, and his themes. It also clearly distinguishes Maugham as preeminently a writer of short fiction. An insightful and brief introduction to the author that also includes an index of his available short stories.

Holden, Philip. *Orienting Masculinity, Orienting Nation: W. Somerset Maugham's Exotic Fiction*. Westport, Conn.: Greenwood Press, 1996. Examines the themes of homosexuality, gender identity, and race relations in Maugham's works.

_____. "W. Somerset Maugham's Yellow Streak." *Studies in Short Fiction* 29 (Fall, 1992): 575-582. Discusses Maugham's story "The Yellow Streak" as a dialectical tale made up of the opposites of civilized/savage, male/female, and racial purity/miscegenation. Considers the treatment of the relationship between the two men in the story.

Jonas, Klaus W., ed. *The Maugham Enigma*. New York: Citadel Press, 1954. An informative background collection of articles, essays, biographical notes, and book reviews by numerous authors on Maugham. It covers the author as dramatist, novelist, "teller of tales," and essayist, and it also includes some interesting reminiscences and notes on writing from Maugham himself.

Loss, Archie K. *W. Somerset Maugham*. New York: Ungar, 1987. The chapter on short fiction in this general introduction to Maugham's life and art focuses largely on his most familiar story, "Rain," as the best example of his short-story technique and subject matter. Discusses Maugham as a tale-teller and argues that the voice of the narrator is the most important single element in a Maugham short story.

Naik, M. K. *W. Somerset Maugham*. Norman: University of Oklahoma Press, 1953. The underlying concept of Naik's approach to a discussion of Maugham's life and work is that it reveals a basic "conflict between the two strains of cynicism and humanitarianism" in the author himself. Naik begins with a definition of this conflict, discusses biographical data, and then examines the various genres of the author in terms of his overall premise.

Rogal, Samuel J. *A William Somerset Maugham Encyclopedia*. Westport, Conn.: Greenwood Press, 1997. Contains information on Maugham's life as well as his works. Includes bibliographical references and an index.

Kenneth Funsten
updated by Sherry Morton-Mollo

GUY DE MAUPASSANT

Born: Château de Miromesnil, France; August 5,
1850
Died: Paris, France; July 6, 1893

PRINCIPAL SHORT FICTION

La Maison Tellier, 1881 (*Madame Tellier's Estab-
lishment and Short Stories*, 1910)
Mademoiselle Fifi, 1882 (*Mademoiselle Fifi and
Other Stories*, 1922)
Clair de lune, 1883
Contes de la bécasse, 1883
Les Sœurs Rondoli, 1884 (*The Sisters Rondoli and
Other Stories*, 1923)
Miss Harriet, 1884 (*Miss Harriet and Other
Stories*, 1923)
Contes du jour et de la nuit, 1885 (*Day and Night
Stories*, 1924)
Toine, 1885 (*Toine and Other Stories*, 1922)
Yvette, 1885 (*Yvette and Other Stories*, 1905)
Monsieur Parent, 1886 (*Monsieur Parent and
Other Stories*, 1909)
La Petite Rogue, 1886 (*Little Rogue and Other
Stories*, 1924)
Le Horla, 1887 (*The Horla and Other Stories*,
1903)
Le Rosier de Madame Husson, 1888
L'Inutile Beauté, 1890 (*Useless Beauty and Other
Stories*, 1911)
Eighty-eight Short Stories, 1930
Eighty-eight More Stories, 1932
Complete Short Stories, 1955

OTHER LITERARY FORMS

Although he became famous above all for his wel-
l-crafted short stories, Guy de Maupassant also wrote
poems, plays, and three successful novels: *Une Vie*
(1883; *A Woman's Life*, 1888), *Bel-Ami* (1885; English translation, 1889), and *Pierre et Jean* (1888; *Pierre and Jean*, 1890). His preface to *Pierre and Jean*
has attracted a considerable amount of attention over
the years because it reveals the profound influence
that Gustave Flaubert exerted on Maupassant's devel-

opment as a writer. Maupassant was not, however, a
major literary theoretician, and many critics have
agreed with Henry James's perceptive comment that
Maupassant as a "philosopher in his composition is
perceptibly inferior to the story-teller." Maupassant
also wrote several volumes of fascinating letters to
such eminent writers as Flaubert, Ivan Turgenev, and
Émile Zola.

ACHIEVEMENTS

Guy de Maupassant is generally considered to be
the most significant French short-story writer. Unlike
other important nineteenth century French prose writers such as Honoré de Balzac and Flaubert who are
better known for their novels than for their short stories, Maupassant created an extensive corpus of short
stories that reveals an aesthetically pleasing combination of wit, irony, social criticism, idealism, and psychological depth. Although his short stories deal with
readily identifiable situations and character types in
France during the 1870's and 1880's, they explore
universal themes such as the horrors of war and the
fear of death, hypocrisy, the search for happiness, the
exploitation of women, and contrasts between appearance and reality. His characters illustrate the extraordinary diversity in modern society, from prostitutes to adulterous husbands and wives and from
peasants to aristocrats. Even during his lifetime, his
short stories were appreciated both within and beyond the borders of France. He had the special ability
of conveying to readers the universal elements in everyday situations. He used wit and an understated
style in order to create aesthetically pleasing dialogues. His work exerted a profound influence on
many major short-story writers, including Thomas
Mann, Katherine Mansfield, and Luigi Pirandello.

BIOGRAPHY

Henri-René-Albert Guy de Maupassant was born
on August 5, 1850, in the Château de Miromesnil in
the French province of Normandy. He was the first
child of Gustave and Laure de Maupassant. Guy de

Maupassant spent his childhood and adolescence in Normandy. His parents grew to dislike each other intensely, and they eventually separated. Laure did not want Gustave to play any role in rearing either Guy or their second son, Hervé. She was an overly protective mother, and she did not allow Guy to attend school until he was thirteen years old. Until he became a student in 1863 at a Catholic seminary school, Guy's only teacher was the local parish priest. Guy became indifferent to religion, and at the age of seventeen he was expelled from the seminary school because of behavior judged to be unacceptable by his teachers. He completed his secondary studies in 1869 at a boarding school in Rouen.

In 1867, Maupassant met the celebrated novelist Flaubert, whom Laure had known for almost twenty years. Some fanciful critics have suggested that Flaubert was not only Maupassant's literary mentor but also his biological father. Although there is no evidence to support this hypothesis, Maupassant did react with extreme displeasure and perhaps with excessive sensitivity to the frequently repeated remark that Flaubert had been his father.

Maupassant began his law studies at the University of Paris in 1869, but with the outbreak of hostilities in the Franco-Prussian War in 1870, he enlisted in the French army. He served in Normandy, where he experienced firsthand the humiliation of the French defeat and the severity of the Prussian occupation. After his return to civilian life, he became a clerk in the Naval Ministry. He remained in government service until 1880, when he resigned his position in the Ministry of Public Instruction so that he could dedicate all of his efforts to writing.

Starting in 1875, Flaubert became Maupassant's literary mentor. At first, Maupassant slavishly imitated his master's style, but gradually he began to explore themes and situations such as the tragic effect of war and occupation on French society, which Flaubert had chosen not to treat. Maupassant received further intellectual stimulation by frequenting Flaubert's weekly literary salon, which was attended at various times by such eminent writers as Turgenev, Zola, Alphonse Daudet, and Edmond de Goncourt. In late 1879, Maupassant and five other French authors

Guy de Maupassant (Library of Congress)

agreed that each would write a short story on the Prussian occupation of France for a volume to be entitled *Les Soirées de Médan* (1880; the evenings in Médan). Maupassant's contribution was "Boule de Suif." The other contributors to this volume were Zola, Joris-Karl Huysmans, Paul Alexis, Henry Céard, and Léon Hennique. Almost all critics agreed with Flaubert's assessment that "Boule de Suif" was "a masterpiece of composition and wit." This extremely favorable reaction encouraged Maupassant to become a very prolific writer of short stories and novels. During the 1880's, he earned a good living as a writer, but gradually his health began to deteriorate as a result of syphilis, which he had contracted in the 1870's and which his doctors had failed to diagnose until it was too late for him to be cured. On January 2, 1892, Maupassant tried to kill himself. After this unsuccessful suicide attempt, he was committed to a psychiatric asylum at Passy, in Paris, France, where he died on July 6, 1893.

ANALYSIS

Although his active literary career began in 1880 and lasted only ten years, Guy de Maupassant was nevertheless an extraordinarily productive writer whose short stories dealt with such diverse themes as war, prostitution, marital infidelity, religion, madness, cultural misunderstanding between the French and the English, and life in the French provinces, especially his native Normandy. His short stories varied greatly in length from only a few pages to more than forty pages. His stories are extremely well organized, and there is much psychological depth in his insights into the complex motivations for his characters' behavior. His work explores the full spectrum of French society. He describes characters from various professions and social classes with sensitivity and humor. Although Maupassant was himself very pessimistic, rather chauvinistic, and also distrustful of organized religions, his characters do not simply mirror his own philosophy. He wrote about topics of interest to his French readers in the 1880's, but he also enriched his short stories with psychological and moral insights, which continue to fascinate readers born several generations after his death. Maupassant examined how ordinary Frenchmen and Frenchwomen, with whom readers can readily identify, reacted to unexpected social, historical, moral, and business situations. His short stories mirror life because in fiction, as in life, things never turn out exactly as one thinks they will.

Although Maupassant wrote on a wide variety of topics, the major recurring themes in his short stories are war, prostitution, and madness. Why Maupassant explored these themes instead of others is problematic. In their excellent biographies of Maupassant, Paul Ignotus and Francis Steegmuller showed that the Prussian occupation of France had been a trumatic experience for him. Even his mentor Flaubert realized that Maupassant was promiscuous, and he warned his disciple of the physical consequences of sleeping with prostitutes. By the middle of the 1880's, Maupassant began to write very frequently about characters who fear losing their minds. This would, in fact, happen to Maupassant himself, but not until late 1891. Although it is tempting to interpret Maupassant's short stories in the light of his personal experiences, such an approach is not very useful for literary criticism. Other Frenchmen of his day were scarred by the Prussian occupation of France or frequented houses of prostitution, but they did not possess his literary talents. His biography may well explain his preference for certain themes, but it does not enable readers to appreciate the true value of his short stories.

Maupassant wrote more than two hundred short stories. Even in a relatively long essay, it would be impossible to do justice to all of his major works. This article will examine four representative short stories in order to give readers a sense of Maupassant's refined artistry. These works are "La Folle" ("The Madwoman"), "Boule de Suif," "La Maison Tellier" ("Madame Tellier's Establishment"), and "Le Horla" ("The Horla").

"THE MADWOMAN"

"The Madwoman" and "Boule de Suif" both describe personal tragedies that can result from war and military occupation. These two short stories are significantly different in length. In Albert-Marie Schmidt's 1973 edition of Maupassant's short stories, "The Madwoman" is four pages long, whereas "Boule de Suif" fills forty pages. Both, however, describe women who are victimized by the arbitrary abuse of power during the Prussian occupation of France. The structure of "The Madwoman" consists of a story within a story. The narrator is an unnamed man from Normandy. He tells his listener, Mathieu d'Endolin, that hearing woodcocks reminds him of a terrible injustice that took place during the Prussian occupation of Normandy. This odd reference to woodcocks is explained only at the end of this short story. The narrator speaks of a woman who went mad from grief after her father, husband, and baby had all died within a month of one another in 1855. She went to bed, became delirious, and screamed whenever anyone tried to take her out of her bed. The narrator is a sensitive man who feels pity for this woman. He wonders if she still thinks about the dead or if her mind is now "motionless." Her isolation from the world is absolute. She knows nothing about the world outside her room. During the Prussian occupation of the town in which the narrator and this madwoman live, German soldiers were assigned to the various houses. The madwoman and her maid had to receive twelve soldiers.

For reasons that are totally incomprehensible to the narrator, the German officer in charge of the soldiers in this house convinces himself that the madwoman will not talk to him because she holds Germans in contempt. He orders her to come downstairs, but the madwoman cannot understand his demand. He interprets her silence as a personal insult, and he orders his soldiers to carry the woman in her bed toward a nearby forest. For nine months, the narrator learns nothing about the fate of this woman. During the fall hunting season, he goes to the forest and shoots a few woodcocks. When he goes to retrieve these woodcocks, he finds a human skeleton on a bed. The awful truth is revealed to him. The madwoman had died from exposure to the cold, and "the wolves had devoured her." The narrator does not end this tale by denouncing the Germans but rather by praying that "our sons will never again see war" lest other innocent victims suffer similar tragedies. Readers from any country or generation can identify with the hopes of this narrator. Readers and the narrator know all too well that many innocent victims have been killed in war. "The Madwoman" is a powerful short story that expresses one's revulsion over the death of any innocent victim of war.

"BOULE DE SUIF"

Although his most famous short story, "Boule de Suif," also deals with the horrors of war, "Boule de Suif" is a much more complicated tale, and it has eleven major characters. At the beginning of "Boule de Suif," Maupassant evokes the terror felt by many French citizens who came to fear the abuse of power by the occupying soldiers. This short story begins in the Norman city of Rouen. The Prussian general in Rouen grants ten inhabitants of this city special permission to travel by coach from Rouen to Dieppe. Their intention is to reach the port of Le Havre from which they can leave France for safety in England.

Their motivaton is clear. They hope to lead better lives in a free country.

The ten travelers are from different social classes. There are three married couples. Mr. and Mrs. Loiseau are wine merchants whose integrity has been questioned by many of their customers. Mr. and Mrs. Carré-Lamodon are well-to-do owners of cotton mills, but Maupassant describes Mr. Carré-Lamodon as a hypocritical politician. The Count and Countess of Bréville are very rich, but their noble title is of questionable value. Rumor has it that King Henry IV of France had impregnated an ancestor of the Brévilles. In order to avoid an unpleasant situation, he made the lady's husband a count and appointed him as the governor of Normandy. This placated the husband. In the coach, there are also two nuns, an inoffensive leftist named Cornudet who is more interested in drinking beer than in reforming society, and finally a prostitute named Boule de Suif. Her name, which means "ball of tallow," evokes her rotund figure. Although the three respectable couples feel superior to Boule de Suif, they do not hesitate to accept food from her once they realize that she alone has brought food for this trip.

When their coach stops in the village of Tôtes, a German officer orders the ten passengers to stay in the local inn until Boule de Suif agrees to sleep with him. As a patriotic Frenchwoman, she refuses to yield to this blackmail. The next day she goes to church and asks God to grant her the strength to remain faithful to her moral principles and to France. She assumes that the other passengers will support her, but she is wrong. The married couples and the two nuns conspire to put pressure on Boule de Suif. The elder of the two nuns is especially reprehensible because she distorts the clear meaning of several biblical passages in order to convince Boule de Suif that it would be praiseworthy for her to sleep with the Prussian officer. Boule de Suif feels abandoned by her fellow citizens and by two representatives of her church. In despair, she yields to the Prussian's ultimatum. The three married couples and the two nuns celebrate this action by drinking champagne. Their insensitivity and general boorishness are obvious to the reader, who feels much sympathy for the victim.

As they are traveling from Tôtes to Dieppe, Boule de Suif begins to weep, and the others take out their newly purchased picnic baskets filled with cheese, sausage, and bread, but they do not offer to share their food with Boule de Suif, who had been so generous during the earlier trip. A silent rage builds within her, but the proud Boule de Suif says nothing. She realizes that they are unworthy of her.

Ever since its publication in 1880, "Boule de Suif" has been considered Maupassant's masterpiece. Its structure is admirable, and the parallel scenes of eating in the coach serve to reinforce in the reader's mind Boule de Suif's alienation from the other passengers. Her patriotism causes her to sacrifice herself for them, but now they want nothing to do with her. Both "Boule de Suif" and "The Madwoman" reveal Maupassant's artistry in describing the unpredictable and destructive effect of war and occupation on innocent victims.

"MADAME TELLIER'S ESTABLISHMENT"

Although the title character in "Boule de Suif" is a prostitute, the story's main theme is war and not prostitution. In Maupassant's equally celebrated short story "Madame Tellier's Establishment," the principal theme is prostitution, but Maupassant develops this theme with much sensitivity and wit. Madame Tellier runs a bordello, but she is a shrewd businesswoman who does a fine job in marketing. She hires prostitutes representing the different types of feminine beauty "so that each customer could find there the satisfaction" of his sexual fantasies. The men in her town feel very much at ease in her bordello, and she treats her prostitutes and clients as members of her extended family. One Friday evening, however, the routine is disrupted when her customers see a sign with the words "Closed Because of First Communion" at the entrance of her business. Madame Tellier has decided to close her bordello for a day so that she and her five employees can attend the First Communion of her niece, who lives in the rural community of Virville.

The train ride to Virville contains a marvelously comic scene. Seated with Madame Tellier and her five prostitutes are a traveling salesman and an elderly peasant couple, who are transporting three ducks not in cages. The husband and wife watch with disbelief as the five prostitutes take turns sitting on the salesman's lap while playing with the ducks. The salesman then takes out brightly colored garters, and he cajoles the prostitutes and even Madame Tellier into allowing him to place the garters on their legs. All of this is accompanied by much laughter. The peasants cannot believe their eyes. As they get off the train with their ducks, the wife tells her husband: "They are sluts on their way to the wicked city of Paris." She is partially correct, but their actual destination is the nearby village of Virville.

After they have breakfast on her brother's farm, Madame Tellier leads her prostitutes into the local church for the First Communion services. The parishioners have never before seen such gaudily dressed women. The worshipers find it difficult to concentrate on the Mass. The prostitute named Rosa thinks of her First Communion; she begins to cry, and her tears become contagious. First the other prostitutes, then Madame Tellier, and finally all the adults in the church begin to weep uncontrollably, and the tears do not end until the elderly priest has distributed Communion to the last child. He is so moved by their tears, which he interprets as the expression of profound religious emotion, that he decides to give a sermon. For him, this is "a sublime miracle" that has made him the "happiest priest in the diocese." He speaks of the "visible faith" and "profound piety" of the out-of-town visitors. Although this priest would most probably have expressed himself differently had he known of their profession, readers cannot question his sincerity or the reality of the religious emotions experienced by the worshipers in this small church.

After the Mass, life returns quickly to normal for the ever-practical Madame Tellier. She tells her brother that they must take the midafternoon train so that she can reopen her business within a few hours. That evening, there is a festive atmosphere in her bordello. Much champagne is drunk, and Madame Tellier is unusually generous. She charges her customers only six francs for a bottle of champagne instead of the normal rate of ten francs. This is a well-structured short story in which scenes in the bordello precede and follow the First Communion sequence. Maupassant describes characters from widely different professions and social classes in a nonjudgmental manner. The refined artistry and style of "Madame Tellier's Establishment" may explain why Thomas Mann, who was himself renowned for his short prose works, concluded that Maupassant "would be regarded for centuries as one of the greatest masters of the short story."

"THE HORLA"

"The Madwoman," "Boule de Suif," and "Madame Tellier's Establishment" are all effective third-person narratives, but Maupassant also experimented with other narrative techniques. In 1886, he wrote two versions of a short story that he entitled "The Horla." Both versions describe the mental illness of a Frenchman who believes that an invisible being called "the Horla" has taken possession of his mind. In the first version, a psychiatrist named Dr. Marrande asks seven colleagues to listen to a patient who is sure that the Horla entered his locked bedroom, drank milk and water, and then took over his personality. The psychiatric patient assures his listeners that he "saw" the Horla: He looked in a mirror but did not see his own image. After the patient stops talking, Dr. Marrande makes a very strange remark for a psychiatrist: "I do not know if this man is mad or if we are both mad or if our successor has actually arrived." The first version of "The Horla" is ineffective for several reasons. First, it lacks a clear focus because both Dr. Marrande and his patient speak of their reactions to the Horla. Second, Dr. Marrande's comment that he may have gone mad does not inspire much confidence in him. Third, the very nature of this narration does not enable readers to experience the gradual development of the patient's psychiatric problems.

Maupassant wisely decided to revise this short story into a first-person narrative presented in the forms of diary entries written by the patient himself. In his first entry, dated May 8, the diarist seems to be a calm individual who mentions in passing that a Brazilian boat has just passed by his house, which overlooks the Seine. He soon develops a fever, has trouble sleeping, and writes of a recurring nightmare. He dreams that a being is on his bed and is

trying to strangle him. This nightmare returns several nights in a row. For the month of June, he is on an extended vacation, and he considers himself cured. When he returns home, however, he has new nightmares. This time, a being is trying to stab him. Although he keeps his bedroom locked at night, a spirit always drinks the water and the milk left in carafes by his bed. Gradually, he comes to accept the presence of this thirsty spirit. By mid-August, however, he concludes that a spirit has taken over his mind. The spirit orders him to read a book and an article on invisible spirits from Brazil that like to drink water and milk. In a desperate effort to free himself from the Horla, he traps the Horla in his bedroom and then burns down his house. It does not occur to him to think of his servants, who are asleep in his house. They die in the fire, and the diary does not indicate what happened to the diarist. Has he been arrested for murder or has he been committed to an insane asylum? In his very last entry, the diarist assures the reader that if the Horla is still alive, he will have to commit suicide. The second version of "The Horla" is very effective because it enables the reader to experience the gradual transformation of the diarist from a sensible person into a terrified and self-destructive individual who no longer appreciates the value of human life.

Although some critics have hypothesized that the second version of "The Horla" somehow prefigures the serious psychological problems that Maupassant himself would develop five years later, this is a fanciful interpretation. Maupassant did not try to kill himself until January, 1892, and he was still perfectly lucid when he wrote "The Horla" in 1886. This first-person narrative is a powerful short story that enables readers to experience the process by which a person can develop a serious mental illness. "The Horla" had a profound effect on generations of readers. In 1938, Arnold Zweig wrote of his recollection of this short story, which he had read years earlier:

> I still remember my emotion and admiration. I do not even need to close my eyes to see the white ship passing his country-house from which the strange guest, the split ego, invaded the life of the sick person.

Maupassant is still admired for his well-structured and beautifully written short stories. He is generally considered to be the best French short-story writer, although since the early years of the twentieth century, his works have been held in much higher esteem outside France (especially in England, the United States, and Germany) than in his homeland. It is not clear why so many French critics have been less than enthusiastic in their assessment of his short stories. Perhaps the critical standing of Maupassant would be higher than it is among modern French critics if he had explored a wider variety of themes. Readers should not forget that Maupassant died at the relatively young age of forty-two. His short literary career of only ten years did not give him sufficient time to develop the extraordinary breadth and diversity of a writer such as Victor Hugo, whose literary career spanned more than six decades. Despite the relatively limited number of themes that he explored in his short stories, Maupassant wrote short stories of such stylistic beauty and psychological depth that they still continue to please readers and to inspire creativity in short-story writers from many different countries.

OTHER MAJOR WORKS

LONG FICTION: *Une Vie*, 1883 (*A Woman's Life*, 1888); *Bel-Ami*, 1885 (English translation, 1889); *Pierre et Jean*, 1888 (*Pierre and Jean*, 1890); *Forte comme la mort*, 1889 (*Strong as Death*, 1899); *Notre cœur*, 1890 (*The Human Heart*, 1890).

POETRY: *Des Vers*, 1880 (*Romance in Rhyme*, 1903).

NONFICTION: *Au Soleil*, 1884 (*In the Sunlight*, 1903); *Sur l'eau*, 1888 (*Afloat*, 1889); *La Vie errante*, 1890 (*In Vagabondia*, 1903).

MISCELLANEOUS: *The Life Work of Henri René Guy de Maupassant*, 1903 (17 volumes); *The Works of Guy de Maupassant*, 1923-1929 (10 volumes); *Lettres de Guy de Maupassant á Gustave Flaubert*, 1951.

BIBLIOGRAPHY

Artinian, Artine. *Maupassant Criticism in France, 1880-1940*. New York: Russell & Russell, 1941. Despite its title, this important book explores critical reactions to Maupassant's works both in France and outside France. Artinian also includes thoughtful comments on Maupassant by some of the most important American and European writers of the 1930's. An essential work for all critics interested in Maupassant. Contains a very thorough bibliography.

Fusco, Richard. *Maupassant and the American Short Story: The Influence of Form at the Turn of the Century*. University Park: Pennsylvania State University Press, 1994. Argues that Maupassant was the most important influence on American short-story writers in the late nineteenth and early twentieth centuries. Focuses on his effect on Kate Chopin, Ambrose Bierce, Henry James, and O. Henry. Arranges Maupassant's stories into seven categories based on narrative structure.

Harris, Trevor A. Le V. *Maupassant in the Hall of Mirrors: Ironies and Repetition in the Work of Guy de Maupassant*. Houndmills, England: Macmillan, 1990. A critical evaluation of Maupassant's use of irony and repetition.

Ignotus, Paul. *The Paradox of Maupassant*. London: University of London Press, 1966. In this fascinating but subjective interpretation of Maupassant's genius, Ignotus believes that Maupassant was a paradoxical writer because he was obsessed with sex and was nevertheless a creative genius. At times, Ignotus's arguments are not terribly convincing, but this book does discuss very well Maupassant's ambivalent attitudes toward his literary mentor Gustave Flaubert.

Jobst, Jack W., and W. J. Williamson. "Hemingway and Maupassant: More Light on 'The Light of the World.'" *The Hemingway Review* 13 (Spring, 1994): 52-61. A comparison between Hemingway's "The Light of the World" and Maupassant's "La Maison Tellier." Discusses how both stories focus on a single prostitute rising above stereotypes.

Lloyd, Christopher, and Robert Lethbridge, eds. *Maupassant conteur et romancer*. Durham: University of Durham, 1994. A collection of papers, in both French and English, commemorating the centenary of Maupassant's death in 1993. Papers in English on Maupassant's short stories include an essay on "Mademoiselle Fifi," David Bryant's paper "Maupassant and the Writing Hand," and Angela Moger's essay "Kissing and Telling: Narrative Crimes in Maupassant."

Steegmuller, Francis. *Maupassant: A Lion in the Path*. New York: Random House, 1949. In this extremely well-documented biography of Maupassant, Steegmuller describes very well both the nature of Flaubert's influence on Maupassant and the contacts of Maupassant with such major writers as Émile Zola, Ivan Turgenev, and Henry James.

Sullivan, Edward. *Maupassant the Novelist*. Princeton, N.J.: Princeton University Press, 1945. This volume is a very thoughtful analysis of Maupassant's novels. Sullivan argues persuasively that Maupassant's novels do deserve as much critical attention as his more famous short stories have re-ceived over the years. Contains a solid bibliography.

_____. *Maupassant: The Short Stories*. Great Neck, N.Y.: Barron's, 1962. A pamphlet-length introduction to some of Maupassant's basic themes and story types. Particularly helpful are Sullivan's attempts to place Maupassant's short stories within their proper generic tradition.

Wallace, Albert H. *Guy de Maupassant*. New York: Twayne, 1973. Wallace presents an excellent analysis of recurring themes in Maupassant's major works. He discusses with much subtlety Maupassant's representations of war and madness. This well-annotated book is an essential introduction to the thematic study of Maupassant's major works.

Edmund J. Campion

CHRISTOPH MECKEL

Born: Berlin, Germany; June 12, 1935

PRINCIPAL SHORT FICTION

Im Land der Umbramauten, 1961 (novella)
Tullipan, 1965 (novella)
Die Noticen des Feuerwerkers Christopher Magalan, 1966 (novella)
Die Gestalt am Ende des Grundstücks, 1975 (novella; *The Figure on the Boundary Line*, 1983)
Licht, 1978 (novella)
Suchbild: Über meinen Vater, 1980 (novella; *Image for Investigation About My Father*, 1987)
Ein roter Faden: Gesammelte Erzählungen, 1983
Der wahre Muftoni, 1982 (novella)
Plunder, 1986 (novella)
Snow Creatures and Other Stories, 1990
Zünd and Other Stories, 1990

OTHER LITERARY FORMS

Christoph Meckel first gained renown and critical acclaim for his poetry, which appeared in such collections as *Nebelhörner* (1959), *Wildnisse* (1962), and *Säure* (1978); he is continually praised as one of the leading poets in contemporary German literature. Furthermore, his graphic art has appeared in more than thirty one-man exhibitions on three continents and has been published in various cycles as woodcuts, engravings, and drawings under several titles, such as *Moël* (1959) and *Das Meer* (1965), which consist of prints, and *Anabasis* (1982), which consists of prints and poetry. He has also written several radio plays and essays. His long fiction includes *Bockshorn* (1973), *Die Messingstadt* (1991), and *Shalamuns Papiere: Roman* (1992).

ACHIEVEMENTS

Christoph Meckel has been most highly regarded for his poetry, having received the prestigious Rainer Maria Rilke Prize for Poetry (1979) and the Georg Trakl Prize of the City of Salzburg (1982), as well as a dozen other prizes or subventions for his writings and honors for his graphic art. In fact, as early as the 1950's, he began creating prose fiction, as well as poetry and visual art. Meckel's early prose works drew curious interest and mixed critical acclaim, earning for him the reputation of a fantast, a comic, even a dilettante. Individual short stories were initially placed with various periodicals or appeared in special printings with small publishing houses. The success of his more serious fiction, such as *Licht* and *Suchbild*, has caused him to be recognized as a major writer, and his works have regularly appeared with major West German publishers.

BIOGRAPHY

Christoph Meckel was born in Berlin on June 12, 1935, son of the German poet Eberhard Meckel. His early years were spent in the warmth of a loving and well-to-do family, but within ten years he had experienced the collapse of the Third Reich, and with it that of his stable family life. While waiting for his father's return from a French prisoner-of-war camp in North Africa, the family became refugees, frequently moving between Berlin, Erfurt, and Freiburg. Despite poverty and a contentious father, Meckel survived the tumultuous early postwar years.

Though standard biographies report that he studied painting and graphics at the art academies in Freiburg (1954-1955) and in Munich (1956), he admits in *Bericht zur Entstehung einer Weltkomödie* (1985) that he was duly unimpressed with the quality of instruction and thus taught himself the intricacies of his craft through patience and experience. With the exception of the Near East, he has traveled extensively throughout the world: Besides Munich, Paris, and Rome (and his alternating residences in Berlin and southeastern France), he has lived for brief intervals in the United States, Mexico, Africa, Australia, and Southeast Asia. These travels are mirrored in the majority of his works as—in his own term—"vagabondage," the wandering from one landscape or climate to another.

Although Meckel has not written an autobiography as such, several of his works seem to be based on events or experiences from his life. *Suchbild*, for ex-

ample, relates his childhood, his experiences as a youth at the end of World War II, his relationship with a distraught father, and the eventual literary successes which overshadowed the father's earlier poetry. If the biological father is here rejected, Meckel discovers a more suitable progenitor in *Nachricht für Baratynski* (1981); the forgotten nineteenth century Russian poet is resurrected through biography and fiction as literary kin to Meckel to clarify the latter's aesthetics and support him in his undertaking. (Incidentally, *Nachricht für Baratynski*, while composed of fictional elements, can best be understood as an essay, rather than as a "story" or literary prose fiction.)

Further biographical information can be gathered in the *Bericht zur Entstehung einer Weltkomödie*. Like other works by Meckel, this so-called report on the origins of a world comedy is not easily categorized in literary terms. While it purports to be a biography of Meckel the graphic artist (and pointedly not that of Meckel the writer), it is scarcely the objective work that a "report" would insinuate, and it is woefully incomplete as a biography: Names and dates are frequently omitted, and the entire narration is superficially divided into three parts, the "report," followed by "notebooks" and an "appendix." Indeed, the reader finds mention of the external events of Meckel's life, his development as a graphic artist, his methods and ultimate goal: to create a world comedy consisting of nine hundred etchings (*Radierungen*), from the origins of the early collection *Moël* in 1959 to the completion of *Anabasis* in 1982—a period of twenty-three years.

Still, the literary aspects, the taste of fiction, are familiar to Meckel's readers. He reproduces in words and images the themes that are evident in his visual art: the moods, weather, people and objects, personal recollections, and historical events which underlie his work. This prose piece, like *Suchbild*, can be read as flawed autobiography—though the style and narrative techniques, the evocation of subjectivity through brief anecdotes and mood pictures make a "good story." As autobiography it is disappointingly incomplete; as a report it is fragmented and too subjective. Yet as literature it is evocative and revealing, creating character, mood, and impact which engage the reader.

With its irony and humor, *Bericht zur Entstehung einer Weltkomödie* is similar to another of Meckel's fictional biographies, the notes of Christopher Magalan, the fireworks maker.

ANALYSIS

Christoph Meckel's preoccupations with both graphic art and literature have proven to be mutually beneficial. In preparation for an illustration, for example, Meckel collects moods and events in written form as the basis for his visual art. Conversely, his literature benefits from the images that he has seen or "dreamed," as he so often expresses it. To the repeated frustration of literary critics and scholars, Meckel's prose works also elude traditional literary categories. Each is frequently a composite of his complete artistic expression: A prose work may be introduced or illustrated with his own engravings and further enhanced by the inclusion of poems or songs. Especially in his longer fiction, Meckel has insistently avoided the term "novel," preferring instead the broader category of "narration," which allows him more auctorial freedom to combine poetry and graphics with his prose.

Meckel and his works are often characterized as clever, witty, and inventive. Perhaps the most concise description of Meckel's traits comes from his translator and collaborator, Christopher Middleton, who emphasizes Meckel's exuberance. This term is meant to convey not only Meckel's enthusiasm for writing but also his inventiveness and the resultant variety of characters, themes, and forms. A common misconception of Meckel's works centers on precisely this exuberance, this playful aspect of much of his prose. Here several critics have noted that this abundance of imagination often results in no more than interesting tableaux, devoid of a cohesive plot and sustained tension. Others have complained about the aspect of "play," finding no redeeming value in these fanciful creations. In Meckel's defense, this imaginative world is created spontaneously, and, when successful, encourages a similar spontaneity of thought and action on the part of the reader. The world of routine and boredom suddenly is infused with new life; much in the traditional Romantic sense, each reader can create his or her own world through imagination and active participation. It is in this vein that a reader can begin to appreciate Meckel's unique contribution to modern literature.

Meckel's short prose includes both the realistic and the tragic, as well as the fantastic and fanciful. The latter clearly are fictive; with the former, however, the temptation to consider them autobiographical is irresistible: Indeed, they deal with writers or storytellers and are set in locations where Meckel himself has resided. This is the nature of his art: The stories are sensitive, seemingly based on personal experience, thus convincing, yet they must be recognized as fiction.

IM LAND DER UMBRAMAUTEN

Meckel's first significant piece of short fiction, *Im Land der Umbramauten*, contains three short stories and twenty-one anecdotal prose pieces centering on the thoughts and deeds of Herr Ucht, a confessed magician. Ucht invents objects and scenarios, purportedly the title story of this volume. Here, in the land of the Umbramauts, the reader learns the geography, topography, characteristics, traditions, and myths—in short, everything one would wish to know in this imaginative travelogue, so reminiscent of Tacitus's *De origine et situ Germanorum* (c. 98; also known as *Germania*; *The Description of Germanie*, 1598). Unusual features of this country include wandering mountains and lakes amid the generally barren landscape of a perpetual twilight, fierce winds and giant dogs that threaten the inhabitants. The pivotal chapter, placed exactly in the middle of the narration, concerns Sambai-Sambai, the wandering storyteller. His yarns captivate and entertain the Umbramauts yet also activate and engage their imaginations, much as Meckel himself attempts to do with this slim volume. Though these stories are the result of a clever and active fantasy, they are not, finally, memorable. They concern the magician's creations—wisps of fancy—not individual characters or events that might capture the reader's sympathy or interest, with which he or she might identify.

Still, noteworthy in this prose work are the descriptions of the artists, Ucht and Sambai-Sambai, and their function. They are storytellers, creators, and magicians who make life more interesting and thoughtful. Yet their responsibility does not end with the creation of their characters (as is repeated later in the story "Tullipan"). In short, authors must be completely aware of their characters' capabilities before they set them into the world, for otherwise they might inadvertently harm themselves or others.

"THE CROW"

Following this first major prose publication, Meckel wrote "Die Krähe" ("The Crow"), arguably the most popular and frequently anthologized of Meckel's short pieces. One fine summer day, the narrator happens upon a hunter in the forest, who is seeking to capture a tiger. Agreeing to help, the narrator soon learns that the tiger has metamorphosed himself into a bear, then into an elephant, a wolf, a black fox, and finally a man-sized crow. Eventually, the narrator meets and becomes friends with the crow; together they elude the hunter and make their way through the forests and villages. When they come to a city, however, the crow's unusual size attracts attention, and the two are chased through the streets by an unruly mob. Attempting one last transformation, the crow slowly becomes a huge black cat, blind and thus harmless. The city dwellers, overcome by suspicion and fear, stone the helpless cat to death, while the unharmed narrator quickly leaves the city, never to return. In "The Crow," Meckel's strength as a narrator is evident: Characterized by simplicity of style, an innocent and magical narrative stance leads the reader into a fairy-tale world. This atmosphere of naïveté and innocence, the wondrous mood, are unexpectedly dashed by a grotesque scene of senseless murder, thus earning for the piece the designation as an anti-fairy tale. Regardless of its literary categorization, the story's implications reflect a timeless moral, as well as a possible reference to contemporary world events.

TULLIPAN

Tullipan is literally a figment of the narrator's imagination—an invented personality through whom the author can live vicariously—who appears one day at the door. Though harmless and lovable, Tullipan is not a "mature" character; his refreshing innocence estranges him from the townspeople and the narrator. Though Tullipan is able to survive and live happily

ever after in a remote castle, the townspeople and the narrator ultimately regret their loss.

DIE NOTICEN DES FEUERWERKERS CHRISTOPHER MAGALAN

Another artist-figure of note is outlined in *Die Noticen des Feuerwerkers Christopher Magalan*, a humorous encomium to the fictitious nineteenth century genius of fireworks. Magalan's brilliant career is cut short during an aerial display, when he suddenly disappears in smoke and flames; the worst is assumed, since he is never seen again. Magalan's biography, written by a certain C. E. McKell, is accompanied by original sketches and an interview with the scholar L. Kuchenfuchs. This playful sketch scarcely conceals its author, Christoph Meckel, in the guises of Christopher Magalan and C. E. McKell, while recalling the Romantic age, Meckel's true artistic and spiritual home.

THE FIGURE ON THE BOUNDARY LINE

A more serious investigation of life's meaning is presented in *The Figure on the Boundary Line*. Alone as the houseguest of an absent friend, the protagonist, a writer, observes a lone figure in the woods bordering his property. The writer discovers that this person, seemingly poor and hungry, is perfectly content, that he wants and needs nothing. Gradually, the writer becomes more deeply involved with this man's simple routine, spending more time each day on the border of the property, until one day he completely disappears with the unknown figure, leaving only his diary as a clue to his fate. Metaphorically speaking, both men live at the extreme, at the boundary of property and a complicated, modern lifestyle. It is precisely this lifestyle, from which the writer was originally recuperating, that the writer ultimately rejects when he joins the outsider's uncomplicated existence.

LICHT

The appearance of *Licht* in 1978 marked a new departure for Meckel; this is the first serious narrative of extended length since the novel *Bockshorn* (1973). Its plot is simple: Upon the discovery of a love letter from his companion Dole to an anonymous recipient, the narrator, Gil, sees his world destroyed. Both Gil and Dole, globe-trotting journalists dedicated to their careers, share their spare moments and thus create a separate world of love, hope, and trust. This world is dashed by the presence of the letter. Before Gil can accept and begin to reconstruct their relationship, he receives yet another letter, this one announcing theaccidental death of Dole. Reviewers chastised Meckel for the lack of epic narration at the center of the story, while overlooking its necessity: The subjective memories of the narrator throughout the piece purposely clash with the objective reality of the love letter at the beginning and the death notice at the conclusion. Despite the negative reviews, this work established Meckel as a serious writer of prose fiction.

SUCHBILD

With his next work, *Suchbild*, Meckel enjoyed his greatest success. Perhaps his most ambitious, complex, and compelling work, this "wanted poster" is an attempt to identify his own deceased father, the poet Eberhard Meckel. Initially, the son recounts those many childhood memories that constitute his love for his father. Upon the discovery of his father's war diaries, however, Meckel realizes that the father had compromised his principles and become a conformist to Nazi ideology. The son's faith and trust are shattered, and he must find adequate means of expressing his loss. In addition to introductory quotes, his own engraving as frontispiece, the diary entries, and his personal memories, Meckel expands the scope of the work by including an afterword composed as a fairy tale; in it, the father as magician ultimately destroys the world he loves through thoughtless acts. This narration represents the high point of many "father books" published around 1980, in which children of Nazi sympathizers took their parents to task for betraying their professed ideals under pressure or out of conviction.

DER WAHRE MUFTONI

Der wahre Muftoni provides a humorous respite for Meckel and his readers, following the two previous narratives. The dead brother of Suzanne, the narrator, reappears as a diminutive figure reminiscent of Tom Thumb. As he grows to his former adult size, the two siblings become lovers and lead a scandalous life of glamour and adventure. The brother is a perfect charlatan and lovable thief, a "Muftoni." Finally, however, he begins to shrink, until he is no larger than Suzanne's little finger. His final request is that he be placed in a bottle and cast out to sea until he can return once again in adult size. While Meckel's story can be seen as a delightful parody of sensational adventure novelettes, the "immoral" freedom and spontaneity of the Muftoni inject vitality into an otherwise pedestrian tale.

PLUNDER

As defined by Meckel, *Plunder* are those superfluous objects that inhabit one's world. Neither consumer items nor those with practical value, they are the useless, impractical mementos that one invests with value and that in turn provide one's life with its distinctive meaning. These objects by their subjective appeal—for example, a mildewed spoon, tin soldiers long lost, a stolen bath towel from a favorite hotel—represent a healthy chaos in the ordered ennui of modern society. Interestingly, much of the book consists of anecdotes or stories that the narrator and his companion Caroline tell each other. Like plunder, these stories are unique, without utilitarian value, yet in their very telling they represent at once play, trust, mutual esteem, and affection between the man and woman. Aside from content and intent, the act of narration provides a valuable human bond between narrator and listener.

When asked why he writes, Meckel once replied that the best of all possible worlds was not good enough for him, that he wanted to create his own heaven on earth and to communicate the fact that he was alive. This he has done, even in his less successful works. Though he has written short fiction as brief as a 1-page anecdote and as long as a 120-page novelette, his most memorable works are those that engage the reader's sense of play or sympathy, the contemplation and involvement with his fictional world. Only through this shared spontaneity, this exuberance, can people actively create their own worlds and thus escape the stifling regimentation of everyday existence.

OTHER MAJOR WORKS

LONG FICTION: *Bockshorn*, 1973; *Die Messingstadt*, 1991; *Shalamuns Papiere: Roman*, 1992.

POETRY: *Tarnkappe*, 1956; *Nebelhörner*, 1959;

Wildnisse, 1962; *Säure*, 1978; *Anabasis*, 1982; *Souterrain*, 1984; *Anzahlung auf ein Glas Wasser*, 1987; *Das Buch Shiralee*, 1989.

NONFICTION: *Nachricht für Baratynski*, 1981; *Bericht zur Entstehung einer Weltkomödie*, 1985.

MISCELLANEOUS: *Moël*, 1959; *Das Meer*, 1965; *Werkauswahl: Lyrik, Prosa, Hörspiel*, 1971.

BIBLIOGRAPHY

Bedwell, Carol B. "Bread and Brilliance: Utility Versus Poetic Ecstasy in Meckel's 'Der Zünd.'" *Seminar: A Journal of Germanic Studies* 20 (November, 1984): 290-298. The author provides a close reading of an early story by Meckel and focuses on the creative process as one of its themes.

Grant, Alyth. "When Is Biography an Autobiography? Questions of Genre and Narrative Style in Christoph Meckel's *Suchbild.*" *Seminar: A Journal of Germanic Studies* 26 (September, 1990): 189-204. Grant finds that Meckel's *Suchbild* is a mixed genre work, that it not only presents his father's story but also reveals much about the author himself. An analysis of Meckel's narrative style reveals that he employs two distinct styles, one for the biographical and one for the autobiographical sections of the book.

Hanlin, Todd C. "A Biography for the 'New Sensibility': Christoph Meckel's Allegorical *Suchbild.*" *German Life and Letters* 39 (1986): 235-244. Hanlin discusses Meckel's *Suchbild* as a merging of two forms of biography, that of the artist and that of the parent, and sees the work both as an allegory of the behavior of the fathers during the Nazi period and an allusion to the potential danger in the "indifference" and "inertia" of the author's own contemporaries.

Rockwood, Heidi M. "Writing as a Magician's Game: The Strange Early World of Christoph Meckel." *Studies in Twentieths Century Literature* 8 (Spring, 1984): 197-210. Rockwood focuses on Meckel's use of the metaphor of "playing a game" in four of his short stories and concludes that the author, while recognizing its possible dangerous implications, nevertheless regards the element of play as essential for retaining one's "basic humanity."

Shapiro, David. "The Figure on the Boundary Line." *The New York Times Book Review* (November 25, 1984): 8. This review of the first book-length English translation of Meckel's work provides a good insight into a limited selection of the author's better known stories.

Todd C. Hanlin, updated by Stella P. Rosenfeld

HERMAN MELVILLE

Born: New York, New York; August 1, 1819
Died: New York, New York; September 28, 1891

PRINCIPAL SHORT FICTION
The Piazza Tales, 1856
The Apple-Tree Table and Other Sketches, 1922

OTHER LITERARY FORMS

Herman Melville's sixteen published books include novels, short stories, poetry, and sketches. He is best known for his novels, particularly *Moby Dick*

(1851), *The Confidence Man* (1857), and *Billy Budd, Foretopman* (1924).

ACHIEVEMENTS

By the middle of the twentieth century, names such as *Moby Dick* and captain Ahab were well known in the popular culture of the United States. Yet, one must look to the 1920's and the revival in Melville's work (notably *Moby Dick*) to see the beginning of what came to be Melville's immense stature in American literature. His most significant works received little popular or critical acclaim in his lifetime. One reason for this may have been friction with nineteenth century American tastes. Problems also stemmed, however, from Melville's fascination with forces that seemed (to him) to lie below the placid optimism of his contemporary American culture. Readers were disturbed by the author's tendency to view outward appearances as pasteboard masks that concealed a truer, darker reality. It should come as no surprise that modern students sense an invitation to allegorize Melville's works. Many believe that Melville, himself, perceived life in a symbolic way.

Many of the short pieces that Melville wrote for various magazines represent conscious attempts, through symbol and irony, to express disturbing layers of meaning beneath a calm surface. In 1855-1856, Melville finished a novel, *The Confidence Man*, rendering a bleak view of the possibility of faith in the world as he knew it. Although Melville openly wrote verse throughout his life, the manuscript that would become his novella, *Billy Budd, Foretopman*, was packed away by his widow and not discovered until the 1920's.

Melville completed *Moby Dick* some forty years before Sigmund Freud began to penetrate the veneer of conventional surfaces in his quest for the causes of hysteria—the salient behavioral aberration of repressive nineteenth century Europe. Yet, Melville (like his contemporary Nathaniel Hawthorne) had already begun to probe beyond the level of mundane appearances in his fiction. Even though some of Melville's stories are lengthy by modern standards, the finest of them exhibit exceptional merit in the short-story genre. "Benito Cereno" and "Bartleby the Scrivener," for example, reveal a rich complexity and density which rival those of modern masterpieces of the form.

BIOGRAPHY

Herman Melville withdrew from school at the age of twelve after the death of his father. He worked in various jobs—in a fur and cap store (with his brother), in a bank, on a farm, and as a teacher in country schools. He made two early sea voyages, one on a merchant ship to Liverpool in 1839, and one to

Herman Melville (Library of Congress)

the South Seas aboard the whaler *Acushnet*, in 1841. After about eighteen months, Melville and a friend deserted the whaler, and Melville spent a month in the Taipi Valley on the island of Nuku Hiva. Melville escaped the island aboard an Australian whaler but was imprisoned when he and ten other crewmen refused service. Again, he escaped, spent some time on the island of Mooréa, then several months in Hawaii. Eventually, he joined the U.S. Navy and returned home in 1844.

Out of these early sea adventures came Melville's two successful early novels, *Typee: A Peep at Polynesian Life* (1846) and *Omoo: A Narrative of Adventures in the South Seas* (1847). His experiences aboard the whaling ships led to a novel that was not to be successful in his lifetime, *Moby Dick*. The failure of *Moby Dick* and *Pierre: Or, The Ambiguities* (1852) left Melville financially and morally drained, but he would continue to produce fiction for a while, including the short stories that were guardedly constructed to seem unruffling to the sensibilities of the time but carried submerged patterns and disturbing undertones.

While still in the limelight of his early success, Melville married Elizabeth Shaw, daughter of a Massachusetts chief justice. They were to have four children; three died in young adulthood and the eldest son committed suicide in his eighteenth year (1867).

Melville was continually plagued by doubt, unrest, and marital problems. His later years were spent trying to adjust to his decline in status and seeking a comfortable living. In 1856, his father-in-law subsidized Melville's travels to the Mediterranean, the Holy Land, and England, where he visited Nathaniel Hawthorne. Unable to secure a naval commission during the Civil War, Melville sold his estate in Massachusetts and settled in New York. Finally, in 1866, he became an inspector in the New York Customs House until, some twenty years later, an inheritance enabled him to retire. He died September 28, 1891, at the age of seventy-two.

ANALYSIS

After the critical and commercial failure of *Moby Dick* and *Pierre*, Herman Melville, who was then supporting his wife and children, his mother, and his four sisters, was desperate for money. So when he received an invitation from *Putnam's Monthly Magazine* to contribute short stories at the rate of five dollars a page, he accepted. He also sold short stories to *Harper's New Monthly Magazine*. Both magazines, however, had very strict editorial policies banning any material which might conceivably offend even the most sensitive reader on moral, social, ethical, political, or religious grounds. This was a shattering limitation to Melville, whose deepest personal and artistic convictions were bound up in the defiant heroes and themes of highly unconventional metaphysical speculation of *Mardi and a Voyage Thither, Moby Dick*, and *Pierre*. He genuinely questioned many of the ideas which, although they came to be freely debated, were sacrosanct in the nineteenth century. These included the existence of a personal God outside the human spirit, the importance of material goods, the existence of absolute good and absolute evil, and the right of established civil and religious authorities to impose sanctions against those who expressed ideas that differed from the ideas of the majority. Obviously, neither *Putnam's Monthly Magazine* nor *Harper's New Monthly Magazine* would publish stories which dealt openly with opinions that would be objectionable to many of their readers. This left Melville in an apparently unresolvable dilemma: ignore his own strongest beliefs, or allow those dependent on him to live in poverty.

Not only did Melville find a solution, but also he found one which, while not ideal from an artistic standpoint, gave him a great deal of rather diabolical satisfaction. Melville's short stories—all of which were written during this period and under these conditions—present bland and apparently harmless surfaces under which boil the same rebellion and the same questioning of established ideas that characterize his most controversial novels. Furthermore, these stories reflect, in allegorical terms, the same dilemma that produced them. Beneath apparently innocuous surface plots, Melville's short stories center on the image of an anguished human being who is cursed with the ability to see more than the world sees; faced with the hostility that results from his challenge to the established beliefs of a complacent majority, his protagonist either fights against, withdraws from, or surrenders to the world.

"BARTLEBY THE SCRIVENER"

One of the most effective devices that allowed Melville to achieve his artistic purpose was his use of reassuringly respectable elderly gentlemen as narrators. In the very act of allowing them to tell their own stories, Melville injected a subtle but savage mockery which both expressed and concealed his own attitudes. For example, the narrator of Melville's best-known short story, "Bartleby the Scrivener" (1856), which was collected in *The Piazza Tales*, is an elderly lawyer reminiscing about an incident which had occurred some time earlier. The lawyer's own blindness to the deeper meanings of life is suggested in the first paragraph of the story, when Melville describes Bartleby as "one of those beings of whom nothing is ascertainable." As the reader discovers, it is primarily the physical, external facts of Bartleby's life that are unknown; but to the materialistic lawyer, these are everything. He sees only surface reality, never inner truth, a point which is underlined in the narrator's next sentence: "What my own astonished eyes saw of Bartleby, *that* is all I know of him."

The lawyer begins his story by describing the office on Wall Street which he occupied at the time of Bartleby's appearance. The significance of "Wall Street" becomes apparent immediately; the lawyer has surrounded himself with walls, and his windows command no other view. When the lawyer hires Bartleby as a scrivener, or copier of law documents, he assigns Bartleby a desk near a window which faces a wall only three feet away. On one side of Bartleby's desk is a ground glass door separating him from the other two copyists, and on the other side, the lawyer places a folding screen. Having imposed upon Bartleby his own claustrophobic setting, the lawyer gives him law documents to copy. For a while all goes well; Bartleby copies documents neatly and efficiently. On the third day, however, the lawyer asks Bartleby to examine his writing.

In ordering him to examine his writing, the lawyer means that Bartleby should read through the copy he has made while someone else reads aloud from the original. This is an extremely boring task, but an accepted part of every scrivener's work. Bartleby replies, "I would prefer not to." The lawyer reacts with characteristic indecision: He feels impelled to expel Bartleby from his office, but does nothing because he is unnerved by Bartleby's total lack of expression, by the absence of "anything ordinarily human about him."

Several days later, when Bartleby again refuses to examine his copy, the lawyer appeals to him in the name of two ideals which are of great importance to the lawyer himself: common usage and common sense. Bartleby is unmoved. Instead of asserting his own authority, the lawyer appeals not only to his other two scriveners but also to his office boy. All these uphold the lawyer's view. He then calls upon Bartleby in the name of "duty"; again, Bartleby fails to respond to the verbal cue.

The lawyer's inability to cope with Bartleby is anticipated in the story by his tolerance of the Dickensian eccentricities of his other two scriveners. The older one, Turkey, works well in the morning, but after a lunch which is implied to be mostly liquid, he becomes reckless, irascible, and messy. The younger copyist, Nippers, is dyspeptic. His irritability takes place in the morning, while the afternoons find him comparatively calm. Thus, the lawyer gets only one good day's work between them. Nevertheless, he always finds some rationalization for his lack of decisiveness.

The first rationalization he applies to his indecision regarding Bartleby is the difficulty of coping effectively with passive resistance. The lawyer feels that Bartleby's unaccountable displays of perversity must be the result of some involuntary aberration, and he reflects that tolerating Bartleby "will cost me little or nothing, while I lay up in my soul what will eventually prove a sweet morsel for my conscience." Even on the comparatively rare occasions when he is sufficiently irritated to confront Bartleby with a direct order to do something which Bartleby "would prefer not to," the lawyer always retires with dire resolutions, but no action.

One Sunday morning, as the lawyer walks toward Trinity Church "to hear a celebrated preacher," he decides to stop at his office. There he finds Bartleby in his shirt sleeves, together with evidence that he has been using the office as his home. The lawyer feels at first a sense of melancholy and pity at Bartleby's loneliness; but as the full realization of Bartleby's isolation dawns on the lawyer, his feelings turn to fear and repulsion. He reflects that Bartleby never reads, never converses, but only works and stands for long periods staring out at the dead walls. Bartleby's presence in the office at night and on Sunday, when the usually bustling Wall Street is silent and uninhabited, reminds the lawyer of Bartleby's essential difference from his own concept of humanity, which revolves around surface society. The lawyer rationalizes his unsympathetic response to these circumstances by reflecting that such depths of soul-sickness as Bartleby's repel the human heart because common sense rejects the idea of pity where there is no realistic hope of offering aid.

The lawyer makes an attempt, on Monday morning, to bring Bartleby inside the narrow circle of external reality which is all the lawyer is capable of comprehending. He asks Bartleby for details of his life: place of birth, family, and the like. Bartleby re-fuses with his usual "I prefer not." The lawyer notices that he and his other copyists have begun to use that expression, and he fears that the influence of Bartleby will spread throughout the office. Bartleby further ir-ritates the lawyer the next day by refusing to do even the one task he had, until then, been willing to do: copying law documents. When the lawyer asks the reason, Bartleby replies, "Do you not see the reason for yourself?" The lawyer does not see; and ironi-cally, he attributes Bartleby's refusal to copy to trou-ble with his eyes. When Bartleby finally makes it clear, some days later, that his refusal is final, the lawyer decides to order him to leave. Yet he feels a sense of pity for the scrivener because "he seemed alone, absolutely alone in the universe."

The lawyer gives Bartleby six days in which to get ready to leave; at the end of that time, Bartleby is still there. The lawyer gives him money, and, ordering Bartleby to be gone by the next day, leaves the office assuming that he will obey. The lawyer's self-congratulations on his masterly application of the doctrine of assumption end abruptly the next day when the lawyer discovers the scrivener still in the of-fice. Then the lawyer rationalizes that it is his predes-tined fate to harbor Bartleby, and that his charity will be amply repaid in the next world. The gibes of his friends and professional associates, however, under-mine his resolve, and again he orders Bartleby to de-part. When he does not, the lawyer finally takes deci-sive action. He packs up his own belongings and moves to a new office, leaving Bartleby alone in an empty room.

The lawyer soon finds, however, that he is not yet free of Bartleby. The landlord of the lawyer's former office, unable to move Bartleby from the building even after the new tenant has expelled him from the office itself, applies to the lawyer for help. The law-yer offers Bartleby several different jobs, and even suggests that he make his home with the lawyer for a time. Bartleby, however, replies that he "would prefer not to make any change at all." The lawyer flees the building and stays incommunicado for several days. When he cautiously returns to his office, he finds that Bartleby has been removed to the Tombs, a prison in New York City. The lawyer visits the Tombs to offer comfort, but Bartleby will not speak to him. He ad-jures Bartleby to look at the blue sky and the green grass, but Bartleby replies, "I know where I am," and refuses to speak again. The lawyer leaves Bartleby in the prison yard, and on his way out arranges for him to be well fed but Bartleby refuses to eat. When the lawyer visits Bartleby again, several days later, he finds the scrivener curled up in a ball with his head against the prison wall, dead.

The narrator concludes the story by relating a ru-mor he has heard to the effect that Bartleby was once employed in a Dead Letter Office. He reflects on the melancholy nature of such work, handling letters containing messages of charity and hope which ar-rived too late to relieve those to whom they had been sent. "On errands of life," reflects the lawyer, "these letters speed to death." The story ends with the line, "Ah Bartleby! Ah, humanity!"

Although the lawyer seems to be an honest and humane man, he is actually guilty of what Melville considers society's most prevailing sin: self-deception. He labels his pusillanimity prudence, his indecisiveness tolerance, his curiosity concern, as if by doing so he can create a reality which corresponds to his own illusions. He goes to a fashionable church not to worship the God in whom he professes to be-lieve, but "to hear a famous preacher." When he is up-set by Bartleby's presence in his office on a Sunday, he does not turn to God for help. Rather, he stays away from church because his perturbation makes him unfit for the only function of church-going that he is aware of: the social function. He constantly thinks in terms of material entities, particularly money and food. Yet the lawyer is not an evil man. By the standards of the world, he is exceptionally charitable and forbearing. He feels for Bartleby's suf-fering, even if he never understands it; and if the help he offers his scrivener is not what Bartleby needs, still it is all the lawyer has to give. That is Melville's point: Even the best of those who think conventional thoughts, order their lives by conventional rules, and never question conventional commonplaces like "common sense" and "common usage," are incapable of understanding a man like Bartleby. Bartleby is the only character in the story who makes a point of looking at the walls, who is actually aware of the limitations with which society, represented by the lawyer, has boxed him in. Bartleby's refusal to value meaningless tasks simply because they are important to a shallow and materialistic society reflects Melville's own rage at being ordered to produce literary pabulum by a society which will not even try to understand his ideas. Bartleby is placed in the same economic dilemma which produced the story in which he appears: Produce what society values, regardless of individual needs and beliefs, or die. The solitary Bartleby died; and Melville, equally oppressed by being tied down to a family of dependent women and children, wrote "Bartleby the Scrivener."

"THE FIDDLER"

Not all the protagonists of Melville's short stories withdraw from the world. The narrator-protagonist of "The Fiddler," for example, responds to the world's contempt for his poetry by abandoning his art and attempting to become a happy failure. The story opens as the young poet, Helmstone, storms out of doors after reading an unfavorable review of his recently published work. He meets a friend, Standard, who introduces him to Hautboy. The three attend a circus, where Helmstone rages at seeing the applause which the world has denied to his poetry being awarded to the antics of a clown. He marvels at the evident enjoyment of Hautboy, whom Helmstone identifies as a man of taste and judgment. Helmstone and Standard later visit Hautboy's home, where he entertains them by playing common tunes on a fiddle. Despite the simplicity of the tunes, Helmstone is struck by Hautboy's style; and Standard finally explains that Hautboy is actually a musical genius who has given up the fame he once had and retired to happy obscurity. The poet, resolved to imitate him, tears up his manuscripts, buys a fiddle, and goes to take lessons from Hautboy.

In "The Fiddler," Hautboy serves as a lesson in the worthlessness of fame because, having had it and rejected it, he is so outstandingly happy. This allows the poet to rationalize his own failure into a deliberate choice to turn his back on the world's opinion of his poetry. In this story, however, as in "Bartleby the

Scrivener," the narrator's conformity to the standards of the world (in this case, by ceasing to produce poetry which the world does not appreciate) is an act of self-deception. Either Helmstone's poetry is meritorious but misunderstood by a world whose applause is reserved for clowns, in which case he has betrayed his art by abandoning it, or his poetry is genuinely inferior, in which case he has renounced nothing because he has had nothing, and his attitude of choice is a sham. This reflects another aspect of the situation that produced "The Fiddler." If the kind of literature Melville would have preferred to write was in fact the truth, then in ceasing to write it he was betraying himself; if it was not the truth, he was deceiving himself.

These two examples illustrate the complexity and depth which underlie the surface smoothness of Melville's short tales. His stories are allegorical in nature, expressing his ideas as parables rather than as expositions. Melville often makes his points by means of emblematic symbols, such as the walls in "Bartleby the Scrivener" and the clown in "The Fiddler." In his short stories, as in his novels, Melville emphasizes subjectivity, relativity, and ambiguity. Different characters see the same situation from different perspectives, and there is no omniscient force within the story which can resolve the resulting conflict. Reality is not static and absolute, but shifting and relative; ultimate truth, if it exists at all, is unattainable.

OTHER MAJOR WORKS

LONG FICTION: *Typee: A Peep at Polynesian Life*, 1846; *Omoo: A Narrative of Adventures in the South Seas*, 1847; *Mardi and a Voyage Thither*, 1849; *Redburn: His First Voyage*, 1849; *White-Jacket: Or, The World in a Man-of-War*, 1850; *Moby Dick: Or, The Whale*, 1851; *Pierre: Or, The Ambiguities*, 1852; *Israel Potter: His Fifty Years of Exile*, 1855; *The Confidence Man: His Masquerade*, 1857; *Billy Budd, Foretopman*, 1924.

POETRY: *Battle-Pieces and Aspects of the War*, 1866; *Clarel: A Poem and Pilgrimage in the Holy Land*, 1876; *John Marr and Other Sailors*, 1888; *Timoleon*, 1891; *The Works of Herman Melville*, 1922-1924 (volumes 15 and 16).

NONFICTION: *Journal Up the Straits*, 1935; *Journal of a Visit to London and the Continent*, 1948; *The Letters of Herman Melville* (1960; Merrill R. Davis and William H. Gilman, editors).

BIBLIOGRAPHY

Bryant, John, ed. *A Companion to Melville Studies.* New York: Greenwood Press, 1986. Articles contributed by various scholars compose this thorough volume, which includes a biography, and discussions of the short stories and other works. Some articles give insight into Melville's thought on religion and philosophy and discuss his impact on modern culture.

Burkholder, Robert B., ed. *Critical Essays on Herman Melville's "Benito Cereno."* New York: G. K. Hall, 1992. Includes a few early reviews and sixteen previously published articles on Melville's novella, as well as three new articles written especially for this volume. Essays range from Newton Arvin's claim that the work is an artistic failure to more contemporary historicist critiques debating whether the work presents African Americans in a positive or a negative light.

Dillingham, William B. *Melville's Short Fiction 1853-1856.* Athens: University of Georgia Press, 1977. Dillingham provides footnoted, readable explications of the stories, with moderate allusion to possible sources and other works.

Fisher, Marvin. *Going Under: Melville's Short Fiction and the American 1850's.* Baton Rouge: Louisiana State University Press, 1977. Explores the short fiction works with Melville's cultural milieu of the 1850's as a backdrop. Fisher discusses "The Fiddler," "The Lightning Rod Man," and "Bartleby the Scrivener," among other short works.

Kirby, David. *Herman Melville.* New York: Ungar, 1993. A short yet comprehensive guide to Melville's career, including chapters on his life, his early novels, *Moby Dick*, the later novels, and the tales and poems. Includes a chronology and a bibliography.

Levine, Robert S., ed. *The Cambridge Companion to Herman Melville.* Cambridge, England: Cambridge University Press, 1998. An indispensable tool for the student of Melville. With bibliographical references and an index.

Leyda, Jay. *The Melville Log: A Documentary Life of Herman Melville, 1819-1891.* New York: Harcourt, Brace, 1951. This compilation of documents (letters, diary entries, and other materials) is carefully prepared chronologically with pages headed by year. It is published in two volumes and includes biographical sketches of Melville's associates.

McCall, Dan. *The Silence of Bartleby.* Ithaca, N.Y.: Cornell University Press, 1989. An extensive survey and analysis of criticism on "Bartleby."

Newman, Lea Bertani Vozar. *A Reader's Guide to the Short Stories of Herman Melville.* Boston: G. K. Hall, 1986. Newman includes "The Encantadas." Each chapter is divided into sections: publication history, circumstances of composition, relationship to other works, profile of interpretive criticism, and bibliography.

Parker, Hershel. *Herman Melville: A Biography.* Vol. 1, 1819-1851. Baltimore: Johns Hopkins University Press, 1996. The first volume of a two-volume biography of Melville by the most distinguished authority on his life and art covers his life from birth in 1819 until the publication of *Moby Dick* in 1851. Especially helpful on the early life of Melville and the controversies that arose from his early novel's being labeled obscene and blasphemous.

Robertson-Lorant, Laurie. *Herman Melville: A Biography.* New York: Clarkson Potter, 1996. The best one-volume biography, in a lively and sensitive format. Robertson-Lorant deftly explores the origins of Melville's themes in his family life and travels.

Updike, John. "The Appetite for Truth: On Melville's Shorter Fiction." *The Yale Review* 85 (October, 1997): 24-47. Discusses Melville's magazine short fictions of the mid-1850's, which Updike finds to be stiffer than Melville's earlier novels; claims that as a novelist he was exalted by Shakespearean possibilities, but as a short-story writer he saw failure everywhere.

Joan DelFattore, updated by Mary Rohrberger

PROSPER MÉRIMÉE

Born: Paris, France; September 27, 1803
Died: Cannes, France; September 23, 1870

OTHER LITERARY FORMS

While Prosper Mérimée is best remembered as an important innovator of the short-story form in France, he was, as befits a member of the French intelligentsia of the mid-nineteenth century, a contributor to all of the literary genres. He dabbled in poetry; wrote astonishing plays, romances, and a major novel; contributed as a journalist to the art and literary criticism of his time; distinguished himself as a translator of Russian literature into French; and is largely responsible for introducing Russian literature to the French reading public.

ACHIEVEMENTS

In Prosper Mérimée, readers encounter an amazingly versatile writer, scholar, and public official. Best known for his short stories, which, as Henry James once commented, are full of "pregnant brevity" and a "magical after-resonance," Mérimée also belonged to the French Romantic generation. With the Romantics, he shared a taste for exoticism, folk culture, and local color, and he practiced unsparingly that uniquely Romantic form of irony, whereby writers distance themselves from their work, mocking themselves and their own creations. In his desire, however, to shock the bourgeoisie, indulge in complex wordplays, and mock Romantic conventions, he resembles the writers of the later Young France movement. Simultaneously, his objectivity and the concision of his narratives link him with realism. Renowned as a writer of short fiction, he has also been praised for his painstakingly researched reconstruction of the past in his historical works and his innovations in dramatic theory and practice. Named to the French Academy in 1844, Mérimée was a cosmopolitan figure in the cultural life of Europe. His work was favorably reviewed by contemporary English periodicals.

BIOGRAPHY

Prosper Mérimée was the son of a wealthy art professor and painter; his mother was well known for her own work in the arts as a child-portraitist. Therefore, early in his life, Mérimée was surrounded not only by the arts but also by the atmosphere in which art thrives: There were constant discussions and arguments among friends, an intermingling of art forms, and, above all, an acknowledgment of the art of living. Like his close friend Stendhal, he lived through the Romantic period in France without ever becoming too deeply involved himself, although some of his plays show discernible tendencies to cater to the public's taste of the moment. For many Romantics, art was a game, and in this sense Mérimée excelled: His first publications were elaborate put-ons. *Le Théâtre de Clara Gazul* (1825; the theater of Clara Gazul) purported to be a collection of plays by a Spanish actress and enjoyed great success in Paris. Two years later, Mérimée published *La Guzla* (an anagram of Gazul), a collection purporting to be translations into French of Balkan ballads and folk songs; his techniques were so sophisticated that Alexander Pushkin translated the collection into Russian and published it in his own country before the hoax became known. The success of these anonymous works as well as of others confirmed to Mérimée that his true artistic talent lay in the development of shorter fiction since the genre permitted him to exploit his quick wit, cleverness, and extraordinary powers of observation.

In 1829, at the age of twenty-six, Mérimée signed his real name to several short stories that took the

Prosper Mérimée (Library of Congress)

reading public by storm: "Mateo Falcone," "Tamango," and "Le Vase étrusque." Several plays were equally successful, bringing Mérimée more and more into the public eye, where his family, friends, and connections paid off with a series of political posts. In 1833, he was appointed chief inspector of historical monuments; the position provided his aesthetic preoccupations an outlet. Thanks to his energetic dedication to his task, which required him to sacrifice his own personal artistic ambitions, Mérimée was instrumental in helping to preserve and upgrade French treasures of Roman and gothic art.

Mérimée's life was filled with successes, including being elected a French senator, remaining close to the emperor Napoleon III and his wife Eugénie, and being elected early (1844) to the Académie Française. Although he was able to indulge himself in every way, his upbringing in the world of art helped guide him instinctively toward ventures that were both noble and aesthetic; he was a learned critic, linguist, and historian with many diverse interests. While his detractors criticized his calm dispassion, contemporary critics, armed with Mérimée's vast correspondence, perceive that this dispassion was also a pose, concealing an artfully nurtured sensitivity.

ANALYSIS

Typical of Prosper Mérimée's art is "Mateo Falcone," first published in 1829, and included in the volume *Mosaïque*. Set in Corsica, it is a story of rigorous family pride and personal honor. While Mateo Falcone and his wife are away caring for their flocks, their ten-year-old son Fortunato remains at home alone. A bandit, however, pursued by soldiers, arrives and gives the young boy some coins in exchange for the latter's promise to hide him. Moments later, the soldiers arrive and question Fortunato, who disavows any knowledge of the bandit. The captain, nevertheless, is a clever person; he shows the boy a lovely silver watch that will be his if he reveals the presence of the fugitive. Unable to resist, Fortunato grasps the watch and reveals the hiding place. Mateo and his wife return at this point and hear the bandit cursing the greedy child and his family. Profoundly shocked, Mateo asks his wife if Fortunato is truly his son, for if so, Fortunato is the first member of his race to have betrayed another. Consanguinity confirmed by the mother, father and son walk into the underbrush where Fortunato is ordered to pray and is shot. One of Mérimée's first published works in prose, this short story is powerful precisely because of the author's meticulous control of the material. There are no digressions, no self-serving descriptions, no gratuitous details. Mérimée's sober and rigorous discipline is in marked contrast to the exuberant mood of Honoré de Balzac, his contemporary. The tone of detachment heightens the intensity of primitive passion, giving a mythical quality to the story.

COLOMBA

Another tale of Corsican passion is *Colomba*, which deals with the notion of vengeance that overpowers all other considerations. After Napoleon's defeat at Waterloo, Lieutenant Orso returns to his native Corsica to learn that his father has been killed. Rumors suggest that the Barricini family is responsible, although the official accounts exonerate them. Because of his European experience and culture, and because his long absence from the island may have dulled his native instincts, Orso's first response is to accept things as they are. His sister Colomba, however, has been eagerly awaiting his return to avenge her father, and she will not allow Orso's complacency. Similar to Electra in Jean-Paul Sartre's *Les Mouches* (1943; *The Flies*, 1946), Colomba drives her brother to action, and thus the cycle begins again. With all the classical intensity of such a work as Pierre Corneille's *Horace* (1640), Mérimée's story builds as the characters fall victim to a terrifying and overpowering thirst for blood.

CARMEN

Perhaps the best known of Mérimée's short stories is *Carmen*, the story of the love of a soldier, Don José, for Carmen, the bohemian he is supposed to escort to prison. Infatuated, he allows her to escape and then suffers the humiliation of being demoted for his ineptitude. His love for Carmen prompts him to abandon his career and seek her out, join her, and earn his livelihood as a smuggler. Since he exults in his love for her, he can accept his new life, and he savors his exclusive possession of such a fascinating woman. She, on the other hand, is a bohemian, both capricious and willful, dominated by fate and tradition. When Carmen's husband reappears unannounced, Don José kills him from jealousy since he cannot endure the sight of Carmen with another man. Later, when Carmen throws down her wedding ring in a temper, Don José kills her in a fit of jealous rage. Mérimée adopted for this story the point of view of a young archaeologist, whose scientific detachment makes these extraordinary characters more believable and the overpowering presence of fate in the story more compelling. *Carmen* had many imitators and served as the basis for Georges Bizet's opera of the same name, presented in Paris in 1875.

THE VENUS OF ILLE

Finally, *The Venus of Ille* must be mentioned because it develops Mérimée's notions of the supernatural and marks an important step in the evolution of the genre toward its climax in the works of Guy de Maupassant. On the Spanish border in the foothills of

the Pyrenees, a collector discovers a lovely statue of Venus, which he cherishes all the more strongly when the local townspeople express their fear of it as an omen of evil. The collector's son is a devotee of the game of *pelote*; on his wedding day he joins some friends in a game, and in order not to be encumbered by the wedding ring which he will soon be placing on his bride's hand, he places the ring on the hand of the statue, where it is forgotten. Later, at the wedding ceremony, another ring must be used. That same afternoon, he returns to the garden to attempt to recover the ring, but it will not come off the statue's finger. In panic because he feels bewitched, the son joins his bride in their room, where he hopes to be comforted and distracted. Once in bed, however, he is kissed by the statue, whose embrace kills him in full view of his bride, who then goes mad. The dispassion of the author in leading the reader from the festive atmosphere of the opening pages to the horror of the conclusion, and his subtle foreshadowing of the hand of fate are excellent examples of Mérimée's art.

Contrary to Gustave Flaubert and his preoccupation with subject matter that could be considered normal, ordinary, or plausible, Mérimée was fascinated by the *élan vital* of the Mediterranean world. Strong, colorful people from Italy, Corsica, and Spain inhabit his universe; they have violent, primitive passions and are imbued with tradition and a keenly developed sense of honor. In contrast to his contemporaries, Mérimée applied to his prose that dispassionate artistic perspective that neither praises, condemns, nor judges.

OTHER MAJOR WORKS

LONG FICTION: *La Famille de Carçajal*, 1828; *Chronique du règne de Charles IX*, 1829 (*A Chronicle of the Times of Charles the Ninth*, 1830).

PLAYS: *Le Théâtre de Clara Gazul*, pb. 1825 (*The Plays of Clara Gazul*, 1825); *La Jaquerie*, pb. 1828; *L'Occasion*, pb. 1829; *Le Carrosse du Saint-Sacrement*, pb. 1829; *Les Deux Héritages*, pb. 1850.

POETRY: *La Guzla*, 1827.

NONFICTION: *Histoire de don Pedre Ier, roi de Castille*, 1848 (*The History of Peter the Cruel*, 1849; 2 volumes); *Les Faux Démétrius*, 1852 (*Demetrius, the Impostor*, 1853); *Lettres à une inconnue*, 1874 (*Letters to an Unknown*, 1874); *Correspondance générale*, 1941-1964 (17 volumes).

MISCELLANEOUS: *The Writings of Prosper Mérimée*, 1905 (8 volumes).

BIBLIOGRAPHY

Bowman, F. P. *Prosper Mérimée: Heroism, Pessimism, and Irony*. Berkeley: University of California Press, 1962. Provides an analysis of the heroes depicted in Mérimée's works, a study of his basically pessimistic ideas about life and human fate, and a discussion of the way Mérimée's concepts of hero and life express themselves in the formal aspects of his writing. The comic and the ironic, Bowman claims, mask a deep sensitivity. Instead of trivializing the role of the writer, they allow him to maintain an intense awareness of his emotions and fears and to achieve a balance between sensitivity and will. Includes a bibliographic note and extensive references throughout the text.

Cogman, P. W. M. "Cheating at Narrating: Back to Mérimée's 'La Partie de trictrac.'" *Nineteenth-Century French Studies* 26 (Fall/Winter, 1997/1998): 80-90. Argues that the tale embodies a tension between psychological content and the narrative technique, which seems to mock storytelling and both exploit and subvert narrative expectations; claims the story has two centers.

_____. *Merimée, Colomba, and Carmen*. London: Grant & Cutler, 1992. An examination of the two stories.

Dale, R. C. *The Poetics of Prosper Mérimée*. Paris: Mouton, 1966. An exploration of the creative theory that underlies Mérimée's practice. Although the focus is more on Mérimée's theory as revealed in his letters and criticism than on his fictional works, the study does offer a number of insights that can be applied to the fiction. According to Mérimée, Dale concludes, the writer's fictional works incorporate a worldview that reflects his own psyche or inner self. The study is well substantiated by references to the author's voluminous correspondence and includes a brief bibliography.

Gould, Evlyn. *The Fate of Carmen*. Baltimore: Johns Hopkins University Press, 1996. A thoughtful study of *Carmen*.

Mickelsen, David. "Travel, Transgression, and Possession in Mérimée's *Carmen*." *Romantic Review* 87 (May, 1996): 329-344. Argues that the story should be viewed as an unequal meeting of cultures in which the central figure is not the Gypsy Carmen but the French narrator visiting Spain; claims that examining the role of the narrator helps reveal the cultural imperatives operating within the story, especially its hidden colonialist stance.

Raitt, A. W. *Prosper Mérimée*. London: Eyre and Spottiswoode, 1970. An essential study of the life, times, and works of Mérimée, for both the specialist and the general reader. Raitt combines a biography with critical chapters analyzing Mérimée's major writings. Illustrations, appendices, a comprehensive bibliography, and an index enhance this book as an invaluable source of material on the French author.

Rigolot, François. "Ekphrasis and the Fantastic: Genesis of an Aberration." *Comparative Literature* 49 (Spring, 1997): 97-112. Discusses "The Venus of Ille" as an illumination of the fantastic as a displaced mode of ekphrastic representation.

Seidler-Golding, Marianne. "Destablized Security in Mérimée's Short Stories." *Paroles-Gelées* 13 (1995): 63-73. Discusses the relationship between explicit violence in Mérimée's stories and implicit violence in the ways the violent actions are depicted, with reference to "Mateo Falcone" and "The Venus of Ille."

Smith, Maxwell A. *Prosper Mérimée*. New York: Twayne, 1972. A readable introductory study of the author's life and works. Especially relevant to the study of the short prose fiction are chapters 6 through 11. Biographical and critical material are supplemented by a chronology of Mérimée's life, a select bibliography, and an index.

Stowe, Richard. "Prosper Mérimée." In *European Writers*. Vol. 6 in *The Romantic Century*, edited by Jacques Barzun and George Stade. New York: Charles Scribner's Sons, 1985. This brief study combines a biographical overview with a discussion of the style and content of Mérimée's major works, including the short fiction. The select bibliography includes editions, collected works, bibliographies, translations, correspondence, and biographical critical studies.

Tilby, Michael. "Languages and Sexuality in Méri-mée's *Carmen.*" *Forum for Modern Language Studies* 15, no. 3 (1979): 255-263. An analysis of the fictional world of *Carmen*, focusing on its tight and natural organization.

Robert W. Artinian, updated by
Anna M. Wittman

LEONARD MICHAELS

Born: New York, New York; January 2, 1933

PRINCIPAL SHORT FICTION
Going Places, 1969
I Would Have Saved Them If I Could, 1975
A Girl with a Monkey: New and Selected Stories, 2000

OTHER LITERARY FORMS

Leonard Michaels is as well known for his 1981 novel *The Men's Club* as he is for his much admired short-story collections. He is also the author of the autobiographical *To Feel These Things: Essays* (1993) and *Sylvia: A Fictional Memoir* (1992). *Shuffle* (1990) is a collection of essays and what Michaels calls "autobiographical fiction." He has collaborated with artist Frances Lerner on a coffee-table book entitled *A Cat* (1995), filled with almost a hundred observations about cats accompanied by Lerner's line drawings.

ACHIEVEMENTS

Leonard Michaels's first collection of stories, *Going Places*, was nominated for the National Book Award in 1969. He was a John Simon Guggenheim Memorial Foundation fellow in 1969 and a National Endowment for the Humanities fellow in 1970. He received a National Institute of Arts and Letters Award in Literature in 1971 and *The New York Times Book Review* Editor's Choice Award in 1975. His novel, *The Men's Club* (1993), was nominated for the American Book Award and the National Book Critics Circle Award in 1982.

BIOGRAPHY

Leonard Michaels was born in lower Manhattan on January 2, 1933, to Polish-Jewish immigrant parents; he grew up during the Depression in New York, where his father was a barber. He received his B.A. from New York University in 1953 and an M.A. in English literature from the University of Michigan in 1956. He entered the Ph.D. program at the University of California at Berkeley, but withdrew and moved back to Manhattan to devote his time to writing. During this time he married Sylvia Bloch, about whom he has written a memoir, and made a living by teaching English classes at Paterson State College in Wayne, New Jersey.

After separating from his wife, who later committed suicide, Michaels went back to graduate school, this time at the University of Michigan, where he earned a Ph.D. in English and married Priscilla Older, with whom he had two sons. He published his first collection of short stories, *Going Places*, in 1969 while teaching English at the University of California at Davis; based on the reception of that book, he was hired to teach at the University of California, Berkeley. In 1977, he divorced his second wife and married poet Brenda Lyn Hillman, with whom he had a daughter. In the late 1980's his third marriage also

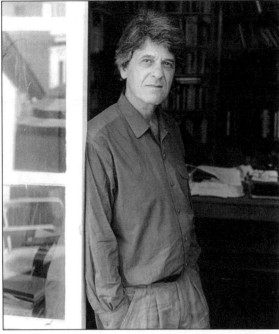

Leonard Michaels (©Miriam Berkley)

ended in divorce. Michaels has written extensively about his marital difficulties in his fictional and autobiographical works.

ANALYSIS

Leonard Michaels's stories are most often admired for his whimsical style, his erotic satire, and his comic treatment of sexual violence. More than one critic has noted that his stories raise the old aesthetic/moral question of how it is possible to write about something horrible and hideous that is simultaneously hilarious and beautiful. Citing the influence of Bernard Malamud, Philip Roth, Isaac Babel, Jorge Luis Borges, and Franz Kafka, reviewers admire Michael's fantastic plots and metaphorical style, which has been characterized as poetic realism. Combining fantasy and concrete realism, Michaels creates darkly terrifying worlds that keep readers laughing until they become appalled at what has made them laugh. As Michaels's recurring autobiographical persona, Phillip Leibowitz, encounters Conradian hearts of darkness and secret sharers in the jungle of New York City, he is always amazed at the mysterious multiplicity of the world around him.

"THE DEAL"

In this account of an encounter between a young woman and a group of fourteen- to fifteen-year-old boys over the woman's dropped glove, threat and tension shift back and forth between the boys and the young woman. The dangerous little dance between the woman and the gang (described by Michaels as a "monster of boys") begins harmlessly enough as she asks them if they have seen her dropped glove. The teasing game of "keep away" that the boys play shifts to a possible threat to the woman when she takes control by asking them what they want for the glove. Pushed to "make a deal," banter changes to barter as they demand ten dollars and she offers twenty-five cents.

The balance of power in the struggle shifts again when one of the boys demands a kiss for the return of the glove. Although she responds at first with nervousness, the woman switches to a businesslike tone as she agrees to the deal and goes with the boy to the doorway of her apartment. Female fear of male violence shifts to adolescent fear of female sexual power as the boy resists and is chided by the woman for being a chicken. The story shifts once more when after the kiss, the rest of the boys crowd into the doorway also demanding a kiss, pushing and shoving and knocking the woman down. The story ends with one of the leaders of the gang helping the woman open her door. When, once again reverting to a combination of childlike plea and male threat, he yells, "You give me something," she shuts the door in his face.

"MURDERERS"

Because of its combination of boyish Peeping-Tom comedy and horrifying, sexually stimulated violence, this has been Michaels's most anthologized story, appearing in contemporary American short-story anthologies edited both by Tobias Wolff and by Raymond Carver. The narrator of the story is Phillip Liebowitz, a young Jewish boy featured in a number of Michaels's stories, a preteen who, along with a small group of friends, climbs up to the roof of a building to watch a bearded young rabbi and his sacramentally bald wife make love in their apartment across the way. As the boys become excited watching the couple, one begins to slide down the roof, his ring catching on a nail; while the ring finger remains, "the hand, the arm, the rest of him, were gone." At this point the rabbi sees them and calls out the window, "Murderers," shouting their names. The story ends abruptly with the boys being sent to a New Jersey camp overseen by World War II veterans.

A mere summary of the plot of the story does not convey its lyrical quality as the narrator, a grown man recollecting the event, places it within the context of coming of age and coming to terms with the terrible conjunctions that constitute human experience. He says that when the event occurred, he wanted "proximity to darkness, strangeness." Phillip considers the boys' voyeuristic observation of the rabbi and his wife the "beginning of philosophy." The rabbi he sees as "Mr. Life" as he dances to a rhumba on the phonograph, and the wife, with her many wigs, is for him "the world's lesson"; it little matters that one does not know what she "really" looks like, he says, for "what [i]s *reality*?" At the end of the story, Phillip lies in his bunkhouse listening to owls. Considering the mystery of the lessons he has learned about desire and death, mystery and danger, he listens to a sound he has never heard before, "the sound of darkness, blooming, opening inside you like a mouth."

"CITY BOY"

Second only to "Murderers" as an anthology favorite, "City Boy" also features Phillip Liebowitz, this time somewhat older and having sex with his girlfriend on the living room floor while the girl's parents sleep in the adjoining bedroom thirty feet away. Although the girl repeatedly says, "Phillip, this is crazy," he is so caught up in the encounter that he "burns" with the violence of it. Afterward, the two fall asleep, only to be awakened in the middle of the night by the girl's father who steps on Phillip's naked bottom in the dark.

The broad comedy of the encounter is emphasized by Phillip's reaction, springing "up like a frog out of the hand of a child"; he stands "spread-legged, bolt naked, great with eyes" face to face with the father, a sudden secret sharer, like two men "accidently met in hell." As the father threatens to kill him, Phillip runs out the door "naked as a wolf." The comedy increases as Phillip realizes that he needs poise, that without it

the street was impossible; consequently he walks on his hands and pushes the elevator button with his toes, feeling he is in control of the situation. "I was a city boy," he thinks. "No innocent sh—-kicker from Jersey. I was the A train, the Fifth Avenue bus. I could be a cop. My name was Phillip, my style New York City."

Thinking he can be cool, for a naked man is mysterious, Phillip goes out on the street, is turned away at the subway change booth, and runs into his girlfriend, who gives him his clothes and tells him that her father has had a heart attack and is in the hospital. As he accompanies her back to the apartment, Phillip feels as though he were in a trance, thinking, "This was life. Death!" When she gets a phone call that her father is going to be all right and that her mother is going to stay all night with him in the hospital, the story ends with her urging him to make love to her, as they "sank into the rug as if it were quicksand."

The fact that the story ends where it begins, with the primal sexual encounter, as if everything in between was inconsequential, suggests that this is another coming-of-age lesson for Phillip Leibowitz, who encounters in typically comic fashion basic elements of desire and danger. Being cast onto the city streets stark naked in the middle of the night is the ultimate comic image of vulnerability, punishment for transgressions, and the unaccommodated self.

OTHER MAJOR WORKS

LONG FICTION: *The Men's Club*, 1981; *Shuffle*, 1990; *Sylvia: A Fictional Memoir*, 1992.

PLAY: *City Boy*, pr. 1985.

SCREENPLAY: *The Men's Club*, 1986.

NONFICTION: *To Feel These Things: Essays*, 1993; *A Cat*, 1996; *Time out of Mind: The Diaries of Leonard Michaels, 1961-1995*, 1999.

EDITED TEXTS: *The State of the Language*, 1980, 1990 (with Christopher Ricks); *West of the West: Imagining California*, 1989 (with Raquel Sheer and David Reid).

BIBLIOGRAPHY

DeCurtis, Anthony. "Self Under Siege: The Stories of Leonard Michaels." *Critique: Studies in Modern*

Fiction 21 (1979): 101-111. Argues that in his first two collections of stories the most pressing problem Michaels's characters confront is maintaining their humanity in face of the brutalization of modern life. Says his stories reveal the tenuous props that sustain continuity in the modern world. Discusses Michaels's imagery, his style, and his treatment of violence.

Ditsky, John. "A Men's Club: The Fiction of Leonard Michaels." *The Hollins Critic* 28 (December, 1991): 2-11. A survey of Michaels's work through *Shuffle*; discusses autobiographical elements of his fiction, which he argues is energized by a tension between academic intellectuality and indulgent sexuality embodied in his characters. Says that in his work sex becomes a language at odds with the purely verbal.

Donoghue, Denis. "Couples." *The New York Review of Books* 13 (July 10, 1969): 17-20. A review of *Going Places* in which Donoghue claims that the paradigm for Michaels's fiction is two people locked in violence, in which the people hardly matter except as conduits for the violence. Argues that the most powerful story in the collection, "The Deal," makes more stringent demands on the gothic genre than usual.

Lyons, Bonnie, and Bill Oliver. "An Interview with Leonard Michaels." *New England Review* 15 (Fall, 1993): 129-140. Michaels discusses his blurring of the lines between fiction and autobiography, his characters as embodiments of Jewish New York, and the influence of Isaac Babel on his fiction. He also comments on the frequent comparison made between him and Philip Roth and the obligation writers have to speak the truth when writing about the Holocaust.

Segal, Lore. "Captivating Horrors." *The New Republic* 161 (July 19, 1969): 31-33. A review of *Going Places* that surveys several of the stories in the collection and concludes that the book poses the question of how it is possible to write about hideous things in a hilarious and beautiful way.

Woiwode, Larry. "Out of the Fifties." *The Partisan Review* 44 (1977): 123-130. Fellow writer Woiwode praises *I Would Have Saved Them If I Could*, as a mature, dense, complex work of fiction. Summarizing several of the stories in the collection, Woiwode notes Michaels's debt to Isaac Babel, Ernest Hemingway, Franz Kafka, and Samuel Beckett. Argues that Michaels's use of cultural figures such as Sigmund Freud, Georg Wilhelm Friedrich Hegel, and Karl Marx suggests that history pursues him.

Zweig, Paul. "Delicate Intentions." *Harper's Magazine* 251 (September, 1975): 68-69. Argues that in *I Would Have Saved Them If I Could*, Michaels uses a poet's twist to reduce civility to elements of sex, perverse daydreams, and inventive resentment. Calls the essaylike fragments in the book its thematic heart, placing it in the tradition of William Burroughs, Donald Barthelme, and Phillip Roth.

Charles E. May

SUE MILLER

Born: Chicago, Illinois; November 29, 1943

PRINCIPAL SHORT FICTION

"Given Names," 1981
"Leaving Home," 1982
"Tyler and Brina," 1985
"The Lover of Women," 1986
"Calling," 1986
Inventing the Abbotts and Other Stories, 1987
"The Moms of Summer," 1991

OTHER LITERARY FORMS

Sue Miller's first novel *The Good Mother* was published in 1986 to effusive praise from many reviewers; it was on a number of best-seller lists for much of that year. Her second novel, *Family Pictures* (1990), also was a best-seller. Her subsequent novels, *For Love* (1993) and *The Distinguished Guest* (1995), have generally been well received but not so enthusiastically as her first two. Her novel *While I was Gone* (1999) has sold well and received modern critical praise.

ACHIEVEMENTS

Sue Miller's novel *Family Pictures* was nominated for the National Book Critics Circle Award in 1991. She has received a Bunting Institute Fellowship from Radcliffe, a McDowell Fellowship, and a John Simon Guggenheim Memorial Foundation Fellowship.

BIOGRAPHY

Sue Miller was born on the south side of Chicago in 1943, into what she calls a family "ecclesiastical to its roots"; both grandfathers were preachers, and her father, also a minister, taught church history at the University of Chicago. She entered Radcliffe College at the age of sixteen and majored in history. By the time she was twenty, she had graduated and married a medical student. She taught high school English for a time, worked in a Head Start program, was a cocktail waitress, a research assistant, and a model.

When her marriage failed, she supported her son as a preschool teacher and helped found the Harvard Day Care Center. She has said that one day she read a review of Robert Coover's first novel and was stunned because she remembered Coover as a boarder in her parent's basement apartment when he was a graduate student at the University of Chicago. "Suddenly," she says, "publishing a book was not such a remote thing."

In 1979, Miller attended the creative writing program at Boston University on a fellowship and began to publish stories in literary magazines; she also taught as an adjunct faculty member at Boston University, Tufts University, Emerson College, and the Massachusetts Institute of Technology. In 1983, she won a Bunting Fellowship at Radcliffe, during which time she finished half of *The Good Mother*. Her first novel was a best-seller and in 1988 was made into a successful film, staring Diane Keaton and Liam Neeson. Miller remarried, writer Douglas Bauer this time; they settled in Boston's south end.

ANALYSIS

Sex is the center of most of Sue Miller's short stories. In practically every story, men and women engage in quite explicitly described sex, but seldom is the act successful as a sign of intimacy and union. More often, whether Miller is describing sex from the point of view of a female or a male character, sex is an attempt at control or an act of desperate illusion. For example, the story "Slides" is structured around seven nude slides taken of a woman by her former husband early in their marriage, which become irritating illusory images that get in the way of genuine intimacy. In Miller's best-known story, "Inventing the Abbotts," a young man has sex with a wealthy young woman to try to climb the social ladder, while she has sex with him to rebel against her parents' control. In "Leaving Home," sex is a desperate attempt to hold on and hold things together.

One of the most fascinating aspects of Miller's short stories is her ability to assume the role of a male character and tell his story in the first person. Four of the eleven stories in *Inventing the Abbotts and Other Stories*, including the title story, are told from the perspectives of male characters. This bit of gender ventriloquism has been all the more intriguing to readers because of the sexual drives of the men Miller creates as her personae. The effect on male readers is somewhat of a mild shock, as if one's gender secrets have been found out. As Jonathan Penner noted, in a review of the collection, "When a female author employs a male viewpoint character to regard women, we are in a hall of mirrors, where sometimes we surprise or frighten ourselves."

"TYLER AND BRINA"

The central character in this story, Tyler, is a typical Miller male; the first couple of sentences delineate his central characteristic: "Tyler loved women. He was in love with women." Told in a straightforward, unadorned way, the story seems almost prototypical of a man who cannot resist women. What

Sue Miller (©Miriam Berkley)

plot there is in the story centers on the disruption Tyler's obsession creates in his marriage to Brina. She wants a divorce and leaves him; he woos and pursues her; she gradually forgives him, accepting that he cannot help himself; he continues secretly to have sex with another woman; Brina moves back in with him; the other woman comes to the house; Brina sees her, and the story ends with Brina smashing the bottle of champagne she had bought to celebrate their reunion.

One side of Brina's face is dead, injured in a childhood accident. Miller uses this detail throughout the story as a metaphor to suggest that for her "some deep sorrow . . . lay under every fleeting joy." The metaphor allows Miller to evoke a striking conclusion to the story when Brina sees that Tyler will never change. She looks at him for a moment, the muscles shifting in the "live" side of her face, but when she turns, all he can see is the dead side, which shows a "vacant serenity as she looked down at the mess that lay around her feet." Brina will probably stay with Tyler, but she will have to turn her dead side to him and the world to make it possible.

"LEAVING HOME"

One of the shortest and most lyrical stories in *Inventing the Abbotts and Other Stories*, "Leaving Home" is about a middle-aged woman, Leah, who has come to baby-sit for the young daughter of her son Greg and his wife Anita while they put on a twenty-fifth birthday party for Anita. Leah lives alone but has been seeing a man, enjoying her "long-awaited freedom, her claim to sexuality." The external conflict of the story is the friction in Greg and Anita's marriage, but the more significant emotional interest lies within Leah, who fears that Greg's marriage is going to fail and that he will lose not only his wife but also his daughter.

When Leah overhears Anita complaining to Greg about all the "mommy-daddy-baby" endless threesomeness of their life, she identifies with her daughter-in-law's lament that she does not exist as a woman anymore, even as she resents the younger woman's self-centered disregard for her child and husband. The story ends with Leah overhearing Greg and Anita making love, but knowing that even though they still have sex it is not enough. Left with a sense of help-lessness to guard her son against pain, she desires Joe, the man she has been seeing, for, like her son, she needs the "illusion of wholeness, of repair." The story poignantly portrays the difficulty of creating and sustaining intimacy when intimacy demands a sacrificial loss of self.

"INVENTING THE ABBOTTS"

Primarily because it was made into a 1997 Hollywood film, this is Miller's best-known short story. More like an abbreviated novel than a short story, the title story of Miller's collection focuses on the social-climbing desire of Jacey, a relatively poor young man, alternately, for the three Abbott sisters, who represent the wealthiest family in a small town. The narrator of the story is Jacey's younger brother Doug, who scorns the Abbotts and Jacey's social aspirations.

The story is a relatively conventional one, the basic conflicts arising from Jacey's sexual encounters with the Abbott sisters over the years and the Abbott family's socially snobbish reaction to those relationships. At a key point in the story, Jacey and Doug's mother, a working woman who raises her boys with good humor and common sense, tells Doug that if Jacey had not met the Abbotts, "he'd have had to invent them, one way or another." The story ends when, at Jacey and Doug's mother's funeral, the mother of the Abbott girls tells Jacey, "Well, I've no more daughters for you."

A recurring motif throughout the story is the theme of pretense or role-playing, something at which Doug is able to succeed more easily than Jacey is. For example, early in the story, when Doug is first invited to one of the Abbotts' parties, he draws side-burns on his cheeks, like singer Elvis Presley, and Jacey refuses to go, saying that Doug will be the only one there "pretending to be someone else"; the mother simply tells Jacey to pretend he has never seen Doug before in his life. Near the end of the story, Doug, always on the fringes of Jacey's affairs, feels he is just "some bit actor in some part of their family drama." Later in the story when Doug goes off to Harvard University and becomes involved in theater groups, Doug feels he has chosen the right pro-fession, saying, "I'm really much better at pretending than at being."

Throughout the story, the characters are involved in playing certain roles, yearning to be something they are not, and using others to achieve these goals. At first, while Jacey uses Eleanor Abbott to try to climb the social ladder, she uses him to rebel against her family. Later, when Doug falls in love with the oldest Abbott daughter, Alice, he feels she is using him for her own purposes. Finally, he has an affair with Phoebe, the youngest daughter, in order to revenge himself for ill treatment by the other sisters.

"Inventing the Abbotts" is derivative of a common F. Scott Fitzgerald theme—the attempt of a young man of modest means to leap across from one social class to another on the backs of wealthy young women. Jacey is not simply after money; for him the Abbott girls represent some sort of ideal; in fact, he tells his mother at one point, "Eleanor was just an *idea* I had." Originally entitled "The Lover of Women" when it appeared in *Mademoiselle*, the story is about a man who needs women, particularly young women unreachable because of their higher social class, in order to create an acceptable self-image.

OTHER MAJOR WORKS

LONG FICTION: *The Good Mother*, 1986; *Family Pictures*, 1990; *For Love*, 1993; *The Distinguished Guest*, 1995; *While I Was Gone*, 1999.

BIBLIOGRAPHY

Ebert, Roger. "Joie de Vivre Missing from Cardboard 'Abbotts'." *The Chicago Sun-Times*, April 4, 1997, p. 37. In this review of the film version of "Inventing the Abbotts," well-known film critic Roger Ebert says the picture's story and its values and style are inspired by the 1950's. Argues that the film is haunted by a story problem, for it is not about anything but itself; the characters are so preoccupied by the twists of the plot they have no other interests.

Gussow, Mel. "Sue Miller Discovers a Trove of Domesticity." *The New York Times*, March 8, 1999, p. E1. This general article, based on an interview and written on the occasion of the publication of

Miller's *While I Was Gone*, provides a biographical sketch, discusses critical response to Miller's work, and comments on the novel's source in the life of Katherine Ann Power, a 1960's activist involved in a robbery and the killing of a policeman in Boston.

McNamara, Mary. "Authors—The People Behind the Books We Read." *Los Angeles Times*, April 14, 1999, p. E1. An interview-based article and discussion of Miller's *While I Was Gone*. Reacts against critics who characterize Miller's work as "domestic"; discusses her literary career; summarizes *While I Was Gone*, and provides a brief biographical sketch. Miller says that she does not understand why she is perceived as a women's writer or a family writer, but says that at least women are still reading, asking: "Where are the people who were reading Philip Roth and Norman Mailer?"

Miller, Sue. Interview by Rosemary Herbert. *Publishers Weekly* 229 (May 2, 1986): 60-61. Miller discusses the evolution of her novel *The Good Mother* from a short story about a teenager's preoccupation with an aunt. She says she was dissatisfied with the simplistic answers of much postfeminist fiction and wished to trace the devel-

opment of a woman who wanted to be someone other than who she became.

_____. "Virtual Reality: The Perils of Seeking a Novelist's Facts in Her Fiction." *The New York Times*, April 12, 1999, p. E1. Miller's contribution to the series "Writers on Writing" focuses on the common reader question about how much of her fiction is autobiographical. Miller insists that you can make a story out of anything and what is interesting about a story is not the thing that is in it, but what the writer makes of that thing; shaping is what writing is all about, she says, the struggle for meaning allowing the writer to "escape the tyranny of what really happened."

Penner, Jonathan. "Sense and Sensuality." *The Washington Post*, May 17, 1987, p. X9. In this review of *Inventing the Abbotts and Other Stories*, Penner praises Miller for her ability to capture the male viewpoint, especially male sexual views of women. Singles out the stories "Tyler and Brina" and "Leaving Home" for special praise, but argues that the title story, although the most ambitious, is too conversational, too engaged in summary and analysis.

Charles E. May

STEVEN MILLHAUSER

Born: New York, New York; August 3, 1943

Principal short fiction
In the Penny Arcade, 1986
The Barnum Museum, 1990
Little Kingdoms: Three Novellas, 1993
The Knife Thrower and Other Stories, 1998
Enchanted Night: A Novella, 1999

Other literary forms
Edwin Mullhouse: The Life and Death of an American Writer, 1943-1954, by Jeffrey Cartwright, A Novel (1972) was Steven Millhauser's acclaimed debut novel. His next two novels, *Portrait of a Ro-*

mantic (1977) and *From the Realm of Morpheus* (1986), were less successful, to the point of relegating him to relative obscurity. *Martin Dressler: The Tale of an American Dreamer* (1996), however, restored his reputation; early collections of his short fiction were brought back into print, and new ones became easier to publish.

Achievements
Martin Dressler won the Pulitzer Prize for fiction in 1997. Steven Millhauser has also been given an Award in Literature from the American Academy of Arts and Letters in 1987, and received a Lannan Fellowship. He also received a Prix Médicis Étranger in

1975, a World Fantasy award in 1990, and a Lannan Literary Award for fiction in 1994.

BIOGRAPHY

Steven Lewis Millhauser, like the hero of his eponymous first novel, Edwin Mullhouse, was born in early August of 1943, the son of a college English professor. As the events of that novel show, however, it is unwise to conflate the events of an author's life with those of his characters. When Millhauser unexpectedly won the Pulitzer Prize for his novel *Martin Dressler* in 1997, most news stories stressed Millhauser's deliberate avoidance of publicity, in a word, his shyness. Nevertheless, the salient features of his life can be noted.

Growing up in Connecticut, Millhauser wanted to be an author from an early age. After receiving his undergraduate degree from Columbia University, he wrote fiction while living with his parents and working. He attended graduate school at Brown University, pursuing a Ph.D. in medieval and Renaissance studies, and left after the success of his first novel. A series of academic appointments followed, including one at Skidmore College, where he has shared a teaching position with his wife. He settled in Saratoga Springs with his wife and two children.

ANALYSIS

It seems clear enough at first where to place Steven Millhauser's short fiction. In its use of the fantastic and grotesque, it springs directly from the American tradition of Edgar Allan Poe and Nathaniel Hawthorne, with traces of Herman Melville thrown in. Millhauser's European forebears include E. T. A. Hoffmann and Franz Kafka; more recent international influences include Jorge Luis Borges and Vladimir Nabokov. That his work also coincides with that of other American postmodernists, such as Robert Coover and John Barth, is not surprising either. Yet his work cannot be so easily pigeonholed.

As in the work of Borges and Nabokov, Millhauser's work is filled with doubles, slightly obtuse scholarly narrators, and at times a seemingly infinite series of regressions. Yet the metafictional aspects of Borges's and Nabokov's work often leave readers feeling that they have missed out on some cosmic point or joke that only the authors and their acolytes share. In Millhauser's work, this layered effect gives his readers a sense of depth and a clear indication of the questions he is asking about the interrelationships of art, life, dreams, and reality. Similarly, the anguish that Kafka's characters undergo in his parables often seems too personal for readers to share; in Millhauser, such suffering arises not only out of the human condition but also out of the artistic dilemmas in so many of his stories. In short, Millhauser's fictional worlds, while often as mysterious as those of his predecessors, are both more accessible and more comprehensible—and admitting this removes none of their accompanying sense of wonder. His fantastic kingdoms, albeit rooted in reality, defamiliarize the mundane world of daylight and habit. Nevertheless, he is quite capable of writing the typically anthologized type of epiphanic, realistic short story, such as "A Protest Against the Sun" or "A Day in the Country."

Even though Millhauser has admitted that he often writes about "failures," they are often specifically American failures, who share a sense of vision with such quintessentially American figures as Thomas Edison and Walt Disney; his dreamers' machineries and domains are always doomed to failure, because they attempt to engulf and break down the borders between their experience and their dreams.

"AUGUST ESCHENBURG"

Some of Millhauser's most important stories are miniature portraits of the artist. This story is the first of these. Eschenburg is a designer and constructor of miniature automatons, and, like many of Millhauser's other artistic protagonists, explores with his lifelike creations the interstices between real life and the artificiality of the imagination; in Eschenburg's work, "realism itself [is] being pressed into the service of a higher law." Eschenburg's triumphs are overshadowed by the successes of his artistic double (a characteristic Millhauser device), Hausenstein, whose figures are unabashedly sensual and satisfy the baser instincts of their audience. Thus it seems as if Hausenstein's appeal to the degraded tastes of the audience, the "Untermensch," as he calls them, has triumphed. Yet even as Eschenburg wanders out of the plot, the inner fire that has led him to construct his analogues of life has not deserted him. "His ambition was to insert his dreams into the world, and if they were the wrong dreams, then he would dream them in solitude." He has failed, like so many of Millhauser's artistic protagonists, but he is not defeated.

"A GAME OF CLUE"

One of the most striking aspects of Millhauser's short fiction is his ability to stretch the form by making a narrative out of the most unlikely subjects. In this case it is the juxtaposition of a normal, realistic narrative concerning four young people playing a popular board game with, in alternating paragraphs, descriptions of the actions of the well-known characters in that game, such as Colonel Mustard and Miss Scarlet. They and their surroundings are described with a scrupulosity bordering on the laborious. Even though the action "in" the game veers towards the licentious, as the Colonel attempts to seduce Miss Scarlet, the action is also paradoxically moving toward a sense of stasis. The mansion itself becomes a characteristic Millhauser edifice, with a series of rooms and secret passages branching off into labyrinthine infinity. The human characters playing the game are also trapped in a sense of stasis, as they each silently wonder about their present problems and their futures: playing the game itself provides a balm, "a spot of time" as it were. A chance passerby looks on the game "and feels a yearning so deep that he wants to cry out in anguish, though in fact he continues steadily, even cheerfully, on his way."

"THE LITTLE KINGDOM OF FRANKLIN J. PAYNE"

Franklin Payne is the first of Millhauser's early twentieth century American dreamers. His career loosely resembles that of pioneering American cartoonist Winsor McCay. Payne begins as an illustrator for that favorite site of Millhauser, the dime museum. Becoming an editorial cartoonist, Payne also draws comic strips, in which he explores the boundaries of reality and the imagination. When his characters become too unconstrained, deconstructing the panels that enclose them, they feel "a craving for the lines and shadows of the actual world." Payne soon meets his artistic double, Max Horn, whose own work is derivative

and characterless. When Payne begins creating his own silent black-and-white cartoons, Horn, Disney-like, sets up his own assembly-line cartoon studio, which Payne rejects. His laborious technique of drawing each frame individually gives "the shimmer of a dream" to his work. Max ends up stealing Payne's wife, but he cannot steal Payne's soul. Payne's last work ends with his main character erasing himself; even though reality must be served, it is imperative

> to smash through the constriction of the actual, to unhinge the universe and let the impossible stream in, because otherwise—well, otherwise the world was nothing but an editorial cartoon.

"CATALOGUE OF THE EXHIBITION"

This portrait of the artist is presented in the form of a catalog commentary on the works the artist has created. Millhauser's triumph is to create a completely fictitious yet nonetheless highly believable major nineteenth century American painter. However, unlike August Eschenburg's automatons or Franklin Payne's cartoons, Moorash's work is not grounded in realism; he is, according to Millhauser, a sort of American J. M. W. Turner—his paintings are romantically, fantastically abstract. Many of Millhauser's artists inhabit both the mundane day and the transfigured night, but Moorash is totally an inhabitant of the night. In his work "the world and the dreamer intermingle and dissolve." Moorash's menage echoes William Wordsworth's in England's Lake District: He lives with his sister, with whom he is uncomfortably close. The plot is out of Poe via Nabokov. Not only is Moorash doubled in the character of William Pinney, but also his sister is duplicated in Pinney's sister. As the catalog progresses, Moorash's work becomes more fantastic: "It is as if only by smashing what he once called 'the mimetic fetters' that Moorash could release into paint the human mystery." While others of Millhauser's artists walk into the sunset, the ending of this unabashedly romantic artist is suitably lurid and melodramatic.

THE KNIFE THROWER AND OTHER STORIES

Millhauser's collection of stories shows him moving further away from the classic realistic mode of the short story. Some stories at first resemble that mode, such as "The Visit," in which the narrator visits an old friend, but the story soon takes a turn toward John Collier's *His Monkey Wife* (1930) as the friend turns out to be married to a large frog, who shows no sign of becoming a princess. Many of the stories are communally narrated, as a voice only known as "we" wonders what the young girls in the town are doing ("The Sisterhood of Night") or describes subterranean passageways ("Beneath the Cellars of Our Town").

The most significant stories in the collection characteristically concern artists, and in each case, Millhauser's vision has grown darker. In the title story, the knife thrower deliberately and artfully wounds his target, culminating in death. The theme is subtly linked to current American preoccupations with violence: "If such performances were encouraged, if they were even tolerated, what might we expect in the future?" "The New Automaton Theater" is a development of "August Eschenburg," but here the artist, Graum, deliberately enhances the artificiality of his creations and invites the audience to become one with them: "We yearn to mingle with these strange newcomers, to pass into their clockwork lives." Such a dissolution, the story hints, would be "terrifying." In "Paradise Park," Charles Sarabee, creator-designer of an early twentieth century amusement park, must resort to ever-increasing thrills to lure his audience. He becomes a modern Pied Piper, working toward "a magical or mystical park from which the unwary visitor would never return." In the dreams of Millhauser's artists begin not responsibilities but an escape from them, and his work increasingly identifies their siren-song lure and danger.

OTHER MAJOR WORKS

LONG FICTION: *Edwin Mullhouse: The Life and*

Death of an American Writer, 1943-1954, by Jeffrey Cartwright, A Novel, 1972; *Portrait of a Romantic*, 1977; *From the Realm of Morpheus*, 1986; *Martin Dressler: The Tale of an American Dreamer*, 1996.

BIBLIOGRAPHY

Byatt, A. S. "Reports from the Edge of Reality." *Washington Post Book World* (June 14, 1998): X1. A penetrating review of *The Knife Thrower and Other Stories* by a fiction writer who explores much of the same territory as Millhauser does. Compares him to Hawthorne, Hoffmann, and Kafka.

Fowler, Douglas. "Steven Millhauser, Miniaturist." *Critique* 37 (Winter, 1996): 139-149. Places Millhauser firmly in the postmodernist tradition of Donald Bartheleme et al. Finds him "a fabulist disguised as a realist and a parodist."

Howe, Irving. "An Afterword." *Salmagundi* 92 (Fall, 1991): 110-114. An admittedly swift evaluation of "Catalogue of the Exhibition" by the eminent critic, who finds the story "a masterpiece." "The subject may be Romantic, the treatment is not." Contains an interesting note by Millhauser about his intentions.

Kinzie, May. "Succeeding Borges, Escaping Kafka: On the Fiction of Steven Millhauser." *Salmagundi* 92 (Fall, 1991): 115-144. Despite its title, this essay concentrates on Millhauser's second story collection, *The Barnum Museum*. Finds Borges's influence on Millhauser much stronger than Kafka's.

Millhauser, Steven. "Steven Millhauser: The Business of Dreaming." Interview by Jennifer Schuessler. *Publishers Weekly* (May 6, 1996): 56-57. One of the few interviews that Millhauser has given.

William Laskowski

SUSAN MINOT

Born: Manchester, Massachusetts; December 7, 1956

PRINCIPAL SHORT FICTION

Monkeys, 1986
Lust and Other Stories, 1989
"Green Glass," 1991
"House of Women," 1991
"Japanese Lanterns," 1992

OTHER LITERARY FORMS

After her first two collections of short fiction, Susan Minot wrote two novels: *Folly* (1992) and *Evening* (1998). She also collaborated with film director Bernardo Bertolucci in writing the screenplay for *Stealing Beauty* (1996) and has written travel articles and an *Esquire* essay, "No Woman Is Convinced of Her Beauty."

ACHIEVEMENTS

Susan Minot's stories have been anthologized in *The Best American Short Stories*, *Prize Stories: The O. Henry Awards*, and *The Pushcart Prize*. She was awarded the Prix Fémina Étranger for *Monkeys*, which has been optioned for a film, and in 1994 she was named *Victoria* magazine's first writer-in-residence.

BIOGRAPHY

Susan Minot was born in a north Boston suburb and grew up in a family of seven children that bears a strong resemblance to the one portrayed in *Monkeys*. She attended preparatory school at Concord Academy, where she worked on the school's literary magazine and spent summers with her family in North Haven, Maine. After beginning her college career at Boston University, Minot transferred to Brown University, where she studied creative writing and art, earning her B.A. in 1978. During her senior year, her mother was killed in a car accident; after graduation she returned home to care for her father and youngest sister.

Minot earned an M.F.A. in 1983 from Columbia University, where she began writing the stories that would be collected in *Monkeys*. While attending Columbia she worked as an editorial assistant for *The New York Review of Books* (1981) and as an assistant editor for *Grand Street* (1982 to 1986), whose editor Ben Sonnenberg had published her first story, "Hiding." Before committing herself to writing full time, Minot worked as a carpenter, waitress, Greenpeace canvasser, and bookseller. After the critical success of *Monkeys*, she retreated to a small village in Tuscany for a brief sojourn, during which she wrote many of the pieces in *Lust and Other Stories*. She married filmmaker Davis McHenry in 1988, and they made their home in New York, where she occasionally teaches writing workshops at Columbia.

ANALYSIS

In an eloquently understated style, Minot explores the enigmas of familial and romantic love under stress. Her short-story cycle *Monkeys* focuses on the tensions within a large patrician family, whose mother provides a model of how to maintain love and joy in the midst of a troubled marriage. Even as the anxieties of adolescence, the growing need to express independence, and loss threaten family unity, new rituals and allegiances can work to mitigate and even transcend these forces. Her depictions of heterosexual relationships in *Lust and Other Stories* are less optimistic, however, as her female protagonists exhibit problems in coping with the gulf between the stirrings of desire and its romantic fulfillment in an ongoing relationship. Searching for commitment, they discover male attachment to be ephemeral and warily enter subsequent relationships emotionally wounded, seemingly fated to repeat self-destructive patterns.

Minot's family portrait in *Monkeys* has been likened to J. D. Salinger's Glass family, and her stories are clearly influenced by *The New Yorker* school of fiction. Her careful, polished, and somewhat understated style is marked by descriptive economy and a skillful use of detail, both of which provide oblique glimpses of her characters and develop ideas by implication. She notes that many of her stories begin in images and concurred with one interviewer's observation that her work contains numerous images of hiding and secrets.

With her 1998 novel *Evening*, Minot noted that she had diverged from the direction of her previous work, moving toward exploring material she had sought out "rather than a sorting through of material or concerns which life had presented me." The focus in her short fiction on the latter, however, has resulted in finely nuanced stories that exactingly anatomize the perplexities of uncertain relationships, whose contours are subtly shaped by influences of family and gender.

MONKEYS

Monkeys, although labeled a novel by some critics, is a collection of nine interrelated stories—seven of which were previously published in *The New Yorker* and *Grand Street*. Singly, each story conveys a significant incident that threatens the precarious unity of a large, privileged New England family; together the stories chronicle the ebb and flow of that coherence, which threatens to undergo dissolution when the mother, who has served as its nucleus, dies.

Rose Vincent, the mother whose nickname for her children provides the collection's title, provides love and continuity as she devises adaptation strategies to her husband Gus's alcoholism. Gus is most often flummoxed by, distracted by, or indifferent to his active brood, although he must ultimately take charge after Rose's death two-thirds of the way through the volume. The stories' most frequent point of view is that of Sophie, the second daughter, although other stories are related in the third person or through the eyes of other family members, all struggling to discover themselves, while at the same time maintain the ties that knit them together.

"Hiding," the volume's best story, artfully depicts the family's typical routine, with Gus characteristically aloof from its Sunday morning chaos before church. Later, on a skating excursion, the parents' difference is highlighted in their styles on the ice: Gus, a former Harvard University hockey player, powers determinedly in strong straight lines, while Rose, a for-

Susan Minot (©Miriam Berkley)

mer figure skater, glides stylishly in figure eights, which the impatient Gus fails to appreciate. Back home, Rose leads the children in an impromptu game of hiding from their father; his failure to seek them out, however, leaves Rose to hide her disappointment from the children in a sudden burst of domestic activity.

Subsequent stories foreshadow the breaches in the family that will widen as the children mature: In "Thanksgiving Day," a holiday dinner at the grandparents' goes awry as Gus's father's memory fails and his temper flares; "Allowance" sketches a family vacation during which Gus's drinking, impatience with the children, and inability to leave work behind similarly spoil the family holiday. Little wonder that in "Wildflowers," the children perceive Rose's adoration of vacation neighbor Wilbur Kittredge, although the story's final scene depicts her more overwhelming exhilaration with motherhood.

In "Party Blues," Sophie's concluding memory of

the aura of safety she relished as a child in the story "Madeline" contrasts with the confusion and chaos that adolescent love, alcohol, and drugs create during a party she and her siblings throw in their parents' absence—one which emulates the parties from which her parents have withdrawn as Gus's alcoholism worsened. Danger of a return to this pattern in "The Navigator" provokes intervention by his children, who may harbor some hope that his former abilities at a ship's helm will carry over into the family. Although some hope momentarily emerges that he will regain such capabilities, the story concludes with the dramatic shattering of a tranquil family picnic by the sound of his opening a can of beer.

While the "Accident" announced in the climactic story's title initially refers to son Sherman's drunk driving, the car accident that claimed Rose Vincent's life six months before is behind the family's current turmoil. With no mother to comfort him and a father who will not step forward to assume authority, Sherman's ache culminates in a wail that signals the danger of breakdown and despair. After the family muddles through the first Christmas after Rose's death in the penultimate story, "Wedlock," the volume concludes with the award-winning story "Thorofare," in which a provisional unity results after Gus takes the helm and leads the family on an improvised ceremony to dispose of Rose's ashes—a year and a half after her death. Illustrating individual style with a common purpose, each family member scatters a handful of ashes in a moving farewell; on shore, they regroup in an order that emulates their lineup in youth—a unity that is as evocative and promising as it is transitory, a loose coherence similar to the form of the collection as a whole.

LUST AND OTHER STORIES

Minot's 1989 collection, *Lust and Other Stories*, which contains twelve stories divided evenly into three sections, traces the curve of male-female relationships from early attraction through incipient breakups to the aftermath, when despair and desperation lead to the initiation of new relationships. Her female protagonists' instincts lead them in directions contrary to fulfillment, toward self-centered and distracted men threatened by commitment. The collec-

tion received somewhat mixed reviews, with *The New York Times Book Review* praising it as "superbly organized, poignant, and profound" and noting how the stories resonate and progressively accumulate meaning. *Time* magazine remarked that Minot's eye for "clinching detail" was less acute than in earlier short fiction and that the collection exhibited sameness in its focus on unmarried people in their thirties in "modish urban lofts and restaurants."

"Lust" opens the volume with an assembly of vignettes concerning sensuality and passionate encounters, where betrayal by the senses and by the male partners the narrator chooses seems inevitable. She melts easily into sensual abandon, although the results of her encounters gradually shift from erotic bliss and relief to the feeling that she is "sinking in muck," surrendering to sadness after desire is consummated and her partners disregard her. Passion thus gives way to ennui, and ultimately wary defensiveness: "You open your legs but can't, or don't dare anymore, to open your heart." Subsequent stories carry forward the same theme, as their protagonists drift through relationships with abandon, often ending up like Ellen in "City Life," who "felt like something washed ashore after a shipwreck" after succumbing to a perfunctory seduction.

The slighter stories of the middle section project an autumnal ambience, as indifferent men seeking to maintain their emotional distance close down relationships before they become too involved. In "The Feather in the Toque," a bird that has unwittingly flown into the house becomes the metaphor for the girl who makes plans to extricate herself from such static relationships, with her only satisfaction being her plan to leave behind some small item as a warning to the next woman that others have preceded her.

"The Knot," which sketches the dissolution of a relationship through a series of conversational vignettes, is typical of the final group of stories. While the man is unable to provide the woman with the concentrated attention she desires and accuses her of craving unhappiness, even after they separate and establish equilibrium in new relationships, she discovers that her attraction to him still remains. "A Thrilling Life" perhaps best depicts Minot's female characters' tendency to seek men who will inevitably fall short of their hopes, even in the aftermath of a relationship that has failed for similar reasons. As the story's narrator confesses, her partner, Frank Manager,

> was not a candidate for the long run. He might just as well have been wearing a banner which said FRIVOLITY. . . . It was just what I was looking for.

Intrigued by his thrilling life, his tendency to be easily annoyed, and the rage that lurks beneath his charm, she sets herself up for jealousy and disappointment, even as she attempts to reason away her emotions and expect less.

Ultimately, Minot's female characters resign themselves to fatalistic acceptance that desire's vagaries will lead them astray, deluding themselves—as does the narrator of "The Man Who Would Not Go Away"—that they can settle for "one of those loose easy things." Thus, they drift through relationships, emotionally wounded and perpetually unfulfilled. As "dispatches from the sexual wars," *Time*'s reviewer remarks, Minot's stories show that "the news is not good for either side."

OTHER MAJOR WORKS

LONG FICTION: *Folly*, 1992; *Evening*, 1998.
SCREENPLAY: *Stealing Beauty*, 1996.

BIBLIOGRAPHY

Picker, Lauren. "Talking with Susan Minot: A Private Affair." *Newsday* 15 (November, 1992): 34. Minot notes how her stories begin in images and reflects upon the genesis of her novel *Folly* in a vision of a woman on her deathbed. Though unwilling to discuss her private life in interviews, she recalls how success generated expectations that affected her relationship with her work. She concludes by contrasting the more focused and intense form of the short story with the novel, which depicts a larger world, in which one can live.

Pryor, Kelli. "The Story of Her Life: Writer Susan Minot Begins a New Chapter." *New York* 12 (June, 1989): 52-55. Pryor reviews Minot's career and praises *Monkeys* for its "coiled, understated language," "meticulous rendering of childhood," and "painful penchant for detail." She contrasts the "grand loss" of the mother depicted in *Monkeys* with *Lust*'s focus on "desire's smaller wounds." Minot notes how happiness is a "constant struggle" and "just does not last."

Minot, Susan. "Interview with Susan Minot." Interview by Robley Wilson. *Short Story*, n.s. 2, no. 1 (1994): 112-118. Minot discusses her early experiences with writing, as well as the influence of early reading in Ernest Hemingway, F. Scott Fitzgerald, William Butler Yeats, William Faulkner, and Salinger. After experimenting briefly with metafiction, she discovered that it was not her "natural bent." She reviews her early career and experiences in Columbia's M.F.A. program, as well as the influence of New York City in stimulating her writing. Minot confirms the presence of numerous images of hiding in her work and comments on the relation they might have to her growing up in a large family.

_____. "Susan Minot: Understatement Is the Novelist's Preference, in Her Writing as Well as in Her Conversation." Interview by Marcelle Thiebaux. *Publishers Weekly* 16 (November, 1992): 42-43. Minot discusses her novel *Folly*, set in the patrician world she "always resisted" and her identification with her protagonist, who clings foolishly but bravely to slavish adoration of a man who spurned her. She comments on her "decorative" painting and her understated style. After remarking about her writing routine and future projects, Minot concludes, "There's more fictional material in unhappiness and disappointment and frustration than there is in happiness."

Robert M. Luscher

YUKIO MISHIMA
Kimitake Hiraoka

Born: Tokyo, Japan; January 14, 1925
Died: Tokyo, Japan; November 25, 1970

PRINCIPAL SHORT FICTION

Hanazakari no mori, 1944 (includes plays)
Kaibutsu, 1950
Tōnorikai, 1951
Manatsu no shi, 1953 (*Death in Midsummer and Other Stories*, 1966)
Eirei no Koe, 1966 (includes essays)

OTHER LITERARY FORMS

Yukio Mishima wrote more than eighty short stories; twenty novels; more than twenty plays, several in the manner of the classical Nō dramas, as well as plays for the Kabuki theater; several essay collections; two travel books; a bit of poetry; and a handful of works that defy clear-cut classification.

ACHIEVEMENTS

The collected works of Yukio Mishima form thirty-six volumes, more than the literary production of any other writer of his time. The Japanese writer best known outside Japan, from the viewpoint of Western critics he is the most gifted of the post-World War II writers. Mishima also combined his knowledge of classic Japanese literature and language with his wide knowledge of Western literature to produce plays for the Kabuki theater and the first truly successful modern Nō plays.

While uneven in some volumes, style is the most distinctive feature of Mishima's work. His writing is characterized by beautiful but rarely lyric passages. Figures of speech, notable in his later works, are also present in his juvenilia. He consistently used ornate language, though he could also write realistic dialogue.

A Nobel Prize hopeful at least two times, Mishima is among those Japanese writers closest to attaining the rank of master of twentieth century fiction.

BIOGRAPHY

Kimitake Hiraoka, who began using the pseudonym Yukio Mishima in 1941, was the son of a middle-class government official who worked in Tokyo. When Mishima was less than two months old, his paternal grandmother, Natsu, took the boy to her living quarters; his mother, Shizue, felt helpless to protest, and his father, Azusa, appeared to be totally subjected to his mother's will.

In 1931, Mishima was enrolled in the Gakushūin (the Peer's School), a school attended largely by young aristocrats. In due time, he was graduated at the head of his class and received a silver watch from the emperor personally at the imperial palace. By this time, his literary gifts had already become evident, and "Hanazakari no mori" ("The Forest in Full Bloom") was published in 1941.

In 1946, Mishima entered the Tokyo Imperial University to study law. After being employed for a time at the Ministry of Finance, he resigned in 1948 to devote full time to writing. The publication of *Kamen no kokuhaku* (1949; *Confessions of a Mask*, 1958) established him as a literary figure.

The 1950's were eventful years in Mishima's life. During this decade, he produced several novels, two of them major successes. He also traveled to the United States, Brazil, and Europe, and his visit to Greece in particular was a highlight because of its classical associations. During these years, *Shiosai* (1954; *The Sound of Waves*, 1956), a best-seller, was published and film rights were sold, and *Shiroari no su* (1956; the nest of the white ants) established his reputation as a playwright. He also began a bodybuilding program (having been a spare, sickly child) and married Yoko Sugiyama in 1958.

During the first half of the 1960's, writing plays occupied Mishima's time. He trained at the Jieitai (Self-Defense Forces) bases and traveled periodically. He was a strong contender for the Nobel Prize in 1968, the year that his mentor Yasunari Kawabata won. The short story "Yūkoku" ("Patriotism"), in which the hara-kiri (ritual suicide by disembowelment) of a young patriot is described, was published in 1961. He also acted in his first film, a gangster story.

By this time, Mishima's obsession with death was manifested both in word and in deed. He developed a plan for organizing a private army to be used somehow in his death, a step labeled foolish by his friends and ignored by others. During the final five months of his life, he completed the third and fourth books of his tetralogy *Hōjō no umi* (1969-1971; *The Sea of Fertility*, 1972-1974), and on November 25, 1970, he delivered the final volume to the magazine that was publishing it in installments. Later that day, following his plan and schedule implicitly, Mishima went to the Ichigaya Self-Defense headquarters with a group of his Shield Society (a private legion) and, following a nationalistic speech, committed ritual seppuku.

ANALYSIS

The world will never know what course the literary career of Yukio Mishima might have taken had he not died at age forty-five. Nevertheless, he was the best known of post-World War II writers among critics and readers outside Japan, and he received a fair share of attention within his own country. Not all of his work was of equal literary merit, but a certain unevenness is almost certain for a prolific writer.

Apart from his style, usually ornate and meticulously wrought, Mishima's success stemmed in part from his effectiveness in capturing the sense of void and despair that typified many Japanese during the postwar period. Another key to his success lay in his unusual interest in Japanese cultural tradition. His abilities, unique among his peers, enabled him to write in the genre of classical Kabuki and Nō plays.

"THE FOREST IN FULL BLOOM"

Mishima's early works represent a period that both clarified the directions in which his talents would go and developed features that would become trademarks of his later works. He came to realize that poetry was not to be his major effort. In 1941, the year he was graduated from the Peer's School, he published his first long work, "The Forest in Full Bloom" in October, at the age of sixteen. The matu-

Yukio Mishima (CORBIS/ Bettmann)

rity of style in this juvenile work amazed his mentors and peers. The sophisticated word choice is noteworthy, but its maturity goes much farther; it establishes the major theme of his life's work, for he was well on his way to evolving the aesthetic formula that would distinguish his work: Longing leads to beauty; beauty generates ecstasy; ecstasy leads to death. Likewise, the sea, an important motif throughout his writing, is associated with death. Indeed, as Donald Keene has noted, Mishima seemed to be "intoxicated with the beauty of early death."

DEATH IN MIDSUMMER AND OTHER STORIES

Preoccupation with death is obvious even in the title of the short-story collection that constitutes Mishima's major short fiction, *Death in Midsummer and Other Stories*. The title story, "Death in Midsummer," takes an epigraph from one of Charles Baudelaire's poems that translates as "Death affects us more deeply under the stately reign of summer." The psychological realism of Mishima's presentation of the family's reactions to three deaths in the family is the focus of the story. Masaru and Tomoko Ikuta have two sons, Kiyoo and Katsuo, and a daughter, Keiko. Yasue, Tomoko's sister-in-law, is baby-sitting the children while Tomoko takes an afternoon nap. Despite warnings to the children against wandering away, during a brief moment when Yasue is preoccupied with other thoughts, two of the children disappear, leaving the three-year-old Katsuo alone, crying. When Yasue realizes what has happened, she is stricken with a heart attack and dies. Informed of Yasue's accident, Tomoko "felt a sort of sweet emptiness come over her. She was not sad." (This is only one of several passages in which a dearth of feeling is expressed.) Only then does she inquire about the children; she finds Katsuo, who informs her that "Kiyoo . . . Keiko . . . all bubbles." Tomoko is afraid; she sends her husband a telegram telling him that Yasue is dead and that the two children are missing, although by now it is clear that the children have drowned.

Masaru prepares to go down to the resort where the family was vacationing. Devoid of any emotion, he feels more like a detective speculating on the circumstances of death than a distraught father. Intuitively, he senses that the children are dead, not simply missing. When he arrives at the resort, he hears that three people have died, and his thoughts turn to how to approach his wife. Funeral preparations are made. Tomoko is conscious of the incongruity of her almost insane grief alongside her businesslike attention to detail and her large appetite at such a time. She vacillates between a feeling of guilt and her knowledge that she did not cause the deaths. Dissatisfied, she believes that Yasue is lucky to be dead because she does not have to feel that she has been "demoted and condemned" by relatives. Mishima here intrudes to comment that although Tomoko does not know it, it is her "poverty of human emotions" that is most troubling her.

On the surface, life returns to normal, but Tomoko associates almost everything with the tragic accident, while Masaru takes refuge in his work. Tomoko questions the fact that "she was living, the others were dead. That was the great evil. How cruel it was to have to be alive." Autumn comes and goes; and life becomes more peaceful, but Tomoko comes to feel as

if she is waiting for something. To try to assuage her empty feelings, Tomoko seeks outside activities. She asks herself why she had not "tried this mechanical cutting off of the emotions earlier." Winter comes. Tomoko, who is to have another child, admits for the first time that the pain of the lost children was gone, but she cultivates forgetfulness in order not to have to deal with her feelings further. After two years, one summer day, Tomoko asks Masaru to return with her to the beach. Grudgingly, he consents. Tomoko is silent and spends much of her time gazing at the sea, as if she were waiting for something. Masaru wants to ask but then realizes that "he thought he knew without asking."

As with much Japanese literature, the cycle of the seasons is prominent. Deaths come in midsummer, when things should be flourishing and in full bloom. When winter comes, the final ritual of burying the ashes of the dead is completed. Tomoko becomes pregnant, and Momoko is born the following summer. Again, it is summer when she returns to the beach. The cryptic ending is typical of some, not all, of Mishima's work. One may speculate that the return to the beach in the summer is a sign of acceptance or an effort by Tomoko to come to terms with her own identity. Possibly, her waiting represents some sense of communication with the spirits of the dead or even indicates a longing for her own death. A less gloomy interpretation of the return to the beach, however, may recall Baudelaire's line suggesting that death in summer is out of place; death is for the winter, when nature too is desolate.

"THE PRIEST OF SHIGA TEMPLE AND HIS LOVE"

More often anthologized, the story "Shigadera Shōnin no Koi" ("The Priest of Shiga Temple and His Love") manifests Mishima's familiarity with classical Japanese literature. At the same time, the central theme of the story is one that is common in the West but relatively rare in Japanese literature: the inner conflict between worldly love and religious faith. A brief account in a fourteenth century war chronicle of an elderly priest falling in love with the imperial concubine provides the subject matter of the story.

It is the motivation of the concubine and the

priest—rather than the events—that is the focus of the story. The priest is an exemplar of virtue; he is old and doddering, physically a "bag of bones"; it is unlikely that he would become infatuated with a beautiful young woman. When the concubine comes to the area to view the springtime foliage, the priest "unwittingly" glances in her direction, not expecting to be overwhelmed by her beauty. He is, however, and he realizes that "what he had imagined to be completely safe had collapsed in ruins." Never had he broken his vow of chastity, but he realizes that this new love has taken hold of him. The concubine, having forgotten their meeting, is reminded of it when she hears a rumor that an old priest has behaved as if he were crazed after having seen her. She, too, is without blemish in that, while she performed her duties to the emperor, she has never given her love to any suitor.

The priest is now tormented by the implications of this love in relation to his attaining enlightenment. He longs to see the lady once more, confident in his delusion that this will provide escape from his present feelings. He goes to her garden, but when the concubine sees him, she orders that his presence be ignored; she is frightened when he continues to stand outside all night. The lady tells herself that this is a one-sided affair, that he can do nothing to her to threaten her security in the Pure Land. Finally, she admits him, and her white hand emerges from beneath the dividing blind that separates them, as custom decrees. She waits, but the priest says nothing. Finally, he releases her hand and departs. Rumor has it that a few days later, the priest "achieved his final liberation" and the concubine begins copying rolls of religious sutras. Thus, the love story between these two who both are faithful to the tenets of *Jōdo* Buddhism focuses on the point at which the ideal world structure that each one envisioned was in this incident "balanced between collapse and survival." If nothing more, the story reflects the aesthetic formed early in Mishima's life, which holds that beauty causes ecstasy which, in turn, causes death.

"PATRIOTISM"

The story "Yōkoku" ("Patriotism") which was made into a film, is the first of several that focus on ideals of young military officers of the 1930's. To understand this work, it is important to grasp the meaning of the translation of the word "patriotism." The word *yōkoku* means grieving over a country rather than loving a country (*aikoku*), which is a positive emotion. Thus, it is autobiographical in that it expresses Mishima's own grief over the country that he perceived to be in disorder. "Patriotism," according to Mishima's own evaluation, contains "both the best and the worst features" of his writing. The story concerns a young lieutenant, Shinji Takeyama, who commits seppuku because he feels that he cannot do what he has been ordered to do: lead an attack on the young rebels in the Ni Ni Roku Incident, an unsuccessful coup d'état that occurred on February 26, 1936, in Tokyo. Although Mishima was only eleven years old at the time of the incident, its influence on him provided the germ for two other works, a play *Tōka no Kiku* (1961; tenth-day chrysanthemums) and *Eirei no Koe* (voices of the heroic dead). These works confirm Mishima's growing dedication to imperialism. The story contains what is possibly the most detailed account of the samurai rite of seppuku in all of Japanese literature.

Almost everything spoken or written by Mishima fits into a personal cosmology that evolved and was refined throughout his life; the living out of this system led to his death: Beauty leads to ecstasy, ecstasy to death. Literature was central to Mishima's cosmos and was virtually inseparable from it. To understand one is to comprehend the other. Mishima was obsessed with death, and to create beauty in his works, in his system, led inevitably to his death.

OTHER MAJOR WORKS

LONG FICTION: *Kamen no kokuhaku*, 1949 (*Confessions of a Mask*, 1958); *Ai no kawaki*, 1950 (*Thirst for Love*, 1969); *Kinjiki*, 1951 (translated with *Higyō* as *Forbidden Colors*, 1968); *Higyō*, 1953 (translated with *Kinjiki* as *Forbidden Colors*, 1968); *Shiosai*, 1954 (*The Sound of Waves*, 1956); *Kinkakuji*, 1956 (*The Temple of the Golden Pavilion*, 1959); *Kyōko no ie*, 1959; *Utage no ato*, 1960 (*After the Banquet*, 1963); *Gogo no eikō*, 1963 (*The Sailor Who Fell from Grace with the Sea*, 1965); *Hōjō no umi*, 1969-1971

(*The Sea of Fertility: A Cycle of Four Novels*, 1972-1974; includes *Haru no yuki*, 1969 [*Spring Snow*, 1972], *Homba*, 1969 [*Runaway Horses*, 1973], *Akatsuki no tera*, 1970 [*The Temple of Dawn*, 1973], and *Tennin gosui*, 1971 [*The Decay of the Angel*, 1974).

PLAYS: *Kantan*, wr. 1950, pb. 1956 (English translation, 1957); *Yoro no himawari*, pr., pb. 1953 (*Twilight Sunflower*, 1958); *Dōjōji*, pb. 1953 (English translation, 1966); *Aya no tsuzumu*, pr. 1955 (*The Damask Drum*, 1957); *Shiroari no su*, pr., pb. 1955; *Aoi no ue*, pr., pb. 1956 (*The Lady Aoi*, 1957); *Hanjo*, pb. 1956 (English translation, 1957); *Sotoba Komachi*, pb. 1956 (English translation, 1957); *Kindai nōgakushū*, pb. 1956 (includes *Kantan*, *The Damask Drum*, *The Lady Aoi*, *Hanjo*, and *Sotoba Komachi*; *Five Modern Nō Plays*, 1957); *Tōka no kiku*, pr., pb. 1961; *Sado kōshaku fujin*, pr., pb. 1965 (*Madame de Sade*, 1967); *Suzakuke no metsubō*, pr., pb. 1967; *Wa ga tomo Hittorā*, pb. 1968 (*My Friend Hitler*, 1977); *Chinsetsu yumiharizuki*, pr., pb. 1969.

NONFICTION: *Hagakure nyūmon*, 1967 (*The Way of the Samurai*, 1977); *Taiyō to tetsu*, 1968 (*Sun and Steel*, 1970); *Yukio Mishima on "Hagakure": The Samurai Ethic and Modern Japan*, 1978.

EDITED TEXT: *New Writing in Japan*, 1972 (with Geoffrey Bownas).

BIBLIOGRAPHY

Keene, Donald. *Fiction*. Vol. 1 in *Dawn to the West: Japanese Literature of the Modern Era*. New York: Holt, Rinehart and Winston, 1984. Keene's section on Mishima contains both biographical data and critical evaluations of a large number of Mishima's works. He quotes important passages from various works and from conversations that he had with Mishima. Includes notes, a bibliography, and a detailed index.

_____. *Landscapes and Portraits: Appreciation of Japanese Culture*. Tokyo: Kodansha International, 1971. The section on Mishima and his work comments on a variety of his works but especially on *Confessions of a Mask*, because, atypically, this novel is autobiographical, providing insight into his thinking and his relation to his own work. As in most works, Mishima's preoccupation with death is explored. Includes a short reading list but no index.

_____. "Mishima in 1958." *The Paris Review* 37 (Spring, 1995): 140-160. Keene recalls his 1958 interview with Mishima, in which Mishima discussed influences, his delight in "cruel stories," the importance of traditional Japanese theater for him, and his novels and his other writing.

Miyoshi, Masao. *Accomplices of Silence: The Modern Japanese Novel*. Berkeley: University of California Press, 1974. Chapter 6 in part 2, "Mute's Rage," provides studies of two of Mishima's major novels, *Confessions of a Mask* and *The Temple of the Golden Pavilion*, as well as comments on works that Miyoshi considers to be important. Includes notes and an index.

Napier, Susan J. *Escape from the Wasteland: Romanticism and Realism in the Fiction of Mishima Yukio and Ōe Kenzaburō*. Cambridge, Mass.: Harvard University Press, 1991. Napier uncovers shocking similarities as well as insightful dissimilarities in the work of Mishima and Ōe and ponders each writer's place in the tradition of Japanese literature.

Nathan, John. *Mishima: A Biography*. Boston: Little, Brown, 1974. In this very readable biography, Nathan's personal acquaintance with Mishima as one of the writer's several translators is evident. The chapters are organized according to chronological periods in Mishima's life. In addition to a chronological listing of the major plays and novels, this volume contains a helpful index.

Scott-Stokes, Henry. *The Life and Death of Yukio Mishima*. Rev. ed. New York: Noonday Press, 1995. Following a personal impression of Mishima, Scott-Stokes presents a five-part account of Mishima's life, beginning with the last day of his life. The author then returns to Mishima's early life and the making of the young man as a writer. Part 4, "The Four Rivers," identifies the rivers of writing, theater, body, and action, discussing in each subsection relevant events and works. Part 5 is a "Postmortem." Supplemented by a glossary, a chronology, a bibliography, and an index.

Starrs, Roy. *Deadly Dialectics: Sex, Violence, and Nihilism in the World of Yukio Mishima*. Honolulu: University of Hawaii Press, 1994. A critical and interpretive look at sex and violence in Mishima's work. Includes bibliographical references and an index.

Ueda, Makoto. *Modern Japanese Writers and the Nature of Literature*. Stanford, Calif.: Stanford University Press, 1976. Mishima is one of eight Japanese writers treated in this volume. While Ueda discusses certain novels in some detail, for the most part his discussion centers on philosophical and stylistic matters and suggests that Mishima's pessimism derived more from his appraisal of the state of human civilization than from his views on the nature of literature. Includes a brief bibliography and an index.

Wolfe, Peter. *Yukio Mishima*. New York: Continuum, 1989. Wolfe asserts that common sense explains very little about motives in Mishima. "What makes him unusual is his belief that anything of value exists in close proximity to death."

Victoria Price

GEORGE MOORE

Born: County Mayo, Ireland; February 24, 1852
Died: London, England; January 21, 1933

PRINCIPAL SHORT FICTION

Parnell and His Island, 1887
Celibates, 1895
The Untilled Field, 1903
Memoirs of My Dead Life, 1906
A Story-Teller's Holiday, 1918
In Single Strictness, 1922
Peronnik the Fool, 1924
Celibate Lives, 1927
A Flood, 1930
In Minor Keys: The Uncollected Short Stories of George Moore, 1955

OTHER LITERARY FORMS

George Moore began his career as a poet with *Flowers of Passion* (1878) and was to go on to write dramas and several novels, the most enduring and accomplished being *Esther Waters* (1894). He also wrote art criticism, such as *Modern Painting* (1893), and autobiography, the best known being *Hail and Farewell: A Trilogy* (1911-1914; *Ave*, 1911; *Salve*, 1912; *Vale*, 1914).

ACHIEVEMENTS

One of the most prolific of the Irish writers of the late nineteenth and early twentieth centuries, George Moore published seventeen books, which included several novels, books of literary and art criticism, poetry, autobiography, and social criticism. On his eightieth birthday the London *Times* praised his contribution to literature in an article, signed by many of the major writers of the day, which recognized his long and serious service to literature, and his contribution, in particular, to the art of narrative. The Irish Academy was founded in 1932, and Moore was included in the first list of members.

BIOGRAPHY

George Augustus Moore was born to a wealthy family at Moore Hall, the family estate in County Mayo, in the west of Ireland on February 24, 1852. The family was originally Protestant but through marriage had become Roman Catholic. He had a spotty education, due to health problems, spending some time at Oscott, a Catholic boarding school in England. When he was seventeen, he joined the family in London, and his formal education ceased. In 1871, he went to Paris to study painting and began his close association with the French painters and writ-

George Moore (Library of Congress)

ers. By 1875, he gave up painting as a possible career but not his interest as a critic of contemporary French painters. He was an acquaintance of Edouard Manet and Edgar Degas, and the French naturalistic writer Émile Zola, who was a major influence on him. In 1880, he returned to London and began to write for a living. His first novel, *A Modern Lover*, appeared in 1883. Always concerned with the problems of style and content in fiction, he was determined to follow the French naturalistic writers and to bring their simplicity and intellectual honesty to British fiction. He also became a successful art critic, and social man-about-town in London. Lively and outgoing, he was an outrageous self-promoter, often extolling his skills in his various texts. He became more and more interested in Irish letters and politics in the 1890's and became a director of the Irish Literary Theatre, returning to live in Ireland in 1901. He returned to London in 1911 and lived there until his death, continuing his interest in Ireland and writing about Irish life in several genres. He kept up his sometimes abrasive relationships with other artists throughout these years,

quarreling with William Butler Yeats in 1902, with Æ (George Russell) in 1918, and later with Frank Harris. He died in London in 1933, and his ashes were deposited on Castle Island within sight of Moore Hall in Ireland.

ANALYSIS

George Moore brought to his short fiction the same theories and intentions that were the mark of all of his work. He wanted to write about ordinary people, and, in particular, about ordinary Irish people. He was determined to follow the late nineteenth century French writers, such as Zola and Gustave Flaubert, and the Russian writers, such as Ivan Turgenev, in attempting a realistic portrayal of life without artistic cleverness or dramatic heightening. His aim was to develop an "oral" style in which the reader would be presented with a sense of intimacy, as if the writer were talking to a friend.

The stories were chosen to avoid extravagant or violent action. The plots were simple and direct, with no intrusion of interior exploration of a character or of narratorial monologue. They were to be objective, not judgmental. It was a matter of showing, not telling the reader how to react. He followed Turgenev in using landscape to convey mood and to strive for a lyric simplicity, a flow of narrative with an avoidance of dramatic shaping, obvious climax, or clear conclusion.

He was to have a strong influence on the short story and particularly on the Irish writers. His determination to draw the short story away from eccentric, heightened behavior and incident to "real life" with a kind of subtle artlessness was to be an example followed by James Joyce in his collection *Dubliners* (1914). A further aspect of his career as a short-story writer appeared in his series of Irish folk tales, in which the fairy world comes into play and wherein he made a serious attempt to retrieve and reshape Irish literary heritage.

"WILFRID HOLMES"

Moore often published his stories in sets exploring a single theme. In *In Single Strictness*, the characters live repressed lives, and Moore uses a minor incident to explore such unhappiness, very quietly, in stories leading to subdued, and often, inconsequential endings. Wilfrid Holmes is the youngest son of a middle-class family. He has a comfortable childhood but tends to be lazy and dreamy. The older children gradually go off to normal lives in business and marriage. It becomes obvious, however, that Holmes's aimlessness carries on into maturity. He tries a number of possible careers, but nothing quite works. He likes music and finally settles on composing operas, but he never attempts to learn the finer aspects of composition; his skill is in melody. He exists on a regularly paid allowance from an aunt.

Rubbing along, working on his opera, Wilfred is suddenly aware that his allowance has not come. Several days go by, and he becomes worried, not knowing if he should write his aunt. He gets a small amount from a brother. He attempts to get a job as a music critic, but it is obvious that he simply does not know enough for such work. The allowance comes. The aunt has simply forgotten to send it and to make up for her forgetfulness, she sends him considerably more than usual. He is happy again, continuing on his feckless, incompetent way with his opera.

Moore, who spoke and wrote often of his literary theories, liked to think that the arts had strong connections and could be helped by cross-reference; this story is an example of his use of "minor keys," a kind of story that goes nowhere but explores without comment a hopeless life. Aside from a very quiet heightening in the story when Wilfrid begins to fear that he will not be able to survive, the rest of the work is as lazily quiet as he is, an example of the idea that style is meaning.

"SARAH GWYNN"

In this story (from *Celibate Lives*), Moore brings together his interest in the quiet desperation of humans and his admiration for the Irish working class. Sarah is taken on as a housekeeper by a Dublin doctor, moved by the story that after years of service as a lay sister in a convent, she was dismissed for complaining about the working conditions. She proves to be an excellent worker, and it looks as if she and the doctor's gardener will marry.

Suddenly she announces she must leave, and he discovers that she has a mission and cannot marry.

Years earlier, alone and helpless in Dublin, she was befriended by a girl, Phyllis, who got her work in a biscuit factory. The pay was far too meager, however, and some of the girls also worked at night as prostitutes. Phyllis does this and uses her extra money to keep both of them from starvation, refusing to let Sarah join her in the profession. When the chance comes for Sarah to enter an English convent, Phyllis raises the money for her passage.

Since then, Sarah has been searching for Phyllis. Now the chance of marriage is too much for her; it is not her right to have a decent life until she finds and rescues Phyllis, although she knows this is highly unlikely. The doctor tries to dissuade her, but she will not relent, and the story ends, as the doctor says, with three people unhappy, the doctor, Sarah, and her hopeless lover, the gardener.

"SO ON HE FARES"

Moore believed his best work as a short fictionist was in *The Untilled Field* and with characteristic immodesty said that "So on He Fares" was the best short story ever written by anyone. Moore was determined to avoid the caricature of the Irish peasant and the exaggerated plot in favor of the simplicity of the rambling tale, told quietly and intimately, about ordinary people. The style is strongly rhythmic, called by Moore his "melodic line."

Ulick Burke, with his father in the army, lives with his mother in rural Ireland. She dislikes him, and often punishes him severely. At the age of ten, he runs away, and almost drowns, but he is rescued by a passing barge. He becomes a sailor. In his twenties, he returns. His father is away again, and his mother has another son, also called Ulick. His mother is cool toward him but clearly has considerable affection for the brother. He senses her old dislike of him growing the longer he stays. He leaves, wondering if it might not have been better had he died when he fell in the river on first leaving home. He thinks of drowning himself but rejects the idea, since a man, unlike a child, cannot kill himself because his mother does not love him. He must get on with life. The quietly sombre conclusion, playing off the right of a child to die for lack of love against the adult's obligation to endure is the only touch of short-story cleverness in the work. It does, however, function as proof of Moore's idea of how life plays itself out, not in tricky endings, but in sad acceptance.

A STORY-TELLER'S HOLIDAY

This work avoids one of the problems of the short-story collection, the fragmentary nature of one story following another. Here Moore solves that difficulty by immersing the stories in a wider, slightly novelistic tale of the writer (a fictional representation of Moore himself) going from London to Ireland, meeting travelers on the way, and gradually reaching the rural world of the old Irish tales. The stories come out of innocent conversations, allowing for different kinds of tales, individual characters offering them as modest entertainment. The Story-Teller tells some of the stories in educated English, but the locals use their native accent and sentence style. The frame is set slowly with the early material being comment upon the political, religious, and social problems of Ireland after the Easter Rebellion of 1916. When he gets into the country, the tales become closely related to rural life, and once he meets Alec Trusselby, a wandering storyteller, the stories shift into the genre of the Irish medieval tale, often with fairy connections.

By 1918, depressed by World War I and the political troubles of Ireland, Moore had lost interest in modern life, and this collection marks a return to the solace of ancient Ireland, narrated by storytellers emotionally and intellectually connected to the bards, telling tales rather than writing them, which Moore, somewhat illogically, was attempting to duplicate in print. The love story of Liadin, the wandering singer, and Curithir, the wandering storyteller, doomed to fail since their gifts of enchanting the people must come before any private happiness and their eventual reunion, side by side in death, is an example of the kind of tale Moore wanted to use to enrich the artistic and social fabric of a modern, violent Ireland.

OTHER MAJOR WORKS

LONG FICTION: *A Modern Lover*, 1883; *A Mummer's Wife*, 1884; *A Drama in Muslin*, 1886; *A Mere Accident*, 1887; *Spring Days*, 1888; *Mike Fletcher*, 1889; *Vain Fortune*, 1891; *Esther Waters*, 1894;

Evelyn Innes, 1898; *Sister Teresa*, 1901; *The Lake*, 1905; *Muslin*, 1915; *The Brook Kerith*, 1916; *Lewis Seymour and Some Women*, 1917; *Héloise and Abélard*, 1921; *Ulick and Soracha*, 1926; *Aphrodite in Aulis*, 1930.

PLAYS: *Martin Luther*, pb. 1879 (with Bernard Lopez); *The Strike at Arlingford*, pr., pb. 1893; *The Bending of the Bough*, pr., pb. 1900; *Diarmuid and Grania*, pr. 1901 (with William Butler Yeats); *The Apostle*, pb. 1911; *Esther Waters*, pr. 1911; *Elizabeth Cooper*, pr., pb. 1913; *The Making of Immortal*, pb. 1927; *The Passing of the Essenes*, pr., pb. 1930 (revision of *The Apostle*).

POETRY: *Flowers of Passion*, 1878; *Pagan Poems*, 1881.

NONFICTION: *Confessions of a Young Man*, 1888; *Impressions and Opinions*, 1891; *Modern Painting*, 1893; *Hail and Farewell: A Trilogy*, 1911-1914 (*Ave*, 1911; *Salve*, 1912; *Vale*, 1914); *Avowals*, 1919; *Conversations in Ebury Street*, 1924; *Letters from George Moore to Edouard Dujardin, 1886-1922*, 1929; *The Talking Pine*, 1931; *A Communication to My Friends*, 1933; *Letters of George Moore*, 1942; *Letters to Lady Cunard*, 1957 (Rupert Hart-Davis, editor); *George Moore in Transition: Letters to T. Fisher Unwin and Lena Milman, 1894-1910*, 1968 (Helmut E. Gerber, editor).

TRANSLATION: *Daphnis and Chloë*, 1924 (Longus).

BIBLIOGRAPHY

Burkhart, Charles. "The Short Stories of George Moore." In *The Man of Wax: Critical Essays on George Moore*, edited by Douglas A. Hughes. New York: New York University Press, 1971. A clear and sensible discussion of the short stories in general terms without academic jargon. A good way to look at the entire list in the context of his other work. There is also an essay by Enid Starkie on Moore and French naturalism, which helps immensely in understanding the movement and how Moore adapted it to his work.

Dunleavy, Gareth W. "George Moore's Medievalism: A Modern Triptych." In *George Moore in Perspective*, edited by Janet Dunleavy. Totowa, New Jersey: Barnes & Noble, 1983. Moore used medieval themes in both his novels and short stories. This is a straightforward discussion of this kind of story, with *A Story-Teller's Holiday* receiving special attention. This volume also contains an interesting discussion, written by Melvin J. Friedman, of the similarities between Moore and Samuel Beckett, which also brings the short stories into consideration.

Farrow, Anthony. *George Moore.* Boston: Twayne, 1978. Includes a bibliography and an index.

Jeffares, A. Norman. *George Moore.* London: Long-mans, 1965. One of the British Council series and the best short introduction to the author and his work, including his short stories. A good place to start.

Seinfelt, Frederick W. *George Moore: Ireland's Unconventional Realist.* Philadelphia: Dorrance and Company, 1975. A discussion of Moore's women; includes comment upon his use of women in the short stories.

Charles Pullen

LORRIE MOORE

Born: Glen Falls, New York; January 13, 1957

PRINCIPAL SHORT FICTION
Self-Help, 1985
Like Life, 1990
Birds of America, 1998

OTHER LITERARY FORMS

Lorrie Moore is the author of the novels *Anagrams* (1986) and *Who Will Run the Frog Hospital?* (1994). She has also published a children's book, *The Forgotten Helper* (1987).

ACHIEVEMENTS

Lorrie Moore's stories have appeared in *The New Yorker*, the annual *The Best American Short Stories*, and *Prize Stories: The O. Henry Awards* series. In 1976, at the age of nineteen, she won *Seventeen* magazine's fiction contest. She has also received a National Endowment for the Arts Fellowship (1989) and a Granville Hicks Memorial Fellowship (1983).

BIOGRAPHY

Lorrie Moore (born Marie Lorena Moore) was born in Glen Falls, New York, in 1957. She is the second of four children born to professional, middle-class parents (her father an insurance executive and her mother a nurse-turned-housewife). Although both of her parents had harbored literary ambitions in their youth, neither of them was particularly supportive of Moore's decision to become a writer, both believing that she should do something more practical.

Moore won a regents scholarship and attended St. Lawrence University in New York, which she followed by two years of paralegal work. In 1980, she enrolled in Cornell University's M.F.A. program; there she had the good fortune of studying under the novelist Alison Lurie, who proved to be very supportive of her work. Upon Lurie's recommendation, Moore's work was accepted by literary agent Melanie Jackson, and in 1983, when she was twenty-six, Moore's first collection of short stories, *Self-Help*, was accepted for publication by Knopf.

Moore moved to Madison, Wisconsin, to accept an assistant professorship in the Department of English at the University of Wisconsin. She had some difficulty adjusting to life in the Midwest, so for a while she continued to spend her summers in New York. Moore advanced to the position of full professor at the University of Wisconsin and settled in Madison with her husband, an attorney, and her son, Benjamin.

ANALYSIS

Lorrie Moore's work is often compared to that of such literary notables as Raymond Carver, Bobbie Ann Mason, Ann Beattie, and Flannery O'Connor. There are definitely overtones of O'Connor in the comic despair that pervades Moore's work. One can also perhaps find traces of Carver and Mason in her characters and subject matter. However, no one has written more convincingly and poignantly about the angst of our modern world than Lorrie Moore. Her characters—an assortment of housewives, mothers, and career women (usually academic)—are typically isolated or disconnected from the larger world through no real character flaws of their own. These women can be bitingly sarcastic in their speech, but without fail they are eminently likable, sweet characters. In this world of upwardly mobile Americans, there are very few panaceas for women who both think and feel. They cannot convince themselves to believe in God or the sanctity of marriage; relationships with the opposite sex offer little real comfort, and all efforts at self-help fail.

Given Moore's early success as a writer, it is not surprising to find some lack of maturity in her earliest work. Moore herself calls *Self-Help* (her first collection of short stories) and *Anagrams* (her first novel) apprentice work. The stories in *Self-Help* bear the marks of graduate workshop writing; all seem designed primarily to evoke laughter and thus have a stand-up comedic effect. These stories are saved, however, by the sad, underlying truths that slowly make their way to the surface and leave a lasting impression on the reader. Similarly, stories in *Like Life* are often too self-consciously clever. However, evidence of Moore's mature writing is present in the stories "You're Ugly Too" and "Places to Look for Your Mind." Her novel *Who Will Run the Frog Hospital?* has some early pacing problems, but it proves to be a hauntingly sweet story of the friendship between two teenage girls, a friendship that nothing in adult life can quite match. Finally, the stories in *Birds of America* are breathtakingly good. Her mordant sense of humor is still present, but she does not allow humor to eclipse plot and character development. Nearly every story is about characters in relationships (mothers and daughters, husbands and wives, or lovers) who just cannot really connect or experience true intimacy. The last three stories of the collection are especially stunning: "Real Estate," in which a dying woman is saddled with her husband's choice of a house that needs massive renovation; "People Like That Are the Only People Here: Canonical Babbling in Peed Onk," in which a couple is faced with the cruel ironies of a baby with cancer; and "Terrific Mother," in which a childless woman accidentally kills a friend's baby and is left to struggle with this irreparable grief.

"REAL ESTATE"

The story "Real Estate" from *Birds of America* is one of many stories by Moore that explores the futility of marriage. Ruth, who has already lost one lung to cancer, gets a premonition that she will die in the spring "after much boring flailing and flapping and the pained, purposeless work that constituted life." She also discovers yet another of her husband's love affairs and laughs for over two pages. At Terence's (her husband) instigation, they begin to shop for a new house. Ruth finally consents to buy an old farmhouse with which her husband falls in love, but as with all his flings, he soon abandons the house. Ruth, a dying woman, is left to oversee the house's renovation. She also begins to battle the house's infestation with racoons, ants, bats, crows, squirrels, and finally a teenage punk.

Meanwhile, in a parallel plot, Noel, a lawn care person, is left by his girlfriend because, among other cultural deficiencies, Noel does not know a single song all the way through. Noel begins to drink a lot, gets fired, sleeps all day, and wanders the streets at night. Noel soon turns to burglary, but his motivation is not the acquisition of worldly goods. He holds a gun to his victims' head, demanding that they sing a song all the way through. He ends up in Ruth's house, where Ruth shoots him, killing him. The plot of "Real Estate" is as inevitable as the return of Ruth's lung cancer (she still smokes occasionally). Ruth shows us what can happen when basically kind, gentle women are pushed too far by the utterly selfish people around them.

"PEOPLE LIKE THAT ARE THE ONLY PEOPLE HERE"

"People Like That Are the Only People Here," from *Birds of America*, has also appeared in *The New Yorker*. Although Moore keeps the details to herself, this story is probably her most autobiographical. Her son, Benjamin, suffered through a similar ordeal. In this story, the main characters do not receive names; they are known as the Mother, the Baby, the Father, etc. The Mother finds a blood clot in her baby's diaper and rushes him to a clinic at the children's hospital. She soon discovers that he has a cancerous lesion on his kidney and will require a nephrectomy, probably followed by chemotherapy. The story explores the various stages of parents faced with catastrophic illnesses in their children: self-blame, attempts to pray or bargain with God, thoughts of suicide or escape, and finally, just getting through the illness. As usual, Moore's humor is intact. God looks like a manager at Marshall Field's, who only offers the reassurance that not knowing the future is what makes us human. The narrator, a mother who writes, offers a number of succinct commentaries on what can only be Moore's own craft. For example, she says, "I do *the careful ironies of daydream*. I do *the marshy ideas upon which intimate life is built*." The Baby of this story survives the nephrectomy and does not have to go through chemotherapy, but other characters in the story are not so lucky. A child named Joey is expected to live only three more weeks after battling cancer for four and a half years. His father Frank has given up everything to save Joey—his career and his marriage—but now Joey is going to die anyway. One cannot help but wonder if Joey's mother did the right thing by leaving Frank and Joey, remarrying, and having a healthy child. Frank's sacrifice is one of the cruelest ironies in this story.

"TERRIFIC MOTHER"

In "Terrific Mother," also found in *Birds of America*, Adrienne, the thirty-five-year-old protagonist, accidentally kills a friend's baby (the picnic bench upon which she is sitting topples and the baby hits his head against a stone wall). Adrienne withdraws for a period of seven months until a friend and lover, Martin Porter, offers to marry her for purely practical reasons. He is going to a conference in Northern Italy for a month, and if Adrienne is married to him, she can go also. Ironically, this marriage of convenience turns out to be one of the best marriages in Moore's fiction. There is little to no romance between the couple, but Martin is infinitely kind and patient. At the conference in Italy, Adrienne finds academics mean-spirited and pretentious, so she escapes into the company of the other spouses and discovers an American masseuse named Ilke. Through massage, Adrienne begins to let go of some of her horrendous guilt. She even half falls in love with Ilke, but then realizes that Ilke is bored while she, Adrienne, is having a religious experience. When Adrienne discovers that Martin is also going to Ilke, she is as infuriated as she would be over a sexual infidelity. The story ends with Adrienne asking for Martin's forgiveness, and the reader is left to believe that here is a relationship that will work.

"YOU'RE UGLY TOO"

"You're Ugly Too," found in *Like Life*, is one of Lorrie Moore's most successful short stories. It has been published in *The New Yorker*, the *Prize Stories: The O. Henry Awards*, and *The Best American Short Stories*. As in many of Moore's stories, the protagonist, Zoë Hendricks, finds it nearly impossible to connect with those around her. Zoë, an American history professor at a small liberal arts college in the Midwest, feels that she is dying, and she may, in fact, be dying because she has a tumor in her abdomen. Her students find her sarcastic, and she finds them inane. All of her efforts at romance or self-help have failed her. One refuge is her sister's place in New York, so Zoë heads for New York just after she discovers her tumor but before she hears the diagnosis. There she learns that her sister is getting married to her live-in boyfriend just at the point at which all the romance of their relationship has obviously died. At a Halloween party, her sister's boyfriend is already beginning to flirt shamelessly with other women. Zoë, dressed as a bonehead, is slated to meet Earl, a boorish man dressed up as a naked woman with rubber breasts and steel wool placed strategically over a body suit. Earl is, in many ways, a prototype of men who fail at intimacy. He interrupts Zoë's joke, changes the subject when she mentions her health (a serious concern), and then suggests ways to improve herself (wear the color blue). Finally, he whines that he prefers women with part-time jobs over professional women. Zoë nearly pushes him off the balcony, twenty floors up.

OTHER MAJOR WORKS

LONG FICTION: *Anagrams*, 1986; *Who Will Run the Frog Hospital?* 1994.

CHILDREN'S LITERATURE: *The Forgotten Helper*, 1987.

BIBLIOGRAPHY

Blades, John. "Lorrie Moore: Flipping Death the Bird." *Publishers Weekly* (August 24, 1997): 31-32. In this preview for the upcoming publication of *Birds of America*, Blade provides an overview of Lorrie Moore's successes. Moore defends herself against assumptions that she has had it too easy as a writer, and she defends her use of humor, which some critics have found excessive. Moore considers both *Anagrams* and *Self-Help* apprentice books.

Lee, Don. "About Lorrie Moore." *Ploughshares* (Fall, 1998): 224-229. An overview of Moore's life and work.

Moore, Lorrie. "The Booklist Interview: Lorrie Moore." Interview by Molly McQuade. *Booklist* (October 15, 1998): 402-403. Moore discusses the use of absurdity in her work, her pessimistic rather than cynical worldview, and the craft of writing stories.

Nancy E. Sherrod

ALBERTO MORAVIA

Born: Rome, Italy; November 28, 1907
Died: Rome, Italy; September 26, 1990

PRINCIPAL SHORT FICTION

La bella vita, 1935
L'imbroglio, 1937
I sogni del pigro, 1940
L'amante infelice, 1943
L'epidemia: Racconti surrealistici e satirici, 1944
Due cortigiane, 1945
L'amore coniugale e altri racconti, 1949
I racconti, 1927-1951, 1952
Bitter Honeymoon and Other Stories, 1954 (selections from *I racconti*)
Racconti romani, 1954 (*Roman Tales*, 1956)
Nuovi racconti romani, 1959 (*More Roman Tales*, 1963)
The Wayward Wife and Other Stories, 1960 (selections from *I racconti*)
L'automa, 1963 (*The Fetish*, 1964)
Una cosa è una cosa, 1967 (*Command and I Will Obey You*, 1969)
I racconti di Alberto Moravia, 1968
Il paradiso, 1970 (*Paradise and Other Stories*, 1971; also as *Bought and Sold*, 1973)
Un'altra vita, 1973 (*Lady Godiva and Other Stories*, 1975; also as *Mother Love*, 1976)
Boh, 1976 (*The Voice of the Sea and Other Stories*, 1978)
La cosa e altri racconti, 1983 (*Erotic Tales*, 1985)

OTHER LITERARY FORMS

Alberto Moravia was a very prolific writer, with the novel and short story his preferred forms. His most famous work, *Gli indifferenti* (1929; *The Indifferent Ones*, 1932; also as *The Time of Indifference*, 1953), called Italy's first European novel, is also the first distinctively existential literature of the twentieth century. In addition to penning several translations, plays, and screenplays, Moravia wrote critical essays about drama and the cinema and adapted several of his novels—*Il conformista* (1951; *The Conformist*, 1952) and *La ciociara* (1957; *Two Women*, 1958), for example—to film. Besides his travelogues covering disparate locations and some thirty years, in the final decade or so of his life he created some delightfully irreverent children's literature.

ACHIEVEMENTS

In *The Indifferent Ones*, Alberto Moravia created the first existentialist novel. With the success of that book, Moravia emerged as one of Italy's leading literary figures, and with the translation of *La romana* (1947; *The Woman of Rome*, 1949) twenty years later, his reputation spread to the English-speaking world. He received a number of awards for his writing: the Corriere Lombardo Prize in 1945 for *Agostino* (1944; English translation, 1947), the Chevalier de la Légion d'Honneur (1952), the Strega Literary Prize for *Il disprezzo* (1954; *A Ghost at Noon*, 1955), and the Viareggio Prize for *La noia* (1960; *The Empty Canvas*, 1961). Although his fiction rarely strays far from Rome and his themes hardly vary in his many works, he created an impressive body of work that depicts the plight and struggles of modern humans regardless of geographical location.

BIOGRAPHY

Alberto Pincherle Moravia, son of Carlo and Teresa de Marsanich Moravia, was born in Rome, Italy, on November 28, 1907. His Jewish father was an architect, and his Catholic mother was a Dalmatian countess. Hence, he grew up in an affluent and cultured family that kept a box at the opera and retained a chauffeur. Moravia's home life was not happy, though, and his descriptions of bourgeois family conflicts in his fiction mirror his own childhood.

One early escape was storytelling. In 1937, he recalled that as a child,

> I would go off into the fields, or stretch myself out . . . on a couch in a room of the summer villa, and talk to myself. I cannot remember the plots of these solitary narratives; I think they were adventures, dangerous episodes, violent and improbable incidents; I do remember very well, however, that I took up the thread of the

story every day at the precise point where I had left it the day before.

At sixteen, tuberculosis of the bone forced him to leave school, and he spent the next several years in bed. A later short story, "Inverno di malato," written in 1930, draws upon his experiences in a sanatorium, and the protagonist, Girolamo, suffers, like his creator, from tuberculosis of the bone. During this long convalescence, Moravia read extensively, and, according to his essay of 1945 "Ricordo degli Indifferenti" ("Recalling *Time of Indifference*"), he was also already demonstrating his writing fluency. In October, 1925, he began *The Indifferent Ones*; by the time he finished the work, he had, in addition, written poems, short stories, and two other novels. "Cortigiana stanca," his first publication, appeared in French in the avant-garde magazine *'900* in 1927. At the time, his sex-obsessed stories and the novel *The Indifferent Ones* were considered pornographic, so

Alberto Moravia (Library of Congress)

much so that some critics insist "Moravia" is a pseudonym Alberto Pincherle assumed after the clamorous—and scandalized—reception of the novel, which made his reputation as a leading Italian writer. Although having no basis in fact, this interpretation gives a good indication of the novel's impact. In fact, much later, Moravia himself recalled, "Certainly no book in the last fifty years has been greeted with such unanimous enthusiasm and excitement."

When his next novel, *Le ambizioni sbagliate* (1935; *The Wheel of Fortune*, 1937; also as *Mistaken Ambitions*, 1965), angered Italy's Fascist government, Moravia left for the United States, where he taught Italian for a time. A trip to Mexico provided the background for *La mascherata* (1941; *The Fancy Dress Party*, 1947), his only novel set outside Italy. Returning to his native country in 1937, he was soon traveling again, this time to China. Subsequently, he went to the Soviet Union, India, back to China, and to Africa; he wrote about each of these places in his various travelogues.

Moravia's difficulties with the government of Benito Mussolini did not end with the 1930's. Il Duce himself ordered the publication of *The Fancy Dress Party*, but he soon recognized the book's anti-Fascist satire and ordered it withdrawn. *Agostino*, Moravia's next novel, was also banned and not published until Italy was liberated in 1944. Following the collapse of the Fascist government on July 25, 1943, Moravia rejoiced in the *Popolo di Roma*, publishing two articles critical of the former regime. Consequently, when the Germans established another fascist government shortly afterward, Moravia had to flee for his life.

He took refuge in the mountains of Ciociaria, and the nine months he spent there had a deep effect on his writing. As he explained in *The Guardian* (May 31, 1962),

> I had an experience which usually intellectuals don't have. I lived with peasants, ate their food, slept with them, stayed with them all day. So I conceived a great interest in the people, the people who work hard, [and] I tried to write about them.

Heretofore, his characters had been drawn from the middle class, but in the short stories of *Roman Tales*

and More Roman Tales, and in the novels *The Woman of Rome* and *Two Women*, he drew upon his newfound familiarity with peasantry.

In 1944, Moravia initiated his lengthy career as a film critic; he held his position as a reviewer for *L'Espresso*, obtained in 1955, until the late 1980's. The 1950's were, however, not as stable as his employment: His marriage to Elsa Morante dissolving and his affair with Dacia Maraini beginning, Moravia took to travel and the critical reassessment of his concept of the novel. Two works from the 1960's—*La noia* and *L'attenzione* (1965; *The Lie*, 1966)—are the results.

In the 1970's, Moravia's perennial theme of sexual relations, this time presented from the woman's point of view, became tinged by his own commitment to the woman's liberation movement in Italy, as the stories in *Il paradiso*, *Un'altra vita*, and *Boh* reveal. The elements of ambivalence, elusiveness, and perversities of human yearning—and passion—shared by these tales are equally strong in certain works, such as *La cosa e altri racconti* and *L'uomo che guarda* (1985; *The Voyeur*, 1987), produced during the 1980's.

A longtime resident of Rome, Moravia received the honor of being elected to the European Parliament in 1984. Two years later, after the death of his estranged wife, Elsa Morante, he married Carmen Llera. Still deeply engaged in his culture and his writing, Moravia died in his apartment in Rome on September 26, 1990.

ANALYSIS

In his "Frammento d'autobiografia" (fragment of autobiography), Alberto Moravia wrote, "The dominant theme of my work seems to be the relationship between man and reality." Michele, an autobiographical character in *The Indifferent Ones*, elaborates on the difficulty this relationship poses for modern humans:

> Once upon a time . . . men used to know their paths in life from the first to the last step; but now . . . one's head was in a bag; one was in the dark; one was blind. And yet one still had to go somewhere; but where?

That is the question that Moravia's characters repeatedly attempt to answer. Often the correct response is, "Nowhere."

What Moravia said about his first novel in "Recalling *Time of Indifference*" applies equally well to his early short stories, in which he sought to render the "boredom and impatience" of the Roman middle class, feelings to which he himself was subject. Later stories often deal with the lower classes rather than the bourgeoisie; here, too, though, the characters are trapped by their fears, desires, and lack of direction in a world that has lost all sense of values.

On the cover of *L'imbroglio*, Moravia wrote that if the short story "is to rise again from its present state of inferiority, compared with the novel, it must regain its former character, turn back to plot and anecdote, exploit its possibilities for violent dénouements and rapid synthesis, and condense events into natural and concise narrative." In fact, Moravia used plot and action only as a means of revealing character. Many of his most successful stories revolve around mundane activities—a drive into the country, for example, or a picnic at the seashore—and provide only sufficient detail to demonstrate the characters' moods, usually alienation and existential anxiety.

Moravia used the family, or male-female relationships, to express this sense of isolation, showing the inability of men and women to communicate with one another. Arguing in 1961 in "Erotismo e letteratura" (eroticism in literature) that sex is "among the few ways of expression and communion available to man," he thus explains what some regard as his obsession with the erotic. *Erotic Tales* might serve as the title to any collection of his fiction, but sex is a means, not an end, for his characters. Their goal is to cure what Adriana in *The Woman of Rome* describes as "absurd, ineffable anguish," and physical coupling is the only way for them to achieve spiritual union. In other cases, sex serves as an escape. Again, *The Indifferent Ones* explains the motivation of many of Moravia's fictional characters when Carla tells why she will accept her mother's lover as her own:

Virtue would merely throw her back into the arms of boredom and the distasteful trivialities of everyday

habit . . . this present adventure . . . was the only epilogue her old life deserved; afterwards, everything would be new—both life and herself.

"INVERNO DI MALATO"

This desire for escape from the present, whatever the cost, is evident in the story "Inverno di malato" (a sick boy's winter), published in 1935. Girolamo is staying in a sanatorium in the mountains because he is suffering from tuberculosis of the knee bone. A greater affliction, though, is his roommate, Brambilla. This coarse traveling salesman relieves his own boredom by mocking Girolamo as effete. To prove himself, Girolamo decides to seduce Polly, an English girl who has been a sympathetic companion. As so often happens in Moravia's stories, this effort to escape leads only to greater alienation. Girolamo's sexual adventure results in the loss of Polly, and Brambilla still despises him. When Brambilla departs, cured, Girolamo is even more isolated than he was before.

"CRIME AT THE TENNIS CLUB"

Another early story that exposes the ennui and callousness of the middle class is "Delitto al circolo di tennis," published in 1927 and translated in 1960 as "Crime at the Tennis Club." Members of a tennis club invite an aging countess to a party because they know that she will get drunk and entertain them by making herself ridiculous. This indifference to another's dignity and sensibility turns even more vicious when five of the men lure the countess into a room and try to undress her. Her resistance so angers the self-centered Ripandelli that he hits her on the head with an empty champagne bottle and so kills her. Jancovich easily persuades his colleagues to dispose of the body in the river to make the crime look like an accident, and the young men return to the party to become "indistinguishable . . . from the other male dancers." They are indistinguishable not only because of their dress but also because none of the other partiers would have behaved better; all seek an escape from the present, whatever the cost may be.

In technique, these stories show Moravia as the contemporary and admirer of Marcel Proust and James Joyce, using realistic details to expose the unreality of man, whose existence is bounded by and composed of bits of time and the objects he perceives. Thus, Moravia details Ripandelli's "starched shirt-front" and the countess's "black shawl embroidered with birds, flowers and arabesques of every possible color." The story "Fine di una relazione" ("End of a Relationship") notes the furniture in Lorenzo's apartment, which includes "the yellow marble top of the sham Louis XV table in the hall." Such description not only grounds these stories in reality but also frequently reveals character. The countess's behavior is as bizarre as her shawl; Lorenzo's sham table and ground-floor apartment in a "small new building at the far end of a still unfinished by-road" indicate the falseness and incompleteness of the character's life.

L'EPIDEMIA

In the 1940's, Moravia experimented with another form of fiction: Surrealism. Frequently, these pieces are thinly veiled social or political satire. In *L'epidemia*, people's heads begin to give off a putrid odor, but the victims regard the stench as perfume. Moravia here comments on the moral decay that fascism causes. "Primo rapporto sulla terra dell' Inviato speciale della luna" (1944; first report on Earth of the special envoy from the Moon) purports to be an analysis by a lunar delegate on the two races of humans, the rich and the poor. Because this delegate understands nothing about money, he assumes that everyone behaves as he wishes. He therefore concludes that one race prefers "rags to new clothes, . . . cheap furniture to good makes, . . . municipal pools to the sea." Beneath the humor lies the message that the middle class often shares the same attitude as the delegate, for both are equally ignorant of the true nature of the class struggle.

Although Moravia adopted this surrealistic mode to avoid censorship under the Fascists, it also appealed to his playful nature. Much later he reverted to this form. "Celestina," for example, treats a robot as if it were a girl. The title character "grows up" in a middle-class home, but, despite her own brilliance and her parents' social and economic status, she elopes with an old water heater.

In the postwar period, Moravia's writing changed in two important ways. His earlier writings had concentrated on the middle class, and his protagonists were generally effete intellectuals incapable of acting. Their stories were presented in the third person by an omniscient narrator. Without permanently abandoning any of these literary devices, Moravia in *Roman Tales* and *More Roman Tales* allowed his characters to tell their own stories. The use of the first person allowed Moravia to capture more fully the language of the characters and to demonstrate the limited vision that the individual possesses, thereby indicating that omniscience is too great a fiction even for fiction.

The other change lies in the social class that Moravia turned to consider. As he said in an interview with the *Paris Review* in 1958, "I've tried in these stories . . . to depict the life of the subproletariat and the très petite bourgeoisie in a period just after the last war."

The 130 stories collected in these two volumes first appeared in the Milan daily *Corriere della sera* beginning in 1952. This form of publication imposed a brevity and concentration upon these pieces. Yet the sparseness of detail mirrors well the empty lives of the characters and concentrates the reader's attention upon them: A length of some six pages allows for no distractions. While a lesser writer might find this format confining and the large number of stories exhausting, Moravia thrived on the challenge, and these two books contain some of his best stories.

"THE LORRY DRIVER"

Though the form and characters differ from Moravia's earlier work, the theme does not. Like their prewar bourgeois counterparts, the bartenders, barbers, and dishwashers are trapped in a meaningless world. Typical is the narrator of "Il camionista" ("The Lorry Driver"), who, with his partner, Palombi, regularly drives between Naples and Rome. On one of their runs, they pick up an attractive hitchhiker, Italia. She becomes a frequent passenger, and the narrator quickly falls in love with her. On their drives, he puts one arm around Italia, and they exchange "mere trifles and jokes and lovers' talk." Meanwhile, Palombi "either . . . noticed nothing or . . . pretended not to notice."

One night, the drivers have a minor accident. When they enter a café to get help, they find Italia cleaning up; they also learn that she has a lover, or husband, who is a seafaring hunchback. This discovery is one of two that the narrator makes that night. On the way back to Rome, Palombi tells him, "We were more or less engaged." The narrator correctly observes that "Italia had fooled us both," but the partners have also deceived each other. Though all three sat so close together in the cab of the truck, no one understood the others; their communication indeed consisted of trifles. At the end of the story the two drivers separate, thus confirming the spiritual isolation that had existed all along.

THE FETISH

The Fetish, which followed the two collections of Roman stories, returns to third-person accounts of the middle class. The title story reveals one of Moravia's fictional devices, in which a seemingly insignificant event such as a dream at the beginning of a narrative serves as a trenchant commentary on the action that follows. In this case, as Guido waits for the rest of his family to get ready for a picnic, he puts a disc on the phonograph. The machine malfunctions, ruining the record; when Guido tries a second time, the record player works flawlessly.

By now, the family is ready, and as Guido drives he tells about this unusual experience. Jokingly, his wife responds, "Obviously, machines sometimes get fed up with being machines and want to prove that they're not." Nearing the lake that is to be their picnic site, Guido suddenly gets the urge to drive the car off a cliff into the water and so kill himself, his wife, and his two children. He drives off the road but lands in a meadow, an ideal spot for having lunch. Like the record player, Guido had momentarily malfunctioned. He had wanted to assert his individuality, to demonstrate that he is not a machine. In the end, though, he returns to being the predictable husband and father he has always been, unable to escape.

"THE MISANTHROPE"

"Il misantropo" ("The Misanthrope") from this collection again stresses a character's entrapment. Another Guido sets off with an acquaintance, Cesare, for a day at the Lagi di Vico. Cesare has provided a date for each of them, but Guido soon tires of his and secretly asks Cesare to trade. His companion agrees, but Guido quickly tires of her, too, and asks to sit beside Cesare. By the time they reach their destination, Guido hates him as well. As they walk to the restaurant overlooking the lake, he sees his reflection in the water and feels such disgust that he throws a stick at it. Once more characters have failed to communicate; Guido is alienated even from himself.

Command and I Will Obey You and *Paradise and Other Stories* serve as companion volumes, the former told by first-person male narrators, the latter by women. The social world of the characters varies: In *Command and I Will Obey You*, Tullio, from the story "Tu mi conosci, Carlo" ("You Know Me, Carlo"), is a beggar; the narrator of "Le cose che crescono" ("The Things That Grow") is a lawyer; and the protagonist of "La cognata" ("The Sister-in-law") is a teacher. Similarly, in *Paradise and Other Stories*, some women are married to rich husbands, others are middle class, and some, such as the protagonist in "L'immaginazione" ("Imagination"), are impoverished. Whatever their social class, though, they are alienated and feel reduced to machinery, like Guido in "The Fetish."

A prominent image expressing this condition is the double; like objects, people in the modern world are mass-produced rather than individual. In "Doppioni" ("Doubles"), a student thinks about taking a second apartment in another part of town. He discovers that this place exactly resembles the first, the second landlady has the same name and appearance as the first, and her daughter, who bears the same name as the daughter of his present landlady, behaves exactly like her counterpart. In "Tipo medio" ("A Middling Type"), the narrator regards his apartment, his furnishings, and himself as unique. A flower girl whom he lures to his apartment disabuses him, telling him that everything, even the device he used to attract her in the first place, is identical to the behavior and possessions of the previous occupant.

In his 1941 essay "L'uomo e il personaggio" ("The Man and the Character"), Moravia had remarked, "Modern man seems a mere cipher within mass groupings which are amongst the most formidable humanity has ever known." The narrator of "Doubles" repeats this observation: "We're identical with millions of other people in the world."

The idea of mass-produced humanity informs *Paradise and Other Stories* as well. In "I prodotti" ("Products"), the narrator sees herself as a producer of various kinds of love, such as maternal or conjugal. Even when she sits on her husband's lap, kisses him, or jokes with him, she feels no emotions. Instead, she is like a machine or robot. Hence, when she learns of her husband's infidelity, she remains unmoved, simply deciding to produce one item more—murder. "I am a pretty young woman, wife of a rich young man," the narrator says in "Venduta e comprata" ("Bought and Sold"). Her husband, too, has been unfaithful, indicating that in Moravia's vision of the modern world, fidelity is lacking because the bonds between friends, lovers, and spouses have vanished. Each character is trapped within himself, unable to connect meaningfully and permanently with anyone else. In this story, the woman does not contemplate murder, though; she seeks instead something more fundamental than revenge: herself. Viewing herself as a beautiful object that has been discarded by her husband, she goes into the country each Sunday and pretends to be a prostitute. After a man picks her up, she first takes his money. Then, just as he is about to have sex with her, she feigns illness and returns his payment. In this obsessive way, she tries to buy herself back, selling herself to regain her selfhood.

Moravia's subsequent short fiction has continued to explore questions of sex, interpersonal relations, and humans' quest for self-expression "within mass groupings."

The title story of *Erotic Tales* again considers the theme of entrapment; here Diana cannot free herself from her cruel lesbian lover. In "La cintura" ("The Belt"), the female narrator had once been struck by her father when she resisted his efforts to save her from drowning. That experience has turned her into a masochist, so the only way she can relate to her husband is to anger him until he beats her. "Il diavolo va e viene" ("The Devil Comes and Goes") expresses a recurring theme in this and other books of Moravia's

when the Devil says, "Hell isn't suffering more; it's repeating what's already been done."

That is indeed the hell of modern life that Moravia depicts. Characters repeat what they or others have already done. They may think that they are escaping the past, that through violence or love they are breaking out of the circle of repetition, but the reader sees their mistake. Moravia's clinical prose never comments on the plight of humans; it merely portrays it. In "Recalling *Time of Indifference*," Moravia observed that he had wanted to write tragedy, plays that involved "crime, bloody and insoluble conflict, passion, violence." Although making his reputation as a writer of understated fiction rather than of melodramatic plays, in one sense he remained true to that early ambition. His stories and novels do in fact reveal the tragedy of modern humans, trapped within themselves with no way of finding the exit, if indeed an exit exists.

OTHER MAJOR WORKS

LONG FICTION: *Gli indifferenti*, 1929 (*The Indifferent Ones*, 1932; also as *The Time of Indifference*, 1953); *Le ambizioni sbagliate*, 1935 (*The Wheel of Fortune*, 1937; also as *Mistaken Ambitions*, 1965); *La mascherata*, 1941 (*The Fancy Dress Party*, 1947); *Agostino*, 1944 (English translation, 1947); *La romana*, 1947 (*The Woman of Rome*, 1949); *La disubbidienza*, 1948 (*Two Adolescents*, 1950; also as *Disobedience*, 1950); *L'amore coniugale*, 1949 (*Conjugal Love*, 1951); *Il conformista*, 1951 (*The Conformist*, 1952); *Il disprezzo*, 1954 (*A Ghost at Noon*, 1955); *La ciociara*, 1957 (*Two Women*, 1958); *La noia*, 1960 (*The Empty Canvas*, 1961); *L'attenzione*, 1965 (*The Lie*, 1966); *Io e lui*, 1971 (*Two: A Phallic Novel*, 1972); *La vita interiore*, 1978 (*Time of Desecration*, 1980); *1934*, 1982 (English translation, 1983); *L'uomo che guarda*, 1985 (*The Voyeur*, 1987); *Il viaggio a Roma*, 1988 (*Journey to Rome*, 1990).

PLAYS: *Gli indifferenti*, pr., pb. 1948; *La mascherata*, pr. 1954; *Beatrice Cenci*, pr. 1955 (English translation, 1965); *Teatro*, pb. 1958, 1976; *Il mondo è quello che è*, pr., pb. 1966; *Il dio Kurt*, pb. 1968; *La vita è gioco*, pb. 1969; *L'angelo dell' informazione e altri testi teatrali*, pb. 1986.

NONFICTION: *Un mese in U.R.S.S.*, 1958 (travel sketch); *Saggi italiani del 1959*, 1960; *Un'idea dell'India*, 1962 (travel sketch); *L'uomo come fine e altri saggi*, 1964 (*Man as an End: A Defence of Humanism, Literary, Social and Political Essays*, 1965); *La rivoluzione culturale in Cina*, 1967 (travel sketch; *The Red Book and the Great Wall*, 1968); *A quale tribù appartieni?*, 1972 (travel sketch; *Which Tribe Do You Belong To?*, 1974); *Impegno controvoglia: Saggi, articoli, interviste*, 1980; *Lettere dal Sahara*, 1981; *L'inverno nucleare*, 1986; *Passeggiate africane*, 1987.

CHILDREN'S LITERATURE: *Tre storie della preistoria*, 1977; *Quando Ba Lena era tanto piccola*, 1978; *Un miliardo di anni fa*, 1979; *Cosma e i briganti*, 1980; *Cama Leonte diventò verde lilla blu*, 1981; *Storie della preistoria*, 1982.

BIBLIOGRAPHY

Aillaud, Charlotte. "A Visit with Italy's Man of Letters." *Architectural Digest* 45 (March, 1988): 210. Discusses Moravia's childhood, during which he read extensively while convalescing from tuberculosis; Moravia contends he would like to have been a painter because painting is "closer to reality than writing."

Dego, Giuliano. *Writers and Critics: Moravia*. New York: Barnes & Noble Books, 1967. A valuable overview of Moravia's early production, with discussion centering on his naturalistic presentation, his remarkable descriptive ability, his major theme of alienation, and his ceaseless exploration of crisis.

Haberman, Clyde. "Obituary." *The New York Times*, September 27, 1990, p. B10. A brief but useful retrospective of Moravia's life and work. Includes many quotes from the author and from those, such as the president of Italy, who have long appreciated his fiction.

Heiney, Donald. *Three Italian Novelists: Moravia, Pavese, Vittorini*. Ann Arbor: University of Michigan Press, 1968. Concentrates on Moravia as creator and craftsman, not as political thinker, psychologist, sociologist, or philosopher. Contains some discussion of characters, themes, and techniques in the short stories, which Heiney considers "models" of the novels. Notes, bibliography, index.

Kozma, Janice M. *The Architecture of Imagery in Alberto Moravia's Fiction*. Chapel Hill: University of North Carolina Press, 1993. A monograph in the North Carolina Studies in the Romance Languages and Literatures series (no. 244). Kozma carefully examines how Moravia organizes his imagery into simple and complex forms, and into "discrete and seemingly discrete" categories. A set of appendices analyzes the imagery of women, men, war, nature, architecture, machines, the body, food, and sex. Includes a bibliography.

Lewis, R. W. B. "Alberto Moravia: Eros and Existence." In *From "Verismo" to Experimentalism*. Bloomington: Indiana University Press, 1969. Lewis, describing Moravia as a minor master of the strategy of "*artistic* conversion, of the transformation of one set of values into another," succinctly analyzes the "sexualization" of objects, values, and relationships in Moravia's fiction.

Paterson, Harriet. "Mourning the Maestros." *The Independent*, July 7, 1991, p. 26. A tribute to, and discussion of, four of Italy's late, great postwar authors. Notes that the deaths of Moravia, Italo Calvino, Primo Levi, and Leonardo Sciascia signal the end of a generation who stood for the new left-wing ideal in Italy; with Moravia's death, Paterson asserts there is no one left to make angry judgments in the country.

Peterson, Thomas E. *Alberto Moravia*. New York: Twayne, 1996. Part of Twayne's World Authors series, this volume offers an excellent introduction to Moravia's life and works.

Rebay, Luciano. *Alberto Moravia*. New York: Columbia University Press, 1970. This very abbreviated introduction to Moravia's life and novels offers insight into the short stories as well; Rebay emphasizes that Moravia gladly accepted the charge of being "monotonous" in his concentration on tragic human emptiness, spiritual crisis, and sex. Supplemented by a bibliography.

Ross, Joan, and Donald Freed. *The Existentialism of Alberto Moravia*. Carbondale: Southern Illinois

University Press, 1972. Placing Moravia in the context of the literature and philosophy of existentialism, this thoroughly conducted analysis underscores the considerable significance of the concepts of love, suffering, and reality within this broader framework. Complemented by notes and an index.

Schifano, Jean-Noel. "A Moravian Perspective." *World Press Review* 32 (August, 1985): 59-60. In this interview, Moravia discusses his collection of stories entitled *The Thing*, as well as his novel and play; also discusses the Catholic Church, Rome, and travel.

Weaver, William. "Roman Candle." *The New York Review of Books* 45 (June 25, 1998): 49-52. Discusses the life and works of Moravia, whom Weaver befriended for four decades; notes that Moravia claimed the determining factors in his life were his aversion to Fascism and a childhood illness that denied him both a normal adolescence and a traditional education; notes how the antifascist stance and sexual candor of his novels antagonized both the church and the wartime government.

Wood, Sharon. *Woman as Object: Language and Gender in the Work of Alberto Moravia*. London: Pluto, 1990. Cogent and sensitive, this excellent study explores the relationship of language to sex and power, and to experience—both gender bound and intimately individual—in Moravia's work. The author concludes that Moravia's attempts at representing experience from the female perspective ultimately fail. Includes excellent, extensive notes, a bibliography, and an index.

Joseph Rosenblum, updated by Terri Frongia

WRIGHT MORRIS

Born: Central City, Nebraska; January 6, 1910
Died: Mill Valley, California; April 26, 1998

PRINCIPAL SHORT FICTION
Green Grass, Blue Sky, White House, 1970
Here Is Einbaum, 1973
The Cat's Meow, 1975
Real Losses, Imaginary Gains, 1976
Collected Stories: 1948-1986, 1986

OTHER LITERARY FORMS

In a career that began in 1942, Wright Morris has published everything but plays and poems. Known primarily as a novelist, he is also a photographer and has created books of photographs such as *The Inhabitants* (1946), with accompanying text, which present his view of the artifacts of American lives. He has even incorporated his photographs into a novel, *The Home Place* (1948). He is an essayist, offering his interpretations of literature and culture in general in works such as *The Territory Ahead* (1958, 1963). The first fifty years of Morris's life are examined in *A Cloak of Light: Writing My Life* (1985). He has also published *Time Pieces: Photographs, Writing, and Memory* (1989), a nonfiction work.

ACHIEVEMENTS

Though often compared to Midwestern writers such as Sherwood Anderson and Willa Cather, Wright Morris is hardly a mere regionalist. He has written about all sections of the United States and many parts of Mexico and Europe. What most distinguishes his fiction is a distinctly original American writing style rooted in the vernacular and a consistently amused response to the efforts of his characters to cope with the daily reality of an increasingly complex world. Frequently categorized as unfairly unheralded, Morris has been given many honors by the literary establishment. *The Field of Vision* (1956) received the National Book Award, and *Plains Song*, for Female Voices* (1980) won the American Book Award. He was elected to the National Institute of Arts and Letters and the American Academy of Arts and Sciences in 1970 and was made an honorary fellow of the Modern Language Association in 1975 and a senior fellow of the National Endowment for the Humanities in 1976. He won the Western Literature Association's Distinguished Achievement Award in 1979 and the Robert Kirsch Award of *The Los Angeles Times* in 1981. Morris's most notable achievement is the consistent quality of his writing. He is one of the few American authors to have written as well after he turned fifty as he did before.

BIOGRAPHY

Wright Marion Morris was born in Central City, Nebraska, on January 6, 1910. His mother, Ethel Grace (Osborn), died six days after his birth, and his father, William Henry Morris, reared his son (mostly alone) in rural Nebraska, Omaha, and Chicago. His father's efforts to find a new mother for Morris and to make a fortune in the egg business were rewarded with only limited success.

Between 1925 and 1930, Morris worked on a farm in Texas with his uncle. He later crossed the country in several run-down cars and lived in Chicago with his father, whose ill-fated enterprises encouraged Morris's early financial and emotional independence and propelled him into his long and productive writing career.

After briefly attending the City College of Chicago and Pacific Union College, Morris transferred to Pomona College and remained there from 1930 to 1933. In 1933, Morris traveled to Europe, where he remained for one year. He married Mary Ellen Finfrock in 1934. He supported himself by teaching drawing and swimming, while he learned the arts of fiction-writing and photography. After he had published several novels, Morris taught at several universities, including Princeton University, Sarah Lawrence College, Swarthmore College, and others. Divorced in 1961, Morris married Josephine Kantor that same year. He was a professor of English at San Francisco State University from 1962 until his retirement in 1975.

Wright Morris (Jo Morris)

In 1992, Morris, then in his eighties, told an interviewer he had ceased writing. Only two more stories were published after the definitive *Collected Stories: 1948-1986*. One was "Uno Más" (one more), appearing in *The New Yorker* (February 6, 1989). The other was "What's New, Love?" (about a waitress with a secret crush on a famous movie star who frequents her coffee shop), published in *American Short Fiction*.

ANALYSIS

Wright Morris's novels, to a large extent, are about what it means to be American. They examine the unrelenting grasp of the American Dream and the often bizarre ways in which people attempt to live up to this ideal, which they only vaguely understand. His stories are more concerned with the everyday details of life, though these may be bizarre as well. They are stories of character and mood more than plot or theme, written in a style which manages to be distinctive without calling attention to itself.

While the majority of his novels have Nebraska and California as their settings, Morris's short fiction roams all over the United States and Europe, presenting characters with extremely varied social, economic, educational, and ethnic backgrounds. Morris wrote stories sporadically for the first quarter century of his career, taking up the form in earnest only in 1969. Unusual among American writers for having refined his short-story skills after becoming firmly established as a novelist, he has produced his best stories since turning seventy.

These stories look at the quiet side of the emotional turmoil people put themselves through each day. Such themes as the inability to communicate with or understand or feel for one another, loneliness, and the failure of relationships are presented without nostalgia for some simpler past, with little sentimentality or anger. Morris's objective stance toward the world of his characters creates a comic, compassionate, quirkily individualistic body of short fiction.

"THE RAM IN THE THICKET"

"The Ram in the Thicket," Morris's first published and best-known story, is an early version of what became the first two chapters of *Man and Boy* (1951), but it stands on its own as a memorable portrait of one of Morris's frequent subjects in his early fiction: a weak husband in the grasp of a domineering wife. Roger Ormsby and his wife, known as Mother, are depicted preparing to go to the christening of the SS *Ormsby*, named for their only child, Virgil, missing in action during World War II.

The need to conceal emotions characterizes Ormsby and Mother, neither of whom allows the other to guess how they feel about their son's death. Although hearing that Virgil has been killed seems strangely "natural" to his father, Ormsby has "not been prepared to feel what he felt. Mother need never know it unless he slipped up and talked in his sleep." Mother, without saying so, blames Ormsby for the boy's death, since he gave Virgil an air rifle years earlier, thereby conditioning him for war. Since that time, she has considered them united against her, calling them *they* or *you* plural as if they were twin halves of a conspiracy: "Though the boy had been gone two years he still felt him *there*, right beside him, when Mother said *you*."

From the time of the air rifle, both father and son felt greater emotional distance from Mother, Virgil spending as much time as possible out-of-doors, Ormsby seeking solitude with his pipe in the basement. Once, Ormsby is surprised to find his son in his refuge, and the experience becomes the closest they ever share: "For two, maybe three minutes, there in the dark, they had been what Mother called them, they were *they*—and they were there in the basement because they were so much alike." When Ormsby receives the telegram he knows will tell him of Virgil's death, he takes it to the basement to read.

Mother is nationally prominent for her interest in bird-watching and is constantly involved in that activity, the League of Women Voters, and other organizations and causes. She understands wildlife and politics better than she does those closest to her. She enjoys saying, in jest, that she prefers shoes to men but is actually truthful, since clothing is less complicated than people. Causes are her shelter as much as the basement is her husband's. Yet neither character is being held up to ridicule; the typical Morris character looks for excuses to hide his feelings, for ways of ignoring failures of communication.

The characters in "The Ram in the Thicket" could easily be comical caricatures, but Morris is not concerned with types. His creations come alive through their idiosyncrasies, such as the Oriental rug Mother puts in the bathroom and the leftovers she refuses to throw away, carefully storing them in jars in the icebox, then forgetting about them, leaving Ormsby, when the contents have become moldy, to bury them behind the garage. Such details help create a sense of ordinary lives closely observed.

"THE SAFE PLACE"

"The Safe Place" is another Morris story incorporated into his longer fiction, appearing in a different form in *Ceremony in Lone Tree* (1960); it also has characters and situations resembling those in the short novel *War Games* (written in 1951-1952 but not published until 1972). A retired army colonel lives a dull Brooklyn existence with his wife until he is hit by a pie truck and almost killed. The cynical colonel spends his recovery in the hospital contemplating how life is full of senseless violence which ceaselessly swoops down upon the unsuspecting and innocent: "Life, to put it simply, was a battleground." He decides that the only way to avoid the world's dangers and foolishness is to stay in bed—"the only safe place." In many ways, the colonel's view of the absurd world outside the hospital foreshadows that in Joseph Heller's death-obsessed *Catch-22* (1961).

The colonel becomes interested in another patient, Hyman Kopfman, who has had an arm and a leg amputated because of a blood ailment. When Kopfman identifies the problem in his body as America, the colonel senses a kinship between them: "What Hyman Kopfman knew was that the world was killing him." While the colonel is reserved, Kopfman enjoys talking about himself—apparently to himself—"as if he were somebody else." The colonel listens in fascination to Kopfman's account of how his family left Vienna for Chicago when he was a boy, of how Kopfman, as he grew, began wearing his small father's clothes while his brother Paul wore their mother's old skirt and peasant blouse. The boys rarely left their apartment, making it into a self-contained world, a safe place. Below their apartment was another safe place: a walled garden where blind people came to walk.

The colonel decides that Kopfman's life has always been rather hopeless and that this hopelessness makes him lovable. That he is not aware of how hopeless he is touches the colonel even more. The colonel realizes that all Kopfman has ever wanted is to lead "the useless sort of life" that he has himself had. Kopfman's case inspires the colonel to get well despite having nothing to live for, while Kopfman, with his hunger for life, gets worse.

"The Safe Place" displays some of the common concerns of Morris's fiction. His characters always seem to be seeking safe places, as with Ormsby's basement, which might not seem to be havens to others. Man survives in this absurd, violent world by tricking himself into believing that he has found a refuge, whether it be a place, a person, a job, a role in society, or a philosophy. "The Safe Place" is also one of several Morris stories contrasting American and European views of life; others include "The Character of the Lover," "Drrdla," "Fiona," "Here Is Einbaum," "In Another Country," "The Customs of the Country," and "Things That Matter." Whether Europeans in America or Americans in Europe, these characters always experience a feeling of dislocation.

Pets are central to Morris's delineation of character. Cats, dogs, and birds appear in the majority of his stories to help underscore certain facets of the humans around them, humans who belong to the pets more than vice versa. Morris's use of animals ranges from the poignant, as in "Victrola," in which an elderly man's dog dies, to the comic, as when a man develops an affection for his neighbors' leghorn pullet in "Fellow Creatures."

Because his characters are independent and eccentric yet crave attention and love, it is appropriate that several Morris stories involve cats. The stray feline in "The Cat in the Picture" causes a marriage to break up. "Drrdla" explores how cats and women are alike, as a husband becomes attached to another stray, who rejects him for the man's unfaithful wife. "The Cat's Meow" is one of Morris's most effective humorous stories. A writer and his seventeen-pound cat are virtually inseparable, the cat lying on the man's desk during the four hours he writes each day: "The cat faces him, his eyes blinking in the desk light, and the look he gives Morgan, and Morgan returns, is not something to be lightly dealt with, or even when soberly and thoughtfully dealt with, put into words." Morris's animals and humans share this enigmatic quality.

"GLIMPSE INTO ANOTHER COUNTRY"

With its whimsical acceptance of the unusual, the unexpected, and the inexplicable, "Glimpse into Another Country" is most representative of Morris's later stories. On the plane from San Francisco to New York, Hazlitt, an elderly academic, is treated rudely by Mrs. Thayer, a fellow passenger, when he tries to make casual conversation with her and her husband. Soon after he arrives in Manhattan, Hazlitt goes to Bloomingdale's Department Store, seeing Mrs. Thayer on the way. In Bloomingdale's, he loses his driver's license and, in a sense, his identity, when the store is closed because of a bomb threat while a clerk is having his check approved.

The next day, he learns from a medical specialist that the health problem about which he has been worried is nonexistent. Considering himself "free of a nameless burden," Hazlitt returns to Bloomingdale's to retrieve his driver's license and impulsively buys an expensive strand of pearls to give to his wife. He cannot afford the gift, but "writing the numbers, spelling the sum out gave him a tingling sense of exhilaration."

Going to the Metropolitan Museum of Art, Hazlitt sees the ubiquitous Mrs. Thayer in the gift shop. In the museum's basement rest room, a group of boys, seemingly under the influence of drugs, force him to give them the pearls. He returns to the gift shop for an Etruscan pin, the type of gift his wife will consider "sensible." From a bus outside, Mrs. Thayer waves to him, her now-friendly eyes giving him "all the assurances he needed."

Hazlitt, as opposed to the colonel in "The Safe Place," is not perturbed by these events, being slightly bemused by them. Unlike the stereotypical elderly person, Hazlitt also accepts the inevitability of change, as when he discovers that the museum's once-striking Fountain Court lunchroom has been renovated into blandness. More important are the usual Morris concerns, such as the protagonist's inability to communicate with either the relatively nonthreatening Thayers or the drugged youths. In the taxi from the airport, Hazlitt wants "to chat a bit with the driver, but the Plexiglas barrier between them seemed intimidating."

"Glimpse into Another Country" is primarily a comic view of contemporary life. Hazlitt, like many Morris characters, travels through life with an amused tolerance and detachment, refusing to take anything seriously since so many others are willing to assume that burden for him. The unusual and the everyday merge as he moves about as if in a dream. He sees a television picture of a milling crowd in India indifferently passing by dead or sleeping bodies: "The film gave Hazlitt a glimpse into a strange country where the quick and the dormant were accustomed to mingle. Perhaps . . . it was not the walkers but the sleepers who would range the farthest in their travels." For the Hazlitts of the world, so-called real life is carried on with even less logic than a dream.

"THE ORIGIN OF SADNESS"

With its characters stoically enduring the pains of emotional isolation on the Plains, "The Origin of Sadness" is the Morris story most like his novels, particularly recalling *The Works of Love* (1952). Growing up in Osborn County, Kansas, shy, brooding, self-absorbed Schuler enjoys playing with an Indian companion because they do not have to talk much. He has as a pet a coyote pup, freed from a steel trap, who treats everyone else as an enemy. Schuler is expected to become a country doctor like his late father but is more interested in nature and becomes a paleontologist. Schuler's temperament is suited to an obsession with the remains of the distant past: "He did not find the immediate and shifting flux of time present real at all." As such, he is one of the few Morris characters with some understanding of his sense of displacement.

He marries one of his students, Doreen Oakum, who is part Cherokee, because she shares "both his passion for bones and his talent for silence." Their life becomes "a matter of shared but secret communications." Typically for a Morris couple, there is little romance in their marriage. Doreen seems to feel more strongly about her parrot than her husband. Yet what Schuler loves about her is "her detachment from the world that hummed and buzzed around her, her attachment to the invisible world within her."

Doreen's sudden death drives Schuler back to his birthplace as he experiences despair for the first time. As a snowstorm begins, Schuler, an Ice Age expert, makes his way to the arroyo where he had freed the coyote and discovers it to be full of tiny fossils, seemingly undisturbed since his last visit years before. He is concerned that he must bring destruction to the ageless setting by climbing the arroyo. His obsession with the past, his despair at the present, and the innocence of his youth converge as he falls, breaks his hip, and calmly lies awaiting an icy death. His final discovery is that the "deep freeze of all freezes was time itself." By understanding the past and its significance for the present, Schuler has sought to arrest time, and at the end, he recognizes the futility of his efforts.

During a public lecture, Schuler is once asked what he is really seeking; he replies, "What interests me is the origin of sadness." This search is similar to what motivates Morris as he takes ordinary people and situations and peels back the surface layers to uncover the human elements—or their absence—underneath. Morris's stories are unsentimental yet strangely moving, unusually amusing explorations into what it means to be human in the twentieth century.

"UNO MÁS"

Many of Morris's best short stories originally appeared in the nation's most prestigious literary magazine, *The New Yorker*. The title "Uno Más" might be taken to have the double meaning of a farewell to his readers. It concerns the problems of a California couple who have hired Maria, an illiterate Indian immigrant from Oaxaca, Mexico, as an all-around cook, maid, and babysitter for their three small children. The story owes its broader implications to the fact that the United States is experiencing a deluge of immigration from south of the border, with the resulting impact on every aspect of American life, including language. The youngest family member becomes so strongly attached to Maria that his mother and father become alarmed: "Once Peanuts clutched the rope of Maria's braids, he would not let go. He only likes the food she prepares for him. He wants only Maria to bathe and dress him. He only wants to speak Spanish." His conventional middle-class parents fear they are losing their son. They were pleased that he was learning Spanish but fear he is in danger of becoming a non-English-speaking alien in his own country. The Drysdales themselves have become attached to Maria, who is so honest, devoted, industrious, and inexpensive. They do not have the heart to fire her but think they have found the solution when they recommend her to the wife of a successful avocado rancher who has three hellcat tomboys to raise and would like her daughters to grow up with Spanish as their second language. Mr. Drysdale railroads Maria on the pretext of taking her to a Mexican movie. He drives for five hours to the Fresno ranch and dumps her on

her new family. "Drysdale did not generally consider the Third World to be his personal problem, but the settling of Maria—into one place or another—gave him the disquiet of a winner's shame."

Peanuts is desolate. All the physical and psychological problems he exhibited before Maria's arrival reappear. The panicked parents capitulate. Drysdale drives all the way back to Central California and returns exhausted after a nonstop round-trip. Maria, who has not tried to understand the changes these "gringos" have made in her life, calmly goes to the kitchen and washes the dishes stacked in the sink. Mrs. Drysdale, pregnant with the couple's fourth child, gives in to the inevitable. The whole family is obviously destined to succumb to the influence of a culture more ancient, and in some respects more humane, than their own.

Morris's short stories have a distinctive touch, a characteristic humanity and wisdom. They deal compassionately and humorously with seemingly incidental events in the lives of ordinary people which reflect in microcosm the growing complexity of the greater world.

OTHER MAJOR WORKS

LONG FICTION: *My Uncle Dudley*, 1942; *The Man Who Was There*, 1945; *The Home Place*, 1948; *The World in the Attic*, 1949; *Man and Boy*, 1951; *The Works of Love*, 1952; *The Deep Sleep*, 1953; *The Huge Season*, 1954; *The Field of Vision*, 1956; *Love Among the Cannibals*, 1957; *Ceremony in Lone Tree*, 1960; *What a Way to Go*, 1962; *Cause for Wonder*, 1963; *One Day*, 1965; *In Orbit*, 1967; *Fire Sermon*, 1971; *War Games*, 1972; *A Life*, 1973; *The Fork River Space Project*, 1977; *Plains Song, for Female Voices*, 1980.

NONFICTION: *The Inhabitants*, 1946; *The Territory Ahead*, 1958, 1963; *A Bill of Rites, a Bill of Wrongs, a Bill of Goods*, 1968; *God's Country and My People*, 1968; *Love Affair: A Venetian Journal*, 1972; *About Fiction: Reverent Reflections on the Nature of Fiction with Irreverent Observations on Writers, Readers, and Other Abuses*, 1975; *Wright Morris: Structures and Artifacts, Photographs, 1933-1954*, 1975; *Earthly Delights, Unearthly Adornments:*

American Writers as Image-Makers, 1978; *Will's Boy*, 1981; *Photographs and Words*, 1982; *Picture America*, 1982; *Solo: An American Dreamer in Europe, 1933-1934*, 1983; *A Cloak of Light: Writing My Life*, 1985; *Time Pieces: Photographs, Writing, and Memory*, 1989.

MISCELLANEOUS: *Wright Morris: A Reader*, 1970.

BIBLIOGRAPHY

Bird, Roy K. *Wright Morris: Memory and Imagination*. New York: Peter Lang, 1985. An excellent appraisal of self-consciousness in Morris's fiction. Bird moves from a discussion of Morris's use of the past, namely the author's ambivalence toward it, to an analysis of his linguistic technique. The final chapter contains a detailed analysis of *The Fork River Space Project* and *Plains Song, for Female Voices*. Contains a bibliography.

Booth, Wayne C. "The Shaping of Prophecy: Craft and Idea in the Novels of Wright Morris." *American Scholar* 31 (1962): 608-626. An excellent reappraisal of Morris's work, focusing on *Love Among the Cannibals, The Territory Ahead*, and *Ceremony in Lone Tree*. Booth argues that Morris's fiction is structured around a distinction between the everyday time-bound world of "reality" and a more timeless world of platonic reality.

Crump, G. B. *The Novels of Wright Morris: A Critical Interpretation*. Lincoln: University of Nebraska Press, 1978. In an effort to demonstrate Morris's importance and clarify his contribution to modern fiction, Crump begins his study by addressing the major critical positions toward Morris's writing, thus isolating significant features of the author's work. Then he offers a new theoretical groundwork for criticizing the author's fiction: a major dualism between the real and the ideal.

Hamilton, James. "Wright Morris and the American Century." *Poets and Writers* 25 (November/December, 1997): 23-31. In this extended interview, Morris discusses his decision to stop writing, his feelings about America, and his family.

Hollander, John. "The Figure on the Page: Words and Images in Wright Morris's *The Home Place*." *Yale Journal of Criticism* 9 (Spring, 1996): 93-108. Discusses how Morris's *The Home Place* mixes text and photographs; examines the work's original way of presenting word and image in a mode that appears to mix ekphrasis and illustration.

Howard, Leon. *Wright Morris*. Minneapolis: University of Minnesota Press, 1968. In this brief but insightful pamphlet surveying Morris's novels, Howard asserts that no other American novelist has approached Morris in the variety and shaping of the raw materials. According to Howard, the novelist's unique medium is the high seriousness of brilliant comedy in which the absurd is laid bare with neither bitterness nor hope.

Knoll, Robert E., ed. *Conversations with Wright Morris: Critical Views and Responses*. Lincoln: University of Nebraska Press, 1977. This collection of lectures, interviews, critical essays, and photographs is one of the best sources of information about Morris and his work for the general reader. Much is illuminated in the discussions of Morris the novelist and Morris the photographer. Extensive bibliography.

Madden, David. *Wright Morris*. New York: Twayne, 1964. This work assumes little or no prior knowledge of Morris's writing. Its main purpose is to examine each of Morris's novels (ending with *Cause for Wonder*) in quasi-chronological order so that the reader might see how the author's themes and methods develop from novel to novel. Madden also discusses characterization and the influence of setting (the Midwest) on Morris's work. Bibliography of primary and secondary sources.

Morris, Wright. *A Cloak of Light: Writing My Life*. New York: Harper & Row, 1985. In this extremely informative and insightful autobiography, Morris sheds light not only on the formation of his character but also on his writing. Among other things, Morris discusses his faculty of image-making or what he calls time retrieval—a faculty that has served him well both as a photographer and as a writer.

Trachtenberg, Alan. "Wright Morris's 'Photo-Texts.'" *Yale Journal of Criticism* 9 (Spring, 1996): 109-

119. Discusses Morris's mixing of words and photographs in three works of fiction in which image and text stand beside each other in quite unexpected ways; shows how each work addresses

similar questions about the role of images in the making of fiction.

Michael Adams, updated by
Genevieve Slomski and Bill Delaney

EZEKIEL MPHAHLELE

Born: Marabastad township, Pretoria, South Africa; December 17, 1919

PRINCIPAL SHORT FICTION

Man Must Live, and Other Stories, 1946
The Living and Dead, and Other Stories, 1961
In Corner B, 1967
The Unbroken Song: Selected Writings of Es'kia Mphahlele, 1981
Renewal Time, 1988

OTHER LITERARY FORMS

Ezekiel Mphahlele's 1962 collection of essays, *The African Image*, was an important early discussion of the "African personality." His autobiography was published in two volumes, *Down Second Avenue* (1959) and *Afrika My Music: An Autobiography* (1984), and brought international attention to the oppression of blacks in South Africa. He has edited or coedited important volumes, including the landmark anthology *African Writing Today* (1967), *Perspectives on South African English Literature* (1992), and *Seasons Come to Pass: A Poetry Anthology for Southern African Students* (1994).

ACHIEVEMENTS

Ezekiel Mphahlele is widely considered the most significant black South African writer of the twentieth century and the most balanced critic of African literature. His autobiographical novel *The Wanderers* (1971) was awarded the *African Arts* magazine prize in 1972. He received a Carnegie Foundation grant in 1980 and has been awarded honorary doctoral degrees from the University of Pennsylvania, the Uni-

versity of Natal at Pietermaritzburg, the University of Denver, and the University of Cape Town.

BIOGRAPHY

Ezekiel Mphahlele was born in Marabastad township, Pretoria, South Africa, on December 17, 1919. His father left the family early in Mphahlele's life, and he was raised by his mother, a housemaid, and his grandmother, who struggled to keep him in school in spite of economic hardship and an oppressive, strictly segregated social structure. His birth name was Ezekiel, but he later changed his name to Es'kia; both names appear on his works.

In 1945, employed as a high school teacher, he married Rebecca Mochadibane. His first collection of short stories, *Man Must Live, and Other Stories*, was published in 1946. In the early 1950's, he was fired for protesting the segregation of schools, and in 1957 he chose exile from South Africa over life under apartheid. His autobiographical volume *Down Second Avenue* (1959), describing South Africa's black townships, was an international success, but led to the official banning of his work in that country.

For twenty years, Mphahlele moved about Africa, Europe and the United States, teaching at various universities and writing highly acclaimed fiction and criticism. He was allowed to return to South Africa in 1977, and the ban on his writing was lifted two years later. His next several books were published in South Africa and were addressed to an African audience. After the end of apartheid in 1990, he continued to teach and write about political and cultural imperialism.

ANALYSIS

Ezekiel Mphahlele's fiction and other writing have been important bridges between African and Western societies. As an African in a segregated South Africa dominated by Western whites, and later as an African living in exile in Europe and the United States, Mphahlele has been in a unique position to present to many Westerners a picture of black South African life that they would not otherwise have had. Because his writings were officially banned by the South African government in 1961, making it illegal for South Africans to read or even quote his work, most of his stories were not read in his own country until the ban was lifted in 1979. While Mphahlele has always considered himself an African author writing for an African audience, he also recognized the opportunity to address Western oppressors at the same time that he celebrated the strength and beauty of his own people.

Trained in a European-based school system, Mphahlele had as literary models only Western fiction writers, including Charles Dickens, Miguel de Cervantes, and Fyodor Dostoevsky. He writes in *Afrika My Music* that he had never read an "artful" short story before he began writing them, "so I had no genuine models." He traces his realism to Dickens, William Faulkner, and others and his tendency to focus on a single character in a single intense situation to Scottish and English ballads. Over these European frameworks he drapes the cloth of South African experience and sensibility. His stories typically focus on one African character struggling to survive.

Critics often point to Mphahlele's prevailing sense of hope and optimism, even as he writes about racial tension. This optimism comes from Mphahlele's immersion in African humanism, a belief in the essential connection between human nature and the natural world, strengthened by the presence of ancestral spirits and the spirit of community.

MAN MUST LIVE, AND OTHER STORIES

Mphahlele's first short-story collection, *Man Must Live, and Other Stories* included five short stories about characters struggling to survive in a difficult world. The theme of survival grew out of his own childhood in a segregated black township, always under a cloud of poverty and oppression. In the title story, a black railroad policeman named Khalima Zungu adopts a philosophy that he chants to himself, "man must live." He marries a woman of means, then treats her poorly and squanders her money, always telling himself that he is entitled to whatever he can get because "man must live." After his new family leaves him and he burns down their house out of revenge, he lives alone in a tin shack, still believing that his need to live is more important than how he treats others. Zungu's life has been a hard one, but his decline is due more to his character than to his circumstances.

Mphahlele knows that survival in a racist society is a struggle, but his underlying belief in community informs this story and many later stories. Community is a central pillar in the belief system Mphahlele has called African humanism. The seven hundred copies of *Man Must Live, and Other Stories* sold quickly in and around Cape Town, establishing Mphahlele's early reputation. As he grew as a writer, however, Mphahlele rejected most of the stories as clumsy and immature. Only "Man Must Live" retained his approval, and he included it in his next collection, *In Corner B*.

"GRIEG ON A STOLEN PIANO"

One of Mphahlele's most likable characters is Uncle, the central character in "Grieg on a Stolen Piano" from *In Corner B*. Uncle, like many black South Africans, has been shaped by a rich blend of traditional and Western cultures. He is a school inspector who moves between the white and black worlds, sometimes playing Edvard Grieg on the piano and using the services of medical doctors, sometimes playing African music and calling for a traditional herbalist and witch doctor. He shares with Zungu of "Man Must Live" a strong will to survive, but Uncle is amusing and gentle, harmful only to himself.

As the story unfolds, Uncle hatches a get-rich-quick scheme to pay off a gambling debt by coaching pretty Mary-Jane to victory in a beauty contest. His plan includes bribing the judges, but Mary-Jane loses anyway. Uncle feels no remorse for his crookedness, nor for the fact that many of his possessions, including his piano, were bought as stolen property. "Don't we steal from each other," he asks, "lie to each other every day and know it, us and the whites?"

"In Corner B"

The title story of *In Corner B* shows the richness of life in South Africa's black townships, a world that is invisible to whites, who encounter blacks only as employees and know nothing of them socially. The story is a simple one, about the recently widowed Talita and her troubled memories of her husband of nineteen years on the day of his funeral. Just before her husband's death, Talita learned that he had a mistress, Marta. Marta comes to the funeral and wails loudly but later writes Talita a letter to say that the husband never gave Marta his love. The story again shows Mphahlele's concern with community, and includes scenes of township people laughing, drinking, and preparing for a funeral. "In Corner B" does not deal with racial tension; whites appear only in the background. Mphahlele would write later, in the essay "Renewal Time," that whites would appear less and less in black African writing because they are "simply irrelevant to the black man's understanding of himself."

"Mrs. Plum"

Mphahlele has called "Mrs. Plum" "the best thing I ever pulled off." First published in *In Corner B*, it tells the story of the black housemaid Karabo and her white employer Mrs. Plum. Told from Karabo's viewpoint, the story is one of the first pieces of fiction to feature a black African woman as the central character. Karabo is young and eager to take her place in the world. Like Zungu in "Man Must Live," she carries a refrain with her: "I learned. I grew up." What she learns is that Mrs. Plum, a typical white liberal in segregated South Africa, is as hypocritical as she is well meaning. Mrs. Plum allows herself to be arrested to protest the injustice of discriminatory laws but will not allow her daughter to marry a black intellectual, who has been a guest in their home. Additionally, she is never able to see Karabo as an equal. Gradually Karabo develops the confidence to demand fair treatment from her employer.

Mphahlele's indictment of white liberal hypocrisy and his detailed true-to-life scenes of South African domestic life are typical of his fiction. Also typical is the story's focus on one central character, struggling to survive in an oppressive society. Karabo's story is set in a real place, at a real time, and the civil injustices she faces are historically accurate.

Renewal Time

Renewal Time is especially significant because it was the first collection of Mphahlele's short fiction published and reviewed outside Africa. Issued in 1988 by Readers International, it made the short fiction more easily available to American and European readers who already admired Mphahlele for his autobiographical volumes and criticism. *Renewal Time* comprises the eight stories Mphahlele considers his best, including "Man Must Live," "Grieg on a Stolen Piano," "In Corner B," and "Mrs. Plum"; all of the stories were included in *In Corner B*, and most were written during Mphahlele's exile from South Africa.

Mphahlele begins and ends the volume with new essays reflecting on the stories in the context of his own exile and return. "The Sounds Begin Again–Essay, 1984" (actually the first chapter of *Afrika My Music*) is a narrative account of the author's return to South Africa, interwoven with memories of his youth. In the episodic structure and poetic language of fiction, the piece traces the educational system and the writers—mostly Western—who shaped Mphahlele's own writing. Discovering the short stories of Richard Wright in the 1940's, Mphahlele learned "how to use the short story as a way of dealing with my anger and indignation." In "Renewal Time–Essay, 1981," Mphahlele addresses the reader directly, calling for revolution and renewal.

OTHER MAJOR WORKS

LONG FICTION: *The Wanderers*, 1971; *Chirundu*, 1979; *Father Come Home*, 1984.

NONFICTION: *Down Second Avenue*, 1959; *The African Image*, 1962, rev. 1974; *A Guide to Creative Writing*, 1966; *Voices in the Whirlwind and Other Essays*, 1972; *Afrika My Music: An Autobiography*, 1984; *Poetry and Humanism*, 1986.

EDITED TEXTS: *African Writing Today*, 1967; *Perspectives on South African English Literature*, 1992; *Seasons Come to Pass: A Poetry Anthology for Southern African Students*, 1994.

BIBLIOGRAPHY

Akosu, Tyohdzuah. *The Writing of Ezekiel [Es'kia] Mphahlele, South African Writer: Literature, Culture and Politics*. Lewiston, N.Y.: Mellen University Press, 1995. An important overview of the critical reception of Mphahlele's work and an assessment of his literary achievements. Akosu claims that aesthetic questions about African writing are inappropriate because they do not take into account the sociopolitical environment in which the work is created. Mphahlele's work should be analyzed in terms of its value as protest against apartheid.

Barnett, Ursula A. *Ezekiel Mphahlele*. Boston: Twayne, 1976. Although published before Mphahlele's return to South Africa from exile in 1977, this volume is still the best introduction to Mphahlele's early and middle life and work. Includes a chronology, biography, and close reading of the major writings.

Egejuru, Phanuel Akubueze. *Towards African Literary Independence: A Dialogue with Contemporary African Writers*. Westport, Conn.: Greenwood Press, 1980. Interwoven interviews with several important writers, including Mphahlele, on the importance of African literature for Africans and for Westerners. Mphahlele discusses the challenges of being both an African and an exile, and of writing for an African audience but being published and read by Westerners.

Hodge, Norman. "Dogs, Africans, and Liberals: The World of Mphahlele's 'Mrs Plum'." *English in Africa* 8 (March, 1981): 33-43. A close reading of "Mrs. Plum," emphasizing the indictment the story makes of white liberals in South Africa under apartheid. Hodge believes that "Mrs. Plum" is Mphahlele's most important piece of short fiction and demonstrates his ability to depict characters in the process of intellectual and moral development.

Manganyi, N. Chabani. *Exiles and Homecomings: A Biography of Es'kia Mphahlele*. Johannesburg, South Africa: Ravan Press, 1983. An insightful biography written by a clinical psychologist with full cooperation from Mphahlele and his family. This biography is unusual in using a first-person narrative voice.

Obee, Ruth. *Es'kia Mphahlele: Themes of Alienation and African Humanism*. Athens: Ohio University Press, 1999. Mphahlele has often discussed African Humanism, rather than European influences, as it underlies the writings of the black consciousness movement. Obee extracts the basic values that describe African humanism and traces these values as they appear in Mphahlele's major works and in other important works of South African literature and criticism.

Pitok, Todd. "An Interview with Es'kia Mphahlele." *Poets and Writers Magazine* 22 (November/December, 1994): 64-71. A brief overview of Mphahlele's life and career, important because of its glimpse of the author's life since the end of apartheid. Pitok discusses Mphahlele's political role in democratic South Africa, including his missed chance to help Nelson Mandela complete an autobiography.

Ruth, Damian. "Through the Keyhole: Masters and Servants in the Work of Es'kia Mphahlele." *English in Africa* 13 (October, 1986): 65-88. An examination of the theme of the white employer and black employee in South Africa under apartheid, as it plays out in three of Mphahlele's short stories. In each case, the white employer is blind to the humanity of the employee, while the employee is able to see and to grow.

Cynthia A. Bily

CRITICAL SURVEY
OF
SHORT FICTION

GEOGRAPHICAL INDEX

GEOGRAPHICAL INDEX

GEOGRAPHICAL INDEX

CATEGORY INDEX

CATEGORY INDEX

CATEGORY INDEX

CATEGORY INDEX

SOCIAL SATIRE. *See also* MANNERS, FICTION OF, SOCIAL REALISM

SOUTH AFRICAN CULTURE

SOUTHERN UNITED STATES

SOUTHWESTERN UNITED STATES

SPANISH CULTURE

SUPERNATURAL STORIES. *See also* GHOST, GOTHIC, GROTESQUE STORIES, HORROR, MAGICAL REALISM, OCCULT, SUSPENSE

CATEGORY INDEX

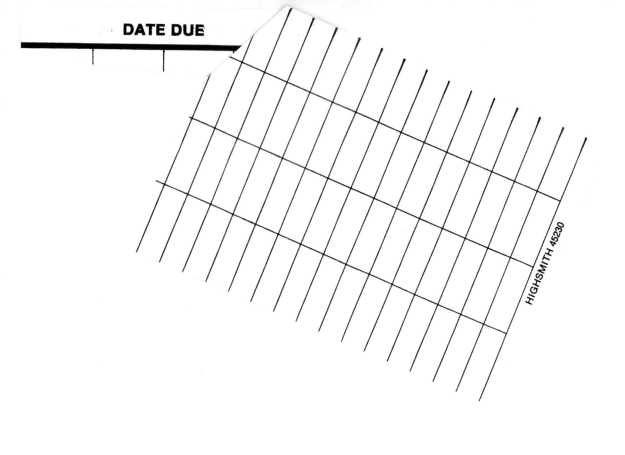

HIGHSMITH 45230